From Ideologies to Public Philosophies

D1423743

ONE WEEK LOAN

for
Lynnie

From Ideologies to Public Philosophies

An Introduction to Political Theory

Paul Schumaker

with

Will Delehanty

Dwight Kiel

Thomas Heilke

Blackwell
Publishing

© 2008 by Paul Schumaker

BLACKWELL PUBLISHING
350 Main Street, Malden, MA 02148-5020, USA
9600 Garsington Road, Oxford OX4 2DQ, UK
550 Swanston Street, Carlton, Victoria 3053, Australia

First published 2008 by Blackwell Publishing Ltd

1   2008

Library of Congress Cataloging-in-Publication Data

Schumaker, Paul.
    From ideologies to public philosophies : an introduction to political theory / Paul Schumaker
with Will Delehanty . . . [et al.].
      p. cm.
    Includes bibliographical references and index.
    ISBN 978-1-4051-6836-6 (hardback : alk. paper) — ISBN 978-1-4051-6835-9 (pbk. : alk.
paper).   1. Political science—Philosophy. 2. Ideology. I. Delehanty, Will. II. Title.
    JA71.S298 2008
    320.01—dc22

                                                                                    2007037808

A catalogue record for this title is available from the British Library.

Set in 10/13pt Sabon
by Graphicraft Limited, Hong Kong
Printed and bound in Singapore
by Markono Print Media Pte Ltd

The publisher's policy is to use permanent paper from mills that operate a sustainable forestry
policy, and which has been manufactured from pulp processed using acid-free and elementary
chlorine-free practices. Furthermore, the publisher ensures that the text paper and cover board
used have met acceptable environmental accreditation standards.

For further information on
Blackwell Publishing, visit our website:
www.blackwellpublishing.com

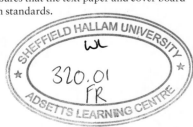

Table of Contents

Preface

This book is an introduction – albeit an ambitious one – to political theory. It seeks to give students (and citizens generally) a framework and a wide array of concepts for thinking seriously about politics. It invites you to enter into conversations with others in search of public philosophies that can guide the political communities to which you belong and that can add to the breadth, depth, and validity of your own political beliefs, values, and principles.

This book emerged out of my desire to enhance the learning, enthusiasm, and involvement of students who are encountering political theory in a serious manner for the first time. One common approach to introducing students to political theory is to jump into the great works of Plato, Hobbes, Marx, Rawls, and many other seminal thinkers. I got my feet wet about 40 years ago with such an approach, and I have used it many times in teaching political theory. The downside is that students invest a lot of time trying to comprehend these theorists, and they often see "the canon," or great works in the history of political thought, as too dated and abstract to be of much use in helping them generate a set of political ideas that can guide their political lives and the politics of the communities in which they reside.

A second common approach is to assign a textbook covering major ideologies. About 15 years ago, I tried this approach, but was soon disenchanted with the quality of the available texts, so I co-authored one of my own, *Great Ideas/Grand Schemes: Political Ideologies in the 19th and 20th Centuries* (*GIGS*, as my students affectionately called it). I think *GIGS* was successful at providing students with a fairly comprehensive, clear, and deep understanding of various ideologies. However, this approach also had a downside. Students tended to be preoccupied with the question, "Which ideology best captures my ideas?" Students too often used *GIGS* to find defenses for the political ideas that they had been socialized to accept, rather than use the book as a vehicle for finding ideas that challenged old ways of thinking and for carefully evaluating the worth of both familiar and unfamiliar ideas.

This book provides an alternative approach. It is organized to encourage students to think deeply about the most basic political questions, sometimes called the perennial questions or the great issues of politics. With which political communities should we identify? Who should be granted citizenship in these communities? What should be the rights and obligations of citizens? What should be the roles of economic markets, cultural values, voluntary organizations, and governments in structuring our communities? Who should rule? In what areas of personal, social, and economic life should governments be authorized to use their coercive powers? How should social goods, like education and wealth, be distributed? How much and what kind of change is needed? Political theory also addresses some even larger philosophical issues that are often the basis of our political thinking. Ontological questions address assumptions about ultimate reality. Questions of human nature deal with basic characteristics and motivations of men and women. Questions of society deal with the origins and characteristics of social life. Epistemological questions deal with how we can attain reliable knowledge of politics – if such knowledge is even possible. This book provides students with a wide array of answers to these questions in a way that encourages them to ask which answers they should embrace both as individuals and as members of various communities. It is intended to force students to see their current beliefs in relationship to alternative answers, encouraging their thoughtful evaluation of competing ideas.

Political ideologies and quasi-ideologies provide a wide range of thinking on the perennial questions. Chapters 2 and 3 introduce eight major ideologies that have been most influential in American and world politics during the nineteenth and twentieth centuries, paying attention to how these ideologies arose historically and what their central ideas have been. In these chapters, classical liberalism is distinguished from contemporary liberalism, and traditional conservatism is distinguished from contemporary conservatism. Despite their affinities as "far left" ideologies, anarchism, Marxism, and communism are distinguished from each other. Despite their similarities as totalitarian "far right" ideologies, the differences between fascism and Nazism are also considered. Such distinctions help provide historical perspectives on how ideologies have evolved, and they allow us to broaden the range of answers to the perennial questions.

But it is important to move beyond the most familiar ideologies of the past. Chapter 4 introduces a wide variety of radical and extremist voices that seek to be heard in contemporary politics, perspectives that are called quasi-ideologies because they are less comprehensive than ideologies. For organizational purposes, these many voices are classified into four categories: the radical right, the radical left, the extreme right, and the extreme left. Such a classification scheme is described and defended in chapter 4, and subsequent chapters show the utility of that scheme by applying it to widen alternative perspectives on the perennial political questions.

The stage is thus set for considering the great issues of politics. Each of the next 11 chapters (5 through 15) focuses on a set of questions dealing with a basic topic. The views of each ideology and various quasi-ideologies on each set of questions are presented. Such presentations can be regarded as the opening statements of various participants in political conversations seeking to come to consensus on the perennial questions, even while stressing their differences.

This format furthers two objectives. First, deeper, cumulative understandings of each ideology and quasi-ideology are attained as students proceed from the basic introductions in chapters 2–4, through the philosophical foundations of these perspectives, and then into more in-depth presentation of their basic political principles. As the semester goes on, students gain a deeper internal understanding of the various perspectives, enabling them to see politics from many vantage points. Second, students have the resources needed to engage in informed discussions of the perennial questions. I assign students to be spokespersons for particular perspectives, requiring them to assume viewpoints often far from those with which they are most familiar and comfortable, asking them to bring an internalized understanding of their assigned perspective to group conversations, and ensuring that all views will be taken into account during these conversations. (Students are, of course, assigned different ideological perspectives throughout the semester.) I ask them to seek as much agreement as possible during their conversations, to clarify the major conflicting ideas, to think about the reasons why they disagree, and to evaluate their different answers.

In the conclusions of these chapters, I suggest that there is some agreement on the perennial questions, if only among most ideologies and quasi-ideologies and if only on some basic and general matters. In settling political disputes, mediators typically begin by searching for those most basic matters on which they can get the conflicting parties to agree. The agreements that I propose in the conclusions are called the underlying consensus of pluralism. Taken together, the consensual agreements on the various perennial questions comprise pluralist public philosophy, which is proposed here as the most basic philosophy guiding politics in the United States and many other countries today. While it is one purpose of this book to provide a fairly comprehensive account of pluralism, it can initially be understood as a public philosophy that affirms the legitimacy of many interests, identities, and ideas that often compete with one another and emphasizes democratic procedures for reconciling differences, if only tentatively and temporarily. (Thus, pluralist public philosophy should not be confused with a much more focused orthodox pluralist theory that rose to prominence in political science at the beginning of its behavioral revolution almost a half century ago and that has given pluralism a negative connotation among many political theorists and political scientists.)

The consensus within pluralist public philosophy is proposed with the tentativeness that is a central feature of pluralism. Perhaps the suggested underlying consensus on each perennial question is too optimistic, rejected not only by extremists but also by some outlooks that are generally friends of pluralism. Or perhaps the suggested underlying consensus is too timid, as the friends of pluralism can actually have more substantial agreements than those proposed here. Conversations among spokespersons for various ideologies – including those that are normally regarded as affirming pluralism and those that are normally regarded as questioning and rejecting it – are useful tests of the adequacy of pluralist public philosophy as depicted here.

Even if there is widespread consensus on pluralist public philosophy, more specific public philosophies are also needed. Pluralism is too general to provide much guidance on the specific issues that arise within political communities, and thus more specific perspectives may be helpful to orient individuals to political life and to provide more specific guidance to how various political communities should be governed. Students can profitably discuss the more specific contested ideas of various ideologies and quasi-ideologies to try to construct public philosophies that should govern the various political communities to which they belong.

The search for such public philosophies might begin with two very basic orientations. First, searching through the available ideological alternatives and selecting among them may not yield the most suitable public philosophy for an individual or a political community. Indeed, it seems unlikely that the specific public philosophies to guide us are lying around waiting to be discovered. Comprehensive public philosophies that we can embrace may need to be constructed by carefully evaluating the alternative philosophical foundations of public philosophies, choosing among competing political principles addressing the perennial political issues, and integrating them into a coherent set of principles. Second, different public philosophies may be best suited for different political communities. The best public philosophy for a city may be different from that for a nation, which may be different from that for the global community. And different public philosophies may be most suitable for different cities and nations. This text does not endorse any specific public philosophy, but rather seeks to provide helpful resources for their construction by those individuals who seek to become deeper political thinkers and by political communities seeking the benefits of a public philosophy.

While this book is structured thematically rather than historically, I have adopted some strategies for giving readers basic information on the origins and evolution of ideas. First, the introductions to the various ideologies in chapters 2, 3, and 4 pay considerable attention to the historical contexts that gave rise to the ideologies. Second, the perennial issues are discussed by presenting the ideological responses to them in a basically chronological manner. However, there is no single historical sequence to ideologies, and so I sometimes change the order of presentations so as to provide the clearest flow of ideas. A third device used to aid in understanding the history of political ideas is to indicate the lifespan of non-living contributors to an ideology, whenever he or she is first introduced.

The fairly extensive endnotes are intended to clarify issues that may occur to thoughtful and informed readers and to provide some sense of the related work being done by political theorists on the ideas sketched in the text. The bibliography at the end of the book provides complete citations to the authors and abbreviated titles presented in the text and footnotes. (I have used the convention of citing authors' first and last names with the first reference to a specific work, but only last names for subsequent references to that work.)

There are many people whom I would like to acknowledge for their direct and indirect contributions to this book, but I fear that any effort to list everyone would only offend those who were inadvertently omitted. Beyond the many great, good, fair, and poor political thinkers whose ideas are cited below, I am indebted to many former teachers and mentors who developed my interests in the issues pursued here, hundreds of students who provided suggestions on earlier drafts of the text, numerous colleagues who advised me on particular issues, fellow panelists and reviewers who provided feedback on parts or all of this text, and friends and family who listened and commented on ideas presented here.

While this text is distinct from *GIGS*, I want to acknowledge the contributions of my co-authors in that enterprise – Dwight Kiel and Thomas Heilke. I have occasionally drawn on materials in that earlier text, and so their contributions to *GIGS* remain interwoven into the present text. While their primary interests have changed, they have read and commented extensively on the current manuscript. I also want to acknowledge the contributions of Will Delehanty, who has served as my teaching assistant during the semesters when this text was developed and tested. He both provided valuable feedback on the text and facilitated many conversations in discussion sections – conversations that generally produced both consensual support for the pluralist public philosophy proposed here and civil disagreements about the best principles that should guide the resolution of the issues that all political communities confront.

But my greatest debt is to my wife, who inspired and has greatly supported my undertaking of this project. This book is dedicated to her.

Paul Schumaker
Lawrence, Kansas

Chapter 1

Constructing Our Public Philosophies

The overall quality of life in our political communities is often undermined because our governments are overly responsive to the requirements of economic growth in a capitalist economy, to the interests of the powers-that-be, and to the shifting moods of an ill-informed and prejudicial public. As an antidote to such debilitating forces on our political life, the residents and rulers of political communities are often urged to deliberate on the political principles that should guide their governance, and then develop structures and processes and enact and deliver policies and programs consistent with these principles.[1]

The main purpose of this book is to provide resources enabling thoughtful discussions about such principles – about the public philosophies that should guide how we live together in political communities.

Public Philosophies and Political Ideologies

Public philosophies, like political ideologies, provide fairly comprehensive and coherent sets of core ideas about politics. Both provide beliefs about how political communities are governed, ideals about the goals that should be sought by political communities, and principles providing broad guidelines for achieving these goals. While the term "political ideology" is more familiar – it is widely used to designate many competing sets of political beliefs and values such as liberalism, conservatism, socialism, fascism, and so forth – it has very contested meanings and implications. For example, political scientists usually maintain that people who hold an ideology have much more developed, complex, and coherent political ideas than the vast majority of citizens who are ideologically innocent.[2] In contrast, many other social theorists think of ideologies in derogatory terms – as providing biased ideas furthering particular interests, as oversimplifying and distorting reality, and as promoting rigid, utopian, and extreme thinking.[3] While the term "public philosophy" may suggest an abstract and academic preoccupation with mere theorizing about the good society and good government

– with little relevance to political reality – this book seeks to convince you that such philosophies address issues of great practical significance, that they can avoid the pitfalls of ideologies, and that ordinary people can enter into important conversations with one another in search of both a general public philosophy that can guide the politics of all communities and more specific public philosophies that can guide the politics of the various particular communities to which they belong.

To generate a public philosophy, community members must address a variety of important issues – the perennial political and philosophical questions presented in the next section.[4] Different ideologies provide a wide range of perspectives on these questions and thus are important resources for conversations in search of public philosophies. By comparing and analyzing the answers to the perennial questions of competing ideologies, it is possible to locate their agreements and disagreements. Thoughtful comparative analyses of the ideas of alternative ideologies are the building blocks of public philosophies.

This book proposes that conversations among contemporary liberals, contemporary conservatives, and some other older and emerging ideologies can generate consensus on some ideas. This consensus comprises the most general public philosophy of advanced societies. All adherents to *pluralist* public philosophy understand (among other things) that modern societies are composed of people having different biological and social characteristics, different religious beliefs and moral principles, and different interests, that individuals have rights to express and pursue these differences, and that governments should thus foster mutual toleration.

Conversations involving spokespersons for different ideologies nevertheless produce more disagreement than agreement. Communists, fascists, and various religious fundamentalisms illustrate ideologies that reject many tenets of pluralist public philosophy. Communitarians, libertarians, and greens usually agree with most tenets of pluralism, but they would like to extend or reform pluralism in various ways – for example, by insisting that pluralist societies give greater attention to the moral development and political obligations of citizens, to the property rights of individuals, or to achieving a sustainable natural environment. Even those ideologies that are most committed to pluralism – contemporary liberalism and contemporary conservatism – seem to share few ideas beyond a thin and abstract consensus on the perennial questions. Indeed, today's liberals and conservatives so emphasize their differences and forget their commonalities that they are often characterized as contributing to the unnecessary polarization of pluralist societies.

In brief, thoughtful deliberations among spokespersons for various ideologies can result in many benefits for political communities. They can result in consensus on at least some basic and general principles that can guide all pluralist societies. They can produce additional agreement on more specific principles that can guide particular communities. They can provide forums for considering modifications and even radical reforms of prevailing public philosophies. They can result in better understandings and amicable reconciliation of ideological differences within pluralist politics. They can identify the ideas of certain ideologies that endanger pluralist societies. These are among the primary tasks of political theory.

Political Theory

The subject matter of political theory is vast, because it seeks general understandings of all things political. Like the term ideology, the meaning of politics is widely contested.

Politics

Some see politics as involving human conflict. In David Easton's famous formulation, politics involves "the authoritative allocation of values" among people seeking larger shares of scarce social goods.[5] Others see politics as involving human cooperation. According to another eminent political scientist, Karl Deutsch (1912–92), politics "deals inescapably with the collective self control of human beings – their joint power over their own fate."[6] To include and emphasize both human conflict and coopera-tion, politics can be understood as involving the production and distribution of social goods (things that most people value but can attain only through relationships with others, such as protection from enemies and diseases, safe and attractive environ-ments, transportation and communication systems, various products and services, education, occupational opportunities, power, and money). Community members often initially disagree about the collective actions appropriate for producing and dis-tributing social goods and resolve their disagreements in various ways. They may resort to war, violence, or coercion; some people may overpower others, forcing the weak to abide by the ideas of the strong. They may employ propaganda; some people may manipulate information in ways that achieve widespread compliance with their goals through a "false" consensus that others would reject if they had fuller informa-tion and unrestricted access to competing ideas. They may agree to employ certain procedures for resolving disagreements; they could flip a coin, put issues to a vote, take issues to court, or use any other procedure they believe is a legitimate method of resolving their disagreements. Or they can try to resolve their disagreements by coming to agreement; they might engage in collaborative efforts to work through their conflicts, to find common ground, and to arrive at understandings that are widely regarded as acceptable.

Such a conception of politics is useful because it recognizes the conflicts we all experience in community life, because it recognizes diverse ways of handling conflict, and because it recognizes that politics is a feature of all communities. Politics occurs in families, churches, schools, and other associations in civil society, as well as in various states.

The perennial questions of politics

Figure 1 provides a schematic diagram containing eleven broad categories of very general concerns that are central to politics and thus to developing public philoso-phies. The seven categories at the top of the figure deal with the beliefs, values, and principles that most directly bear on political life.

Political Principles

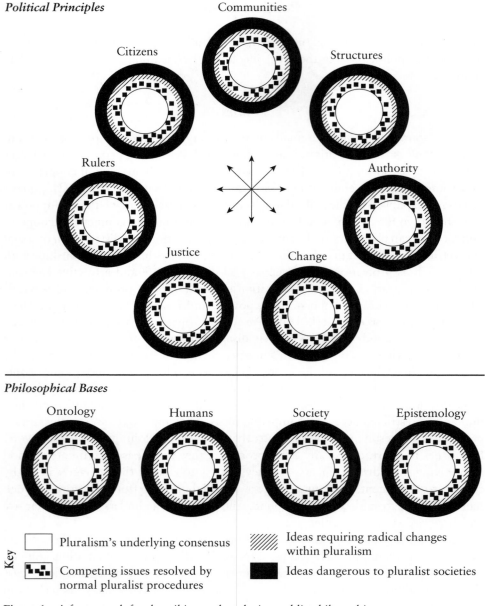

Figure 1   A framework for describing and analyzing public philosophies

Communities   People reside in, identify with, and have obligations to many political communities or *polities*: territorially defined states having governments that make laws and develop programs affecting the production and distribution of social goods. Such polities include: the global community; various civilizations defined by the ethnicities, religions, and cultures of people; regional political systems like the European

Union; nations; provinces, metropolitan areas, cities, and towns within nations having decentralized political systems; school districts and other specialized associations for the delivery of specific public goods; and local neighborhoods.[7] With which of these kinds of communities do people most strongly identify? With which of these kinds of communities should they identify?

Citizens   Political communities are composed of residents and citizens. Who can become residents and citizens of various communities? Can there be legitimate differences in the status of residents (e.g., full citizens, partial citizens, mere residents)? What benefits are provided to citizens, and should such benefits be extended and guaranteed as rights or should they be reduced? What duties must citizens perform, and should citizen obligations be strengthened or diminished?

Structures   Many institutions and processes structure polities by giving meaning and purposes to people's lives, and by producing, distributing, and controlling social goods. Such institutions include governments (or various sorts), corporations and other business organizations, labor unions and other associations of workers, religious institutions, schools, voluntary and charitable organizations, and families. Such processes include market transactions and governmental regulations. Cultures (broadly accepted norms and values within political communities) are non-institutional structures that affect social life in important ways. Should our lives be highly structured, or should such structures – or at least certain structures – be dismantled or at least diminished? Which of these structures are the most important? What is the existing balance of power among these structures? Should this balance be modified?

Rulers   Elected representatives, appointed office-holders (bureaucrats), owners and managers of economic organizations, producers and disseminators of ideas and information, leaders of community groups, active participants on community issues, and ordinary citizens are among the kinds of people in a community who exercise political power. Who really rules and who should rule? What is the distribution of power within a community, and should power be distributed differently? What are the mechanisms for limiting the power of rulers and the occasions for holding rulers accountable?

Authority   Matters of economic behavior, social interaction, environmental protection, religious worship, cultural values, and personal lifestyles are among the many facets of community life that are potentially subject to governmental authority. For what purposes should government authority be exercised? What constraints on individual freedom can governmental authorities legitimately impose? In what areas should government authority be expanded or contracted?

Justice   People normally adhere to cultural norms and governmental laws. What principles of justice should be reflected in such norms and laws? People should treat each other in a just manner, and social goods should be distributed fairly. What principles of justice should guide the distribution of social goods? What distributive procedures and outcomes are just?

Change   Political change can be resisted, or it could be sought in small and large doses, and through peaceful and violent means. How much and what kind of change is desirable? What tactics used by agents of change are legitimate? To what extent and under what conditions is repression of those who seek change legitimate?

Beyond these seven categories, figure 1 directs attention to four kinds of philosophical assumptions – to ideas that are broader than political principles and often foundational to them. These assumptions tend to be unarticulated in political discussions and are often poorly understood by political actors, but that does not diminish the extent to which they are firmly held and the basis of people's political beliefs, values, and principles. Philosophical assumptions are hard to contest, because there exists no agreed-upon method for validating or falsifying them, but that does not diminish our need to think rigorously about their merits and limitations. They concern:

Ontology.   People hold different conceptions of ultimate reality. Ontological assumptions deal with the most basic source(s) of the world we experience. Are there supernatural beings or a Supreme Being (Yahweh, God, or Allah) that created the natural world? Are there transcendental beings (such as God or Platonic forms) that provide absolute standards specifying what is good and evil in the natural world and human conduct? Or is ultimate reality simply the most basic materials and forces in the natural world? Ontological assumptions also deal with ultimate ends. Is what will become of the world determined by divine or supernatural causes? By material and natural causes? Or are ultimate ends undetermined, subject to human ideas, will, and power?

Human nature.   People hold different beliefs about the essence of humans. Are humans fundamentally equal and, if so, in what ways and on what basis? In what ways are humans unequal? What constitutes the good life for individuals? What are basic (and desirable) human motivations and purposes? Are humans autonomous and rational in choosing their own ends, or are their conceptions of the good life and their motivations socially and politically influenced?

Nature of society.   People have different notions about the origins of social life and different images of society. What are the basic characteristics of a good society? To what extent should societies be homogeneous, and in what ways are they heterogeneous? What are the fundamental bases of conflict within societies?

Epistemology.   People have different conceptions of what we can know politically and how we can know it. To what extent can we have certain knowledge or tentative knowledge about politics? Or must we accept complete uncertainty about fundamental political questions? How can we achieve political knowledge?

To answer these questions and to develop public philosophies, we must become political theorists. Political theory seeks to understand how humans live and should live in community with others. It encompasses all the conflicting ideas of the great (and less great) thinkers about how our various communities are governed and how they should be governed. Because everyone has such ideas, everyone is, to some degree, a political theorist. But at least two qualities are found in the ideas of serious political thinkers or theorists.

First, the ideas of theorists are expressed in terms of *abstract concepts* and *generalizations*. Non-theorists often focus on concrete and specific cases. For example, they might express the notion that Smith is an important person in the community and describe the ways he attained and used his control over others. Such descriptions can be fascinating and illuminating, because of the particular nuances and unique features of community relations that are revealed by the case of Smith. Political theorists, however, deal with concepts that encompass many cases and generalize across cases and about differences among cases. For example, political theorists may regard as a key political concept – which they denote as power – the differences among people in their capacity to affect the production and distribution of social goods. After observing power relations in various communities, theorists might regard gender as an important concept in understanding power and propose as generalizations such ideas as "the powers-that-be tend to be men," or "the greater power of men than women in communities is due to the different socialization experiences of boys and girls in childhood," or "communities are best governed when power is distributed equally between men and women." Theorists believe such generalizations make comprehensible the basic patterns of human life that underlie concrete cases.

Some theorists are most interested in producing generalizations about political reality, about how political communities are actually structured and function. Such *empirical* theorists provide descriptions about most cases, explanations for variations among cases, and predictions about future cases.[8] Other theorists are interested in producing generalizations about how political communities ought to be structured and function. Such *normative* theorists envision ideal – or at least better – political communities, evaluate how well specific cases correspond to their ideals, and prescribe ways of achieving desirable outcomes in most cases. The idealizations, evaluations, and prescriptions of normative theorists always involve value judgments. Feminist theorists, for example, would likely regard male dominance over women as morally and politically unacceptable.

Second, compared to most people, political theorists are more deeply concerned about the basis and *validity* of their ideas. Theorists usually present their descriptions, explanations, predictions, idealizations, evaluations, prescriptions, and other such ideas with a measure of tentativeness and humility.[9] They often suppose that the questions they address about politics have true answers in the eyes of God or from some ideal, all-knowing, unbiased, or transcendent perspective. But recognizing their humanity, they acknowledge the limits of their knowledge and the potential biases in their perceptions and analyses. Theorists ask about the underlying assumptions that must be accepted to support their ideas, and reflect on the usefulness and validity of these assumptions. According to the Austrian-born British philosopher Karl Popper (1902–94), empirical theorists check the validity of their descriptions and explanations by employing scientific methods that seek to falsify hypotheses by analyzing observable evidence concerning their ideas; such methods filter out various biases to thinking and allow others to examine the procedures used to test their ideas. According to French philosopher Simone Weil (1909–43), normative theorists check the validity of their idealizations, evaluations, and prescriptions by regularly employing as methods of investigation a search for the contrary to their ideas and they inquire into the validity of these opposing views. In short, both empirical and normative theorists look for counter-evidence and counter-arguments to their ideas, revising their conclusions as required. Being reflective about the validity of ideas, theorists conduct an open-ended and tentative search for what is true in political life and what is good in political life.[10]

While it is conventional to stress the different goals and methods of empirical and normative theorists, the distinction between them is perhaps overdrawn. Political scientists emphasize the development of empirical theory, but they often make normative claims. Political philosophers emphasize the development of normative theory, but they often make use of empirical generalizations. Moreover, public philosophies contain both empirical and normative ideas, and the development of public philosophies that merit our allegiance requires the tools of both political science and political philosophy.[11] Political ideologies provide a host of interesting and plausible ideas for possible inclusion in public philosophies, but skepticism about the validity of their ideas is always in order. Some ideologies may distort political reality to camouflage how existing practices benefit particular class interests at the expense of the public good. Other ideologies may be based on paranoia. Still other ideologies may invite people to make unreasonable sacrifices in the present for utopian future goals. Political science and political philosophy provide approaches for evaluating the claims of contending political ideologies.

Political science

As a scholarly discipline, political science aspires to impartial analysis of political beliefs; it provides methods for guarding against the influence of various biases in determining the validity of our descriptions and explanations of the workings of actual political communities. Nevertheless, the capacity of scientific methods to overcome ideological biases about how the political world functions has often been questioned. For example, our ideological orientations are alleged to shape the questions we ask about the empirical world, the hypotheses we form about it, and the observations we make about it. Such allegations suggest that we cannot transcend ideology in forming political beliefs, because ideologies are particular and narrow sets of lenses that channel and distort our perceptions and thoughts about the empirical world, making inter-subjective agreement impossible.

Ideologies undoubtedly do shape the questions we ask about how the political world actually works. For example, Marxism is an ideology that claims that democratic governments are merely "the executive committee of the capitalist class," leading Marxists to raise questions about the distribution of power in communities that are formally democratic. Who really rules? Who really has predominant power in American cities and other political communities that are claimed to be democratic? If ideologies prompt scientific investigations of such important questions, that may be an asset rather than a liability.

Ideologies may also influence the hypotheses that one chooses to investigate. In response to the question of who really rules, liberals normally suppose that elected representatives are the most powerful actors in a democratic society, but Marxists argue that various business interests – members of the capitalist class – have extensive power over such officials,[12] while contemporary conservatives suggest that a "New Class" of intellectuals and bureaucrats may be the real rulers. Thus, ideological predispositions often result in the formulation of not only one hypothesis regarding an important topic, but of alternative or rival hypotheses. At least in principle, these rival hypotheses can be tested scientifically, resulting in more precise and valid descriptions and explanations about such matters as the actual distribution of power within communities.

Ideological preconceptions may, however, affect the evidence that people marshal on behalf of their hypotheses and theories. For example, it is claimed that those Marxists who believe that capitalists really rule in liberal democratic communities employ research methods that reinforce the perception of capitalist dominance, but fail to distinguish adequately between that perception and the actual and very significant limits on capitalist power.[13] Meanwhile, Marxists claim that liberals, who believe that elected representatives rule, use methods that are unable to capture the hidden control that capitalists exercise over representatives.[14] Such arguments about the biases of the methods used to collect evidence in support of rival hypotheses about the distribution of power have led some observers to conclude that there is little likelihood of attaining objective answers to "who rules?" because the field of study is hopelessly muddied by ideological preconceptions and biases.[15]

Despite such difficulties, *the scientific method* is designed to overcome ideological biases. While ideological positions may influence the evidence that is brought to bear on such hypotheses, science has developed many procedures – such as insisting on the replication of findings – to winnow out questionable empirical claims and to increase our confidence in the validity of scientific findings. When ideologically derived beliefs are subjected to scientific examination, the controversy that usually ensues about the adequacy of the methods employed often leads to the development of more complicated – and ultimately more adequate – answers to such questions as "who rules?"

Scientific analysis of "who rules?" has resulted in more adequate understandings of the concept of power. Rather than simply conceptualizing and measuring political power in terms of who holds office in governmental institutions, persons from different ideological perspectives now acknowledge that power has several, more subtle, faces or dimensions. There is a first face of power that appears when some people are able to get other people to defer to their preferences when policy decisions are made.

There is a second face of power that appears when some people are able to establish and control the agenda of issues that come before a community, providing a context in which the first face of power can be effective. And there is a third face of power that appears when some people are able to shape the preferences of other people so that those whose preferences have been shaped will use their power to help secure the goals of those who shaped their preferences.[16] Perhaps liberals developed the concept of the first face of power – and methods for analyzing the first face – because they anticipated these methods would reveal that elected officials have more such power than capitalists. And perhaps neo-Marxists developed the concepts of the second and third faces of power because they anticipated that analyses would reveal that capitalists usually set the agenda to which elected officials respond and that the ideological dominance of capitalist values shape the preferences that elected officials (and even the working class) pursue in the policy-making process. While ideological motivations perhaps gave rise to the conceptualizations of these different dimensions of power, both liberals and neo-Marxists now acknowledge that power is multidimensional, involving at least these three separate facets.[17] Additionally, the ideological debate over who rules has led to a scientific consensus that neither elected representatives nor capitalists rule entirely, but rather that the distribution of power varies across communities and even within communities, depending on the kinds of issues that are being addressed. Business interests do predominate in some communities that are formally democratic, but interests that oppose business predominate in other communities. Indeed, scientific investigations suggest that business interests are particularly likely to predominate under specific conditions such as when communities employ institutions that de-politicize government (for example, by having nonpartisan elections for office).[18] Such investigations also indicate that business interests are likely to predominate on economic development issues, but have much less influence on issues concerned with the provision and allocation of governmental services such as libraries, recreation facilities, and trash removal.[19]

In summary, scientific analyses of ideologically motivated debates over such questions as "who rules?" show the inadequacy of the simple answers provided by various ideological perspectives. While some persons – commonly referred to as ideologues – bring unshakeable ideological beliefs to such debates, and while they resist more complex scientific advances on these topics, ideological blinders have not prevented the development of more sophisticated and accurate understandings of power and other key political concepts. The example of community power studies suggests that more adequate political knowledge can be attained by asking the questions about political reality posed in our framework depicted in figure 1, by entertaining as rival hypotheses the contrasting beliefs held by those from different ideological perspectives, and by analyzing these hypotheses using normal scientific methods. This is not to claim that such scientific investigations will be free of ideological biases and thus result in objective or true generalizations. Instead, the claim of political science is that the examination of the rival hypotheses provided by different ideologies through the most adequate scientific methods available leads to progressively better descriptions and explanations of political reality.

Political philosophy

Scientific methods are of little help in overcoming partiality when we are analyzing idealizations, evaluations, and prescriptions, because such methods are intended to detect biased beliefs about reality rather than biased ideals about what is good in life. According to ancient philosophers like Socrates (470–399 BCE) and Plato (427–346 BCE), the best method for informing our political ideals is the dialectical method, and this method still has its defenders.[20]

Most simply, *the dialectical method* involves submitting one's political principles to the critical inspection of others. When the dialectical method is employed, the goal is not simply to win a debate against those having opposing views; instead, the goal is to attain better knowledge, even if this entails modifying one's initial position. Plato's *Republic* illustrates the application of the dialectical method to the question, "What is justice?" Conventional Athenian ideas, the Sophistic views of Thrasymachus, and Socrates' conception of justice are presented and subjected to critical examination by others. Despite Plato's standing as a great thinker, contemporary philosophers may regard his dialogue as an unsatisfactory attempt to discover unbiased principles of justice. Absent from his discussion are various contemporary conceptions of justice. And, although there is an appearance of critical analysis of the various positions presented by his interlocutors, Socrates' own views seem to be rather meekly accepted. Thus, employing the dialectical method in a contemporary attempt to resolve the issue of "What is justice?" might be a much more demanding enterprise than that presented by Plato.

What is involved in moving beyond holding ideologically derived ideals of justice (or of other big issues regarding communities, citizenship, structure, rulers, authority, and change) to choosing justice ideals on the basis of philosophical inquiry employing the dialectical method? According to David Ricci, this method involves engaging in "a great conversation":

> What this requires, in effect, is a great conversation, larger than any small conversations that members of particular social groups, such as professions, or learned disciplines, are accustomed to conducting among themselves. The goal of this large-scale dialogue is, in fact, for various groups to express diverse aesthetic, moral, and scientific opinions and somehow thrash them out on common grounds, in intelligible terms, so that a slowly moving consensus on truth and decency can be worked out and maintained over the generations, to serve as a framework of social cement binding members of the community to one another and enabling them to live good lives together. Withal, it is an intellectual enterprise intent on examining a great many facts by comparing them to canons of right and wrong, good and evil, sin and virtue, rights and obligations.[21]

Such a conversation would attempt to discover the public philosophy that we would choose to govern our politics generally. It might also seek to discover those public philosophies we would choose to govern each of our political communities. Because of the differences among political communities – for example, in their purposes and in the values of their citizens – we should expect consensus on a general public philosophy to be minimal, and we should expect different communities to choose somewhat different public philosophies.[22] Because public philosophies must address many questions, it would be most manageable to have a series of conversations, each aimed at answering for various types of communities a particular perennial question, such as who should rule or how should social goods be distributed? To conduct such conversations, we can imagine representatives of various ideological perspectives assembling with the intention of somehow achieving consensual answers to a perennial question. We would expect proponents of each ideology to express clearly their principles on the issue. We would expect proponents to explain, as fully as possible, the philosophical bases for their principles and to show their implications for the overall structure and governance of community life. We would expect proponents to explain how these principles would solve (or reduce) various social, economic, and political problems, achieve (or approach) various political goals, and reflect various moral concerns. Each of these arguments would, of course, be subjected to the critical scrutiny of persons from all other ideological perspectives gathered at the assembly, leading to extensive discussions about the adequacy of each argument.

As Ricci suggests, such conversations would be *great* in terms of the importance of the issues being discussed and in terms of the diversity of views under consideration. They would also be of great – perhaps interminable – duration. Given the magnitude of the perennial political questions, we should not expect any oral discussions to quickly resolve such questions and produce consensus. Indeed, while oral discussions can be valuable, it is important to recognize that the great conversation is also a metaphor for the kind of analyses that characterize contemporary political philosophy. To conduct such conversations or to engage in the dialectical method, people need not actually assemble in one place or present their arguments orally. Indeed, because of the complexity of this task, precision is surely enhanced by writing down one's arguments in a manner that clarifies ambiguous terms and lines of argumentation, and that allows one's audience ample opportunities to reflect upon and analyze these arguments. In short, the great conversation occurs through books and articles where people present and defend their ideas, where others respond to perceived shortcomings, and where authors then rework their claims.[23]

To this point, our discussion of the analytical framework presented in figure 1 has focused on how political science and political philosophy can be used to address the perennial issues. We have thus far ignored the concentric circles associated with each of these issues. It is now time to turn our attention to these circles, which are intended to convey what we can hope to achieve by engaging in theoretical reflections. As already suggested, our first objective – depicted by the innermost circles – is to attain as much consensus as possible on the perennial issues – if not a universal and eternal consensus, at least one within the kinds of pluralist political communities that we presently have. Our second objective – depicted by the next innermost rings – is to identify the perennial issues that continue to be the source of disagreement within pluralist societies and that are frequently discussed and debated in the ordinary politics of such societies. The third objective – depicted by the next to outermost rings – is to identify those ideas that *radicals* introduce in order to bring about what they regard as fundamental improvements to pluralist politics. Our fourth and final objective – depicted by the outermost rings – is to identify those ideas held by *extremists* – ideas that normally seem misguided, at least to those committed to pluralist politics. The remainder of this chapter discusses these objectives.

Searching for an Underlying Consensus Within Pluralism

Our framework directs attention to the centrality of pluralism in contemporary political thought. Like politics, pluralism is a contested term in political theory. For many political scientists, pluralism is understood as a largely empirical theory of politics, based upon questionable understandings of American politics. During the behavioral revolution in political science during the middle of the twentieth century, this orthodox pluralism emerged as a (perhaps *the*) mainstream political theory. According to orthodox pluralists, American politics could be described as embracing such normative goals as tolerating a wide variety of interests, organizing various interests into political groups, and having a wide dispersion of power among competing groups. Most importantly, orthodox pluralists claimed American political communities had institutions and processes that enabled the realization of these goals, and thus approached achieving democracy and justice.[24] However, for several decades this orthodox theory has been criticized as a narrow conception of pluralism because it focused too strongly on the distribution of power and ignored other normative concerns of political communities composed of citizens having diverse interests and moral and political principles. It was also criticized for failing to see that pluralism was an evolving political theory, having historical roots that preceded the ideas of orthodox pluralism and having the capacity to absorb many modifications in both its normative concepts and empirical generalizations.[25] A variety of neo-pluralisms emerged that focused on troubling deficiencies in current political arrangements, such things as the lack of adequate opportunities for many citizens to convert their concerns into political issues, the inadequate representation of various groups at crucial stages of decision-making, and the systemic biases and inequalities in treatment of people in the policies and programs of pluralist regimes.[26] The varieties of pluralism that have emerged indicate that it is a theory of politics that is in constant evolution. Updating pluralism as a normative, empirical, evaluative, and prescriptive theory is one concern of this book.

As conceived here and by other neo-pluralists, pluralism (broadly understood) is a public philosophy having wide allegiance among academics, governmental leaders, political participants, and ordinary citizens – especially in the United States and other Western nations, but increasingly among non-Westerners as well. Although political communities incorporating the ideas of pluralist philosophy have many shortcomings, pluralism is thought to provide a modicum of peace and prosperity. Although pluralism contains no recipe for producing heaven on earth, pluralism is thought to avoid the most hellish politics that too often afflicts human life. While some political communities are not governed by pluralist ideas and ideals, they are thought to lack the social, economic, and cultural conditions needed for pluralist politics. Pluralism is a great, but only partially realized, political achievement of many modern societies.

Figure 1 shows that at the core of each category is a limited set of ideas that are essential to pluralist public philosophy; these comprise a basic underlying consensus among all people committed to pluralism. Scholars have often insisted on the existence of a certain consensus within the United States and other pluralist societies. Historians like Richard Hofstadter and Louis Hartz have claimed that there is a broad consensus that has guided American political development, involving an emphasis on individualism, equal opportunity, democratic rights, and other such liberal values.[27] Drawing on public opinion polls, political scientists like Herbert McClosky and John Zaller have claimed that there is widespread support in the United States for the basic institutions of capitalism and democracy.[28] Cross-national surveys, such as those conducted by Ronald Inglehart and his associates, also indicate that most citizens in many developed countries support political reform over maintenance of the status quo or revolutionary change, as well as other orientations that seem consistent with a pluralist public philosophy.[29] Political philosophers have also suggested the existence of a consensus within pluralism. For example, George Klosko claims that pluralist societies have achieved consensus on procedural justice – the principles and procedures for resolving disputes fairly.[30]

Perhaps the most important theoretical contribution in this regard is that of John Rawls (1921–2002), who proposed in *Political Liberalism* that the primary characteristic of a pluralist society is that it is made up of people who hold a wide variety of "comprehensive moral doctrines." Precisely because various religions, ideologies, ethics, and lifestyles are embraced within pluralist societies, their citizens require a *political* agreement to tolerate each other and abide by minimal widely held principles enabling their peaceful coexistence in a stable political community. Pluralist societies require an "overlapping political consensus" that will curtail endless battles for political dominance. This consensus must include a basic agreement that victors in battles for power cannot impose their particular morality on others; whoever governs must respect the moral autonomy and basic rights of all citizens. Rawls does not specify the contents of this consensus in detail, but he does claim:

> Its breadth goes beyond political principles instituting democratic procedures to include principles covering the basic structure as a whole; hence its principles also establish certain substantive rights such as liberty of conscience and freedom of thought, as well as fair equal opportunity and principles covering certain essential needs.[31]

This book seeks to discern whether a broader consensus within pluralism is possible than that yet specified by these historians, political scientists, and philosophers. By considering the answers that various ideologies give to the perennial political issues, we can discover areas of agreement, as well as disagreement, among them. As suggested above, it seems unlikely that there will be universal consensus among all ideologies on the perennial questions, but there will be some agreement on each perennial question among those ideologies that are *friends of pluralism*. Bernard Crick included conservatives, liberals, and (democratic) socialists among such friends, but – as we will see – these ideologies have various strands and newer ideological perspectives have come into prominence.[32] By considering how a wide range of ideological perspectives answer the perennial issues of politics, we will argue that there is much more consensus within pluralism than is often acknowledged.

Just as we do not expect to find any universal consensus, any agreements that we find among the friends of pluralism should not be regarded as eternal or absolute. Some analysts doubt that there will ever be significant changes in a pluralist consensus endorsing capitalism and democracy, and thus proclaim that debate about the big issues of politics is over, that we are at "the end of ideology," or "the end of history."[33] Pluralists, however, do not insist on an enduring underlying consensus, and instead suppose that the pluralist consensus will evolve over time, as new problems, goals, and understandings come to the attention of people in pluralist societies. Pluralism does not require that all people within pluralist societies agree on this consensus; dissent is honored within the pluralist consensus, and this means that only *most* people in existing pluralist communities have allegiance to some core ideas.[34] While chapters 5–15 will conclude by specifying the underlying consensus among pluralists in each issue area, these conclusions are asserted with the tentativeness that is a central feature of pluralism.

To anticipate a key conclusion from chapter 8 dealing with epistemological questions, we will conclude that pluralists reject the idea of certainty concerning political knowledge and instead seek socially constructed tentative understandings.[35] Pluralists agree that moral and political knowledge arises from social agreements that find their way into constitutions, laws, and international agreements and treaties. While these agreements may be imperfect expressions of "truth" (of what is absolutely best for political societies), they provide a tentative consensus on right and wrong conduct that can only be revised by parties to the agreements in light of new conditions and understandings. This assumption is so critical that it defines the essential common outlook of the friends of pluralism. It is important to recognize at the onset, however, that tentativeness is not the same thing as skepticism. Pluralists are confident that pluralist societies and philosophies are better than non-pluralist ones.[36] Pluralists reject extreme skepticism because such skepticism leads to embracing the idea that politics is nothing but the application of pure power. Skeptics become cynics when they see domestic politics as having no basis in shared understandings and hence as purely a struggle for power among various interests. Skeptics also become cynics when they see global politics as nothing but a struggle for power among various countries, each in pursuit of its national interests. If those countries with superior power are unrestrained by the negotiated understandings that are the bases of international law and organizations, their applications of power will be interpreted as oppressive and dangerous by others in the global community.

Ideas Beyond the Underlying Consensus of Pluralism

Pluralists are committed to the abstract ideas within the pluralist underlying consensus. Pluralists are also committed to many political values – especially security, freedom, morality, solidarity, prosperity, equality, and democracy – and they recognize obligations to exhibit such political virtues as tolerance, civility, and reciprocity. However, such commitments and obligations are insufficient to enable people to take principled stands on most contemporary issues. To be able to locate one's political identity within pluralism, take stands on current issues, and move from being a passive pluralist spectator to an engaged and passionate activist, people need a more specific public philosophy than pluralism; they need a perspective such as a political ideology that provides an initial place to stand without being so rigid as to preclude understanding alternative ideas or negotiating differences. While the general and abstract public philosophy of pluralism affirms many political values, specific outlooks bring to the pluralist process clearer priorities among values. While pluralism contains very general principles for structuring political life and for reconciling and ordering competing values, specific outlooks contain more substantive principles. In short, we need widespread allegiance to pluralism, a public philosophy writ large. But people can also have – and indeed can be encouraged to embrace – secondary commitments to more specific public philosophies that are "friends of pluralism."

Figure 1, in the concentric circles just beyond the core underlying consensus, depicts the competing beliefs, values, and principles of the friends of pluralism. During most of the twentieth century, conservatism, liberalism, and (democratic) socialism have been regarded as the leading friends of pluralism, but perhaps distinct strands within these ideologies (such as social conservatism and neoliberalism) and new ideologies (such as environmentalism and feminism) have emerged in recent years, and such outlooks may also agree with many tenets of the underlying consensus of pluralism. Nevertheless, such friends of pluralism bring different principles to ordinary issues that must be resolved through pluralist politics. Great political conversations should attempt to identify the competing principles that are contested in ordinary pluralist politics and they should assess their merit. Achieving agreement on the best (and worst) of these competing principles is made difficult because their proponents often represent competing interests, have alternative underlying philosophical assumptions, and seek different values – or give the core values of pluralism different priorities and interpretations.

Consider the basic issue of property rights. Those on the right side of the pluralist spectrum believe that property rights should be relatively free from governmental control and taxation, while those on the left side of that spectrum believe that property rights should often be regulated and taxed for broader public purposes. Obviously, those with the most property will normally assert their extensive property rights and those with the least property will normally assert the need for limiting property rights. However, suppose that we could somehow get participants in the great conversation to overlook their interests and resolve their differences in an unbiased fashion.

At this point, participants might invoke different philosophical assumptions in defense of their contrasting principles. For example, defenders of property rights might argue that such rights arise because society is a collection of specific individuals, that social production reflects the contributions of specific individuals, that different individuals make unequal contributions, that these contributions reflect resources (such as labor, inventiveness, and energy) owned by individuals, and that individual owners of these resources therefore have a right to the fruits of their contributions. But critics of extensive property rights might argue that society is a collectivity that surpasses any specific individuals comprising it, that social production reflects contributions from many resources (such as the public infrastructure) within the broader community, that these contributions reflect social and historical investments as well as individual labor, that such investments are publicly owned, and that the public thus has claims on property that has been socially produced. Moreover, even if some people contributed less to social production than others, their lesser contributions often arise from unjustified natural and social inequalities that require compensation. The merits of such different assumptions need to be discussed in order to have any hope of resolving the disagreement among the friends of pluralism over property rights. Thus, great conversations must identify the competing principles that are at stake on the ordinary issues that arise in pluralist politics, they must identify the different underlying assumptions behind these principles, and they must try to assess the merits of these assumptions.

Even if agreement on the underlying assumptions were achieved, however, agreement on the best principles may still be allusive. Some people will say that the underlying assumptions that are the basis of political principles are less important than the implications or consequences of adopting one set of principles over its competitors. For example, defenders of property rights might say that (even if their underlying assumptions are inadequate), property rights must be affirmed because they are essential to the overall prosperity of the political community. But those who would limit property rights might say that (even if their philosophical assumptions are inadequate) property rights must be limited to provide equal treatment to all people within the community. Pluralists would admit that many values – including achieving prosperity and equal treatment – should be furthered in the resolution of ordinary issues in pluralist politics. To guide conversations on the consequences of adopting alternative principles to resolve such issues, it would help if there were agreement on which values – such as democracy, security, morality, freedom, social solidarity, as well as prosperity and equality – are most important. But pluralists recognize at least three problems that thwart consensus in determining what principles have the most valued impacts.

First, the many values that may be affected by our choice of principles are at least partially conflicting, and there exists no common standard for choosing among competing values. For example, the values of overall prosperity and equality among individuals are conflicting and incommensurable.[37] My overall judgment may be that overall prosperity (for the community as a whole) is more important than equality, but your judgment may be that equality is more important than aggregate prosperity, and though we might both be able to mount impressive arguments for our judgments, there is no single objective criterion for determining whose arguments are best.[38] Thus, we are unable objectively to rank-order competing values.

Second, the very meanings of fundamental pluralist values are contestable. Ronald Dworkin's comments about the difficulty of agreeing on the meaning of equality illustrate this problem:

We might say that individuals have a right to equal concern and respect in the design and administration of the political institutions that govern them. This is a highly abstract right. Someone might argue, for example, that it is satisfied by political arrangements that provide equal opportunity for office and position on the basis of merit. Someone else might argue, to the contrary, that it is satisfied only by a system that guarantees absolute equality of income and status, without regard to merit.[39]

Similarly, prosperity can be conceived as private prosperity (the total income that all individuals in a community have available to spend on their personal needs and wants) and as public prosperity (the quantity and quality of public goods and services that are available to everyone in the community). Extensive property rights might enhance equal opportunity and private prosperity. Restrictive property rights might enhance equal conditions and public prosperity. If there are different conceptions of equality and prosperity (as well as other pluralist values), which conception ought to be used in evaluating alternative principles?

The third problem that can thwart consensus on the consequences of alternative principles is the difficulty of reaching firm conclusions about relationships between principles and pursued values. Contemporary liberals and contemporary conservatives may both agree on the importance of freedom and they might even agree that freedom occurs when individuals have real choices about how to live their lives, but they could still disagree about the role of governmental programs in achieving or undermining such individual choices. In contemporary pluralist politics, liberals often support more governmental programs extending schooling and health benefits to all citizens, because they say that people need more education and better health to pursue their chosen life plans. Conservatives often support fewer governmental programs in these areas because they stress the importance of individuals choosing among (public and private) schools and among various health providers, rather than having single public providers of such programs. The complexity of the link between extensive or limited government programs and individual choice complicates judgments about whether liberal or conservative principles best further individual freedom.

Despite the difficulties that confront pluralists who seek to evaluate the competing principles that various ideologies bring to politics, conversations on these matters can introduce much greater understanding of those who think differently and thus can enable the friends of pluralism to reconcile their differences with as much mutual toleration, civility, and reciprocity as possible. Reconciliation among the friends of pluralism is facilitated when people avoid dogmatism, absolutism, and rigidity in their ideological beliefs. To avoid dogmatism, pluralists must be willing to subject their beliefs about social, economic, and political reality to empirical testing and falsification and to rational critiques concerning limitations of and alternatives to these beliefs. To avoid absolutism, pluralists must recognize the existence and worth of many values, some of which conflict with one another. Because efforts to achieve certain values usually come at some cost of other things that are valued, pluralists must often limit their pursuit of specific values. To avoid rigidity, pluralists normally recognize that the principles that they hold sometimes conflict with other legitimate principles held by themselves or by others whom they respect. Principles are broad prescriptions about the best course of action that are based on beliefs and values. But the courses of action to which principles apply are always specific cases, and pluralists recognize that a particular principle may prescribe a course of action that leads to inadequate handling of particular cases. For example, those on the left of the pluralist spectrum normally hold progressive tax principles. They believe taxes that are borne most heavily by those with the most income and wealth are necessary to generate revenue for necessary public goods and are desirable because they produce a more equal distribution of social goods within society. But in a particular community, a particular progressive tax proposal may threaten the overall economic prosperity of the community, generate rancorous social conflict, encourage dishonest behavior (cheating) by citizens, be cumbersome to administer, and involve other negative features that outweigh being true to principles. Principles are important for providing initial predispositions and stances on specific issues, but pluralists listen attentively to concerns that undermine the application of their principles in particular cases, and they do not become slaves to rigid principles.

However, proponents of some ideologies hold their ideas with greater certainty or rigidity than is typical among most pluralists. The ideas of radical pluralists are depicted as falling within the third ring of political ideas answering the perennial political issues in figure 1. Radical pluralists do not reject the underlying consensus of pluralism, but they have firm beliefs about fundamental deficiencies within pluralism. They identify what they regard as the root causes of problems within pluralism that prevent pluralist politics from achieving important social goals. Radical pluralists do not want to subvert pluralist politics, but they want to transform pluralism in ways that they regard as superior to existing pluralist politics. Some radical pluralists are strong egalitarians who believe that the pluralist norm of equal treatment involves much more equal distributions of social goods than currently exists in pluralist societies. Some radical pluralists are strong libertarians who believe that pluralist norms of liberty are too often compromised by the regulations of pluralist governments. Some radical pluralists are strong moralists who, while recognizing that the state should remain neutral among competing comprehensive moral doctrines, nevertheless insist that the governmental silence on moral issues promotes moral decay on matters that concern people who have a variety of moral outlooks. In addition to identifying areas of consensus and conflict among pluralist ideologies, our conclusions in chapters 5–15 will indicate those ideas of radical pluralists that might transform and improve pluralism. Because pluralism is an evolving public philosophy, radical ideas should not be automatically discredited as being dysfunctional for pluralism.

In the outermost layer of circles in figure 1 are the ideas of perspectives that reject and may endanger pluralism. Right-wing extremists normally seek to replace pluralist democracy with authoritarian regimes that would be oppressive to at least some groups in a pluralist society. Left-wing extremists are normally so cynical about pluralism that they invite people to drop allegiance to pluralist principles and to give up the battle to improve pluralism through sustained political action, or they are so utopian that they have little chance of being persuasive to most people or of being successful if ever attempted. Dealing with the ideas of extremists provides many challenges for pluralists.

Conclusions

Political theory addresses the perennial political and philosophical questions seeking to discover better understandings about how political communities are and should be structured. Absolute truth about these questions has eluded political scientists and philosophers,[40] but some consensus about these questions – at least at a highly abstract level – may be possible among those committed to pluralist politics. However, pluralists will disagree about more specific answers to political issues. Conservatism, liberalism, socialism, and other pluralist ideologies may all help people who need more specific guidance to political issues than the broad consensus within pluralism can provide. But pluralism needs to be defended against those who would undermine the useful political ideals that it upholds. As an alternative to public philosophies that seek to legitimate monistic regimes that are structured and governed according to a fixed authoritarian public philosophy, pluralist theory and philosophy assume that no one has a monopoly on truth in the realms of morality and politics.

In the realm of morality, pluralism can be contrasted with perfectionism – an alternative ethical approach that claims humans should live a good or ethical life, that contains substantive versions of a good life, and that holds society and the state responsible for helping people achieve that good life.[41] Ethical pluralists agree that humans should live an ethical life, but question the existence of an objectively specified good life and right ethical choices. They thus deny that the state should use its coercive power to enforce a particular moral doctrine. Ethical pluralists recognize that different ethical traditions are evident throughout the world and within subcultures of most countries; these different ethical traditions provide alternative assessments of practical moral questions and often imply alternative modes of reasoning to defend their judgments.

In the realm of politics, pluralism is defined in contrast to monism – an alternative political approach that insists that there is one best way of structuring the inter-relationships among people, so that people can live good and virtuous lives and treat other people justly. Political pluralists question the existence of an objectively specified good society and just government. They recognize that various groups of people have different political beliefs and interests and thus disagree on how to govern their interpersonal (collective or social) lives. Pluralists maintain that such disagreements are best resolved peacefully through democratic processes. All citizens – often in association with others who share their interests and ideals – should have full opportunity to bring concerns or issues to the attention of the public and political officials. If these issues are viewed (and often specified by prior fundamental agreements embodied in constitutions) as being within the purview of government, they are deliberated employing public reasons in full, open, and fair hearings. Disagreements lead to negotiations, bargaining, and compromises, and are resolved by democratic voting processes having procedures that have been subject to prior (often constitutional) agreements. Pluralism thus involves achieving negotiated understandings among people with (initially) different ideas and interests.

Pluralism is thus a normative theory of politics, but the norms that it most clearly affirms are highly abstract and often process-oriented or procedural. The substantive ends or end-state ideals of pluralism are not well defined, because the ends sought by pluralist politics depend on the values that participants bring to pluralist processes and on the goals that they ultimately affirm through their deliberations. Democracy provides fair procedures for deliberation and decision-making and is thus the primary procedural value of pluralism, though the friends of pluralism have different conceptions of the requirements of democracy. Justice is the primary substantive goal of pluralists, but the friends of pluralism give different degrees of emphasis to various principles of justice that are reflected in the laws, policies, and programs of pluralist governments.

PART I

PARTICIPANTS IN OUR POLITICAL CONVERSATIONS

The National Museum of American Art contains a painting entitled "Ideals are Like Stars," by Joseph Cornell. A decade ago, Mary Chapin Carpenter recorded a song with a similar title, "Ideas are Like Stars." In either case, stars can serve as apt metaphors for envisioning the universe of political ideas and ideals.

Just as there is an infinite number of stars, so the political universe contains countless political ideas, many dealing with widely cherished political ideals. Perhaps astronomers treat the discovery of even the dimmest star as important, adding to our map of the physical universe. Perhaps political theorists should treat every political conception, generalization, or other abstract idea about political life as important to a complete map of the universe of political theory. But like stars, some ideas within political theory shine more brightly than others. And just as particular stars become intelligible to most observers only when they are seen as part of larger configurations with other stars into constellations and galaxies, so do particular political ideas become intelligible when they are seen in relationship to other ideas within political theory.

Some analysts insist that each person regards the universe of political ideas differently and organizes these ideas into a coherent perspective in his or her own unique way.[1] This may be the case, but to achieve some sort of coherence to the universe of political ideas, political theorists (at least for the past few centuries) have seen the value of organizing political ideas into ideal types of coherent systems, especially into ideologies, which they name and regard as characterizing the political beliefs and values not just of particular individuals but of larger groupings of people. Political ideologies emphasize larger ideas answering perennial political issues, much like constellations emphasize the larger and most visible stars. Political ideologies emphasize the logical interrelationships of certain ideas, in a manner parallel to the way in which constellations emphasize how stars are arranged into recognizable patterns. Every constellation is merely a human construction; the "big dipper" only looks like a ladle from the vantage point of humans on earth. In a similar manner, every ideology is merely a human construction; each is a particular set of ideas that many theorists and analysts, from their historical and social perspectives, have come to regard as interrelated and important.[2] Just as constellations help us make sense of the stars in the universe, political ideologies help us make sense of some of the major political ideas that various groups of people have embraced.

Regarding political ideas as stars suggests two important lessons. First, the recognition that constellations and ideologies are both human constructions enables us to see that there is nothing *essential* about political ideologies. Accordingly, there is no need for a political thinker to ask: which ideology best reflects how I see the world? Indeed, pursuing that question is probably dysfunctional as it encourages us to seek ideological identities that have been constructed by powerful political interests to serve their interests. Perhaps developing your own political ideas or choosing carefully among ideas that you encounter and then organizing these ideas as you see fit are the tasks that you must undertake to be an effective political thinker. Seeking to name your ideology may encourage us to regard our political ideas as somehow fixed. Political theorizing is not about finding reasons for clinging to the political ideas that we have come to believe without much critical reflection, but rather is about considering alternative answers to the perennial issues, analyzing these alternatives, and deciding which ideas we should embrace because we can communicate and defend these ideas in the company of others. This book will not be successful if, upon its conclusion, you are satisfied to proclaim yourself a Marxist, a contemporary conservative, or an adherent to any other ideology that you will encounter here. Instead, this book will be successful only if, upon its conclusion, you have some tentative understanding of which answers to the perennial questions seem most worthy of your allegiance, knowing that your allegiance to these ideas may well change as the world changes and as you acquire deeper political understandings.

But the second lesson from seeing political ideas as stars is that there is indeed value in organizing political ideas into various constellations, into ideologies. During the past two centuries, political life has been deeply affected by political ideologies. We cannot understand how people come together to form political organizations and movements if we do not understand ideologies. We cannot understand how political parties and political regimes govern, unless we grasp the ideological orientations that give a certain direction to their policies and actions. Ideologies enhance political understanding – as long as we do not get trapped into seeing the political universe from a single ideological perspective but instead value seeing politics from a wide variety of ideological perspectives. Having proponents of a wide range of ideologies participate in conversations addressing the perennial political issues seems an excellent way to understand and evaluate the universe of political ideas.

The ideologies introduced in chapters 2 and 3 as participants in the great conversation are easily defended.[3] Most treatments of the major ideologies of the nineteenth century focus on classical liberalism, traditional conservatism, anarchism, and Marxism. Classical liberalism was the first ideology, and conservatives developed from traditional ideas a coherent alternative political outlook. Classical liberals and traditional conservatives provided the most prominent governing ideologies as modernizing nations struggled with the forces of industrialization and democratization that defined the major political issues of Western civilization during that century. But both classical liberalism and traditional conservatism seemed hopelessly reactionary to those further to the left. During the second half of the nineteenth century, anarchism and Marxism emerged as protest ideologies that criticized the new political economy that was developing in the most advanced industrial societies of the period. Classical liberalism, traditional conservatism, anarchism, and Marxism are introduced in chapter 2 (and deeper understandings of these ideologies will come into view as their answers to the perennial questions are considered in chapters 5–15).

During the twentieth century, two totalitarian ideologies – fascism (and its especially evil twin Nazism) and communism – appeared, whose ideas must be considered in any survey of the universe of political ideas. While there were some important differences between German Nazism and Italian Fascism – indeed, there are such differences also among fascists in Italy, Spain, Romania, and elsewhere – these ideologies had many similarities that enable them to be studied as a related perspective that is very different from previous ideologies. While the communists who came to power in the Soviet Union, China, and elsewhere may have cited Marx to justify their authoritarian and often totalitarian rule, they departed from Marx in developing their strategies for how to rebel against capitalism and then went beyond Marx in developing ideas on how to govern communist societies.[4] In response to the new problems that fascism, Nazism, and communism posed for democratic societies, and to a wider variety of changing circumstances, the governing ideologies of liberalism and conservatism were modified to such a degree that it is useful to regard contemporary liberalism and contemporary conservatives as distinct from their nineteenth-century precursors. The need for these distinctions is evident when we consider only a couple of evolutions in these ideological traditions. While limited government was central to classical liberalism, contemporary liberalism came to embrace strong government. While skepticism about the virtues of capitalism was central to traditional conservatism, contemporary conservatives now give two cheers – if not three – for capitalism.[5] Introductions to fascism, communism, contemporary liberalism, and contemporary conservatives are provided in chapter 3 (while deeper understandings of these perspectives will again be attained in subsequent chapters).

As we survey the contemporary universe of political ideologies and try to peer into the future, a wide variety of political perspectives comes into sight. Democratic socialism, feminism, environmentalism, and Islamic fundamentalism are just a few of the many other perspectives having ideas that must be understood and included in political conversations. Because full consideration cannot be given to all such perspectives, we adopt the device of organizing such alternative perspectives into four categories: the radical right, the radical left, the extreme right, and the extreme left. This categorization is sufficiently unconventional that it deserves a broader justification, but we will defer that discussion until the beginning of chapter 4. We introduce there a variety of perspectives that can be regarded as *quasi-ideologies* rather than as full-blown ideologies. If ideologies are well-recognized constellations of inter-related political ideas, quasi-ideologies are constellations of ideas whose complete configurations remain somewhat obscure, but which may well come into clearer focus during the twenty-first century.

Chapter 2

Voices from the Major Ideologies of the Nineteenth Century

Although there are many important political ideas that predate modernity, we can limit our analysis to those that became incorporated into ideologies, the comprehensive political perspectives that began to emerge at the end of the eighteenth century.[1] Prior to the age of ideology, Thomas Hobbes (1588–1679), John Locke (1632–1704), Adam Smith (1723–90), and other worldly philosophers of that period developed many new ideas for organizing society, enhancing economic production, and ensuring good government. Many of these ideas found their way into the first modern ideology, classical liberalism. In this chapter, classical liberalism and its major critics during the nineteenth century are introduced.

Classical Liberalism: Building Democratic Capitalism

Classical liberalism provides a basis for many contemporary liberal ideas, but to enter into the worldview of this ideology, it is important to recognize that its ideas are distinct from those that are normally identified with liberalism today. Although the term "liberalism" was first coined in 1810 by the *Liberales* in the Spanish legislature, most of the ideas of classical liberalism were developed decades and even a century or two before then. Classical liberals were products of the Enlightenment, who sought to develop a "science of politics," and this project is often thought to have begun with Hobbes and Locke. The philosophers of the Enlightenment thought that political ideas could no longer be based on traditional and religious beliefs. Traditional beliefs, religious dogma, and metaphysical speculation had contributed to unnecessary restrictions on individual freedom, to archaic economic practices, and to the justification of political absolutism. Inspired by Francis Bacon (1561–1626) and René Descartes (1596–1650), Enlightenment philosophers in general and classical liberals in particular hoped to eliminate these "idols of the mind." They sought to base political, social, and economic thought on rational deductions from minimal assumptions about the natural world.

Classical liberals did not deny that God existed or had created the universe, but they believed that He no longer controlled it. Natural rather than divine laws were thought to govern the world and human behavior. Such behavior could be explained in terms of the pursuit of pleasure and the avoidance of pain. Society could be described by the social and economic interactions of individuals and these were largely governed by the natural laws of the marketplace. Humans who are free to pursue their own happiness would naturally enter into mutually beneficial economic and political exchanges. Social progress would occur as a result of natural human interaction, because such free exchanges make each person better off. For classical liberals, such natural laws led to endorsement of capitalism, an economic system of open competition in a free market. Classical liberals also endorsed governments led by democratically elected representatives, because electoral accountability encourages rulers to provide for the happiness of citizens in exchange for their votes. Thus, classical liberals became advocates of democratic capitalism.

Liberal ideas were developed during the seventeenth through nineteenth centuries in response to a variety of problems confronting Europe as it abandoned its feudal and medieval past and embraced modernity. Particularly eager for a more progressive, scientific, and industrial society were economic entrepreneurs and traders, proponents of more political rights and freedoms, and the intellectuals of the Enlightenment. Several features of European society during the Middle Ages impeded the development of modern societies, which emphasized commercial activity, political liberty, and scientific progress.

First was the problem of a static social structure. During the Middle Ages, people had little chance of being able to move upwards from the rank in society into which they were born. Most commoners were serfs (peasants or agricultural laborers) who lacked basic freedom and political representation and who were bound by law and custom to the land they worked and the lord they served. Some commoners, who became known as the bourgeoisie, engaged in commerce in the emerging medieval towns. More privileged than serfs and the new bourgeoisie were the clergy and nobility. Even as late as the eighteenth century in France, the nobility were exempt from most taxes and had almost exclusive rights to hold governmental and religious offices. Such privileges were greatly resented by commoners. And the restrictions on serfs deprived the emerging capitalist industrial order of mobile labor. Liberals wanted greater social mobility that would give individuals opportunities to move beyond the class into which they were born.

A second problem concerned the restrictions on economic activity that were imposed by the Catholic Church and many European governments during the late Middle Ages. Rules controlling economic exchanges and the production of goods included prohibitions against *usury* (charging interest on lent money), the establishment of "just prices" (or permitting local religious officials to set the price of goods at a level that limited profits), and prohibitions against competing with monopolies supported by monarchs. Classical liberals joined commercial and craft interests in attacking such barricades to freedom in the marketplace, and they eventually celebrated the ideal of free competition.

A third problem that worried those of liberal temperament were the scope and power of government. Initially, the decentralized nature of feudal society hindered economic development, and the merchant class welcomed the emergence of such nation-states as England, France, and Spain, and the centralization of power in the monarchies of these nations. Such centralized governments provided traders with greater security from robbers as they transported goods to distant markets, and they facilitated economic transactions by replacing complex and diverse local rules and regulations with common laws, measurements, and currency. But as the authority of these monarchies increased during the sixteenth and seventeenth centuries, so too did the problem of political absolutism. Kings gathered for themselves the powers that were previously dispersed among the landed nobility and church leaders, placed themselves above the law, practiced censorship and inquisition into private affairs, gave patronage to favored industries, and imposed taxes and oppressive regulations on the rising middle class. Louis XIV of France may have declared "*L'état c'est moi*" (I am the state), but his absolute rule was regarded as rapacious government by leading philosophers of the Enlightenment. Liberals sought to curb such political tyranny and the abuses of concentrated political power.

A fourth problem was that of religious orientation and conformity. The Middle Ages were characterized by the domination of the Catholic Church, which encouraged people to be oriented toward spiritual salvation. Practicing Christian virtue and saving one's soul were considered much more important than such worldly concerns as attaining scientific knowledge, producing economic goods, or acquiring wealth. During the sixteenth century, the Protestant Reformation challenged the domination of the Catholic Church by declaring that religious belief was a private affair between the individual and God and that the clergy had no special authority to interpret and declare God's will. The reformation also helped instill the *Protestant ethic*.[2] This ethic suggested that, in addition to enhancing one's private enjoyment, economic production and material acquisition were virtues that identified those with spiritual excellence and contributed to the greater glory of God. Protestantism helped reorient people toward secular life, but it did not solve the problem of religious conformity. Both because of religious conviction and because of a desire to strengthen support for their regimes, the monarchies of the era often required subjects to conform to particular religious doctrines, and heretics were suppressed. This resulted in a series of civil wars (sometimes between Protestants and Catholics and sometimes amongst Protestants) throughout Europe. Persons of liberal temperament, like England's John Locke, called for religious toleration and a wall of *separation between church and state*.[3] They argued that social stability required the church to concern itself solely with spiritual salvation and the state to concern itself solely with people's secular interests, such as their liberty and their property.

The religious wars exemplified a more fundamental problem: social and political disorder. Nascent liberals believed that life, liberty, and property were fundamental individual rights, but they understood that these rights were insecure. For example, Hobbes emphasized that each individual's security was threatened by the actions of other individuals. To overcome social disorder (or anarchy) and to deter individuals from infringing each other's rights (for example, by stealing their property), a sovereign government was needed to punish those who invaded the rights of others. However, subsequent liberals like Thomas Paine (1737–1807) argued that such governments were themselves great threats to individual rights. To secure individual liberty, societies should constrain arbitrary and rapacious government.[4] Believing that the British had succeeded in restraining government, John Stuart Mill (1806–73) argued that public opinion was also a great threat to individual liberty. For Mill, individual liberty could only be secure when government protected and fostered individualism from the views of the majority.[5] Given such diverse views, it can be said that the greatest problem for classical liberals was how to construct a government that would secure individual liberty without, at the same time, encroaching on individual rights.

This discussion of the problems that concerned classical liberals suggests that they have been – and remain – primarily concerned with enhancing individual liberty, promoting capitalism, establishing constitutional democracies, and developing a scientific understanding of social life.

Hobbes provided a typical liberal conception of liberty when he declared, "[A] free-man is he that in those things, which by his strength and wit he is able to do, is not hindered to doe what he has a will to."[6] In general, the classical liberal conception of liberty emphasized three things. First, the value of freedom is that it enables each individual to choose and pursue his own ends. Classical liberals assumed that each person wants happiness – that he wants to maximize pleasure and minimize pain – but they recognized that each person has a different conception of happiness because everyone experiences pleasure and pain in different ways. Only the individual can define his own good, and liberty involves the right to pursue a self-defined conception of happiness. Second, freedom is given to each person at birth; it is a natural right of everyone. Third, while everyone is born with an equal right to pursue his own happiness, such liberty can and should be constrained. Most generally, liberals understood that complete natural liberty results in a state of disorder. To be part of society, people must give up some liberty. The classical liberal conception of how far liberty should extend was best articulated by John Stuart Mill: "The only freedom that deserves the name is that of pursuing our own good in our own way, so long as we do not attempt to deprive others of theirs or impede their efforts to obtain it."[7] Such a formulation is intended to give individuals an absolute right to think and worship as they wish and to act on their own inclinations within a private sphere. But absolute freedom ends when individuals encounter other people. People are not free to harm others or infringe on their rights. People are not free to renege on their agreements and contracts with others. The purpose of law is to specify precisely the limits on individual freedom, and government exists to enact and enforce laws regulating individual actions in the public sphere.

Developing a capitalist economy is a second liberal goal, and the most celebrated expression of this goal is Adam Smith's *Wealth of Nations*, published in 1776. Capitalism was seen as enhancing such liberties as the freedom to make contracts with other people, the freedom to acquire, exchange, and maintain private property, the freedom to sell one's labor for the highest wage one can secure, and the freedom to invest one's capital in those areas having the greatest potential for profit. In short, classical liberals sought the liberty to trade, work, invest, produce, and consume in a free market. They wanted a society where people have the capacities and motivation to produce material abundance. They value economic freedoms, in part, because they permitted each individual to increase personal economic prosperity, enabling society as a whole to become wealthier.

Developing constitutional democracies is a third liberal goal, and this goal is related to enhancing individual freedom and economic progress. As replacements for monarchies and aristocracies (that often regarded various freedoms as threats to their traditional privileges), democratic governments would protect individual rights and economic freedoms in order to obtain the consent of the governed. In seeking democratic governments, classical liberals did not endorse the highly participatory democracies practiced in ancient Athens or advocated by radicals such as Jean-Jacques Rousseau (1712–78). Instead, liberals sought the kind of democratic governments that would protect the rights of even those citizens who do not actively participate in governmental affairs. To the extent that citizens can minimize their political involvement, they are free to pursue their economic interests as producers and consumers in a capitalist society. Rather than citizen involvement, classical liberals regarded constitutions (that would establish periodic elections holding officials accountable to citizens; that would divide and thus limit the powers of various governmental officials; and that would provide restrictions on how officials behaved after elections) as the key device to prevent democratic governments from infringing on individual rights and intervening too extensively in the capitalist economy.

Classical liberals sought to develop a science of politics that would be a rational basis for a political economy that would provide extensive individual freedoms, facilitate a capitalist economy, and would govern as a constitutional democracy. This rational and scientific basis will become apparent when we discuss the philosophical assumptions of classical liberalism in chapters 5–8. The comprehensiveness of this science will become apparent when we discuss the logically interrelated political principles that classical liberalism is able to provide in response to the perennial political issues in chapters 9–15.

Classical liberalism was the first systematic ideology and it remains a powerful voice today. In chapter 4, we will see how recent libertarians have drawn upon and indeed radicalized, classical liberalism. In that chapter, we will also encounter "neoliberalism," or "globalism," a contemporary version of democratic capitalism that may well be the dominant ideology among elites throughout the world today. And in chapter 3 we will see that contemporary liberalism – while developing philosophical assumptions and political principles that make it a distinct ideology – has also drawn upon many ideas of its precursor in ways that make it part of the broad liberal tradition that has dominated political thought in the modern era.

Traditional Conservatism: Defending the Old Social Order

At its inception, the ideas of classical liberalism were often resisted. The second American President, John Adams (1735–1826), rejected liberal ideology as "the science of Idiocy. And a very profound, abstruse, and mysterious science it is. . . . It is the bathos, the theory, the art, the skill of diving and sinking government. It was taught at the school of folly."[8]

Traditional conservatives argued that reason and science could not comprehend such matters as God, human spirituality, moral consciousness, and the intricate aspects of political communities. They believed that traditional understandings of ultimate reality, human nature, and society provided better guidance for governance than did the so-called scientific constructions of these matters provided by classical liberals. Traditional conservatives considered the liberal celebration of individualism to be misguided because it undermines traditional social units such as families, churches, guilds (associations of craftsmen), and local communities. The growth of capitalist economies at the expense of earlier feudal and mercantile economies encouraged individuals to take self-interested rather than public-regarding actions, and it encouraged innovation and competitiveness, both of which undermine social order. Strong political and religious authority – located in the monarchs, the landed aristocracy, and religious leaders – were necessary to guide society toward the public good. Most generally, the *traditions* and *conventions* of societies must be respected because they serve as more prudent guidelines for individual, social, and political conduct than do the scientific theories of classical liberals. Such traditional conservative ideas live on under the influence of more recent political philosophers like Michael Oakeshott (1901–90) and Russell Kirk (1918–94), but most contemporary conservatives endorse only a limited number of the ideas of their predecessors and have developed a distinct ideology – to be introduced in the next chapter.

Throughout world history, social order had been preserved and societies had often prospered by applying conservative ideas. For example, Confucianism, a moral philosophy with striking similarities to traditional conservatism, guided the Chinese Empire for more than 2000 years until its collapse in 1905.[9] Most Europeans between the Middle Ages and the late 1700s accepted the ideas of traditional conservatism, and these ideas served to legitimate the existing political regimes and the traditional social order of this period. Traditional understandings were challenged by such developments in the early modern period as the Renaissance, the Protestant Reformation, the scientific revolution, and the Enlightenment, and these developments evoked criticisms from those of conservative temperament. Nevertheless, these criticisms and impulses required a defining moment in order to emerge as a full-blown conservative ideology.

The French Revolution provided such a defining moment. In 1789 the absolutist state of King Louis XVI was overthrown, and a National Assembly issued its Declaration of the Rights of Man and of the Citizen. By 1791 a constitutional monarchy was established and citizen rights were extended to tax-paying property-holders. During 1792 and 1793, radical politicians abolished the monarchy and executed the King and Queen, giving birth to the French Republic. But this Republic was soon overthrown by an even more radical provisional regime that initiated the "Reign of Terror" to suppress enemies of the Revolution and to achieve a "Republic of Virtue," where popular education would mold ethical citizens. The most radical aspects of the French Revolution had run their course by 1795, when its leader, Robespierre, was executed.

These events in France and the threat that such revolutionary events would be repeated elsewhere in Europe were sufficient to give rise to traditional conservatism as a set of counter-revolutionary principles. Indeed, by 1790, the basic ideas of traditional conservatism were set forth in *Reflections on the Revolution in France* by the central figure in conservative thought, the English philosopher and statesman Edmund Burke (1729–97). For Burke, the Revolution revealed the dangerous consequences of basing politics on abstract rights, of guiding political reforms by Enlightenment rationality, and of rejecting established authority. One way of understanding traditional conservative ideas is by looking at Burke's criticisms of those liberal ideas that he thought had given impetus to the turmoil in France.

The rallying cry of the French Revolution, "*Liberté, Egalité, Fraternité,*" drew upon liberal thought by demanding such *abstract rights* as liberty, property, security, and resistance to oppression. While these might sound appealing, it is unclear what they signify in practice. Does everyone have unlimited liberty to do what they wish? Even if all citizens should have equal freedom from arbitrary arrest or equal freedom of speech, should political power be equally apportioned between the wise and the foolish or between the virtuous and the corrupt? Should economic wealth be equally distributed between the industrious and the lazy?

Burke argued that radical demands for such abstract rights as liberty and equality ignored the historical development of *real rights*, which were different in each country. Throughout Europe, local and national political communities had developed their own unique set of rights and obligations over a long period, and they often applied to specific groups. The imposition of abstract rights, Burke claimed, would undermine these real rights.

Like other traditional conservatives, Burke criticized the deployment of Enlightenment rationality as a guide for social and political reforms. Classical liberals believed that rational individuals could calculate those courses of action that maximized their happiness and that rational societies could discover those political reforms that best served most people in society. Traditional conservatives rejected such claims that untainted reason could serve as a guide for individual choices and for political changes. Burke thought humans have *prejudices* – emotions, habits, and attachments – that do not allow for the pure use of reason. His concept of prejudice does not mean that humans cannot use reason, but that habits and traditions must supplement liberal "rationality" when political decisions are made.

Just as humans are not calculating machines, neither is society simply a contraption to be easily altered, fixed or improved. For Burke and other traditional conservatives, societies are best understood as *organic* entities. It may be possible and necessary to improve society, but such improvements must be made slowly and carefully. The confidence with which the French revolutionaries introduced drastic interventions struck Burke as dangerous *hubris* that could have grave consequences for organic societies.

Traditional conservatives also deplored the liberal rejection of traditional authorities, especially in government and in the church. In his *Reflections on the Revolution in France*, Burke expressed his dismay over the composition of the National Assembly.

For the most part, its members were undistinguished, untalented, and without evident virtue. Most importantly, "of any practical experience in the state, not one man was to be found. The best were only men of theory."[10] For Burke, governing requires practical wisdom or *prudence*. Only men of experience *and* historical knowledge can exercise good political judgment. Prudence cannot be reduced to simple theories and mathematical formulas. Those who have acquired good judgment, wisdom, and virtue constitute a natural aristocracy. It is foolhardy to remove such men from office and entrust political authority to representatives of various interests within society or to liberal theoreticians who claim to know the best course of action on the basis of abstract principles and rights.

For traditional conservatives, it was also foolhardy to undermine religious authority or to believe, as liberals do, that religion is purely a private and personal matter. Burke, who was an ardent Anglican, viewed with horror the attacks on the Catholic Church during the French Revolution and defended established religions as essential social institutions.[11] The authority of a single religion supports the state by promoting social harmony, establishing a set of common religious practices, and reinforcing public and private morality. Traditional conservatives viewed demands for religious freedom and for a separation between church and state as dangerous steps toward social decay.[12]

Burke feared that liberal reason and support for abstract equality could lead to proposals to redistribute land. Traditional conservatives supported the practice of most land being in the hands of a few noble families and the church, in the belief that they were respectful caretakers. This unequal right to land, they argued, led to a commensurately greater obligation to preserve it for future community use. For conservatives, land was not simply a commodity, but had value far beyond any price established in the market. Under capitalism, it becomes a commodity to be bought and sold, often for the sole pursue of gaining future profits. Such speculation severed the sacred connection that traditional conservatives believed should exist between the land and its owners.

Traditional conservatives also rejected arguments for the redistribution of other forms of property and wealth because they believed that the natural inequalities in the abilities of people made acceptable economic inequalities. Inequality is made less painful, according to traditional conservatives, by the doctrine of *noblesse oblige*: elites must practice the art of charity out of a sense of compassion and obligation to help the less fortunate.

As the nineteenth century evolved, traditional conservatives gave only grudging support to the developing capitalist economies. They believed that capitalism would undermine the traditional fabric of society, produce relentless and distressing change, uproot individuals from the traditional and secure places they had previously enjoyed, produce undue poverty, and encourage elites to neglect their social responsibilities. Because, from the start, the captains of industry in capitalist economies rarely lived up to the notion of *noblesse oblige*, traditional conservative politicians occasionally used government to provide some goods for the poor and some services to the entire population. For example, the Conservative British Prime Minister, Benjamin Disraeli

(1804–81), revised the labor laws to recognize some rights for workers and supported legislation that attempted to provide public housing, public healthcare, and clean air and water. During his reign as the first Chancellor of the German Empire, Otto von Bismarck (1815–98), established accident insurance for workers, pension plans for the elderly, and healthcare programs for all. In both countries, this social legislation was designed to promote the public good *and* to defuse the appeal of radical social movements.

It might seem that the main goal of traditional conservatives was the protection of the status quo or even a return to the good old days of the Middle Ages. There is certainly nostalgia for the Middle Ages in much of the traditional conservative literature,[13] but the primary goal was to cultivate deep respect for tradition and convention. Traditions are understandings that are the product of the accumulated knowledge of previous generations. Conventions are habitual social practices that similarly provide social bonds and give life a predictable rhythm. During the seventeenth and eighteenth centuries, many traditions and conventions were threatened by scientific thought, by liberal innovations, and by radical aspirations. By restoring respect for traditions and conventions, conservatives sought to bestow on individuals and communities the wisdom of the ages and restrain the vexations that occur through the pursuit of every (sometime fleeting) scientific theory and radical belief.

Many goals of traditional conservatives can be expressed in ways that appeal not only to the social elite, but also to most members of society. First, they sought a well-ordered and peaceful community governed by laws and rules of conduct that are clear and reflect the current beliefs of most people in society. Governance should be "a specific and limited activity . . . enabling people to pursue the activities of their own choice with minimum frustration."[14] A principle duty of government should be to reduce friction and conflict among groups; rather than seeking to perfect society, governments should focus on reducing passions and minimizing conflict. Traditional conservatives believed that governments should avoid grand theories and utopian dreams and instead rely on established rituals, traditional practices, and common sense to provide for a stable and well-ordered political community.

A second goal of traditional conservatives is the preservation and development of a variety of voluntary organizations. Associations such as churches, community groups, charity organizations, and schools provide regular attachments among familiar people and provide individuals with shelter from the storms of human life. Voluntary associations remind people of their social life, shake them out of a narrow self-interested perspective, and provide opportunities for citizens to practice their social obligations and responsibilities in a supportive environment. Voluntary organizations also mediate the relationship between the national government and the individual, reducing the need for governmental intrusion into private life and lessening the power that governments might have over people.

Third, traditional conservatives want to cultivate and nourish individual character and excellence. They seek to develop citizens with social virtues and civic commitments. Traditional conservatives promote individual excellence not only because it will contribute to the betterment of society, but also because excellence is threatened by both capitalism and socialism. Capitalism threatens to reduce excellence to whatever the market will bear, and socialism threatens excellence by celebrating the average person.[15] High culture should not descend to the masses, but, rather, individuals with talent should ascend to the heights of culture.

Fourth, traditional conservatives encourage individuals to engage in activities that are non-instrumental. Michael Oakeshott argued that modern individuals too often limit their activities to those that provide rewards, such as honor and profit.[16] A conservative disposition is cultivated, and human happiness is expressed best in relationships and activities that are enjoyed for themselves, without concern for future benefits. Friendship is an obvious relationship to be enjoyed for its own sake. Leisure activities also may be enjoyed without concern for their success. In short, conservatives remind people that there is more to life than the great preoccupations of classical liberals: economic productivity and the accumulation of wealth.

In pursuing these goals, traditional conservatives reasserted the importance of social cooperation. They have argued that society is more important than the individual. They have reminded us that excessive individualism in politics, science, economics, and religion threatens a well-ordered and peaceful community. They seek to attach the individual in a concrete, rather than abstract, way to society and thus provide a *rooted* individualism whereby citizens have a sense of belonging to something bigger than themselves and something more important than their immediate self-interest.

During the nineteenth and twentieth centuries, traditional conservatives accepted some new developments in politics and economics. They accepted certain aspects of democratization, such as an increase in the number of elected officials and a wider franchise, but they never forgot the need for strong political authorities. They accepted certain aspects of capitalism, but they never celebrated capitalism (as did classical liberals), because they feared its morality and its disruption to society. Resisting the rapid social, economic, and political changes of the nineteenth and twentieth centuries, traditional conservatives sought to protect the world against this avalanche of change. When protection provided impossible, as was often the case, traditional conservatives fought to slow down the modernization of society.

The twentieth century produced immense changes that have greatly troubled traditional conservatives and have made their public philosophy seem outdated. Many of them have made their peace with such a world by cultivating a conservative temperament rather than championing a traditional public philosophy. Michael Oakeshott's description of this temperament reveals the distance between traditional conservatism and the other ideologies we will consider in this text:

> The man of conservative temperament believes that a known good is not lightly to be surrendered for an unknown better. He is not in love with what is dangerous and difficult; he is unadventurous; he has no impulse to sail unchartered seas; for him there is no magic in being lost, bewildered or shipwrecked. If he is forced to navigate the unknown, he sees virtue in heaving the lead every inch of the way. What others plausibly identify as timidity, he recognizes in himself as rational prudence; what others interpret as inactivity, he recognizes as a disposition to enjoy rather than to exploit. He is cautious, and he is disposed to indicate his assent or dissent, not in absolute, but in graduated

terms. He eyes the situation in terms of its propensity to disrupt the familiarity of the features of his world.[17]

Anarchism: Rebelling Against Authority

In addition to being attacked from the right by traditional conservatives, classical liberalism was attacked during the nineteenth century from the left by anarchists (and other more radical voices for the working class and the poor).[18] Although anarchists are often regarded today as unprincipled terrorists, adherents to anarchism have held principles that have attracted people – such as Henry David Thoreau (1817–62), Leo Tolstoy (1828–1910), and Mohandas Gandhi (1869–1948) – who have been deeply committed to justice, freedom, and nonviolence.

The main ideas of anarchism include the following. It is possible for individuals to live freely, unconstrained by man-made laws; only natural constraints should limit human freedom. Most existing institutions – especially governments, churches, schools, (patriarchal) families, factories, and the private property that is essential to a capitalist industrial system – repress human freedom. Such institutions corrupt the social and cooperative instincts within human nature and undermine harmonious natural societies. The old social order must be replaced by a new social order that is highly decentralized, voluntary, and communal. In such an order, the injustices that arise from traditional authority and the ownership of private property can be replaced by a new ethic of justice under which individuals treat each other with dignity and respect and attend to the needs of one another.

The term "anarchism" is derived from the original Greek word *anarchos* which means "without a ruler." Thus, the central idea of anarchism is that it is possible for humans to live together in social communities having neither rulers nor governing institutions. Emma Goldman (1869–1940) provides the following definition of anarchism: "Anarchism: The philosophy of a new social order based on liberty unrestricted by man-made law; the theory that all forms of government rest on violence and are therefore wrong and harmful, as well as unnecessary."[19]

Anarchism is not as systematic an ideology as classical liberalism (or Marxism). Indeed, anarchists have libertarian attitudes that resist dogma and systematic theory. Persons having quite different political outlooks have been regarded as important contributors to anarchist thought. Thus, there is a highly individualistic strand of anarchism, exemplified in the writings of Max Stirner (1806–56). But there is also a collectivist strand of anarchism, exemplified in the writings of Peter Kropotkin (1842–1921).[20] In this brief description of their common themes and ideas, such differences among anarchists are de-emphasized.

The term "anarchism" first appeared in modern political thought during the French Revolution to characterize, disparagingly, the Enragés, an unorganized but like-minded group of revolutionaries who urged the development of communes, rather than democratic governments, as the means of alleviating the suffering of the poor. At approximately the same time (in 1793), the first important anarchist treatise appeared: William Godwin's *Enquiry Concerning Political Justice*. But Godwin (1756–1836) did not call himself an anarchist; indeed, he seemed to see his ideas as simply a logical extension, or radicalization, of the ideas of classical liberalism. It was not until the 1840s that Pierre Proudhon (1809–65) recognized that the word *anarchos* implied a deep criticism of authority without, at the same time, advocating disorder, leading him proudly to embrace the term anarchism. For Proudhon, "Order is the genus: Government is the species"[21] – meaning that social order could be attained in more ways than by government authority. He suggested that governmental authority was perhaps the most ineffective and unjust means of attaining order. Nevertheless, most followers of Proudhon rejected the label of anarchists and preferred to call themselves *mutualists* – a term that implied that order could be attained not by governmental authority, but by the mutual cooperation of free individuals. It was not until the 1870s that the term "anarchism" was fully embraced by followers of Mikhail Bakunin (1814–76) who wished to distinguish themselves from Marxists. At the end of the nineteenth century, anarchists competed with Marxists for leadership in the revolutionary movements against liberalism and its institutions of capitalism and representative democracy. Although Marxist ideas were more influential than those of anarchists during the twentieth century, anarchism is nevertheless an important political ideology that adds distinctive ideas to political conversations.

Historically, anarchism has provided the ideological impulse behind prominent social movements. On the European continent at the end of the nineteenth century, anarchism was a significant force among the working class, as anarchists urged labor unions to go beyond the struggle for better wages and working conditions and to employ the *general strike* as a weapon for destroying capitalism and the state. In America at the beginning of the twentieth century, the Wobblies (the Industrial Workers of the World) adopted the principles of anarcho-syndicalists and played a vital role in organizing miners, loggers, and other unskilled workers.[22] In Russia, anarchists played a significant role in the mass uprisings that destroyed the Provisional Government in 1917 and resisted the statist regime established by the Bolsheviks. In Spain, anarchists were a major force in the Civil War of 1934–9, and succeeded in controlling much of eastern Spain for several years. In Italy and Germany, anarchists were adamant in their opposition to fascism and Nazism. During World War II, anarchists like Georges Bataille were involved in the French Resistance because they despised the Nazis' thick notion of the state, their cult of leadership and hierarchy, and their emaciated sense of citizen responsibility. During the 1960s and early 1970s, anarchist thought was prominent among student *new left* radicals in both the United States and France. Today, some protestors against globalization initiatives proudly proclaim their allegiance to anarchism. In general, whenever there is widespread discontent with capitalism and government and when cultural values stress the importance of unfettered individualism and freedom and a desire for more natural and voluntary associations than presently exist in a society, the principles of anarchism are attractive.

Anarchism can be seen as both an important radicalization of liberalism and a precursor of Marxism. Like classical liberals, anarchists look to nature and the individual to develop political principles that they believe will lead to human progress. But , find nature to be more social and benevolent than do classical liberals, and they believe that individual fulfillment derives less from the freedom to secure one's own interests than from the opportunity to pursue one's own understanding of the public good. Such philosophical foundations lead anarchists to believe that no government at all is better than the limited government endorsed by liberals, that self-rule is better than that of democratically elected representatives, and that an egalitarian ethic is better than the inequalities of wealth and power that occur under capitalism. Like Marxists, anarchists call for the abolition of liberal, capitalist societies. And, as we shall see next, Marx believed that the decentralized, voluntary, and non-coercive social order sought by anarchists could and would actually be achieved after a transitional period of socialism.

Marxism: Pursuing a Classless Society

During the nineteenth century, the most acerbic critic of capitalism and representative democracy was Karl Marx (1818–83), who developed a two-pronged attacked on classical liberalism. First, he argued that liberalism's science of politics that aimed to provide universal knowledge about the ideal political economy was a mistaken preoccupation, since the human condition was not directly affected to any significant degree by such ideals. Instead, he claimed that the human condition was determined by economic forces and the social and class relations that flowed out of economic developments. Second, he regarded classical liberalism as propaganda, as a mask for the interests of industrial capitalists, rather than as a true set of principles for effective government.

Among his followers, Marx is regarded as the founder of a new science of political economy, not as an advocate of an ideology. This science sought to analyze the workings and deficiencies of capitalist economies and the fraudulent nature of liberal democracies. Yet Marx did not see his intellectual task as claiming that capitalism should be rejected because of its shortcomings. Instead, his intellectual task was to provide a scientific theory of revolution. He sought to uncover the laws of history and economics, which would show how economic changes produced predictable changes in human behavior, society, and politics. In short, he sought to *predict*, rather than *prescribe*, the demise of democratic capitalism and the eventual emergence of a communist society. While Marx denied that he was developing an ideology containing principles for how to govern societies, his ideas, along with those of his collaborator Friedrich Engels (1820–95), provide a coherent set of political beliefs and values that can be characterized as the ideology of Marxism.

For many people, Marxism embodies foolish ideas that were embraced by communist regimes in the Soviet Union, "Red China," Vietnam, Cuba, and elsewhere during the Cold War. In this view, Marxism was responsible for the international hostilities between "the East and the West" and the lack of freedom for people who lived behind "the Iron Curtain." It is often thought that Marxism justifies despotic government and contains failed economic doctrines that undermine productivity and human initiative in order to enforce a drab equality among people. Perhaps there is some truth to such characterizations of Marxism, but a less biased assessment of this ideology requires a deeper understanding of its many concepts and generalizations. At minimum, Marxism cannot be correctly understood or assessed by equating it with the philosophy behind the communist revolutions and regimes of the twentieth century. Marxism and communism are related but distinct ideologies, as will become clearer when communism is introduced in the next chapter.

Marx and Marxists generally held the following. Human beings are naturally laboring beings, and all human activity is ultimately economic activity. All societies are divided into classes on the basis of economic activity: the ruling classes own the means of production (such as land, factories, and equipment), and the subordinate classes provide the labor of production. This division causes all human beings, but especially working men and women, to be alienated from their labor and from their essential human nature as creative workers. This is especially true in capitalist society, in which there are only two significant classes: a small group of capitalists who own all the means of production, and the large mass of the proletariat, who own only their own labor. The laws of history and political economy reveal that capitalism is doomed and will be overthrown by the proletariat. This revolution will pave the way to a classless, communist society. Private property will be abolished, and the political state (which upholds the interests of the ruling class) will cease to be necessary and will wither away. In this future society, all human beings will achieve their potential as creative laborers, and none will be alienated from their labor, from themselves, or from each other.

The *Manifesto of the Communist Party*, the most celebrated writing of Marx and Engels, which was published in 1848, was an attempt to unite the working classes throughout Europe and inspire them to engage in coordinated revolutionary activity at a time when revolutions were sweeping the continent. These revolutions, however, were uprisings of liberals, essentially targeted against the monarchies and autocratic regimes of the period, and not against the capitalist regimes that Marx and Engels despised. During the 1850s, Marx began extensive studies of capitalism and the problem of how to develop class-consciousness among working men and women, sketching out a grand theoretical system that placed capitalism into broad historical and economic perspectives. His notebooks written during this time are called the *Grundrisse*, from which he published the first volume of *Das Kapital* in 1867. Two subsequent volumes were published posthumously, under Engel's editorship, in 1885 and 1894.

Marx was active in working-class politics. In 1864, he participated in founding the International Workingmen's Association, and remained active in it into the 1870s. He often competed with anarchists such as Mikhael Bakunin for doctrinal leadership in the Association (later known as the First International). By 1872, his influence in the International had waned, as many former allies deserted him.[23]

Despite his limited influence during his lifetime, Marx bequeathed to opponents of classical liberalism a number of economic, sociological, political, and philosophical doctrines. Even before his death, intellectuals sympathetic to the revolutionary overthrow of capitalism began to interpret and, to some extent, alter Marx's theories. These activities showed that they regarded his theories as an authoritative beginning point. Engels was perhaps the most enthusiastic interpreter of Marx's frequently complex and chaotic writings; his interpretations are now described as *orthodox Marxism*. The central idea of this perspective is that capitalism is plagued with contradictions that doom it to self-destruction. Orthodox Marxists believe that a revolution against capitalism is inevitable when "conditions are ripe" (when economic productive capacities have matured to the point where they can produce widespread affluence but where the unequal distribution of economic goods leaves most people poor and unable to purchase the goods that capitalism produces). They believe that an egalitarian socialist order will eventually appear after the revolution. Orthodox Marxists remained influential in many communist and socialist parties in Europe throughout the twentieth century, but other critics of capitalism who believed they were true Marxists gave Marx's writings other interpretations.[24]

Marx and Engels stressed many problems with capitalism and thereby provided a body of criticism that has remained useful even for those who do not subscribe to all aspects of Marx's "science" of history. They describe how capitalism produced economic and social misery in the working class, particularly among women and children. At the advent of capitalism, adult men often worked long hours doing unsatisfying, repetitive work in unsafe and dreary working conditions for subsistence wages, and the plight of women and children was often worse. Thousands died of diseases and ailments that were contracted in the steamy, dusty, dark, and filthy conditions of the factories, or from injuries caused by machines and unsafe working conditions. Meanwhile, successful industrialists often lived in opulent luxury. Those who prospered under capitalism often attributed their success to their high moral character, their great energy and stamina, and their superior intelligence. Marx rejected such explanations, calling them an ideology that the bourgeoisie used to justify its oppressive role.

Marx also stressed the ethical shortcomings of capitalism. In 1843, the young Marx wrote "On the Jewish Question," in which he argued that capitalism emphasized the self-interested and materialist aspects of human motivation at the expense of more public-regarding and spiritual concerns. He recognized that capitalism encouraged competition rather than cooperation among people. More generally, capitalism enhanced the alienation of human beings, causing individuals to be estranged from their fellow workers, the products they produced, and the process of production. Rather than making work an enjoyable, creative process, capitalism led to people seeing work as a drudgery that they had to endure to obtain wages necessary for their survival.

Marx and Engels were highly concerned with the disunity of the working class, which weakened their political power. According to Marx, most people were objectively members of the working class because they did not own the means of production, but they were unaware – or lacked subjective consciousness – that they were oppressed, that other members of the working class shared their oppression, and that becoming class-conscious was an essential precondition to a successful revolution against capitalism. Many factors contributed to this lack of working-class consciousness. The great poverty of the workers resulted in their preoccupation with satisfying immediate, material needs like food and shelter, leaving them with scant time and energy to understand their role as a revolutionary force in history. The prevailing liberal ideology also diminished class-consciousness, because it prompted the working class to view society not in class terms, but as an aggregation of individuals, to believe that individuals had equal opportunities for advancement, and to hope that the capitalist system produced economic progress benefiting everyone, including the working class. Religion, "the opiate of the masses," also helped to curtail class-consciousness. Not only did religious differences divide the working class, but they also turned attention away from worldly oppression to the hope of heavenly salvation. Because the working class was unable to overcome these factors and become conscious of its common oppression under capitalism, it failed to acquire a realistic understanding of how to escape this oppression. Most socialist alternatives to capitalism were, according to Marx and Engels, utopian. They involved the creation of small-scale socialist communities – such as the industrial cooperatives created by Robert Owen (1771–1858) in New Lanark (Scotland) or New Harmony (Indiana) or the phalanxes envisioned by Charles Fourier (1772–1837), which provided the basis for such social experiments as Brook Farm, the utopian community established in Massachusetts. While such utopian communities might have some romantic appeal to those members of the working class who were aware of their own oppression under capitalism, they took their attention away from understanding their historical role as a revolutionary force.

For Marx, the historical role of the working class was not to break itself into little self-sufficient communities within a larger capitalist system. Instead, it was to bring about a universal revolution that would transform a capitalist society into a transitional socialist one. In such a society, human beings would overcome alienating, oppressive conditions and start to live more authentic, satisfying lives as creative laborers and be much more productive than in the past. In such a society, the technological innovations initiated under capitalism would come under state ownership and control and become even more productive. In time, a highly affluent society – one capable of satisfying the economic needs of everyone – would be attained. This, in turn, would lead to the transformation of human nature, as men and women would become communal, public, and social in their basic motivations. When such human transformations and economic affluence had been achieved, a utopian communist society would emerge, which would be classless, as productive property would be publicly owned and managed and no class of people would be able to use its control of such property to exploit others. In such a society, the state would be abolished as the coercive and oppressive instrument of the property-owning classes, and true anarchism would be achieved.

Conclusions

The nineteenth century saw the development of four important ideological perspectives that not only affected political life in that century but have continued to have lingering impacts today. Each of these ideologies has seen the partial incorporation of some of their ideas into contemporary politics and newer ideological perspectives. But each contains important and unique ideas that still resonate. Each deserves to be heard during conversations on the perennial political issues.

The principles of classical liberalism have brought many social, economic, and political benefits to those countries – especially in North America and Europe – where they been applied. The opportunity for social mobility has replaced societies based on fixed social status. Religious intolerance and religious wars have receded. Absolutist governments have given way to constitutional democracies. Political liberties – such as freedom of the press and freedom of speech – are widely permitted. Capitalism has greatly increased material wealth. And individuals enjoy an extensive private sphere in which to think, act, and live according to their own wishes.

But classical liberalism has not been without its detractors. Perhaps the philosophical assumptions of liberalism are inadequate. Is the material world our only world? Are the pursuit of pleasure and avoidance of pain the most fundamental human motivations, or is there something nobler in the human spirit? Are societies nothing but the interactions of individuals, or do they exist prior to individuals, imposing social roles and obligations on everyone? Do people really have extensive individual rights? When liberal assumptions about these questions are rejected, numerous criticisms of liberal principles emerge. Perhaps governments should do more than secure individual rights; perhaps they should regulate morality and the economy. Perhaps the inequalities of income and wealth that are produced in a free market are unfair to those who fail in the marketplace for reasons beyond their personal control. Perhaps limited and divided government diminishes the capacity of political authority to achieve the public good. Perhaps representative democracy is unable to provide strong national leadership or ample opportunities for citizen participation in government. And perhaps liberal principles have excused citizens from taking an active role in public life and exercising more social responsibilities. While classical liberals can become ideologues who are blind to the limitations of their philosophical assumptions and political principles, most liberals have engaged in continuous reflection on and discussion of their ideas, and they have developed a variety of liberalisms to accommodate their evolving political principles.[25]

Traditional conservatism has declined as a potent ideology in the twentieth century. This may be because few people today are nostalgic for the elitism, ignorance, poverty, and other deprivations that characterized life in earlier times. Perhaps traditional conservatism has few supporters because the life that its adherents find familiar and enjoyable is only available to the privileged few, while most people encounter various social, economic, and political problems that they are eager to reform. Perhaps the traditional conservative fear of the unknown betrays a pessimism about the possibility of achieving a better future that most people find unwarranted. Perhaps the values of individual freedom, more equality, and more democracy are too appealing for most people to be attracted to an older perspective that seems at best reluctant to embrace these values. Even though most traditional conservatives have come to seek the preservation of the present rather than a return to the past, any political program they come up with may simply be too unreceptive to the progress that people have come to expect and demand. Certain ideas of traditional conservatives – like the importance of human excellence, the vital role of voluntary associations, and the need for social cooperation – retain wide appeal and have thus been incorporated into other political ideologies. But most contemporary conservatives find too many embarrassments in the ideas of their precursors, and have therefore developed their own unique perspectives on the perennial political questions, as we shall learn in subsequent chapters.

Anarchism continues to have many attractions. It recognizes how traditional societies, capitalist economies, and even democratic governments can dominate and coerce individuals, and it urges us to question conventional authorities, institutions, and ideas. It prompts us to expand our vision and conceive of new social orders, where individuals have extensive freedom, yet use that freedom to pursue just relationships with one another. It describes a simple and natural life that better supports the moral development of humanity and the ecological survival of the world than does our current obsession with material possessions and economic development.

Despite these appeals, anarchism has not attracted as many followers and has not had as broad an historical impact as the other ideologies we are examining. Perhaps anarchists depend too heavily on the benevolence of people, failing to have a realistic conception of the self-interested aspect of human nature. Perhaps anarchists ignore various positive benefits that governments can provide for members of society. Perhaps the destruction of existing institutions, especially by means of violence, demands a more convincing alternative society than anarchists provide.

At the beginning of the twenty-first century, Marxism seems to have more appeal to academics interested in analyzing the shortcomings of capitalist society than for political activists interested in creating an ideal society. Marxism does provide useful concepts, explanations, and criticisms of societies dominated by democratic capitalism, but Marx's systematic analysis of economics and history seems to imply that we should simply wait for the material order of things to unfold, as it inevitably will, bringing capitalism to an end and generating an ideal communist society. While some enthusiasts for Marxist goals attempt to interpret or revise Marxism to allow for deliberate political action to achieve communism, their ideas have lost much of their appeal.

The collapse of the communist regimes of Eastern Europe and the former Soviet Union and the development of more market economies in such countries as China and Cuba have led to a general discrediting not only of communism, but also of Marxism, which served as the ideological basis of these regimes for much of the twentieth century. However, Marx would likely have been very critical of communist attempts to bring about revolution in these countries, before his science would have considered it historically possible. He (and his followers) might argue that the "crude communism" practiced in the twentieth century had to be abandoned and that such countries as Russia and China must fully experience democratic capitalism before they can hope for the achievement of true communism.

However we may interpret Marxism's practical political failure at the hands of communism, Marxism does nevertheless raise many theoretical questions. Is it true that labor and material processes of production are the essence of human beings? Or is this materialist supposition suspect? Are spiritual and intellectual phenomena only the epiphenomena of material forces, or do they have their own ontological importance? Is it truly possible to understand the forces of history in the way that Marx claims? If so, why has the revolutionary consciousness of the proletariat not developed in ways that he predicted? Does Marx's projection of a future communist society not become just one more utopia that is essentially a "castle in the air," as Jonathan Swift might have called it?

Despite these troubling questions, Marxism clearly offers insights that are still useful. His analysis of the ways in which the ruling classes use ideology and religion to suppress dissent and to mollify their subjects, his insight that class conflict is a perennial aspect of politics, and his examination of human exploitation and alienation under capitalism may all be aspects of his ideology that endure in an era where competition in the global marketplace imposes ever greater imperatives on people to devote their energies to satisfying economic desires and ensuring the profits of others.

Chapter 3

Prominent Totalitarian and Pluralist Voices of the Twentieth Century

The twentieth century somehow survived the development and predominant role of two major totalitarian ideologies: communism and fascism (and its especially evil relative, Nazism). Totalitarianism involves the claim that governmental leaders – such as Lenin, Stalin, Mao, Mussolini, and Hitler – should be given total control over all aspects of society (including the economy, religion, the arts, and even families) in order to achieve great transformations in social and human life.[1] Drawing upon many Marxist ideas, yet departing significantly from orthodox Marxism, communists fomented revolutionary movements in many developing nations, came to power in Russia in 1917, generated a larger Union of Soviet Socialist Republics (the USSR, or Soviet Union) during the 1920s, and subsequently governed throughout Eastern Europe and much of Asia until the "Iron Curtain" began to be lifted in 1989. Fascists first came to power in Italy in 1922 and Hitler was appointed Chancellor of Germany in 1933, securing the dominance of the Nazi Party in that country; only the victories of Allied forces at the end of World War II in 1945 dismantled these regimes.

The demise of these totalitarian regimes is normally regarded as a victory for ideologies that are friends of pluralism, especially contemporary liberalism and contemporary conservatism. Other ideologies that include commitments to pluralism and democracy have also played roles in the defeat of totalitarianism and the spread of democracy, but liberals and conservatives have been particularly prominent in the governance of those pluralist democracies that have opposed and often replaced totalitarian regimes.

The waning of totalitarianism and the growth of pluralism have resulted in a vast increase in the number of democratic nations, where citizens have basic political rights and the ability to control governmental officials through competitive and free elections. Prior to 1900, only 6 (of 43) countries met criteria that enabled them to be characterized as democratic.[2] But by 2006, the number of democracies had increased significantly (much faster than the number of independent countries throughout the world). By one count, 89 of 192 countries (46 percent) could be regarded as fully democratic by 2006 and another 29 percent are counted as partially democratic.[3] Within these democracies, many parties have competed for political power and most have done so by appealing to electorates using the principles of contemporary liberalism and contemporary conservatism.[4] Acknowledging that they must win democratic elections in order to govern according to their political principles, contemporary liberals and conservatives (along with radical pluralists) have a shared commitment to constitutional government and representative democracy that supersedes their disagreements on more immediate issues. Whenever pluralist democracy is threatened by non-democratic enemies (such as the Nazis during World War II, the communists during the Cold War, or Islamic fundamentalists during the current "war on terrorism"), liberals and conservatives have been able to set aside their differences and agree to defend democracy and pluralism – even if they disagree on the best means of doing so.

Communism: Fighting Imperialism in Developing Societies

Communism can be understood as a distinct ideology that sought many of Marx's goals but rejected the idea of deferring revolution until the conditions that Marx thought necessary were ripe. When the Bolshevik Party, under the leadership of Vladimir Ilyich Lenin (1870–1924), seized power during the Russian Revolution of 1917, communism took on a new meaning. Previously, communism referred to a vague future ideal: a freer, equal, and cooperative society that could replace liberal regimes after the Marxist revolution or after anarchists had demolished existing governments. But Lenin declared himself a Marxist and initiated the process of transforming Marxism from a protest ideology into a governing one. In the Soviet Union (and later in Eastern Europe, China, Cuba, and several other developing nations), the Communist Party ruled, drawing extensively on Marxist-Leninist ideology (or, in other countries, on revisions to Marxist-Leninism). Such revisions were introduced in Yugoslavia by Josip Broz Tito (1892–1980), in China by Mao Zedong (1893–1976), in Cuba by Fidel Castro (1926–), and in Vietnam by Ho Chi Minh (1890–1969). The major modification to Marxist thought introduced by these leaders was that communism could be pursued in underdeveloped, or weakly industrialized, societies. Despite Marx's assertions that capitalism had to be strongly developed in a society before a revolution could occur, and that ideal communism could thrive only in affluent societies having the industrial capacities to satisfy everyone's material needs, quite a few communist parties acquired governing power in underdeveloped societies during the twentieth century.

Between World War II and the collapse of the Soviet Union in 1991, the debate between communism and democratic capitalism structured much of international politics. Recent world history and the current conditions of many countries cannot be understood without having some grasp on the ideas that were central to communism, such as the following. Worldwide imperialism constitutes a higher stage of capitalism than Marx had foreseen, and this development requires that certain modifications are necessary in his predictions about the processes that will bring about a communist society. Instead of revolutions occurring automatically in mature industrialized societies, they must be initiated by a *vanguard* of intellectuals and activists in nascent industrial societies and in developing nations that suffer most under imperialism. Nations that experience successful revolutions must temporarily be ruled by this vanguard – organized as a Communist Party – that will act on behalf of the proletariat (and peasants) and whose duty it is to pave the way for a future ideal communist society. In order to achieve economic affluence and to eliminate human alienation – which are required for ideal communism – party leaders must plan economic investment, production, and distribution, nationalize private property, and prevent the dissemination of counter-revolutionary (liberal and conservative) ideas. While the rule of communist parties may involve some temporary sacrifices by the general population, communist ideology provides reassurance that these sacrifices are worthwhile, because they are necessary for the future achievement of a stateless, classless, and affluent society.

While communism is a direct descendant of Marxism, two major differences stand out. First, (orthodox) Marxists are less politically active than communists. While Marxists do not seek to foment revolutions, because they believe capitalism will inevitably fall when conditions are ripe, communists accept the necessity of human initiative to bring about revolutions. Second, Marxism is essentially a protest ideology, while communism is often a governing ideology. Marxists are primarily concerned with criticizing capitalist societies, and their principles about socialist and communist societies are not well developed, because Marx and his immediate followers never had to govern or justify their governing principles. In contrast, when communists came to power, they had to transform Marxism into an ideology that legitimated their rule. Given these differences, communism can be regarded as a kind of applied Marxism.

Lenin most fully developed a communist ideology out of the writings and thought of Marx. He wrote *What Is to Be Done?* in 1902, became the leader of the Bolshevik Party in Russia in 1903, and founded the communist Soviet State after the Russian Revolution in 1917, guiding it through its formative years. Communist ideology has also been shaped by other twentieth-century Marxists, such as Rosa Luxemburg (1879–1919), Leon Trotsky (1879–1940), Antonio Gramsci (1891–1937), Ernesto (Che) Guevara (1928–67), and the leaders of various parties and regimes calling themselves communists.

Such communists revised Marx's theory of the revolution against capitalism. They observed that capitalism had become more adaptable than Marx had predicted. According to Marx, there is a fundamental contradiction within capitalism that will eventually result in its demise. Capitalist forms of production (factories, new technologies, workers who specialized in particular tasks, etc.) create more material goods than the workers who produce them need in order physically to survive. These extra goods are *surplus value*, which, in capitalist societies, is not retained by the laborers who produce it but rather by the (capitalist) owners of the means of production. This surplus value allows for *capital accumulation*, investment, economic efficiency, and the production of an increasing abundance of consumer goods, but this process is accompanied by the enlargement and impoverishment of the working class. Because most workers are paid only a subsistence wage and cannot afford the goods that capitalism produces, economic stagnation and the revolutionary overthrow of the capitalist system is, according to Marx, inevitable. By the end of the nineteenth century, however, the massive economic dislocations that Marx predicted had not occurred. In 1902, an English economist, John Atkinson Hobson (1858–1940), wrote a book, *Imperialism: A Study*, which suggested the failure of Marx's theory. According to Hobson, the limited purchasing power of most citizens made it rational for capitalists to restrict production for domestic markets and to limit domestic investment. Thus, to continue to accumulate wealth, capitalists would have to sell their goods in foreign markets and discover profitable investment opportunities in less developed nations. In short, the life of capitalism could be extended by *imperialism*, which is the practice by more advanced capitalist societies of establishing economic domination over less developed nations. To ensure ready markets for their products and to facilitate investment, the imperialist nations could either acquire these countries directly, making them their colonies, or they could put great economic and military pressure on the formally independent governments of these nations to ensure their subservience.

In 1913, Rosa Luxemburg, a Polish revolutionary theorist, wrote *The Accumulation of Capital*, which further explained how imperialism extended the life of capitalism. She proposed that capitalism could no longer be regarded as a closed system within particular nations; capitalism had become a worldwide phenomenon. Capitalists no longer depended on the surplus value attained from their workers to fuel capital accumulation. In worldwide capitalism, surplus value is attained from sales and profitable investments in nascent capitalist (or developing) societies. According to Luxemburg, mature capitalist societies would thrive as long as their workers could be appeased by benefits that capitalist societies attained by exploiting developing nations.

A few years later, in 1917, Lenin wrote *Imperialism: The Highest Stage of Capitalism*, in which he agreed with and extended Luxemburg's analysis. According to Lenin, capitalism had taken on a new character. The capitalist system that Marx had analyzed was *industrial capitalism*, in which large corporations increasingly developed into oligopolies and monopolies, as market competition led either to bankruptcies or mergers. The capital to finance the mergers and the investments of these corporations came from the surplus value that each corporation extracted from its workers. Lenin, however, discovered a new form of capitalism, which he called *finance capitalism*. In this system, financiers and bankers supplied capital to corporations, making such industrial capitalists increasingly dependent on finance capitalists, until the banks actually gained control of industry. This new form of capitalism concentrated great power in the hands of a small group of financiers, most of whom were not associated directly with the processes of production.

Internationally, the concentration of financial wealth in a small number of banks in the most mature capitalist nations resulted in these few imperial powers dominating less developed nations. By exporting capital to developing nations, by investing in large operations to extract mineral and other natural resources from them, by developing profitable collaborations with the indigenous "national bourgeoisie," and by employ-ing the poor (at minimal wages), the imperial nations gained economic and political control over the developing nations. Lenin called this new phenomenon "imperialism or the domination of finance capital," and he considered it the "highest stage of capi-talism." During Lenin's time, liberal democracies often engaged in such imperialism. British and American oil companies, for example, became active in the Middle East, and the Dutch rubber companies built huge plantations in Southeast Asia.[5]

Lenin and other communists recognized that colonial people often responded to imperialism with various kinds of nationalism. They treated these nationalist move-ments as allies of communism and sought to mobilize colonial people to take part in communist revolutions. If such revolutions were successful and Western capitalists were to lose their colonies, they would be forced to turn back to exploiting their own proletariat, which would rekindle the crises and produce the revolutions in the indus-trialized nations that Marx had predicted.

However, prior to such revolutions in the undeveloped world, instead of becoming more impoverished, as Marx had predicted, workers in advanced capitalist societies achieved notable improvements in their own standards of living and working condi-tions. The surplus value achieved by capitalists through the exploitation of the workers and natural resources of the developing nations meant that they had less need to exploit their own workers back home. To defuse the revolutionary consciousness of the proletariat in advanced industrial societies, capitalists could share their profits from the colonies with their workers and permit the development of trade unions at home. Trade unionism undermined revolutionary consciousness because it encouraged workers to be preoccupied with attaining better wages and benefits and improving their working conditions. Accordingly, Lenin regarded trade unionism as essentially a capitalist tactic of throwing a bone to the proletariat, since, under capitalism, the proletariat would never receive a fair share of the proceeds from industrial produc-tion, and humans in general would continue to be alienated beings. Imperialism and trade unionism were merely ingenious means by which the bourgeois capitalists could realize their aim of domination over the proletariat.

Such changes in capitalism prompted communists to revise Marx's theory of class-consciousness. While Marx believed that the objective conditions of capitalism would result in the maturing of the revolutionary consciousness of the proletariat, Lenin believed that workers by themselves lack the ability to develop a proper revolutionary consciousness. In mature capitalist societies, the benefits of trade unionism and imperialism resulted in the proletariat being "bought off" or co-opted. In pre-capitalist societies, peasants outnumbered industrial workers, and they lacked the experiences with capitalist exploitation that would engender any revolutionary consciousness. Lenin thus stressed that the masses of people without productive pro-perty would require leaders – the Communist Party – to guide and shape the revolu-tion. Communism clearly distinguishes itself from Marxism by proclaiming the possibility that party leaders can act on their own initiative as an elite vanguard on behalf of the proletariat, fomenting a revolution and guiding history toward com-munist goals.

Communists also expanded on Marxist ideas about the first stage following the revolution – which both Marxists and communists characterized as the *dictatorship of the proletariat*, though this term meant different things for them. For Marx, the dictatorship of the proletariat would be a rather democratic process. In his theory, the proletariat would constitute a significant majority within society, and a united proletariat would use democratic means to inflict its will on the bourgeoisie. But for communist theoreticians, leaders of the Communist Party, acting on behalf of the proletariat, would take over the apparatus of the state and use its instruments of coercion against the capitalists to prevent a counter-revolution. In the Soviet Union, this led to the Communist Party taking complete control of all state institutions, the media, all economic planning, and most industries. All privately held land, factories, and other resources for producing economic goods were confiscated and socialized; their ownership and control were transferred to the state. According to communist doctrine, these measures would cause economic classes gradually to disappear and the second stage of communism to emerge. Eventually, production and distribution of goods would be transferred from the party-led state to the community as a whole, where equal citizens would administer economic matters. In this way, the state would "wither away."

Joseph Stalin (1879–1953), who was the de facto dictator of the Soviet Union after Lenin's death, saw as a central problem for the communist revolution the need to transform the underdeveloped society that he ruled into an affluent industrial society with citizens who were trained to be productive laborers. Marxists had anticipated no such problem, because Marx predicted that revolutions would occur in advanced industrial societies with both a technological base to sustain an affluent society and a skilled (though alienated and impoverished) proletariat. Communists in Russia and other agrarian countries had to generate the industrial capacities that Marx presupposed, by de-emphasizing the production of consumer goods and emphasizing state investment in the physical infrastructure required for industrialization. Additionally, such communists had first to generate a proletariat – or working class. The peasants, who made up the vast majority of these populations, were unsympathetic to Marxist goals and were instead preoccupied with obtaining ownership of the land on which they worked. The state thus had to force peasants to work on collective farms and to relocate to urban centers in order to provide factory labor. Stalin also developed an extensive system of labor camps, which could be seen as a way of preparing the Soviet population for the rigor, discipline, and relative homogeneity of industrialized life. Communists maintained that, if properly directed by state authorities, only one generation of Soviet citizens would be required to suffer these deprivations, compared to the several generations of British workers who had to endure inhumane conditions during its process of industrialization.[6]

The communist regime in the USSR had originally proclaimed world leadership in matters of interpretation of Marxist and communist doctrine. However, many of the communists who came to power in other countries after World War II – especially the Chinese and Yugoslavian regimes – revised such doctrine in ways that reflected their specific political, social, and economic situations. Communist parties in Western

Europe increasingly distanced themselves from what they perceived to be Soviet self-interest. Even Eastern European regimes differed from Soviet leaders on many doctrinal issues. Increasingly, communism began to lose its appearance as a unitary science of history and set of governing principles. By the 1950s, the Soviets could no longer presume to dictate communist doctrine. During the 1980s, the rulers of the communist countries recognized the need to introduce reforms in their doctrine to revitalize increasingly stagnant economies and mollify increasingly restless populations. Such reforms were, of course, followed by a general repudiation of communism in much of the former Soviet Union and Eastern Europe, and it is often claimed that governing communist parties in China and Cuba and communist movements elsewhere have paid little more than tepid lip service to the version of communism that the world knew as Marxist-Leninism throughout much of the twentieth century. Still, communism retains supporters in Russia and other former communist states and enthusiasts in some parts of the developing world. Its ideas – both as expressed by Lenin, Mao, and other founders and as revised by Mikhail Gorbachev and other reformers in the late twentieth century – require consideration in the great political conversations.

Fascism and Nazism: Totalitarian Control to Strengthen the Collective

During the first half of the century, fascists and Nazis presented an enormous challenge to democratic capitalism. Rather than emphasizing economic freedom and political equality, they sought national power and world domination, and they thought that national strength was advanced by giving absolute authority to Il Duce (Benito Mussolini, 1883–1945) and the Fuehrer (Adolf Hitler, 1889–1945). Most thoughtful people regard the events associated with the rise of German Nazism and Italian fascism – the Holocaust and World War II – as the darkest hour in human history. While humans have long acted in a cruel and barbarous manner, the magnitude and scope of evil that these ideologies wrought on the world in general and the Jews in particular was unprecedented. Perhaps most chilling is the fact that such evil could be committed by citizens of highly educated and cultured societies.

While there are some important differences between Italian fascism and German Nazism, what ideas did they share that won the acceptance, and often the allegiance, of such people? Both rejected liberalism, stressing the supremacy of the collectivity over the individual and the need for totalitarian state authority that controlled social, economic, religious, and family life for the overall good of the political community. Both rejected communism, believing that the Marxist notion of class conflict undermines the unity of society and retards the attainment of the common good. Both rejected democracy, arguing that it panders to human weaknesses and special interests. Both endorsed rule by authoritarian leaders who mobilize the masses on behalf of elite-defined goals. Both believed that human reason can play only a limited role in political life, and stressed that collective greatness depends on intuitive understandings of human destiny and on energizing human emotions and will behind such goals as military conquest and national unity. Most fundamentally, both fascists and Nazis sought *communal solidarity* – the end of competition between classes or individuals within the state, and a redirection of competitive energies toward other states in the international system. A fundamental goal was to have all segments of society working in unison in order to enhance state power and produce social and political order. The disputes between management and labor that resulted in work stoppages and strikes had to be replaced by employer–employee cooperation. Hostilities between rural and urban areas had to be replaced by collaborative efforts to build society as a whole. Legislators rallying around the communal objectives articulated by Hitler and Mussolini needed to replace the partisan disputes and competition among special interests that accompany the disorderly democratic process. In effect, communal solidarity was sought in order to achieve efficiency: the trains would run on time; economic and military goods would be produced on schedule and according to social needs. The achievement of social solidarity also implied the development of a more uplifting human ethic. The material and selfish preoccupations of individuals in liberal capitalist societies would be replaced by more communitarian values. Individuals would become more dutiful and responsible to others as they learned the gratification of contributing to the good of the collective, and would become more heroic as they set aside their own smug and comfortable bourgeois existence and embraced the great adventures that awaited them as soldiers in pursuit of collective greatness.

Nazism and fascism are not, however, the same ideology. While fascism celebrated the nation as the collectivity that its members should venerate and serve, Nazism celebrated the so-called "Aryan race" as the collectivity to be promoted.[7]

The foundations of fascism can be found in the ideas and governing practices of Benito Mussolini, who was dictator of Italy from 1922 to 1945. Fascist philosophers, such as Giovanni Gentile (1875–1944), made clear that true fascists reject the racist ideas of Nazism and were instead primarily nationalists who put the power, prestige, and expansion of the nation at the center of their principles.[8] In Italy, this meant recapturing the glory of the Roman Empire. But Mussolini and his party de-emphasized the development of a well-formulated set of principles and programs for achieving such national greatness. According to Mussolini, "Our program is simple; we wish to govern Italy. They ask us for programs, but there are already too many. It is not programs that are wanting for the salvation of Italy, but men and willpower."[9]

The origins of Nazism – sometimes called "national socialism" – can be found in the ideas and governing practices of Hitler, who became influential in Germany during the 1920s and was dictator of the German Third Reich from 1933 to 1945.[10] Hitler stressed racial struggle as the central problem of politics. Nazism proclaimed that many German problems were the result both of Jewish ownership of many businesses and of Jewish conspiracies.[11] The Nazis also thought that the intermixing of the descendents of the Aryan race with Jews, Gypsies, and other so-called "sub-human" races had been tragic. They believed that the development of a pure Aryan race would bring greatness to humankind, and that this required the subjugation and ultimate elimination of the subordinate races. Accordingly, the Nazis pursued what they came to call *the Final Solution* – the physical destruction of all Jews and other "inferior" races. Indeed, they sought the *genetic cleansing* of the Aryan race itself by the elimination of those with physical and mental handicaps or any of a long list of illnesses, physical "defects," or "deviant" behaviors.[12] In the resulting *Holocaust*, about six million Jews and six million other "undesirables" and opponents of the Nazis were systematically killed. Nazi racial policies make clear the decisive political difference between Nazis and fascists: whereas the state is an end in itself for fascists, it is merely a means to a higher end for Nazis – namely, Aryan supremacy.[13]

Although Italian fascism and German Nazism were greatly discredited following the defeat of Axis powers in World War II, many of their ideas have been the basis of various governing regimes and of many extreme right-wing movements throughout the latter half of the twentieth century. The Spanish fascist party (the Falange) led a rebellion against the Spanish Republic in 1936 and brought Francisco Franco to power until his death in 1975. Argentina's Juan Perón incorporated many fascist ideas into the Peronist Party, which ruled Argentina from 1945 to 1955 and from 1973 to 1976. Various third world military dictatorships – such as that of Saddam Hussein (1937–2006) in Iraq – have also incorporated fascist principles into their regimes, although they usually avoid claiming allegiance to fascism as a whole. Until it was overthrown in the 1990s, the Nationalist Party in South Africa used the racist policy of *apartheid* – the complete separation of all whites and all "coloreds" – to guarantee white minority rule and the repression of black Africans. The Serbian policy of ethnic cleansing in Bosnia is the most conspicuous reminder that racial goals similar to those of the Nazis are alive and well in the post-Cold War era.

These diverse manifestations of fascist and Nazi principles make clear that it is an oversimplification to see these ideologies as ad hoc responses to specific and unusual circumstances; indeed, elements of these ideologies can reappear under many conditions. Nevertheless, it is useful to understand the particular social, economic, and historical developments that seem to have prompted the rise of fascism in Italy and Nazism in Germany.

The first condition was a sense of international injustice embodied in the punitive measures of the Treaty of Versailles, signed in 1919 and ending World War I. Many Germans in particular believed that the treaty unfairly blamed and punished Germany for the war. Germany lost roughly 1 percent of its pre-war arable land, 10 percent of its population, all overseas colonies and other investments, and much of its military and merchant fleets. It was also forced to pay large reparations to France and Great Britain. Signing the treaty at all was an unpopular measure among the German populace. The Italians, who had broken their treaty with Germany and joined the Allies in 1915, putting them on the winning side of the war, also had grievances stemming from the post-war settlement. In a secret treaty with the Allies, Italy had been promised territory in modern-day Slovenia if the Allies were victorious. After the war, however, the Allies reneged on the agreement. This decision insulted the Italians, wounded their sense of national pride, and produced in them a sense of betrayal. In short, widespread perceptions of international injustice stirred intense nationalist sentiments to which Nazis and fascists could appeal.

The second historical condition involved rising economic expectations combined with economic instability. Italians and Germans had accepted extensive economic sacrifices during World War I; when it ended, demands for economic comforts were widespread. Although there were significant gains in economic productivity and the standard of living in both Italy and Germany rose during the 1920s, economic problems persisted.

In Italy industrialization was confined to a small number of northern cities, and the rural and southern areas remained economically weak. Extensive budgetary deficits by Italy's liberal-democratic government necessitated higher taxes and reduced expenditures. Italy also suffered from a balance-of-payments deficit in international trade, and the lira dropped significantly in value. Such problems caused widespread disillusionment and resentment among Italians, stimulated a rapid growth in trade unionism, and precipitated many labor disputes. In this climate, the middle class sought an alternative to the various liberal and socialist parties then competing for power, while the working class sought a party that promised economic self-sufficiency for Italy. The fascists appealed to both.

The German economy immediately following World War I was devastated by several factors, including the need to pay reparations that were far beyond its capacity, the imposition of extensive restrictions on its international trade, and the eventual French occupation of the Ruhr region in response to German failure to keep up reparations payments. The government of the Weimar Republic (1919–33) responded by printing money to meet expenses, and from 1922 to 1923 this policy resulted in runaway inflation, which wiped out savings and pensions and other bases of economic investment. Although there was a temporary recovery in the mid-1920s, the worldwide depression that began in 1929 caused unemployment to rise to more than 25 percent of the German labor force. In this economic climate, the allegiance of German citizens to liberal democracy was eroded. The lack of a stable liberal-democratic tradition provided a receptive audience for the authoritarian rhetoric of the Nazis, who implied that Germany's economic problems could be solved by attacking the alleged source of these problems (the Jewish domination of the economy) and by instituting a program of national socialism involving extensive governmental control of the economy while retaining private production and enterprise.

A third problem to which fascists and Nazis responded was the apparent ineffectiveness of parliamentary government. After World War I, Italy and Germany adopted proportional representation electoral laws that led to the proliferation of small parties in their legislatures. For example, 38 parties appeared on the ballot during the 1932 German election and 18 obtained parliamentary seats. No party in the Weimar Republic ever won an absolute majority, so coalitions governments had to be created. However, cooperation among parties proved difficult; political infighting, petty jealousies, and genuine differences of policy continuously undermined coalitions, so that governments fell frequently. The spectacle of political wrangling and instability under this system of government did little to enhance popular confidence in democracy. The electorate and legislators became polarized into right-wing and left-wing extremes. These problems enabled Nazis and fascists to point to liberal democracy as faction-ridden and unworkable. According to both fascists and Nazis, effective government required institutions of national unity, a one-party state with a supreme leader.

A fourth problem to which Nazism and fascism responded was the uprooting of many Germans and Italians from their rural communities, local parishes, and extended families that occurred as these countries underwent industrialization. People found themselves immersed in large urban masses, with few group loyalties and attachments. The alienation of the urban masses, particularly under conditions of widespread unemployment, led them to search for a secure, meaningful place in the world. Nazism and fascism appealed to the "higher" purposes of race or state in order to satisfy this need for meaning.

These problems of international injustice, economic instability, political ineffectiveness, and social alienation contributed to German and Italian receptivity to Nazi and fascist appeals. But widespread public support did not propel Mussolini into power in Italy in 1922, or Hitler to power in Germany in 1933. The fascists had won less than 20 percent of the vote in Italy in 1921, and Mussolini attained power when the King asked him to take office during a threatened general strike staged by socialists, communists, and other left-wing organizations. Hitler received less than 37 percent of the vote in 1932, and while the Nazis became the largest party in the German parliament after that election, they did not have an absolute majority. Preceded and followed by considerable intrigue and extra-constitutional manipulations, this election result encouraged the aged, nearly senile president Paul von Hindenburg to make Hitler the chancellor of a conservative-nationalist government on January 30, 1933. Within two months, Hitler was granted dictatorial powers, and the abbreviated tenure of the Thousand-year Reich began.[14] Perhaps historical accidents – as well as social, economic, and political conditions – can prompt political communities to succumb to the temptations of fascism and Nazism.

Contemporary Liberalism: Reforming Capitalism and Democracy

Contemporary liberalism evolved from classical liberalism when many people began to realize that government could promote liberty as well as reduce it. While classical liberals assumed that the free market system and minimal government maximized individual freedom and happiness, contemporary liberals recognized that democratic governments needed to be strong in order to defend the liberties of their citizens from communism, fascism, and Nazism. They also thought that strong government could address some of the problems of pure *laissez-faire* capitalism. Contemporary liberals thus called for a strong state to provide more security, stable economic growth, and more equal economic opportunities for all citizens. Additionally, they sought a variety of political reforms to equalize the distribution of political power and, generally, look for ways to solve a variety of social problems – such as racial and sexual discrimination – through a more expanded use of governmental authority than was envisioned by classical liberals.

We have seen that liberalism – at least in its classical articulation as a defense of democratic capitalism – was subjected to relentless criticism throughout the nineteenth and early twentieth centuries. Such criticisms prompted many European political theorists with a commitment to liberty and democracy to fuse these liberal ideals to other ideologies (such as democratic socialism) rather than reform or reframe liberalism. In America, however, liberalism remained a respected, if somewhat flawed, doctrine. Efforts to retain core liberal ideas while recasting the ideology to answer its critics were, therefore, primarily an American enterprise. Such liberal intellectuals as John Dewey (1859–1952) and such liberal politicians as Franklin D. Roosevelt (1882–1945) were instrumental in redefining liberalism in the following ways. While political, social, and economic liberties are of prime importance, they are more likely to be supported than threatened by democratic governments. While there is no injustice in owning private property or in the inequalities in wealth that emerge under capitalism, it is desirable and fair for governments to regulate certain uses of private property, impose progressive taxes that fall most heavily upon the rich, and develop public welfare programs that help the poor. While governments must act within constitutional limitations and electoral mandates, strong and active national governments are needed to stimulate and regulate the economy and to extend liberty and equality. While social change and progress are important, they should occur through reform, not through revolution.

Although classical liberalism emerged at the beginning of the industrial revolution to justify capitalism and limited government, liberals acknowledged many problems with unfettered capitalism as industrialism matured. The seeds for the emergence of *reform liberalism* were sown as early as 1848 when John Stuart Mill suggested, in *Principles of Political Economy*, that goods should be produced and exchanged according to capitalist principles, but that governments could play a role in distributing (or redistributing) these goods in a more equal manner. It was not until the twentieth century, however, that reform liberalism emerged as a coherent public philosophy.

The idea of reforming capitalism is a two-edged sword. On the one hand, it involves a fundamental commitment to capitalism. Like classical liberals, contemporary liberals believe that the good life requires material prosperity that can best be attained through a capitalist economy. By promoting steady economic growth and facilitating business interests, contemporary liberals are sometimes seen as advocating *corporate liberalism*.[15] On the other hand, the idea of reforming capitalism involves commitments that are often regarded as hostile to capitalism. By imposing regulations on businesses and by enlarging welfare rights, contemporary liberals are sometimes regarded as *welfare-state liberals*. These two tendencies within contemporary liberalism have led to extensive debate and some confusion regarding political principles. Theodore Lowi has suggested that contemporary liberals have sought to resolve these tensions by becoming *interest-group liberals*.[16] Such liberals regard the demands of many groups in society as sufficiently legitimate to warrant a positive governmental response. If businesses important to national prosperity or national security face bankruptcy, then liberal governments should provide subsidies that bail them out of their financial difficulties. If the wealthy need encouragement to invest in new economic enterprises, then liberal governments should provide appropriate tax incentives. If labor needs safer working conditions, liberal governments should regulate the workplace. If minorities are discriminated against, liberal governments should enforce civil rights legislation. If the poor need better healthcare, liberal governments should improve their access to medical services. Such examples could be multiplied endlessly. While contemporary liberals seldom identify themselves as interest-group liberals, they have evolved principles and policies that they hope appeal to corporate leaders, welfare recipients, minorities, and many other groups and interests within society.

Reform liberalism, corporate liberalism, welfare-state liberalism, and interest-group liberalism are thus the main designations used to differentiate contemporary liberalism from classical liberalism. While classical liberalism can be seen as a conscious attempt to create a science of politics in which political principles are deduced from philosophical assumptions, contemporary liberalism is much more pragmatic. Contemporary liberals attempt to develop political principles that address various specific problems and thus attract widespread political support.

There are, of course, many problems confronting political communities, and the primary issues on the liberal agenda have changed over time. But it is useful to discuss some important and recurring economic, social, and security issues that have pre-occupied liberals during the twentieth century.[17]

Liberals have come to recognize that the benefits of capitalism – its capacity to promote economic freedom and material prosperity – are partially offset by certain *market failures*. First, it was apparent by the end of the nineteenth century that an unregulated marketplace can result in concentrations of economic power that undermine economic competition, increasing the exploitive capacity of corporate giants and reducing their incentives to become economically efficient. In America, capitalists like John D. Rockefeller and J. P. Morgan were able to squeeze competitors out of their industries, establishing monopolies and oligopolies that dominated such markets as oil and railroads. Second, liberals (like Marxists) realized that an uncontrolled market economy exhibits business cycles producing economic inefficiency and insecurity. During periods of economic growth, the price of goods often rises in an inflationary manner and the values of currencies and savings are reduced. During periods of economic stagnation – such as the worldwide depression that occurred during the 1930s – many workers become unemployed and are thrown into poverty. Third, liberals understood that pure market systems are unable to provide many beneficial services – or public goods – such as national defense, education for the poor, universal immunization against contagious diseases, and mass transportation. Fourth, liberals recognized that the wealth created by a capitalist economy is not distributed widely or equally. Some people – the very young, the very old, the severely handicapped, and so forth – cannot participate in a market economy. Other people who are capable of economic productivity may become unemployed during depressions and recessions. While liberals do not regard economic inequality as a problem, they do regard poverty as one.[18] When people live in poverty, they are unlikely to acquire the education and skills necessary to become productive, they are likely to be a source of other social problems (like crime), and their opportunities for intellectual and moral development and for fulfilling lives are limited. Fifth, liberals realized that the self-interested actions of participants in the marketplace often create externalities harming the broader public. The tendency of industries to reduce their costs of production by dumping their waste byproducts into rivers, into the air, or underground – spoiling the environment and causing public health problems – illustrates the externality problem. By recognizing the need for governmental regulation of industry to prevent environmental abuses, contemporary liberalism has provided a comfortable home for many environmentalists.[19] Contemporary liberals believe it is legitimate for governments to address environmental problems and other market failures.

Like classical liberals, contemporary liberals believe that individuals should have an equal opportunity to employ their talents and energies in order to advance socially and economically. Indeed, they have made central to their public philosophy the fact that many people have been denied equal access to jobs, education, housing, and public accommodations because of their race, ethnicity, gender, sexual preferences, and so forth. During the early stages of the civil rights movement, liberals sought to eliminate explicit discriminatory laws (such as those creating racially segregated schools) and practices (such as when realtors "redline" white neighborhoods and discourage black home ownership in such areas). Formal equal opportunity has been furthered by the passage of laws forbidding such discrimination, but liberals recognize that the historical legacies of racism, sexism, and homophobia continue to constrain the upward mobility of minorities, women, and gays. Liberals also recognize that certain cultural values and traditional practices constitute subtle forms of discrimination. For example, standardized tests to determine admission to universities appear to disadvantage minority students, and promoting people at work on the basis of continuous years of employment tends to discriminate against women who temporarily interrupt their careers to raise children. Contemporary liberals are therefore concerned with detecting and changing those social norms and practices that constitute significant barriers to fair equal opportunity for all. Such commitments have made contemporary liberalism a comfortable home for many people in the movements for civil rights, gay rights, and women's rights.[20]

Although contemporary liberals have focused on such economic and social problems, they have not forgotten the main problem that concerned classical liberals: providing security for citizens. Liberals have recognized many international threats to security and have thus endorsed military power that is sufficient to deter potential aggressors. US liberals like Franklin D. Roosevelt and his War Secretary, Henry L. Stimson, rallied America behind Allied efforts to defeat Nazism and fascism during World War II; George Kennan created the policy of containment to check communist expansion; and Robert McNamara sought a "second-strike" capability to deter nuclear attacks on liberal democracies. When liberals believed that American security and national interests were threatened by the Axis powers during World War II, by a communist regime in North Vietnam, and by Islamic terrorists after September 11, 2001, they endorsed military action. Liberals have also recognized many domestic threats to security and have called on governments to declare war against organized crime and drug dealers and to enact gun control legislation.

Beyond addressing various market failures, forms of discrimination, and security threats, contemporary liberals believe that governments must address an expanding and evolving set of problems. Indeed, liberals have recognized that some of their "solutions" to the problems of previous decades have created new problems. For example, to integrate schools that were largely segregated racially due to housing patterns, liberals initially supported busing black students into predominately white schools and white students into predominantly black ones. But when this caused "white flight" out of the school districts serving largely inner cities populated by minorities, liberals turned to other approaches, such as building magnet schools with special programs that attracted students throughout the area.

To address these many problems, contemporary liberals have moved away from the limited government advocated by classical liberals and have instead embraced active government. But, for the most part, they do not repudiate the goals of their forerunners. Rather, they extend and give somewhat different interpretations to the ideals of enhancing liberty, sustaining capitalism, promoting constitutional democracies, and creating a science of politics.

Classical liberals sought to secure individual freedom, but according to T. H. Green (1838–82), a British philosopher who is regarded as one of the precursors of reform liberalism, they were preoccupied with *negative liberty*. For them, liberty was the absence of restraint, especially by coercive governments and oppressive majorities. Liberty in this sense means being left alone to do as one wants. While respecting negative liberty, contemporary liberals have also sought what Green called *positive liberty*. Rather than being left alone, positive liberty allows for the capacity to make choices that enhance one's ability to live according to one's own conception of the good life. If left alone, a poor, ignorant, or ill child has few real choices. Such a child may wish to become a doctor, lawyer, or scientist, but she is not really free to pursue such aspirations given the formidable obstacles standing in her way. Positive liberty occurs as these obstacles to individual choices are reduced or eliminated.[21]

Endorsing positive liberty has important implications. First, the amount of positive liberty that people have is unequal, because it is highly dependent on their external environment. If people are surrounded by poverty, racism, disease, and other environmental constraints, freedom of choice is restricted. People living in such circumstances are likely to be preoccupied with fulfilling their minimal economic and security needs, and the choice of developing themselves intellectually, morally, and spiritually will be foreclosed to them. Second, by promoting the health, education, and welfare of its citizens, governments can play important roles in overcoming environmental restraints to real choices and individual development.

Contemporary liberals usually assert that societies, acting through their governments, have not only the capacity but also the obligation to promote positive liberty. Such obligations are discharged by enacting and implementing laws and policies expanding *citizen (or welfare) rights*. For example, liberals assert that all young people have a right to an equal education, claiming that the public schooling provided for poor and minority students must be equal to that provided for affluent white students. Liberals also assert that all citizens have the right to be protected from certain health hazards and that governments should provide such basic health services as immunizations, sanitation, and access to doctors through public health clinics; increasingly, liberals seek expansion of citizen rights in this area by calling for national health insurance. Liberals often assert that the poor have a right to various forms of welfare, such as food stamps, subsidized housing, and cash transfer payments. While contemporary liberals debate among themselves the content and extensiveness of various citizen rights, they agree that governments are the appropriate vehicles by which societies can extend welfare in order to facilitate the positive liberty of all citizens.

Classical liberals sought to develop a capitalist economy in order to produce material prosperity. Contemporary liberals want to retain a basically capitalist economy, but they want greater governmental control over it. They want steady economic growth and believe governments must act to prevent both economic stagnation and excessive growth. They recognize that economic stagnation throws people into poverty and limits their real choices for personal development. They believe that some growth is needed to provide new economic opportunities and to provide additional revenues for governmental expansion of citizen rights. And they believe that economic development is a prerequisite for attaining stable liberal democracies in many less developed nations around the world.[22] However, contemporary liberals also recognize that economic growth can be excessive and costly. Rapid economic growth involves vast changes in where and how people work, and there may be more losers than gainers from rapid growth.[23] Unregulated rapid growth can also erode the natural environment, resulting in aesthetic losses and health dangers. Given the dangers of economic stagnation and of rapid growth, contemporary liberals hope to achieve steady, managed growth.

Contemporary liberals want to retain the constitutional democracies developed by classical liberals, but they have sought some democratic reforms. First, they have sought a steady increase in representation within democracies, bringing previously excluded groups such as minorities and women to the voting booth and into governmental offices. Because liberals have become increasingly skeptical that "neutral" experts can determine those policies that best serve the public interest, they have concluded that the policy-making process must be open to all viewpoints and interests. Second, contemporary liberals have argued that constitutional limitations – while necessary to restrain capricious and tyrannical government – must be reinterpreted over time to enable governments to address contemporary problems.[24]

Additionally, contemporary liberals seek a form of government that operates in a scientific fashion, but their understanding of scientific politics differs from that of their forerunners. Classical liberals sought a scientific theory of politics in which general principles of government were deduced from self-evident philosophical assumptions. Contemporary liberals are more concerned with applying the scientific method to analyses of social and economic problems. For contemporary liberals, the principles of classical liberalism – the desirability of an unregulated market, the inviolability of property rights, the prohibition against legislating morality, and so forth – are too dogmatic. No principles – not even liberal principles – can always provide appropriate guidance to policy-making. As suggested by John Dewey, problem-solving and policy-making are pragmatic sciences.[25] The best solution to a problem is not deduced from a set of principles that are themselves deduced from assumptions about the nature of the universe, humans, society, and knowledge. Instead, the best solution to a problem can only be known experientially and perhaps experimentally. What works? What policies are effective? What policies produce the most desirable consequences while having the fewest adverse affects and costs?

Classical liberalism suggested that everyone had to decide such questions for themselves, and that they could register their individual intelligence as producers or consumers in the marketplace and as voters at the ballot box of democracy. But contemporary liberals argue that intelligence is not purely an individual quality. Just as a larger community of scholars must validate the insights and discoveries of individual scientists, so must the broader democratic community collectively use "organized intelligence" to solve human problems.[26] The democratic community must continually entertain innovative solutions to old problems. It must continually study and debate the effects of existing programs and policies. Just as scientific inquiry can never be legitimately blocked, the door to social and policy change must never be closed.

Perhaps the principle of *toleration* best summarizes the outlook of contemporary liberals, but their idea of toleration extends well beyond the religious toleration emphasized by the founders of classical liberalism. Contemporary liberals are more tolerant than classical liberals because they recognize the fragility of their own philosophical foundations. They understand that liberal principles cannot be proven based on indubitable conceptions of how the universe, humans, or society work. They recognize that allegiance to liberal principles depends upon acceptance of certain liberal values that can be questioned by those who are attracted to other ideologies. While contemporary liberals have a low opinion of absolutist and intolerant ideologies like communism and fascism, they regard democratic socialists and contemporary conservatives (and such emerging ideologies as feminism and environmentalism) as their friends as long as these ideologies remain tolerant and friendly toward them. Contemporary liberals share some principles with their friends. Like contemporary conservatives, they are committed to the maintenance of capitalism. Like democratic socialists, they are committed to more equality. Like feminists, they support equal rights and opportunities for women. Like environmentalists, they recognize the need to address our environmental problems. And all these ideologies share with contemporary liberalism a commitment to constitutional and representative democracy. Such overlapping principles provide the bases for broad support for fundamental liberal institutions and for building temporary coalitions on specific policy issues.

In addition to being tolerant of other pluralist ideologies, contemporary liberals are tolerant of the diversity within liberal societies. They tolerate life plans and lifestyles that differ from their own; they tolerate the expression of various viewpoints regarding religion and morality; and they disagree among themselves about many practical political issues. For example, which social and economic problems should rise to the top of the political agenda? Which reforms best address important problems? Which competing principles (e.g., efficiency or equality, security or civil liberty) should be stressed when dealing with a particular problem? Because answers to such questions cannot be deduced from the abstract principles of contemporary liberals, those who think of themselves as liberals are often in conflict over these practical matters. Contemporary liberals tolerate other liberals who disagree with them on specific issues, hoping to reach accommodations through further deliberation and hoping to reconnect on future issues. The fact that internal disagreement on specific issues is implied by the principles of liberal ideology dashes any hope for a united and disciplined liberal party, but it does not diminish the attractiveness of toleration and other such principles for those who are committed to contemporary liberalism.

Contemporary Conservatism: Opposing Liberal and Socialist Programs

Many people with classical liberal principles think that contemporary liberals have betrayed liberalism's fundamental principles by drifting toward egalitarianism and the strong state. Such people have entered into an uneasy alliance with those who hold traditional conservative principles and those who fear such international menaces as Soviet communists and Islamic fundamentalists to frame a contemporary conservative viewpoint. Borrowing from classical liberals the idea that big government strangles individualism and individual rights, these conservatives want more freedom in the marketplace and, therefore, less governmental intervention in the economic realm. Drawing upon the traditional conservative belief in a natural hierarchy among humans, they reject the egalitarianism that underlies the welfare state.

Nevertheless, contemporary conservatives want governments to retain the authority to act decisively in pursuit of collective goals, such as providing security against external threats. Indeed, US government has grown extensively in recent years under conservative leadership. Especially since September 11, 2001, President George W. Bush and others in the Republican Party have enhanced military capacities. They created a large new Homeland Security bureaucracy to deal with terrorist threats and natural disasters, and expanded the role of the national government in public education in order to ensure that the next generation of US citizens has the skills to compete in the emerging global economy. Some analysts believe that Bush has transformed contemporary conservatism by abandoning (or at least downplaying) its reduction of government theme. Perhaps conservatives have come to believe that it is not government per se that is bad, but only government that reduces individual choice and responsibility.[27] Perhaps conservatives not only accept but even embrace governmental programs that encourage people to become more responsible (such as the welfare reforms of 1996 that put time limits on people's eligibility for welfare services) or that provide citizens real choices (such as old age insurance programs that allow people to invest mandatory payroll – social security – taxes in various investment opportunities that become privately held retirement accounts).

In general, the big governments that contemporary conservatives denounce are those that are expected to solve all social problems. Contemporary conservatives – including such prominent political leaders as Margaret Thatcher in the UK and

Ronald Reagan and the Bushes in the US, as well as such well-regarded academics as Thomas Sowell, Jeane Kirkpatrick, James Q. Wilson, and Dinesh D'Sousa, and such media pundits as George Will, William Kristol, David Brooks, Rush Limbaugh, and Ann Coulter – believe that communists, democratic socialists, and contemporary liberals create unrealistic expectations about what can be accomplished in political life. They assert that governments cannot solve a wide variety of human problems. While some governmental authority is needed to provide national security and social order, more expansive governments threaten individual liberty, the autonomy of civil society, and the economic prosperity provided by free markets. If there is to be progress, it will come about by the hard work of individuals who exhibit traditional virtues and who are motivated by the rewards available to them in the marketplace and from their involvements in voluntary associations.[28]

Contemporary conservatism is thus a reaction against contemporary liberalism, democratic socialism, and various external threats to democratic capitalist societies.[29] To counter the threats posed by these forces, contemporary conservatives rely on the pro-market ideas of classical liberalism. To condemn the assault on traditional social customs by the left, contemporary conservatives also draw on the pro-culture ideas developed by traditional conservatives. They, too, are concerned that cultures reflect and individuals exhibit traditional moral values. Contemporary conservatism is a mix, then, of portions of two ideologies that were historically and philosophically antagonistic. Contemporary conservatism is able to overcome some of the contradictions and tensions between traditional conservatism and classical liberalism by focusing very sharply on the problems generated by those pursuing the political agendas of the left.

The publication of the first issues of the *National Review* in 1955 may have been a defining moment in the birth of contemporary conservatism as a coherent ideology, especially in the US. Its first editor, William F. Buckley Jr., provided a magazine in which conservative intellectuals could air their grievances about the advances made by contemporary liberals, socialists, and communists after World War II. Many of these intellectuals were uncomfortable with what they perceived as a blatant liberal bias in journalism, the entertainment industry, government bureaucracies, and universities. Buckley's magazine was the first of what would become many forums where contemporary conservatives could develop their public philosophy.[30]

Throughout the 1950s, conservatives mostly made up an intellectual elite outside the mainstream of academic and political affairs. In the 1960s, these intellectuals (most of whom resided in the eastern US) began to deliver their criticisms to the public and soon found allies among western Republicans who celebrated rugged individualism and the competition in free market economies. These forces helped launch political campaigns, such as the Goldwater quest for the presidency in 1964. While most western conservatives were much more committed to reducing the role of the federal government than were eastern conservatives, agreement that communism abroad and liberal social engineering at home were threatening American society enabled this coalition to grow.

During the 1960s, several developments in the US gave momentum to the conservative movement. The growth of the welfare state, the free speech and anti-war demonstrations on college campuses, the women's movement, the civil rights movement, and the riots in urban areas were just some of the developments that prompted many citizens to rethink their allegiance to contemporary liberalism. In the early 1970s, many intellectuals who had originally been supportive of contemporary liberal programs, especially those of President Lyndon Johnson's "Great Society," joined the conservative movement, because they considered those liberal programs naive and dangerous failures. These intellectuals were dubbed "neoconservatives," and they brought innovative ideas to conservatism by suggesting ways of using the market to achieve many of the goals that had previously been sought by governmental regulation of, and intervention in, the free market.[31]

Since the 1970s, there have been many conservative victories at the polls on both sides of the Atlantic. The elections of Ronald Reagan, George H. Bush and George W. Bush in the US, Brian Mulroney in Canada, Margaret Thatcher and John Major in Great Britain, Helmut Kohl and Angela Merkel in Germany, and Nicolas Sarkozy in France are the most visible examples of the popularity of conservatism in recent years. Such politicians succeeded at the polls, in large part, because of their incisive criticisms of the failures of communism, socialism, and contemporary liberalism to deliver the good life for citizens.

Conservatives have identified four general problems facing pluralist societies in recent years: (1) the failure of Western foreign policy to promote the interests of the "free world" and democracy; (2) the promotion of liberal and socialist domestic policies by increasingly strong central governments; (3) the prominence and power of radical reformers, social engineers, and socialist utopians in educational institutions, especially at universities and colleges; (4) a culture of permissiveness that combines a relativism of values with an acceptance of multiculturalism, producing a society where there is confusion about citizen virtues and an inadequate common culture to sustain political stability. Conservatives have not always agreed on solutions to these problems, but these areas of concerns have served as rallying points for different perspectives within the conservative movement.

Conservative criticisms of liberal foreign policy can be summarized in four "C's." First, they argue, the United States and its pluralist allies have too often practiced *capitulation*. After World War II, they failed under liberal leadership to respond vigorously to the Soviet Union's establishing its sphere of influence in Eastern Europe and to Mao's communist takeover of Mainland China. Today, many allies of the US are viewed as too soft in dealing with the "axis of evil" – Saddam's Iraq, Iran, and North Korea – as well as international terrorists that threaten security and global interests. Second, when threatened by communists or terrorists, liberals have relied too heavily on a policy of *containment* in which first Soviet aggression and now Islamic terrorism is thought to be effectively checked by showing a willingness to take counter-measures that will be so costly to potential aggressors as to deter future encroachments on pluralist societies; conservatives charge that liberals are satisfied with containing aggression, rather than counter-attacking and eliminating the hostile powers. Third, liberals have been insufficiently vigilant concerning *conspiracies* against Western interests. In the early 1950s, conservatives suspected that communist spies and sympathizers had penetrated Western governments and research projects. The Soviet

Union's rapid development of an atomic bomb at that time was viewed as evidence by conservatives that a communist conspiracy existed within the security systems of the US.[32] Today, conservatives stress that liberals are not concerned enough about foreign industrial saboteurs who steal our technologies and about shadowy extremist movements whose adherents infiltrate Western societies, positioning themselves for terrorist attacks on them. Finally, conservatives claim that US liberals and their allies have often naively accepted international *cooperation* and the United Nations as vehicles for conflict resolution. US conservatives have always been highly critical of the United Nations, arguing that such institutions deprive nations of their rightful sovereignty and pave the way for a "one world government." Such a world government would be controlled by nations and bureaucrats whose worldviews would be hostile to the best interests of the US and her allies and would undermine the traditional cultures and institutions that have served pluralist societies so well.

The presidency of Ronald Reagan during the 1980s gave conservatives their first opportunity to change foreign policies in ways that reflected these criticisms. Reagan put in train the massive military build-up that was necessary to set in motion the forces that resulted in Eastern European nations breaking free from Soviet communism and the dismantling of the Soviet Union in 1989–91. Conservatives have remained vigilant against the remnants of communism that persist in Cuba and elsewhere, but they have found in international terrorism a new hostile force demanding their attention. While some see Bush's "war on terrorism" as a new conservative foreign policy, there are few differences between conservative principles in their battle against communism and their battle against terrorism. Containment of the enemy is seen as insufficient in a context where suicide bombers apparently care little about the retaliatory capacity of their targets. For conservatives, such threats cannot be contained and so preemptive strikes must be considered. International cooperation and the initiatives of the United Nations are seen as weak and inadequate; unilateral military action must be used to ensure that the interests of the US are not compromised by the naive conciliatory responses of potential international allies in the war on terrorism.

Contemporary conservatives view the pursuit of liberal and socialist policies that empower centralized bureaucracies as the most serious domestic problem. In Europe, conservatives deplored the nationalization of industries and the development of elaborate welfare schemes. In the US, Franklin D. Roosevelt's New Deal was seen not as an attempt to save capitalism during the Great Depression of the 1930s, but as an assault on business interests and on individual choice. The US social security system, established by FDR in 1937, has been a favorite target of conservatives, because it compels citizens to participate, relieves them of the need to make thoughtful and independent decisions to ensure their own futures, and (mildly) redistributes income from the rich to the working poor. Although social security is now seen by most conservatives as too politically sensitive to assault directly, it remains an indirect target, and many conservatives continue to call for privatized social security accounts.

For conservatives in the US, domestic policies from World War II until the 1980s were too anti-business and too pro-union to enable the capitalist economy to be fully effective. Government regulations are seen as costly, intrusive, and excessive. Support for labor unions by FDR and subsequent Democratic presidents is seen as having driven up wages beyond the market price for labor, thus contributing to inflation. This together with costly and unnecessary regulations on businesses has weakened US businesses competing in the world economy. The owners of small and medium-sized businesses have been particularly attracted to contemporary conservatism by such anti-regulatory views.

Especially after the growth of federal expenditures in the late 1960s that accompanied the pursuit of the Great Society, conservatives have been very critical of programs that expand the functions of central governments. They argue that governmental interventions often compound or complicate the original problems. According to George Gilder:

> Unemployment compensation promotes unemployment. Aid for Families with Dependent Children (AFDC) makes more families dependent and fatherless. Disability insurance in all its multiple forms encourages the promotion of small ills into temporary disabilities and partial disabilities into total and permanent ones. Social security payments may discourage concern for the aged and dissolve the links between generations. . . . All means tested programs (designed exclusively for the poor) promote the value of being "poor" (the credential of poverty), and thus perpetuate poverty.[33]

According to conservatives, liberal domestic policies not only tend to be counter-productive; they are also often based on profoundly mistaken analyses of the roots of social problems. Conservatives claim that social problems are all too often seen as the result of structural problems, rather than as the result of a failure of individual character.[34] For example, drug-use is a problem that conservatives blame on the lack of individual character and the inability to "just say no." The willingness of liberal policy-makers to place the blame on structural matters like poverty over-extends government and ignores the crucial role that individual responsibility and virtue must play in a civil and well-ordered society.

Conservatives argue that the increasing scope of government activity spawned by liberal policies results in both vast centralized bureaucracies and huge government expenditures, forcing governments to rely on high and progressive tax rates. High taxes stall general economic growth by diverting money from the private economy, and progressive rates discourage the wealthy from making more money that they can invest in private ventures that spur economic growth.

Like Adam Smith and other classical liberals, contemporary conservatives hold that government should keep its role in economic matters to a minimum and allow the economy to steer itself. Attempts by liberals to steer the economy and avoid recessions through fiscal policies that create budget deficits have only created sluggish economies prone to inflation. Conservatives believe that liberal policy-makers since the 1930s have had much too little faith in capitalist economies.

Citizens also need to have faith in capitalist economies, but such faith is undermined by the liberal and radical biases within higher education. Conservatives believe that universities, at least those in the US and Great Britain, have, since World War II, become havens for liberal and socialist scholars. Academics in the social sciences have encouraged the belief that social engineering is both necessary and easy and have ignored the fact that vast structural reforms only enhance the power of national governments at the expense of local governments and private actors. During the 1980s, Prime Minister Margaret Thatcher accused English universities of harboring socialists and communists. Her primary targets were sociology departments in publicly funded universities, which her Conservative Party tried to weaken or eliminate. Conservatives in the US have complained that universities are no longer institutions celebrating and transmitting the ideals of Western civilization. Rather, they have become settings for unrelenting criticism of capitalism and traditional beliefs and practices.

The universities and colleges were also blamed for creating a "culture of permissiveness" that has permeated society since the mid-1960s. The argument is that teachers have given priority to turning out students who are independent critical thinkers sensitive to cultural differences, and in so doing, they have produced spoiled children who consider all values to be relative and who are disrespectful of authority.[35]

This culture of permissiveness reflects the relativism of liberalism, which fails to provide clear moral standards proclaiming the virtues necessary to live a good life. For conservatives, many of the problems facing pluralist societies are the result of liberal neglect of the importance of virtue and personal character. Crime, social disorder, single parents, large welfare rolls, and excessive public spending are traceable to this culture of permissiveness. According to James Q. Wilson: "For most social problems that deeply trouble us, the need is to explore, carefully and experimentally, ways of strengthening the formation of character among the very young. In the long run, the public interest depends on private virtue."[36]

Since the 1980s, this permissiveness has often taken the form of multiculturalism. Particularly in public schools and on university campuses, there has been a liberal willingness to accept the strident demands of racial minorities and immigrate groups for their own programs (such as Black Studies programs) and for opportunities to practice lifestyles that reflect the values of minority cultures (such as in multicultural centers on campus). Conservatives allege that there is an attitude of *political correctness* on campuses that prevents any challenge to the desirability of such multicultural initiatives.[37]

While stressing the problems caused by the programs of the left, contemporary conservatives believe it is a mistake to articulate visionary and utopian goals. They stress that their goals are modest and realistic, involving the redirection of economic, moral, and social life. Three general goals seem to unite contemporary conservatives and, to some extent, set them apart from traditional conservatives: defending free market capitalism, promoting a work ethic, and sustaining the family.

While traditional conservatives had some fears and reservations about capitalism, contemporary conservatives, like Milton Friedman, embrace the free market, stressing in particular two of its virtues.[38] First, minimal governmental intervention promotes dynamic domestic economies. When governments refrain from regulating economic activities, domestic economies are most efficient: they produce more economic growth, and national wealth is enhanced. Second, free markets among nations promote a harmonious international order; free trade among nations produces maximum economic benefits (in the long run) for all parties to international trade and thus reduces tensions among nations.

In defense of domestic free market economies, conservatives champion *privatization*. They claim that compared to nationalized industries, privatized industries are more competitive, more innovative, less bound by bureaucratic inertia, and less prone to labor disputes. In Western Europe, conservatives have re-privatized industries that had been nationalized by socialist regimes after World War II. During the Thatcher years, over half the industrial assets that had been owned by the British state were converted to private enterprises, including British Petroleum, Jaguar, Rolls Royce, and British Steel. In America, conservatives have privatized various public programs. Believing that public bureaucracies are often inefficient, they have supported initiatives to allow private educators to compete with public schools (giving vouchers that can be redeemed by private educators). They have even privatized significant elements of the US defense establishment by having private contractors assume many of the support activities that were traditionally performed by soldiers, sailors, and others who have served in the country's armed forces.

Conservatives have also focused on the benefits of *deregulation*, claiming that governmental regulations reduce innovation, discourage investment, raise costs for consumers, and damage the international competitiveness of US companies. Some regulation may be necessary, but most is excessive, creating costly mounds of bureaucratic red tape. Domestic economies are healthy when privately owned companies compete in markets in which they are unfettered by rigid regulations.

While traditional conservatives emphasized a sacred morality that placed reverence to God as their core ethical value, contemporary conservatives emphasize a more secular morality that stresses a work ethic. Conservatives fear that hard work has lost its luster in societies that are constantly increasing welfare and imposing high taxes on those who work hardest. Motivating young people to forgo immediate gratifications and instead become educated, skilled, and productive workers has become a central moral concern. According to conservatives, students are inadequately challenged in public schools to develop skills that make them effective contributors to society. To counter this trend, the Bush administration and a Republican Congress enacted a "No child left behind" educational policy that has created greater pressures on both schools and students to perform at higher levels.

While traditional conservatives believed that an organic society depended on the existence of many smaller voluntary associations, contemporary conservatives have focused on the family as the most important social unit where individuals can be nurtured. Sustaining the family has become the central social goal of contemporary conservatives. According to one conservative group:

> Marriage and the family – husband, wife, and children joined by public recognition and legal bond – are the most effective institution for the rearing of children, for the directing

of sexual passion, and for human flourishing in the community. . . . It is necessary to discriminate between relationships; gay and lesbian "domestic partners," for example, should not be recognized as the moral equivalent of marriage. Marriage and family are institutions for our continual social well-being. In an individualistic society that tends to liberation from all constraints, they are fragile institutions in need of careful and continuing support.[39]

The traditional family, though – according to conservatives – has been assaulted by government policies, schools, feminists, and children's rights advocates. Government welfare policy, which was designed to aid children without paternal support, encouraged the emergence of female-headed single-family households. Schools employ curricula and teach practices that undermine the role of the family in inculcating values in children. Feminists criticize the division of labor in the traditional family, and discourage women from playing their traditional domestic roles in the family. Children's rights advocates question (and limit) the authority traditionally exercised over children by their parents.

Conservatives believe public policy, culture, and institutions must all be reformed in ways that strengthen the family. The trend toward liberalized "no-fault" divorce laws must be reversed. Children must be taught to respect the authority of their parents, and parents must recognize that their responsibilities include instilling proper moral values in their children.

Conclusions

By the end of the twentieth century, the potency and appeal of the totalitarian ideologies of communism and fascism had waned. Of these ideologies, fascism fell from favor first, as the defeat of the German Nazis and the Italian fascists at the end of World War II in 1945 discredited them in the minds of most people. But many of their ideas continue to attract followers to neo-Nazi and fascist parties and other extreme right-wing movements that have emerged in Germany, the US, and elsewhere. These parties and movements remind pluralists not to disregard the non-rational and non-economic dimensions of human life. Human needs for a feeling of belonging, for a sense of purpose that transcends the individual, and for a sense of glory and power will continue to make fascism and even Nazism attractive to some. The historical legacies of Italian fascism and German Nazism serve as warnings about the power of chauvinism and nationalism, and reveal the dark side of desires for immersion in community life. Nazism continues to warn us of the power of racist thinking as a way of constituting a sense of community.

The appeal of communism has waned with the fall of communist regimes in Eastern Europe and the Soviet Union. Despite its vision of developing a stateless society, communism created an overly centralized, bureaucratized, and closed economy directed by a strong state, which may have been the single most important factor in its decline as a viable governing ideology. Despite its vision of a classless society, communist countries became stratified into two groups: those within the party and those outside it, generating privileges for Communist Party members that were deeply resented by others.[40] Whereas communism promised to bring prosperity for all, the populations of Eastern Europe and the Soviet Union experienced extensive poverty compared to those living in societies with free markets. Whereas communism was supposed to create a worker's paradise, life expectancy in communist societies was generally lower and environmental degradation from industry much higher than in Western, industrialized societies. In those states in which communism is still the official ideology, we may observe that the regimes increasingly act according to market principles to the neglect of ideological purity.

The apparent demise of Soviet and East European communism, economic reforms in China, and an aging Cuban leadership give communism an uncertain political future. For the most part, free market economics or the mixed economies supported by democratic socialists are replacing centralized planning. The "dictatorship of the proletariat" has been exchanged for various versions of either benevolent authoritarianism or parliamentary democracy. Communism may become an ideological relic of the very history it sought to transform. Whereas Marxism may live on in the form of various critiques of capitalism and liberal society, communism appears, for now, to be politically and intellectually discredited.

Although contemporary liberalism arose and achieved dominance in the United States before contemporary conservatism emerged as a coherent pluralist alternative to it, such conservatism has achieved rapid and dramatic success. Conservatives have won many elections and governed in many pluralist societies. Once highly critical of the media from which they felt excluded, conservatives now command much space on the editorial pages of newspapers and magazines, and control much time on the radio and television.

This, of course, does not mean that conservatism is without difficulties as an ideology. Conservatives still confront the challenge posed by their defense of dynamic market economies *and* their desire for social stability. Can communities be cohesive and stable when markets create innovation and dislocation? Can the nuclear family survive when economic conditions force, or at least make it attractive for, both spouses to work? Can the self-discipline that conservatives applaud be generated in market economies that often laud immediate gratification?

In foreign policy, conservatives must respond to a world in which their archenemy, communism, is no longer so powerful or threatening, and it is unclear whether terrorists lacking sponsorship of a powerful state can serve as a long-term adversary against whom conservatives can rally. Conservatives are now arguing among themselves over how to carry out foreign policy objectives.

Conservatives have also to decide whether they can broaden their appeal in Western nations without diluting their ideology. The environmental concerns of young people are not well addressed by conservative free market priorities. Conservatives must also confront their limited support among women and minorities. Conservative leaders have not been very effective so far in making their ideology more inclusive. Can they do so, without threatening the base of their support?

Despite these many challenges, conservatism remains a potent ideology with many ideals that must be entertained in our great conversations. Its defense of the economic ideas of classical liberalism will continue to find adherents in a world in which disillusionment with governments' role in planning and regulating economies is widespread, in terms of providing generous public welfare programs and imposing extensive taxes. The search for more moral societies with less permissive cultures is likely to have continued political appeal.

Currently, contemporary liberalism is both enjoying unprecedented success and experiencing an enormous crisis. On the one hand, the demise of fascism and communism has led some observers to argue that ideological conflict is at an end because liberal principles and values now reign supreme over much of the world.[41] Capitalism has been established in former communist societies. Constitutional and representative democratic regimes govern an increasing number of nations. Support for expanding citizen rights is widespread. The secular and material values that accompany liberalism seem increasingly to dominate cultures throughout the world. Despite conservative attacks on their excesses, liberal welfare policies remain operative in much of the world. On the other hand, liberalism is under attack, denigrated as the awful "L-word," and avoided as a label by even those politicians having liberal principles, because liberalism has become associated – at least in many minds – with big and intrusive government, bureaucratic domination, excessive business regulations that strangle the economy, reverse discrimination, coddling of criminals, moral permissiveness, and (especially) higher taxes.[42]

Perhaps liberalism is implicated in these problems, but addressing such problems is what liberals like to do best. Given their commitment to and experience with reform, contemporary liberals may well be up to the task of reforming their own political principles. Which principles to stress remains a topic of broad concern amongst them. For example, Michael Tomasky has recently proposed two major "big ideas" that contemporary liberals – or at least those within the American Democratic Party – should increasing adopt. First, they should employ the language of the "common good" and pursue policies that serve the interests of most citizens, de-emphasizing their responsiveness to the concerns of smaller (minority) segments of society. Second, they should articulate more clearly the duties that citizens owe society and one another, de-emphasizing the liberal stress on individual rights.[43] His ideas have provoked much comment and reflection among liberals in their continuing search to develop a more progressive liberal philosophy that can attract more adherents and voters than a liberalism that has been increasingly defined by its opposition to President Bush and a Republican Congress.[44] By considering the central ideas that have comprised contemporary liberalism throughout the twentieth century and how these ideas relate to a broader pluralist public philosophy, we can get a better understanding of whether such reform proposals as those put forward by Tomasky can be accommodated without sacrificing ideas that are essential to liberalism.

Given the great changes that occurred in the politics of the nineteenth and twentieth centuries, it would be naive and foolish to suppose that pluralism, the dominant roles of liberal and conservative ideologies, and the sorts of democratic processes that now attempt to resolve the differences between conservatives and liberals will continue to structure politics throughout the twenty-first century. Powerful and seductive ideologies are already fairly well developed that seek radical changes within pluralism. And extremist worldviews are also available that seek profound political changes that would threaten the very existence of pluralism. In the next chapter, these ideas are introduced.

Chapter 4

Radical and Extreme Voices in Contemporary Politics

The eight ideologies introduced in chapters 2 and 3 are but a few of hundreds of political perspectives that have been identified as important in political theory and practice.[1] Libertarianism and communitarianism have taken center stage as important perspectives discussed by contemporary political theorists. Neoliberalism, neoconservatism, egalitarian liberalism, and social conservatism are among many important strands within the ideologies we have already discussed that have their own distinct concerns. Feminism and environmentalism (of various sorts) have become prominent during the past several decades. Islamic fundamentalism and Christian evangelicalism are only the most obvious among many religious orientations that have entered political arenas. Various nationalisms seek to rally African-Americans, French Canadians, Basques, Ukrainians, and many other culturally related people around racial and ethnic identities and aspirations. While such right-wing extremist groups as the John Birch Society, the Ku Klux Klan, and the Aryan Nation have receded in importance, various white nationalist, hate, and survivalist groups – such as Posse Comitatus, Christian Identity, and the Patriot movement – still raise havoc in pluralist societies, as witnessed by the bombing of the Alfred Murray Federal Building in Oklahoma City in 1995. While most of the left-wing extremists of the 1960s have faded from the political scene, many anti-globalist groups – such as the Ruckus Society, the Direct Action Network, and Tutte Bianche – now use disruptive street tactics to express their deep hostility toward many aspects of pluralist societies. No introductory text can possibly give adequate coverage to all such voices, but it is important that our conversations be highly inclusive of the diversity of political perspectives that compete for attention today and that might become prominent in the twenty-first century.

To provide some way of organizing and presenting a wide sample of such voices, a classification scheme is needed. While many such schemes have been used to identify and label particular political ideologies,[2] the sort of typology that is needed here is one that organizes a wide variety of perspectives beyond the ideologies already discussed. The classification scheme employed here locates such perspectives on two dimensions.

The first dimension distinguishes other voices by their orientations toward pluralism. Our analytical framework suggests that broad agreements on the perennial issues among contemporary liberals and contemporary conservatives provide an initial specification of pluralist public philosophy. But other voices that are potentially friends of pluralism must be considered before pluralist public philosophy can be confidently defined. Additionally, pluralist public philosophy should be able to withstand challenges from its ideological opponents. We must therefore examine those perspectives that seem to fit into the third and fourth rings of the concentric circles of figure 1 (in chapter 1). Recall that the third and fourth rings distinguish between the orientations toward pluralism of radicals and extremists.

Radicals see significant deficiencies within pluralism that they believe must be corrected to achieve better pluralist societies. Such perceived problems include unjustified inequalities among citizens and inadequate attention to morality. Radicals doubt that ordinary pluralist politics – involving choices between liberal and conservative candidates for office and between liberal or conservative policies – will rectify these deficiencies and significantly improve pluralist politics. To do this, radicals want to get at the *root causes* of these problems. They want important alterations in the underlying structures of pluralist societies; they want changes in economic and governmental institutions, the quality of civil society, and cultural values. But such alterations do not involve revolutionary changes. Radicals may want to tame capitalism, but they do not envision destroying it. Radicals may propose constitutional amendments and new political institutions, but they are unlikely to seek an entirely new political system. Radicals might seek to strengthen various parts of civil society (e.g., labor unions or churches), but they would not prohibit or impose extensive controls on various associations within civil society. And radicals may seek a culture that is more receptive to minorities or more reinforcing of religious or traditional values, but they do not seek to impose uniform cultural values on society. Radicals propose to pursue such changes through pluralist politics.

In contrast, *extremists* believe that pluralist ideals as well as pluralist practices are deeply flawed. They want to abolish pluralism or at least some of the structures that are essential to pluralism. While pluralists see the importance of many values, identities, and institutions, extremists often hold particular values, identities, and institutions in such high regard that they see competing ones as evil. And while pluralists recognize some problems with current arrangements, extremists often see these arrangements as evil. Some extremists may be extremely devoted to the unity and strength of a particular community, and pursue goals that are oppressive to sub-communities or that deny obligations to larger ones. Others may be extremely devoted to a religion, and seek to establish a theocratic state that supports that religion, to the detriment of others. Yet others may be extremely devoted to some particular cause and seek to abolish those things that impede the realization of their goal. As these examples suggest, extremists are *true believers*, if not in the sacredness of some goal, at least in the wickedness of prevailing ideas. They despise the multiple voices, the competing agendas, and the continuous compromises of pluralism. Extremists have no desire to work within what they see as the fatal corruption of pluralist politics.

The second dimension of our classification scheme employs the commonplace distinction between the left and the right, defining them in terms of their orientation toward the many inequalities that exist in pluralist politics. *The right* accepts existing hierarchies within and between societies – whether or not these are based on differences in talents and energies, in ownership of property, in access to other material goods, in racial and ethnic characteristics, in religious virtue, or on any such inequalities. Believing such inequalities to be natural and desirable, those on the right reinforce existing hierarchies, and they would often like to return to the past, when conventional hierarchies were less frequently challenged. In contrast, *the left* usually criticizes existing hierarchies; rather than thinking inequalities are natural, those on left see them as constructed by powerful persons in order to extend their own privileges. Those on the left believe that more enlightened human beliefs and values point toward essential human equalities, and that collective action can be taken to reduce social and natural inequalities.[3]

To capture the ideas of those who challenge pluralism, this chapter introduces some of the more important and interesting voices that fall into four categories defined by differences on these two dimensions: the radical left, the radical right, the extreme right, and the extreme left.[4] Each of these categories contains many perspectives and specific groups, all of which stress somewhat different concerns and principles. In this chapter, I introduce major theoretical perspectives within each category but ignore various nationalisms and specific groups. By omitting such voices here, I do not wish to imply that they are unimportant; indeed, some of their main ideas will be mentioned in subsequent chapters. Rather than catalogue the diverse nationalisms and specific groups, it will be sufficient to discuss various perspectives committed to articulating a philosophy to defend their goals.

It is important to stress that some of perspectives discussed in this chapter are limited in their scope and that perspectives within a category are frequently hostile to one another. Perspectives that are limited in scope can be called *quasi-ideologies*. For example, "deep greens" distinguish themselves from liberal environmentalists by providing an "ecocentric" alternative that regards humans as only part of nature and subordinates individual aspirations to the requirements of a sustainable environment. Deep greens are seeking to develop a comprehensive perspective providing coherent and persuasive answers to the full range of perennial political issues. However, it is doubtful that they have achieved a full-blown ideology, as they continue to debate among themselves such important questions as what their ideals demand for the organization of society.[5] As another example, there are large differences among liberal, radical, and extreme feminists.[6] Each of these feminist perspectives has its own specific concerns, and its advocates have largely focused on such concerns rather than address the full range of perennial questions. Some deep greens and feminists have undoubtedly addressed most, if not all, of the perennial issues of politics, but these quasi-ideologies can be understood for now as offering distinct ideas on only some of these issues. In our treatment of quasi-ideologies, we will address only those issues on which they primarily focus, and ignore those areas where internal disagreements have yet to be worked out or where the dominant ideas differ little from those of other longer-standing ideologies.

The categories of the radical left, the radical right, the extreme right, and the extreme left do not themselves constitute full-blown ideologies. Instead, each of these categories contains a variety of perspectives that are distinct from one another and sometimes hostile to one another. In our treatment of the extreme right, for example, we focus on Islamic fundamentalists and Christian fundamentalists. Both seek the sort of cultural uniformity that is antithetical to pluralism, but they disagree intensely on the contents of the religious values they would impose on societies. In our treatment of the radical right, we include both global neoliberals (those who seek to push pluralism toward greater acceptance of a global free market) and national protectionists (those who seek to insulate particular pluralist societies from global markets). Clearly such differences and conflicts within categories mean that the discussions in the remainder of this chapter can only describe important but distinct perspectives within and across our four categories; any effort to present perspectives within the four categories as merely different strands of a common and coherent ideological perspective would be futile and, indeed, inaccurate.

The Radical Left: Seeking More Egalitarian and Communal Societies

Democratic socialism has been the most prominent perspective within the radical left in countries throughout the world during the twentieth century, but many prominent socialist leaders – like Great Britain's Tony Blair and Germany's Gerhardt Schroeder – have moved their parties and ideologies toward the center of the pluralist continuum in recent years. Perhaps democratic socialism is as much a full-blown ideology as the perspectives introduced in chapters 2 and 3,[7] but other quasi-ideologies have emerged as more staunch radicals in certain areas. Political philosophers advocating egalitarian liberalism actually seem to be stronger proponents than many social democrats of equal distributions of social goods within pluralist societies. Proponents of cosmopolitan global justice seem stronger critics than today's socialists of inequalities across nations. Civic communitarians have taken up and extended the longstanding concerns of socialists with increasing social solidarity and with promoting in citizens the political virtues needed for more socialist communities. Advocates of radical democracy seem clearer spokespersons for deepening democracy within pluralist societies than many social democrats today. Radical greens provide new reasons for constraining capitalism – reasons that may be more compelling today than the longstanding arguments of socialists. Each of these quasi-ideologies will be introduced in this section.[8]

Democratic socialists rose to prominence as revisionist Marxists, but they have mostly advocated and pursued programs that simply strive to push pluralist societies further to the left.[9] While providing a more radical critique of capitalism than contemporary liberals, democratic socialists reject the idea of orthodox Marxists that revolution is necessary to solve the problems of capitalism. Instead, they have formed socialist parties that compete in democratic elections to use governmental power to achieve such Marxist goals as enhancing public control of the means of production, distributing social goods more equally, and developing deeper democracies.

Socialist sentiments are probably as old as human life, but the ideology of democratic socialism is a reaction to capitalism. In 1884, the Fabian Society was founded in England by a group of intellectuals led by Sidney Webb (1859–1947), his wife Beatrice Webb (1858–1943), and the famous playwright George Bernard Shaw (1856–1950). The *Fabians* shared Marx's indictment of capitalism but wanted to move gradually away from capitalism and toward socialism through non-violent, consensual processes. As support for socialism increased, the Fabians believed that democratic socialists could be elected to Parliament, where they could introduce socialist reforms. In 1901, they cooperated with leaders of the major British trade unions to form the Labour party, but it was not until the end of World War II that Labour controlled the House of Commons and formed the government. While in power, Labour implemented a number of socialist policies, such as nationalizing the production of electricity, steel, and coal, and socializing medical care. Throughout the twentieth century, the Fabian Society continued to develop and defend democratic socialism. The Labour Party has been the principal competitor of the Conservative Party and thus a major force in British politics. Under Tony Blair and, since 2007, Gordon Brown, the Labour Party – often now called "New Labour" – governs Great Britain today, though some complain that too often it has compromised its socialist principles.

A variety of other socialist parties and movements formed toward the end of the nineteenth century in continental Europe, including the Sozialistische Partei Deutschlands (SPD) in Germany. By 1895, the SPD was divided between orthodox Marxists and **revisionists**, whose views were influenced by the Fabians. The most prominent revisionist, Eduard Bernstein (1850–1932), argued that orthodox Marxists had misinterpreted Marx, making his theory of change too deterministic.[10] According to Bernstein, the orthodox Marxist doctrine that capitalism would collapse when conditions were ripe gave the SPD little to do but sit around and await the revolution. In 1899 Bernstein wrote *Evolutionary Socialism*, which argued that capitalism was not about to collapse, that the working class was becoming less revolutionary, and that increases in democratization enabled the SPD to achieve political power and institute reforms leading to socialism. While the SPD adopted revisionist principles, it did not ascend to power until the 1970s, when it became the dominant party in a coalition that ruled West Germany, and its leader, Willy Brandt, became Chancellor. Between 1998 and 2005, the SPD was the dominant party in a coalition governing a united Germany, but its leader, former Chancellor Gerhard Schroeder, was (like Blair) often regarded as a timid proponent of socialist principles.

With the exception of the United States, all industrialized Western democracies have significant social democratic parties, and the ideology of democratic socialism remains a major voice in the pluralistic politics of these nations.[11] At one time or another since 1975, social democratic parties have ruled Britain, Germany, France, Spain, Portugal, Greece, Norway, Denmark, and other Western European democracies. Since 1989, leaders with social democratic orientations have governed many of the former communist nations in Eastern Europe. Social Democratic parties have also formed governments in several provinces in Canada since the 1950s. In 2006, Michelle Bachelot became Chile's first female and socialist president, and Hugo Chávez was elected to another term as President of Venezuela, promising to lead his country in a more socialist direction. Parties with socialist tendencies currently govern several African countries – such as Tanzania, Cameroon, Mozambique, and Zimbabwe. However, Sweden has been social democracy's greatest success story.

The Social Democratic Labor Party (SAP) first came to power in Sweden in 1932 and still receives more votes than any other Swedish party, although a poor showing in Fall 2006 resulted in the resignation of the SAP Prime Minister and the formation of a moderate governing coalition. By governing almost continuously for 75 years, the SAP helped transform Sweden from one of Europe's poorer nations to one of the world's most affluent. Simultaneously, Sweden has achieved one of the world's most equal distributions of income. In pursuit of economic prosperity and income equality, the SAP developed an extensive welfare state, but it has eschewed public ownership of the means of production. Today about 85 percent of Swedish industry remains privately owned. While the SAP has thus abandoned one of the main programs of the Fabians and revisionists, its successes have helped to reorient the focus of democratic socialism from economic production to economic distribution.

Like contemporary liberals, democratic socialists – who will, for brevity, be referred to as socialists in the remainder of this book – believe that a pure capitalist system is plagued by various market failures: business cycles that produce deep economic recessions; inadequate provision of public goods; negative externalities in which the public absorbs significant costs of production; and so forth. But socialists believe that a critique of capitalism that focuses solely on market failures is superficial. They believe that liberals fail to see how the capitalist system dominates all aspects of human life, socializing people to be excessively materialistic and selfish, making their governments far less democratic than popularly believed, and forming the foundations of many social divisions and hierarchies. Still, socialism remains within the pluralist tradition, because socialists do not seek to abolish capitalism. Instead, they wish to limit its domination over economic, social, and political life. Rather than abolishing private property, they wish to limit the benefits that accrue to those who own property. Rather than seeking absolute economic equality, they wish to limit the excessive pride, luxury, and power that accompany the concentration of wealth.

To alleviate the problems of capitalism without eliminating capitalism, socialists seek a transformation of cultural values. Unlike orthodox Marxists, socialists believe that the basic values supported by democratic capitalism can be reformulated in a socialist manner and incorporated into the culture of a society where capitalist institutions play an important role. For example, socialists seek liberty, but a liberal conception of liberty that focuses on economic freedoms and the rights of property-owners is, in their view, a crimped conception. Minimally, political communities as a whole have liberty only when they are free of domination by capitalists. If socialists can expand the public's understanding of such liberal values as liberty, they can achieve broad popular support for curbing the abuses of capitalism, and this popular support can form the basis for democratic control of capitalism.

While socialism has been a leading ideology of parties on the left within plur-alist societies, *egalitarian liberalism* has been a leading political philosophy among academics. Developed primarily in *A Theory of Justice*, published in 1971 by Harvard philosophy professor John Rawls, egalitarian liberalism proposes a more equal dis-tribution of social goods within pluralist societies than is the central tendency among contemporary liberals; perhaps it is more egalitarian than democratic socialism. Egalitarian liberals point out that distributions of wealth, income, education, and other opportunities for success in pluralist societies are highly influenced by natural inequalities (such as genetic differences in intelligence and energy) and social circum-stances (such as the difference in resources that families and communities provide to help or hinder one's prospects). Because people cannot choose their natural endowments and the social conditions in which they are raised, both favorable and unfavorable distributions of these preconditions for success are undeserved. Egalitarian liberals believe social justice includes providing fair equal opportunity to the poorly endowed, and this requires that political communities should make extensive efforts to com-pensate those with natural and social disadvantages. Egalitarian liberals also believe that greater than average shares of wealth, income, education, and other opportunities are justified if and only if these inequalities benefit the least well-off. Rawls's theory will be considered in more detail in chapter 14, when we address questions of justice, but here it is important to note the seminal importance of *A Theory of Justice*, which revitalized political theory and sparked extensive academic discussions that have yet to be resolved. While Rawls's work accompanied a shift in contemporary liberalism to the left – to the embrace of a more extensive welfare state – such liberals have generally drifted back toward a less demanding commitment to equality.[12] While *A Theory of Justice* seems to contain a more extreme commitment to equality than most contemporary liberals have been willing to embrace, egalitarian liberals like Rawls cannot be classified as part of the extreme left, because they have tried to reconcile a strong commitment to equality with other pluralist values like individual liberty and because they have always pursued more equality through methods no more militant than trying to persuade other pluralists of the justice of their egalitarian principles.

Many people on the radical left believe that inequalities in social goods across societies are even more disturbing than those within pluralist societies. About one-quarter of the world's population subsists below the international poverty line, living on less than $140 a year.[13] According to Kai Nielsen:

> The ratio of the richest countries in the world to the poorest has steadily increased under capitalism. In 1913 the ratio of the wealth of the richest countries in the world to that of the poorest was 11 to 1, in 1950 it was 35 to 1, in 1973, it was 44 to 1, in 1992, it was 72 to 1.[14]

Such global poverty and inequality has given rise to another radical left perspective: *cosmopolitanism*. Cosmopolitan theorists of global justice essentially believe that Rawls's principles of egalitarian liberalism apply not only to how social goods should be distributed within particular pluralist societies but also to people everywhere. Cosmopolitan theorists argue that where one is born creates undeserved opportunities for some and undeserved constraints for others. They argue that justice requires that the undeserved disadvantages that plague those born into poor countries be redressed and they make a variety of proposals for reducing global inequalities. We will consider some of these in chapter 14.[15]

To clarify the difference between moderate and radical approaches to global justice, consider the work of Bill and Melinda Gates and Bono – *Time* magazine's three "persons of the year" in 2005. The Gates have established a charitable foundation with a $29 billion endowment from which they make lavish donations to help young and sick people in Africa and elsewhere. As noble and extensive as these efforts are, they are moderate in the sense that they involve no radical changes in pluralist policies, as people in those societies have always been free to give away their money. In contrast, Bono (the rock star who leads U2) has charmed and bullied leaders of the G-8 countries to provide over $50 billion in debt relief, foreign aid, and access to HIV-treatment drugs.[16] The changes brought about by Bono (and his associates) represent more radical shifts in pluralist politics, because they imply that wealthy countries have political obligations to assist poor ones that extend beyond the voluntary actions of individuals. While cosmopolitan theorists often want some international political entity to establish distributive principles that regulate economic inequalities among nations, the willingness of an international group of wealthy nations (the G-8) to pursue redistributive programs is a significant, perhaps radical, step toward acceptance of the cosmopolitan conception of justice that pluralist theorists and societies have previously been slow to embrace. Even Rawls denied that rich countries must help poor ones on an extended and prolonged basis: "Well-ordered peoples have a duty to assist burdened societies. It does not follow, however, that the only way, or the best way, to carry out this duty of assistance is by following a principle of distributive justice to regulate economic and social inequalities among societies."[17]

While most pluralists – and even some radical pluralists – believe that the application of redistributive principles on a global basis would undermine the capacities of people organized into national communities to determine their own future, cosmopolitan justice theorists continue to argue that justice requires such redistribution and that pluralist countries must recognize such obligations.

Civic communitarians provide another set of ideas that would entail radical changes in pluralist societies. They believe that contemporary liberals and egalitarian liberals like Rawls have been too individualistic and have given insufficient attention to the common good. By developing a theory to ensure individual autonomy (the capacity of individuals to choose and pursue their own life plans), egalitarian liberals forget that the choices made by individuals are greatly influenced by the social context. Michael Sandel, a Harvard political scientist, reminds us that the left has always recognized individuals as being embedded in society, has sought more social solidarity, and has encouraged citizens to develop a deep commitment to the common good. Sandel and other civic communitarians believe governments should pursue policies that develop a strong sense of citizenship, where people exhibit trust and indeed love for one another and where they understand that they have greater obligations to respond to the needs of others than would be the case within liberal, capitalist societies. For civic communitarians, the most promising setting for developing more communal orientations among citizens is within a "revitalized civic life nourished in the more particular communities we inhabit."[18] In short, civic communitarians call for a radical restructuring of civil society – a resurrection of the voluntary associations that Tocqueville had observed in American in the early nineteenth century and that Robert Putnam has chronicled as being in decay during the past half century.[19] The voluntary associations within such a society are the necessary seedbeds for developing virtuous citizens with a strong sense of solidarity that a welfare state requires and with the skills to participate in stronger forms of democracy than currently are found in pluralist polities. Such ideas are neither "right" nor "extreme." While the radical right – including more traditional communitarians – also seeks more citizen virtue, it defines virtue in terms of embracing traditional values. In contrast, the civic communitarians want citizens to pursue more socialist values, including being highly participatory on behalf of the common good. While the extreme right wants a homogeneous national culture where there is great conformity to dominant values, civic communitarians embrace heterogeneity and pluralism.[20]

Radical feminism constitutes another quasi-ideology having ideas that should be included in political conversations. While liberal feminists are content to seek equal opportunity with men within the institutions of pluralist society, radical feminists like Catharine MacKinnon contend that equality between the sexes cannot be achieved by allowing men to construct pluralist institutions that serve their interests and then giving women equal opportunity to succeed within these institutions.[21] For radical feminists, real gender equality requires a deeper reconstruction of basic social and political institutions.

The family is perhaps the most basic of these institutions. Even after liberal feminists succeeded in creating more equal opportunities for women in education and employment, women have remained subordinate to men in the patriarchal family. Even women with full-time jobs have continued to assume the lion's share of childrearing and housekeeping chores. Wives are often the targets of physical violence and verbal intimidation by their husbands. More often than men, women sacrifice their professional careers, taking maternal leaves that adversely affect promotion opportunities and quitting jobs to accommodate husbands who receive promotions and transfers to different locations. Such inequalities are often cumulative. For example, the accommodations that women make in their private lives often mean that they accrue less seniority on the job than men and thus are among the first to be laid off when companies use "last in, first out" rules to downsize. Radical feminists adopted the slogan "the private is the political," and seek transformations of private family life that will allow them more equality than occurs through the mere application of liberal nondiscrimination policies.[22]

Radical feminists understand that male dominance is not confined to the family but extends throughout pluralist society in how social roles have become defined. Even though women are increasingly admitted to medical and law schools, these professions continue to be regarded as male professions, and women are more likely to go into the fields of nursing or conflict mediation. The roles of doctor and lawyer are more prestigious and are given more remuneration than are those in nursing and mediation roles. According to MacKinnon, the curtailment of male domination requires empowering women so that they can create and define social roles reflecting female values and orientations.

Radical feminists thus seek a more expansive politics than implied by the public–private distinction invented by liberals, which has become commonplace in pluralist societies. They want women to achieve equal power with men in all the institutions of pluralist societies.

Radical democratic theorists provide yet another radical left perspective, one that challenges the adequacy of the democratic institutions and processes that currently prevail in pluralist societies. For such radicals, democracy is not achieved when citizens can choose between liberal and conservative candidates for office, when various groups have sufficient power to have at least some of their interests reflected in political outcomes, or when governments respond to the will of the majority. For such radicals, democracy is never achieved but represents a continuous horizon, a moving target of more free and equal communities. Radical democracy is an endless series of social movements to emancipate those who are marginalized, excluded, and oppressed.[23] Even if the governments of pluralist societies were to bestow equal treatment on blacks, women, and gays, democracy would still require new contentious political actions to empower those who have become subordinate to others in any of the many particular groups that exist within pluralism.[24] Even if patriarchal families were to fade away, many families would marginalize some members (for example, by abandoning elderly parents to nursing homes), giving rise to demands for more equal power and treatment in such social units.

Radical democrats thus call for "more democracy" within all pluralist institutions, ranging from the national legislature to the local parish and the nuclear family. More democracy can involve fewer restraints on what is regarded as political and thus subject to democratic determination. For example, decisions regarding the relocation of businesses are political as well as economic, because they involve entire communities that are destabilized by plant closings. More democracy in each and all sites can involve more inclusion. Those groups that have been historically marginalized can be provided with special group rights, including help in forming new organizations to represent their interests and reserving positions for members of marginalized groups on decision-making bodies.[25] More democracy can involve more deliberation. Premature up-or-down votes that reflect the preconceived interests of majorities can mean domination over the legitimate concerns of minorities. Radical democrats often want to replace "vote-centric" conceptions of democracy with "talk-centric" ones, because minorities require ample opportunities to persuade others of the justice of their concerns and interests.[26] In general, radical democrats want "strong" democratic processes that encourage wide and extensive citizen participation in all communities.[27]

Limiting the importance of capitalism and the power of capitalists in pluralist societies is important to everyone in the radical left. *Radical green* movements and parties also want to control capitalism, albeit primarily for environmental reasons. If left to their own devices, capitalists pursue new economic developments that have deleterious effects on the environment. While liberal environmentalists have tried to persuade governments to manage some of the environmental problems that result from corporate activity and economic development, they have recognized the need to balance environmental and economic concerns. For example, they have supported governmental regulations on automotive pollutant exhausts and mandated fuel improvements, but these regulations have always been relatively modest and imposed gradually in order to minimize economic costs. Liberal environmentalists have long supported what are now called "smart growth" policies that seek more compact building designs, create land-use patterns that reduce the need for automobiles, provide mass transit alternatives to automobiles, and preserve open spaces and farmland, but they have backed away from policies that create such extensive burdens on developers that economic growth is threatened or that shut down industries that might provide significant future economic benefits. Radical greens are more aggressive. The German Green Party has sought to put an end to nuclear energy as a power source. Radical greens in Brazil have tried to prevent the clearing of Amazon rainforests that enables corporate soybean production. And radical greens in America have strongly opposed oil and gas drilling in the Arctic National Wildlife Refuge. In brief, radical greens believe that environmental protection is a higher priority than economic efficiency, economic development, energy independence, and other such goals that compete for attention within pluralist politics. They believe that a sustainable environment cannot be compromised. However, they are also of the view that the economic developments that most seriously threaten the environment can best be thwarted through pluralist politics, ranging from filing law suits to block particular economic developments to building green parties that elect radical greens to public office. Ralph Nader's candidacy for the American presidency in 2000 with the backing of the Green Party illustrates the willingness of greens to engage in pluralist politics and the strong connection between battling corporate elites and achieving environmental goals. Nader, after all, had attained national prominence as an advocate of consumer interests and as a critic of the globalist agenda, articulating deep criticisms of free market capitalism that have long resonated with the radical left. While Nader was not identified with narrowly environmental concerns, most greens saw little inconsistency between his anti-corporate views and their concern for protecting the environment.[28] Those who believe that a sustainable environment can be attained by engaging in pluralist politics and placing governmental restrictions on corporate interests may be radicals, but they are not extremists. Later in this chapter, we will see that deep greens pursue a more extreme left politics that would abandon pluralism rather than work within it.

The Radical Right: Seeking More Economic Freedom or Moral Consensus

While those on the left challenge the inequalities within and across pluralist societies, those on the right believe that inequalities have legitimate explanations, moral justifications, and social benefits. The radical right embraces political ideas and policies that would enhance such inequalities or at least protect those in dominant positions from encroachments on their privileged positions. Libertarianism, global neoliberalism, national protectionism, neoconservatism, cultural (or social) conservatism, traditional communitarians, and the religious right are important contemporary voices on the radical right that are introduced in this section. Supporters of these quasi-ideologies often criticize the willingness of moderate conservatives to compromise their ideals, but because they are willing to work within pluralist politics for their goals, they are mere radicals rather than extremists. As we will see, the extreme right holds their views with such certainty that they try to suppress and even eliminate their opponents and they reject pluralist politics as a means of sustaining their preferred hierarchies.

The label given to an ideology directs us to its central goal. *Libertarianism* is an outlook that seeks to maximize liberty in all its forms. Libertarians believe people are economically free if there are no governmental restrictions on acquiring and controlling property, on where and how one is employed, on how one invests one's money, and on the goods and services that people buy and sell. They believe people are socially free when they have opportunities to improve their social positions and to move to preferred locations, when their life plans are unconstrained by social prejudices and biases, and when they can act on their own beliefs as long as they respect the rights of others. They believe people are intellectually free when they have opportunities to be exposed to a wide variety of perspectives on moral and political issues, access to the widest possible amount of information on these issues, and access to the sort of education that will enable them to analyze and use effectively various perspectives and types of information. They believe people are politically free if they have various political liberties such as the right to participate in elections and oppose the policies of rulers and if their political rulers have limited authority and are accountable to the citizenry. Libertarians in authoritarian and totalitarian societies especially protest governmental restrictions on their intellectual and political liberties. Libertarians in pluralist societies especially protest governmental limitations on their economic and social liberties.

Many students on American campuses think of themselves as libertarians because they dislike the constraints on social liberty that conservatives have enacted or support; such students are drawn to libertarian proposals to decriminalize marijuana, eliminate all governmental restrictions on abortion, and generally end governmental infringements on the rights and privacy of individuals. They regard enhancing social liberties as a project of the left, and thus are probably surprised to find libertarians categorized among the radical right.

Although libertarian commitment to social liberty is important, a broader understanding of libertarianism reveals that it emerged to defend individual property rights, capitalism, and extensive inequalities of income and wealth. Friedrich von Hayek (1899–1992), a Nobel prize-winning economist, provided an early formulation of libertarianism. He argued that humans have limited rationality and are unable to know what is best for society as a whole, or even for themselves. Because we live in ignorance, we should have liberty to experiment with our own lives. In his classic book published in 1944, *Road to Serfdom*, Hayek argued that no efforts by governments to engage in social engineering – especially the economic planning of governments – can succeed at being more effective and efficient than the results that arise from the free choices that ordinary people make in free markets. Ayn Rand (1905–82), a refugee from Communist Russia, popularized libertarian ideas with novels like *The Fountainhead* (1943) and *Atlas Shrugged* (1957), which glorified individualism, especially the self-absorbed actions of talented and creative individuals. In *The Virtues of Selfishness* (1964) and *Capitalism: The Unknown Ideal* (1966), Rand's libertarian ideals were given philosophical expression and she defended a radical form of capitalism that disparaged private charity as well as governmental welfare programs. In 1974, Robert Nozick (1938–2002), a professor of philosophy at Harvard, published perhaps the most influential single defense of libertarianism, *Anarchy, State, and Utopia*, which criticized all taxation by government to provide public programs and welfare beyond essential security (police and military protection). His minimal government – or "nightwatchman state" – would protect the property that people had justly acquired by their own efforts and by fair exchanges with others, rather than confiscate some of it through taxes and redistribute it to the poor. While libertarians have sought a great reduction of government authority in the name of individual liberty, they cannot be considered extremists, because they recognize some limits on economic liberties: that an individual's right to accumulate wealth must occur through processes that provide other individuals equal opportunities to accumulate wealth, that property accumulated unjustly (through force or fraud) is subject to claims of redress, and that the wealthy are obligated to pay taxes to provide security for all. Furthermore, libertarians pursue their goals of radically enhancing free market capitalism and radically reducing governmental programs through pluralist politics.

Less well known than libertarianism, but much more important, is the related ideology of *global neoliberalism*, which contains some of the key ideas that have come to unite the governing elite of many pluralist societies during the past three decades. Perhaps few of these world leaders identify themselves as global neoliberals, but scholarly observers and analysts find in their rhetoric and policies a public philosophy that essentially applies libertarian ideals beyond existing nation-states to the global community. Global neoliberals favor and promote globalization – the processes of increasing economic, social, and political interaction and interdependence among peoples living in different countries and cultures throughout the world. Global neoliberalism – which we will shorten to globalism – is emerging as a full-fledged ideology centered on the desirability of free market capitalism everywhere. Globalists believe that global capitalism results in many advances throughout the world – ranging from increased economic prosperity to the spread of democracy – that more than justify any increase in inequalities of income and wealth that have occurred by removing restrictions on the freedom of global capitalists.

Advocates of globalism include academics like Francis Fukuyama and Jagdish Bhagwati, journalists like Thomas Friedman, libertarians like Johan Norberg, leaders of global organizations like the World Trade Organization, the International Monetary Fund, and the World Bank, and political leaders like Margaret Thatcher, Ronald Reagan, and Bill Clinton.[29] George W. Bush's initiatives on behalf of immigration reform, tax reduction, and privatizing social security are among the reasons he can be seen as continuing and perhaps deepening the globalist agenda.

Perhaps Manfred Steger has offered the most comprehensive conception of globalism thus far.[30] According to Steger, globalists make several major claims: that the global deregulation and integration of markets benefits everyone economically, that globalization also encourages democratization, and that the processes of democratization and generation of free markets can no longer be thwarted by political rulers – even those of the most powerful countries. Thus, globalists see the processes of globalization, the development of free markets and democracy, and the increases in prosperity, freedom, and equality of opportunity that accompany these processes as being "inevitable and irreversible." In a recent update of his depiction of globalism, Steger contends that Bush's promotion of a permanent war on terrorism adds a significant new plank to globalist ideology.[31]

Globalists share with libertarians the goal of radically reducing state regulations on economic activity and redistributions of wealth, but they add that economic freedom requires that people and the goods they seek are not "fenced in" by political borders as well as state regulations. Globalists seek an open global community that has blown away the walls and boundaries that divide people.[32] Thomas Friedman, a foreign correspondent for the *New York Times*, has called this vision a "flat world" – one where barriers to commerce and innovation have given way to extensive and equal opportunities for global collaboration and a level playing field enabling entrepreneurs and workers in India, China, and other emerging societies to compete on an equal basis with those in the US and Western Europe.[33]

Globalists are also committed to spreading democracy around the world – probably more so than libertarians. While libertarians fear that democracies can be overly responsive to special interests that demand extensive governmental benefits and public majorities that could demand the redistribution of wealth, globalists see constitutional democracies as the key to economic prosperity. Democratization holds political leaders accountable, requiring them to develop policies that promote widespread economic gains. Many countries are poor because they have bad governments characterized by autocratic and corrupt rule.[34] Constitutional democracies replace arbitrary decrees with the rule of law. Such laws secure property rights and provide the stability that encourages investment and economic development. Globalization has resulted in huge increases in the number of countries that are democratized – that have genuine electoral competition with extensive political rights, and the rule of law.[35] Democratization, along with the spread of capitalism, has reduced the frequency and intensity of wars, because "democracies simply do not make war on each other."[36]

Some globalists suggest that democratic capitalism is the best form of political economy everywhere and cannot be improved upon, and thus globalist principles should be universally and eternally embraced. In their view, the superiority of globalist principles so overwhelm opposing ideas that ideological competition can be projected as a thing of the past and that we are thus approaching "the end of history."[37] If this were true, pluralist societies would be radically transformed. The role of global capitalism would dramatically increase. The importance of nation-states and democratic governments in regulating capitalism and furthering egalitarian values would be greatly reduced. However, many features of a pluralist society would remain, including the diversity of groups and moral philosophies that are defining features of pluralism. Globalists can also be seen as pluralists, because they work within the institutions and processes of pluralist societies in pursuit of their goals. But while globalism may be the dominant governing ideology among the world's elite, and though it may result in profound changes in pluralism, it is doubtful that we are at "the end of history" – that its principles will be consensually embraced. Many perspectives on the left regard globalism as an ideology that provides a benevolent mask for the efforts of global capitalists to achieve unprecedented concentrations of wealth and power.[38] Indeed, other voices within the radical right would question and strongly disagree with globalist ideals in conversations on perennial issues.

Neoconservatives generally celebrate global capitalism, but they also fear that the centrifugal forces of capitalism, if unabated, can melt the social glue that keeps political communities together. The neoconservative movement dates to the early 1970s, when former leftists who became disillusioned with the policy failures of liberal and socialist governments founded it. To refine their ideas, they captured control of influential journals like *Commentary*, when Norman Podhoretz became its editor, and they formed their own journal, *The Public Interest*, under the editorship of Irving Kristol. As they developed their criticisms of liberalisms and socialism, they became increasingly supportive of capitalism. But they recognized that capitalism could produce increasingly self-interested citizens and thus saw the need for strong governments that could exercise social control and discipline citizens in the face of domestic and international threats. Neoconservatives have thus often supported the militarization of political communities.[39] "Neocons" recognize the desirability of political authorities mobilizing citizens on behalf of such national purposes as bringing democracy to the Middle East. They seek to instill moral purpose into citizens, prompting widespread adherence to traditional cultural and religious values. Some analysts think that the ideas of neoconservatism have become so enmeshed with those of contemporary conservatism that it no longer provides a distinct voice. But some leaders in the Bush administration – especially Dick Cheney, Donald Rumsfeld, and Paul Wolfowitz – retained the label "neoconservative" especially in regard to their distinctive foreign policy views. Their emphasis was on the need to clearly distinguish America's friends from its foes and to use military force against foes, in a pre-emptive fashion if required, for vital national interests and security. Compared to many other conservatives, they were more idealistic, believing the US has a moral duty to spread democracy even if that imposes significant burdens on the country.

National protectionists are the most obvious opponents of globalism among the radical right. While globalists praise multinational corporations and global capitalism for their economic innovations and efficiencies, national protectionists demonize them. National protectionists fear that globalization threatens the old world order: the dominance of the US in that order and the special places that European nations have had in Western civilization.

During the early 1990s, Ross Perot claimed that global capitalists used their power to undermine self-made entrepreneurs like himself, and he noticed that increasing global exchanges had resulted in massive trade deficits that would ultimately undermine the American economy. His opposition to the North American Free Trade Association (NAFTA) found a receptive audience and earned him 19 percent of the votes for the American presidency in 1992. Pat Buchanan argued that globalization meant that American companies were relocating in countries having much lower labor costs than those in the US, with devastating consequences for the employment prospects and wages of the American worker. Such ideas resulted in his succeeding Perot as the Reform Party candidate for president in 2000.[40] Since then, Buchanan has called on Americans to stem "the invasion" of immigrants into the US.[41] Jean-Marie Le Pen and Gerhard Frey have attained significant followings in France and Germany by criticizing the extensive immigration of foreigners into their countries that has occurred under global capitalism. Such spokespersons for this strand within the radical right reject the globalist movement toward open borders; they want to use the powers of national governments to reduce the flow of trade, investments, jobs, and immigration across national boundaries. To preserve what they see as the unique virtues of their countries – really, the superiority and privileged positions of their countries – they wish to isolate their nations from the pressures and disruptions of globalization.

Cultural conservatives emphasize the social and cultural disruptions of global capitalism. Echoing national protectionists, they recognize that globalization results in the arrival of new cultural subcommunities within nations, exemplified by the concentration of Hispanic immigrants (both legal and illegal) in particular localities in the US.[42] While pluralist societies have always been open to some immigrants, the current patterns of immigration are, according to Samuel Huntington, much more extensive, derive more extensively from a single source (Mexico or perhaps Latin America generally), and are much less likely to result in assimilation into the dominant culture. Compared to previous immigrants, Latinos are said to be less willing to become proficient in English and are less supportive of American values.[43]

Additionally, cultural conservatives believe that globalization has increasingly oriented people – not just immigrants but other citizens of pluralist society, especially the young – to material values. The spread of a market mentality orients people to a life of production and consumption, and many of the goods and services that global corporations provide and peddle are without redeeming moral value – indeed they are often morally debasing. A culture of decency and high standards has given way to a pop culture that appeals to people's lowest impulses.

The concerns of cultural conservatives have, of course, predated the ascendance of global capitalism. People have long worried that pluralist societies endorse a moral relativism that is unable to distinguish good lifestyles and values from degrading ones. During the 1980s, an important academic perspective – *traditional communitarianism* – became prominent, providing a philosophical basis for such concerns and contributing to a larger communitarian movement. Alasdair MacIntyre (a philosophy professor at Notre Dame) and Mary Ann Glendon (a law professor at Harvard) have been the most well-known contributors to this perspective.[44] Traditional communitarians see pluralist society as largely dominated by liberal ideas, and they believe that liberalism has been a disastrous political philosophy throughout the modern era. Under the influence of liberalism, individuals have become uprooted from the local communities that had previously provided social roles and identities, giving meaning to life. Liberalism is responsible for people trying to find moral truths and virtues in some source other than traditional understandings. Because efforts to find alternative bases for morality and justice have produced no consensus, we flounder in a sea of confusion and disarray.

Traditional communitarians also maintain that we often claim rights to things we simply want, even if there is no legal or moral basis for these rights.[45] Such communitarians try to encourage us to think more seriously about the obligations that we owe to others and to the communities of which we are part. If all this sounds familiar, it is because there is significant overlap between the ideas of traditional conservatives, contemporary conservatives, and traditional communitarians. However, contemporary conservatism has been a powerful governing ideology, while traditional communitarianism is much more an outlook of protest against liberalism and the deficiencies of pluralism. Traditional communitarians would like to move pluralism to the right by awakening its citizens to traditional moral values and vices. For example, Glendon argues that the right of couples to dissolve an unhappy marriage, which liberals have increasingly recognized in legislation and court rulings, ignores the traditional responsibilities that parents have to their children.[46]

In contrast to other radical right perspectives and to traditional conservatives, traditional communitarians are little concerned with defending economic inequalities and social hierarchies. In contrast to cultural conservatives, they recognize that there are many, often competing, traditional values, and they doubt that political disputes can be resolved by guidance from any particular moral tradition. Traditional communitarians try to negotiate the problems that pluralist societies have inherited from liberals by consulting the many ideas that various cultural traditions have bequeathed to us and by using our reasoning capacity to do the best we can to create more substantial communities and more ethical individuals. By recognizing the variety of moral traditions that exist within pluralist societies and the relevance of pluralist politics for sorting out our moral conflicts, traditional communitarians clearly operate within pluralist politics, but the society that would emerge from application of their ideas would probably be radically transformed from the current one that stresses liberal freedoms.[47]

Finally, it is important to acknowledge that there are many prominent religious groups that contribute to the radical right. Like cultural conservatives and the traditional communitarians, the *religious right* pursues a politics of morality, but it finds morality in religious teachings more than in cultural values and tradition. Its adherents are among the strongest opponents of abortion rights, gay rights, and the teaching of evolution as "scientific truth" in American schools. During the 1980s, Jerry Falwell of the Moral Majority was the most prominent spokesman for the religious right. During the 1990s, Ralph Reed of the Christian Coalition assumed center stage for this outlook. According to Damon Linker, *theoconservatism* has now emerged as a powerful outlook among the religious right in America, and its leaders – Richard John Neuhaus, Michael Novak, and George Weigel – have the ear of George W. Bush, Antonin Scalia, Sam Brownback and many other political leaders.[48]

Because the religious right and religious fundamentalists both stress the authority of sacred texts like the Bible, they are often confused, but those on the religious right are merely radicals within pluralism, while fundamentalists can be seen as extremists who want to eliminate the pluralism of our political communities. Those adhering to the religious right believe strongly that God's will on moral issues and His role in the creation of the world is evident in sacred texts, and they believe that it is their duty to bring God's voice into political discussions and to try to resolve political disputes in ways that He would approve. But they stop short of proclaiming that there can be no correct interpretation of God's will other than their own, and thus they refrain from seeking to have their religion established as the only religion approved by the state. They stop short of seeing all people who disagree with their views as sinners who should receive divine punishment. The religious right uses pluralist processes to try to create a more religious and devout society, though that society can exhibit some differences in religious beliefs.[49] As we shall see, some religious groups have more extreme views than these.

The Extreme Right: Returning to More Homogeneous Societies

Since 9/11/01, Osama bin Laden, al-Qaeda, and Islam have been the focus of attention as central threats to pluralist societies. Widening our focus from particular individuals and organizations responsible for acts of terrorism to a consideration of broader political viewpoints that give rise to overt attacks on pluralist societies is needed, but Islam is both an overly wide and overly narrow target of attention. Islam is a religion that trails only Christianity in the number of adherents it has worldwide, and it is an extremely diverse outlook; few of its adherents espouse political and philosophical ideas that are hostile to pluralist societies. Consequently, most analysts narrow their focus to *Islamic fundamentalism*, or what is sometimes called "political Islam." Here the focus is only on those Islamic groups that are hostile to pluralism, who regard pluralism as being synonymous with globalization, Westernization, or Americanization, and who despise these forces because they seem to impose cultural values alien to traditional Islamic culture.[50] But a focus on Islamic fundamentalism is too narrow, because it misses other forces on the extreme right that contain ideas dangerous to pluralism. In this section, we begin with a discussion of Islamic fundamentalism and then consider these other voices on the extreme right.

According to Gilles Kepel, a professor specializing in Arabic and Islamic Studies at the Institute for Political Studies in Paris, political Islam came into existence during the 1960s when Arabic intellectuals became dissatisfied with Arab leaders – such as Egypt's Gamal Nasser (1918–70) – who had helped free Arab societies from colonial rule but had allegedly governed in secular, corrupt, and often brutal manners.[51] To generate revolutionary opposition to such leaders, they stressed a more fundamentalist set of political and religious ideas than had come to characterize mainstream Islam. They emphasized that the answer to the problems of the Arabic world was to rebel in accordance with tactics of *jihad* (to struggle against the forces of evil, using violence if necessary) and to govern according to the *sharia* (Islamic law). The 1979 revolution in Iran was the initial success of Islamic fundamentalism, as it resulted in the collapse of the American-supported Pahlavi regime and the creation of an Islamic theocracy under Ayatollah Khomeini (1900–89). Despite the successes of political Islam in Iran and a few other countries, this perspective remained a minority voice in the Arabic world and in other Muslim societies. According to Kepel, its appeal was in decline when al-Qaeda struck the World Trade Center and the Pentagon, the most visible symbols of Western and American economic and military power. While the attacks were intended to demonstrate to the Muslim world the continued saliency of political Islam, most Muslims initially rejected their views. But, as is often the case, when the leaders of a pluralist society respond to such extremists, they often over-react (as Kepel claims has been the case with American involvements in Iraq), giving credence to the claim that America is more an imperial force than a democracy that respects the sovereignty of other nations. In any event, Islamic fundamentalism has regained momentum as a threat to (Western) pluralist societies. The major role of the United Iraqi Alliance (led by Ayatollah Ali al-Sistani) in post-Saddam Iraq, the ascendance of Mahmoud Ahmadinejad to the Presidency of Iran, and the resurgence of the Taliban in Afghanistan illustrate the continuing appeal of Islamic fundamentalism in the Middle East.

If Islamic fundamentalism arose out of a broader Islamic religion to become an external threat to pluralist societies, could Christian fundamentalism arise out of a broader Christian religion to pose an internal threat to pluralist societies? *Christian fundamentalism* in America has been mostly a nonpolitical phenomenon. When its doctrine was spelled out in the *Fundamentals*, a 12-volume book published between 1910 and 1915, mainstream churches were criticized for being too involved in politics. The most important event that thrust Christian fundamentalists into politics was the *Roe v. Wade* decision by the US Supreme Court in 1973: the idea that the govern-ment could sanction "killing babies" convinced many fundamentalists that the time had come to speak out on political issues and be involved in political campaigns. Some Christian fundamentalists joined Operation Rescue and other militant foes of abortion.[52]

Christian fundamentalists believe in the inerrancy of the Bible; they claim that it provides an absolutely true narrative of history and absolutely correct guidelines for what humans should believe and how they should behave. If fundamentalist churches wish to impose biblical claims on their own members, pluralists should not object, because pluralism tolerates groups that practice a wide variety of comprehensive moral doctrines.[53] Pluralists only fear that fundamentalists may seek to impose their views on all members of a pluralist community through the coercive powers of government. Few Christian fundamentalists proclaim a desire to create a Christian theocracy in America, but some episodes are not reassuring. For example, Judge Roy Moore defied a US Supreme Court ruling requiring him to remove a granite monument of the Ten Commandments from state property, as a violation of the separation of church and state principle. While that defiance resulted in Moore's removal as Chief Justice of the Alabama Supreme Court, it gave rise to a crusade to generate public support for a Christian fundamentalist theocracy.[54] In short, Christian fundamentalists can move from being right-wing radicals to being right-wing extremists if they seek to transform pluralist societies into homogenous Christian ones whose governments privilege Christian organizations, beliefs, and behaviors.

Not all right-wing extremists are motivated by religion. For example, white nationalists may simply want to create separate white and black nations because they believe, like Nazis, that only racially pure countries can provide people with secure identities and achieve greatness for their peoples.[55] Other right-wing extremists can be motivated by a belief that their government is controlled by hidden conspirators, such as a Zionist Occupational Government, that must be opposed in many ways.[56] The ideas of such groups must be heard and answered in conversations addressing great political issues.

The Extreme Left: Deconstructing Global Neoliberalism

It is doubtful that left-wing extremism threatens pluralism today as much as it did in the past. Leading contemporary spokespersons for the extreme left are often scholars ensconced in universities who are content to write about the evils of capitalism and globalization and who have no real program for political change; as Richard Rorty has claimed, theirs is a politics of "spectatorship."[57] Additionally, today's extreme left seems less hostile than the extreme right to pluralist public philosophy, as many of their spokespersons can be interpreted as saying that a pluralism that respects all human differences is laudable, but that the pluralism that exists in America and many other Western societies is a sham, fatally corrupted by capitalist, corporate, and bureaucratic power. The extreme left is more anti-globalization, anti-capitalism, and anti-government than the radical left that works within pluralist institutions. The extreme left is comprised of a host perspectives and organizations that position themselves as strong opponents of some aspect of pluralist societies.

Perhaps the most noteworthy theoretical and philosophical expression of left-wing extremists is that of Michael Hardt and Antonio Negri. *Empire*, published in 2000, has been hailed as the "Communist Manifesto of our time," incorporating themes of *autonomism*, a movement within Italian communism stressing direct local participation and popular resistance, in which Negri has occupied a central role.[58] Hardt and Negri claim that globalization is the latest mutation of the capitalist system, a more advanced form of global economic and political domination than imperialism, with even greater capacities to co-opt those who struggle against domination. Written in a dense and opaque manner that eludes clear interpretation, *Empire* can be seen as a deep critique of any suggestion that the global order that currently exists is a pluralist one. While Empire may be governed according to globalist ideology, its governing institutions and practices can scarcely be regarded as democratic.

In 2004, Hardt and Negri published an important sequel, *Multitude*. Among the many ideas introduced in *Multitude* is that the Empire that sustains globalist principles now depends on people accepting that we are in a permanent state of war against terrorism. They also suggest that the only way out of the states of war and domination that Empire sustains is the generation of a grand democratic movement that simultaneously embraces "singularities" (the uniqueness of all individuals) and "the common" (cooperative arrangements whereby ordinary people collaborate in producing both material and, especially, nonmaterial goods for public use). But just as Marx and Engels were less concerned with advocating a revolution against capitalism than explaining the forces that *will* result in such a revolution,[59] Hardt and Negri are less concerned with advocating a great democratic movement than analyzing the current forces that are producing a movement that *could* overcome Empire. According to Hardt and Negri, the forces of globalization that make Empire necessary also are planting the seeds that may result in the destruction of Empire, by creating new networks of cooperation and communication among ordinary people – the multitude – that make possible their resistance to Empire. Such resistance need not take the form of violent revolution against Empire and the sham pluralist societies that it governs. Instead, resistance can take the form of "exodus" in which the multitude becomes enraged with how powerful actors within Empire expropriate the common. Resistance will involve the invention of new weapons that simultaneously emasculate the *biopower* of Empire (its political control over all life) and generate a *biopolitics* by the Multitude (the social production of the real ends of life, rather than the mere material means of life). The exodus that Hardt and Negri predict – if not advocate – must be from the institutions and values that dominate the (sham) pluralist societies that Empire now governs. Perhaps the networks of collaboration that will remain after the old oppressive institutions and processes of Empire are vacated will provide some sort a new postmodern structures that will be sufficiently decentralized and democratic to be in some sense pluralistic. These structures may even provide a higher stage of pluralism than exists in the most democratic societies that now exist. All that seems clear in this extremist left vision is that any exodus from Empire that dominates the (sham) pluralist societies that exist would be a blessed event and should thus be encouraged. Buying into any consensus that currently exists about how pluralist societies should be governed would reflect the biopower of Empire and thus would be both sad and reactionary.

In developing their extreme left vision, Hardt and Negri draw on poststructuralists such as Michel Foucault (1926–84), Jacque Derrida (1930–2004), and Chantal Mouffe

(1943–). *Poststructuralists* position themselves as critics of the various friends and assumptions of pluralism. They would be the first to question the very idea of any underlying consensus within pluralism, at least if that consensus is said to encompass the diversity of interests, ideals, and identities that exist but are often unrepresented within actual pluralist societies.[60] Poststructuralists regard the task of political theory as bringing into question the concepts and understandings that pluralists accept as foundational to their politics. They inquire into how these understandings have been imposed by powerful interests and how these understandings ignore the interests of people who are marginalized by existing pluralist understandings. They oppose any stable understanding of what politics is, how political processes should be structured, or what the goals of politics ought to be. For poststructuralists, politics is a continual process of "deconstructing" and contesting all understandings and arrangements.

Postmodern feminists such as Mary Daly – a professor of theology at Boston College – and Judith Butler – a professor of comparative literature at the University of California, Berkeley – can also be seen as part of the extreme left, with close ties to poststructuralism. While liberal feminists seek to pursue the interests of women through current pluralist politics, and while radical feminists seek to pursue the interests of women by radically reforming pluralist institutions, postmodern feminists stress that the real interests and needs of women can be satisfied only through a complete transformation in how we think.[61] The ideas that we have about how we should live and the languages that we have developed to express and analyze our ideas are male creations, and they are biased toward male interests. For such feminists, pluralist politics was also developed by men to reflect male understandings of politics. Thus, postmodern feminists seek both to detect the hidden male values of pluralism (and its friends) and to discover what is distinct in the excluded female experience that should be included in a more genuine pluralist politics or in a politics that transcends pluralism.

Another important voice on the extreme left comes from *deep greens* like Andrew Dobson and William Ophuls. Deep greens dismiss the band-aid solutions that liberal environmentalists would apply to particular environmental problems and even the extensive restrictions that radical greens would have national governments impose on capitalism and economic development.[62] As long as global capitalism exists, large corporations will develop the capacity to work around environmental restrictions. Profit motives will always prompt corporate capitalists to generate consumer demands for goods that can only be satisfied by exceeding the earth's ecological limits.[63] Large pluralist governments will always respond to the interests of capitalists and the desire of voters for more material consumption. Consequently, corporate interests that produce goods for profit must be replaced by local and small-scale enterprises that produce only those goods needed to sustain local communities.[64] National governments must be replaced by decentralized and highly democratic communities, in which citizens who understand the earth's ecological limits are encouraged to participate in making community decisions because they will realize they can make a difference in such local governance. Even extensive global agreements to address environmental deterioration will not work without revolutionary changes both in the economic and political systems that depend on exploiting the environment and in the consumerist values and lifestyles that globalization is spreading around the world. Deep greens thus propose extensive changes in human habits and practices. Humans must reduce significantly their consumption of material goods. Humans must control their populations. Humans must accept a deep sense of duty to the preservation of nature. In short, humans must give up significant autonomy, the capacity to live as they wish, which is the hallmark of a pluralist society. At the very minimum, the range of responsible lifestyles that would be acceptable within pluralist society should be greatly reduced. The governments of the societies proposed by deep greens could not be neutral on questions of what constitutes the good life. They would have to proclaim that the good life was a simple one, in which people lived in spiritual harmony with nature. They would need to find ways to induce people to live by an ecological ethic and punish those who departed from such an ethic. Deep greens can be seen as having the most developed left-wing public philosophy that stands in clear opposition to current pluralist politics.

Any listing and categorization of the extreme left is highly contestable. Certainly, these schools overlap and influence each other in many ways, and many voices on the extremist left – like Noam Chomsky – simply elude any of the categories that we have named. What all voices on the extreme left stress is the need to confront the existing systems of domination, and thus the contemporary extreme left can collectively be termed *neo-anarchists*. This label has been applied, for example, to Chomsky, and it seems to fit.[65] Most of Chomsky's writings stress the imperialism of American corporations and government. He details how American policies are designed to ensure America the lion's share of the world's wealth and how the US has wreaked havoc on others throughout the world. But Chomsky argues that any government or any other institution that imposes "arbitrary authority" over individuals is illegitimate. Authority that is based on anything other than truth is arbitrary. But if truth is hard to come by in politics, then every effort of institutions to apply authority can and must be questioned. It is doubtful that neo-anarchists like Chomsky would accept the consensual understandings of pluralists as truths, as they could always propose some hidden power that prompts people to reach consensus.

Conclusions

Globalism is probably the most potent of the perspectives introduced in this chapter. Its ideas are prominent among political and corporate elites throughout the world and its ideals are embedded in the practices of governments and multinational corporations, greatly influencing the extensive changes that are remaking economic, social, cultural, and political life everywhere. Nevertheless, it is probably a mistake to regard globalism as an emerging hegemonic ideology, as its influence is undermined by many competing voices throughout the political spectrum, even within the radical right.

Globalists are strongly opposed by voices on the radical left (as well as by extremists on both the right and the left). While globalists are prepared to unleash capitalism, the radical left reminds us of the limitations and dangers of that approach. It is difficult to dismiss as unreasonable the concerns of the radical left for reducing capitalist domination, providing more global justice, and enhancing citizenship. When various radicals on the left pursue their goals through democratic processes and persuasion, their efforts certainly fall within the realm of acceptable pluralist politics.

However, the radical left must respond to many criticisms. Perhaps their views of capitalism could encourage the dismantling of the world's most productive and prosperous economic system. Perhaps their goals require a dominating state that threatens citizen liberties. Perhaps their ideas of social justice create unrealistic expectations about a more egalitarian society than is achievable. Perhaps the radical left seeks too much democracy, forgetting that when citizens are overly empowered they end up electing charlatans and demagogues and pursuing policies that undermine the public good and the rights of minorities. Perhaps the projects of the radical left are founded on naive and overly optimistic assumptions about human nature and society. Such are some of the challenges that await the radical left when they enter into political conversations.

Islamic fundamentalism currently is seen as posing the greatest challenge to the emerging dominant ideology of globalism and to the general public philosophy of pluralism. Islamic fundamentalists proclaim that globalization is really Westernization and even Americanization, the imposition on their cultures of hedonist values that are foreign to their cultures, and they claim pluralism is a recipe for moral and religious decay. While many leaders of Western societies employ rhetoric claiming the political Islam is the newest danger to pluralism, such rhetoric may reveal the extent to which such leaders actually recognize the opportunity that Islamic fundamentalism provides for pluralism. The very diversity of pluralist societies means that they have relatively few common bonds that help sustain the solidarity, loyalty, and patriotism needed for collective strength and stability. Having an external enemy can be seen as important to pluralist societies, and the attacks of 9/11 surely provided George W. Bush and other leaders of such societies with an occasion for rallying patriotism. The end of the Cold War deprived pluralist societies of their traditional enemy – Soviet-led communism – and so Islamic fundamentalism may serve as a useful substitute. Without depreciating the damage and disruption that Islam fundamentalism can impose on pluralist societies, this simple substitution is less than convincing. Soviet communism was directed by a national superpower, while Islamic fundamentalism has no unifying state and the states that are most clearly governed by its ideals – Iran, Syria, and Sudan – are far less developed and powerful than the former Soviet Union. Islamic fundamentalism is a relatively small movement within the much larger Islamic community. Its resort to terrorism as a tactic for pursuing its political agenda is evidence of its general weakness, as terrorism is, of course, a tactic of the weak, of those who fail to possess more conventional political and military resources.

Islam is not the only religion with fundamentalist factions that would like to replace pluralist communities with theocracies. Christian, Jewish, and Hindu fundamentalists may also wish to dominant political life in ways that privilege their religious outlooks.

Indeed, some observers believe that the twenty-first century will be an era in which a vast profusion of apocalyptic and messianic movements will seek to bring about various Kingdoms of God on earth through militant and violent means.[66] Pluralists must recognize that they are engaged in a "war of ideas" with such outlooks; they will have to persuade people everywhere that it is better to adopt pluralist public philosophies that can accommodate various religious outlooks than it is to pursue theocracies that would privilege particular religions.

Opponents of globalism might be attracted to the views of the extreme left, especially the idea that globalism is an ideological mask that disguises the more oppressive forces of Hardt and Negri's *Empire*, which dominates life throughout the world in ways that undermine freedom, equality, justice, and democracy. Indeed, pluralists having various left-leaning orientations can find in most extreme left perspectives many ideas to admire, but they must be wary of the portrait that the extreme left paints of pluralists and the politics they support. The extreme left argues that pluralist societies are so infused with corrupt values and so dominated by powerful economic actors and forces that they are incapable of achieving the values that pluralists proclaim. It is doubtful that pluralist societies can survive if their citizens develop the deeply cynical attitudes that left-wing extremists propagate. While there might be little danger that the extreme left would overthrow pluralist societies, the ideas of such extremists can still be dangerous to pluralism if they induce us simply to abandon pluralism because of *our* cynicism about it. The extreme left contributes to cynicism by questioning our identities as individuals bound together in political communities, by rejecting any legitimate role for capitalist institutions and market justice, by denying the possibility of effective democratic authority, by suggesting a conspiratorial and all-embracing set of rulers, by disparaging the capacities of ordinary citizens, and by embracing a nihilistic approach to political change. The extreme left may also endanger pluralism if its underlying philosophical assumptions include an extremely skeptical epistemology that denies the possibility of any valid socially constructed consensus.

Radicals on both the right and the left may provide important insights that can deepen pluralist understandings. From globalists, pluralists might come to better understand the positive aspects of globalization, modifying their public philosophy to accommodate such developments. From communitarians, pluralists can develop greater sympathy for the religious and moral concerns of many citizens, seeking ways to help bridge some of the culture wars that currently divide pluralist societies. From these outlooks, as well as from cultural conservatives and democratic socialists, pluralists can come to understand that citizens are well served by being more embedded in community life, and that community life would be well served by citizens having a greater sense of their social and political obligations. From various voices on the radical left, pluralists can recognize the many questionable inequalities that arise in pluralist societies and the deficiencies that are evident in many democratic processes and institutions. They might see the value of greater infusion of cosmopolitan redistributive principles into the international policies of pluralist nations. But while pluralism might well be improved by listening to the concerns of the radical right and radical left, pluralists can claim that such radicals too often misunderstand what pluralism stands for and the legitimate concerns of other ideological perspectives that remain friends of pluralism. The remaining chapters in this book are intended to address such misunderstandings.

Pluralists are more wary of extremists. Pluralists don't want to be inhospitable to those on the extremist right with deeply religious views, so they could propose a compromise: we will tolerate you, if you will tolerate others. Pluralists don't want to be self-righteous and proclaim that that their policies are always just and noble, so they might propose a compromise with the extreme left: we will examine some of your criticisms more carefully, if you will express these criticisms in a less cynical manner. And it is certainly plausible to believe that attaining a clearer understanding of the ecological limits within which all communities must operate would improve pluralism.

PART II

PHILOSOPHICAL ASSUMPTIONS: THEIR IMPORTANCE AS FOUNDATIONS FOR POLITICAL PRINCIPLES

The political principles of various ideologies are rooted to a significant degree in underlying ontological, anthropological, sociological, and epistemological assumptions; in other words, these principles are based in large part on what their proponents assume to be the *essence* or fundamental character of the broader universe, humans, society, and knowledge. For example, classical liberal principles ensuring extensive individual liberties are grounded in the ontological assumption that the universe is basically understood as comprising many separate material entities including individual human beings, the anthropological assumption that humans are motivated to pursue their own interests, the sociological assumption that society is merely a collection of individuals organized so as to pursue the interests of individuals, and the epistemological assumption that each human has the best understanding or knowledge of her own interests. In contrast, traditional conservative principles proclaiming that each individual should conform to his social role are grounded in the ontological assumption that each person is a link in "a great chain of being" that extends from God to the humblest insect, the anthropological assumption that the proper goal of humans is to perform dutifully the roles expected of each one in his or her station in life, the sociological assumption that societies come before their individual inhabitants (both in time and in importance), and the epistemological assumption that traditional cultural understandings provide the best knowledge available to humans about how to think and act. The next four chapters will explore in some detail the ontological, anthropological, sociological, and epistemological assumptions that underlie alternative political principles.

Before beginning this task, it is useful to consider the difference between the *principles* to be discussed in the last seven chapters of this book and the *assumptions* discussed here and in the next four chapters. Principles are general guidelines for politics that can be examined through experience. Principles proclaim what ought to be done to achieve specified goals. Certain ideologies proclaim we ought to have an unregulated capitalist economy to maximize human freedom and material prosperity. Other ideologies proclaim that we ought to have extensive governmental provisions of many social goods to ensure that humans have more equal access to the good life. While the goals sought by such principles are simply *givens*, the means specified by these principles can be examined empirically for their effectiveness in achieving the given goals. It is the desirability of the given goals that is most informed by the underlying assumptions of a political outlook. Why are the goals specified in the examples above (freedom, prosperity, and equality), as well as other ideological goals, important in the first place? Underlying philosophical assumptions form a primary basis for justifying these goals.

Such underlying assumptions are philosophical in that they cannot be examined through experience in the same way that principles can. Consider the statement, "humans are equal." There is a sense in which this statement can be examined empirically, in the light of experience. For example, experience suggests that every human will suffer pain if stabbed with a sharp knife, so in a certain sense all humans (and other animals) are equal in their capacity to suffer pain. But perhaps different humans feel pain to different degrees. And perhaps humans are different in other ways that are far more significant than their (equal) capacity to suffer pain. Such complexities make appeals to experience less than convincing in examining the validity of such a statement as "humans are equal."

One way to think about philosophical assumptions is that the universe, human beings, societies, and knowledge are simply far too complex to be reduced to statements about their natures or essences. People stress different aspects of this complexity depending on such things as their having different backgrounds and objectives. If I say that "humans are rational" and you say "humans are irrational and emotional," we are both partially right, given the complexity of human beings. From my perspective, focusing on human rationality may be a better basis than focusing on human irrationality for thinking about a political problem and a set of principles for dealing with that problem. From your perspective, focusing on human irrationality may provide a better basis for thinking about similar problems and principles. Neither of our beliefs about human (ir)rationality is completely right or wrong, but both beliefs may prove useful in developing theoretical understandings about political principles. In this way, simple assumptions that capture only part of the complexity of the broader universe, humans, societies, and knowledge are the building blocks of political theory.

Some political perspectives are fairly self-conscious about their philosophical assumptions. Classical liberals invented *the state of nature* as a devise for clarifying assumptions that they thought would be free of traditional prejudices and would thus lead to political principles that would be more universally valid. As we shall see in chapter 14, John Rawls invented the device of an *original position* to tease out the underlying assumptions of his theory of justice.[1] Other political perspectives are less self-conscious about their philosophical assumptions. Indeed, conservatives normally assert that they reject "grand theories" of politics based on rational deductions of principles from philosophical assumptions. But conservatives and those committed to other less philosophical political perspectives do assert political principles, and their writings do provide clues about their underlying assumptions. It is a task of political theorists to uncover these assumptions.

Understanding the underlying assumptions of political principles is important for both explanatory and evaluative purposes. The underlying assumptions of political principles provide perhaps the most satisfying explanations of why such principles are held and pursued. Suppose that I claim allegiance to the principles of John Rawls, proclaiming that inequalities in the distribution of social goods are justified only if they advantage the poor. If you asked me to explain my allegiance to that principle, I could provide many plausible explanations dealing with my circumstances (I am poor, and the poor would fare well under Rawls's scheme), my values (I have compassion for the poor), the influences on my thinking (my parents and church taught me to be compassionate toward the disadvantaged), and so forth. But the explanations that would be most general, that could apply to anyone holding Rawls's principle, and that could lead to the most fruitful discussion between us about the validity of the principle would be those that address the underlying assumptions. I might explain my views by referring to my assumptions of human nature; I could claim to support Rawls's principle because I assume all people are equal in their desire and capacity to pursue their own meaningful life plans, and that I therefore conclude that societies ought to allow everyone the opportunity to pursue such plans and to have access to those resources guaranteed by Rawls's principle to achieve their conception of the good life. Or I might explain my position by relating it to my assumptions about the nature of society; I could claim to support Rawls's principle because I assume that a good society is a mutually beneficial one, and that a society governed according to Rawls's principle would best achieve a society that everyone would willingly join because it would serve everyone's most fundamental interests to do so. These assumptions, along with related ontological and epistemological assumptions may all be part of why people hold – and should hold – Rawls's liberal egalitarian principles.

Of course, alternative and competing principles proposing more unequal distributions of social goods, such as those articulated by libertarians like Robert Nozick, may be explained by people holding alternative philosophical assumptions. You might explain your support for the principle that people are entitled to unequal holdings of wealth by your assumptions about human nature. You claim that humans are the sole rightful owners of their own labor and that those who labor most extensively and effectively are therefore entitled to more income and wealth. But you might also explain your support for libertarian principles because you assume, *like Rawls*, that a good society is one of mutual advantages that should enjoy the universal consent of all citizens. Moreover, you argue that such mutual benefit and universal consent would better be attained in a society governed by libertarian principles than one governed by Rawls's principles.

   These examples suggest that explanations referring to underlying assumptions also provide important information for evaluating these ideas. Lacking any analysis of the underlying assumptions of these theories, I might say I prefer Rawls's principles over those of Nozick because I value Rawls's focus on equality more than Nozick's focus on liberty, and you might say that you prefer Nozick over Rawls because you value liberty more than equality.[2] Such evaluations get us nowhere in terms of coming to agreement; we would simply agree to disagree because of our different values. But revelations about our underlying assumptions give us something to discuss in a meaningful way that might get each of us to think more clearly about our positions and possibly revise them in light of our deeper understanding. I might see in your explanation for just inequalities some truth in your assumptions about each individual being the rightful owner of their labor and the fruits of that labor. And you might see in my explanation for wanting more equal wealth some truth in my assumptions about each individual having a right to pursue their own legitimate life plans and having access to the minimal resources needed for this purpose.[3] Such new understandings might encourage us to engage in an open discussion about whether the principles of Rawls or of Nozick best lead to a society of mutual advantage and universal consent, which we both assume is important. Such a discussion would probably lead us both to realize that our conclusions here depend on epistemological assumptions about Rawls's famous "veil of ignorance" (to be discussed in chapter 14). If we are ignorant of our own circumstances and fear that we could turn out to be disadvantaged, we would see that our interests (as potentially poor people) would be furthered by more equalitarian principles. But if there is no veil of ignorance and we know we are well endowed, we would see that equalitarian principles would not be beneficial to those of us whose rights to their wealth would be limited by the application of egalitarian principles, and we would be unwilling to join a society that could deprive us of the fruits of our labor. At this point, our disagreement on principles would have deepened from a shallow and apparently irresolvable disagreement about values (our feelings about liberty and equality) to a deeper understanding of human nature and society and the role of assumptions about the veil of ignorance in resolving our disagreements. Perhaps you could convince me that the veil of ignorance is a ridiculous assumption because it is unrealistic for people to be ignorant of their natural talents and social backgrounds that would color their interests in choosing principles. But perhaps I could convince you that the veil of ignorance is a necessary epistemological assumption for getting people to look at principles objectively, in a way that is not colored by their interests.

   Once we uncover the underlying assumptions involved in our principles and come to realize the importance of these assumptions as a basis for these principles, we can discuss with each other the merits of our competing assumptions. Whether or not the assumption of a veil of ignorance (or any other assumption) has merit is perhaps dependent on a host of considerations that are beyond our capacity to explore fully here, but political philosophers agree that at this point there is no escaping various appeals to "our considered moral judgments."[4] If you and I share the moral judgment that people should choose their principles as if they were choosing for everyone and not just themselves, we would see that asking us to choose principles under the veil of ignorance would be a useful device for getting us to look beyond our self-interest and choose principles that would be desirable for everyone. If we agreed on this, we might also agree that Rawls's egalitarian principles have more adequate philosophical foundations than those inegalitarian principles of Nozick and his fellow libertarians.

Of course, this example is incomplete, as other underlying assumptions are involved in the Rawls–Nozick debate, and the analysis provided here about the veil of ignorance can be greatly extended. The point is not to answer the question of whether Rawls or Nozick provides the best theory of justice, but to demonstrate how analysis of underlying assumptions can move political conversation beyond unsatisfying and premature disagreements based on our different values to deeper reflections that can lead to greater agreement. In this way, the understanding of philosophical assumptions is crucial for deepening what we know about how political communities should be governed. In this way, understanding and analyzing the philosophical foundations of our normative theories can lead to greater intersubjective agreement about the good political community in a manner that parallels scientific analysis of our empirical theories about the actual practices of the flawed political communities in which we live.

With this introduction of the role and importance of philosophical assumptions in political thought, we are ready to turn to such assumptions about the nature of the universe, humans, society, and knowledge. As we do so, it is important to keep in mind that this text is only an introduction to political theorizing. Showing precisely how the various assumptions described here explain the principles of their adherents is an enormous task; all that can be done in this and the next few chapters is to describe the basic assumptions of people holding various principles and provide some examples of how these assumptions might connect to their principles. When we get to Part III and focus on principles, the process will be reversed. We will then describe various principles and reflect on the philosophical assumptions that might be the bases of these principles.

Analyzing the merit of these competing assumptions is an even more complex task. All we can expect is to be fascinated by the many assumptions that are available to us and to understand their importance for theorizing about politics. If this happens, you should want to enter into conversations with others about their relative merit. Hopefully, you will find fulfillment in pursuing these matters over a lifetime of becoming a deeper political thinker.

Chapter 5

Questions of Ontology

Is ultimate reality (being) essentially material, ideational, or supernatural? Are our ultimate ends (what becomes of us and of the world) determined by divine or supernatural causes? By material and natural causes? Or are ultimate ends undetermined, subject to human will and power?

Witnessing the escalating culture war over whether or not to introduce in public schools the idea that there is an "intelligent designer" of life on earth suggests the impact of ontological assumptions on political thought. Perhaps our two most basic worldviews are at stake in this issue. For those who believe that the world was made about 6,000 to 10,000 years ago by God, that He both created life on earth and controls our destiny, and that our destiny includes an afterlife in God's heaven or in the Devil's hell, the theory of evolution is inadequate and the teaching of evolution as fact in the public schools betrays a liberal and secular bias; we must therefore enact laws requiring that the concept of intelligent design be introduced (along with evolution) into science classes. For those who believe that the universe evolved naturally during the past 14 billions years, that life changes as a result of natural forces including human intervention, and that life in this material world is the only certainty for humans, science classes are no place to introduce issues of faith; political efforts to introduce intelligent design into public schools is a violation of the *sacred* principle of the separation of church and state.

As important and as widely held as they are, questions of ontology do not reduce to these two simple worldviews. In political theory and philosophy, the concept of ontology has often been used more broadly than is implied by the ontological debate between creationists and Darwinists. It is sometimes claimed that ontological assumptions refer to the basic unit of analysis and value in a public philosophy. In this usage, the ontological basis of liberalism is the individual, and all liberal principles are justified in terms of the rights and good of individuals. In this usage, the ontological basis of socialism is the community, and all socialist principles are justified on the basis of community-wide considerations. In this usage, the ontological basis of green political thought is nature as a whole, and all green principles are justified in terms of "the totality of relationships between organisms and their environments."[1] It is also sometimes claimed that ontology refers to the most fundamental force in human existence, and that this force must be identified and made the centerpiece of public philosophy. In this usage, race is seen as the ontology of Nazism, because racial struggle is seen as the ultimate basis of political action and racial supremacy is seen as the ultimate political goal. Also in this usage, war is identified as "the ontological dimension" in the left-wing extremism of Hardt and Negri; accordingly, they maintain "When genocide and atomic weapons put life itself on center stage, then war becomes properly ontological."[2]

Perhaps in its broadest usage, any foundational argument for a political principle is ontological. According to Stephen White, "strong ontologies are foundational in the traditional sense: they promise some sort of solid truth – about human nature, science, God, and so on – upon which ethical and political views ought to founded."[3] Perhaps the most prominent example of such a strong ontology is Plato's theory of the forms. In *The Republic*, Plato describes "the Good" as a transcendental, essential, and divine form of ultimate reality. The Good exists independently of human perception and thought. If humans are to approach living a truly good life, they require guidance from the form of the Good (as well as the forms of other important but lesser virtues such as Wisdom, Courage, Temperance, and Justice). In some interpretations of *The Republic*, Plato presented his ontological assumption about the Good (and other forms of virtue) as the foundation upon which he justified his principle that political communities should be ruled by philosopher-kings, since such people best knew the Good and could govern in ways that enabled people to live according to the Good. Because contemporary philosophers often doubt the existence of Platonic forms of the Good or even the capacity of humans to come to agreement about the meaning of the good life, they often turn to so-called *deontological* approaches to theory construction in which they avoid any assumptions about the meaning of the good except that its content is radically subjective; each person must have the right to define and pursue her own conceptions of the good life.[4]

Understanding these many usages of ontology helps to grasp the importance of ontological assumptions in political philosophy, but the use of this term will be more narrow and specific here. Assumptions of human nature, the nature of society, and even epistemology are ontological in the broadest sense of that term, and these assumptions can be seen as providing the ontological foundations of many political principles. But these various foundations are so important that the differences among them should be clearly acknowledged. Chapters 6, 7, and 8 will discuss various "ontological" assumptions about human nature, the nature of society, and knowledge. But these assumptions do not directly address conceptions of ultimate being in the world and indeed the universe. Nor do they address the fundamental (perhaps cosmic) forces that might work on humans and society. In this book, the concept of ontology is reserved to refer to these more ultimate beings and forces, and this chapter focuses on such ultimate realities that are foundational to various ideologies.

In general, we expect the friends of pluralism to have *weak ontologies* while non-pluralists will have strong ones. A *strong ontology* focuses on the existence and importance of a single ultimate reality – whether that be God, economic necessity, the will of elites, the will of the people, or any other basic foundation for politics. A strong ontology insists that what happens in political life and what becomes of our world is or must be determined by this ultimate reality. In contrast, a weak ontology is one that claims that humans can bring their own ideas to bear on politics and history, and the future is undetermined.

Traditional Conservatives: Emphasizing the "Great Chain of Being"

In medieval Europe, it was generally assumed that God constituted ultimate reality. God had created the universe, and His will determined the course of human history. These assumptions about how the world works obviously empowered religious authorities, especially church leaders, who claimed to know God's will and His divine laws. These assumptions also empowered the monarchies that grew in power during the sixteenth and seventeenth centuries, and that claimed *the divine right of kings* – that God had chosen them to rule.

Traditional conservatives originally maintained similar ontological assumptions by believing in the existence and political relevance of the *"great chain of being."* God, who embodies perfect goodness, is at the top of this chain (and insects, or even dust, are at the bottom). God's will creates, but does not wholly determine, reality. Humans are lower on this chain (below angels and other heavenly bodies), though not all humans are at an equal level. Some humans of high birth have virtues that are closer to the divine, while most are further removed from God's wisdom and goodness. But all individual humans have imperfections, including an imperfect understanding of how God wants humans to live. Society is intermediate between God and individual humans in the great chain of being. Society is created by God to help humans to live a good, though hardly perfect, life. Society offers insight into the good life, because it is the collective reservoir of human knowledge developed over a long period of time. Society comprises social norms and conventional cultural understandings that are superior to the insights attained by the reasoning of particular individuals and groups. This is why traditional conservatives rely on tradition and custom as the best guides to human activity. And this begins to explain why these conservatives resist changes to our traditional ways of life.

This idea of a great chain of being also includes the idea of the interconnection of all members of a society. The connection is not just among all those living; it includes a link between the living and the dead and between the living and those yet to be born. The living are connected to the dead, because the dead have bequeathed their social knowledge to the living. The living have obligations to future citizens, who are part of the ongoing history of society.

As secular and egalitarian ideas became more prominent, traditional conservatives began to downplay their belief in the great chain of being. Those few people who hold traditional conservative principles today are unlikely to claim that these principles are based on assumptions about God's plan and will. According to Michael Oakeshott, conservative principles do not rest on philosophical foundations, and conservatives need make no reference to God or religion to sustain their arguments. Conservatism is a disposition to enjoy the world as it exists, and governments are justified not by their role in the divine scheme of reality but because they ensure stability and social harmony.[5] Religious beliefs may improve morality, and religious organizations may be useful as mediating institutions in society, but conservative dispositions and beliefs no longer are based on ontological claims about God.

Classical Liberals: Deism, Naturalism, and Materialism

Many classical liberals, such as John Locke, were devout Christians who never questioned God's existence, but the founders of liberalism often embraced *deism* – the view that God created the universe and the laws governing the universe, but no longer exercised any influence over it. According to deist assumptions, God created a material world that works according to precise laws – a world of mechanical and mathematical regularity. After creating a well-ordered world, God "retired." Deists reject the medieval assumption that God actively intervenes in the world, arguing that it was absurd to think that He would alter the natural order that He created and set in motion. Deism was an important liberal assumption because it allowed liberals to view the world in completely naturalistic terms. Science could be used to observe nature and discover the order that God had created. If God's laws are completely reflected in nature and if God does not exercise His sovereignty over the universe except through the working of natural laws, the roles of religious dogma and religious authority in political life could be eliminated. For example, deism laid to rest the idea of the divine right of kings – that God bestowed and thus legitimated monarchical power. In short, liberal deism assumed that while God continued to be the ultimate being in the universe, He is not the ultimate force in the world or the ultimate cause of what becomes of the world.

In order to understand the material world that God created but no longer controlled, liberals developed the idea of *the state of nature*, a hypothetical situation of cultural, social, and political nothingness – a pristine condition of material and human existence that we could observe in an unbiased manner, without lenses introducing distortions from traditional prejudices or powerful interests. Envision a world without cultural heritages providing basic ideas about God, virtue, justice, and human potentialities. Envision a world without social structures (like families and churches). Envision a world without political and economic institutions. What remains in a world lacking such ideas and institutions? The founders of liberalism believed that what remains in an unadorned state of nature is simply matter-in-motion. Their doctrine of *ontological materialism* holds that the world is composed of physical objects set in motion, and thus subject to change, according to natural laws of causation. As we will see in more detail in the next chapter, humans too are simply material beings subject to material forces. While philosophers have often posited the existence of ultimate realities greater than that of the material world – such as Platonic forms and the divine spirit – liberals view such ultimate realities as beings that can only be grasped by metaphysical speculation and religious faith. Outside public life, such speculation and faith can provide much meaning in people's lives, but when people enter public life, they become sources of great conflict that often get resolved only by bloody religious wars. In public life, it is better to focus on the obvious reality of the material world, and use human reason and science to understand natural forces, and to apply such understandings to make the world a better place.

By reflecting on nature, classical liberals concluded that individuals had many equal natural rights – the right to life, liberty, the fruits of their labor (property), and happiness. Capitalism and representative democracy were regarded as natural means of protecting and furthering these natural rights. By seeing history as a result of natural processes, rather than as a result of God's will, liberals became receptive to the theory of Charles Darwin (1809–82) that processes of natural selection can explain the evolution of life. Many nineteenth-century liberals also embraced the theory of Herbert Spencer (1820–1903) that human evolution depends on the playing out of unchecked forces of human competition; human progress requires the *survival of the fittest* in which those humans best adapted to the environment prosper and multiply, and the weak and unfit become extinct.

As classical liberalism evolved, its advocates became less committed to strong ontological assumptions of materialism and naturalism, as they began to wonder if political practices *should* reinforce the laws of nature. Even if nature demonstrated that the fit are most likely to survive and prosper and that those with few natural endowments were most likely to suffer and perish, many liberals began to think that human life would be made better by resisting natural forces and assisting the poorly endowed. As liberalism matured, it downplayed the need for politics to reflect natural forces, much like traditional conservatives came to downplay the need for politics to reflect a supernatural order.

Anarchists: Natural Interconnections, Ideas, and Conflicts

For anarchists, the natural world is ultimate reality. Because they rejected the existence of a supernatural divinity and the sanctity of conventional society, the ontology of anarchists is much closer to that of classical liberals than to that of traditional conservatives. However, anarchists believed that classical liberals had misunderstood the natural world. While such liberals equated the natural world with material reality, anarchists viewed nature in much broader terms. The earth, the plants and animals that live on the earth, energy, social life, moral values, and even "god" can all be natural and thus important aspects of reality.

While God does not play a central role in the ontology of most anarchists, the god of such religious anarchists as Tolstoy is a natural rather than a supernatural being. Tolstoy's god does not reside outside humans or nature, but rather resides within all living beings.[6] This *pantheistic god* does not control nature or dominate human beings, but rather is a vital natural force within humans connecting man to man and man to nature. The existence of such a natural force ensures that the consciousness of each person is but part of a larger collective consciousness.[7]

Nature also provides for social life. By creating a fictitious state of nature that portrays human beings as solitary material beings, liberals underestimated the natural social qualities of human beings and the possibility of a natural society. Anarchists maintained that if one looks at humans in nature and outside conventional society, it is clear that they are not just a bundle of atoms pursuing their self-interest but are also fundamentally social beings. If one looks at natural human interactions, when these actions are unconstrained by conventional authority and institutions, there can be little doubt about the existence of natural societies, in which individuals cooperate and help each other in response to instinctual fellow feelings.[8]

In general, anarchists believed that human ideas are derived from the external environment. Ideas can be natural if they are derived from a natural environment, or they can be artificial if they are derived from conventional sources. Many human values and beliefs – such as the inherent desirability of material progress or the need for governmental authority – arise from convention and are rooted in the interests of those people who dominate conventional institutions. But other ideas – such as the need to respect the freedom of others and the desirability of living a simple life uncluttered by material luxuries – arise from natural instincts and rational reflections concerning natural processes. Conventional ideas are not part of ultimate reality because they are mere reflections of artificial power relations. But *natural ideas* are an independent aspect of ultimate reality because they exist outside the material world and conventional society and because they can have an independent impact on the course of history.

According to the Russian anarchist Alexander Herzen (1812–70), "life does not try to reach an aim," but allows for many possibilities.[9] The historical process is marked by conflict, as humans struggle against such natural forces as drought and disease, against other animals, and against each other. The outcomes of these struggles are not predetermined by natural laws. Contrary to Herbert Spencer's view that the strongest necessarily survive the struggle for existence, anarchists maintained that the characteristics of sociability or solidarity are positive resources in historical struggles. In the struggle for existence among species, humans have survived not because they are strong but because they have exhibited cooperation or mutual aid – for example by providing food and safety to one another and by helping each other raise progeny.[10] But if social cooperation fades, humans can fail in their struggles against nature and other species.

Anarchists recognized struggle as a natural force. They believed that a desire for material accumulation and private property among some people is at the root of human conflict. Anarchists assumed that the rich created institutions of domination – governments, corporations, churches, and so forth – to protect and enhance their wealth. But such institutions offend and suppress the natural desire for liberty and sociability that exist in all humans. The natural spark of freedom in each human leads the oppressed to struggle against domination, and the natural spark toward sociability leads humans to band together for collective action against their oppressors. Thus, struggles between the oppressors and the oppressed characterize the course of history. Whether the oppressors or the oppressed win the struggle is indeterminate. But natural wants, such as the desire for liberty, are potent, and they can enable the oppressed to succeed in destroying the institutions of domination. When this occurs, destruction is natural and good. It enables humans to be lifted from their oppression and permits natural social instincts to flower. If conventional institutions of domination are destroyed, natural society can emerge. If natural society emerges, human competition will diminish and perpetual struggle will cease.

Marxists: Economic Determinism

By rejecting God (as the "opiate of the masses"), Karl Marx adopted ontological foundations that resembled the materialist assumptions of classical liberals. Like anarchists, Marx regarded the natural world as our only ultimate reality, but he believed that natural forces were unfolding in a much more predictable and determinate way than anarchists presupposed. Marx also believed that the materialism emphasized by classical liberals – while thus far a great determinant of human history and life – could and would be transcended in the future.

Marxist ontology stresses three basic ideas. First, Marx embraced historicism, the assumption that human life progressed through distinct historical stages. Second, he assumed that dialectical processes involving conflicts between competing historical forces determined changes from one stage to the next. Third, he assumed that these conflicting forces were material. To understand Marxist ontology, we must clarify these three assumptions.

Historicism is the idea that history is made up of major events that mark the beginnings and endings of various historical stages, and that these events are strongly influenced by conditions and processes that are beyond intentional human control. While historicist schemes had been developed long before Marx,[11] he held a particular view that human history has three stages – pre-historical, historical, and post-historical – and several periods within the historical stage. In the pre-historical stage, humans lived in an uncorrupted natural condition, in a classless and relatively destitute society in which everyone took care of his or her own needs by hunting, fishing, and gathering. The second stage encompasses those historical periods in which private property and power are the bases for social organization. Within this historical stage, three important periods can be identified. The slaveholding period emerged during antiquity when people began to employ a division of labor in order to attain a higher economic standard of living. Rigid class systems with patricians at the top and slaves at the bottom evolved to ensure necessary but unpleasant economic activities were performed. The feudal period arose during the Middle Ages when a relatively small number of nobles acquired landed estates and dominated the serfs or peasants who labored on these manors and produced necessary agricultural goods. A third historical period of capitalism emerged in the modern era emphasizing industrial production and featuring a class structure dominated by a small number of capitalists (the bourgeoisie) who owned and controlled industrial technology and factories, and a large working class (the proletariat) who owned only their own labor. However, just as previous class structures had eventually broken down, the dominance of the bourgeoisie over the proletariat in capitalist society would also eventually come to an end. Therefore, Marx predicted a post-historical period – a future communist society – in which private property, power, and historical conflict would be eliminated.

Marx thought that change from one stage and period to the next would occur as a result of a *dialectical* process. Marx's stress on dialectics also had a long history going back to the ancient Greek philosophers. As we saw in chapter 1, dialectic meant for Plato a conversational debate between two opposing conceptions of reality; in the course of a dialectical conversation, these oppositions would be clarified and resolved, so that we might arrive at better understandings. During the early nineteenth century, the great German idealist philosopher, G. W. F. Hegel (1770–1831), applied something like this dialectical concept to the historical process. In very general terms, Hegel proposed that historical progress occurred as societies acquired ever better understandings of such values as freedom and equality through the conflict of old ideas (called *theses*) with their opposites (*antitheses*). The ideas that supported the highly un-free and unequal conditions of slaveholding societies were opposed by antithetical ideas of freedom and equality, and the first *synthesis* of these contrasting ideas occurred in feudal society where serfs remained bound to their masters (the nobility) but the domination of nobles over serfs was less complete than that of slaveholders over slaves and the inequalities among these classes were attenuated by the greater obligations that nobles owed serfs (as expressed by the traditional conservative idea of *noblesse oblige*). In time, a new antithesis arose in opposition to the inequalities and lack of freedom that remained in feudal society, and this conflict resulted in a new liberal synthesis that understood freedom in a more expansive way – for example, as the right to enter freely into contracts with employers – and that defined equality in a more expansive way – such as the equal right to accumulate property through free enterprise. In short, Hegel thought that better social and political ideas emerged when deficient understandings (theses) encountered their opposite understandings (antitheses) and were resolved by better understandings (syntheses). The dialectical process of ever improving ideas would, according to Hegel, result in a post-historical stage – an "end of history" – where all deficient ideas would have been overcome and humans would be governed by absolutely correct ideas, by pure rationality.[12]

Marx took up Hegel's grand schema of the historical dialectic, but made a fundamental change to it, substituting *materialism* for Hegel's idealism:

> The mystification which dialectic suffers in Hegel's hands, by no means prevents him from being the first to present its general form of working in a comprehensive and conscious manner. With him it is standing on its head. It must be turned right side up again, if you would discover the rational kernel within the mystical shell.[13]

According to Marx, better ideas did not bring about fundamental changes and improvements in the material world. To the contrary, changes in the material world brought about fundamental changes in ideas. In short, while Hegel believed that historical progress was the result of better *ideas*, Marx inverted this ontological assumption and argued that historical progress was the result of material conditions and the resolution of conflicts arising from economic contradictions rooted in these conditions.[14] Marx assumed that material conditions were the root cause of our ideas and our politics.

In the pre-historical and historical periods, humans confronted – and still confront – a world of material scarcity. Under such conditions, humans must provide for their subsistence before they can freely choose to do anything else. This means that economic necessity is the force that motivates human behavior and that economic conditions are therefore the root causes of everything that humans produce, from religions to governments. This ontology – that the ultimate realities and root causes of human life in the historical eras are economic or material and not intellectual or spiritual – has been called *economic determinism* by orthodox Marxists. And the process by which opposing economic forces bring about change has been called *dialectical materialism* by orthodox Marxists. Although Marx never used these terms, he did think that economic determinism would cease at "the end of history." The natural laws of economics, especially those governing capitalism, would lead to economic affluence for a few. The conflicts and contradictions between the great productive capacity of capitalism and the unequal distribution of capitalism's wealth would lead to a new economic synthesis: communism.[15] Communism would retain and even exceed the productive capacity of capitalism, but it would distribute economic goods in a manner that satisfied everyone's needs. Such a communist society would be post-historical, because humans would now be freed from economic necessity. Human history would no longer be economically determined but could take on the many possibilities sought by anarchists. Freed from economic necessity, humans could at last generate a post-historical world reflecting the full range of human desires.

By inverting Hegel – by standing the dialectic on its feet rather than allowing Hegel's idealism to stand it on its head – Marx believed that he could replace all of the previous speculative historicist accounts with a scientific historicist account. The ideas that Hegel emphasized were wisps of clouds, ephemeral and non-observable phenomena that eluded scientific investigation. In contrast, Marx thought that material conditions and economic forces were subject to scientific investigations that could yield empirically verifiable patterns in history and predictions of future historical conditions.

We can elaborate Marx's ontological assumptions by applying them to various understandings of capitalist society. To simplify, we will consider how dialectical change gave rise to capitalism. Then we will consider how the economic conditions of capitalism affect other aspects of capitalist society. Finally, we will consider the implications of dialectical materialism for predicting and bringing about the demise of capitalism and the arrival of the next, post-historical stage in Marx's historicist scheme.

Dialectical processes account for the changes from a feudal society to a capitalist society. The feudal economy produced subsistence for the lower class of serfs and enough economic affluence for the upper class of nobles to generate economic demands for the more luxurious goods that the nobility could afford. A new middle class, the urban bourgeoisie, came into existence with the invention of new technologies and the building of new factories to produce these goods. But the bourgeoisie required a new class, the proletariat, to labor in these factories, and the creation of this class required freeing the serfs from bondage to their lords. The resulting conflict between the nobles and the bourgeoisie over the fate of such workers did not result in a reversal of class structures (the bourgeoisie never dominated the nobility), but it did result in a new synthesis. In short, the economic forces that were in play to transform a feudal agricultural economy into a capitalist industrial economy created conflicts that resulted in a new class structure. Whereas feudalism was characterized by a class structure in which the nobility dominated the serfs, capitalism gave rise to a new class structure in which the bourgeoisie dominated the proletariat.

The needs of capitalism and the bourgeoisie that gave rise to industrialization have produced a large number of changes in other aspects of capitalist society. In Marx's terms, the economic *infrastructure* has produced changes in the *superstructure* of society. Capitalist processes produce a class structure in which the bourgeoisie dominate the proletariat. The bourgeoisie use their dominant position to develop a superstructure of ideas, institutions, and regulations that sustain their privileges and the needs of the capitalist system. Religious ideas mollify the masses by promising the reward of a heavenly afterlife as compensation for their miserable existence as workers in capitalist factories during their time on earth. Classical liberalism developed as an ideology proclaiming that capitalism benefited everyone, including the proletariat. Representative democracies came into existence, proclaiming political equality but responding to the needs of capitalism. New liberal laws proclaimed universal protection of everyone's rights but in fact protected the property interests of the bourgeoisie. In short, economic and material forces produced the religious ideas, the political ideology, the form of government, and the basic content of its laws of capitalist society. All these changes in the superstructure of capitalist society reflected the power and interests of capitalism as a system and bourgeois capitalists as a class. Life in capitalist society has been economically determined.

Marx's ontological assumptions also provide a basis for theoretical predictions about the next and final stage of history and for guiding the political actions necessary to achieve changes from a capitalist to a communist society. However, the implications of dialectical materialism for predicting the demise of capitalism and for bringing about the arrival of communism are perhaps contradictory. On the one hand, Marx's theory of economic determinism seemed to proclaim that capitalism will fall and socialism arrive when (and only when) the economic conditions are ripe: when capitalism has developed the capacity to provide economic affluence for all, but when inequalities in distribution prevent most citizens from having the income to purchase the goods they need and that capitalism can produce. On the other hand, Marx's theory also seemed to recognize that the proletariat must acquire a revolutionary class-consciousness and act out its historical role in bringing about the revolution. This tension between the importance of economic conditions and the role of proletarian actions has generated much debate regarding Marx's ontology of economic determination, even among Marxists. While orthodox Marxists maintain a "hard" determinism – that economics determines everything – many other followers of Marx maintain that he provided for some indeterminism (allowing that historical change is not completely determined by economics, but is also influenced by individuals and ideas). How one chooses sides in this debate is in part determined by which texts of Marx and Engels one chooses to emphasize. Engels' *Anti-Duehring* provides the most persuasive basis for a hard economic determinism.[16] One source for the "soft" interpretation of Marx is his introduction to *Contribution to the Critique of Hegel's Philosophy of Right*. There, Marx wrote that "just as philosophy finds its material weapons in the proletariat, so does the proletariat find its intellectual weapons in philosophy. . . . Philosophy is the head of this emancipation, and the proletariat is its heart." Those who stress the soft Marx claim that Engels, by systematizing Marx, made his theory more deterministic than Marx had intended. How one interprets this matter is not trivial. If Marxists have a determinist ontology and if assumptions of economic determination are correct, then there is little that humans can do to promote a communist society (or to otherwise change political life for the better). If, on the other hand, Marxism allows for a "soft" or less deterministic ontology, then Marxism can serve as a source of inspiration for the communists and other left-wing radicals who have been highly involved in the politics of the twentieth century.

Communists: Revising Dialectical Materialism

The basic ontology of communism is essentially a modification of Marx's theory of dialectical materialism. During the twentieth century, communists revised the orthodox Marxist position that successful revolution is only possible in advanced capitalist societies by introducing four important claims.

First, communists recognized that capitalists were not merely prisoners of history, but could also act to modify economic conditions in ways that sustained capitalism and reduced the threat of revolution. Lenin's contributions were particularly important in this regard, as he identified several capitalist practices that seemed to show that human initiative played a greater role in world history than a strict interpretation of dialectical materialism suggested. For example, capitalists developed imperialism as an adaptive system to extract wealth from colonies, buy off the proletariat, and sustain the capitalist system. In addition, capitalist states introduced unemployment insurance and other governmental programs that attenuated the inherent contradictions of capitalism. Communists viewed such initiatives as efforts to keep the system going by making minor concessions to the grievances of the proletariat while keeping the essential features of domination in place. It would eventually collapse, Lenin thought, but it could be kept artificially alive for much longer than orthodox Marxist theory implied. Lenin reasoned that if capitalists could take initiatives to forestall a revolution, then revolutionary leaders could take counter-initiatives to speed it along.

Second, communists acknowledged changes and variations in economic structures that Marx did not foresee. In Marx's ontology, capitalism had become the most fundamental structural force in human life, and Marx conceived of capitalism as a monolithic economic system. For him, all capitalist societies were essentially identical. However, Lenin argued that capitalism was a *differentiated world-system* in which there were important differences in capitalism throughout the world. For example, Russia was a semi-feudal society that was only beginning to industrialize. Its two major classes continued to be the nobility and the peasants. The United States was a much more industrialized society, but it possessed a vast, open frontier containing many independent family farms and providing an option other than revolution for indebted urban workers. To bring the revolution to Russia or the US would thus require different measures from those in England, which was heavily industrialized and had a large, partially self-conscious proletarian class. In short, differences within the capitalist system, even amongst industrialized societies, implied different opportunities in different places for challenging capitalism.

Third, while communists like Lenin, Trotsky, and Mao agreed with Marx's theory that the fundamental direction of history was towards communism, they challenged his assumption that history had to proceed through the precise stages he had identified. While dialectical materialism insisted that the laws of economic development required that history go through specific and prolonged periods, communists who tried to implement his ideas saw the possibility of shortening certain periods; Mao even speculated that the capitalist period could be completely bypassed in China. When combined with the idea of a differentiated capitalist system, the idea that certain historical periods could be bypassed led to vast transformations in accounts of where and when successful revolutions could occur. According to the doctrine of *telescoping the revolution*, capitalism was strongest at the core – in the heavily industrialized countries like Germany, Great Britain, and the United States – and weakest at the periphery – in countries like Russia, China, and the colonies of European countries. Communists thought that it would be easiest to "snap the chain at its weakest link," in those areas of the periphery where capitalism had not yet fully developed and was, therefore, most vulnerable. In contradiction to Marx, who argued that the revolution would first come to the most industrialized nations and then spread as other nations subsequently industrialized, Trotsky argued that the revolution might be easiest to accomplish in the least industrialized nations. This argument had a threefold implication. First, the transition from feudalism to communism could be "telescoped" into one long revolution, rather than enduring a two-step process of a bourgeois and then a proletarian revolution with a long period of capitalism in between. Second, this process would require a *permanent revolution*, a period of time in which the communist revolutionaries (the vanguard) would engage in a series of revolutionary activities, both while they seized power and while they governed, that would transform feudal societies into communist ones in one extended step. Third, it seemed that the revolution was not a historically necessary event, determined by precise historical and material factors, as Marx had thought. Because it was *not* inevitable in the economically peripheral states ("the weakest link"), it would have to be brought about by deliberate human intervention.

In a fourth modification of orthodox Marxist thinking, Lenin's doctrine of a *vanguard of the proletariat* implies a theory of revolutionary voluntarism that seems at odds with Marx's claim that revolutions necessarily unfold as specified by the doctrine of dialectical materialism. Marx had recognized that intellectuals could assist the revolution by helping the proletariat to develop class-consciousness, but he foresaw no other significant task for intellectuals or other professionals who were not clearly part of the proletariat. In contrast, Lenin argued that a small group of intellectuals – whom he called the vanguard – understood the historical moment when revolution could occur, the requirements of the revolution, and the needs of the proletariat; the vanguard could act on behalf of the proletariat and greatly hasten the coming of the revolution.[17] By giving this vanguard a greater role than Marx did, Lenin made much more room for the role of voluntary human will in the political realm than even a soft determinist interpretation of Marx allowed. In short, communists developed an ontology of *voluntarism* that claimed that humans could shape history.

Fascists and Nazis: Heroic Will and Racial Struggle

The ontological assumptions of fascism and Nazism have certain similarities with those of communism and Marxism. Like communists, fascists emphasized the role of the human will in making history. Like Marxists, Nazis emphasized a conflict between demographic groups of people in the making of history. But both these right-wing ideologies make important modifications in the ontological assumptions of their left-wing adversaries.

Mussolini, who had been a Marxist-Leninist until at least 1914, was influenced by Lenin's stress on the role of human will in affecting the course of human history. Like Lenin, Mussolini rejected the idea that revolutions were completely determined by social and economic conditions; instead, he maintained that elites could decisively influence history. He found in the writings of Friedrich Nietzsche (1844–1900) a helpful emphasis on the role of the will in human affairs. In Mussolini's reading, Nietzsche seemed to argue that a great person is able to transcend his immediate environment and reconstruct the world according to his will. In this reading, human will is the determinant of history, at least when it is the will of heroic humans. Extracting from Nietzsche this emphasis on creative, willful human action, Mussolini transferred it from the individual to the collective.[18] While Lenin saw the heroic individual as mobilizing a *class* to bring about political change, Mussolini saw the heroic individual as mobilizing the *masses* – the entire body of a nation – to bring about changes that empower a nation. Thus, in Mussolini's theory of voluntarism, the strong national leader must mobilize the masses, and, with their cooperation, shift the course of history.

Nevertheless, fascists and especially Nazis do not claim that humans are completely free to shape history as they wish. Circumstances constrain how humans can manipulate historical processes in accordance with their will. According to Mussolini:

[T]o act among men, as to act in the natural world, it is necessary to enter into the process of reality and to master the already operating forces. . . . Man could not be what he is without being a factor in the spiritual process to which he contributes, either in the family sphere or in the social sphere, in the nation or in history in general to which all nations contribute. Man without a part in history is nothing.[19]

Thus, the historical process limits, or at least channels, the will.

For fascists, the historical process to which both leaders and the masses could contribute was the realization of Italian national unity and power. For Nazis, this process involved the emergence of the Aryan race as the dominant force in world history. Thus, the ontology of Nazism focuses on the fundamental role of race in defining political life and bringing about change. The history of the race idea in European intellectual history is complex, but the Nazi appropriation of the idea can be told briefly by summarizing three streams of racialism.

The first stream in Europe was most closely tied to the natural scientific study of man, and writers in the other two streams often appealed to it for validation of their racial speculations. Central to this "scientific" tradition was the theory of evolution. Darwin's theory led to the idea that some species were higher on the evolutionary scale than others, and this in turn lead to speculation that some subspecies, or races, were more evolved and intelligent than others. For example, Samuel Morton (1799–1851) had developed the pseudo-science of *craniology* that maintained that there were significant correlations between race and the size of the cranium (the portion of the skull enclosing the brain) and between the size of the cranium and intelligence. According to this "science," whites were more intelligent than other races because they had the largest craniums. When subsequently combined with Darwin's ideas about evolution, the "science of craniology" led to the idea of white supremacy. Such ideas received a positive public response in the period leading to Nazism.[20]

The second stream of racialism involved social theories that employed broad ethnographic and historical studies that attempted to explain political and historical development on the basis of vaguely defined notions of race. The principal originator of such *ethnographic studies* was Joseph Arthur Comte de Gobineau (1816–82), a French diplomat and social theorist. In Gobineau's speculation, there existed a hierarchy among the human races, with whites having the most fully realized human traits. Gobineau argued that racial and ethnic impurity explained the historical decline of civilizations. When a superior race began to mingle with others, Gobineau thought, its civilization began to decline. Most of the ethnic groups within the white race were the products of such racial mingling. Those that were ethno-racially the purest had the best potential for developing civilization. The greatest of these were the Teutons – Germans, Scandinavians, or English. Those that were ethnically mixed (such as the Slavs and Celts) were capable only of transmitting cultural decay, which hastened the collapse of civilization. To sustain human culture at its best, the Teutons would have to keep themselves racially pure.[21]

Volk is the central idea of the third stream of racial thinking. It is German for "folk," or people, and came to suggest the importance of a biologically, culturally, spiritually, and linguistically homogenous people, giving rise to German nationalism. Inspired by Johann Fichte (1762–1814), an early German Romantic philosopher who developed a political concept of *Volk*, many Germans used the term in art, literature, and political rhetoric. At rallies and other party events, Nazis used *Volk* terminology to evoke immediate feelings and images of German unity, greatness, and capacity to overcome external threats.

These three streams of racialism converge in Nazism to create a kind of ontology of race. Although the Nazis never developed a deep theory of the historical forces giving rise to racial struggle to match Marx's theories about the history of class conflict, their emphasis on race resembles the Marxist emphasis on class. As with the Marxist idea of class, the idea of race served for the Nazis as an explanation for a full range of socio-political phenomena. The essence of history is the struggle for supremacy between races, a conflict that has culminated in a struggle between the "purest," "most civilized," or "highest" race, which is the so-called Aryan race, and such "sub-human" races as Slavs, Gypsies, Negroes, and, especially, the Jews. In the midst of this struggle, the Aryan race itself must also be "purified" of those with genetic deficiencies. All is to the glory and strength of the race.[22]

Contemporary Liberals: Deemphasizing Ontology and Embracing Contingency

Contemporary liberals have abandoned the goal of classical liberals to achieve a universal theory of politics based on firm, incontestable, philosophical foundations. Rather than seeing liberalism as a fixed doctrine based on a true understanding of nature, they see it as an evolving historical and political achievement – an inheritance of a valuable political tradition that is justified by its successes and potentialities, not its metaphysics.[23]

Like classical liberals, contemporary liberals view the world in natural or secular terms, as they regard ideas about God's role in the universe as serving only private, spiritual concerns and as being irrelevant for constructing political principles. But while classical liberals believe that the natural world works according to precise natural laws, contemporary liberals doubt that there is a natural order that determines social and human life. Social arrangements are not naturally ordered; they are human creations. Human capacities are not defined by nature, but rather are shaped by social contexts and human choices. History will not unfold according to predetermined social and natural forces, but rather will be of our making. The social world and the future take on many possibilities and are not subject to iron laws, but rather can be modified culturally and politically.[24]

The emphasis that contemporary liberals give to human choice has sometimes led to the impression that they believe that what happens in political life and what determines history ought to be based on the *popular will*. Just as the existence of "the Good" was the foundation for Plato's elite guardianship, so too the "will of the people" is sometimes seen as foundational to liberal democratic societies.[25] In this interpretation, the "will of the people" exists as the dominant desires of all people in a political community, and it is the ultimate reality that must be discovered and followed. In this interpretation, politicians act as "liberals" and "populists" when they justify an action or policy because it is "the will of the people," or when they claim that "the people have spoken" by electing them to office, giving them a mandate to act of their campaign promises. In fact, contemporary liberals do not believe there is such a thing as "the will of the people" that is the ontological foundation of democratic politics.[26] For liberals, the methods used to proclaim the content of the public will are deeply flawed. Public opinion polls, for example, often record "non-attitudes," as many people have no meaningful preferences on the issues to which they are asked to respond. Elections simply tell us which of the candidates presented to the voters was most preferred by those who turned out to vote; they tell us little about what citizens as a whole prefer on the major issues for which winners claim a "mandate." Even if citizens had genuine preferences on political issues, there exists no method for aggregating individual preferences into a coherent and consistent conception of "the public will," unless there is broad public consensus on the issue.[27] In general, liberals fear that appeals to the public will are a great mischief that politicians of all stripes invoke to claim greater power and legitimacy for imposing their desires on a complacent and confused political community. Minimally, liberals recognize that the will of the people provides no ontological foundation for their ideology or public philosophy.

To claim that there are no ontological foundations in the public will and no iron laws of capitalism, politics, or social life is not to say that developments in these areas are completely unshaped by either ideational (Hegelian) or material (Marxian) forces. Contemporary liberals seem to assume that the achievement of progress will be influenced by both human values and organizational power. Liberals understand that people have many, often competing, values. The values that are strongest within individuals, groups, or societies will influence their goals and achievements. Liberals thus understand that the maintenance and progress of liberalism require the fostering of certain liberal values – for example, a respect for the well-being and accomplishments of individuals, a concern for the rights of others, a commitment to forms of justice other than the distributions of social goods provided through capitalism, and a willingness to fight against threats to a liberal society.[28] Liberals also understand that in order for values to have an impact, political power must be exercised on their behalf. In modern societies, significant political power resides in well-structured organizations of people and material resources. Organized power affecting historical progress may reside in governments, in corporations, in labor unions, or in other large-scale organizations.[29] In short, contemporary liberals believe that there are many possibilities for human history and that our fates are contingent on the values we choose to emphasize and on how power is organized. If liberal ideals are to be more fully realized, liberal values must be encouraged and political power must be democratically and effectively organized on behalf of such values.

Contemporary Conservatives: Appreciating the World As It Is

Questions about the nature of ultimate reality have not been of much interest to contemporary conservatives. Such conservatives usually avoid metaphysical assumptions about the world, and they do not want to ground their political principles in foundational assumptions about ultimate reality or the most essential forces that influence history. They pride themselves in being realists who accept the world as it is. The world is indeed made up of material objects, including humans, and individuals have material interests and motivations; the materialism of this world must be respected. But our world is also defined by human ideas – by the broad beliefs and values of people within different cultures. It is possible to claim that dominant cultural beliefs and values comprise "the spirit of the people" and – as long as that characterization is not so metaphysical as to be disconnected from what most citizens actually believe (as it can be in fascism) – these ideas within existing cultures must be respected. Thus, rather than seeing ultimate reality as defining our ultimate destinations, conservatives see the realities of material goals and cultural values as guides for human choices. Rather than seeing humans as constrained by ontological forces over which they have no control, conservatives see humans as responsible for both their personal and political choices.

Contemporary conservatives generally agree that it is not productive politically to presume that God comprises ultimate reality or that His divine will determines human history. Bringing strong and specific religious convictions to political life is destabilizing, given the diversity of religious outlooks that are evident in modern pluralist societies. Nevertheless, religion remains important for contemporary conservatives and can be useful for politics. Given the reluctance of pluralist societies to impose communitarian conceptions of a good life on all citizens or to legislate various moral codes, contemporary conservatives regard beliefs in God and adherence to the moralities of various religions as helpful in encouraging individuals to abide by the sorts of moral restraints that pluralist governments are reluctant to impose. Religion is useful for helping people believe that they are united as one people under God, however differently people in pluralist societies conceive of God and His teachings.

In the US, much of the conflict between *moderate conservatives* and the radical right grows out of efforts by social conservatives to invoke stronger religious assumptions and to have political communities governed according to their convictions. Perhaps all conservatives have deep reservations about actions that are broadly regarded as immoral: premarital sex, homosexuality, abortion, euthanasia, and so forth. The religious right often regards such actions as sins, as violations of God's will; indeed, some originally claimed that AIDS was a disease sent by God as a punishment for the sin of homosexuality. Moderate conservatives are more inclined to view "sins" as vices – as violations of culturally accepted norms that do social harm – and they distance themselves from claims that God intervenes in human affairs and vents

His wrath on those who do not conform to His will. Moderates have also been unsupportive of attempts by the religious right to introduce creationism and intelligent design into the curricula of public schools, acknowledging that theories about God's role in creation and evolution rely on particular contestable readings of the Bible. Conservatives generally agree that contemporary liberals have been insufficiently supportive of religious life, but moderates believe that the guidance humans receive from God and religion must be subjected to human and social analysis. If religious teachings are consistent with broad cultural values, then we should impose regulations in accordance with our cultural norms. If religious teachings are consistent with our understandings of actions that cause social harms, then we should impose regulations that provide social benefits. For conservatives, ontological speculations about God's will can inspire us to do good and to create a good society, but these speculations by themselves cannot be the basis of political decisions. Such speculations must be tempered by traditional cultural beliefs, common sense, and concerns about the unanticipated consequences of following particular interpretations of God's will.

Contemporary conservatives also have reservations about naturalist ontologies which claim that nature is an ultimate value or that nature provides absolute guidance to human affairs. Conservatives accept that there may be some limits on the carrying capacity of the earth, but they believe humans have imperfect ability to understand such limits; instead, experience teaches that the earth is fairly resistant to human abuses of nature. Perhaps nature provides some common sense lessons – for example, that we should conserve non-renewable resources – but the claims of some people that nature is pacific and teaches humans the importance of nonviolence are assumptions that cannot provide an adequate basis for those who must rely on police power and military force to maintain security in a world that is more "red in tooth and claw" than pacific. Conservatives thus have little sympathy for the environmental movement. In their view, the doomsday prophecies of deep greens on such issues as global warming underestimate the resilience of nature, and the attempts by environmentalists to "protect" nature from human uses prevent the effective human management of natural resources. Nature is there for us to use, and, with careful management, both nature and humans can benefit. The proper approach to nature, according to conservatives, includes conservation and managed use. It is based on common sense, and does not rely on any metaphysical assumptions.

The Radical Right: Refuting Charges of Economic and Divine Determination

We find among the radical right a variety of interesting ontological foundations and issues, but no sustained ontological arguments and certainly no commonality in ontological assumptions. Perhaps most noteworthy is that others attribute strong materialist or religious ontologies to the radical right, but these attributions may be misplaced.

Libertarians revert back to the ontological assumptions of classical liberalism. Their focus is on the individual and his or her natural rights.[30] Like their libertarian allies, globalists also focus on the individual and the material forces that affect human behavior and human history, but the question has arisen as to whether they have a deterministic ontology or whether they think the future remains open to human choices. Some globalists suggest that their principles are based on economic inevitability and thus involve a strong economic determinism that resembles that of orthodox Marxism. Francis Fukuyama is explicit about this, as he claims that people everywhere are gravitating toward globalist principles proclaiming the desirability of liberal democracies and capitalism, because the economic and political sciences make plain that capitalism and democracy are the only reasonable options. Fukuyama maintains that modern science is "the regulator or mechanism that explains the directionality and coherence of history" and this is "in effect an economic interpretation of historical change, but one which (unlike its Marxist variant) leads to capitalism rather than socialism as its final result."[31] In a similar manner, the most prominent popularizer of globalism, Thomas Friedman, insists on the importance of the "golden straightjacket" in globalization, that governments have no real alternative to pursue policies that support a global free market; they must reduce business regulations, welfare spending, corporate taxes, and budget deficits; they must pursue such policies as privatization that make their countries attractive to mobile capital – that encourage multinational corporations to locate in their country and provide jobs.[32] Margaret Thatcher, one of the architects of the new global order featuring globalist principles, famously declared "there is no alternative" (TINA) to people accepting the logic of free market capitalism. Such themes have prompted analysts of the emerging globalist ideology to declare that one of its foundational claims is that "globalization is inevitable and irreversible."[33]

However, it is unclear whether claims about the economic inevitability of following globalist principles reflect a deep belief that the world *must* operate according to the logic of economic determinism or whether such claims are made to justify governmental policies favoring the needs of global capitalism. Some globalists back away from the former interpretation. For example, Fukuyama also asserts that "economic interpretations of history are incomplete"[34] and draws upon Hegel's emphasis on the importance of ideas in world history to argue that the victory of the ideals of freedom and equality ensure a future where democratic capitalism will prevail everywhere.

Johan Norberg seems to express typical globalist assumptions about historical inevitability when he insists:

> [T]he future is not predetermined. There is no single path, and there is nothing forcing us to accept globalization. Capital can be locked up, trade flows blocked, and borders barricaded. This happened at least once before, following the globalization of the late nineteenth century. . . . It is not "necessary" to follow the globalization trend; it is merely desirable.[35]

Such claims suggest that the ontological foundations of globalism are not based on a thick ontology of economic determinism and are instead consistent with the thinner idealistic ontology of pluralists. By recognizing the importance of ideas and moral judgments in the evolution of history, globalists avoid dogmatic assertions that globalism is "inevitable and irreversible," despite certain claims to the contrary.

Other voices on the radical right stress the importance of God and culture, but it is doubtful that they believe that God or cultural values determine history. Instead, their claim seems to be that political communities would be better off if they were more receptive to traditional religious teachings and to traditional cultural values. They claim that communities would be more successful if their citizens were steeped in the values of Christian and Western cultures, but they see these communities as engaged in culture wars with other value systems, where the outcomes of these culture wars are undetermined. Social conservatives, traditional communitarians, national protectionists, and the religious right all pursue political measures to strengthen the role of traditional religions and cultural values in their political communities, but most adherents to these perspectives stop short of proclaiming that God's will or "American values" comprise some sort of foundational force that justifies their principles.[36] For such voices among the radical right, religious beliefs and cultural values are important for their desirable consequences, not because of their ontological foundations.

The Extreme Right: Expecting a Divine Apocalypse

The extreme right seems to embrace two related ontologies: divine determinism and cultural determinism. The most extreme belief among the far right – not only of religious fundamentalists but also among various white nationalists and survivalists – is that God is ultimate reality, that He is all-powerful, and that his intervention in the world is expected. Such voices believe that humans had freedom and the capacity to determine their own destiny, until Eve was seduced by Satan (the serpent in the Garden of Eden). Eve's seduction gave rise to a human history where Satan (and his followers among humans) thwarted God and his plan. However, there will soon be a day of reckoning when God's Kingdom – normally conceived as a white Christian nation – will be established on earth. On that day, God will actively intervene in human history, destroying the unrighteous and saving the righteous.[37] Since this apocalypse is approaching, it behooves people to get straight with God in order to be among the saved.[38]

A related set of ontological assumptions among the extreme right invokes a sort of cultural determinism. In this worldview, God has defined the moral code that individuals should follow and that should be reflected in a nation's culture, but individuals and communities can decide whether or not they will abide by God's moral code. This choice determines each person's position in society and his ultimate fate in the Kingdom of God. Those individuals who strive most unwaveringly toward God's goodness will be strongest, and the strongest shall prevail. Similarly, the cultural and religious values that define a nation determine its fate in the international struggle for power, prestige, and wealth. Those communities that adhere to cultural norms consistent with God's goodness will prevail in the inevitable competition among peoples. If a country is divided and docile in its political culture, others can overcome it. It is at this point that the extreme right can become more extreme than the radical right in its political beliefs. Here, the only human choices are to unite a people on the basis of a godly culture and to impose one's godly culture on others. A failure to pursue these choices allows others to dominate and even exterminate you.

The Radical Left: Tempering Material Forces with Socialist Ideals

Neo-Kantianism is an ontological view that some analysts have attributed to democratic socialism,[39] and it would seem applicable to other voices on the radical left as well. *Neo-Kantianism* attempts to synthesize Hegel's idealism and Marx's materialism. In brief, Immanuel Kant (1724–1804) was an influential German philosopher who distinguished facts and values. For Kant, facts – like Marx's laws of economics and history – are part of the phenomenal world of appearance and can be known by humans through experience and reflection. But morality is part of a deeper ultimate reality (including God and immortality) that lies beyond the phenomenal world and is independent of factual and material considerations. Early democratic socialists like Eduard Bernstein turned to Neo-Kantianism because they did not want to reject completely Marx's economic determinism but rather wanted to subordinate it to a deeper reality of morality. Neo-Kantianism permits humans to will freely certain moralities – such as socialist principles – simply because they are judged to be desirable, rather than necessary.

Such an ontology allowed democratic socialists to believe they could change the world of capitalist domination by pursuing socialist values through democratic applications of political power. This outlook more closely resembles the ontology of contemporary liberals than the Marxist ontology of economic determination. For orthodox Marxists, the economic infrastructure determines social values. Because capitalism requires and supports liberal values of competition, rugged individualism, and equal opportunity, Marxist ontology asserts that socialist values cannot spread as long as capitalism persists. But Bernstein viewed this orthodox Marxist ontology as being too materialist and too deterministic. He argued that ideology, ideas, and ethical considerations were important aspects of ultimate reality, could influence the future, and were at least partly independent of economic factors.[40]

Democratic socialists also were drawn to neo-Kantianism as an alternative to the naturalism of classical liberalism. As we have seen, such liberals thought that historical progress was determined by natural laws. According to Herbert Spencer, for example, human progress required the survival of the fittest, implying that progress was best served by letting the weak and unfit become extinct. But socialists refuse to be governed by such natural laws. According to T. H. Huxley (1825–95), "social progress means a checking of the cosmic progress [of natural selection] at every step and the substitution for it of another, which may be called the ethical process."[41]

Instead of submitting to a natural world of self-assertion, competition, and domination, humans can use their moral will to impose self-restraints, help their fellows, and create a just society.

It seems reasonable to attribute a neo-Kantian ontology to radical left perspectives beyond democratic socialism. Egalitarian liberals like Rawls stress their roots in Kantian philosophy; they provide normative arguments for why egalitarian principles are consistent with our considered moral judgments, and implicit in their whole enterprise of developing an ideal theory of justice is the presumption that moral ideals can play a role in human affairs. Cosmopolitan justice theorists recognize that their principles for global justice are ideals whose realization is strongly constrained by the prevailing economic forces in the world, but such constraints do not totally negate the capacity of their ideals to influence decisions of global leaders that redistribute some resources from wealthy to poor nations – no matter how modest these redistributions may be. Civic communitarians, radical feminists, and greens also recognize that the realization of communal, egalitarian, and environmental values have long been constrained by economic and material forces, but their theories are aimed at ensuring that moral ideals matter in human history.

By rejecting Marxist materialism and (classical) liberal naturalism, the radical left arguably does not ground its political principles in any particular ontology. The radical left does not claim to know ultimate reality, nor does it assert that human history is determined. Nevertheless, it can be argued that the radical left does embrace certain ontological assumptions. Proponents believe that values are real, that values affect social life, and that values are at least partially independent of economic forces, natural laws, and other constraints on our choices. They believe that humans – and human choices – can greatly influence the course of evolution and history – even if human life and history remain influenced by economic and other material forces. But such an ontology leaves ultimate reality and the course of history fundamentally unknown and undetermined, because human values and choices can embrace many ideological alternatives to those supported by the radical left. It is only *possible* for humans to embrace egalitarian, communal, feminist, and environmental values. The choice is ours.

The Extreme Left: Releasing Human Imagination, Constrained by Ecological Limits

A cursory reading of the writings of those on the extreme left may suggest that they hold strong ontological assumptions. In our introduction to this chapter, we noted that Hardt and Negri claimed that "war has become ontological." By this they seem to mean that in the present world governed by Empire, war is our most fundamental reality. The current "war on terrorism" is ever present. In contrast to prior human history, when wars were conducted by particular nations (or peoples) and had clear beginnings and endings, today we live in a state of permanent war that extends throughout the globe. Not only is war everywhere, but it is the most basic force in our lives, as individuals must constantly fear death at the hands of suicide bombers, as ethnic groups must constantly fear genocide, and as humanity as a whole must fear nuclear annihilation. For Hardt and Negri, this condition of war is the most basic reality of our lives and the Empire that rules over the world tries to legitimate itself by proclaiming its capacity to secure a modicum of peace and stability in a world of permanent war.

Post-structuralists like Michel Foucault can also be seen as having a strong ontology, but they point to power as the foundational reality of our lives. Power is not simply the control that political leaders and captains of industry exercise over our lives; it is always present in all aspects of our lives, as individuals are constantly inspected by others, including lower-level authorities like teachers, doctors, and therapists, and are subjected to regimentation to be "normal." Postmodern feminists agree and point out that men have generated the foundational norms upheld and furthered by these ever-present power-agents. Male-centered values and norms, broad and suffocating networks of social power, and the omnipresence of war are, for the extreme left, various defining realities of human existence today.

But are such defining realities truly ontological forces? Strong ontological forces are *essential*; they are permanent (eternal) characteristics and forces of ultimate reality, and thus they cannot be transcended or eliminated. The extreme left does not regard war, power, and male norms as essential in this sort of way. These forces deeply characterize our present world – our current existence – but earlier periods had different sorts of power arrangements, different kinds of war, and different value systems. Moreover, some on the extreme left imagine that these current realities can be transcended – that eternal peace can replace eternal war, that equality among "singularities"[42] can replace domination, and that androgynous norms can replace male-centered ones. The extreme left exposes repressive aspects of our lives, characterizes these as all-encompassing, and then challenges us to reject these forces.

The extreme left is thus anti-foundational. Its various voices reject any ontological assumptions that claim that our political world *must* be determined by God's will, economic forces,[43] war, power, male-norms, or any other primal force. The extreme left also opposes the ontology of contemporary liberals, contemporary conservatives, and other friends of pluralism who believe that our political future depends on realizing liberal, conservative, and even socialist values and ideals. For the extreme left, such values and ideals cannot be regarded as fixed ends to which political communities should aspire. There simply are no foundational values to guide politics. There is only human imagination. Perhaps the most basic assumption of the extreme left is the importance and power of our imagination. Humans can envision new worlds both in the near and distant future. For example, Hardt and Negri can imagine a world of love:

> Both God's love of humanity and humanity's love of God are expressed and incarnated in the common material political project of the multitude. We need to recover today this material and political sense of love, a love as strong as death. This does not mean you cannot love your spouse, your mother, and your child. It only means that your love does

not end there, that love serves as the basis for our political projects in common, and the construction of a new society. Without this love, we are nothing.[44]

As another example, deep greens can imagine a world in which people live simply in harmony with nature and in local communities that sustain spiritual values while dispensing with the materialism that characterizes current pluralist societies.

The extreme left thus shares with the radical left the belief that humans can and should change our world in fundamental ways, and both reject strong ontologies that claim that humans are subject to God's will and power or are prisoners of economic forces. But while the radical left proposes to change the world by pursuing well-defined liberal and socialist values, the extreme left criticizes even these values and proposes to be guided by human imagination. While the radical left understands that there are important economic, social, and political constraints that always limit the extent to which its goals can be attained, the extreme left sometimes suggests that all constraints can somehow be surpassed. To the extent that others value these constraints, the extreme left appears dangerous. To the extent that others see these constraints as unavoidable, the extreme left appears utopian.

This characterization of the ontology of the extreme left is perhaps least applicable to deep greens. The emphasis of deep greens on the ecological limits of the earth contains a clear conception of an ultimate reality that humans dare not broach. They point out that the laws of thermodynamics assert that the world is comprised of matter and energy, and that neither can be destroyed or created, but only transformed from one form of matter or energy into another. However, every transformation – including the increasing transformations produced by humans as we become more numerous and engage in ever greater levels of economic production – degrades usable nature and energy, resulting in entropy.[45] This means that the more we pursue economic development, "the deeper we go into thermodynamic debt, and the more we ultimately impoverish ourselves."[46] Such notions suggest that humans are not entirely in control of the fate of the world but rather must conform to ecological limits.

Conclusions

Pluralism thrives when people have thin ontological ideas, when they understand that their assumptions of ultimate reality (*Being*) and the ultimate causes of the future of the world (*Becoming*) are of little relevance to political life. Pluralists do not reject the existence of God or the primacy of the material world, nor do they deny that divine or natural forces can influence political events, but they insist that humans can resist these forces and attempt to make their worlds in a manner of their own choosing. Pluralists assume that human ideas are a fundamental part of the world and have an existence independent of either supernatural or material reality. They also assume that these ideas will influence the future of the world, but which ideas will prevail is undetermined. The future of the world will depend on human choices and the resources that humans bring to bear on furthering these choices.

The ontologies of contemporary liberals and contemporary conservatives are clearly within this underlying consensus of pluralism. Liberals, of course, stress the import-ance of liberal ideals, while conservatives stress the importance of conservative values, but both agree that values, culture, and morality matter greatly in human life and history. Thus, battles rage in normal pluralist politics over the competing values that should be given priority in policy decisions. Should we emphasize the civil liberties of individuals or collective security measures? Should we emphasize policies that are tolerant of individual choices or that require greater conformity to tradi-tional moral values? Should we emphasize a more equal distribution of social goods or a growing pie of social goods? But battles also rage at the edges of pluralist politics over its institutional basis. The radical right and radical left focus less on the normal electoral and policy issues of pluralist politics and more on the need for significant changes in the institutions that have the power to pursue values of the left or the right. In general, the radical left wants to strengthen democratic and political institutions that can deliver more equality and social solidarity, while the radical right wants to strengthen corporate and religious institutions that deliver greater property rights and traditional morality.

The strong ontologies that characterized nineteenth-century politics and total-itarian ideologies in the twentieth century were not conducive to pluralist politics. The assumptions that supernatural or natural forces – whether in the guise of a "great chain of being," "natural rights and laws," "economic determination," or "the will of the Fuehrer" – are hard to reconcile with the pluralist belief that political com-munities as a whole should make their own histories, generate their own conception of rights and responsibilities, and be governed through democratic means. The weak ontology of pluralism – that the world is undetermined, that human ideas will influ-ence its direction, but that there are real constraints on what humans can achieve politically – is, in retrospect a very simple set of assumptions, but building a politics based on such assumptions has been a difficult accomplishment. It is an achievement that may be threatened by extremists.

Perhaps Islamic fundamentalism is only the most visible movement of those on the extreme right who would create a politics based on submission to the will of God, as it is sometimes observed that deeply religious assumptions are increasingly potent and assumed to be increasingly relevant as foundations of political life.[47] Perhaps American pluralists should fear Christian fundamentalists who seek to enact laws mandating the teaching of intelligent design in our public schools, perceiv-ing this initiative as the beginnings of a dangerous assault by the extreme right on pluralist politics. But perhaps such a fear is overwrought. From the viewpoint of pluralist ontology, the proponents of intelligent design may be making claims that are resolvable by pluralist politics. They may simply be raising the question of whether secular ideas should be emphasized in our schools, while conceding that humans alone can use our reasoning capacities to determine the validity of the ideas of evolution or intelligent design. But if the proponents of intelligent design claim that God must determine the outcome of this issue and that He will intervene in human history, punishing those who see the greater validity of evolution over the "intelligent design hypothesis," they have become extremists who are indeed frightening to pluralists.[48]

Perhaps the ontological forces that the extremist left perceives as our ultimate realities today – permanent war, vast networks of power, a culture of male values – are tendencies that permeate our existence, but the extreme left provides no basis for testing its beliefs about the all-encompassing impact of such forces on our lives. Its extreme views provide no room for seeing counter-forces that might also be present in the complex realities of our lives, and thus its views invite deep cynicism about the pluralistic world that we inhabit. Perhaps a world of love and harmony with nature imagined by left-wing extremists is inspiring. But human imagination can be unrealistic and misguided and thus particular visions need to be subjected to political processes. The extreme left seems to realize this and thus demands that these political processes be as inclusive as possible. In coming to this realization, the extreme left begins to resemble pluralists who have always wanted a politics that is open to new liberating ideas. The extreme left may grant this account of pluralism's possibilities, but it quickly adds that the pluralism that is currently practiced is hardly the open and inclusive political process that is receptive to the sort of massive changes that those on the far left can envision. But at least the extreme left and pluralists can agree on the ontological assumption that history will always be contingent on what people think and how they act politically.

Chapter 6

Questions of Human Nature

Are humans inherently equal and, if so, in what ways and on what basis? In what ways are humans unequal? What are and what should be basic human motivations and purposes? Are humans autonomous and rational in choosing their own ends, or are their conceptions of the good life and their motivations socially and politically influenced?

Alternative answers to such questions about human nature underlie many political issues. Consider, for example, debates about welfare programs. Those calling for more generous public assistance to the needy normally portray welfare recipients as people who are victims of circumstances beyond their control. They are children living in desperately poor households. They are women struggling to raise children who have been abandoned by their fathers. They are people with emotional, mental, and physical disorders that preclude their employment. Or they are workers who have been laid off in stagnant and restructured economies. In contrast, those calling for reductions in public assistance portray welfare recipients as lazy and irresponsible. Behind these characterizations of (potential) welfare recipients are broader assumptions about human nature. Those supporting welfare seem to regard people as essentially equal in their worth and in their desire to live worthwhile lives, but as having unequal opportunities to live good lives due to undeserved natural and social circumstances. Those opposing welfare seem to regard people as having no greater motivation than to get by on a minimal governmental handout; they seem to assume that if welfare payments were to become too generous, we would all calculate that we'd be well served by living off the public dole, rather than working hard and being responsible for ourselves.

Very simple competing characterizations of human nature are commonplace in political thought. Some claim humans are bad and cannot be trusted; thus extensive coercive authority is needed to keep people in line. Others claim humans are good, and thus need little or no authority to control them. If questions of human nature can be reduced to whether humans are devils or angels, then political theory could focus on a debate between authoritarianism and anarchism. But we need to introduce more complexity into our thinking about human nature.[1]

Consider just one dimension of our assumptions about human nature – that of our essential motivations. Is our most basic purpose in life to be:

- happy, maximizing personal pleasure and minimizing personal pain?
- good, developing our human potential and character?
- successful, accomplishing a series of projects?
- rich, accumulating great material goods and wealth?
- famous, or at least recognized as a person with a particular identity?
- loving and loved in return, especially within a family?
- helpful, serving others and the broader community?
- serene, attaining a blissful freedom from desire? or
- holy, serving God?

Of course there are endless possibilities beyond these. How can we possibly know which motivation is basic to human nature when we see ourselves pursuing different motivations at different times in our lives?

There are many other dimensions of human nature implied by the initial listing of questions. Do we freely choose our motivations, or are they somehow bestowed upon us? Perhaps our "choices" simply reflect economic, social, or divine pressures or other forces that greatly limit our imagined autonomy and freedom of choice. There are also difficult questions about human capabilities. For example, we all seem to have some reasoning ability, but no one seems to have infallible reasoning and intellectual capacities. Perhaps no one can cast a truly intelligent vote on difficult political issues. Reasoning and intellectual capacities seem unequally distributed among us, but only a few people seem to have such severe mental limitations that they should be denied the right to make choices over their own lives or participate in making political decisions affecting community life. Perhaps most people have enough mental capacity to hold powerful political positions, including even the US presidency.

While ideologues cling strongly to particular assumptions about human nature, we propose that the friends of pluralism recognize that people have a wide variety of motivations, but these differences do not undermine an essential equality among them. They recognize that humans have many different capacities, but these do not undermine the assumption that most have sufficient rationality to be responsible for their own lives and to participate in making decisions about the communities in which they reside. Pluralists might also find value in the most basic purpose of this chapter: to consider a wide array of views about human nature in order to gain a greater appreciation of human complexity. The more we appreciate the different motivations, capacities, and circumstances in which humans find them-selves, the more likely we are to see politics as a vehicle for serving human differences rather than as a vehicle for serving one type of human, while depreciating and oppressing others.

Classical Liberals: Humans as Equal and Rational Pursuers of Happiness

As an aid to developing valid assumptions about human nature, Hobbes, Locke, and other early liberals conceived humans in a state of nature, as discussed in the previous chapter. In such a condition, humans can be conceived, like other natural objects, as essentially matter-in-motion. As material beings, humans are ontologically estranged from each other; we are physically separate beings lacking any sort of spiritual interconnections or unity. We are also psychologically estranged from one another, not much concerned with the well-being of others. We are self-interested, primarily concerned with the preservation of our own lives and with our own happiness. Because we are the best judges of our own happiness, we should have *autonomy*, the capacity to pursue our own good, as we understand what is best for us.

According to C. B. Macpherson, the liberal "model of man" is as "a maximizer of utilities."[2] In other words, classical liberals have assumed that the primary human motivation is to achieve as much pleasure and to avoid as much pain as possible. Conceptions of human goodness arise, in the first instance, from self-understandings of what yields utility for oneself. Experiencing pleasure is good and experiencing pain is bad, and thus human pursuit of self-interest is necessary for achieving a good life, not a sign of moral depravity. Indeed, if humans focused on their self-interest – on their own preservation and happiness – they would be less inclined to pursue such morally dubious socially constructed motivations as going to war for national glory.

Nevertheless, liberals understand that excessive human self-interest can be a social problem. If humans pursue their self-interest in ways that undermine the interests of others, they will be in a continuous state of conflict. Consequently, liberals understand that individuals must be constrained in their pursuit of happiness. They need to acquire an understanding that their own pursuit of happiness cannot come at the expense of the happiness of other humans. Thus, liberal conceptions of human goodness incorporate, in the second instance, a moral understanding that individuals must act in ways that preserve the rights of other humans. More broadly, classical liberals concluded that political and economic institutions must be devised that protect humans from the belligerent pursuit of self-interest by others and that channel self-interest in ways that benefit others in society. Criminal laws, police, courts, and prisons help tame the belligerent pursuit of self-interest. Capitalism channels self-interest so that people are rewarded for producing goods that others in society want.

Humans have various qualities that help them maximize their utility. They have, of course, their bodies. With their bodies they can labor, removing from nature those goods, like food, that are necessary for their survival. And through physical labor they can transform nature, providing for basic needs (as when they weave clothing from cotton and build shelter from timber) and pleasures (as when they craft precious jewelry from minerals like diamonds and gold).

Humans also have senses like sight and hearing, which enable them to perceive the external world. According to Locke, our senses receive sensations from the environment.

These sensations impress themselves on our minds, which record these perceptions (as on a *tabula rasa*, or blank slate) and then classify and relate these perceptions to one another, forming concepts, relationships, and abstract theoretical knowledge about the world. Humans are thus endowed with *instrumental reason*, understood as the capacity of the mind to arrive at useful ideas on the basis of sensations and reflection on these sensations. A concrete though mundane example of the liberal conception of reason might be as follows. A human perceives occasional rumblings in her stomach, which in time she classifies as hunger and associates with pain. She also perceives red juicy objects growing in the fields, which she classifies as strawberries, and which she learns are pleasant tasting and satisfy her hunger. The application of reason thus yields the useful generalization that picking and eating strawberries reduces hunger and provides a pleasant experience.[3]

This liberal conception of human reason differed from most previous conceptions of reason. Among some schools of pre-modern thought, for example, reason was thought to be capable of producing *ultimate* knowledge; it enabled people to know what is good or virtuous for all humans. "Right reason" enabled people to know the appropriate goals or ends of life. But in liberal thought, human reason cannot deliver such ultimate knowledge. It can only give us instrumental knowledge about that which gives happiness to ourselves personally. In short, while some ancient philosophers viewed reason as a human capacity to restrain or overcome human desires and appetites in order to attain some higher good or virtue, liberals view human reason as a resource to help fulfill human desires and appetites, which are the primary goods recognized by the individual.

Classical liberals assume an *equality of being* among humans. Each person is matter-in-motion, everyone exists (at least in the state of nature) in the same estranged condition, everyone is fundamentally self-interested, and everyone's happiness is of equal worth. Equality of being means that each individual can rightfully claim that his life, liberty, and happiness is as important as the life, liberty, and happiness of any other individual. The *categorical imperative* of Immanuel Kant gave moral expression to the liberal idea of equality of being. No one is justified in sacrificing the life, liberty, and happiness of others as a means to his own happiness or to advance his own well-being.

Liberals also believe that people have certain equal minimal capabilities. As Hobbes noted, for example, everyone is equally capable of causing others physical harm. Locke's understanding of human rationality implies that all people are fundamentally equal in their ability to learn, because learning is ultimately grounded in experiences that are available to everyone.

It is, nevertheless, a great oversimplification to claim that classical liberals think humans are equal. Liberals understand that humans have different goals and conceptions of happiness. They recognize that people have varying physical and mental endowments and different propensities to make use of these endowments. For example, John Stuart Mill understood that the extent to which people have intellectual capacities and have developed these capacities is unequal. Indeed, his view that people are different in their capacity to reach informed political judgments led him to reject the democratic ideal of "one man, one vote" and to endorse a scheme of plural voting giving more votes to the more qualified. Early liberals also understood that human physical and mental capacities are not fixed. Indeed, as liberalism matured, its advocates thought that a liberal (and democratic) society would provide a fertile context in which each individual could develop her own capacities and powers to the fullest extent possible, but that such development will inevitably be unequal in different individuals.[4]

Traditional Conservatives: Defining Humans by their Places in Society

Traditional conservatives reject the notion that humans are simply material beings motivated by the pursuit of pleasure and the avoidance of pain. Instead, humans are spiritual beings who are tied to one another and God in a "great chain of being," as discussed in the last chapter. Humans make wise choices when motivated by spiritual and social considerations, including the moral sentiments about rights and obligations that are emphasized in the communities in which they reside. Individual human reasoning is an inadequate instrument to guide people toward good choices, but humans have the capacity for prudence, a virtue that guides them by means of lessons learned in a well-ordered society that structures choices through custom and tradition.

Traditional conservatives assume each person has within himself the capacity for evil, for pursuing instinctual and emotional desires that are destructive of self and society. But each person also has within himself capacities for goodness: for developing his character, exhibiting human virtues, and serving the community in beneficial ways. Unfortunately, the propensity for evil can easily overcome the potential for good. The propensity for evil is increased when the pursuit of self-interest is encouraged and when humans rely on their own flawed reasoning, rather than seeking guidance in the customs and traditions of a well-integrated, stable, and organic society. Even within such a society, humans are subject to frailties and prone to vices. No society can create perfect humans, but a well-ordered one can reduce the human propensity for evil, nourish sociability, and enable people to live a reasonably good life.

Traditional conservatives stress that human reason is imperfect; it is tainted with passions, emotions, and habits, and it confronts a world and political communities that are too complex for any human to grasp fully. This does not mean that conservatives think humans should abandon reason, but it must be employed carefully. The best kind of reasoning available to humans is not grand and abstract speculation but a more modest approach that focuses on the concrete and specific and relies on experience. They stress that humans should employ common sense, both as a corrective to overly abstract reason and as a means of being guided by traditional social understandings.

Traditional conservatives question the liberal assumption that human autonomy is possible or desirable. They claim individuals need society to shape their conceptions of the good life. Human goals must be socially defined, so that individuals recognize their place in the "great chain of being" and their role in society, and thus come to understand what gives meaning to their existence. Traditional conservatives assume that humans must be guided toward good actions by following social customs and traditions.

Liberalism promotes an isolated individualism, according to conservatives. Freed from the bonds of custom and from the stability of traditional authority, individuals in liberal societies pursue individual pleasure, but cannot discover a meaningful existence. Liberal societies produce an alienated individual, a self that has no place, no companions, and no purpose. The French sociologist Emile Durkheim (1857–1917) called such alienation "anomie," and he argued that the breakdown of traditional authority and the rise of individualism in Europe resulted in increased anomie, which, in turn, accounted for an increased incidence of suicide.[5]

The cure for isolated individualism is not to be found in abstract claims about human equality. Traditional conservatives argue that people vary greatly in their talents and abilities. The well-ordered society takes advantage of these concrete differences by positioning people in social roles on the basis of their different qualities. Society works best when each individual makes different, but important, contributions to society. Working at different tasks, but all working together for the good of the whole, provides citizens with a sense of belonging and contributing to society.

Anarchists: Seeing Human Altruism as Hindered by Conventional Institutions

Anarchists are much closer to classical liberals than traditional conservatives in their assumptions about human nature. They believe, for example, that each person seeks liberty, that all people have the capacity for reason, and that all humans are equally worthy of respect and dignity. However, they regard as inadequate the liberal assumption that humans are self-regarding utility maximizers.

In general, anarchists maintain that two diametrically opposed impulses coexist in natural man. The Russian writer Alexander Herzen asserted, for example, that man is both an egoist and a social animal: "[K]ill the social sense in man – and you get a savage orangutan; kill egoism in him and he will become a tame monkey."[6] Emma Goldman perceived both individual and social instincts in humans, "the one a most potent factor for individual endeavor, for growth, aspiration, self-realization; the other an equally potent factor for mutual helpfulness and social well-being."[7] By stressing only the self-interested impulse in humanity, liberals miss the often unconscious instinct within humans to help others. Peter Kropotkin is the anarchist who most thoroughly documented this more altruistic impulse within humans (and other animals).[8] Calling this impulse "mutual aid," he argued that it consists of more than feelings of love or sympathy toward others. It is an instinct in humans that makes us respond automatically to cries for help. When others suffer, we often sacrifice some of our pleasures to aid them. When others are in danger, we often risk our own lives to help them.

This view that humans have both self-interested and altruistic impulses resembles the belief of traditional conservatives that humans have capacities for both evil and goodness. But while conservatives believe conventional institutions tame the beast within humans, anarchists believe conventional arrangements crush the altruistic side of humans. When we are subjected to repressive conditions (like great poverty, under which basic needs are unsatisfied) and competitive institutions (like capitalism), our selfish, anti-social instincts come to the fore. Because humans have most often lived under repressive and competitive conditions, the selfish side of human nature has been abundantly evident. As Goldman asks, "When human nature is caged in a narrow space, and whipped into daily submission, how can we speak of its potentiality?"[9] Kropotkin's investigations of the mutual aid instinct were particularly important, because he showed that altruism thrived under more natural conditions. He claimed that primitive humans living in a natural condition were not self-interested aggressors, as liberals like Hobbes had depicted them; instead they practiced the motto "each for all."[10]

According to anarchists, environmental conditions also shape other human characteristics. For example, although humans sometimes appear to be lazy and unproductive, such qualities are not inherent in them but are, rather, the result of large-scale capitalist institutions that provide dreary work environments that people find oppressive and from which they seek to escape. In other environments, humans find satisfaction in creative work that is freely done under pleasant circumstances and that results in socially useful products. Humans can also appear ignorant and unreasonable, but these qualities, too, are a result of living in an anti-social environment. The intellectual facilities of humans are strengthened when humans live in cooperative natural societies where intelligence is developed and communicated by language (the most social of all human inventions) and enhanced by the accumulated experiences of fellow humans.

Thus, anarchists stress human malleability. If conditions are oppressive, the dark side of human nature will prevail. If conditions are natural and humane, the tendency of humans to exhibit mutual aid and treat each other justly will prevail. This does not mean that humans can be made perfect by natural and humane conditions. But when oppressive conditions are overcome, humans can continuously improve toward their better natures.

Marxists: Conceiving Humans as Creative Laborers

Marx assumed that the essence of humans is our capacity for creative labor, for working imaginatively in the world and upon nature in ways that transform the world to our liking. All humans have the potential to exist as creative laborers, but current material and economic conditions prevent us from realizing that potential. Marx was strongly influenced in such views about human nature by Hegel, who developed the notion that labor is the most important way in which humans realize themselves and actualize their potential to be fully human.[11] While other animals can only labor within their environment and extract what they need from that environment, we humans can transform our environment through creative labor. Marx was also influenced by Charles Fourier (1772–1837), who believed that humans are most happy when permitted to use and develop their capacities as laborers, and who claimed that only existing social and economic structures make labor unpleasant, degrading, and alienating.[12]

For Marx, *alienation* was a general concept referring to gaps between humanity's assumed potential and its actual condition. The chief causes of human alienation, according to Marx, have been the economic or material scarcity that accompanies human existence and the division of labor that results from organized attempts to overcome this scarcity. This division of labor includes both vertical arrangements of authority and subordination and horizontal specialization among people in the various tasks they perform. Both have been essential features of every mode of production that humans have historically adopted in an effort to overcome scarcity. In order to maximize production and fulfill the community's interest in satisfying material needs, individuals have been assigned specific social, economic, and gender roles that have varied historically depending on material and technological developments.

The division of labor has contributed to five types of alienation. First, human beings have become alienated from the fruits of their labor. As Marx explained in his *Economic and Philosophical Manuscripts of 1844*, "The worker puts his life into the object; but now his life no longer belongs to him, but to the object."[13] The objects produced through a division of labor do not belong to the individual workers engaged in their production. Instead, those at the top of the hierarchy in the division of labor assume ownership and control over them.

Second, humans have become alienated from nature, which provides objects upon which the laborer can creatively operate. Just as an artist needs a canvas on which to paint, all creative laborers need nature as a canvas upon which they produce pleasing products. According to Marx, "Nature provides labor with the *means of life* in the sense that labor cannot *live* without objects on which to operate."[14] However, when individuals specialize and their products are owned and controlled by others, the individual loses his deep connection to nature, seeing it as a resource to be exploited for the gain of others rather than a resource that he can improve (for his pleasure and the pleasure of others) through his creative labor.

Third, humans have become alienated from laboring itself. They no longer labor creatively for the intrinsic enjoyment or satisfaction of doing transforming work, or for the sake of their own self-actualization. Labor no longer satisfies the immediate human need to labor creatively, but becomes only a means for satisfying human needs that are external to labor itself; we work only to acquire food, shelter, clothing, and so on.

Fourth, humans are separated from fellow human beings. This separation is due to the ceaseless competition among people for the most desirable positions in the division of labor. As competitors for better positions and for scarce goods, humans fail to see others as comrades engaged in collective actions of transforming the environment for their mutual benefit.

Fifth, and as a consequence of these other alienations, humans are alienated from their *species-being*. This means that they fail to experience themselves as members of the creatively laboring human species that they naturally are. They no longer recognize what is unique about humans: their capacity to recreate the environment through enjoyable labor. They get no satisfaction from fulfilling their human potential as effective creative labors.

Cast in historical perspective, capitalist society is particularly divided and competitive, and therefore particularly alienating. At the same time, capitalist society has also provided the means of production that can allow for more authentic living – if these means are socialized. The technology of capitalism allows for great productivity and abundance, reducing the need for a division of labor to overcome material scarcity. Socializing the means of production will preclude the expropriation of products away from the laborers who produce them. Under socialized production, laborers would begin to relate to each other again as comrades rather than as competitors. In the initial stages of socialization, the workers' conception of their species-being will remain stunted because of their long exposure to the alienating effects of capitalism. For a time, laborers will still require a wage as an incentive to work, but as socialist society develops and humans begin to experience the joys of creative and free labor, their consciousness of their species-being will be strengthened. In time, the desire to engage in free and creative labor will surpass the desire for a wage. At this point in history, humans will have overcome their alienation.

Communists: Creating a "New Man"

Antonio Gramsci, an important Italian communist theoretician, wrote:

> Reflecting on it, we can see that in putting the question, "what is man," what we mean is: what can man become? That is, can man dominate his own destiny, can he "make himself," can he create his own life? We maintain therefore that man is a process and, more exactly, the process of his actions.[15]

As this quote suggests, communists believe that humans are essentially malleable. Like Marxists, communists see the core of human identity as being a creative laborer. However, this capacity for creative labor must be brought to full and non-alienated expression by means of a total and revolutionary transformation of society. While communists thus accept Marx's theory of human nature, they reject any assumption that this transformation must occur in a deterministic way, through a specific and necessary historical process. Communists suggest various more expedient means of transforming humans into a "new man."

Lenin and Stalin employed the most notorious of these methods. Political intimidation and murder of dissidents, the internment of millions of Soviet citizens into forced labor camps, and the use of surveillance by a secret police to terrorize the entire society were methods some communists believed would be useful in bringing about the transformation of human consciousness and existence.[16] Such communists seemed to assume that humans who are coerced into working within state-owned and controlled enterprises would become less alienated simply because the state would be a better boss than their previous masters; they assumed that when the means of production were collectivized, workers would be given more incentive and opportunity to work creatively and would gain increasing satisfaction from their work.

The doctrine of *continuous revolution* – which Mao applied to China through such schemes as the Great Leap Forward, introduced in 1960, and the Cultural Revolution, begun in 1966 – was another attempt to bring about a revolutionary change in human motivation and identity. The policies of these revolutionary periods disrupted ordinary life, sending factory workers and intellectuals into the fields and replacing them with farmers. Such policies were intended to break down the "chains of institutionalism," ensuring that no one would become overly complacent in her social niche. By reversing roles, people would acquire a broader social consciousness. People were kept in a continual state of dislocation, so that their fundamental nature could be reshaped in accordance with revolutionary requirements.

A third method for transforming human consciousness as required for an ideal communist society involved self-managed workers' councils. Tito, who ruled Yugoslavia from the end of World War II until his death in 1980, resisted economic and industrial centralization, as well as centralization in the government and the Communist Party. Instead, he gave economic control to worker councils at the local factory level. By giving workers control of their state-owned workplaces, Tito sought to reduce the alienation that occurs when workers are dominated by capitalists or by bureaucrats of the state.

A fourth method of creating a new socialist man involved the use of charismatic leadership in a revolutionary context. For example, Castro has spoken on numerous occasions for hours to crowds of more than one million Cubans. During these talks, he recited the abuses that American imperialists had inflicted on Cubans. Then he would explain how the revolution revealed the potential of Cuban citizens, including their courage, willingness to sacrifice, vision, heroism, and unity of purpose. Castro also believed that human consciousness would be transformed when people experienced socialist programs in action. By providing free electricity, public transportation, and education, Castro believed that Cubans were forging a socialist consciousness that allowed them to live "according to truly fraternal norms, truly human norms, and in which each man and woman will see others as his brothers and sisters. . . . Here work will never be an ordeal, but rather the most enjoyable, noblest, most creative activity of mankind."[17]

Fascists and Nazis: Energizing the Will of "the Herd"

For fascists and Nazis, the central characteristic of all humans is that they possess a will, the ability to pursue a chosen course of action. The will as a part of human nature has a lineage extending back at least to Descartes,[18] but fascists and Nazis made it a core assumption and gave it a distinct meaning. They believed that the human will longs to belong to a coherent, recognizable group that transcends the individual. The human need to belong is fulfilled in the Nazi and fascist emphasis on group values and state authority. Following the commands of state authorities relieves individuals of the "burden of freedom" that liberalism imposes on them.[19] The human will also seeks glory and violence. The need for glory and violent action is fulfilled in war, which, according to Mussolini, "alone brings all human energies to their highest tension and sets a seal of nobility on the peoples who have the virtue to face it."[20] War and violence also serve a unifying role. According to fascist philosopher Giovanni Gentile (1875–1944), "Only war can [unite] all citizens in a single thought, a single passion, a single hope, emphasizing to each individual that all have something in common, something transcending private interests."[21] The human will to pursue such motivations can remain latent in most humans, but strong leadership can energize the human will, provoking it to courageously employ many human emotions and instincts on behalf of national and racial goals.

Thus, fascists and Nazis reject the liberal assumptions that the motivations of individuals are internally derived by looking within themselves to discover sources of pleasure and pain and that each individual is the best judge of his own interests. Instead, fascists believe that most people in mass society are like a flock of sheep. Lacking self-actualization, the will of the herd is malleable or open to being shaped by the motivations and emotional appeals provided by elites. Thus, humankind is essentially bifurcated in its power of will. The inferior masses lack strong wills, and others direct the activities they pursue. The superior leaders of the state possess strong wills that can identify the needs of the collectivity and that can pursue such needs with unyielding determination and courage. Given the herd mentality of most people, it is best that they be directed by the leaders of the state to pursue the interests of society as a whole.

In short, fascists and Nazis reject the idea that humans are characterized by their individualism; rather, humans are defined by their connection to collective entities such as nations and racial groups. They reject the view that humans are fundamentally equal, because some are superior and others inferior in the possession of such human virtues as strength of will, courage, and creative insight. Fascists and Nazis did not publicly articulate the idea that most people were like sheep. But the collective goals they articulated received positive emotional responses from those who found little appeal in liberalism's materialistic and individualistic conception of human nature. By recognizing the emotional elements within human nature, fascism suggested that people could live more authentically outside liberal society.[22]

Contemporary Liberals: Fostering Autonomy, Reason, and Moral Development

Classical liberals assumed that humans have fixed and specific characteristics – people are by nature maximizers of utility, endowed with instrumental reason, and equal in certain fundamental ways. In contrast, contemporary liberals believe that it is a mistake to assume a fixed and invariant human nature. When thinking about human nature, contemporary liberals assume that moral prescriptions of how humans *should* live are better bases for political principles than are assumptions about the natural motivations and qualities of human beings.

Contemporary liberals accept the equality of being of each human as a moral ideal. Despite existing differences in human values, rationality, and other capacities and talents, liberals accept the idea of *intrinsic equality*.[23] The moral imperatives stemming from this idea are that all people are to be treated with equal respect, the interests of all people are to be given equal consideration, and the various life plans of people are to be treated without bias by the state.[24]

Contemporary liberals assume that all humans have an essential interest in leading a good life, but they doubt that the contents of a good life can be specified in the abstract utilitarian terms employed by classical liberals. Some people regard the good life as attaining "bourgeois values," such as material comfort and security, but others might see it as involving different goals, such as being emotionally fulfilled, belonging to various groups, contributing to the public good, experiencing dangerous thrills, and other possibilities. Different people may emphasize different goals, and individuals may alter their life plans when they conclude that their current priorities are mistaken.[25] Individuals do not choose their goals in a completely autonomous manner; they are influenced by community traditions and the values of others. Still, individuals have capacities to choose among the values, traditions, and lifestyles that others offer, and individual choices define and redefine the self.[26] The moral imperative is that all individuals be given opportunities to choose and revise their life plans, with few constraints beyond being responsible for themselves and respecting the rights of others.

Contemporary liberals also believe that humans have the capacity for instrumental rationality – that humans have the potential to make economic, social, and political choices that enhance the possibility that they will achieve their life plans. But in order to be fully rational, one must understand the options that are available, one must have information about the likely consequences of pursuing various options, and one must be able to make discriminating judgments about which options best serve the full range of values that are at stake, over the long haul as well as in a more immediate perspective. The extent to which humans are fully rational varies across individuals and within individuals as they develop intellectually. The moral imperative is to foster the intellectual development of each individual. Rather than denying the rational capacity of people and having authorities paternalistically choose what is best for them, liberals insist that humans must continuously develop their rational capacities by being given opportunities to choose for themselves.[27]

Contemporary liberal theorists also stress other human qualities that should be developed if liberal principles, institutions, and policies are to thrive. For example, William Galston has argued that humans within liberal societies should develop a variety of general virtues (such as being loyal and law-abiding), economic virtues (such as having a work ethic and developing a capacity for delayed gratification), social virtues (such as tolerance and open-mindedness), and political virtues (such as supporting democratic institutions, participating in a reasonable manner, and being sufficiently attentive to politics so as to be able to hold representatives accountable).[28] It is thus important that liberal societies foster such economic, social, and political virtues of humans.

The Radical Left: Stressing our Common Humanity and Individual Differences

The radical left does not disagree with any of these moral imperatives stressed by contemporary liberals, but its various voices point out that contemporary liberals have not adequately understood how liberal institutions thwart the kind of human development that liberals seek. The radical left also believes that contemporary liberals (like their classical precursors) continue to overemphasize the individualistic aspects of humans and their development; humans have a social side that needs to be more fully recognized and developed.

Radical and social democrats understand that each person has a unique identity based on different personal qualities and different socially constituted goals, perspectives, and recognitions.[29] However, our unique identities are not fully appreciated and encouraged to develop in existing pluralist societies. Although people are given some civil liberties to protect certain elements of their personal and private lives, they are encouraged to seek conventional goals that reflect the needs of the capitalist regime and to attain conventional social understandings through an educational system that rewards conformity. Capitalism treats people as replaceable cogs in the machinery of mass production and as interchangeable consumers in mass markets. Representative democracy treats voters as part of broad sociological groupings that can be manipulated by offering various inducements that are thought to be keys to winning the vote of various groups. The radical left claims that powerful actors within capitalist economies and representative democracies shape our preferences and choices to such a degree that individual autonomy is a mere illusion. The culture surrounding capitalism and democracy – while giving lip service to liberal ideas about individuality and individual development – actually represses individual identities and development.

The radical left believes that humans can better develop their identities and capacities in societies that are more equal, cooperative, and cosmopolitan. In a society marked by great inequalities, many people lack the resources to develop their potentialities. But in a society in which people's basic needs are met, there will be fewer social and economic constraints to self-development. In societies marked by competition, people are wary of and thus discourage the achievements of others, because those others are seen as threats to their own well-being. But in a society of communal harmony – of respect and support for others – people encourage others to fulfill their potential in order that society as a whole might prosper. In a society where people are embedded in the parochialism of their immediate associations, the

prejudices and ignorance that abound in any social group will limit human understandings and aspirations. People can develop more challenging goals and deeper
understandings – and thus identities that depart from convention – by joining groups
and communities composed of people who are different from themselves and by
immersing themselves in cultures that are foreign to them. The process of developing
such humans needs to be encouraged, and the identities that emerge need to be recognized and respected.

Drawing on older socialist ideas, civic communitarians have stressed the failure of
liberals to understand how humans, despite their individual differences, are embedded
in society. According to Michael Sandel, the ends that humans pursue are always
deeply affected by the social context in which we find ourselves.[30] If humans live in
societies emphasizing individual rights, self-gratification, and material gain, they will
fail to have an adequate sense of their obligations to others and to the common good.
Humans will become fully developed only when they are deeply embedded in various
kinds of communities that stress collective aspirations. Different voices on the radical
left stress different communal bases of human existence. Civic communitarians like
Sandel emphasize local communities and associations in civil society. Cosmopolitan
theorists point out that we are members of a global community that must develop
institutional means for helping us recognize our obligations to the poor and oppressed
in far away places. Greens stress that we are part of global ecologies that can teach us
to better respect our obligations to other species and the earth.

Radical left assumptions about humans being deeply embedded in communities
lead to a conception of political virtues that is much more extensive than those of
liberals. While contemporary liberals emphasize the need for intellectual and moral
development so that humans can make better personal decisions, the radical left
emphasizes the need for humans to develop their capacities for making collective
decisions; humans are capable not only of instrumental rationality but also *political
rationality*. Social democrats have long recognized that ordinary people are capable of developing political skills, if they are given opportunities to participate in
making decisions in their workplaces and local communities. Egalitarian liberals
have emphasized that people who enter into community decision-making can display
public reasonableness, stating their concerns in a manner that speaks to public
implications and broadly understood public values (rather than their own personal
needs and beliefs).[31] Civic communitarians believe humans can develop abilities to
listen emphatically to the concerns of others and to search for outcomes that are
as broadly acceptable as possible. The radical left thus stresses the importance of
developing the virtues of democratic citizens in all humans. While they recognize that
such virtues are too often underdeveloped, they believe them to be sufficiently evident
in enough citizens to permit considerable confidence in democratic processes and
belief that democracy helps to develop the political rationality of those engaged in it.

Overall, the various strands of the radical left endorse socialist morality and values.
A socialist ethic of equality, fraternity, and democracy helps each person reach her
human potential. Humans are capable of developing a strong sense of fellow feeling
toward others and commitments to social justice and the common good, but such

sensibilities will become strong and active only when they are consciously sustained by social institutions and cultures having socialist and civic communitarian values.

Contemporary Conservatives: Accepting Human Imperfection

Contemporary conservatives are unhappy with what humans have become under the liberal and socialist politics that characterized so much of the twentieth century. People have a moral sense that propels them to virtue,[32] but this has too often been undermined by the excessive egoism and relativism of liberal society and by the failure of socialist and liberal welfare states to make individuals responsible for their choices. Human virtue can be encouraged and human vice can be discouraged by economies that reward hard work and responsible choices, cultures that stress decency, and governments that pursue the public interest. Conservatives assume that conceptions of human virtues and vices are not universal, but that particular moral values are well established in the particular communities in which people find themselves. Because America is a capitalist society, individuals should exhibit a strong work ethic and use their economic freedoms responsibly, making economic choices that ensure they can take care of themselves and their dependents. Because America is mostly Christian, the family values emphasized in the Judeo-Christian tradition should be practiced by parents and taught to children. Because America is a republic, individuals should be community-regarding citizens who put the public interest above their special interests. But corrupted by an increasingly socialist economy, a decadent liberal culture, and a democracy that caters to special interests, humans have lost their moral bearings and require a moral awakening.

Contemporary conservatives have little use for philosophical assumptions about an essential human nature. Like liberals, conservatives believe humans should have autonomy, or the capacity to choose and pursue their own life plans and many other freedoms, but they think liberals have gone too far in making autonomy an essential need of humans. The autonomy of particular humans should depend on how responsibly they use their freedoms. Common sense (rather than philosophical assumptions about the importance of autonomy in human nature) is the best guide to when to permit and when to restrict autonomy, but there is a broad range of views amongst conservatives about how much autonomy should be permitted. The more individualist strain within contemporary conservatism assumes that individuals should have a very wide range of choices in their lives, as long as no one else is harmed by individual choices. But this preference for autonomy is based largely on pragmatic rather than philosophical considerations; by allowing individuals more autonomy, the tyrannical capacities of government can be curbed. More community-oriented contemporary conservatives, though, are not persuaded that humans should have extensive autonomy. They believe that humans will often use autonomy in ways that are self-destructive or that violate established norms; thus, many choices regarding sexual behavior, drug use and how people spend their leisure time are bad for both the individual and society. Irresponsible uses of autonomy have unacceptable social costs. This wing of conservatism believes that the free choices of individuals should be restricted in order to promote human virtue.

Contemporary conservatives are also reluctant to make firm assumptions about human rationality. While they lack the liberal confidence in the capacity of humans to become increasingly rational, they do not stress the limits of human reason to the same degree as traditional conservatives. Contemporary conservatives demonstrate a certain confidence in the instrumental rationality of humans by celebrating the economic marketplace and the ability of individuals to make rational decisions for themselves within the market. The many initiatives of the George W. Bush administration to give individuals more choices in public schooling, among healthcare providers, and within retirement programs are premised on the assumption that individuals can make rational decisions that effectively provide for their well-being. In this way, contemporary conservatives strongly resemble classical liberals rather than traditional conservatives. But the more restrictive controls that many contemporary conservatives are willing to impose on moral decisions, such as those regarding sexual behavior, drug use, and some scientific investigations, demonstrate a familiar conservative lack of confidence in the capacity of individuals to make rational choices that are good for themselves and society.

While assuming that people have adequate instrumental rationality, contemporary conservatives seem skeptical that humans have much capacity for political rationality, for discovering expansive common interests. For the most part, they assume that such rationality is limited to discovering our common interests in physical security. More expansive claims about common interests are normally exercises in economic rationality; such efforts are really just people employing political persuasion and power on behalf of their individual interests.[33] For example, workers in public bureaucracies (like teachers) often claim that they provide essential public goods (like education) and seek increased public expenditures on behalf of this presumed public good. However, if such public goods are not provided effectively or valued by the public, then demands for increased public spending is just "rent-seeking" behavior; they are efforts to attain public compensation for the private interests of people without providing taxpayers with commensurate benefits.[34] In short, contemporary conservatives have a much higher regard for the capacity of individuals to exhibit instrumental rationality on behalf of personal interests than political rationality on behalf of collective goals.

While traditional conservatives were once confident in their beliefs about fundamental human inequalities defined by class, race, and gender, contemporary conservatives are again less willing to cling to these old assumptions. They occasionally demonstrate a belief that men and women have essential differences that sometimes justify different treatment before the law. For example, conservatives in the US opposed the Equal Rights Amendment on the grounds that it would generate egalitarian reforms blind to gender differences. Conservatives often argue that women are less likely than men to be career-driven and more likely to leave jobs for marriage and child-rearing, thus justifying some inequalities between men and women concerning wages and promotions. But increasingly, conservatives have come to believe that men and women should be equal under the law. However, conservative opposition to gay marriage suggests a disinclination to treat gays and lesbians equally under the law, and conservatives typically argue that marriage is by definition a relationship between a man and a woman, and that they support the right of all to enter into such a relationship. They might add that they are, nevertheless, increasingly willing to extend to gays the same political and civil rights that are available to others. With regard to race, conservatives have scrapped most of their assumptions of racial inferiority. In general, they still assume that humans are highly unequal in their talents and virtues, but they no longer stress that these differences are strongly determined by a person's ascriptive traits. Irrespective of their racial, class, and gender characteristics, everyone has the ability to develop talents and virtues, and these qualities should be rewarded. And people of all races, classes, and genders exhibit deficiencies and vices – largely because they have refused to develop their talents and virtues. Conservatives believe that we might have some compassion for such people, but that everyone is responsible for his or her own fate, and the larger political community owes them little or nothing.

Contemporary conservatives are thus primarily concerned with the moral qualities of humans. Attempts to encourage virtue and discourage vice are not the result of conservatives entertaining utopian ideals. Conservatives accept human imperfection. There will always exist the industrious and the lazy, the wise and the foolish, the multi-talented and the ungifted, the witty and the banal. No reforms by egalitarian dreamers can alter the broad differences in proclivities and abilities of individuals without denying freedom and enforcing mediocrity. Conservatives seek to limit bad behavior, not mold perfect humans.

The Radical Right: Embedding Humans in Moral Communities and/or Free Markets

The various voices within the radical right hold diverse views of human nature. Traditional communitarians, national protectionists, cultural conservatives, and the religious right resemble traditional conservatives in the stress they give to the importance of embedding humans in moral communities. In contrast, libertarians accentuate the more individualist strain in contemporary conservatism in the stress they give to individual autonomy.

Like civic communitarians on the left, traditional communitarians emphasize how humans are, and should be, deeply embedded in particular communities. Alasdair MacIntyre claims that liberal conceptions of the autonomous self are flawed, because humans are bearers of particular social identities that strongly influence all human choices.[35] Prior to making choices from among various life plans, humans seek to discover who they are, and this involves discovering the communities to which they already belong. Being embedded in communities is very important and valuable. It is from our community identities and roles that we derive meaning and purpose in our lives; without such social roots, nothing would seem worth doing.[36] It is because of our community obligations that we must limit our excessive selfishness and our preoccupation with satisfying our base material appetites. It is within communities that we can regenerate a sense of our spiritual selves that has been lost in the loneliness and materialism of liberal society. The good life can only be realized within communities that provide moral principles that have withstood the test of time. While civic communitarians often seek the construction of new communities having socialist values or the democratic reconstruction of existing communities so that their values are more egalitarian, traditional communitarians, cultural conservatives, and the religious right emphasize the value of established associations like churches and civic groups that emphasize traditional values.

The radical right also includes libertarians, who de-emphasize the importance of communal roots for humans. Like classical liberals, they see humans as autonomous and self-interested, and thus best able to thrive in free markets. Our primary motivation is to obtain happiness by having freedom to live our lives as we want and to acquire and use material goods in ways that serve our purposes. If we seek community, so be it, but it is not the purpose of government to encourage or discourage our ties to community.

Some among the radical right – particularly global neoliberals and neoconservatives – have attempted to resolve this seemingly irreconcilable debate between communitarians and libertarians by stressing that humans simultaneously occupy both economic and social spheres. In the economic sphere, humans can be autonomous, rational, self-interested actors pursuing material goods and personal happiness. Globalization seems to enlarge the economic sphere, as it expands the goods and services that humans produce and consume.[37] In addition to wanting more freedom and material goods, our satisfaction is measured by how well we are doing relative to others around the world, rather than how well we are doing in terms of some natural (minimal) needs or how well our fathers or immediate neighbors are doing. In addition to ever growing material wants, humans have acquired – especially through exposure to global technologies – enhanced wants to be entertained and amused.[38]

Even as they are self-regarding individualists in the economic sphere, humans need to be embedded in the social sphere. As Thomas Friedman points out, globalization does uproot our "olive trees" – his symbol for human roots in communities – and so globalists and neoconservatives are attentive to restoring our attachments to local communities. This can be partly accomplished through a global marketplace that outsources jobs to workers in their local communities; while industrialized production required uprooting people from their traditional rural communities and locating them in urban centers where manufacturing plants were built, the more service-oriented post-industrial globalized economy allows workers to perform essential service functions through telecommunications from their local communities.[39] Globalists applaud the new web communities that are being generated in cyberspace, and neoconservatives applaud the revitalization of civic society, such as churches.[40] They suggest that local communities and voluntary associations within civil society are becoming more heterogeneous, composed of people of more diverse class, racial, and ethnic characteristics than in the past, contributing to the development of more pluralist societies while also providing people with more choices when it comes to joining and identifying with communities that satisfy the human need for roots.

The radical right generally acknowledges that humans are obviously unequal in many capacities (e.g., intelligence, ambition, etc.) that can be employed in ways that lead to justified inequalities in power, in property, and in the opportunities that people enjoy. But they assume that almost all humans have capacities that enable them to thrive, assuming that they live under conditions that encourage use of these capacities. They believe capitalism rewards the use of these capacities and that democratic governments can provide minimal safety nets for those having inadequate capacities to survive capitalist competition.

The Extreme Right: Regarding Humans as either Good or Evil

A *Manichean* conception of human nature is widely held by the extreme right: humans are either good or bad. For some, this dichotomy is genetic, given to people at birth and indicated by their race. For white nationalists, the good people are Aryans and Anglo-Saxons.[41] The bad or sub-human people are Jews (who are the children of Satan) or nonwhites (who are often labeled "the Mudpeople"). Black Nationalists sometimes have their own racial depictions of human nature, seeing whites as demonic offspring of the evil genius "Yacub."[42]

For others, this Manichean vision is less fixed. Fundamentalists in both the Christian and Islamic traditions stress that humans are by nature depraved. Only God (or Allah) is good and humans can only aspire to his goodness. For Islamic fundamentalists, it is precisely human innate sinfulness that requires humans to submit completely to religious laws and authority. In Islamic theology, humans face a false choice between eternal peace and eternal torture; the right choice is to follow "the Straight Path." Among Islamic fundamentalists, the failure to choose the path toward Allah marks one as an infidel and thus a just target for political punishment. Some Christian fundamentalists may hold similar beliefs, but others seem to hold the Calvinist doctrine that God chooses humans for divine grace rather than humans choosing God. This assumption has less extreme political implications, because of uncertainty about whom God has chosen and why political authorities should punish those who do not receive divine grace.

Right-wing assumptions begin with the belief that humans are inherently evil, but that they can become good by embracing religious doctrines in their thoughts and in their actions. American Christian fundamentalists are perhaps the most optimistic in their belief that most people (regardless of prior religious orientation or racial and ethnic background) can choose God or become chosen by God and thus become good. Fundamentalist Muslims seem to have less optimism about the individual's capacity to make such choices, unless they live in political communities that are independent of subversive secular influences and have the capacity to discipline their members. Because staying entirely on "The Straight Path" is demanding, we need the support and company of other believers in a politically organized setting. By seeking to cleanse Islamic communities of infidels, Islam fundamentalists seek the homogeneous community that will enable people to become and remain good.

The Extreme Left: Rejecting an Essential Human Nature

A consistent theme that runs through all extreme left writing is a refusal to provide an essential characterization of humans.[43] Humans are products of their environments in ways that make futile any attempt to provide a fundamental characterization of humans, and any effort to do so is oppressive, a finite depiction of endless possibilities.

The criticisms that the extreme left has often voiced about citizens are not claims about a deficient human nature. The tendency of the extreme left to see human deficiencies as instead arising from misguided social institutions goes back at least to Jean-Jacques Rousseau, who claimed that arrogance, greed, and ambition were among the human traits that were unleashed by modernity. The extreme left today claims that humans increasingly exhibit consumerist motivations, including insatiable appetites for self- and instant gratification, and that this is due to the increasing influence of neoliberal ideology and capitalist institutions in the current global community. Humans have become increasingly androcentric, as many women now adopt traditional male values of competition and domination and become preoccupied with the exchange-, rather than the use-, value of things. Humans have also become increasingly homocentric, viewing nature and other animals as beings to be exploited for often frivolous human pleasures. The extreme left claims that such orientations leave humans ultimately unfulfilled. We flee from our freedom and our boredom in various anesthetics: religion, drugs and alcohol, dining, shopping, spectator sports, TV, work, and other addictions.

The old left often saw these same negative qualities in humans, and Marx and other radicals can be interpreted as claiming that there is an essential human nature that is radically different from the qualities people manifest in their current existence. As we have seen, Marx saw humans as essentially creative laborers, who gained meaning in life by using their unique human capacities to transform nature in ways that satisfied human needs and desires. The contemporary extreme left – especially post-structuralists – would criticize such conceptions, objecting to any particular human characterization in order to justify a particular course of action. Only by keeping open human possibilities can political possibilities be kept open.

Sometimes the extreme left does suggest some of these possibilities. Deep greens are perhaps most likely to see a human essence that corresponds to Marx's unalienated worker, as they stress that humans would fulfill themselves if they were to live in greater harmony with nature. Those on the far left usually assume that humans can be – and perhaps ought to be – equal social beings, rather than the isolated, atomistic, material beings of liberalism. Some suggest that through rebellion against capitalism and globalism, humans can realize their "higher selves" – their creativity, their autonomy, their generosity, their public-spiritedness, and their unity with "gaia."

While academic leftists reject efforts to categorize humans, fellow travelers on the extreme left sometimes depict people in the same sort of Manichean "good versus evil" terms that are prevalent on the extreme right. Some leftists depict people who do not share their views and who resist their more militant actions in dehumanized terms – as "pigs," "tools of the system," or "puppets of the regime" – as such characterizations enable extremists to diminish the moral quandaries involved in using violence against them.[44] Such depictions, of course, undermine the more lofty philosophical assumptions of left-wing theorists.

Conclusions

The underlying consensus of pluralism contains some minimal assumptions about human beings. We are assumed to be equal in some basic ways. The life of each human is equally valuable and the interests of each human should be given equal consideration in governing a pluralist society.

Pluralists agree that each person should be given opportunities to make autonomous judgments about what would make her life good and be relatively unconstrained by governments in pursuing responsible conceptions of the good life. Pluralists recognize that people have different motivations in life, and thus no fundamental or single motivation – such as maximizing utility or seeking union with God – can be attributed to humans to serve as a basis for pluralist public philosophy.

Pluralists thus tolerate a wide range of human choices. They do not believe that all human choices should be valued and rewarded equally by others in society or in the marketplace, but they believe that government should be neutral among choices that are responsible – that do not directly harm others in society, that are consistent with the just laws of society, and that do not seek to undermine the thin underlying consensus of pluralism.

While pluralists assume that all humans have the right to autonomy, they do not assume that all people want autonomy or that they will achieve it. Some people will be more concerned with living according to a moral code provided for them by some group within society to which they belong – such as a fundamentalist church or a communitarian ethnic group – and pluralists tolerate groups of such non-autonomous individuals. Pluralists recognize that some people – perhaps most people – will be deeply influenced by social factors in deciding what conception of the good life to pursue. But they differ over the question of whether pluralism should encourage more individual autonomy or root humans more deeply into community life. Liberals and those on the radical left believe humans are best served by being exposed to diverse social influences and giving humans the political freedom to escape those social influences and communitarian groups that they believe no longer serve their interests. Many conservatives and most perspectives within the radical right believe humans are best served by being deeply embedded in families, voluntary associations, and communities that provide clear standards about the good life and that ease some of the burdens of human autonomy, prompting individuals to make more responsible choices for themselves and choices that better serve the public good.

Pluralists assume that humans generally have significant but limited reasoning ability that they can and should employ in making personal and political decisions.

Pluralists recognize that all but the mentally impaired have sufficient reason to make most decisions about their own good, and thus to be responsible for most choices that affect only themselves. But pluralists recognize that the instrumental rationality of people is imperfect. They acknowledge that individuals often do not know what is good for them, and they often make erroneous predictions about the means of attaining their desires.[45] Consequently, pluralists do not believe that complete autonomy, even in private life, is essential to the good life, so they can support occasional paternalistic governmental policies, such as requiring people to wear seat belts or mandating participation in social insurance programs.

In addition, pluralists recognize that most people have sufficient reason to enter into decisions about their collective life, but that the imperfect understandings that they bring to public decision-making contribute to flawed public policies. Consequently, political decisions should be challenged and modified in on-going pluralist politics.

However, pluralists disagree among themselves about the degree of rationality that humans can bring to personal and collective decisions. Conservatives and those on the radical right are more skeptical about our collective than about our personal decision-making capacities. In contrast, those on the left are more optimistic about human capacity for political rationality. Such differences will be further explored in chapter 8, when we turn to questions of epistemology.

Beyond differences in rationality, pluralists assume that people have unequal natural talents and unequal access to those social resources that help achieve their diverse goals. They recognize that there is a wide variety of human talents and qualities, that those possessing one great talent in one area may be relatively untalented in other areas, and that no single human quality (such as intelligence) serves as the sole indicator of human excellence. Pluralists also believe that there is greater inequality in the distribution of human talents within groupings (like race and sex) than across these groupings.[46] But they disagree on the moral significance of the real differences in natural talents and social resources that are available to people. Contemporary liberals, and especially those on the radical left, stress that the disadvantaged must be compensated for their undeserved inequalities. Contemporary conservatives and those on the radical right see these inequalities as natural and inevitable, and thus oppose many political remedies.

Some assumptions about human nature are clearly dangerous to pluralist politics. Pluralists fear that communitarian ideas that humans should be motivated toward communal unity, union with God, or some alleged human perfection, such as being a creative laborer – no matter how noble these ideas seem to some – can be the basis for totalitarian control over individuals in order to ensure that humans live according to these noble motivations. Pluralists also believe that the notion that some people are inherently good while others are inherently evil is a recipe for the repression of one group of people by another.

Chapter 7

Questions of Society

What are the origins of social life? What are the basic features of political societies? What should be the characteristics of a good political society? Should a society be comprised of people who are similar in specific ways, and what are the major differences among members of society?

The concept of society is often used interchangeably with the concept of community. However, questions of community are not taken up until chapter 9. Assumptions about the fundamental character of societies generally and political societies in particular are prior to arguments about which sort of communities (e.g., local, national, global) are important. People have widely different ideas about how people have come to live in societies, and they hold very different images of the essence of societies. Before we can think clearly about which communities deserve our allegiance, we need to think about the fundamental nature of societies.

The layer-cake image of society has been prominent at least since Karl Marx stressed that industrial societies were divided between capitalists and the working class. Many people now recognize that societies have more than two layers, as other classes such as those composed of middle-class professionals and skilled blue-collar workers are important features of contemporary society. Additionally, it can be assumed that society is layered not only by class – by such things as ownership of wealth, levels of income and education, and occupations – but also on the basis of race, ethnicity, gender, sexual orientation, and other such differences. Some of the most important political movements during the past half century – the civil-rights, women's, and gay liberation movements – have drawn upon such images of society. Reducing inequalities and hierarchies within society defined by class, race, sex, and sexual orientation remain highly visible issues.

While most people agree that there are some divisions in society, many think these divisions are of minor importance. Sometimes political leaders invoke images of a unified society; a picture of an orchestra composed of strongly interrelated people led by a conductor to produce social harmony comes to mind. At other times, they invoke images of a highly individualist society where people interact cooperatively and competitively in pursuit of their own interests; a picture of a marketplace comes to mind. Different images about society serve different political purposes.

In this chapter, we consider the various assumptions that proponents of major ideologies have about the origins and fundamental characteristics of society. We propose that the friends of pluralism will not be committed to any particular assumptions about the origins of society and will find some utility in images that stress various social divisions and forms of integration, but they will stress the diversity of contemporary societies. Perhaps a salad composed of many fruits and vegetables, though in many combinations, best captures a pluralist image of societies.

Classical Liberals: Individuals Seeking Mutual Benefits Through a Social Contract

For classical liberals, societies arise from agreements among individuals to band together in order to escape the loneliness, disorder, and inconveniences that occur in the state of nature. Classical liberals recognized that humans are bound to one another in many types of societies. The most intimate of these is conjugal society based on a "voluntary compact between man and woman."[1] The most inclusive are civil and political societies based on a *social contract* in which individuals agree with one another to limit the liberties they enjoyed in the state of nature in order "to join and unite in a community, for their comfortable, safe, and peaceable living amongst another, in a secure enjoyment of their properties and a greater security against any that are not of it."[2] There are several important features of this liberal conception of political society.

First, while societies do not exist in the state of nature, they arise from the state of nature through natural processes. Thomas Hobbes viewed the state of nature as a state of war. He assumed that men in the state of nature desired goods that were too scarce for all to attain fully, thus creating perpetual conflict in which each person would try to subdue others to get what he wants. In such a condition, men would live in "continuall feare and danger of violent death; And the life of man solitary, poore, nasty, brutish, and short."[3] To escape this condition and to achieve the goal of security, men would naturally reason that they should make a covenant, or social contract, with other men in which each person would agree not to infringe on the life, liberty, and property of others. For Hobbes, such an agreement (and the simultaneous designation of a potentially authoritarian sovereign power to enforce the agreement) created a commonwealth – or a political society.

John Locke provided a more liberal conception of society. He viewed the state of nature in less conflictual terms than Hobbes, but he agreed with him that people would seek to escape it by entering political society. Locke maintained that individuals in the state of nature comprehend an important law of nature: that "no one ought to harm another in his life, liberty, or possessions."[4] He thought that this understanding would prompt individuals readily to make an agreement with others to conform to this law of nature. This mutual agreement, Locke's first social contract, creates *civil* society. Locke recognized that some people in civil society would nevertheless violate this law of nature, giving injured parties the right to defend themselves and to punish offenders. While the laws of nature specify that the degree of punishment should be proportionate to the transgression and merely be sufficient to deter transgressions, injured parties would not be good judges of these matters. They will be partial to their own interests and vindictive toward the accused. Mere civil society thus remains "inconvenient," because there is no impartial power to adjudicate alleged infringements on each other's rights. To overcome such inconveniences in the state of nature, people may "resign to the public" their power to punish offenders of their rights.[5] When in civil society, people will thus agree to Locke's second social contract, to create a government to act for the public in dealing with such conflicts, thereby creating *political* society.[6] In short, political societies arise because of human desires to escape, in the first instance, from the insecurities of the state of nature and, in the second instance, from the inconveniences of living in a mere civil society without government.

Second, the society established by these natural processes can best be conceived of as an aggregation of the individuals composing it and their interactions. While the ancient and medieval world attributed to society an existence and properties beyond the individuals that comprise it, liberals rejected such an inflated conception of society. Society was not an entity created by God; it was created by man. Society did not define the individual and give him an identity; rather, individuals defined society and gave it an identity. Two metaphors are sometimes employed to capture this characterization of society. Opponents of liberalism often allege that liberals hold a mechanical conception of society, viewing society simply as a sort of machine. Just as humans assemble machines to serve their individual purposes, so do they assemble political societies to serve individual interests. Just as a machine works well when its component parts interact with minimal friction, so a political society works well when the individual components of society do not interfere with one another. Just as a machine works well when there are controlling mechanisms (such as the computers that control many modern devices), so does a political society work well when controlled by a government. But the controlling government should only attend to the smooth interaction of the parts. Just as HAL taking over the spaceship in Stanley Kubrick's film classic, *2001*, exemplifies the controlling device of a machine that is out of control, so does a strong government using its power for its own purposes exemplify the controlling device of a political society that is out of control, failing to serve the purposes of the individuals within it. In addition to a machine, the *marketplace* is another frequent metaphor for the classical liberal conception of society. Just as a marketplace is basically made up of individuals in interaction with each other for their mutual economic benefit, so is political society basically made up of individuals interacting for their mutual social benefit. Just as the marketplace needs only minimal supervision by government, so political society needs only minimal supervision by government.

Third, this individualist image of society suggests that classical liberals put the rights and needs of individuals before the rights and needs of society. In the ancient and medieval worlds, it was thought that individuals should yield to the claims of society. In contrast, liberals assumed that society could not make certain claims against the individual. It could not, for example, ask the individual to die for the good of society or to refrain from exploiting natural resources for the good of the environment. Indeed, the liberal conception of society implied that all societal claims on the individual had to be framed in terms of the needs of other individuals within society, not society itself. If the greater good of most members of society is served by compelling an individual to act in a certain way, such as being drafted into the army, such infringements on individual liberties might be justified. But individuals cannot be compelled to do things against their will simply to serve the needs of "the country," where the country is conceived of as an emergent entity with needs beyond those of its present members.

Finally, the creation of liberal societies implies very little about the institutions of those societies. For Locke, majority rule is the only institutional arrangement implied by the existence of civil society. Each civil society must establish institutions to enact, administer, and enforce laws providing for the peaceful resolution of conflict. It must authorize a particular government to carry out these functions, and, if a particular government is not carrying out these functions adequately, it can be dissolved by civil society. Since members of society may disagree about what kind of government to authorize and when a government should be dissolved, these decisions must be made by majority rule.

In sum, classical liberals have a weak conception of society. Society is merely a collection of individuals who sometimes interact with each other to further their various interests. Civil and political societies arise out of social contracts among individuals. Societies have no emergent properties beyond those of their members. Societies can make only limited claims on their members.

Traditional Conservatism: Organic Societies that Come Before Individuals

Opponents of the French Revolution believed that the liberal image of society helped give rise to popular agitation and threatened the destruction of traditional societies throughout Europe. Edmund Burke became the most forceful and respected public philosopher who defended the earlier medieval conception of society against emerging liberal assumptions. In his *Reflections on the Revolution in France*, Burke declared:

> Society is indeed a contract. Subordinate contracts for objects of mere occasional interest may be dissolved at pleasure – but the state ought not to be considered as nothing better than a partnership agreement in a trade of pepper and coffee, calico, or tobacco, or some other low concern, to be taken up for a little temporary interest, and to be dissolved by the fancy of the parties. It is to be looked on with other reverence because it is not a partnership in things subservient only to the gross animal existence of a temporary and

perishable nature. It is a partnership in all science; a partnership in all art; a partnership in every virtue and in all perfection. As the ends of such a partnership cannot be obtained in many generations, it becomes a partnership not only between those who are living, but between those who are living, those who are dead, and those who are to be born. Each contract of each particular state is but a clause in the great primeval contract of eternal society, linking the lower with the higher natures, connecting the visible and invisible world, according to a fixed compact sanctioned by the inviolable oath which holds all physical and all moral natures, each in their appointed place.[7]

Burke thus maintained that political society is more than a contract that can be dissolved by unhappy individuals. It is more than the sum of its parts. Political societies have an existence of their own; they are living entities with a past and a future.

Traditional conservatives reject liberal mechanistic metaphors for society and prefer organic metaphors like "the body politic." An *organic society*, like a healthy living human body, is composed of many interdependent parts. Organic societies develop institutions that structure various roles that, when properly performed, enable the needs of the body politic to be met. Individuals are assigned roles, and they have duties to perform their roles conscientiously. These institutions and the roles within them have developed over a long period of time, and they should not be tampered with lightly. Social reformers who change structures and roles too often ignore the complex interdependencies in society and thus destroy the natural harmony of the body politic. Just as medications for minor ailments in the human body can have unexpected and disastrous side effects, reforms of minor problems in the body politic can cause serious injury or problems unanticipated by the reformers. Thus, traditional conservatives are wary of interventions in the traditional roles and structures of society.

Organic societies are arranged hierarchically. Just as a human body has some organs (brain and heart) that are more important than other tissues (hair and toenails), the body politic has people and groups who are more important than others in the society. Thus, society is class-based. Traditional conservatives in the eighteenth century sought to maintain the class distinctions that prevailed in medieval society, which gave more privileges (and responsibilities) to the royalty, the landed aristocracy, and the clergy than to the urban bourgeoisie, laborers, and peasants. Although allegiance to a feudal class structure has receded among traditional conservatives, there remains an understanding that class distinctions are important. The doctor, the judge, and the statesman are more important than the farmer, the plumber, and the chimney sweep. However, the latter groups are also essential for a healthy society and their contributions must be acknowledged.

For traditional conservatives, societies – independent of their governments – play essential functions for individuals living within them, functions that liberals overlook. Conservatives believe that when individuals are guided by their self-interest and passions, they make bad decisions, both for themselves and society. People need social guidance in how to understand and achieve a good life. In short, society has an obligation to promote virtue and to protect errant members from themselves. Society requires that the passions and inclinations of individuals should frequently be thwarted. Even if a large majority of individuals – the masses – share the same passion (such as a desire to redistribute wealth), society contains traditional norms and enlightened leadership that can subordinate such passions to the needs of society.

The conservative organic society also contains mediating institutions, such as churches, voluntary associations, neighborhoods, and extended families. Mediating institutions within civil society help individuals acquire a sense of connection and belonging to society and an understanding of social obligations. When such mediating institutions play a large role in society, there is less need for state intervention. These institutions thus protect people from the isolated individualism of liberalism and the dangerous nationalistic appeals of fascism. In the twentieth century, traditional conservatives argued that the spread of liberal anomie created populations highly susceptible to fascism's appeal to unify people in a nation-state seeking national glory.[8] Conservatives championed pluralistic organic society – in which mediating institutions were of fundamental importance – not the unitary societies of fascism that insisted on direct connections between the state and individuals within it.

By assuming the importance of a pluralist organic society, traditional conservatives do not reject individual freedom. However, they insist that the individual be rooted in society and that freedom be exercised within the rights and responsibilities that accompany the (varied) roles occupied by members of the society. Society thus is ontologically prior to the individual, and individualism must be constrained to maintain a healthy society.

Anarchists: Natural Societies Built on Friendship

Anarchists are closer to classical liberals than traditional conservatives in their assumptions about society. Rather than believing that individuals should conform to the traditions of organic societies, anarchists think they should challenge social conventions. Like liberals, they believe that societies arise out of agreements among individuals. But anarchists reject the liberal idea that these agreements include a social contract to create a political society providing security through government. Such political societies are artificial, because they are based on the myth of each individual consenting to give up his natural liberties to attain the spurious benefits of governments. In order to entice rational individuals to enter a social contract, liberals have depicted a state of nature that is much more conflictual and hostile than anarchists believe the natural condition of humanity to be. If people are naturally social, as discussed in the previous chapter, they can form natural societies rather than submit to the coercive forces that governments impose to achieve social order.

While political societies are typically territorial, large, distant, and based on coercion, a *natural society* is small, face-to-face, and voluntary. According to Herzen, left to himself, each person will discover who to love, who to befriend, and with whom to associate, and these discoveries will develop into natural societies.[9] If artificial, centralized, political societies are abolished, people will be more inclined to develop natural societies, various associations among people inhabiting local territories based on their friendships with each other and their need for the support and assistance of others.[10] Through a continuous series of face-to-face encounters, people learn to respect and help each other, and from these encounters arise norms of reciprocity and habits of sociability that are impressed into the consciousness of individuals. These norms and understandings may be augmented by socialist values, leading to the communist societies envisioned by Peter Kropotkin. Or they may be little more than the recognition that others are equally self-contained individuals whose solitude and personal liberties must be respected, leading to the society of egoists envisioned by Max Stirner. In other words, natural societies may exhibit great solidarity (with extensive provisions for mutual assistance) or great individualism (with minimal provisions for mutual assistance), depending on the particular norms and habits of the individuals that freely comprise them. But all societies should be decentralized and voluntary, held together by mutual respect and common interests, not the coercive power and authority found in conventional communities.

Marxists: Transforming Class-Based Societies into Classless Ones

Marxists reject both the conservative conception of society as an organic whole and the liberal conception of society as arising from a social contract among individuals. Instead, they believe that civil societies were formed to satisfy the material needs of people, and political societies were formed by acts of force and power by those who had acquired the most property within civil society. This claim built upon that of Rousseau, who developed the first important radical conception of society almost a century before Marx.[11]

In his "Second Discourse," Rousseau provided a speculative history which intended to suggest how humans have descended to their present deprived condition of living in societies characterized by selfishness, alienation, and inequality. He argued that humans began in a primordial condition (or a state of nature), in which they were noble savages, basically independent beings but with compassion for others. Most importantly, humans were guided by instinct and will and had no language to help them reason their way into forming a social contract with others. However, in the state of nature, humans did become aware of their capacity to control nature for human benefit, and they discovered that limited forms of cooperation enabled them to deal with natural disasters and exploit nature more effectively. Through such cooperation, they formed primitive society, which, Rousseau suggested, was generally "best for man" and marked his "happiest and more durable epoch." But this society contained the seeds of its decline, because humans began to desire more than self-preservation; their wants and needs became enlarged. In order to satisfy more "needs," they created a division of labor. Those who did one thing – for example, farmers – had to acquire their tools from those who did something else – for example, smiths or toolmakers. Humans thus began to exchange goods and services with each other, creating human interdependence, which decreased human independence. Such exchanges also presupposed the concept of private property. The farmer began to claim his harvest as his own, so that he could exchange it for the goods that someone else produced. Given that talent and energy were unequally distributed among people, some were necessarily more successful than others in acquiring property. Thus, the claim to private property inevitably amounted to a claim to unequal quantities of property. The social cooperation that began as a convenience evolved into the institution of unequal property. "The person who, having fenced off a plot of ground, took it into his head to say 'this is mine' and found people simple enough to believe him, this was the true founder of civil society."[12]

The most immediate consequence of humans developing civil societies and holding unequal property was that their interactions became increasingly characterized by competition, jealousy, and rivalry. In time, a state of war between the rich and the poor emerged. To secure their property, the rich wanted to exchange natural liberty for *civil liberty*. They wanted everyone to be subject to the rule of law. Governmental laws would protect the unequal distribution of property, making the poor permanently subordinate to the rich. Thus, the idea of political society based on a social contract is a fraud, as governments are not created by a voluntary compact or social contract. Political societies are, instead, the result of power plays by the rich against the poor.

Marx and Engels generally agreed with Rousseau about the role of power in the origins of political society, but they perceived a larger role for impersonal economic and collective forces in its development. According to Marx:

> It is of course very simple to image that some powerful, physically dominant individual, after having caught the animal, then catches humans in order to have them catch animals; in a word, uses human beings as another naturally occurring condition for his reproduction (whereby his own labour reduces itself to ruling) like any other natural creature. But such a notion is stupid – correct as it may be from the standpoint of some particular given clan or commune – because it proceeds from the development of isolated individuals.[13]

Marx's *Grundrisse* and *Das Capital* provide complex accounts of the historical process by which economic and social forces resulted in the class-based societies of capitalism. For our purposes, it is sufficient to understand that Marx believed that the class-based societies that have come to exist under capitalism are "written in the annals of mankind in letters of blood and fire," rather than by any voluntary process.[14] It is also clear that he, like his colleague Engels, believed that "the state arose from the need to hold class antagonisms in check." According to Engels, "the state that arises in political societies serves as the medium for the dominant class, [which] acquires new means of holding down and exploiting the oppressed class."[15]

Such ideas about the class origins and bases of political societies were given their most famous expression in *The Communist Manifesto*, where Marx and Engels proclaimed that "the history of all hitherto existing society is the history of class struggles." Accordingly:

[F]reeman and slave, patrician and plebeian, lord and serf, guildmaster and journeyman – in a word, oppressor and oppressed – stood in constant opposition to one another, carried on in uninterrupted, now hidden, now open, fight, a fight that each time ended, either in a revolutionary re-constitution of society at large, or in the common ruin of the contending classes.[16]

In short, for Marxists, societies are always characterized by class divisions, by the presence of dominant and subordinate classes.

Marxists stress the importance of both objective and subjective aspects to the class structure of societies. Societies exhibit classes "in themselves" that are defined *objectively* on the basis of which class has the resources to control the other(s). Societies have different class structures, based on their technologies and organization of production. While feudal modes of production featuring agricultural manors produced two distinguishable classes, the landed aristocracy and the serfs, capitalist modes of production featuring industrial factories have produced two objectively distinguishable classes: the bourgeoisie and the proletariat. The *bourgeoisie* (or capitalists) are those who own of the means of production (the factories, equipment, banks, and so forth). The *proletariat* (or working class) is comprised of those who lack such ownership.

Objective class conditions produce the essential characteristics of existing societies (such as their forms of government), but *subjective* class conditions bring about social transformations. Social changes require that objective classes-in-themselves become conscious classes-for-themselves. Such classes emerge when a group of people with common interests and living under common conditions perceives and becomes aware of itself as a unified sector of society. Only when the proletariat acquires class-consciousness can there be a revolution. And only if there is a revolution to overthrow the class domination that exists in capitalist societies will it be possible – after a transitional period where the proletariat temporarily dominates the bourgeoisie – to achieve a classless society. In an ideal communist society, the objective conditions of a class-based society will disappear, because the means of production will be collectively owned. There will no longer be a class of people owning productive property and there will no longer be a class of people who are dependent on its owners. The subjective conditions of a class-based society will also disappear as people's most fundamental interests and outlooks will no longer be determined by whether or not they own the means of production.

Communists: Non-Proletarian Contributions to a Classless Society

Communists during the twentieth century agreed with Marxist ideas about the origins and class divisions of society. They followed the Marxist doctrine that societies are composed of classes that are struggling for predominance. However, while Marx believed that capitalism had produced societies characterized by conflict between the bourgeoisie and the proletariat, communist leaders trying to initiate the revolution discovered a more complex situation. In those societies that had not yet industrialized, they found, as Marx claimed they would, a large number of classes with varying interests. The most important of these were peasants, who made up the vast majorities of the populations in Russia and China. Lenin and Mao argued that peasants were important revolutionary resources. Lenin found that it was impossible for the proletariat in Russia to overwhelm the capitalists and to carry out the revolution without the active support of the peasantry.[17] Mao went even further and established a revolutionary doctrine that was based predominantly on the peasantry. Such a shift in emphasis moved him a long distance from Marx, who had assumed that only the proletariat could lead and accomplish the revolution that would lead to communism.

Even in more mature capitalist societies, communists discovered a more complex social structure than was foreseen by Marx. In countries like Germany, Great Britain, and the United States, a sizable and complex middle stratum was developing – which contained a managerial class, a class of salaried and professional workers, a class of small businessmen, a class of skilled craftsmen, and others. This development seemed to contradict Marx's prediction that capitalism would lead to a polarization of all people into a large mass of proletariat and a small minority of bourgeois capitalists. Since Marxism did not account for this development, new theories and strategies were required. In Europe, communist parties often sought popular unions among various classes and utilized democratic processes of electoral politics in their efforts to acquire power, rather than emphasizing revolution and immediate proletarian domination.

As in Marxism, the communist vision of the ideal society is one in which all class differences will be eliminated. It is a society in which everyone will be a freely creating laborer, no longer alienated from others. It is a society free of class conflict.

Fascists and Nazis: Defining Society in Nationalist and Racist Terms

For totalitarians, societies are homogeneous organic entities. Just as traditional conservatives stress the organic nature of societies, fascism and Nazism stress that societies are characterized by the interdependence of people having well-defined and hierarchical social roles. Individuals within fascist and Nazi societies are connected to each other by their common commitment to national or racial purposes, which are provided by leaders at the top of these hierarchies. While traditional conservatives stressed the role of mediating institutions in their organic societies, fascists and Nazis suppressed diverse associations in civil society. Such associations are permitted only insofar as they are under the control of those at the top of the hierarchy, to ensure they do not undermine citizen allegiances to national and racial goals. Social pluralism is anathema to fascists and Nazis.

For fascists, societies must be organized as nations. Many people who see themselves as a social group have not been organized as nations, and various nationalisms give expression to their desire to do so. But unless these nationalist movements seek to destroy social pluralism, they are not fascists. Fascism has always arisen in societies that had already achieved nationhood, but typically these nations had been undermined historically; as a consequence, recovering the past glory of their nations and giving their nations greater worldwide prominence are the fundamental aspirations of fascists. For Mussolini and other Italian fascists, Italy had a grand history as the center of the Roman Empire, and fascism was a public philosophy intended to unify and strengthen the country. Italian unity involved bringing together all Italian citizens without regard for racial purity.

For Nazis, societies must be organized around the racial group, and they emphasized the creation of a society made up solely of pure Aryans. They developed dubious theories and historical narratives about the Aryan race. According to the Nazi writer Alfred Rosenberg (1893–1946), the Aryans originated in Northern Europe, where the harsh and demanding climate produced a dynamic and superior race of warriors. Despite their Nordic origins, Aryans were said to have occupied Iran and the Indus Valley in ancient times, giving rise to their Aryan name, but eventually they returned to territories in the vicinity of Germany. Aryans were said to have specific facial and physical features – such as large brains – that enabled their distinct identification. Nazism was a public doctrine that claimed that such people should be united in one political society, that this society should be purified of other racial influences, and that this society would then rule the world.

Fascists and Nazis emphasized that people are most fundamentally organized into nations and into racial groups. Each nation or race has a culture that defines the spirit of its people. Each nation or race is more than the sum of its parts. The nation or race, not the individuals that make it up, is "real."

Contemporary Liberals: Promoting Social Pluralism

When thinking about society, contemporary liberals stress the idea of *social pluralism*. They are basically indifferent to traditional conservative, classical liberal, and Marxist accounts of the origins of society; whether political societies were originally constructed by God, by consent, or by force, the organic, individualistic, and class-based societies of the past have now become transformed into more modern societies that can best be characterized as composed of many groups having diverse interests. While political societies can be relatively homogeneous racially, ethnically, and economically, they always have some heterogeneity. People with common interests often form associations to pursue these common interests, or existing associations recruit and socialize members to share the values that become common within the group. Either way, such associations become bases of human identity.[18] The competing interests of different groups, whether they are organized or exist as unorganized collectivities, can be peacefully resolved through established liberal democratic institutions.

Contemporary liberals believe that the social pluralism that exists within liberal societies is desirable. Group attachments root individuals within society. Involvements in a variety of groups enable individuals to appreciate opposing sides of an issue, moderating political demands. Group involvement makes participants less susceptible to authoritarianism and the appeals of demagogues.

Several normative principles flow from this endorsement of social pluralism. First, individuals should be encouraged to associate with a variety of groups, to achieve the personal, social, and political benefits of group involvements.[19] Second, individuals must be permitted to associate with others even if the purpose of their association is to oppose the existing authorities and policies of society.[20] Third, all groups have the right to seek power, and all legitimate interests should receive a fair hearing as issues are resolved. Fourth, while various groups need not have equal power, no group should be able to dominate other groups; existing inequalities in power among groups should reflect how well different group preferences serve the public interest and justice.

In summary, contemporary liberals believe that a pluralistic society composed of many groups and associations should be promoted. Such a pluralistic society should also disperse power broadly, in ways that prevent tyranny and that promote freedom and democracy.

Contemporary Conservatives: Seeing Society as a Delicate Watch

Contemporary conservatives are more leery than traditional conservatives of grounding their public philosophy in any explicit assumptions about the nature of society.[21] They maintain that such assumptions would make conservatism overly ideological; they prefer to present conservatism as an outlook that reacts to the excesses of liberalism, socialism, and other ideologies. This reluctance to specify assumptions about society opens the door for others to proclaim what these assumptions must be. Contemporary liberals, for example, claim that conservatives in the George W. Bush administration view society in overly individualistic and corporate terms. Michael Tomasky claims that two of the central precepts of modern conservatism are:

> First, its sanctification of the individual and concomitant rejection of the community as a foundational unit of social organization (except religious communities, which are a substitute for political action and social investment); second, its glorification of the corporation. . . . Conservatives see America not as a nation but as a corporation. This means, in turn, that we are not citizens but shareholders; and that we're not really equal, because shareholders are not.[22]

Perhaps conservative politicians sometimes behave as if they hold such individualistic and corporate images of the political societies that they govern, but conservative theorists would probably regard these as ungenerous attributions of the images that most contemporary conservatives have of society.

While today's conservatives have stepped back from traditional assumptions about the organic "body politic," they still see society as very complicated and interconnected.

Like their forebears, they fear unanticipated consequences of reforms that might shred the social fabric. And they support mediating institutions, such as families and churches that bind people to local communities and offer protection against centralized government. Contemporary conservatives, though, endorse a dynamic market economy that traditional conservatives viewed with distrust. For contemporary conservatives, a well-structured society must foster the dynamic qualities of the market, without allowing the economic sphere to upset the more stable relations that conservatives value in the politics, culture, and families.

Thus, the good society, for contemporary conservatives, must be a mechanism that runs at different speeds in different spheres of life. In the economic sphere, technological changes and social mobility will generate fairly rapid changes in the ways people live and interact. In the political sphere, change should be much slower, and should be the result of careful and prudent considerations. In the cultural sphere, the pace of change must be slower still, so that religion and traditional values can curb the unsettling changes generated in the economic sphere. Conservative criticisms of the avant-garde in literature and the arts and endorsements of "solid middle-class values," reveal conservative concerns about cultural innovations. In the private sphere of individual and family life, change must be slow so that individuals can expect and enjoy the familiar.

The metaphor of a delicate watch is useful for describing a society that is properly tuned.[23] The second hand is economics, the minute hand is politics, and the hour hand is both cultural and private life. If each works at its proper speed, society as a whole will thrive, but society is delicate, even fragile. Social harmony can only occur as a result of the careful tending of the interaction among different spheres as they move along at their respective speeds. The dynamic changes within a market economy must be permitted, but governments should never promote rapid changes in the cultural and private spheres. Liberal reformers who seek extensive change in the political and cultural spheres of life must be challenged, or they will undermine the achievement of a society that is simultaneously productive and stable.

To illustrate threats to the delicate balances within society and the challenges that conservatives must confront, consider the recent liberal embrace of multiculturalism – the celebration of the richness of various cultures, the promotion of diverse worldviews, and the acceptance of multiple languages. For conservatives, the liberal pursuit of multiculturalism creates rapid changes to that part of the delicate watch that must move slowly. It undermines the shared set of understandings, values, and means of communication required for social cohesion. It invites a cultural relativism that refuses to recognize the superiority of Western middle-class principles. Bilingual education promotes permanent cultural separateness and discourages immigrant groups from conforming to mainstream values necessary for educational and economic success. Liberals may think they are assisting minorities and illustrating respect for other cultures by advocating bilingual education, but conservatives insist that liberals are in fact ignoring the normal patterns of cultural assimilation that all immigrants must face and are harming the futures of immigrant and minority groups. Most importantly, multiculturalism undermines the shared cultural traditions that keep society from flying apart.

The Radical Right: Holding either Communitarian or Libertarian Visions of Society

The radical right is divided between those who are appalled by the rapid changes in culture that are occurring in pluralist societies and those who are fascinated by the beneficial transformations that they see possible by freeing the marketplace from political and cultural controls. To the extent that they accept the metaphor of the delicate watch, the radical right assumes either that the "hour hand" of cultural change has been moving far too quickly and must be slowed or that the "second hand" of the economy could move far more quickly without endangering the stability of pluralist societies.

Traditional communitarians, cultural conservatives, and the religious right are generally in agreement that modern pluralist societies have uprooted people from cultural norms and religious understandings that guide individuals and provide social stability. They believe that societies cannot be held together unless they share a deep commitment to common cultural values.[24] They do not claim that there is one set of cultural values that all societies should affirm, as every society has its own cultural values, and large national societies contain diverse local cultures. What is important is that our connections with others, especially in local communities and voluntary associations, be renewed and that the importance of local communities and associational norms be stressed. Governments must develop policies that sustain local communities, churches, and other voluntary associations, and that respect local cultures.

But the radical right also includes libertarians and globalists, who differentiate between two most basic types of societies: voluntary and coercive. They assume that voluntary ones are preferred. Free markets exemplify voluntary associations, as they are composed of investors, property-owners, workers, and consumers who continually enter and exit associations with others in accordance with their own interests and free choices. States exemplify coercive societies. While some governmental rules and regulations are required for economic and social functioning, libertarians and globalists prefer that these functions be performed as much as possible by voluntary rather than coercive societies.

Libertarians and globalists assume that reducing governmental coercion and constraints on individual freedom will enable people to pursue more effectively their own interests and take initiatives that provide social benefits. For libertarians and globalists, cultural norms and governmental restrictions that restrict individual choices and individual initiatives in the marketplace unnecessarily slow down the beneficial social and economic transformations that are possible if the second-hand of a free-market economy is permitted to move more quickly.

The Radical Left: Searching for More Communal and Egalitarian Societies

The radical left recognizes many types of societies, ranging from global and national societies to local communities, schools, churches, unions, workplaces, and other associations. All of these societies are political in their capacities to produce collective goods and in their capabilities to distribute social goods. Within and across these kinds of societies, there are two main types of differences that should be emphasized and analyzed. First, societies differ in the extent to which their members are committed to one another and seek a common life. Second, societies differ in how power and privilege is distributed among the individuals within the community. It is by holding normative preferences about these differences that the assumptions of the radical left regarding societies differ from those of contemporary liberals.

Societies may minimize or emphasize the collective or common lives of their members. When they minimize commonalities, they may be little more than marketplaces in which individuals pursue their self-interest by exchanging goods with each other. In such societies, the prevailing question is: "How should I live?" In contrast, when societies emphasize their commonalities, the prevailing question is: "How should *we* live?" In such societies, the members (or their representatives) assemble in order to define their collective goals. They decide what communal investments – goods that belong to society as a whole – should be pursued and protected. They decide together what goods are needed by all people within a society and how to provide everyone equal access to these goods. Most importantly, the individuals in such societies are willing to invest their time and commit their resources to improving their common lives. Civic communitarians are perhaps the most vocal proponent of the idea that societies that emphasize the common lives of their members are far more attractive than individualistic, selfish societies.[25] Nevertheless, those in the radical left agree that there is an important private sphere of life that must be recognized and protected. Once individuals have fulfilled their community obligations, they should have extensive opportunities to fulfill their own, perhaps idiosyncratic wishes, because all people are different in important ways and these individual differences must be respected and permitted to flower.

Although societies may strive for relatively equal distributions of power, privilege, and other social goods, the radical left recognizes that there is no such thing as a classless society.[26] Individuals within all societies are stratified in various ways. Marx was right to emphasize stratification based on ownership of productive resources, as the class that owns most productive resources normally dominates those that own few. But inequalities in the distribution of power and privilege in a society can also be based on such other factors as occupational status, access to positions of authority, educational attainment, ethnicity, race, and gender. Thus, even communist societies that abolish private property fail to become classless, because they merely replace stratification based on property with stratification based on authoritative positions. While all societies have inequalities based on such factors, the radical left prefers societies in which these inequalities are minimized and in which the inequalities that exist do not overshadow the recognition that all individuals are equally members of society and entitled to equal respect as humans.

A socialist ethic of fraternity and equality helps to develop societies whose members have a strong commitment to building common lives and to minimizing the domination of some individuals by others. Cosmopolitan theorists preach an ethic that stresses the commonality of all people globally, and they seek to reduce the domination of developed nations over underdeveloped ones. Egalitarian liberals preach an ethic that stresses the commonalities between the well and poorly endowed, and they seek to reduce the domination of the rich over the poor. Radical feminists preach the commonalities between men and women, and they seek to reduce the domination of men over women. Radical democrats have perhaps the most general outlook in this regard; they seek to locate any and all types of domination in society, and they regard democracy as a continuous process of discovering and then diminishing the inequalities that separate people from each other.

The various voices on the radical left can preach such an ethic, but the ethic must be lived on an everyday basis to develop a communal society. Thus, local communities like workplaces, neighborhoods, and schools are places where people can actually work together to define common lives, appreciate their individual differences, and treat each other with equal respect. As these local communities more closely approximate the communal associations that the radical left prefers, it will be increasingly possible for national and perhaps global societies to evolve in socialist directions.

The Extreme Right: Seeking Homogeneous Societies

The extreme right sees our most important societies as involuntary homogeneous groupings of people. They believe that people are fundamentally members of societies such as families, clans, ethnic groups, nations, and even civilizations into which they are born. Like fascists, they see these groupings as historical facts and are little concerned with theories about their origins. Because we cannot escape these societies, we should identify strongly with them and ensure their goodness by purging them of foreign (evil) elements. Societies should be homogeneous, if not in class, race, and ethnicity, at least in religion and cultural values.

Such homogeneity is lacking in pluralist societies. However, instead of stressing a class-divided society, the radical right emphasizes even more emotionally charged divisions between "us" and "them" that reflect their Manichean conception of human nature. For white nationalists, "we" are whites (the people of God) and "they" are nonwhites (the people of Satan). For religious fundamentalists, "we" are the faithful and "they" are the unrighteous. For some right-wingers, international society is divided between "the West" and "the Rest," and the West embodies those superior cultural values that must be fostered.[27] Or they claim that domestic societies are divided between producers (those who work and contribute to society) and non-producers (the lazy, foreigners, welfare recipients and treacherous elites). While Marxists see social divisions as providing important impetus for progressive change, the extreme right see divided societies as having no redeeming value. They are an unfortunate fact of social life and the best outcome is for the dominant group to subdue the subordinate group, not so that society can progress but so that it can return to a prior condition in which the dominant group was less threatened by hostile social forces in society.

The extreme right's image of society has little room for an independent civil society, but one can find in some right-wing movements a greater appreciation of civil society than in the old right-wing extremism of fascism and Nazism. Some right-wing movements have tried to infiltrate and capture civil society, hoping to achieve their goals from the bottom up. Egypt, Algeria, Lebanon, and Palestine illustrate a pattern in which Islamic fundamentalists have established voluntary associations that provide a wide variety of healthcare, housing, employment, and educational services, while also indoctrinating citizens and generating extensive social pressure to conform to Islamic norms.[28]

The Extreme Left: Longing for Societies of "Singularities Pursuing the Common"

Most people identified with the extreme left are no more inclined to essentialize the nature of society than they are the nature of humans. Gone is the old left presumption of a class-divided society. Instead, post-Marxists emphasize the multitude of social identities that people have and how these give rise to numerous social cleavages. Racial, ethnic, gender, and other such differences, including sexual and ideological orientations, can all be bases upon which individuals unite for certain political purposes and engage in conflict with their counterparts. Indeed, post-structuralists caution against essentializing these grand cleavages, as even the gender binary of man–woman is seen as an overly restrictive basis for political thinking, since it forgets the inter-sexed person who is most oppressed in contemporary society.[29] In our global economy, the category "women" (which includes Western white women who have benefited from globalization) is less relevant than the more particularized identity of "non-Western women workers."[30] By giving up their presumptions about class divisions, the extreme left increasingly seems to reflect pluralist views. But there remains in left-wing writings a sense of strong social divisions, if not the same every-where and always, at least in the particular struggles that are necessary for political emancipation.

If there is a general conception of society among the extreme left, it might be like the one Hardt and Negri provide. In their view, global society is the prevailing reality and it is structured by Empire – a broad network of national governments, trans-national corporations, supranational institutions, and other powers that exercise *biopower* over life on earth. Those in authority over the networked institutions of Empire control the lives of everyone, not just our external actions, but also our inner-most consciousness (our self-identities, thoughts, and values). Nevertheless, there exists in everyone a certain rebelliousness against Empire and its domination. Thus, society is also comprised of the multitude – unique individuals having identities, consciousness, and interests that escape any effort to be fitted into the broad norms that the authorities of Empire would impose. The multitude is developing the capacity to communicate and cooperate in ways that stand in opposition to the agenda of *Empire*. At this point, only glimpses of the multitude are possible, as a society in which the *singular* members of society effectively communicate and cooperate to achieve common interests is only beginning to develop. But like anarchists of the nineteenth century, Hardt and Negri have few doubts that a good society would be free of the control of Empire – which is really the totality of all authorities that exercise domination and control throughout global society. Like anarchists of old, they have a utopian vision of a society of individuals who are free, but who have such love for others that community life can be sustained without coercive authorities that impose control on the multitude.[31]

Another image that is prominent among the extreme left is of society increasingly torn asunder. Industrialization, capitalism, and globalization have together destroyed much of our social organization. As older bonds of social interdependence are dissolved, *mass society* emerges and our social organization comes to resemble liberalism's state of nature, a place of solitary and isolated individualism. The extreme left thus agrees with Robert Putnam's characterization of the breakdown of civil society and the loss of social capital, but it does not share his optimism that civil society can be adequately repaired as long as neoliberal institutions and practices dominate our lives.[32] Instead, extreme leftists think that globalization and pro-capitalist policies will make our social interactions increasingly transitory and shallow.

In general, the extreme left – like the radical left within pluralism – would like to see the emergence of a non-hierarchical society with much more dense social relationships than those that currently exist, one that enhances the interdependencies and ethical relationships among humans and between humans and other life forms. Some deep greens, for example, call for a return to Burke's organic society, but a more egalitarian one embedded within ecological systems.[33]

Perhaps the hope of such a highly interdependent society gives rise to the belief that societies should be more homogenous in belief systems. The notion that all must devote themselves to "the communist brotherhood" was usually accompanied by the corollary that absence of such devotion is heretical, threatening to the sustenance of true belief by others, and thus it undermines social harmony. While most of the extreme left today are very much committed to a politics of difference that recognizes the many identities and conceptions of the good life that are – and must remain – present in pluralist societies, there remain wisps of a desire for more monistic societies. In deep green thought, for example there are suggestions that people ought to conform to communitarian beliefs centered on a simple post-material set of values. To the extent that the extreme left seeks a homogeneous society in terms of its moral systems, its conception of a good and stable society differs markedly from pluralist assumptions about society.

Conclusions

There is no deep theory about the origins of society that all pluralists embrace. They may regard as theoretically interesting the question of whether societies were formed by God, by the force and coercion applied by powerful actors, or by the voluntary interactions and/or agreements of individuals, but answers to this question have no real importance to the political principles that should be adopted to defend pluralist societies or to engage in politics within such societies. Pluralists conceive of political societies as composed of many groups having common ideas and interests that are usually organized into stable associations. But such groups can be created, modified, or disbanded.

Pluralists recognize that political societies are very diverse in their characteristics. Some are relatively homogeneous, but most have diverse populations, encompassing people with different amounts of wealth and other social resources, different racial, ethic, and religious backgrounds, different interests, and different comprehensive moral doctrines.[34] Pluralists assume that such differences are organized around a variety of social cleavages (such as class, race, gender, age, ideology, etc.), that the saliency of such cleavages varies in different circumstances and for different issues, and that no cleavage is fundamental.[35]

Pluralists recognize and value the existence of a broad array of voluntary associations within civil society, regarding these groups as providing individuals with important identities, purposes, and social ties. Political societies provide important settings for pursuing the common interests of citizens, while voluntary associations provide important settings for pursuing the common interests of smaller sub-sets of citizens. Pluralists believe that no single voluntary association (e.g., the Roman Catholic Church or the Chamber of Commerce) or even a group of similar voluntary associations (e.g., churches or business organizations generally) should dominate a political society. The political power of voluntary associations should be broadly dispersed in a pluralist society.

According to pluralists, societies are subject to diverse forces, such as those that arise from a capitalist economy, from cultural norms, and from political processes. The extent to which the characteristics of society are affected by economic, cultural, and political forces varies from society to society. In pluralist societies no single force determines the character of society, but all such forces can have important impacts and these should be reasonably balanced.

Differences exist among pluralists on many questions about societies. Those on the pluralist left tend to see strong social cleavages that define unjustified inequalities; they would like to see these inequalities reduced. Those on the pluralist right tend to de-emphasize social cleavages, seeing few unjustified inequalities. They stress the common interests of those within society and see talk of cleavages based on class, race, gender, and so forth as distractions from a society of equal opportunity for individuals. The radical left wants to strengthen political forces to counter what they see as excessive influence by capitalist forces. The radical right wants to weaken political forces so that capitalist forces can produce what they regard as the benefits of a free market economy. All friends of pluralism attempt to alter the culture of political communities so that it better reflects their principles.

Pluralists find danger in those ideas that fail to acknowledge the complexity of a pluralist society and that would undermine important aspects of that complexity. They think that the extreme right's goal of a homogeneous society fails to understand and appreciate the ways different kinds of people contribute to society. They think that the extreme left's vilification of capitalism fails to recognize its important role in pluralist societies. And they think that the anarchist dream of a society without politics and government is completely utopian, misunderstanding the fundamental role that politics must play in governing society and ensuring that it serves well the many interests that comprise any pluralist society.

Chapter 8

Questions of Epistemology

What is the role of truth in politics? Can we have certain knowledge or at least tentative knowledge about politics? Or must we accept complete uncertainty about fundamental political questions? How can we achieve truth – or as much knowledge as is humanly possible – about political issues?

In everyday politics, questions constantly arise about the truthfulness of political actors. Did George W. Bush tell us the truth when explaining why the US military should invade Iraq? Was it true that Saddam Hussein and his regime had embarked on a program to acquire an arsenal of weapons of mass destruction? Was it true that Iraq provided – or intended to provide – a safe harbor for Islamic terrorists? Did Bush give an honest account of his motivations for going to war, or did he mislead Congress and the American public by concealing some other motives – such as responding to the interests of "Big Oil" or seeking revenge on a regime that was alleged to have plotted the murder of his father? In short, what was the truth about the situation in Iraq? What were and remain America's true interests in that country? Was a military invasion the best policy for pursuing these interests there, and what were the true motivations of our political leaders in seeking the overthrow of Saddam's regime? Obviously, such questions are extremely important, and pluralist politics require institutions such as a free press and independent commissions that investigate and seek to uncover instances of deception and acting on fallacious information. But epistemological issues run deeper than the ability of a free press and "truth commissions" to do their jobs.

Perhaps most important are questions about the capacity of political leaders to know what is really good for communities as they attempt to deal with various political issues. Some perspectives believe that politics should involve the selection and training of leaders who have the capacity to know what is good for the community and the instrumental knowledge needed to attain the common good, and that such leaders should rule as guardians of others in the community who accept their authoritative understandings.[1] Other political perspectives believe there is no basis for making informed and ethical judgments about what is best for a political community, as everyone has biased perceptions that reflect his own interests; in the absence of knowledge about what is good for a community, political decisions are made on the basis of who has the power to resolve issues in accordance with his own perceived interests. Still others believe that between the alternatives of being governed by truth and being governed by sheer power there lie a variety of ways of bringing imperfect understandings about what is good to bear on political communities. Perhaps the knowledge necessary for good government can be attained by polling public opinion, by engaging in social science inquiry, by conducting social experiments, by pursuing various thought experiments, by studying history, by discerning conventional wisdom, or by consulting sacred texts.

In this chapter, such sources of knowledge will be discussed and related to three broader kinds of epistemological orientations. First are epistemological approaches that seek fundamental truths *above* politics; the goal of *true believers* is to find and declare some truths about the good life, the good society, and good government that are absolute or beyond contestation. True believers pursue truths that must be acknowledged independently of a political process that might result in agreement about them. These approaches seek to confine and reduce politics – or at least pluralist politics – by claiming that there is a nonpolitical basis (such as a sacred text) for specifying the good life that is sovereign over people, society, and government. These approaches reduce politics to the implementation of those truths discovered elsewhere than in politics.

Second are epistemological approaches that seek basic truths *within* politics; the goal of *partisans* is to provide convincing grounds for accepting (or rejecting) some principles and their applications to the contested political issues within pluralist democracies. Partisan approaches are highly political, as they seek to move pluralist politics toward the further incorporation of the principles that they believe are best. But compared to true believers, partisans are modest in their claims, as they recognize the merits of alternative approaches and their own fallibility. Partisans understand that their approaches and their truths are continuously evaluated within democratic procedures.

Third are epistemological approaches that seek fundamental truths *about* politics. The goal of *pluralists* is to show the superiority of democratic and pluralist politics while developing progressively better characterizations of democratic pluralism. Pluralist approaches do not seek to justify democratic pluralism by using uncontested truths above politics, but rather seek social agreement about the virtues of democratic pluralism itself. Complete agreement on the virtues of democratic pluralism may be desirable, but it remains elusive, because some people will always perceive defects in its practices and envision better practices. For pluralists, the search for truth is the quest for improved understandings of how democratic pluralism should operate so as to attain informed consensus more effectively where that is feasible, and how best to resolve disagreements as fairly as possible. To the extent that such understandings are achieved, the consensus supporting democratic pluralism should be enhanced, perhaps resulting in the widespread belief that it comprises the "true" philosophy and science of politics.

This chapter will consider the epistemologies – the approaches to truth and knowledge in politics – of various ideologies. While partisan approaches command the most attention, the future may well depend on whether the dominant epistemological approach to politics becomes that of true believers or pluralists.

Classical Liberals: Moving from Natural Rights to Utilitarianism

Classical liberalism arose as a political philosophy to challenge the assumption that political knowledge was best derived from tradition, religion, or classical philosophical investigation. Liberals regarded traditional understandings as mere prejudices; lacking any objective basis, they were imposed by authorities as truths. Liberals regarded religious prescriptions as little more than expressions of faith derived from interpretations of sacred texts and proclamations of church leaders. Liberals also rejected as being inadequate the philosophical approaches of Platonists, Aristotelians, and the like; the conflicting knowledge they provided led to confusion and vexation. However, classical liberals were not skeptical concerning the possibility of arriving at objective, universal truths about the good society and the good state that were *above* politics. They were true believers in the possibility of a scientific understanding of politics to be achieved by pure reason. Liberal *scientism* was rooted in the methodology of the French mathematician and philosopher, René Descartes, as expressed in his *Discourse on Method*, written in 1637.[2]

The Cartesian method involves doubting the truth of all propositions except for clear and distinct ideas that are so self-evident that no rational person can deny them. Self-evident ideas form the building blocks of more complex ideas derived or deduced from them. Because ultimate knowledge about politics involves the good life, the good society, and the good state, Cartesian liberals sought a clear and distinct conception of the good. However, self-evident propositions about what is good proved elusive, given the differences in human aspirations, capacities, and circumstances. According to classical liberals, what was self-evident was that each individual must define his own good. The basic clear and distinct idea of the good for early liberals was that each individual knows his own good by his perceptions of that which provides the most personal utility or happiness – defined hedonistically as the sensation of pleasure minus the sensation of pain.

This reasoning led liberals to advocate tolerance of different conceptions of the good life held by various individuals, and to deny that government or any other authority has a legitimate role in promoting particular conceptions of the good life. It also led liberals to conclude that each individual has the right to pursue his own good as he sees fit, as long as he does not violate the equal rights of others. For early liberals, the natural rights to life, liberty, and the pursuit of happiness were immediate deductions from the self-evident truth that only individuals know their own good. And by further deduction, early liberals like John Locke proclaimed the goodness of protective democracies (governments that secured individual rights and that were accountable to citizens if they violated individual rights). Similarly, they proclaimed the goodness of economic free-markets and private property because they allowed people to work, trade, consume, and acquire in ways that were consistent with their natural rights. In short, early classical liberals found in Cartesian episte-mology a method for turning skepticism about any universal ideas about the good life for individuals into universal truths that they thought would compel agreement among people everywhere that good government required protective democracies and good economics required capitalism.

But classical liberal hopes about such consensus were quickly dashed. In the next section, we will see that traditional conservatives raised important objections to the concept of natural rights, prompting liberals to de-emphasize their initial emphasis on natural rights and develop more complex and sophisticated versions of utilitarian-ism in the work of Jeremy Bentham (1748–1832) and his followers.

Bentham's major contribution was to develop an aggregative form of *utilitarianism* as a method for justifying political structures and practices independently of any con-siderations about natural rights. Instead of viewing the happiness or utility of indi-viduals as a foundation for proclaiming rights and seeing the protection of rights as a foundation for political institutions, Bentham developed utilitarianism an analytical technique for justifying political institutions and policies on the basis of their con-sequences, their ability to provide maximum utility for people overall. In other words, he transformed utilitarianism from a technique that looked backwards (to the rights that people were thought to possess in the state of nature in order to maximize their individual utility) into a technique that justified institutional and policy reforms by looking forward (to what would serve the future utility of most citizens). Adam Smith's seminal treatise on capitalism, published in 1776, can be read as anticipating this sort of utilitarianism. Smith's basic argument was not that capitalism was necessary to protect individual rights. Instead, he claimed that capitalism and free trade were justified because they enhanced the "wealth of nations" and thus increased aggregate utility; they produced "the greatest good for the greatest number."

While the earlier liberalism of Locke justified minimal governments that protected individual rights and especially the property rights of the rich, Bentham's new aggreg-ative form of utilitarianism justified governments that adopted laws and policies that served the public good, understood now as the aggregate utility of all citizens in a political community. As industrialization developed, radicals like Karl Marx argued that governmental policies of noninterference in the economic realm (of allowing everyone to have maximal economic liberties) protected the privileges of the wealthy and did little to help the poor. For example, if governments failed to provide public schools, the wealthy could still use their economic liberty and resources to purchase private education (and the economic benefits accompanying such education) for their sons (and daughters), while the only liberty open to the poor (being unable to afford a private education) was to send their children into the workplace. From the immediate perspective of the individuals involved, the utility of the wealthy may be well served by their purchasing private education, and the utility of the poor may be well served by their sending their children into the workplace. But to reform-minded liberals, it was at least arguable that governmental provision of public education for all children could best serve the overall public good by creating a more informed and skilled citizenry.

Bentham did not argue that the public good exists apart from the individuals comprising society. Instead, the public good is simply the aggregation of the utilities of all individuals within society. In our example, the government should estimate the pleasures and pains for each individual in society that would be derived from providing public schools. Public schools would be good public policy if the aggregate amount of utility accruing to all individuals from such public schools were to exceed the aggregate amount of utility that occurs if no public schools were provided. The calculation of aggregate utility is complicated. Such factors as the intensity, duration, and certainty of projected pleasures and pains must be weighed, as must the different susceptibilities or sensitivities to the pleasures and pains of different individuals. The complexity of this *felicific calculus* for determining the public good of policy options led Bentham to acknowledge: "It is not to be expected that this process should be strictly pursued previously to every moral judgment, or to every legislative or judicial operation. It may, however, always be kept in view."[3] By keeping the pleasures and pains of all citizens in mind when enacting laws and policies, Bentham believed that governments would gradually enact laws that provided a steady increase in public welfare (i.e., the overall well-being of citizens).

As liberalism evolved during the nineteenth century, utilitarianism became an increasingly complex approach for discovering the public good. John Stuart Mill introduced three modifications to utilitarianism. First, he thought that Bentham's conception of pleasure was overly sensual and material. For Bentham, drinking a beer can provide more utility than reading an informative book if it produces a more pleasant sensation for the individual. To correct this possibility, Mill argued that some pleasures – especially intellectual ones – are objectively superior to others: "It is better to be a human being dissatisfied than a pig satisfied; better to be Socrates dissatisfied than a fool satisfied."[4] Second, Mill argued that the object of a good life is a pleasurable existence rather than immediate pleasurable sensations. If the attainment of an immediate pleasant feeling increases the risk of significant future losses, the value of such immediate pleasures must be discounted. Third, he suggested that individuals might secure a pleasurable existence if they contribute to the public good rather than maximize immediate personal happiness. For example, if people are forced to pay taxes to increase the education, health, and welfare of other members of society, the loss of utility from the pain of taxes can, in the long run, be compensated for by living in a better society. In short, Mill argued for *enlightened self-interest*. The good life is one in which individuals maximize their intellectual and spiritual pleasures and minimize their pains over the course of a lifetime, and in which people recognize the pleasure of living within a society where other individuals are likewise satisfied. The good state is one that has laws and policies promoting such a good life for individuals within a community.

The implications of the shift within liberalism from an epistemological approach that seeks to identify natural rights to an approach that seeks to determine the public good based on an enlightened utilitarian calculus are immense; as a result Bentham and his followers were regarded as *philosophical radicals*. The successful identification of natural rights would provide a universal foundation for liberal institutions of limited government. It would provide truths about politics that are *above* politics, in that they are non-negotiable within political institutions; politics could not be used to control freedoms within a capitalist marketplace or to expand the functions of governments if the policies required were to violate people's natural property rights. In contrast, determining the public good is an inherently political activity. Bentham and his followers used utilitarianism as a method during political debates to advocate extensive reforms in English laws and trade policies, so they better served utilitarian conceptions of the public good even if they violated proclaimed, but dubious, natural property rights.

In addition to being a method that could justify extensive reforms in public policies, utilitarianism became a method used for advocating reforms of the political process itself. In his *Essay on Government*, James Mill (1773–1836) – a colleague of Bentham – used an aggregative form of utilitarianism as a basis for recommending more democratic government. While only property-holders had the right to vote in Locke's democracy, which protected property (and other) rights, James Mill argued that the franchise should be expanded to most citizens, because then representatives would be encouraged to create policies that furthered the good of all citizens, not just those who held property. James Mill also advocated other reforms, such as more frequent elections and the secret ballot, because he thought such devices would encourage elected officials to produce laws that were for the greatest good of the greatest number. Utilitarianism thus became an epistemological approach that sought to make prescriptions *about* effective democratic procedures.

Liberals have never completely abandoned utilitarianism, but they have come to recognize some of its limitations. Contemporary liberals thus give it a smaller role in defending their political principles, as we shall see shortly.

Traditional Conservatives: Doubting Reason, Stressing Conventional Wisdom

Traditional conservatives rejected both the natural right and aggregative utilitarian approaches of classical liberalism. They viewed them as overly scientific, and they resisted the incursion of science into the political realm, because it makes extravagant claims about reason and causality and underestimates the power of passion, prejudice, and habit. Michael Oakeshott provided an exemplary conservative critique of liberal rationalism, claiming that it seeks uniform practices when sensitivity to unique political circumstances is warranted. For Oakeshott and other conservatives, politics is not a science but an art. Much like a good chef, the practitioner of politics should not consult cookbook rules and formulae; politics involves:

> practical knowledge [that] can neither be taught nor learned, but only imparted and acquired. It exists only in practice, and the only way to acquire it is by apprenticeship to

a master – not because the master can teach it (he cannot), but because it can be acquired only by continuous contact with one who is perpetually practising it.[5]

Traditional conservatives do not think that reason should be abandoned, but rather that it should be employed carefully and with attention to the specific details of the case at hand.

Perhaps many early traditional conservatives objected to a science of politics and abstract reason in order to retain a significant role for religious faith in political life, but such conservatives backed away from relying on religious faith as a guide to politics. Although God is the source of truth, faith is too personal and inarticulate an approach to acquiring knowledge of God's goodness to allow a political community to share common understandings of divine truth. For traditional conservatives, the best guide to political thought and action is reliance on the conventions and traditions developed within specific societies. Tradition embodies the wisdom of the ages, having culled out those ideas that once appeared promising but turned out badly, and having retained those ideas that have proven useful to people within particular societies over long periods of time.

Traditional conservatives did not mount a sustained attack on faith because they realized that many conventions and traditions were rooted in longstanding religious beliefs. Instead, they took dead aim at rationalism and science, seeking to undermine the epistemological assumptions of their liberal rivals. David Hume (1711–76) provided the first important attack on the idea that human reason affirms natural rights. According to Hume, the human mind can only know what it perceives and the perceptions of all individuals are unique; humans can only know their perceptions of nature and not nature itself. Thus, while liberals could reason that humans had natural rights, they could not be sure that nature actually contained or asserted these rights. Edmund Burke concluded that the natural rights proposed by liberals were mere rational abstractions. Whatever natural rights liberals emphasized were without consequence, because nature does not enforce these rights. Only the rights that had been incorporated into social practices and backed up by laws were real. Other conservatives broadened this attack by challenging the assumption that individuals were sufficiently rational to know their own good, suggesting that passion and habit often guided individuals more than reason. If individuals do not know their own good, why would it be reasonable to give them rights to pursue their mistaken impressions of the good life?

Their scientific way of viewing the world led liberals to think in terms of cause and effect, and this led them to think that changes in particular laws could lead to known consequences that were judged desirable. If the causes of economic stagnation included restrictive trade laws, then less restrictive trade laws would increase economic prosperity. Traditional conservatives thought that such human understandings of causal relationships are always limited. Because society is a highly complex organic entity, even a minor change in one area of society may lead to large, unexpected, and undesirable changes throughout the organism. To such conservative criticisms, liberal reformers could respond that while complexity complicates causal understanding, science can become more sophisticated and develop understandings of the many causal relations involved in change, enabling people to understand effects that traditional conservatives claim will always remain unanticipated. Traditional conservative developed a counter-response to this liberal optimism by drawing on the insights of Hume, who argued that humans simply couldn't know how the external world works. Rather, we can only know our ideas about the external world. When we claim that A causes B, what we are really claiming is that our idea of A is connected (or conjoined) to our idea of B. The connections we make about things are really just connections we make in our minds, and these connections are not based solely on accurate perceptions of the external world but are shaped by prejudices, customs, habits, and passions. Liberals mistakenly think that their ideas about causal relationships accurately capture external reality, but the world that exists outside our thoughts of it always remains mysterious.

For traditional conservatives, reason and science are thus inadequate guides to truth. When seeking to understand the best approach to a particular issue, we are best served by relying on tradition and the conventions of our society, our knowledge of history, our concrete experiences, and common sense. The epistemological assumptions of classical liberals are thus misguided, because they neglect the accumulated wisdom that exists within particular societies and are inadequately attuned to the specific cases to be addressed.

Anarchists: Depending on a Vision of Human and Social Possibility

Anarchists have a less developed and uniform epistemological basis than the other leading ideologies of the nineteenth century. They reject the claims of tradition as merely reflecting the interests of those having predominant power in society. They do not completely reject science, but it is doubtful that anarchism has a scientific base. When G. P. Maximoff published a book called *The Political Philosophy of Bakunin: Scientific Anarchism*, a leading student of Bakunin objected, "there is no such thing as 'scientific' anarchism."[6] Indeed, many anarchists reject the desirability of creating a science of anarchism, for all sciences involve highly authoritative and constricted intellectual frameworks.[7] Some anarchists even reject the very idea of truth – whether truths are based on science or any other epistemological foundation. An anarchist prefers to be a thinker of his own thoughts rather than a believer in the thoughts provided by some external source.[8]

Anarchists base their ideas of a good life on a vision of how humans could live in a natural world, unconstrained by existing institutions. For anarchists, truth about the good society was based on

> their vision of the rule of nature. The rediscovery of nature might be immensely difficult to accomplish, but they refused to waver in their hopes, and they constructed their faith on three propositions about nature: the possibility of discerning its truths; that nature was good; and that eventually every soul could know and follow nature.[9]

To discern the truths of nature, anarchists could not completely reject the tools that science provided. Indeed, Peter Kropotkin employed the methods of empirical science to generate evidence for the existence of an instinct for mutual aid that is suppressed in modern society but can be better discerned in natural circumstances. Moreover, Kropotkin proposed, "science be devoted to considering the means by which the needs of all may be reconciled and satisfied."[10] Thus, scientific studies could both support certain anarchist assumptions and serve anarchist goals, but they did not make anarchism scientific. In contrast to the "scientific socialism" of Marx and Engels, anarchists did not conduct careful empirical studies of the capitalist economy or of government, nor did they propose scientific laws of historical development predicting the emergence of anarchism. For anarchists, the deficiencies of capitalism and government were self-evident, and the emergence of anarchism depended much more on human will and action than on the predictions of any scientific theory.

In attempting to provide principles about how people ought to act in relationship to each other in a natural society, anarchists in general and Godwin in particular emphasized the role of reason. For anarchists, reason is not collective deliberation within politics but rather involves individual reflection about nature that is *above* politics. Godwin believed that nature provided a standard for eternal truth regarding moral conduct – for example, that nature commands everyone to act in such a way as to produce the public good. More generally, he believed that if individuals employ their reason, they will come to adequate conclusions on the principles of right and wrong conduct, but he did not see any need for a political determination about such principles and he envisioned no political institutions as being necessary to enforce that understanding.[11]

Anarchists thus do not rely on reason to justify their principles. Instead, their belief in the possibility of an orderly society without governmental authority is based on a vision of human nature and natural society that may be neither unreasonable nor contrary to scientific evidence. The idea that conventional institutions suppress the instinct for mutual aid may be a plausible hypothesis for which scientific evidence can be mustered. The idea that people can live orderly and secure lives free of government control is another interesting hypothesis for which there is some historical evidence.[12] Anarchists believe that the evils of existing institutions are sufficiently evident to warrant abolishing these institutions to test more fully the hypothesis that a natural society provides more liberty, equality, and social harmony than do conventional societies. Those who want to create an anarchist society peacefully face the challenge of convincing others that such a test is warranted.

Marxists: A Science Showing the Inevitability, not the Goodness, of Communism

Marxism is often regarded as a philosophy claiming that a good society is a communist society, but Marx did not work out a scheme of an ideal communist society, nor did he provide a systematic argument for why such a society would be good or just. He thought that previous arguments about the desirability of socialism were simply the product of utopian and wishful thinking. According to Engels, "there is no end to the conflict among absolute truths" about the goodness of particular social systems.[13] Thus, Marx and Engels chose to base their argument for communism on scientific understanding of the laws of history in general and of the laws of political economy in particular. While scientific laws would not demonstrate the moral goodness of communism, they would show its inevitability. In this way, Marx and Engels wanted to replace utopian socialism with *scientific socialism*.[14]

Liberals had earlier sought a science of politics, but their scheme sought to build moral truths *deductively* from indubitable facts about human nature. In contrast, Marx employed an *inductive* science to build factual truths about how history works. According to Marx, "My results have been won by means of a wholly empirical analysis based on conscientious study of political economy."[15] Marx and other Marxists formulated certain concepts that described the world in general terms and then developed generalizations based on what they believed to be empirical observations about the relationships among these concepts. Such generalizations sought to describe and explain social life, and provide the basis for predictions about the future. This scientific approach to the problems of human existence in history ultimately makes Marxian epistemology the lynchpin of Marxism.

Marx's science incorporates various previously discussed ontological assumptions about the world. It assumes historicism: that history proceeds in progressive stages. It assumes economic determinism: that material forces determine social life within stages and bring about changes from one state of history to another. Marx's science is *dynamic*, stressing change, but also provides for *static* analysis concerned with the interrelationships within and among various domains of life of a particular historical period.[16] Static analysis reveals the reality of each historical period, consisting of descriptions of the prevailing means and modes of production and how these economic infrastructures affect the intellectual, cultural, religious, and legal superstructures of the period.

According to Marx, empirical observations of the capitalist stage of history confirm the following scientific propositions. There are two main classes: the bourgeoisie, who own the means of production such as factories and land; and the proletariat, who own only their own labor. Because the bourgeoisie are relatively wealthy and few in number, whereas the proletariat are poor and many in number, the bourgeoisie and proletariat do not confront or bargain with each other as equals, despite their formal legal equality. The greater bargaining power of the bourgeoisie enables them to extract surplus value (profits) from the proletariat and requires the proletariat to sell their labor for subsistence wages. Moreover, market competition forces the bourgeoisie to reduce their production costs in order to survive economically, prompting them to reinvest their profits in labor-saving technological improvements. This competitive process results in ever increasing accumulations of capital and the reduced employment and misery of the proletariat. This competition also reduces the ranks of the bourgeoisie, because the losers in this competition become bankrupt, and descend into the ranks of the proletariat.[17] To get the proletariat and the dispossessed bourgeoisie to accept these wretched conditions, capitalist powers reinforce liberal ideology (including the idea that capitalism improves the condition of everyone) and Christian beliefs (including the ideas that this world is a "vale of tears" and that the poor will receive their reward in heaven).[18]

By themselves, Marx's scientific descriptions of capitalism may invoke criticisms of the prevailing system, but they do not provide a basis for predicting changes in these conditions. In order to achieve predictions of change, Marx developed a dynamic science about the laws of history, or dialectical materialism. We considered the broader outlines of these dynamic changes in our discussion of dialectical materialism in chapter 5, and we will discuss the specific process of change from a capitalism society to a socialist one in our concluding chapter on change. For now, it is sufficient to remember that Marx's dynamic science predicted that capitalism was doomed to fail. Eventually it would develop the capacity to produce the material goods that people needed, but it would fail to employ enough people and pay them sufficient wages so they could purchase these goods. This would result in a huge economic depression that would sour the vast majority of people on the capitalist system, and they would rise up in revolution against it. In this way, Marx used inductive science to generate what he and his followers thought would be objective predictions about the political world, and they thought such knowledge was much more important than philosophical approaches that sought to understand the good society and good governance.

Communists: Generating Truths from Authoritative Readings of Marx

Communists may be described as authoritarians who find political truth in the theories of Marx or interpretations of Marx's theory provided by other ideologues. Their conception of truth is *monistic*. This means that there is one truth, and one authoritative voice to guide political decisions. This authoritative voice is Marx. While interpreters of Marx have introduced variations into the received doctrine, they have done so within the broad Marxist framework and they have found in Marx's writings some basis for their interpretations. Thus, communists consult Marx's writings as a kind of holy writ, which serves as the authoritative guide to all political practice.

The truths asserted by communists have *not*, however, been *monolithic*, because Lenin, Stalin, Mao, Ho, Tito, Castro, and other communist leaders have had different interpretations of Marx, which have led to different versions of communism. These differing interpretations are necessarily opportunistic, since they reflect contextual circumstances and national needs, rather than iron-clad and universal doctrines.[19] Most interpretations are rendered in the context of trying to legitimize the rule of a particular regime. In other words, new interpretations were frequently attempts to explain why things are not developing as predicted by orthodox Marxists, why departures were needed from Marx's revolutionary strategy, or why governing measures that had not been stressed by Marx were needed in order to bring about the new communist order. Communist epistemological assumptions thus reassert the essential truth of Marx's scientific socialism, while allowing for diverse interpretations of Marxist doctrine to make it seem to justify the actions that communist leaders thought necessary in the particular circumstances that they found themselves.

Fascists and Nazis: Finding Absolute Truth in the Intuitions of a Political Leader

Fascists and Nazis may be said to have simultaneously a weak and a strong conception of truth. On the weak side, they do not believe that there is any rational basis for understanding the good life or for determining political principles and actions. Political knowledge cannot be generated by reference to tradition, rational deductions, assessments of public utility, or inductive science; these provide, at most, glimpses of knowledge. For fascists and Nazis, truth is known ultimately through *intuition*, an epistemological approach that leads to a strong sense of truth. The leader intuitively knows the collective good (which is what the community really wills), his intuitions are absolutely correct, and others are obligated to act in accordance with these intuitions. It is the keen intuition of the fascist leader that enables him to grasp the national will, and it then becomes his duty to communicate this will to the masses and to ensure that the nation fulfills its historic destiny in accordance with this will. The truth resides not in any intersubjective understandings, but in the authority of those whose intuitions are accepted as the truth. As ideologies, fascism and Nazism are even more authoritarian than communism, because the intuitions of its leaders were absolutely authoritative and admitted no challenge, while the actions and pronouncements of communists could be challenged as being impossible to reconcile with Marx's writings. This is not to say that Mussolini and Hitler never justified their intuitions. Clearly, Hitler thought the sort of race theories and concepts discussed in chapter 5 justified his racial policies. But fascists and Nazis never felt the need to justify their actions by reference to some external standard in the way the communists felt the need to find in Marx a justification for their actions.

Fascism and Nazism thus rejected the longstanding belief that the actions of political leaders could be ethically wrong. Since the leader's acts were grounded on his intuitions and since his intuitions were presumed to be right, ethical reflection was both impossible and undesirable for everyone under him – ranging from his top aides to the most humble worker in the factory or soldier in the line of fire. In fascism and Nazism, subordinates become either slaves or young children who have no ability to reason ethically or critically about action. They merely obey the injunctions of the leader.[20]

The doctrine of intuitionism has its origin in philosophies that are only distantly related to how intuitionism became incorporated in fascism and Nazism. One such source was German Romanticism, especially as developed in the philosophical writings of Arthur Schopenhauer (1778–1850). Reacting against the perceived excesses of the rationalism and scientism stressed by the Enlightenment and the utilitarianism of liberalism, the Romantics emphasized the importance of the emotions, intuition, and other non-rational forces in human life. They looked to art, music, poetry, mysticism, and the like for "true" knowledge of the world. Another such source was the intuitionism of thinkers like Henri Bergson (1859–1941). Bergson's philosophy was in large part a response to those scientists who claimed that humans could only hope to measure and describe surface appearances; it is impossible for us ever to know the real essence of things. Bergson countered that we could indeed "penetrate the inner core of being."[21] This penetration is not possible through perceptions and intellect, which he agreed could only know surface realities. Instead, we require intuition to inform us about ultimate reality. Bergson's intuitionism was an attempt to carve out space for the emotional and spiritual dimensions of human experience, and to claim that such experiences were more important than those known by the increasingly positivist and technocratic epistemologies of the nineteenth century.[22]

Both Nazis and fascists adapted the mystical concepts of Romanticism and intuitionism to appeal to the irrational side of the human psyche. For example, the Nazis incorporated flags, lights, music, and speeches during the famous Nuremberg rallies to appeal to the emotions of the masses.[23] Such emotional appeals were potent enough to sustain support for these totalitarian regimes for some time. Fascism and Nazism became largely discredited when the Axis powers lost World War II to more democratic regimes, not because their emotional appeals were widely rejected by the subjects of these regimes.

Contemporary Liberals: Emphasizing Pragmatism

Contemporary liberals generally believe that the Cartesian approach to acquire a science of politics built on natural rights is mistaken. There are no self-evident truths about the world and humans from which the political principles of liberalism can be deduced.[24] Many contemporary liberals have also abandoned aggregative utilitarianism as an adequate basis for liberal principles, finding in this approach a host of analytical and moral problems.[25] Analytically, it is unclear whether utilitarians should act so as to maximize the satisfaction of the expressed preferences of everyone, or the informed preferences of everyone (discounting mistaken preferences), or the legitimate preferences of everyone (discounting sadistic and other morally dubious preferences). Or perhaps the good to be maximized is some sort of objective assessment – independent of people's preferences – of what will result in their having a fulfilling existence. Analytically, it is unclear whose interests should be considered in making utilitarian judgments. Should Congress seek to maximize the good of current Americans, current and future Americans, or perhaps people everywhere in the world who are affected by our decisions? Analytically, there are all those impossible measurements and calculations. Morally, it is not clear that political actors should put the greater good of the greater number ahead of their more immediate special obligations. Morally, it is doubtful that the greatest good for the greatest number should be pursued if the rights of any individuals are disregarded in order to achieve utilitarian goals.[26]

If contemporary liberalism is to be defended, it must be done so on some basis other than the Cartesian deductions or the utilitarian claims used to defend classical liberalism. Contemporary liberals have provided a variety of alternative justifications for their political principles.

The most influential defense of contemporary liberalism among political theorists and philosophers is *the deontological contractual justification* of John Rawls. His approach is deontological, because it "gives priority of the right over the good."[27] It claims that conceptions of "the good" and the "good life" are subjective,[28] and thus a state should be neutral with respect to the various conceptions of the good life held by individuals and groups within it. Governments must simply protect a right for citizens to define and pursue their own life plans based on their own view of the good life. If people agree that their highest concern is to secure their autonomy (their right to pursue their own life plans) with as few political, social, and economic constraints as possible, they should also agree that others have the same right. They should form a sort of social contract, an agreement with others to be governed by liberal principles, institutions, and practices promoting that right and giving everyone access to those social goods necessary for pursuing their life plans. According to this argument, a liberal society is the preferred and rational choice of all autonomous individuals. Rawls's argument has certain features in common with the defense of classical liberalism based on the idea of a social contract that yielded what classical liberals thought were universal truths. But Rawls claimed that this argument was "political, not metaphysical" and did not yield a universal justification for liberalism.[29] He acknowledged that his deontological justification depended on people holding (or assuming) certain liberal ideas – such as having equal respect for others, valuing first and foremost their autonomy, understanding the necessity of certain social goods to the realization of their life plans, and being willing to put aside information they might have about their natural endowments and social circumstances. As Rawls and other liberal theorists began to understand that such foundational assumptions are not widely held, they recognized that consensus on liberal principles could not be achieved using Rawls's deontological approach.[30]

A second set of justifications for liberalism claims that liberal principles and institutions are better than competing principles and institutions because their adoption produces positive outcomes. One such claim is that "it is only in a liberal society that human beings can fully flourish."[31] This argument asserts that liberal institutions are best able to provide individuals with the freedoms and opportunities to exercise self-determination, to take responsibility for their actions, to engage in collective deliberations about policy decisions, and thus to stimulate the moral and intellectual development of all individuals within society. A second such claim is that liberal institutions promote social peace.[32] Unless groups with different conceptions of the good life accept the liberal idea of tolerating each other and develop institutions that ensure the fundamental rights of all individuals, they will live in constant fear that the strongest group will impose its vision of the good life on all others and thus engage in "religious wars" to avoid such oppression. A third such claim is that the adoption of liberal principles, institutions, and policies has contributed to social progress in many areas.[33] They have brought about prolonged, stable economic growth. They have been able to regulate economic power, compelling businesses to pay attention to such public interests as protecting the environment. They have reduced poverty. They have increased equal opportunities for minorities, women, and other disadvantaged groups. They have contributed to stable and democratic distributions of power. While such consequentialist arguments are important to the defense of liberalism, they do not provide proof for its desirability, because they make empirical claims that are sometimes contentious, they assume that everyone values the claimed positive consequences, and they ignore or downplay claims about the adverse consequences of liberal arrangements.

A third type of justification for contemporary liberalism is that it provides those principles and practices that are most suited to human fallibility and ignorance. In order to understand this argument, we must briefly consider the connection between science and liberal politics as presented by *pragmatists* like John Dewey. According to Dewey, science is an open-ended activity in which humans who are ignorant of absolute truths and whose knowledge about life is fallible attempt to improve their knowledge through experimentation. Similarly, the politics of a liberal democracy – which is simply the "scientific method writ large"[34] – does not involve the assertion of absolute truth about how to govern but instead involves an open-ended process in which people address the concrete problems that they experience in everyday life. Liberal politics involves organizing people to produce increasingly accurate and useful information, acquired by social experimentation, that helps solve social problems. Karl Popper expanded upon Dewey's understanding of the link between science and liberalism, stressing that science can never verify a theory but only falsifies inadequate ideas; all scientific knowledge is thus tentative and subject to future revision. In *The Open Society and Its Enemies*, Popper argued an "open" liberal society resembles a true scientific community, because people recognize that their political programs can never be verified as "true," alternative ideas must always be tolerated, and institutions must exist that provide for orderly social change. In contrast, authoritarian or closed societies incorrectly presume that authorities can acquire absolute truths about the good society and construct an all-powerful government with knowledge about the means to achieve such a society. More recently, Charles Anderson argued that pragmatic experimentation and appraisal of the results of these experiments provides for continuous social progress even in the absence of absolute liberal principles, despite our uncertainty about what the good society is like, and despite our tentative knowledge about the effectiveness of reforms.[35] In short, because human knowledge about the good society is always limited and tentative, the best system of governance is a liberal one that guarantees human freedom and that continually experiments with reforms in order to address problematic social and economic conditions.

Richard Rorty (1930–2007) emerged as the leading contemporary advocate of pragmatic liberalism. According to Rorty, a liberal society like the US must avoid any externally imposed conception of what the country should be and instead exhibit faith that the democratic process allows it to become whatever it wants to be. When liberal societies stagnate because those on the right think things are already as they should be (and strive to keep intact the present arrangements) and those on the left withdraw from progressive politics (because of disillusionment with the deficiencies and failures of their country), the pragmatic approach is not to provide people with foundational and philosophical arguments about why they should be liberal in their outlooks and in their actions. According to Rorty, the pragmatic approach – the approach that will actually work in bringing nonliberals to liberalism and energizing disaffected liberals – is to tell "sad and sentimental stories" about oppressed people who require the liberation that liberalism offers and to tell "inspiring stories" about liberal achievements.[36]

Contemporary Conservatives: Using a Social Science of Political Failure

Rather than developing deep epistemological approaches, contemporary conservatives employ four forms of reason to guide their politics: tradition, historical knowledge, common sense, and science. Conservatives accept as a given the democratic pluralist processes that exist in their societies, and thus do not employ these epistemological tools to provide a uniquely conservative defense of pluralism. Instead, they use these four forms of reason as partisans who hope to generate support for conservative principles and programs within pluralist democracies.

Contemporary conservatives agree with earlier conservatives like Burke that traditional beliefs and practices are valuable results of human reasoning that have withstood the test of time. However, they doubt that tradition reveals certainties about social life or provide a foundation for an unchanging social order. The traditions that contemporary conservatives respect are not those of the distant past, as they believe that aristocratic regimes, mercantile economies, rigid social classes, established churches, and so forth are now hopelessly out-dated. Contemporary conservatives in the US instead value traditions that they saw practiced perhaps 50–75 years ago: a capitalist system with few governmental regulations, a Supreme Court that interprets the Constitution according to the original intentions of its framers, prayers in schools, and mothers who stay home and raise children.

Attention to the lessons of history is a second form of reason employed by conservatives today. Historical knowledge should prevent the repetition of errors and highlight effective practices. For example, the "lesson of Munich" – when Western allies permitted Hitler to incorporate Czechoslovakia into Germany in return for a promise that he would curtail further expansionary efforts – teaches that democracies must never appease aggression. The tax policies pursued by George W. Bush may well be based on the lesson he learned from watching his father's popularity decline prior to the 1992 election, as people recoiled from his support for tax increases. Historical knowledge is far from perfect, though, because different lessons can be drawn from the same events and previous events may bear little resemblance to current conditions. History is a guide that only charts general directions.

Conservative reliance on common sense as a form of reason is both an acknowledgment of the value of everyday experience and a counterweight to the abstract and theoretical tendencies in scientific thought. For example, common sense taught that the Soviet Union was not to be trusted concerning nuclear weapons, and that it was foolish to pursue arms limitation treaties and, worse, unilateral disarmament policies that depended on theories about Soviet goodwill. Today, common sense is said to teach that squeamish concerns about civil liberties and the rights of terrorist suspects must be compromised for the far more urgent goals of defending the country from future attacks. Such common sense is a form of reason that works without theoretical elaboration, and is centered on the everyday needs of people. Such common sense resists the utopian goals and the high-minded principles of abstract thinkers.

Contemporary conservatives are not as critical of science as traditional conservatives. Many contemporary conservatives, especially domestic neoconservatives, have been trained in the social sciences and are familiar with the techniques and methods used for analyzing social activity. In general, conservatives use social science to show the failures of liberal social engineering; they argue that the experiments of pragmatic liberalism often fail to achieve their goals and instead have adverse unintended consequences. More specifically, the scientific findings of conservatives, according to Albert Hirschman, can be summarized in terms of three basic theses.[37] First is the perversity thesis: conservative social science shows that well-intended social policies produce perverse effects that are precisely the opposite of those intended. For example, the cross-town busing of children was a liberal attempt to integrate schools, but the policy prompted white flight away from inner-city public schools to private schools and the suburbs, resulting in increasingly segregated schools.[38] Second is the futility thesis: conservative social science shows that liberal reformers are oblivious to deep social laws that resist attempts at social improvement. For example, neoconservatives have produced empirical data showing that the distribution of income has a persistent character that cannot be significantly changed by redistributive federal policies.[39] Third is the jeopardy thesis: conservative social science shows that naive attempts to expand prior reforms only undercut the gains that these reforms produced. For example, neoconservatives claim that the equal opportunity laws of the 1960s succeeded in breaking down many barriers to minority employment, but when liberals attempted to expand equality through affirmative action, the unintended results included increased white resistance to minority advancement and a reduction in black employment opportunities.[40]

Despite employing social science to demonstrate the failures of liberal programs, conservatives generally regard most social science with skepticism. Political philosophers Leo Strauss (1899–1973) and Eric Voegelin (1901–85) were particularly influential in questioning the concerns of the contemporary social sciences. They argued that the modern social sciences have forsaken the quest for the good citizen in the good polity – a concern traditionally addressed in classical political philosophy – in order to provide "objective" explanations of how social life works.[41] Social science encourages scholars to assume the world is much more pliable and amenable to reform than it actually is. Social science that only explains, but that cannot judge, leads to relativism in the classroom; giving equal attention and respect to all forms of political life leaves the critical abilities of students impaired and fails to win the allegiance of citizens to the best in the Western tradition.[42] Social science must be tempered by the prudence that classical political philosophy, historical knowledge, and common sense provide.

Conservatives employ reason, but they recognize the limitations of all forms of reason in understanding natural and social worlds that are too complex for human mastery. The best understandings of the human condition will blend the four forms of reason that conservatives employ. These understandings will be rich and multi-faceted, but they will not approach the richness and complexity of our lives.

The Radical Right: Finding Meaning in Tradition and Truth through Science

The radical right contains conflicting epistemological orientations, many of which we have or will encounter in other perspectives. To grasp these conflicts, consider the orientations of libertarians and traditional communitarians. Libertarians revert to the individualistic utilitarianism of early classical liberals, though their conception of utility is broader than mere physical sensations. Because only the individual can know his own good – however that good is perceived – he should have maximal freedom to pursue that which he desires. Libertarians revere Ayn Rand's protagonist Howard Roark, who demanded freedom to pursue his creative impulses, which were far more important to him that any hedonistic pleasure.[43] Of course, this approach allows for the moral relativism that is so problematic to traditional communitarians. For Alasdair MacIntyre, the most pressing problem of pluralist societies is the domin-ance of the libertarian and liberal idea that individuals must be free to develop their own conception of the good life, because this outlook leaves people rudderless and society disordered. What is required is for people to see themselves as characters within communities, especially local communities, which provide narratives about the meaning of life that conform to cultural traditions. Only when people are deeply embedded in these traditions can they acquire the virtues necessary for well-being and for the proper functioning of community.[44]

Many other voices on the radical right – such as national protectionists and cul-tural conservatives – agree with MacIntyre and doubt that political communities can be strong and stable unless people are guided by the cultural traditions that have long prevailed. Like traditional conservatives and communitarians, they do not insist that the cultural traditions of any nation are true, as they recognize the great diversity of cultural traditions. Instead, cultural traditions are functional for communities as a whole and for people within them, providing social glue and identities and social purposes for individuals. The religious right also shares this emphasis on cultural traditions, but of course stresses the religious foundations of cultural norms; for them, any uncertainty in what are the cultural norms of a political community can be easily repaired by consulting the sacred texts of their religions and the proclamations of God's will provided by religious authorities. Compared to contemporary conservatives, these outlooks on the radical right are more insistent on public policy being consistent with cultural (and religious) traditions. Such forces on the radical right become disillusioned with more moderate contemporary conservatives who, they believe, too often sacrifice traditional norms to other concerns, such as giving individuals freedom to pursue their own good.

In general, global neoliberals reject this emphasis on tradition and are libertarian in their epistemological assumptions. However, it is possible to see in globalism an additional approach to attaining knowledge about the good life that justifies globalism. Francis Fukuyama calls this approach "the logic of modern natural science."[45] Clearly, modern applied science is at work discovering many technological and managerial improvements that are fueling the global economy. Private corporations apply such methods to develop new and improved products, and they use the logic of applied science to find more efficient ways of organizing production in order to be competitive in the global market. For example, management sciences have discovered the virtues of outsourcing service work to inexpensive labor markets and "supply-chaining" the components of products so as to lower inventory costs.[46] According to globalists, the logic of applied science is no longer confined to a few Western societies, but is effectively employed by people everywhere, fueling an endless supply of innovations that are available in global markets.

For the most part, the logic of science is applied at the micro-level by businesses within the global economy, but it can also be applied at the macro-level to thinking about what is good for political communities, including the global one. Essentially, such a science admits that people have diverse ultimate values, but there are certain known means to the achievement of penultimate values. You and I may have very different conceptions of what gives us happiness and satisfaction, but we both want security, liberty, opportunity, and wealth. Most importantly, we both want money, which is the most convertible resource enabling its possessors to live the good life (whatever one's conceptions of the good life).[47] Politically, we need concern ourselves only with maximizing things like freedom, opportunity, and wealth. We can apply modern science to discover effective and efficient ways to attain our common interest in penultimate goals like money and security (while leaving aside whether they are effective means to our ultimate but subjective goals of happiness and satisfaction).[48] For example, economics can demonstrate the wealth-generating capacities of free trade (due to the law of comparative advantage), of privatization (due to the advantages of competition over monopoly), and other globalist principles. Similarly, military science can, at least in principle, provide knowledge about the most effective and efficient means of providing global security. Hence, neoliberals are comfortable with professional technicians who can generate and apply scientific knowledge to guide the global community to peace and prosperity.

The Radical Left: Emphasizing Political Rationality

The radical left believes that the knowledge provided by the logic of science is inadequate for pursing the good life and must be supplemented by politics. Two illustrations of the limits of scientific knowledge will suffice. First, the logic of science can only produce bounded rationality; it generates cause–effect relationships among a limited number of theorized variables while ignoring latent cause–effect relationships that are beyond the bounds of one's theory. While conservatives have long been skeptical of science because of this problem, the radical left believes that this only shows that scientific results must be included within a much broader approach to gaining political knowledge. For example, economic rationality might demonstrate a new technique that produces large increases in economic productivity, but that technique might have other effects (such as social dislocations or environmental deterioration) that remain unknown because they are outside the boundaries of the scientific theory. While conservatives would be cautious about adopting the new technique because of fears of consequences that can't be anticipated, the radical left would be more confident that the most important effects could at least be theorized. Even if the environmental impacts could not be completely specified, informed estimates of the environmental risks could be assessed and included in a broader political determination about the desirability of the new technique.

Second, the logic of science might be able to tell us quite a bit about the consequences of a particular policy on our penultimate ends, but when these consequences are positive in some respects and negative in others, it provides no way of rendering an overall judgment. For example, scientific generalizations based on similar cases may conclude that removing a dictator like Saddam Hussein is good for our security but bad for our diplomatic relations with long-time allies, but it cannot calculate whether the gain in security outweighs the diplomatic costs, because there is no ultimate end through which we can make that determination.

The antidote to the limitations of science is politics. Political decision-making can be of various sorts. The various voices on the right stress the worst forms of political decision-making: the power politics that occurs in autocratic and democratic regimes alike whereby the powerful make decisions on the basis of their own interests. Without question, many political decisions are made in this sort of way. However, the radical left believes there is another – a better – form of decision-making that radicalizes the pragmatic epistemology of contemporary liberalism. This can be called *political rationality*.

Like pragmatism, political rationality addresses concrete social and economic problems in the absence of absolute knowledge about the ultimate ends to be achieved. Like pragmatism, political rationality involves a willingness to conduct experiments to relieve social problems and achieve social goals. Pragmatism is completely open about the goals to be achieved by pursuing experimental solution to social problems. For example, pragmatists may agree that existing welfare policies have problems and that states should be given greater flexibility to experiment with their welfare programs to determine "what works," but they are reluctant to specify the goals or criteria to be used in assessing the effectiveness of the programs. Thus, various criteria can be used in assessing effectiveness. While conservatives might apply such criteria as cutting program costs and reducing the number of people receiving welfare benefits, liberals might apply such criteria as reducing the number of people living below the poverty line and reductions in the overall level of economic inequality in the community. Pragmatism is thus liberal, not only in its proactive approach to addressing social problems, but also in its value relativism. Whether experimental programs will serve the goals of the left or the right is left open, at least in principle. But the radical left believes that, in practice, the capitalist aspect of contemporary pluralist society is dominant and thus economic values centered on property rights, economic liberty, and economic growth are consistently given priority in political determinations of what works.

To offset this bias in designing and evaluating experimental reforms, the radical left seeks the inclusion of values that are poorly fulfilled by capitalism: equality, solidarity, a sustainable environment, and a citizenry with the capability to use effectively the democratic process to pursue a good society. The various elements of the radical left have produced strong defenses of the importance of each of these values, but these are justifications *about* political ends, not justifications *above* politics. Perhaps the strongest defense of equality is that of John Rawls, but his liberal egalitarianism is based on political, not metaphysical, reasoning.[49] The work of William Julius Wilson is in a long line of radical left scholarship emphasizing the importance of reducing racial, class and other divisions and thus enhancing social solidarity.[50] Aldo Leopold (1887–1948) was perhaps the first of a long line of ecologists to stress the importance of a sustainable environment.[51] Michael Sandel has provided a strong argument for including the qualities of good citizenship as a central value in formulating and evaluating policies.[52] In short, the radical left recognizes that there may be no epistemology that can demonstrate that the values of the left are superior to those of the right, but it believes that there are many good reasons for political communities to have deep commitments to these values. For the radical left, the question is not how to provide epistemological foundations for these values; the question is how more adequately to include them when making political decisions.

In order to achieve more political rationality in community decision-making, the process of agenda-setting – of identifying problems in the community and possible enhancements to the community – must be highly open to citizens of all walks of life.[53] Because powerful actors often try to suppress issues from arising that threaten their interests, the radical left stresses the importance of citizens hearing and providing alternative messages than those conveyed through channels controlled by the powerful, so that citizens do not mistake the interests of the powerful for their own.

To achieve political rationality, issues on the public agenda need to be deliberated both informally and formally. This requires that people develop civic competencies and virtues that are necessary for deliberative democracy.[54] One such competency is what Wilhelm Dilthey (1833–1911) called *verstehen*: empathetic knowledge or understanding others by living and continuously interacting with them. Citizens and officials should look beyond their immediate and personal interests and ideas, putting themselves "in the shoes" of other community members, seeking to understand others' interests and ideas.[55] This requires that special efforts be made to include in deliberations those individuals and groups that have traditionally been excluded and marginalized, so that their concerns do not remain invisible.[56]

Another civic competency is exhibiting *public reason*.[57] This requires that people express their ideas and interests clearly and competently, so that others might understand, and that they listen intently to others without preconceptions about the merits of their case. To be understood, people need to demonstrate how their concerns adhere to the underlying consensus within pluralism and how their proposals might enhance the attainment of values that are widely embraced: such as prosperity, equality, solidarity, environmental sustainability, and citizenship. Appealing to ideals that are meaningful within a moral, political, or religious doctrine that is embraced by only a limited number of people within a political community should be understood as unproductive or counterproductive to having oneself understood. If only some people in a community regard the Bible as holy writ, quoting biblical verses will not be very productive in persuading others to your position.

After adequate deliberation, political rationality requires resolution through previously agreed-upon decision-rules. These rules will normally empower representatives to vote, but they also ensure that representatives are held accountable for their votes through fair elections.[58] After adoption of a rule, policy, or program, its adequacy must be open to evaluation, so processes must be in place that allow people to give feedback on how well these policies are working and that enable alteration and reconsideration of policies that are widely regarded as inadequate. Such is the tentative nature of the products of political rationality.

Not only are the results of political rationality tentative, but the adequacy of particular efforts to achieve political rationality are always in doubt. In practice, the openness of agenda-setting, the public reasonableness of democratic deliberations, the empathy that people achieve, the fairness of existing decision rules, and the effectiveness of feedback and reconsideration fall short of the ideals stressed by the radical left. Those on the right will always emphasize these inadequacies of political rationality, claiming that they normally make public decisions less rational than the private decisions that drive the free market. But the radical left has two powerful responses to such claims. First, they can maintain that the imperfections in political rationality are no excuse for abandoning efforts to achieve equality, solidarity, and environmental sustainability, and other goals that are inadequately attained by voluntary actions of people acting in free markets and that are best approached through democratic politics. Second, the radical left can agree that both the process and results of political rationality can be flawed, but point out that their tentativeness enables future progress. The radical left is always eager to join others in finding and fixing gaps between the ideals of political rationality and actual practices.

In sum, the radical left concedes that political rationality may not lead to truth in any objective sense, but it can provide temporary understandings of how to proceed in the absence of any higher truths. Political rationality enables a community to use the collective power of the state to take remedial action against problems that remain unaddressed by individual decisions in the market place.

The Extreme Right: Finding Truth in Authoritative Texts and Leaders

The extreme right incorporates large chunks of authoritarian epistemology into its political views. Many right-wing Americans look to the founding fathers and the Constitution, which must be given a *strict constructionist* interpretation, as a foundation for their political beliefs. Such an epistemology assumes that the Constitution is the original political agreement that provides the truths to be reflected in subsequent political decisions, that its authors had great wisdom about how the country should be governed, and that such wisdom should continue to be incorporated into today's politics.[59] Given these assumptions, the extreme right asserts that the Constitution is the sacred text of American democracy and that it must be interpreted not just in terms of the wording of the document itself, but also in terms of the intentions and understandings of the founding fathers. The extreme right thus argues, for example, that any effort to find in the Constitution a right to privacy that extends to reproductive rights is simply an invention of a liberal Supreme Court. The extreme right finds in the Constitution provisions for many of the rights they assert – such as the right to bear arms – and an absence of provisions authorizing the government to undertake many of the programs – like affirmative action and multiculturalism – that they abhor.

The US Constitution, however, is not a reliable source for many principles of the American extreme right, so they look to other sacred texts for guidance about political truths. Perhaps the most infamous such texts are Hitler's *Mein Kampf*, *The Turner Diaries* (written by William Pierce under the pseudonym of Andrew Macdonald), and *White Man's Bible* and *Nature's Eternal Religion* by Ben Klassen. Each of these books provides conspiratorial theories about the hidden Jewish rulers of pluralist societies and promotes racial conflict. The most widespread sacred texts of the extreme right are, of course, the Bible (for Christian fundamentalists) and the Quran (for those committed to Islamic fundamentalism). For the most militant of Islamists, Osama bin Laden's *Encyclopedia of Afghan Jihad* has also become a source of authoritative guidance in the confrontation with Western pluralism.[60] For the extreme right, such sacred texts are to be interpreted literally and are authoritative. The Muslim belief that the Quran contains the exact words of Allah as recited to Muhammad and as recorded precisely by His Messenger is a clear example of the inerrant quality of a sacred text. The belief of fundamentalists that truth resides in sacred texts prompts true believers to ground their moral beliefs "in the book" rather than "in experience." What should guide morality and politics are the words in the sacred text, not how moral beliefs and political principles work out in practice. Of course, the words in sacred texts need to be interpreted to understand how they apply to contemporary issues, but this poses no great problem for the extreme right. People trained in the traditions of these texts are seen as authorities in this regard, and there is no independent basis for challenging their judgments. Such assumptions, of course, exemplify an authoritarian epistemology that finds truths that are *above* political contestation, and should be imposed on people even in the face of wide-spread opposition.

The Extreme Left: Contesting and Deconstructing all Truths

Today's extreme left rejects the authoritarianism of the old left, such as Marx's scientific pronouncements or the various interpretations of Marx provided by communists. The various voices on the extreme left have adopted a number of epistemological stances that distance themselves from such rigidity in the quest for political knowledge. Most famously, they embrace post-structural denial that concepts (structures or categories) have universal meanings that hold for everyone. Instead, the meaning of concepts is always dependent on the experiences of the person exposed to them. There is no determinant good, justice, democracy, or politics – to name some concepts that are widely used but whose meaning always remains elusive.

French philosopher Jacques Derrida (1930–2004) explains why this is so. According to Derrida, the meaning of concepts is *not* determined by the concept's relationship to specific objects. This position contests the positivist claim that concepts like democracy are understood by their operational indicators. For example, positivists maintain that various countries can be classified as democracies if they display specified observable indicators of democracy – such things as genuine competition for office, fair elections, political rights, etc. Derrida rejects such positivism and claims that meaning derives instead from the relationships of concepts to other words. When we encounter a concept like democracy in speech or in texts, we derive its meaning from how it is used in relationship to many other words that surround it. For example, on hearing the word "democracy" used in the context of a discussion of electoral campaigns, party competition, voters, and so forth, I will understand it in one way (as something like liberal democracy). But on hearing "democracy" as used by the radical left in the context of words like transformation, exclusion, marginalized groups, and so forth, I will understand it in another way (as something like radical democracy). Moreover, I will probably attribute some normative judgment or value to a term, depending on the words that surround it and whether I have experienced those words in ways that make me sympathetic or hostile to them. Unfortunately, there are endless possibilities to the meanings and judgments we give to the words that surround the concepts we encounter, and so there can be no stable meaning to these concepts. Whenever we read a text, there will thus be no stable interpretation of that text, because the meanings given to its key concepts will depend on the words surrounding such concepts and the readers' own histories.

This problem of instability grows as our ambitions for acquiring knowledge grows. We want understandings not only of democracy, but also of the historical trajectory of democracy and the conditions that surround it; indeed, we want such understandings of many things of interest and importance to humans. One impulse is thus to create a great system of ideas that acquire their meaning in relationship to other ideas in the system. Such an impulse gives rise to ideologies and broader public philosophies (including those explored in this text). These systems of political ideas may generate greater meaning by the consistency with which their concepts are related, but – according to the post-structural embrace of deconstruction – the gain in clarity comes only through what is excluded in the systems that have been created. The ideas that are absent from any ideology are as critical to understanding what these grand intellectual systems say as what is present in them. No ideology can encompass all human meanings and experience, and thus it is necessary to deconstruct these ideologies, to show their limitations by making apparent that which is invisible (those concerns absent from an ideology).

The extreme left is particularly interested in contesting our most basic political concepts. In the pluralist world we inhabit, capitalism is widely interpreted as providing freedom and affluence. The thin democracy that we have is interpreted as providing popular sovereignty and enabling citizen participation. Politics is seen as an activity confined to a public sphere. Science and reason are widely hailed as objective methods for acquiring the knowledge we need to live our collective existences. Such interpretations are not so much wrong as they are limited. All of these concepts have alternative meanings and implications, but the orthodox ones persist. Why is this so? The answer for the extreme left lies in the distribution of power. As Michel Foucault has argued, knowledge gives rise to power, but power determines knowledge.[61] Given the many meanings or interpretations we can give to concepts, the ones we absorb and accept as true are those that have been brought to our attention most forcefully by powerful agents. While there can be many such agents in a decentralized system of power, the most powerful tend to reinforce each other and provide dominant meanings. The powerless have little capacity to have any alternative understandings taken seriously within pluralist politics.

Conclusions

Pluralists reject the idea of certainty concerning political knowledge and instead seek tentative understandings. They assume that tentative moral and political understandings exist in many forms. They can be broad agreements among political philosophers and theorists, the underlying consensus among pluralists that are the concern of this book. But they can also be widely accepted political norms within and across cultures (which philosophers can scarcely ignore). And they can be the kind of tentative political agreements achieved by political leaders, the understandings that become codified in constitutions, laws, and international agreements and treaties (which ideally reflect the understandings of philosophers and cultural norms). While these agreements may be imperfect expressions of Truth (of what is absolutely best for political societies), they provide a tentative consensus on right and wrong conduct. When new conditions arise and when new ideas are proposed, philosophers can revise their principles, political cultures can generate new norms, and political leaders can revise their constitutions, laws, and treaties. This assumption of tentative understandings is so critical that it defines the essential epistemological assumption of the friends of pluralism.

While pluralists recognize the importance of broad cultural agreement, they have no formula for achieving it. They fear that efforts to generate cultural agreement from above – by religious, governmental, or corporate powers – smack of tyranny, as efforts to impose a set of ideals on people who are entitled to autonomous moral and political judgments. Nevertheless, political communities composed of people having different interests and moral doctrines can still have "an overlapping consensus" on fundamental principles.[62] Such a consensus exists not because it has been imposed but because it is inherent in the understandings of all kinds of people in the community. These are the sorts of ideas that when explicitly expressed are embraced as *common sense* by most people.

Pluralists believe that codified agreements, such as laws and treaties, are most consensual if attained by democratic procedures that are inclusive and deliberative. All views must be heard. All views are listened to sympathetically, with a genuine effort on the part of all participants to understand the value of what is said and why expressed views are important to the speaker. Attention is directed toward seeing where common meanings and understandings can be achieved. While complete agreement often proves illusive, those who dissent should feel that their views have received a fair hearing and that the open and tentative nature of all such political resolutions will allow them future opportunities to revise current dominant understandings. While majority rule may have to be used to resolve difficult issues, laws enacted through process where majorities impose their will on minorities without significant efforts to hear and respond to minority concerns are scarcely the sort of consensual understandings that pluralists seek.

Pluralists believe that the tentative understandings of political philosophers and theorists that form the underlying consensus of pluralist public philosophy are generated through academic procedures that mirror those of pluralist democracy. Through academic discussion and publication, all views are considered and subjected to critical scrutiny. Political philosophy strives for intersubjective agreement among all informed participants involved in "the great conversation" (see chapter 1). But when widespread agreements prove elusive (as they always have), then philosophers strive for as much agreement as possible. This text proposes that in today's world, the widest consensus that political philosophy has been able to attain is among the friends of pluralism.

The underlying consensus of pluralism is an important political achievement, as it has taken political thinkers centuries and even millennia to come to these understandings. But this is not such a great achievement that we can relax and cease further political theorizing. As we will see in the next seven chapters, many fundamental disagreements remain. With further analysis and discussion, some of these disagreements might be resolved and the underlying consensus of pluralism enlarged. Or upon further reflection, some aspects of the pluralist consensus might be challenged, resulting in a reduction of that consensus. Equally important work for political theory, however, will be to understand better the bases of continuing disagreements, to analyze arguments for alternative positions, and to recommend those principles that should be brought to bear on the concrete issues that pluralist communities must resolve as best they can, even in the absence of a consensual understanding about these principles.

The absence of unanimous, universal, and permanent political truths may be regrettable, but it is part of the human condition. Politics is no more plagued by the absence of Truth than are other subjects. It just seems that way because political disagreements are highly visible and important, because they deeply affect the good life and the just society that we all so desperately seek.

In the course of ordinary pluralist politics, major competing positions and the principles behind them often coalesce and harden, and consensus becomes a vanishing hope. If such conflict is to be resolved in a civil manner, people need to understand the limitations of their own principles and the bases of the conflicting principles of their opponents. Part III is intended, in part, to enhance such understandings. But before turning there, it is useful to summarize the epistemologies that are employed to defend opposing positions within pluralist politics, because the friends of pluralism should recognize the limitations of their own truth claims.

Relying on traditional understandings and seeking guidance from the lessons of history to guide our politics may help bring the wisdom of the ages to bear on our contemporary problems, but our political communities seem to be changing quickly and encountering new problems that undermine the relevance of traditional understandings and historical lessons. And even if these might be relevant, which of the many traditions and lessons of history are the best guides for a particular issue?

The deductive reason employed by classical liberals and in such other perspectives as the egalitarian liberalism of Rawls allows for valuable thought experiments to justify many political principles, but such reasoning is based on foundational assumptions. Reasonable people can always contest the adequacy of these assumptions.

The inductive reason employed in such epistemologies as Marx's scientific socialism and globalism's "logic of science" can provide important causal understandings about the means and processes to various goals. But the complexity of the social life makes predictions about the future highly problematic. Certain proposed interventions may not only fail to achieve predicted results, but they can have unanticipated consequences. And science can tell us little about the desirability of various results and consequences.

Utilitarian arguments are an important way of conceptualizing the public good. But statements about what will maximize utility depend on the logic of science and on knowing the consequences of one's proposals. And even if all consequences could be known and their value agreed upon, the pursuit of "the greatest good" may be objectionable if the rights of any individuals must be sacrificed for utilitarian gains.

Pragmatic experiments to address various social problems are hard to fault, but embracing pragmatism leaves unanswered many things that we would like to know. Which problems should be addressed? Which experiment should be tried? By what criteria should we judge whether an experiment works?

The intuitions of political leaders, the proclamations of authorities, and the words in sacred texts might all inspire people to act for noble political goals, but they have also led to great atrocities. By themselves, such approaches lack the sort of intersubjective agreement that is essential for pluralist politics.

The limitations of each of these approaches to political knowledge do not mean that they should be abandoned. Each can be used as a basis for our political claims, but each has to be disciplined through political deliberation. The radical left's emphasis on political rationality seeks to establish an ideal form of such deliberation. While it is an ideal that is seldom realized, it is difficult to object to making greater efforts to understand and implement the requirements of political rationality.

Finally, the epistemological orientations that misrepresent politics as it is practiced and should be practiced must be exposed and rejected. The epistemologies employed by extremists are not only incompatible with pluralism but are also dangerous to it. Perhaps the most dangerous epistemological assumption is that truths exist beyond the comprehension of ordinary people and are known to only a select few who must impose these truths on others. This epistemological orientation is exemplified by the emphasis of the extreme right on sacred texts and the special role of particularly gifted and/or trained persons in the interpretation of these texts. Also dangerous is the epistemological assumption of post-structuralists on the extreme left, at least if we interpret them to mean that political concepts are so subjective in their meaning that intersubjective communication, understanding, and consensus is impossible. Post-structuralists are right to want to contest the understandings that the powerful impose on ordinary citizens, but pluralists insist that ordinary citizens can acquire the understandings they need to advance their aspirations through democratic processes.

PART III

THE GREAT ISSUES OF POLITICS: CONSENSUAL AND CONTESTED PRINCIPLES

The philosophical assumptions that have been considered in Part II are important and interesting for thinking about politics. But it is now time to focus on the perennial political issues.

We must first ask about the communities to which we belong or that we might join, as living within communities is a prerequisite for political life. People belong to many communities, and all communities are political. Families, religious organizations, workplaces, and other such associations pursue collective goals and distribute power and privileges, leading us to speak of family politics, church politics, office politics and the like. Because each of these communities is political, their members could benefit by having conversations on the perennial political questions in order to develop a public philosophy to guide their politics.

Some communities are larger, territorially defined, and have governing institutions for resolving political issues affecting all residents within their territories; these can be called polities. Throughout the modern era, nations have been regarded as our most fundamental polities, although some of their territorial sub-units (such as provinces, states, and cities) and some supranational units (such as the United Nations, the European Community, and NATO) have been seen as highly important. Given the variety and impermanence of polities, theorizing about the political must begin with questions about which of these types of communities are of primary and secondary importance and why people identify with and are loyal to particular polities.

All communities have changing memberships, giving rise to questions about who should be members and what their status is within the community. Polities normally have citizens, though not all residents of polities are necessarily citizens. Outsiders often wish to become citizens – and occasionally communities seek to expel citizens or take away citizen rights from some residents – giving rise to questions of citizenship. Questions about who should be citizens cannot be answered without thinking about what citizenship entails, and this leads to questions about the rights and duties of citizens.

Once we have defined the communities to which we belong and developed principles regarding the members and citizens of these communities, we have to ask how these communities are and should be structured. Perhaps there is almost no structure to particular communities, as people pretty much attend to their own (private) lives. But people within communities potentially affect and interact with others, even as they go about their private lives. People might want to do business with each other and enter economic markets that structure these interactions. People might want to pursue some common purpose – play sports, make music, or worship together – and form various voluntary associations to do so. Communities also contain cultural norms that structure the lives of residents. Some people believe that civil society comprised of economic markets, voluntary associations, and cultural norms provide all – or at least almost all – the structure that a polity needs, and that there is little or no need for governments to structure community life. Questions about roles of government and the components of civil society must be discussed to form a public philosophy.

The multiplicities of communities and the (potential) importance of civil society in structuring polities suggest that we should not assume that governmental authorities necessarily rule communities and thus have the most control over people's lives. Fathers and husbands may rule over their children and wives. Priests may rule over their parishioners. And corporate chieftains and bosses in the workplace may rule not just employees but also broader polities by the decisions they make. While democratic communities may have norms proclaiming that citizens rule themselves through their governments, the extent to which such communities exhibit meaningful democracy is unclear.

Whether citizens, their elected officials, appointed officials, special interests, or others have predominant power within governments, questions remain about the authority of government: for what purposes should the special (coercive) powers of government be used? Should governments use their power to address every conceivable economic, social, environmental, or moral problem? Should governments be prohibited from interfering with private, family, religious, economic, or other aspects of personal and community life?

Our penultimate chapter addresses questions of justice, which is often seen as the primary virtue for any political community. Justice deals with the distribution of those social goods (and burdens) that are produced in communities – not just income and material goods, but such things as educational opportunities, meaningful work, onerous tasks, and power over others. Communities can be destroyed by widespread beliefs that social goods are unfairly distributed, not just by governments but also by free markets and cultural values, and within families, workplaces, and all the other associations of civil society. But what does justice entail, and what are just procedures for allocating social goods?

The final chapter addresses questions of change, which is a useful concept for summarizing many of our previous political ideas. The changes we want depend on the ideals we have regarding communities, citizens, structures, rulers, authority, and justice and our beliefs about whether our political practices are in accordance with our ideals. And if there are gaps between what we believe we have and what we think we should have, we have to think about how to change our politics. But in pursuit of our unfulfilled political ideals, we can harm others and the broader community. When do reformers, revolutionaries, and rebels go too far, justifying acts of repression against those who seek change?

Answers to these questions take the form of political principles, but there are many possible principles that can guide people in their political lives. A major premise of liberal arts education is that we can understand alternative principles and make informed choices between them, both as individuals and collectively, as members of communities. Perhaps both political competence and civility are rooted in awareness of the many principles that people bring to bear on the big and small issues of political life. Perhaps our political communities require that people bring their principles to political issues with the humility of knowing that there are others that pull in opposite directions. Perhaps if we wish to live in peace and prosperity with others, we will have to enter political conversations, large and small, to talk through our differences and achieve as much consensus as possible on how to live in political communities with others.

Chapter 9

Questions of Community

What are the primary polities (and other communities) with which people identify, in which they participate in decision-making on matters regarding their social existence, and in which they incur their primary political obligations? Which sorts of communities – ranging from the local to the global – are most influential in people's lives? Which should be most influential? What prompts people to identify with and be loyal to particular communities?

The longstanding importance of questions of community identity in political thought is illustrated by Socrates' refusal to flee Athens after its citizens had sentenced him to death for corrupting the youth with his tireless questioning of customary opinions; he preferred to die because he could not envision himself as a citizen of any other city (or polis) than Athens.[1] The continuing importance of these questions is illustrated by the break-up of the Soviet Union and the consolidation of the European Union. Clearly political communities continue to arise and fall apart, and with these changes come changes in our political identities and loyalties. The end of the Cold War has diminished the tendency of people to identify themselves as part of "the free world" or "the communist bloc." Globalization may be diminishing the saliency of national identities, but have these developments prompted people to identify increasingly with a universal global community?

Throughout human history, there have been changes in our political maps as political communities have come and gone. Not only has the world witnessed changes in national boundaries, but the importance of nations as political entities has also changed. The centrality of nations as political communities is generally thought to be a modern development, less than 400 years old. Nevertheless, philosophers and theorists have only recently gone beyond making casual assumptions about communities. For example, Robert Dahl noticed in his 1989 comprehensive treatment of *Democracy and Its Critics* that democratic theory was silent on the question of who comprises the people that should govern themselves democratically.[2] It has been generally acknowledged that democracy is something to be practiced by existing nation-states (and their sub-units like states and cities), but the boundaries of these nation-states are normally taken for granted. Paradoxically, democratic processes have seldom, if ever, been used to determine the composition of even democratic nations. Instead, our political maps have been largely determined by military conflict, historical accidents, and a myriad of other factors that seem morally arbitrary.

Because political communities come and go and because the boundaries of communities change, questions arise about the forces that prompt people to hold allegiance to existing communities or prompt them to seek different ones. Most political theorists doubt that political loyalties and identities are grounded in rational calculation.[3] For example, in general Americans are not loyal to the United States because their interests are better served by remaining there than by emigrating to Canada, Sweden, or Thailand. Instead, their political loyalties and identities as Americans are based on emotional feelings and are highly affected by symbolic, rather than tangible, concerns.

Many nationalist movements have arisen during the past few decades composed of people who seek to redefine political maps so that their political communities better encompass those who share common histories, languages, ethnicities, religions, and cultural traditions and who have emotional attachments to one another. But increasingly, processes of global interaction and mobility have made political communities more heterogeneous and pluralistic – not less.

In this chapter, we will see that the friends of pluralism agree that national political identities continue to be of primary importance and that nations having significant racial, ethnic, and religious heterogeneity can be stable. But they generally doubt that national identities should be all-encompassing. Citizens of pluralist nations can and should identify with the global community, various local communities, and various sub-national communities based in ethnicity, religion, and other shared characteristics and interests, even if these communities have no governing institutions. Multiple community identities provide individuals with social bonds and moral values, but each community remains limited in its capacity to dominate both members and non-members, enhancing individual freedom and social stability. Let's look more closely at how various ideologies think about these matters.

Classical Liberals: Presupposing the Primacy of Nations

Thomas Hobbes, John Locke, and other leading precursors of classical liberalism wrote shortly after the Treaty of Westphalia, which consolidated the system of nation-states in Europe in 1648. While such liberals gave little explicit attention to questions of community, it seems safe to assert that they regarded their liberal science of politics as generating political principles for governing nation-states. Both Hobbes and Locke developed their theories as their English homeland was confronting a series of crises. Hobbes's initial social contract theory was written in response to the civil war in England. It implied that the sovereign or dominant power of England (or any other nation) – whether that power resided in the monarchy (as it did before the execution of Charles I in 1649) or in Parliament (as it did during the English

Commonwealth that existed between 1649 and 1660) – was legitimate because English citizens consented to be governed by a supreme authority that would provide order and security throughout the nation. Locke's subsequent social contract theory was written as James II ascended to the English throne amidst great concern that he would impose his Catholicism on people who were largely Anglican in religious orientation; his *Second Treatise of Government* was thought to legitimize England's glorious revolution of 1688, which ultimately lead to parliamentary supremacy in England. Many years later, when Jeremy Bentham, James Mill, and other philosophical radicals sought to ground classical liberal principles in utilitarianism, the individuals whose interests were to be considered in the felicific calculus were apparently members of existing nation-states.

Two colossal events at the end of the eighteenth century – the founding of America and the French Revolution – also point to the primacy of the nation as the sort of political community to be established and governed by the principles of classical liberalism. After declaring their independence from England in 1776, the 13 American colonies could be considered nascent nations in which citizens of each colony identified primarily with the state in which they lived – as Virginians, as New Yorkers, as Pennsylvanians, and so forth. The Articles of Confederation sought to enhance the primacy of the colonies and gave the larger American political community the minimal status of being a confederation. But the limitations of this arrangement gave rise to the understanding that a more substantial national union was required. The American Constitution of 1787 was, in effect, a social contract to create a national polity. In the *Federalist Papers*, James Madison (1751–1836) defended the creation of a stronger national government on the grounds that liberal ideals centered on individual freedoms, property rights, and economic prosperity could best be secured in a national political community. The American Constitution began the great American experiment of drawing on the principles of liberal democracy to govern a nation.

The idea of a national community was also central to the French Revolution. On August 17, 1789, the National Assembly of France approved a *Declaration of the Rights of Man and Citizens*, containing a series of liberal principles as the foundation for a new political community that would replace the absolute monarchy of French King Louis XVI. This document claimed that sovereign governing power resided not in the King but in the Nation as a whole. It declared that all people in the existing French Nation were bound together as free and equal citizens, and that all laws of their political community must represent the will of the Nation. While radicals would subsequently betray many liberal principles contained in the Declaration, that document remains as strong evidence of the importance of the national community to classical liberal thought.

Classical liberals did not necessarily seek a monolithic nation, in which citizens identified solely with the nation-state and owed their sole allegiances to the nation. Some liberals, like Madison, developed principles of *federalism*, in which multiple political communities coexisted as nested boxes. Within large political communities (nations) could be found smaller communities (states). Within states could be found cities, towns, and other local communities. Each type of community had a role to play, and citizens had multiple political allegiances that curbed unbounded identities with nations.

Moreover, liberals embraced the idea that citizens should join many communities within *civil society*. Civil society within a liberal nation comprises many different churches, educational institutions, cultural groups, business organizations, and other voluntary associations, enabling citizens to pursue common interests with little oversight or interference from national political institutions. Liberals may not have declared that multiple community identities were a central element of the liberal outlook, but they accepted the importance of federalism and civil society (with the multitude of communities that they generated), and they often celebrated the fact that liberal citizens belonged to many such communities.

In classical liberal theory, the basis for people's identification with and loyalty to a nation – or any other political community, for that matter – was their self-interest. Liberals believed that their fundamental interests in securing their life, liberty, property, and happiness could only be attained within political communities having governments with the coercive power to enforce laws protecting individual rights. Loyalty to a national government rested on the belief that each citizen would reason that their agreeing to obey governmental laws in return for governmental institutions that protected their rights was a good deal. In short, classical liberals believed that governmental institutions that carried out their end of the bargain of the social contract would win the loyalty of citizens and generate citizen allegiance to the political community, albeit a "thin community" emphasizing individualism.

However, it is not clear that classical liberals believed that support for political institutions that effectively protect individual rights was sufficient for maintaining allegiance to a political community. At least some classical liberals seem to have believed that national identity depended on shared racial and ethnic characteristics. Perhaps most infamous in this regard are the beliefs of Thomas Jefferson (1743–1826) – long regarded as a leading liberal among the founders – that slavery should be abolished and blacks forcefully returned to Africa, as America could only endure as a liberal nation if American national identity was limited to whites.[4] Of course, the provision of equal citizenship to former slaves after the Civil War represented an increasing recognition by liberals that multiracial political communities are possible, but many nineteenth-century liberals seemed anxious about the inclusion of blacks, Asians, Hispanic, and even non-Anglo Europeans into the American community, perhaps believing that national allegiances based on support for political institutions had to be supplemented by common racial and ethnic bonds. Giving up this belief was a key element in the transformation of classical liberalism to contemporary liberalism.

Traditional Conservatives: Patriots Lacking Nationalist Fervor

By the time that traditionalists developed a conservative alternative to classical liberalism, especially in the writings of Edmund Burke, nation-states had emerged as central elements of the political landscape. Traditional conservatives certainly thought that nations were important, as they were the locus of cultural norms giving guidance to people's lives and they provided the central governments that could orchestrate social harmony. Traditional conservatives believed that people within nations had become interdependent in ways that necessitated patriotic sentiments that prompted putting national interests above petty personal interests. Indeed, patriotism – or love of country – is a primary conservative virtue. Based on emotional attachment to larger political communities to which people belong, it involves their enjoying and embracing many inheritances from their national ancestors, and it makes people aware of their responsibilities to their fellow citizens and future generations of national citizens.

But traditional conservatives are not strong nationalists in several senses. First, many nationalists believe that existing nations should be disassembled, because they do not conform to preferred alternative national configurations. *Nationalism* is a perspective that claims that people sharing a particular ethnic, religious, linguistic, and historical heritage are entitled to their own nation; they should govern themselves. If the Scots (or the Welsh) are minorities within Great Britain, and if they have the characteristics of a unique community of people, then their nationalist principles give rise for demands for an independent Scotland (or Wales). If the Quebecois (French Canadians) are minorities within Canada who have a distinct language, ethnicity, and heritage, then their nationalist principles lead to efforts to break up Canada. Ditto the Basques in Spain, the Chechens in Russia, the Native Hawaiians in the US, etc. Traditional conservatives reject such nationalist movements as undermining the stability provided by the maintenance of longstanding nations.

Second, many nationalists seek to strengthen national governments at the expense of smaller political communities (such as provinces and districts) within nations. Traditional conservatives have opposed such nationalisms, because they have long understood that local communities can provide important places for political cooperation, and because they believe that sub-communities within nations have distinctive problems and aspirations and they have their own traditions. Traditional conservatives believe that proclaiming the universality of liberal principles – that there is one best way of governing all nations and all smaller communities within nations – is misguided. Local cultures have distinct traditions that provide better guidance to managing political issues than the one-policy-fits-all approach implied by liberal theory. National communities and their governments have traditionally served important but limited purposes, and national communities must recognize these limitations.

Third, some nationalists seek to strengthen national identity by dismantling other community identities that arise in civil society which can undermine national identities. Certain political theorists – ranging from Machiavelli to Rousseau – sought to replace people's allegiances to the various religions that exist within nations with a single civic religion that encompasses all national citizens, so that religious identities mirrored and reinforced national identities. While conservatives have had fewer reservations than liberals about established churches, they have been wary of efforts to undermine churches and other communities within civil society, as they believe that all the "little platoons" within a nation serve important social functions.

An important difference between traditional conservatives and classical liberals concerns the bases for national identification and loyalty. Traditional conservatives have been even more prone than classical liberals to emphasize that a common culture is a necessary supplement to political institutions as a basis for strong national identities and loyalties. American conservatives believed that members of the political community needed to share in the Anglo-Protestant culture of those Englishmen who originally settled in America. During much of the nineteenth century, they tolerated other immigrants who arrived in America, but only if they were assimilated quickly into the culture that defined what it meant to be an American – if they adopted values emphasizing Christian faith, individual responsibility, the work ethic, and other aspects of Anglo-Protestant culture.[5] They were also slower than liberals to accept African-Americans as equal citizens within the nation.

The traditional conservative often expresses an affection for longstanding nations that is less evident in the discourse of liberals. Traditional conservatives see their nations as embodiments of meaning and virtue, in ways that liberals do not. Traditional conservatives want to honor the unique traditions and accomplishments of their nations, while classical liberals often want to reform what their nations have done and ensure that their nations conform to the abstract liberal principles that they believe all national communities should reflect.

Anarchists: Rejecting Conventional Communities While Seeking Natural Ones

Anarchists have principles about communities that are the polar opposite of those of traditional conservatives. They doubt that people should feel allegiances to any polity, because nations, states, and local political communities all employ governments, and these governments use their coercive power to limit freedom unnecessarily. Other traditional communities of people – whether corporations that organize people for economic production, churches that organize people for devotion, families that organize people for raising children, or any other such association – all have authority structures that dominate people. Anarchism is a political perspective that involves rebelling against all conventional communities.

While rejecting allegiance to conventional communities, anarchists embrace natural communities. Many natural communities already exist, as when people join together and enjoy face-to-face interactions in pursuit of common interests. Perhaps Alcoholics Anonymous (AA) groups exemplify such natural communities. Here people come together to support each other in their common objective of "staying dry," and consist of those who voluntarily come to meetings, which are sufficiently small so that members know each other and treat each other with equal concern and respect; such groups rely on no more than social norms and moral suasion to ensure that the rights of individuals within the community are upheld. Communities like this are small, personal, voluntary, and fluid – people enter and exit them as they like. Anarchists believe that by joining a variety of such voluntary and natural communities, which serve the distinct needs and interests of individuals, each person can satisfy their needs for community identification and achieve the benefits of community life.

People with mere anarchistic temperaments may be inclined to focus on being involved in natural communities while simply ignoring and questioning the dictates that come from their inability to escape from conventional communities, but more political anarchists believe that they must actively engage in destroying conventional communities. Only when freed from the oppression of such communities will people generally thrive as autonomous moral beings who can think and live freely in social harmony with others.

Marxists: Identifying with the Working Class and Eventually Humanity

Marxists share with anarchists a disdain for most conventional communities that are prominent in the capitalist era, but Marxists believe alternative community identities are important. Marx famously sought to unite the working class and instill class-consciousness. In order to have a successful revolution against capitalism, workers would have to overcome the identities that divide them – such as national and religious differences. If German Lutherans, French Catholics, English Anglicans, and American Baptists who worked for subsistence wages provided by capitalists could look past their national and religious identities and see themselves as similarly oppressed by a larger capitalist system, they could begin to attain a sense of class solidarity and their collective role in overthrowing capitalism.

Precisely how class-consciousness would develop remains unclear. Perhaps simply living under such capitalist contradictions would make all members of the proletariat conscious of their common class interests. Perhaps such contradictions would generate class-consciousness among *some* members of the working class, who would become hubs of communication networks and thus be responsible for the diffusion of ideas that would lead to widespread identification with the plight and role of the proletariat. But Marx probably thought that he and other intellectuals could instruct the working classes on these matters. After all, the purpose of the *Communist Manifesto* was to inform the proletariat of their plight and urge them to unite. The thinking of orthodox Marxists about communities focused on developing a cohesive transnational community among the proletariat.

Marxists departed with anarchists in their ideas about communities after the revolution. Marx doubted that the natural communities sought by anarchists would be sufficient to organize people, at least initially. Some capitalists would become counter-revolutionaries and attempt to reconstruct a capitalist system, and these people would have to be suppressed or at least re-socialized; some sort of coercive community would be necessary for this task. Even the proletariat would not immediately overcome the alienation they developed under capitalism; something more than the moral suasion of natural communities would be required to reward and punish

workers so they became productive. The communities that would come to prominence after the revolution would apparently be smaller than nation-states, but they
would continue to be political entities having coercive power to organize and manage
economic and social life. Orthodox Marxists insisted that such coercive communities
would be merely transitional, and would eventually give way to the natural communities that anarchist sought. They apparently believed that citizens would submit
to such coercive communities if they understood that they were merely temporary
but necessary stages that must be endured on the road to a communist community.

Orthodox Marxists can be seen as seeking a global community. Marx himself
helped to organize the first International Workingmen's Association in 1864, and
he had little use for the existing nation-state. In general, Marxists appealed to a
moral ideal where all humans everywhere would be free and equal members of a
global community. To be sure, such citizens would interact primarily with those in
their local natural communities, but those in other such communities would not be
seen as "others" with conflicting purposes and interests that made them enemies.
They would be people with whom we can cooperate if and when it suits our mutual
interests. In this sense, it is possible to see Marxists as proposing a global community
that shares features of the global community sought by neoliberals today. Of course,
such communities would be organized according to socialist rather than capitalist
principles, and so the global community sought by the more utopian elements within
Marxism remains profoundly different from anything that has or does exist, as should
be made clearer as other perennial issues are considered.

Communists: Fighting Imperialism Through Nationalist Appeals

Communists of the twentieth century shared with Marxism many ideas about community. They claimed to be pursuing the eventual classless and stateless global community sought by Marx, but they understood that international realities precluded
rapid movement toward such an ideal. Russian communists practiced "socialism in
one country," as Stalin specified. After the Russian Revolution, communists established councils called *soviets* at national, regional, and local levels to enable extensive
participation in governance and administration, to facilitate social relations and
strengthen social bonds, to promote the emergence of creative laborers, and to guide
those living in Russia toward an ideal communist community.

When communists came to power in other countries, such as China and Eastern
Europe, they continued to operate within the existing system of nation-states. These
communist regimes usually looked to Russia for support and guidance and sought
a larger community of communist nations. However, a united communist bloc was
mostly apparent to Westerners who feared that such a bloc would overrun the West
and impose global communist rule on people everywhere. Governing communist
regimes often experienced national differences that precluded the sort of communist
bloc that the West feared.

Communists also de-emphasized class-consciousness. Most communists operated in countries that saw themselves victimized by imperialism, and thus communists appealed to many people (beyond the working class) within underdeveloped societies who wanted to end their domination by capitalist and imperial entities. In short, communist revolutionaries often emphasized nationalism, reminding Russians, Chinese, Vietnamese, Cuban, and other citizens of colonized nations that the yoke of imperialism could be overthrown only through nationalist uprisings.

Once communists took power in these countries, they sought to have citizens develop strong identities with the governing communist parties and the nations they led. They developed ideological apparatuses to convince citizens that their new socialist communities were threatened by capitalist forces abroad – especially American economic and military power. They also developed programs to dismantle social and political pluralism internally.[6] To the extent that they used both education and coercion to eradicate other community identities than those led by communists, they became totalitarians. But communists never regarded singular identities with communist parties and nations as an ultimate objective, as did fascists. Such singular identities were seen as temporary and instrumental to enabling socialist societies to get through the transition to ideal communism. But as these transitional arrangements persisted, communist slogans about an ideal community just around the corner began to be seen as "the big lie."[7] Eventually, communism lost much of its appeal and most communist regimes lost their legitimacy. The former Soviet Union, Yugoslavia, and Czechoslovakia – political communities that were formerly held together by allegiance to communist ideology and regimes – dissolved as various nationalisms based on ethnicity, language, and culture provided stronger bases of political identity than the political ideas and institutions that had held these larger political communities together during the Cold War era.

Fascists and Nazis: Embracing a Unified Nation and an Aryan State

Fascism is the most nationalist ideology. It seeks to have citizens identify completely with the nation-state. In Italy during the 1920s, the Fascist Party began to create (though they never fully realized) a totalitarian state, as they sought to persuade citizens to identify strongly and completely with the nation. Alternative bases of allegiance were de-emphasized or brought under the control of national leaders, so that citizens would not be cross-pressured by competing community identities. For example, while Italian fascists never sought to dismantle the Catholic Church, they ensured that the Church upheld the ideals and policies of the fascists who controlled the state. Singular identities with the nation-state would generate national unity and power, enabling the fascist state to prevail in international competition with other nations, whether that competition was cultural, economic, or military.

The underlying basis of fascist nationalism consists ultimately of the common bonds provided by history and culture. The citizens of Italy, which had only achieved modern unity between 1815 and 1871, took pride in the former greatness of the Roman Republic and Roman Empire. Italian fascists emphasized the common language and traditions of Italians. They exhorted Italians to regard their national culture as a great resource for recreating a strong Italian nation, which could be attained if Italians set aside their economic, social, and political differences.

In contrast, Nazis emphasized race much more than the nation. They recognized that Germany had different racial heritages – some Germans were particularly pure Caucasians, whom they claimed were superior to others who lived in Germany. Nazis believed that such Aryans should identify and feel at one with fellow Aryans and that the presence of Jews within their community diluted and corrupted the strength of "true" Germans. Of course, some Aryans lived outside of German borders, justifying Nazi efforts to conquer countries where Aryans lived and unite them into a broader German empire comprised of Aryan people. Thus, Nazis opposed communities that were racially, ethnically, and culturally diverse. They believed the racial characteristics of people were the sole necessary and sufficient bases for political identity.

Contemporary Liberals: Nations Built on Individual and Group Differences

Contemporary liberals inherited from classical liberals an emphasis on national communities and the role of federalism and civil society within nations. They too recognize that it is desirable for people to identify not only with the national community in which they reside but also with states, localities, and various voluntary communities within the nation. Increasingly, liberals are likely to take on more global identities, having concerns for people throughout the world and joining international nongovernmental organizations (NGOs) that seek to improve global conditions.

Contemporary liberals are probably more oriented toward the national community than are the other main friends of pluralism today. As we will see, many voices on the left are relatively international in their views, and conservatives are relatively local in their allegiances. For liberals, the nation-state provides the proper location for our primary political identities and obligations. Liberals believe citizens within a nation and its national government must help fellow compatriots first and foremost.[8] For example, all Americans, and not just immediate neighbors, should feel obligated to help the American victims of terrorist attacks, hurricanes, or other misfortunes, and governmental assistance is an important component in fulfilling these obligations. Of course, liberals will contribute their time and money in volunteer efforts to help victims, but they believe governmental assistance paid for by federal tax revenues are a just basis for ensuring that all citizens fulfill their obligations to their compatriots, for only such governmental programs ensure that we too would have a right to assistance should we be victimized. Because they recognize their (secondary) global citizenship, liberals may also be willing for national governments to extend assistance to people outside their national boundaries, but such international obligations are secondary to those one has to fellow citizens.

Compared to conservatives, liberals emphasize that many social and economic problems are national problems requiring national solutions. The racial discrimination that was written into the laws of southern states and that sparked the civil rights movement during the 1950s and 1960s was not simply a regional problem; it was a national problem – a true *American dilemma*[9] – and it required national policies to help those southern blacks who were not just citizens of Mississippi and Alabama but Americans. The pollutants that companies in particular states dump into the air or water foul the environment for those living elsewhere, requiring national environmental standards and solutions. While contemporary liberals recognize the importance of many political communities, they emphasize the national community and the capacity of its institutions for addressing social problems.

For contemporary liberals, the bases of national identity are political institutions. Unlike fascists (and some social conservatives), they do not see a common culture as essential to national identity and patriotism. Unlike Nazis (and some of their classical liberal predecessors), they do not regard common ethnicity or race as important to national identity. Contemporary liberals are comfortable with a multicultural and multiracial nation. They have supported social movements of minority groups, women, gays, and other excluded and marginalized citizens within nations that have been nominally liberal but have failed to realize the liberal ideal of a community that treats all individuals equally.

Contemporary liberals see community solidarity as occurring when individuals join together to cooperate in collective endeavors. Such cooperation can occur in both political communities and in groups within civil society, and these various settings need involve no common moral understandings. Indeed, liberals' deep commitment to the moral autonomy of individuals leaves them suspicious of strongly communitarian associations that insist on common moral outlooks and values. Liberals think individuals can come together for common purposes in spite of their perhaps divergent value systems. Liberals like public schools where kids from various classes, races, ethnicities, and religions come together to acquire a basic education and learn to live together. Liberals like civic associations composed of people with different characteristics and values that join together on specific but limited community projects. Because liberal groups must often resolve differences in order to work together effectively, they will be "procedural" rather than "constitutive" communities.[10] While solidarity within liberal communities is weakened by the different moral values that different individuals bring to community groups, members of the group do experience important connections with others. They develop common allegiance to fair and effective procedures for reaching group decisions. And they get satisfaction that their collective endeavors can achieve successful outcomes that were unattainable alone.

Contemporary liberals believe that such solidarity is approachable in national polities, but liberal nationalism involves thinner social solidarity than conservative nationalism. Liberals are less committed than conservatives to national languages (in the US, they are sympathetic to the burdens that "English-only laws" place on ethnolinguistic minorities) and to national symbols (they will burn flags). Liberals embrace a nationalism of equal rights and responsibilities. Liberal national solidarity rests on the understanding that my fellow citizens have the same rights as I and that I have responsibilities to my fellow citizens that are greater than those to other people. Liberal national solidarity rests on citizens sharing attachments to those national institutions like the Constitution (however flawed its democratic provisions)[11] and the office of the presidency (however limited the incumbent). For liberals, such institutions can bind us together and merit our common allegiance, because they enable us to resolve our differences fairly and to pursue our collective endeavors effectively.

The national (and sub-national) communities with which liberals identify are not as strong as the communities sought by their pluralist friends. Liberals do not seek as many communal provisions for fellow citizens by national governments as do democratic socialists. For example, such socialists usually endorse a system of universal medical care for all citizens, while contemporary liberals have yet to enact such provisions. And liberals do not look to a moral code or set of national values in the ways pursued by many conservatives. For example, while many conservatives seek an amendment to the American Constitution effectively banning gay marriage, liberals are much more comfortable with different moral practices involving marriage. The national communities that liberals love and feel allegiance to are weak communities that tolerate individual differences.

Contemporary Conservatives: Seeking Moral, but not Communitarian, Countries

Contemporary conservatives inherited from both classical liberals and traditional conservatives a deep respect for national communities and an emphasis on the need for citizens to identify with and have patriotic loyalties to that nation in which they have citizenship. American conservatives are likely to have a more positive, romanticized understanding of American history than contemporary liberals. American conservatives love their country because it has had traditions of both economic liberalism (emphasizing free markets and the importance of private property) and social conservatism (of popular movements emphasizing religious awakenings and moral crusades).

But contemporary conservatives – at least in America – were initially more supportive of and involved in state and local communities than in national ones. Conservatives fought for *states rights* not only to resist the national initiatives of liberals on the racial issues of the 1950s and 1960s, but also to resist national regulation of the economy and the imposition of national programs on states, especially unfunded mandates for states to provide costly access for the disabled and other disadvantaged citizens and to meet national safety and environmental health standards. Conservatives resisted such national initiatives, because they thought that Washington politicians and bureaucrats could not grasp local needs and constraints as well as local citizens and officials. They also thought empowering states and localities to develop their own programs to deal with social and economic problems would allow alternative policy approaches. For conservatives, local initiatives are much more prudent than the liberal approach which, according to conservatives, involves social engineering on a national scale – the articulation of national goals, the development of a scheme for achieving these goals based on theoretical reasoning, and an under-appreciation of unintended consequences of national programs on local communities.

While conservatives continue to employ anti-Washington rhetoric, they have moved decisively into the national arena as the conservative movement has matured. This movement toward national politics reflects both their increasing power at the national level and their increasing appreciation of the importance of national issues to their goals. Conservatives have experienced increasing success in national elections; whereas Washington used to be run by Democrats and liberals, Republicans and conservatives have controlled many national institutions during the past 25 years. Conservatives have become increasingly aware of the importance of national politics. Until the mid-1970s, conservatives were more oriented toward local communities than national ones. As the contemporary American conservative movement was gaining momentum, conservatives prided themselves on being realistic and paying attention to the things that actually influenced their lives in their immediate surroundings, rather than being caught up in faraway issues in Washington. Conservatives thought that state and local politics were more involved in the issues that bore on their everyday lives. States regulated alcohol, gambling, and sexual conduct; they established criminal codes regarding these and other vices. Schools educated their children and were subject to local control, and thus conservatives ran for positions on school boards. Local governments regulated land uses in ways that effected property values, and so conservatives dominated city hall. But by the 1970s, national governments were understood to be increasingly involved in such issues. When the Supreme Court issued its 1973 ruling on *Roe v. Wade*, which maintained that women had a constitutional right to abortion, conservatives came to understand that their moral positions would be continuously eroded unless they mobilized in national elections to put conservatives in the White House and Congress, who would, in turn, ensure that the Supreme Court was not packed with liberal judges. Such growing involvement in national politics has increased the capacity of conservatives to pursue their political agenda of reducing discretionary national programs, cutting national taxes, and having their moral values reflected in national social policies.

However, most contemporary conservatives have not succumbed to the temptation to try to impose a singular moral outlook on a nation composed of people holding different moral values. Unlike more radical social conservatives, contemporary conservatives seldom look to the national government to encourage a common culture and a single moral outlook on all Americans. Instead, they are content if national governments simply allow communitarian groups the opportunity to prosper on their own. This means that conservatives seek to have national governments that facilitate the existence and prosperity of many churches and morality-based organizations without endorsing the morality of any particular church or groups as the moral code to be favored or punished by such governments. Of course, such conservatives can at best achieve a thick social solidarity *within* smaller groups (such as within various religious denominations) and perhaps local political communities. Conservatives believe that local communities and even states often contain the moral consensus that is lacking at the national level on such issues as abortion and homosexuality, and that local governments can thus provide greater moral restrictions than is perhaps prudent at the national level.

Beyond sustaining communitarian groups and giving local communities the flexibility to enforce local moral values, contemporary conservatives also want national communities to generate thicker allegiances and loyalties than the liberal procedural republic provides. Conservatives believe that common languages, national symbols, and rooting for the country's Olympic athletes can all build a helpful sense of social solidarity within larger pluralistic political communities, and thus they emphasize such means for building national identities.

The Radical Right: Competing Global, National, and Sub-National Loyalties

On no issue is the radical right more divided than on that of community. Emphases on global, regional, national, and local identities can all be seen in the various perspectives on the radical right. Indeed, one can also see different emphases on the importance of political communities relative to other kinds of associations based on religious and economic ties.

It is tempting to suggest that what unites the radical right is an emphasis on community identities, but libertarians give priority to individual liberties and little attention to what binds individuals to communities. For libertarians, the individual's conception of the good life is internally generated and owes little if anything to the communities in which he resides. For libertarians, the good community is one that has minimal restrictions on the individual, and only those communities that provide maximal liberties deserve support. A libertarian may identify with Las Vegas and be loyal to its politics, but not because he feels it has defined him or that he has obligations to others who reside there; instead, the individual's affection is based on it being the sort of community where "anything goes," where freedom is celebrated and protected.

Traditional communitarians could not be more different. They reject the libertarian emphasis on individual rights and emphasize *the community good*. While liberals and libertarians regard as metaphysical nonsense any conception of the community good beyond that available to individuals living within a community, traditional communitarians think it is meaningful to speak about the community good as being independent of the good that community life provides for specific individuals. Community goods can arise out of the interactions of people, sometimes in the distant past or future.[12] For example, a nation's honor or its reputation for carrying out its commitments may be extremely valuable community goods that reside in no one and that may be attained today only at considerable cost to existing individuals in the community, but their attainment may well affect community life, benefiting present and future generations. Thus, traditional communitarians stress the need for individuals to uphold moral codes that are consistent with the community good, in ways that libertarians would utterly reject.

Traditional communitarians stress local identities and the importance of community roots that are highly particular and that arise from our daily interactions with other people. Being embedded in local communities can offer individuals the clarity of moral purpose that is too often lacking at the national level and it offers real social bonds that can combat the loneliness of existence in the overly individualistic society that liberalism has bequeathed to us and that global neoliberalism currently promotes.

National protectionists, of course, stress national identity. Gerhard Frey's German People's Union stressed "putting Germany first," and the American Reform Party under Ross Perot and Pat Buchanan stressed putting "America first, and not only first, but second and third as well."[13] Such statements might be interpreted as suggesting that national protectionists deny the importance of multiple community identities, but they should be seen in the context of nationalist struggles against globalization and its tendencies to generate economic insecurities for Germans and Americans and to undermine traditional ways of life in these nations. National protectionists are concerned with how globalization can reduce national sovereignty, undermine the economic interests of a nation, and lower the standard of living of domestic workers. They believe that international agreements on trade or environmental protection must be judged not on the basis of their overall impact on the global community but on their specific impacts on the nation. While national protectionists would clearly reduce global and regional identities, they do not call for people to sever their identifications with sub-national communities or associations in civil society.

Social and cultural conservatives also seek to strengthen national identities. In *Who are We?*, Samuel Huntington worries about the decline of cultural homogeneity in the US, because he regards shared values as the key to strong national identities, which in turn are key to national stability, power, and effectiveness. Huntington argues that the Anglo-Protestant culture is central to American identity in ways that Hispanic, African, and Asian cultures are not. To achieve sufficiently strong attachments to America, cultural conservatives emphasize the need for immigrants to be fully assimilated into American cultural values (such as the Protestant work ethic and Christian morality), become familiar with the European literature and arts that have been central to American culture, and become fluent in the English language. Multiculturalism and related liberal programs that fail to emphasize what is unique and exemplary in American culture leads to cultural confusion and a decline in national identity that can lead to a bifurcated society and to questioning the legitimacy of the existing political community.

During the post-Cold War era, civilizational identities have been reasserted, according to Huntington in his provocative *Clash of Civilizations*. Such identities are based on common cultures and religions, but are much broader than the more specific cultural and religious identities stressed by Huntington in *Who are We?*. Westerners – whether they are Catholics living in Rome or Mormons living in Utah – generally share Christian values and appreciate the same literary, artistic, and political traditions. The cultural differences among Westerners are much less than those between Westerners and people from Islamic, Hindu, Chinese, or other civilizations. The differences among civilizations generate many conflicts and complicate efforts by even the strongest world powers to deal with the crises that arise in other civilizations. Although this focus on civilizational identities has been much maligned for suggesting apparently irreconcilable differences among the civilizations of the world, Huntington argues that stronger civilizational identities that honor religious and cultural differences across civilizations can provide a relatively stable global community.[14]

Global neoliberals stress individual freedom in a global marketplace, and thus would seem to have little appreciation for the "embedded self" stressed by traditional communitarians or for strong national identities. However, most globalists do not deny the importance of the nation-state as a contemporary political fact or as a normative force that gives meaning to our lives. For example, while celebrating globalization in his *Lexus and the Olive Tree*, Thomas Friedman maintains, "the nation-state will never disappear, even if it is weakened, because it is the ultimate olive tree – the ultimate expression of whom we belong to – linguistically, geographically, and historically."[15] But globalists believe that a more globalized economy will require reducing the strength of our identities with and allegiances to the nation-state. Overemphasis on nationalism leads to misguided economic decisions such as the pursuit of national self-sufficiency and the erection of trade barriers.[16] Excessive national pride and insufficient national self-esteem are important factors contributing to international conflict and war.[17]

Globalists seek to develop non-nationalist identities more appropriate to the age of globalization, especially with the global marketplace. Globalists would encourage us to identify with the global community and people who live beyond our borders as potential customers, investors, and workers. Such a global community is not a political community that is governed by a state that uses coercion to regulate our lives. It is a voluntary community where people interact with particular others for mutual advantage.

Globalists recognize that globalization has contributed to the disintegration of traditional community ties and thus to a breakdown of social order, but they see such problems as transitory and believe that globalization will soon produce a richer, more diverse community life. According to Fukuyama, the social dislocations that have accompanied globalization have prompted a resurgence of religious communities – not the orthodox and otherworldly churches of the past, but rather new kinds of churches that emphasize providing social activities and social bonds for their members.[18] Johan Norberg sees globalization replacing traditional homogeneous local communities with more heterogeneous and pluralistic cultures. In most cities throughout the world, numerous ethnic and religious sub-communities have arisen to offer diverse cultural choices within easily accessible locations.[19] In short, globalists seek to reorient people, reducing the role of national identities in their lives, enhancing their attachment to people in different countries and cultures, and making their local communities more inclusive and diverse. They believe such communal arrangements should encourage tolerance, social mixing across ethnic and class lines, and mutual gain by peoples throughout the world.

Despite their diversity of views about communities, the various voices on the radical right seem to favor our having multiple community memberships, identities, and obligations. None of these voices seeks the sort of singular community identities stressed by fascists, Nazis, or the contemporary extreme right. It also seems unlikely that any of these strands seek to dissolve the national identities stressed by contemporary liberals and conservatives.

The Radical Left: Pursuing Solidarity Among Diverse People in Many Polities

The radical left is more international than the radical right. While globalists seek a reduced focus on national identities, the global community they stress is a global marketplace, not a political community. In contrast, there are several strands within the radical left that urge people to adopt identities that focus on the international political community. Democratic socialists have long realized that the global community is the ultimate setting for the realization of socialist goals. Socialists are prominent among advocates of cosmopolitan justice who seek to reduce the great inequalities of wealth that exist between industrialized Western nations and developing nations, or between the relatively affluent North and the relatively deprived South.[20] Many voices on the radical left oppose the existing orientations of international organizations – especially the World Trade Organization and the International Monetary Fund – which they see as pursuing a neoliberal agenda of trade policies favorable to corporate interests based in the most advanced societies rather than following policies that would provide developing nations with a greater share of the benefits that flow from globalization; but they see the value of international organizations that would govern on the basis of more egalitarian principles. Radical feminists and radical greens are often involved in nongovernmental organizations that are composed of peoples from many countries and that address the plight of women in traditional societies and environmental issues affecting less developed nations.[21] Such NGOs and movements seek to contain multinational corporate power, organize workers on a transnational basis, promote global justice, further issues of importance to women, and protect the global environment.

However, many voices within the radical left continue to have a strong orientation toward the nation-state. Liberal egalitarians like John Rawls have been explicit in asserting that their principles do not apply at the international level, but only to existing national political communities where citizens have political obligations to one another.[22] While civic communitarians have claimed that liberal egalitarians have not given sufficient attention to ensuring that the citizens of a nation share cultural values that sustain these strong obligations, egalitarian liberals believe that people with diverse cultural values can nevertheless share a political consensus that recognizes the obligations we have to our fellow national-citizens to ensure that their essential needs are satisfied.[23]

Democratic socialists have long been oriented toward national communities. During the twentieth century, they came into prominence and power in those nations that had developed sufficiently democratic processes to provide opportunities for critics of capitalism to eliminate, or at least tame, through political means the major problems and injustices that accompanied capitalism. When elected, socialists sometimes nationalized industries to pursue national objectives such as facilitating transportation and communication throughout a nation. Socialist governments developed and administered extensive programs to ensure that various goods and services – such as education and healthcare – were available universally to all citizens within a nation.

Civic communitarians hope to strengthen citizen involvement in national government, but suggest both larger and smaller community identities should also be strengthened. Michael Sandel seeks to develop at the national level a citizenry that has the civic virtues that enable effective self-governance. He decries the transformation in the understanding of democracy that occurred in America during the twentieth century. Formerly, Americans thought that democracy entailed the capacity of citizens to shape their collective destiny. Now they think democracy entails the capacity of individuals to choose their own values and goals. When national power remained strong, this shift in emphasis from collective to individual mastery was acceptable, because it was hardly noticed. But the need to recapture civic virtue and strengthen our collective capacity to control the destiny of the nation became apparent when national power waned both domestically – as evidenced by the social upheavals of the 1960s and the economic struggles of the 1970s – and internationally – as evidenced during the war in Vietnam and the Iranian hostage crisis. But just as this realization was sinking in, so also was the reality of globalization. Sandel recognizes that even if citizens were to identify more strongly with the national community and acquire the civic virtues necessary for effective national governance, they could not hope to govern the global economy in the absence of global political institutions. Thus, Sandel concludes:

> The hope for self-government today lies not in relocating sovereignty but in dispersing it. The most promising alternative to the sovereign state is not a cosmopolitan community based on the solidarity of humankind but a multiplicity of communities and political bodies – some more extensive than nations and some less – among which sovereignty is diffused. Only a politics that disperses sovereignty both upward and downward can combine the power required to rival global market forces with the differentiation required of a public life that hopes to inspire the allegiance of its citizens.[24]

Sandel continues with the criticism of the national welfare state made by all communitarians – both right and left: "The American welfare state is politically vulnerable because it does not rest on a sense of national community adequate to its purpose."[25] While we need to try to strengthen national identity, Sandel argues that the revitalization of citizenship within local communities, neighborhoods, and civic associations is also important and more feasible.

The radical left thus understands that humans inhabit many political communities and join many voluntary associations. The various forces within the radical left are committed to bringing the values of social solidarity, equality, and strong democracy to all communities. The radical left stresses *engagement* or participation as a means of attaining common experiences and social solidarity in political communities. Both the process of working together politically and the hope of developing a more socialist ethos are seen by the radical left as contributing to forward-looking, rather than conservative backward-looking, communities.[26]

Compared to liberals, the radical left regards community as an intrinsic substantive value. While liberals see communities as places where various common purposes can be sought and achieved, the radical left sees communities as also providing for essential human needs to bond with each other; communities enable people to enjoy a sense fraternity and solidarity with one another. Part of the reason that the radical left values extensive communal provisions like national healthcare, day-care centers, and public transportation is because they are universally available to everyone in the community. When rich and poor, black and white, and those in other social cleavages have similar experiences in socialized medical centers, in community nurseries, on the subway, and in other public spaces, they have opportunities to know others having values and lifestyles that are different from those in their more immediate social circles. Early in the twentieth century, Milwaukee developed the nation's most dense system of public parks under one of the few socialist municipal administrations in American history. These public spaces were created on the premise that, at the end of the day, people from all walks of life could leave their hierarchically organized workplaces and interconnect as equal citizens. For the radical left today, skyboxes in stadiums symbolize a major loss of social solidarity, because they segregate people and diminish common experiences. The goal of common experiences is to learn more about each other, to forge common memories, and to build empathy and solidarity toward those differently situated than oneself.

The Extreme Right: Rejecting Multiple Community Identities

The extreme right contains a wide range of ideas about the kinds of political communities and community identities that are most important. Of course, many voices on the extreme right resemble fascists in their stress on the nation-state. Many right-wing groups like the National Alliance, Posse Comitatus, and the Patriot Movement in the United States seem nationalistic in their disdain for globalization and their fear of a world government, but their patriotism is compromised by their alarm over what has happened to America: they loath our transformation from a white to a multiethnic society, and they believe that the national government has become an oppressive force. Most such right-wingers look to strong local communities as bastions of defense against oppressive global and national forces. In contrast, some movements on the far right, especially outside of the US, seek broader identities than those with existing nations. Islamic fundamentalists, for example, regard the existing nation-states and borders in the Arabic world as colonial impositions. Osama bin Laden's apparent political goal is to unite all Muslims behind one Islamic identity that transcends current national differences.

Despite such differences in the type of political community sought, right-wing extremists have little appreciation for and much hostility toward the notion of multiple-community identities. They seem always motivated by a vision of being part of a singular community – a community where there is unity of purpose and morality – and often of religion, race, and ethnicity. Both black and white nationalists exemplify this belief in the importance of homogeneity. Indeed, white nationalists in America today are less likely than white racists of the past to maintain that the reason for wanting a racially pure national community is so that whites can separate themselves from "inferior" races. Instead, their claim is that people of different races simply have divergent cultures and values that make living together difficult for people of both races.[27] Of course, such insular unity is antithetical to pluralism.

The extreme right is hostile to notions about being part of any singular global community or world government. Perhaps there are still some right-wingers who dream of worldwide domination, of imposing their culture or religion on peoples everywhere, but most in the extreme right today are not universalists. They understand the reality of pluralism among nations and civilizations, and they are willing to accept some sort of modus vivendi among peoples of different cultures, religions, and ethnicities. One might say that the extreme right seeks unity within their primary community and accepts pluralism across communities. However, the pluralism across nations that the extreme right accepts is highly fragile. Given their disdain for peoples from other cultures and for international organizations that might provide rules and venues for dealing with issues that arise among nations, their global pluralism is really a state of competitive anarchy.

Insofar as globalization is accelerating and tearing down the walls that have separated people of different civilizational, cultural, racial, and ethnic identities, and insofar as globalization is destabilizing and threatening to many people, the various voices on the extreme right have a growing and receptive audience for their ideals that would establish homogeneous communities and erect barriers between "them" and "us."

The Extreme Left: Deconstructing Current Identities

The extreme left challenges many community identities. They believe the friends of pluralism privilege nations as the fundamental human association, and they question this centrality both empirically and normatively. They believe that globalization has weakened national cultures, economies, and governments. Global communications, technologies, and markets have homogenized what were formerly distinct national cultures. Transnational corporations have exposed local investors, workers, and consumers to the needs, insecurities, and exploitation of foreign markets. The perceived need to attract mobile wealth has made national governments less responsive to the preferences of their own citizens. Thus, globalization has reduced the role of the nation in people's lives, as we increasingly become workers and consumers in world markets.

The extreme left is more critical of the processes that have reduced the importance of nations than of the actual losses of national identity and allegiance. After all, misguided beliefs in the superiority of Western nations have served as dubious rationales for dominating underdeveloped countries, and strong national identities have promoted international conflict and reduced commitments to global justice.[28]

The extreme left is normally oriented toward the international community, encouraging humans to assume more global identities. Hardt and Negri speak of the "multitude" as a transnational array of people networked by global communications and collaborations. For such left-wing extremists, no one is excluded from the multitude; it is a sort of universal community of people everywhere who seek to resist forces of global domination and to generate more democracy.[29] Hardt and Negri consider a variety of ways of strengthening global political institutions, such as reforming the United Nations so that it would be a truly representative body, forming a global body modeled upon the World Social Forum (WSF), and creating a "global parliament or assembly that is based on peoples, nations, or even civilizations."[30] While urging people to "act locally," deep greens stress the need to "think globally," and sometimes employ the concept of a *planetary community* to underscore the importance of humans perceiving themselves as part of a global ecology that interconnects not only humans but all animals, plants, soils, and other natural resources.[31]

At the same time, the extreme left has little sympathy for how the global community and the earth's ecology are currently structured and governed. For the most part, the international community is dominated by global capitalism; the massive power of the leading economic actors in that system distorts the relations of people within the global community, creating injustices and hostility among them. And the earth's ecological system is too often exploited, depleted, and disrupted by the greed of powerful economic interests and the failure of humans everywhere to recognize their proper role in sustaining the fragility of the planet. Most international organizations are seen as agents of powerful economic interests. Many on the radical left agree with the extreme left in this depiction of the current problem. But while those within the radical left often become activists within the institutions of international civil society – working within various NGOs and organizing international social movements – the extreme left has little hope that such political activity can produce positive changes.

Some left-wing extremists believe a return to local communities is the best solution. For example, deep greens believe that the planet and all its inhabitants are threatened by massive structures – by extensive global markets, big business, and large bureaucratic governments – and thus call on people to "act locally," in decentralized communities. In the "Blueprint for Survival," deep greens call for people to organize primarily into neighborhoods of about 500 people, where they can comprehend changes in and have some sense of control over their environments.[32] Of course, deep greens recognize that these local neighborhoods will need to be associated into larger localities, regions, nations, and a global community. However, the primacy of local communities is emphasized by the principle that no collective task should be done at a higher level than absolutely necessary and by arrangements of confederation ensuring that relationships among local communities are entirely voluntary, rather than supervised under the forceful imposition of more centralized governmental authorities.

In the end, the extreme left wants to "aim high" in thinking about how to restructure our political life. Hardt and Negri speak about "going back to the drawing board" to "formulate a new science of society and politics."[33] Perhaps aiming high is a noble task, and perhaps many changes sought by left-wingers like Hardt and Negri are more radical than extreme. But Hardt and Negri's concluding attack on the concept of sovereignty approaches an anarchistic assault not only on existing governance but also on existing political communities: "It does mean that rulers become increasingly parasitical and that sovereignty becomes increasingly unnecessary. Correspondingly, the ruled become increasingly autonomous, capable of forming society on their own."[34]

Hardt and Negri go on to deny that they are anarchists, by claiming that the "choice is not between sovereignty and anarchy." Rather than calling for the abolition of political communities, they seek to create new social relations and communities.[35] While it is not clear what form these new political communities would take, Hardt and Negri hope that the multitude would stage a grand "exodus," leaving current political communities and resisting all current forms of authoritative relationships.[36] By calling for a politics of revolt against existing political communities rather than a radical reform of these communities, Hardt and Negri make apparent that their politics is extreme in its implications.

Conclusions

People committed to pluralism identify with, participate in, and have obligations to many communities. Such people see themselves within nested boxes ranging from smaller to larger polities. In America, allegiance to federal principles – to simultaneously identifying with one's city, state, and nation – gives an initial expression of this idea. In a more cosmopolitan manner, pluralists can also identify as being part of the Americas, Western Civilization, and the global community. To complicate matters, people have allegiances beyond these territorially defined communities. Pluralists identify with voluntary associations such as churches, workplaces, and educational institutions. They also identify with communities where other members are amorphous strangers except for the fact that they have, if sometimes only temporarily, some interests in common: "We are African-Americans," or "We are part of a chat group on the web" with such common interests as pursuing gay rights or playing fantasy football.

Contemporary liberals and conservatives and those on the radical left and right all believe it important for people to have and appreciate having many community identities. Such friends of pluralism believe that identifying solely with one community, or even a few similar communities, is unhealthy for the individual and for politics.[37] Singular community identities encourage narrow, parochial, and inflexible thinking. If a person is totally enmeshed in one community, he will think that the beliefs, values, and principles that govern that community are unchallengeable, and he will be given little opportunity to evaluate the adequacy of these ideas in relation to those of other communities (of which he is ignorant).[38] Having multiple community identities heightens our sense of connection to others while dampening our zeal for the narrow interests and understandings of any one community with which we might identify.[39] Having multiple obligations reminds us that obeying certain dictates from authorities in one community can undermine our capacity to fulfill our moral and political obligations to others in the broader or narrower communities in which we are members, enhancing our ability to develop moral autonomy. Having multiple memberships enables us to appreciate those communities in which we, as members, have participation rights and those communities in which we are not members and which have a right of self-governance independent of our participation and influence. In contrast, fascists, Nazis, and various right-wing extremists today seek singular identities in order to achieve community unity, and thus have views on community that are well outside the boundaries of pluralism.

Accepting the idea of multiple community identities leaves unresolved many important issues about community, and thus pluralist societies (including a pluralist global order) will experience conflicts between those who would give greater or less priority to global interconnections, national sovereignty, states rights, and local control.[40] But the friends of pluralism do not deny any of these identities or seek to dissolve any of these communities; instead they seek adjustments that either strengthen or weaken our identities with these communities and their influence over our lives.

One issue dividing pluralists is the basis of community identity. All pluralists deny that communities should be homogeneous in terms of race, ethnicity, or religion. But cultural conservatives and communitarians (both right and left) believe that people must share many cultural values in order to achieve necessary identifications and loyalties to political communities. Civic communitarians believe that democratic control of a community's destiny and support for policies of social justice are dependent on citizens understanding and having commitments to widely shared civic virtues like putting the community good ahead of self-interest and being willing to do one's share by giving time, attention, and economic resources to public affairs. Traditional communitarians believe that social stability and public order require that citizens understand and be guided by longstanding moral values centered on work, family, religion, and decency in sexual display and behavior. Cultural conservatives believe that national effectiveness and strength require that citizens of a community speak a common language and take pride in the great achievements of those in their community, in ways that motivate others to seek similar achievements. However, liberals, libertarians, and neoliberals deemphasize the importance of common culture as a basis for community identity. Liberals believe that national communities can be strong and stable if their citizens are simply committed to some common political principles – what Samuel Huntington calls a political creed.[41] If citizens affirm their national identity by supporting a nation's constitution, its political institutions, the equal political rights of all citizens, and such fundamental political values as the rule of law, equal opportunity, and tolerance, that is a sufficient basis for stable pluralist politics.[42]

The cultural unity sought by many communitarians seems contrary to pluralist principles of self-determination and governmental neutrality among moral and religious doctrines. Pluralism holds that each individual should have the capacity to choose and pursue his own conception of the good life and that governments should not privilege any particular moral or religious doctrine. Efforts to create cultural homogeneity are unacceptable to pluralists, who believe that exposure to many cultures furthers the fundamental goal of individual autonomy. Exposure to cultural differences enables citizens to better understand and evaluate their moral choices, to pursue a conception of the good life that reflects their own choice, and to revise unsatisfying life plans in order to pursue alternatives made known through exposure to alternative cultures. For pluralists, political identities built on a general consensus about a community's political creed are sufficient. The efforts of communitarians and cultural conservatives to enforce a stronger sense of community identity by demanding cultural conformity are anathema to pluralism. Governmental efforts to privilege a particular culture are unjust to people from other cultures, as the costs of assimilating to the privileged culture would be disproportionately borne by people not of that culture. In order to remain within the pluralist consensus, communitarians and cultural conservatives must therefore retreat from emphasizing cultural unity and having government privilege a particular culture. Such voices can still seek stronger community identities than currently exist; they can try to embed individuals more strongly in various political communities and voluntary associations and they can even seek to have governments resolve particular moral issues on the basis of consequential arguments about how policies dealing with moral questions promote or hinder results that are good for the community. But they must accept and try to accommodate the inevitable differences in cultural values that exist in pluralist societies.

Another area of disagreement among pluralists is the extent of ties among people within political communities. Classical liberals, individualist anarchists, libertarians, globalists, and many contemporary conservatives de-emphasize strong community bonds that can undermine individual freedoms. Traditional conservatives and communitarians and cultural conservatives seek stronger community ties based on common moral and cultural understandings. Contemporary liberals, egalitarian liberals, democratic socialists, cosmopolitans, radical democrats, and civic communitarians seek stronger community ties and a stronger sense of political obligations based on principles of social justice. These differences will come into clearer focus as we address questions of citizenship, structure, authority, and justice in subsequent chapters.

Pluralists do not agree on the salience and substance of a global community, but unlike the extreme right, who have nothing but contempt for the global marketplace and any institutions of world governance, pluralists are willing to explore mutually beneficial global economic relationships and develop global political institutions to deal with international issues. Pluralists believe that a well-ordered global community is threatened by denying the independent existence of an international community. Pluralists understand that if only nation-states are regarded as legitimate, international agreements will not be binding unless all nations remain committed to them. Lacking a stronger identity with the international community, nations can withdraw from international agreements at any time and act unilaterally in ways that threaten a well-governed global society.[43] Unless international obligations are recognized and international regulations constrain various nationalisms, the danger is that nationalism could spin out of control in the twenty-first century, just as it did during the first half of the twentieth century.

Pluralists are particularly concerned about those right-wing extremists who seek strong nationalist identities based on denigrating or fearing other national groups. Pluralists can be comfortable with national identities that are based entirely on factors about their own political community but involve no comparisons with other communities. But they find very dangerous efforts to build community identities that depend on making invidious comparisons between "them" and "us" – and they dismiss such comparisons as contrary to the spirit of equality and mutual respect necessary for pluralist politics.

Chapter 10

Questions of Citizenship

Who are citizens and who can become citizens of various polities? Can there be legitimate differences in the status of citizens (e.g., first- and second-class citizens)? What rights are provided to citizens, and should citizen rights be extended or contracted? What duties must citizens perform, and should citizen obligations be strengthened or diminished?

Such questions have been subjects of perennial discussion, although their urgency has varied over time. In the ancient world, most people were subjects of governments, not citizens, and issues of obligation were much more prominent than those of rights. For example, almost 2,500 years ago, Sophocles raised the question of whether Antigone was obligated to obey Creon, the King of Thebes, or whether she should disobey him in order to fulfill other, perhaps more pressing, moral obligations (to give her brother a decent burial despite Creon's insistence that he was a traitor).

The modern world has tended to focus on rights. Perhaps no issue has been more discussed than the claim, normally made by those on the left, that citizens have extensive welfare rights ensuring their access to such necessities as food, housing, and healthcare. In opposition to such claims, those on the right often claim that the property rights of citizens should prevent governments from taxing people's justly acquired income and wealth to provide welfare for the poor.

While these ancient and modern issues remain, the current era of globalization has focused attention on the question of extending citizenship to outsiders. For example, it is estimated that there are currently 12 million illegal immigrants in the United States, and this has prompted debates as to which of three general policies should be adopted to deal with this issue. Should we make greater efforts to secure our borders and deport illegal immigrants? Should we develop *guest worker programs* that would register and permit migrants to be resident within the country if gainfully employed for a certain period of time after which they would be required to return to their native lands? Or should we make it much easier for those who wish to come to our country to gain full citizenship? This chapter provides the views of various ideologies on issues of admitting new citizens to a political community, as well as the rights and obligations that accompany citizenship.

Classical Liberals: Curbing Citizenship, Providing Limited Rights and Obligations

As we have seen, classical liberals believed that political communities should be regarded as arising out of social contracts among individuals residing in proximity to one another who agree to authorize a government to protect their rights. They initially assumed that only male property-owners should count as citizens of national communities. John Locke's social contract was an agreement to protect life, liberty, and *property*. Since only those owning property had fundamental interests in the governance of their nation, citizenship was limited to property-owners, and because existing laws prevented most women from owning property, they could therefore be excluded. Classical liberals subsequently debated whether male property-owners should extend citizenship to others.

Classical liberals were slow to provide inclusive answers to these issues. Among liberal philosophers, James Mill was willing to exclude women and the poor. His son, John Stuart Mill, was willing to extend voting rights to women, but he thought it important to exclude recipients of charity and the illiterate. The most basic justification for such exclusions was the belief that people needed certain qualifications to become citizens, otherwise they might use their power in ways that could undermine the effective workings of a liberal society.[1] The poor and the uneducated, for example, might use their voting power to abuse the property rights of the affluent, and in so doing weaken the capitalist economy.

The United States, even under liberal leadership, enacted many restrictions on citizenship. Black slaves and women were denied citizenship and/or the right to vote when the Constitution was written (1787) and when the first naturalization statute was passed (1790). While liberal impulses led to passage of the Fourteenth Amendment in 1868, which granted citizenship to former black slaves, almost a century passed before liberals enacted the Voting Rights Act of 1965, which more effectively secured for Blacks their political rights. Liberals accepted many exclusions from citizenship throughout the nineteenth century. In 1831, the Supreme Court ruled that Native Americans could not be eligible for American citizenship "unless they explicitly detached themselves from their tribes and integrated themselves into American society."[2] Despite an extensive women's suffrage movement that began with the Seneca Falls Declaration in 1848, women remained second-class citizens who were denied voting rights in national elections until passage of the Nineteenth Amendment in 1920. The nineteenth century also witnessed widespread concern about the arrival in America of many Irish, Eastern Europeans (including many Jews), Southern Europeans (mostly Catholics), and other non-Anglos. In 1882, a "Chinese exclusion" act was enacted, but this was just the most visible part of a broader nativism that was engulfing the country. An anti-immigration movement culminated in the very restrictive immigration policies adopted by Congress in 1924. This law capped immigration levels at 150,000 persons per year and established a quota system that assigned most immigration opportunities to applicants from Northern and Western Europe. The clear intent was to ensure that people lacking Anglo and (broadly) liberal values would not engulf America.

Not only did classical liberals endorse restricted citizenship, but they also thought that citizenship conveyed a very limited array of benefits. Classical liberals did not uphold extensive welfare rights for citizens. Instead, their emphasis on limited government and the importance of capitalism meant that those in need of assistance would have to depend on charitable organizations and minimal welfare programs offered by sub-national governments. Classical liberals did not make civil rights – the equal and respectful treatment of people in everyday life within civil society – a significant part of their agenda. Welfare and civil rights would have to await initiatives by contemporary liberals and others.

Classical liberals also showed little interest in extending opportunities for citizen participation in politics. For the most part, they thought limiting direct participation in government was a benefit – not a deprivation – for citizens. Hoping to enlarge the private sphere of life so that citizens could devote their energies to economic production and consumption and other means of satisfying personal interests, they wanted to protect the essential rights of citizens without requiring their extensive involvement in government.

Classical liberals argued for government of and for the people, but not government by the people. Government is *"of the people"* in the sense that its authority is derived from the consent of the people, by means of a (hypothetical) social contract. Government is *"for the people"* in the sense that it exists to protect the rights of each citizen to his life, liberty, and property, as specified by the social contract. Government is *"by the people"* in only the limited sense that citizens participate in selecting representatives. Liberal citizenship meant that citizens need only monitor their representatives and have the opportunity to vote on the basis of their assessment of whether the incumbent or an opposing candidate would best protect their rights and further their interests.

Such a view of citizen participation does not make great demands on citizens to develop or possess political virtue. *Republican* critics of liberal citizenship suggest that democracy requires citizens to act on the basis of the common good, while classical liberals relied on institutions such as regular, frequent, and competitive elections to convert self-interested political motivations into approximations of the public interest.[3] Nevertheless, as liberalism matured, greater emphasis was placed on the acquisition of political virtue. John Stuart Mill thought citizenship rights should be most extensive for those who possessed such virtues as "judgment, discriminative feeling, mental activity, and even moral preference."[4] Liberals also came to appreciate other political virtues, such as being open to new ideas and experiences and having tolerance for individual differences.[5] For the most part, however, classical liberals emphasized the need for citizens to acquire economic virtues. Despite acknowledging that citizens could pursue their personal interests in the marketplace, Adam Smith understood that effective markets required them to have such economic virtues as a work ethic, thrift, and frugality, as well as a desire to invest in the future and – most importantly – to accept responsibility for their own economic needs.[6]

Classical liberals also insisted that everyone within a liberal society, including those excluded from citizenship, must obey the laws of their governments. For liberals, the social contract creates political obligations on all residents. As Locke suggested, everyone who enjoys the security of government – every resident of the territory ruled by a government – "doth thereby give his tacit consent, and is as far obligated to obedience to the laws of government."[7] The obligation to obey is not very burdensome, however, because the laws of liberal governments are limited to protecting everyone's rights. Such governments will not ask citizens to conform to moral principles contrary to individual conscience, because they do not legislate a specific morality. Their laws will not dictate what an individual can think or do in the private sphere, because liberal governments only regulate the behavior of individuals in the public sphere.

What if a liberal government exceeds its legitimate powers and creates unjust laws? For classical liberals, there are two main options open to those who believe that their government has acted unjustly. First, they can vote against the representatives who created the unjust laws, hoping that most citizens share their views and that new representatives will eliminate the offending laws. Second, they can leave – an option that liberals thought was viable for those who believe that governments are infringing their rights, but whose views are persistently in the minority.

In summary, classical liberals have generally favored limited citizenship in three senses. First, they granted citizenship only to certain *qualified* people. Second, they have been satisfied with providing a *short* list of citizen rights, focusing on legal and political liberties. Third, they have made *minimal* demands on citizens, limiting their obligations to such things as obeying just laws and paying minimal taxes.

Traditional Conservatives: Stressing Loyalty and Obedience to Authorities

Traditional conservative have accepted various tiers of membership in the polity; all residents might be entitled to some legal protections, but only a small number of residents are entitled to broader economic and political rights, and only an elite few should directly participate in government. Conservatives have thus been even more reluctant that classical liberals to extend equal citizenship to those who are without property, illiterate, female, or who possess other attributes that have been customarily used to differentiate between full and second-class citizenship. However, traditional conservatives do not raise various exclusions of citizens to the level of principle.[8] As circumstances changed or as democratic norms evolved, conservatives slowly granted rights to more and more people who were formerly second-class citizens. For example, they no longer oppose women's suffrage or voting rights for minorities.

No firm principle seems to control conservative ideas about immigration. Consider the changing views of a leading American traditional conservative, Russell Kirk. As recently as 1989, he took a strong pro-immigration position, claiming that

> [the] peaceful coming of people from abroad is not usually a cause of economic decay. Rather such migrations mean that the host country is acquiring more human resources. Most such immigrants, especially in the history of the United States, have been hard working ambitious people who helped to improve their economic condition. Often immigrants are willing to accept, at least in the beginning, hard, dangerous, or unpleasant work for which it is difficult to find sufficient labor within a country's established work force. In the long run, most immigrants become strong upholders of the culture, the political system, and the economy to which they come.

However, Kirk reconsidered this position and became Pat Buchanan's campaign manager in Michigan during the 1992 presidential primaries, in part because he believed Buchanan would discourage "indiscriminate immigration into the United States, for our country cannot play host to all the world and still maintain its established culture, its successful economy, and its social cohesion."[9]

Kirk's vacillations nicely sum up traditional conservative thinking on the issue: whether or not to have more open admissions policies for immigrants is dependent on its perceived effects on social cohesion in the host community. Applicants who serve the needs of the community should be extended citizenship, but only if their admission does not threaten social stability.

When it comes to thinking about the consequences of citizenship, traditional conservatives emphasize duties over rights. Thus, their view of citizenship is even more passive than that of classical liberals. The good citizen accepts traditionally constituted government institutions, obeys the laws of the land, and performs his allocated role in society to the best of his abilities. Citizen obedience is warranted, because everyone is part of an organic society that binds individuals together and provides roles and purposes for individuals. Conservatives reject the idea that obligations to obey are based on a social contract. They believe that the social contract perspective of liberals encourages citizens to question their loyalty and obedience to a society, as it suggests that citizens need not be obedient if they are dissatisfied with government. For traditional conservatives, the bonds of society are much more than a "mere contract." They are deep moral and cultural understandings that provide social order and prompt individuals to put social duties above individual desires.

Traditional conservatives reject the liberal idea that political rights can be determined by appealing to universal abstract principles. Citizens have only those rights – such as voting or participating in juries – that have been traditionally recognized within particular political cultures and that are specified by law. Conservatives believe that most countries are better governed if citizens are less involved in government, as most people are incapable of achieving the competence, prudence, and virtue necessary for public participation. Citizen participation opportunities should be extended slowly, only as warranted by improvements in citizen competence. Such competence will not increase quickly, as most people are rightly focused on their personal and local concerns, rather than the public good. If ordinary people want to participate in community life, there are sufficient opportunities available in the voluntary associations within civil society.

Anarchists: Comrades Without Political Obligations

Anarchists reject the concept of citizenship. They regard as illegitimate the power of political communities to designate some people as full citizens, others as second-class citizens, and still others as non-citizens. They reject restrictive immigration laws that prevent outsiders from becoming part of a community. They believe the rights that political communities extend to citizens are always less than the rights that all people have by virtue of their humanity. They believe that the obligations that political communities impose on citizens are far beyond what is necessary for people to live in harmony with others. Rather than thinking of how they should relate to other citizens (and non-citizens), anarchists prefer to think about how they should relate to comrades, neighbors, and friends who co-inhabit natural communities.

The natural communities sought by anarchists would not be defined by and confined to explicitly designated citizens. A natural community is composed of people who share, if only temporarily, common interests and a desire to associate with each other in pursuit of those interests. An ongoing natural community would not use coercion to exclude outsiders, but it might well refrain from welcoming outsiders who it suspects would contribute little to the community. A natural community would comprise people who, through their interactions and acceptances, have achieved a mutual, though perhaps tacit, understanding that they are part of a community.

Because anarchists regard citizens as subordinate members of political associations, who are subject to the commands of governmental authorities, they call on people to reject the rights of citizenship that such authorities grant. For example, early anarchists urged people to abstain from voting. According to Pierre Proudhon, an individual effectively surrenders his moral autonomy by voting. Only by abstaining can the individual maintain that the unjust and oppressive acts of government are not his responsibility. Abstention from participation in government reinforces the individual's refusal to obey government; it signifies that the anarchist is the mistress of herself. However, some contemporary anarchists seek to define a participatory anarchism that works to undermine government. For example, the Italian Director of Great Films and anarchist Lina Wertmuller urges other anarchists to vote for small parties having very specific platforms, based on the premise that the representation of such parties in the legislature would complicate the formation of governing coalitions and thus make it more difficult for the state to exercise coercive power.

While rejecting any political obligations to obey the state, anarchists believe that people have moral obligations – to act justly in relationship to others. According to William Godwin, "every man is bound to the exertion of his facilities in the discovery of right, and to the carrying into effect all the right with which he is acquainted."[10] Rather than obeying some external authority, each person should be morally autonomous, obeying the dictates of his own conscience.

Godwin argued that three features characterize a virtuous person. First, she has bene-volent intentions; rather than simply seeking her own interest, she is motivated to do good for others. Second, the effects of her actions actually are beneficial to others, contributing to general happiness. Third, her actions produce benefits that correspond with her capabilities.[11] Thus, for a wealthy person to be virtuous, she must seek to help others, she must actually benefit them, and she must be more generous in her assistance than less wealthy persons. Absolutely just and virtuous persons would distribute their resources (e.g., their time and money) to those who could most benefit from them; if someone else needs a good more than its possessor, the dictates of justice and virtue require that the possessor give that good to the person in greatest need of it.

Anarchists understand that people are unlikely to meet this absolute standard of human virtue, but the disposition of being virtuous should be cultivated. Obedience to external authority undermines such cultivation of moral autonomy and its accom-panying predisposition to be virtuous. Thus, rather than calling for the obedience of citizens to the state, anarchists call for the obedience of persons to principles of moral conduct.

Marxists: Transforming Alienated Workers into Public-Spirited Comrades

Like anarchists, Marxists have little use for the concept of "the citizen." To the extent that liberal or conservative governments use their authority to designate some as citizens, to provide citizen rights, and to instill citizen obedience, they reinforce the national identities that undermine the more fundamental understanding that most people are part of the transnational working class. Marxists think workers should look past their designations as citizens of democratic capitalist societies and scorn their bourgeois rights in liberal society. Instead, they should accept necessary duties as members of working-class movements that will propel them forward into classless, nonpolitical communities where they can live together as comrades.

Marxists argue that citizen participation in a democratic capitalist society is essentially symbolic and ineffectual. Citizen involvement in democratic institutions is part of a *legitimation system* that is intended to induce obedience and loyalty in the masses.[12] The myth of the democratic state makes citizens believe that they are obeying laws of their own making, but capitalists or their representatives in fact make these laws. Marx had little to say about the major vehicles of proletarian participa-tion within capitalist society, because he regarded trade unions and working-class parties as diverting energy from revolutionary action.[13]

Following a capitalist revolution, the proletariat would belong to transitional political communities, such as the Paris Commune, a socialist arrangement that ruled the French Capitol during Spring of 1871.[14] Marx suggested that in workplaces and neighborhoods, the proletariat would have enhanced opportunities to debate and resolve issues, and they would elect and hold accountable their representatives to higher-level political institutions. Still, his emphasis on the dictatorship of the proletariat during this transitional period clearly implied that participation would be limited to those who were qualified by having overcome the false consciousness that predominates in capitalist society. Those who clung to liberal ideas and ways of life would be excluded until they accepted communist ones.

During the transitional period, the socialist state would impose many obligations and command widespread obedience. Former aristocrats and capitalists would be obligated to relinquish their land and factories as the state collectivized and nationalized their property. Those with great wealth would have to pay heavy taxes, and the right of inheritance would be abolished. Those workers who disagreed with their comrades would have to submit to the dictatorship of the proletariat and obey its rule without resistance. While the burdens of obedience might appear extensive during the transitional socialist society, Marxist theory suggests that they are justified as necessary means for achieving a full communist society.

In a communist society, citizenship would be minimal, but membership extensive. Citizenship would be minimal, because the state would have withered away, and members of society would no longer be citizens of a state. They would no longer participate in *governmental* decision-making, and they would no longer be obligated to obey *governmental* authority. People would exchange their identities as citizens of states for those of comrades within communities. In this capacity, they would participate in resolving whatever social issues arose. If members of a communist society are to "hunt in the morning and fish in the afternoon," as Marx proposed,[15] they will need to discuss which animals and fishes should be protected as endangered species, the appropriate hunting and fishing seasons, and the weapons that humans can use to shoot and catch their prey. On such matters, members of communist societies would govern themselves, and this could be a demanding and time-consuming activity.

Most importantly, citizenship would be transformed from that which exists in liberal societies. Rather than viewing citizenship as a means of protecting rights and pursuing self-interests, the communist comrade is envisioned by Marx as someone who possesses an extraordinary public spirit. Such a person would live entirely within the public sphere, always concerned with society, understanding his own good as intertwined with the public good. Rather than viewing themselves as subjects who are required to obey the laws of the state, members of a communist society would submit gladly to the decisions of others in the community. If goods are abundant and if everyone is public-spirited, the decisions of self-governing comrades would hardly be oppressive, but would simply represent the (general) will of free men and women finally making their own history in accordance with their shared understanding of the good life.[16]

Communists: Transforming Oppressed People into Obedient Revolutionaries

Communists would agree with most Marxist ideas about citizenship, including the problematic status of being citizens of pre-revolutionary nation-states and the importance of defying the authorities of these regimes. Still, communists developed some ideas about "citizenship" that both extend and depart from those of orthodox Marxists.

According to communist doctrine, members of subordinate classes have particular roles to play during a revolution and particular obligations in the communities governed by communists immediately following the revolution. Many of these roles and duties were itemized in a list of "21 conditions" at the Congress of the Second Communist International in 1920.[17] The obligations included: an absolute ideological commitment to communism; a duty to establish underground and illegal organizations that would prepare for revolutionary action; aiding revolutionary activities among people in the colonies of the imperialist powers; supporting the USSR even if one were from another country; and adhering to the principle and practice of democratic centralism after a successful revolution, which included eliminating from the party ranks all so-called reformists, revisionists, and trade unionists.[18] Communists everywhere were expected to obey the executive committee of the International.

Communists emphasized considerably more differentiation between leaders and followers at the beginning of the revolution than in subsequent stages of progressing toward an ideal communist society. At the outset of the revolution, communists accepted the Leninist doctrine that followers had an obligation to subject themselves to the authority of party leaders, especially those in the Soviet Union. This strict obedience was largely maintained in the immediate aftermath of a successful revolution, while the Community Party consolidated its control over society. Under Stalin, complete obedience was strictly enforced. However, other governing communist regimes provided more opportunities to diminish the gap between leaders and followers. Under Tito, for example, Yugoslav workers had comparatively greater autonomy and decision-making discretion.

Additionally, as the transition into communism progressed, members of communist parties and regimes were to receive more and more freedom until that point at which they became autonomous laborers and public-spirited comrades. While different communist regimes had somewhat different conceptions of the role of "citizens" during the transition, these conceptions all gained their legitimacy from the belief that each provided a path that led to an ideal international community in which all people would live as comrades in harmony.

Fascists and Nazis: Mobilizing Dutiful Citizens for Purposes of State

Fascists and Nazis were essentially elitists who focused on the power and authority of rulers and gave less attention to questions of citizenship. Nevertheless, some principles can be suggested about who comprised citizens of fascist and Nazi communities.

Fascist and Nazi leaders stressed the importance of a strong nation and, thus, a united citizenry. In the case of Italian fascism, this meant having citizens who shared an Italian heritage and culture. In the case of Nazi Germany, this meant having a citizenry that was racially homogeneous. Both regimes opposed the admission of outsiders who did not conform to cultural or racial requirements, and both regimes attempted to restrict the emigration of those who did. For example, Mussolini's regime passed laws aimed at impeding emigration of those Italians who opposed its growing power during the 1920s.[19]

Both fascists and Nazis regarded citizens as essential resources in acquiring state power. Thus they sought extensive citizen mobilization behind governmental programs and policies. Fascist mobilization of the masses occurs when one leader rules, articulating the will and interests of the nation, and when the Fascist Party then rallies the masses to exert their energies on behalf of those national goals defined by the leader. Such mobilization involves citizen participation, but not in order that citizens could have political influence or secure their personal interests. In these perspectives, citizen participation is a measure of people's attachment, loyalty, and obedience to the regime. To develop loyalty and obedience to the state, citizens were encouraged to participate in party organizations and rallies.

In fascism and Nazism, citizens were expected to exhibit total obedience to state authority, and citizens had ethical virtue if they did their duty. To minimize social conflict, fascists and Nazis suppressed individual self-expression, freedom of speech, and involvements in civic associations. Instead of being given a catalogue of rights that they could claim against the state, citizens were provided with a list of duties specifying how they must contribute to the goals of the state.

Fascists claim to desire liberty but their understanding of liberty is very different from that of the liberals. Mussolini expressed the fascist conception of liberty in the following terms:

> [I]f liberty is to be the attribute of the real man and not of the scarecrow invented by the individualistic Liberalism, then Fascism is for liberty. It is for the only kind of liberty that is serious – the liberty of the State and of the individual in the State. Because, for the Fascist, all is comprised in the State and nothing spiritual or human exists – much less has any value – outside the State. In this respect Fascism is a totalizing concept, and the Fascist State – the unification and synthesis of every value – interprets, develops and potentiates the whole life of the people.[20]

And Alfredo Rocco declared:

> Our concept of liberty is that the individual must be allowed to develop his personality in behalf of the state [so that] freedom therefore is due to the citizen and to classes on condition that they exercise it in the interest of society as a whole and within the limits set by social exigencies, liberty being, like any other individual right, a concession of the state.[21]

Contemporary Liberals: Pursuing Inclusion and Expanding Rights

Contemporary liberals regard classical liberals as fairly reactionary on two matters regarding the composition of the citizenry. First, they think classical liberals did not live up to liberal ideals of equality, because they allowed racial minorities, women, and other marginalized groups to remain second-class citizens. Second, they think classical liberals placed undue emphasis on seeking a racially and ethnically homogeneous citizenry. We begin by considering these two issues.

Classical liberals made full citizenship contingent on competence, slowly extending citizenship rights as various kinds of people were deemed qualified. Contemporary liberals have rejected competence as a criterion for citizenship, asserting that all adults who are affected by political decisions should be citizens. Having adopted the principle of *maximal inclusion* into citizenship of all but the mentally defective, children, and transients,[22] liberals now focus on how many and which "outsiders" should be granted residency and made citizens.

During the twentieth century, liberal societies achieved levels of economic affluence, political liberty, social mobility, and welfare rights that have made them extremely attractive to people outside their borders. Without some restrictions on who could become citizens, those seeking admission would besiege liberal societies. Contemporary liberals understand that unrestricted immigration, whereby outsiders could simply choose to become citizens, raises several difficulties. As outsiders become residents, they can reduce the economic security of existing citizens, because of their willingness to work for wages below prevailing rates. Additionally, unrestricted immigration can threaten the liberal welfare state, because of the reluctance of taxpayers to maintain or extend economic entitlements if they believe that such programs will simply entice the poor from other countries to arrive on their shores to receive welfare. Most basically, unrestricted borders threaten the very idea of national sovereignty – that every nation has a right to decide, according to its own values and its own procedures, which outsiders to admit.[23]

Contemporary liberals nevertheless reject nativist conceptions of restricted admissions (or largely closed borders) in favor of extensive but qualified immigration. They admire the qualities of many newcomers to society, find morally appealing the idea of admitting the oppressed from other parts of the world, and recognize the extraordinary economic and cultural contributions that immigrants make to society. Liberals believe that admission criteria should give preference to those who seek asylum from political oppression in their native lands, whose extended families are already citizens, whose occupational skills are most likely to contribute to the economy, and whose political values and language lead to easy assimilation into society. However, such criteria should not be used to exclude certain applicants on racial, ethnic, or religious grounds, as the immigration policies of a liberal society must promote diversity, rather than nativist, prejudices.

Being or becoming a full citizen is important for three principal reasons: citizens acquire rights; citizens incur public obligations; and citizens obtain opportunities for political participation. Compared to classical liberals, contemporary liberals have developed fairly extensive conceptions of citizen rights, obligations, and participatory opportunities.

Contemporary liberals have expanded citizen rights, and they have tried to ensure that these rights have been extended to the lower classes, minority groups, women, and other previously marginalized citizens. Some of these extended rights – such as providing women and minorities with the right to vote – can be regarded as political rights to participate more fully in the democratic life of a liberal society. However, for the most part, the broader rights that contemporary liberals have supported involve claims that individuals have *against* the state (e.g., the right to privacy) or *upon* the state (e.g., the right to consume various public goods and services). By emphasizing such private and welfare rights, contemporary liberals have remained faithful to the conception of citizenship held by classical liberals. They view citizens as individuals who devote most of their lives to private enjoyments and to economic production and consumption. They have sought to emphasize and enhance the private sphere of life through public protections and provisions. Accordingly, they have de-emphasized those aspects of citizenship that propel individuals more strongly into the public realm.

Nevertheless, contemporary liberals – perhaps liberal theorists more than liberal politicians – recognize that citizens have political obligations, a term they prefer over "duties." While duties can be disconnected from rights, as in fascism, liberal obligations are intimately connected with citizen rights. Most basically, the rights that governments secure for each citizen impose obligations on other citizens to obey those laws that secure these rights. Each person's property rights impose an obligation on all other citizens to obey no-trespass laws. Each person's right to due process if accused of a crime imposes an obligation on all citizens to serve as jurors if called. The right of citizens to be secure from foreign invasion may impose military obligations on citizens. During World War II and the Korean and Vietnam wars, American liberals supported a draft, and toward the end of the Vietnamese conflict, they supported a lottery as a means of making young men equally vulnerable to the draft. However, they now support reinstituting a draft only in cases of national emergency, and believe that citizen obligations in support of more limited military conflicts, such as that in Iraq, can be met by paying the taxes necessary to recruit a voluntary army.

The expansion of welfare rights by contemporary liberals is, at least in principle, accompanied by parallel obligations on citizens to pay for welfare entitlements through higher taxes. Citizens may express their welfare rights as claims against the government, but they are really claims on fellow citizens, as governments are merely relatively efficient and fair instruments for delivering these rights and collecting the tax obligations of citizens. Of course, most citizens want rights but not responsibilities, giving liberal politicians incentives to emphasize rights while minimizing obligations. When contemporary liberals have stressed obligations, they have usually encountered hostile responses. When President Kennedy said, "Ask not what your country can do for you; ask what you can do for your country," he was chastised in the press for forgetting that government was the servant of the people. When Walter Mondale promised to raise taxes when accepting the Democratic nomination for President in 1984, he sealed his defeat during the general election. During the 2000 and 2004 presidential campaigns, the more liberal candidates – Al Gore and John Kerry – felt the need to be more restrained than Mondale had been on taxes.

In summary, liberal theorists insist that the welfare state is based on an implicit social contract in which citizens define rights corresponding to their perceived basic common needs, develop governmental programs fulfilling these needs, and obligate themselves to contribute their fair share to the costs of these programs. But, in the everyday world, liberals "have not had a well-developed public language of responsibility to match our language of rights."[24] Minimally, liberal theorists hope to reestablish the intimate link between rights and responsibilities.[25] Obedience to just laws, involvement in public service, and payment of necessary taxes are responsibilities that citizens must discharge if they hope to retain the rights provided by a liberal state. Additionally, some liberal theorists sense the need for a conception of citizen responsibilities that goes beyond those obligations that are merely the flip side of our rights. Certainly, citizens have obligations to future generations and to the preservation of the natural environment, even if there are no living human rights-holders on the other side of these obligations.[26] However, it remains an unresolved question whether such responsibilities can be reconciled within an ideology that is as rights-oriented as contemporary liberalism.

While many contemporary liberals seek to develop a thicker conception of citizen obligations, they normally reject a duty to engage in political participation. For liberals, there can be no duty to vote, because the right to vote also implies the right not to vote. Rather than impose penalties for non-voting, liberals are content to increase opportunities for citizens to vote and engage in other modes of participation, believing such opportunities will make it easier for them to acquire such virtues as toleration and public spiritedness.[27]

While classical liberals focused on voting, contemporary liberals have encouraged citizens to participate between elections in organized interest groups, in ad hoc protest groups, and in social movements. None of these forms of participation requires prolonged, continuous, or extensive involvements, and they are thus suited to liberal citizens whose goals remain outside the realm of politics, but who wish to pursue particular interests or ideals politically. Citizens can join those organizations that lobby on behalf of their interests, even if they do nothing more than pay annual dues. Citizens whose primary interests are threatened by such things as an economic development project or by a particular governmental program can temporarily join with other threatened citizens to protest these projects and programs, and then return to their apolitical lives when the issue has passed. Citizens who seek larger but specific ideals can become part of social movements, as liberals have been deeply involved in labor, civil rights, women's, GLBT (gay, lesbian, bisexual, transgender), environmental, and anti-war movements.

As members of protest groups and social movements, liberals have sometimes engaged in *civil disobedience*. Acts of civil disobedience are carried out for limited public ends using premeditated but nonviolent methods that are recognized as being illegal or of contested legality.[28] Martin Luther King, Jr. and his followers in the civil rights movement provide the most prominent example of civil disobedience in American history.[29] King sought limited goals by calling for an end to segregation laws but not for the overthrow of the racist regimes that created such laws. Rather than seeking some private advantage, he addressed the rights of a large but oppressed group. He employed limited means, as his direct action tactics sought to create an atmosphere of crisis without involving violence. He acknowledged that his actions violated existing laws and was prepared to accept the penalties for his disobedience, even while pointing out the injustice of these laws.

While liberals believe that citizens normally have an obligation to obey the laws of government, they also regard civil disobedience as morally legitimate. Liberals recognize that citizens have multiple obligations. Sometimes their obligations to their families, to fellow members of oppressed groups, or to humanity may conflict with their obligation to obey governmental laws. In such situations, disobeying questionable laws may contribute to a good society. Existing liberal societies, of course, fail to realize perfectly their liberal principles. Within liberal societies, tyrants can acquire political power, and well-motivated public officials can create oppressive and unjust laws. Liberals believe that a society that does not respect and even encourage courageous acts of civil disobedience runs the danger of producing citizens who will submit to tyranny and injustice. Civil disobedience serves both to educate liberal citizens about civic virtues and to correct departures from liberal ideals.

Contemporary Conservatives: Developing More Responsible Citizens

It is hard to find in contemporary conservatism a set of principles that provide unambiguous guidance on most questions of citizenship. Indeed, their sometimes conflicting predispositions can cut both ways on the question of admitting outsiders as citizens. On the one hand, their celebration of free markets has led some contemporary conservatives to support the reduction of governmental restraints on the free flow of workers across borders.[30] On the other hand, worries about cultural cohesion have prompted other conservatives to want to limit immigration, particularly of persons coming from those parts of the world that do not share the values that have historically predominated in the US. Perhaps conservative views here can best be characterized as favoring immigration of those who contribute to the national economy (for example, by accepting low-paying jobs) as long as such immigrants assimilate reasonably well into the national culture.

The issue of citizen participation has also divided contemporary conservatives. Conservative populists have called for empowering "average citizens" and have developed sophisticated techniques for identifying and mobilizing conservative voters. In America, they have developed a broad network of national lobbies to further conservative causes on Capitol Hill. They have called on their supporters to become active in local politics, especially on such social issues as allowing prayers in schools and denying access to abortion clinics.

Nevertheless, many conservatives – especially conservative intellectuals – have rejected calls for greater citizen involvement, questioning the capacity of citizens to have the wisdom, technical knowledge, and virtue to support appropriate policy choices.

In his classic work, *Capitalism, Socialism, and Democracy*, Joseph Schumpeter (1883–1950) developed a realistic theory of democracy that claimed that the proper role of citizens is limited to choosing a government among competing parties.[31] According to Schumpeter, greater citizen involvement in politics should be discouraged because citizens tend to be motivated by irrational mob impulses and because their preferences can be manipulated by demagogues. During the 1970s, many conservatives endorsed writings by Samuel Huntington that warned against a "democratic distemper" in societies with too much citizen participation, which was seen as a disruptive force in politics.[32] From this perspective, citizen participation is citizen demand-making. The interests of various groups of citizens become demands for rights and claims on the public purse, which involve an expansion of governmental activity. But government cannot and should not satisfy all the competing claims on it. When citizen participants fail to have their supposed rights satisfied, they become cynical and disrespectful of government, leading to a crisis of governmental authority. Thus, except for voting, citizen participation in governance should be discouraged.

Citizen involvement in voluntary associations is something all contemporary conservatives support. Rather than demanding that government be expanded to provide assistance to various needy populations, citizens ought to join various local charitable and service organizations that provide help to the disadvantaged, that build character, and that create a sense of community among those who participate. George H. Bush described such voluntary groups as a "thousand points of light." Both he and his son, George W. Bush, believe that citizen involvement in such groups evoked the true spirit of American citizenship. Of course, contemporary liberals also celebrate citizen involvement in voluntary associations, but they see voluntarism as only a complement to political action; when conservatives reduce state welfare, the decent thing for a liberal to do is to work to restore welfare programs *and* increase contributions to the United Way.[33] In contrast, contemporary conservatives see citizen involvement in voluntary organizations as an alternative to the liberal "nanny" welfare state.

Contemporary conservatives, of course, recognize the importance of citizen obligations, but many increasingly subordinate the political obligations of citizens to the cultivation of responsible citizens. They believe that an emphasis on political obligation implies an authoritative government that issues commands which citizens must obey. Of course, all conservatives agree that citizens must obey those laws that governments pass to achieve an orderly society and that citizens must meet their public obligations by paying necessary taxes. But governments too often impose excessive tax obligations on citizens in order to provide dubious governmental programs. Many of these programs, such as excessive welfare provisions, enable citizens to pursue irresponsible lives. Contemporary conservatives want a government that encourages responsible individual behavior. Conservatives celebrated the replacement of welfare programs like AFDC (Aid to Families with Dependent Children), which encouraged irresponsible behavior,[34] and the creation of programs like TANF (Temporary Assistance to Needy Families), which encourage people to become responsible for their own needs instead of making them dependent on government. Contemporary conservatives seek to reform old-age insurance programs – like Social Security in the US – to give citizens responsibility for making their own investment choices.[35]

Conservatives generalize this emphasis on creating responsible citizens to encouraging citizens to acquire a wide range of moral virtues. Conservatives agree that liberal societies have done far too little to cultivate the virtue of citizens. Conservative philosophers like Leo Strauss condemn what they call the moral relativism of liberalism, claiming that liberals in effect teach "that there is nothing a man should be ashamed of . . . denying that there are some things that are intrinsically high and others which are intrinsically low."[36] A cottage industry of conservative "virtuecrats" – including William Bennett, Laura Savage, and Lynn Chaney – have written endlessly on this theme. They claim that liberals have preached an ethic of self-expression, but what is needed is an ethic of self-control.

Nevertheless, conservatives are wary of proclaiming a thick communitarian ethos, or a particular conception of citizen virtue, that all must follow. Rather than enforcing a strict list of virtues, mainstream conservatives believe that governments have only a limited role to play in developing the virtue and character of citizens. Legislatures can pass laws regulating behaviors that almost everyone regards as vices: prostitution, drug abuse, pornography, and so forth. Legislatures can reform those public policies – such as no-fault divorce laws – that provide opportunities for persons to abandon responsible behavior. Schools can promote good character in children by emphasizing academic achievement, by instilling discipline through homework, and by praising conduct that conforms to agreed-upon standards of human virtue. The police can apprehend and the courts can punish those who violate the rights of others and who undermine social order. Stiffer sentences for crimes, fewer opportunities for parole, and increasing the size of police forces may be the best way to deter deviant behavior, letting people know that crime does not pay and that access to the good life requires being a lawful and hard-working citizen.

Nevertheless, conservatives believe that individual liberty and social order can be threatened when state power is used for moral crusades.[37] According to James Buckley, for example, government ought not to prohibit smoking; instead, the legitimate role of government ends when it alerts the public to the dangers of smoking. Ultimately, the individual must choose.[38] Rather than strict governmental controls, most people will respond to familiar guidelines such as those noted by conservative columnist George Will: "There are three not-at-all recondite rules for avoiding poverty: graduate from high school, don't have a baby until you are married, and don't marry while you are a teenager. Among people who obey these rules, poverty is minimal."[39]

James Q. Wilson argues that citizens do not require government to instruct them on the moral virtues, as most people have deep intuitions about the importance of self-control, sympathy, fairness, and duty. What is required is that citizens confidently acknowledge their moral sensibilities, repudiate the false skepticism and tolerance that liberals have promoted, and speak out against immoral behavior. It is the role of robust social institutions – families, churches, schools, and other voluntary associations – to reinforce our innate sense of virtue and to strengthen the character of citizens.[40]

The Radical Right: Privileging Property Rights and Instilling Virtue

The libertarian and communitarian voices within the radical right stress very different concerns about citizenship. Libertarians seek open borders and extensive rights. Communitarians seek to restrict admission into citizenship and emphasize the responsibilities of citizenship.

Many libertarians seek *open admissions* policies that would allow people everywhere the liberty to reside and work where they wish and to become citizens of the political communities governing those locations.[41] The CATO Institute's Dan Griswold has been quoted as saying, "The problem with illegal immigration is not the immigration; it's that it's illegal."[42] In general, libertarians support open borders, because they are morally committed to accommodating the freedom of people to locate where they want, and because they see immigrants as positive contributors to both the cultures and economies of the countries where they locate. Libertarians see immigration restrictions as "a form of socialism. They involve bloated budgets, bureaucracy, central planning, taxation, abusive police powers, intrusions in the marketplace, and widespread corruption."[43] American libertarians also point out that the Constitution makes no provision for the federal government to limit immigration.

Similarly, global neoliberals believe territorial boundaries should be relatively permeable. According to Norberg, "It is a profound error to regard immigrants as a burden on a country. They represent a manpower and consumption boost that leads to market growth. More immigration means more people to work, spend, and hatch new ideas."[44] Norberg adds that the US and Europe will need more immigrants in the future to pay taxes to finance public programs for aging and retiring populations. Yet most globalists stop short of calling for open admissions. Instead, they want nations to have fewer restrictions on immigration.

Libertarians and globalists adopt principles of citizen rights and obligations that they regard as appropriate to the era of globalization. Their conception of citizen rights – the accesses, services, and goods that are equally available to all members of the community – focus more on opportunities than conditions. People should have equal legal opportunities to acquire property, employment, and profits, but they have no right to equal – or even minimal – economic resources. In short, libertarians and neoliberals seek to return to the more limited citizen rights emphasized by classical liberals. In an age of globalization, they believe the welfare rights supported by the left must be reduced. They regard welfare rights as undesirable, because they infringe on the property rights of others, they reduce work incentives, and they distort markets. The reduction of welfare rights would ease fears that relatively unrestrictive immigration policies would attract unproductive poor people.

Libertarians and globalists do not deny that people are obligated to abide by the laws, economic regulations, and tax codes of the political communities in which they reside or do business. But these should be far less onerous than the excessive regulations and taxes imposed by contemporary liberal and socialist governments.

Like liberals, libertarians and globalists do not uphold idealist conceptions of citizenship – that citizens should be highly informed, community-regarding, and participatory in politics. For example, in the UK Margaret Thatcher accepted a "public choice" theory of democracy that assumed citizens should vote on the basis of their interests – and that such sporadic involvement in elections is sufficient to hold democratic officeholders accountable.[45] Such voices claim that community members are not so much citizens as economic actors (consumers, investors, and workers). They "vote" most effectively with their wallets, spending their incomes on the goods they prefer and investing their wealth in those opportunities throughout the world that will be most profitable.[46] Globalists stress that investor decisions to move their capital in and out of countries are more apt indicators of the effectiveness of public policies than are the votes cast by citizens.

The more communitarian voices within the radical right strongly disagree with libertarian and globalist views of citizenship. Rather than open borders and reduce citizen obligations, cultural conservatives and traditional communitarians generally wish to restrict immigration and emphasize our political obligations. National protectionists like Pat Buchanan are particularly concerned with the rising levels of illegal immigrants in America, maintaining that their presence contributes to unemployment among American citizens and puts downward pressure on wages. Cultural conservatives fear that the heavily Latino characteristics of illegal immigrants – almost 80 percent have arrived in the US from Latin American countries, especially Mexico – can lead to a bifurcated country, because Latinos often retain their Spanish language and Latino cultures, do not assimilate into the existing culture as readily as previous immigrants, and are fairly concentrated in the American southwest where they have historical territorial claims.[47] For national protectionists and cultural conservatives, such immigration is a recipe for national political weakness, social instability, and perhaps secessionist movements.[48]

Traditional communitarians believe that citizens need to have allegiance to a substantive conception of the common good in order for them to have meaningful lives. In the United States, this would be the culture and values that Americans have inherited from their Anglo ancestors. They bequeathed to us a culture that stresses such things as Christian morality, the work ethic, the rule of law, and conceptions of human excellence represented in European art and literature.[49] If citizens are not deeply embedded in cultures that stress such values and instead are set adrift in a liberal world that stresses the equal worth of all cultures and an individualism that refuses guidance from the dominant culture in a society, they will be doomed to lives lacking clearly defined purposes and meanings.[50] But the ultimate grounds for widespread allegiance to a communitarian conception of the common good may be that political communities perish if "the fount of public virtues has run dry."[51] Political communities weaken and become unstable if cultures do not provide instruction about social deviance, teach respect for authority, specify appropriate roles, and emphasize the importance of loyalty and fulfilling one's duties. Fearing that the fount of public virtues has indeed run dry, traditional communitarians believe that it is time to make clear that citizen rights must be accompanied by citizen responsibilities, and that our Bill of Rights may require a complementary Bill of Duties.[52]

The Radical Left: Embracing Multiple and Deep Citizenships

Like other pluralists, the radical left acknowledges that people are primarily citizens of a nation-state (and its various sub-national units), but it emphasizes that most people are in some sense citizens of many communities. People belong to the global community and to non-state communities (e.g., industrial enterprises, trade unions, minority groups, and women's groups). These multiple belongings are all part of our public life, as they are political in their effects. Like polities, non-state communities pursue collective goals, distribute social goods, and impose obligations on their members; thus membership in non-state communities resembles citizenship in states. While all pluralists are in favor of people having multiple community memberships, the radical left is inclined to call these "multiple citizenships" and to stress the extensive rights and obligations that attend them.

With regard to the question of "who are citizens?" of a nation, most outlooks on the radical left look forward to the day when national borders no longer prevent people from living where they wish, but they recognize the same conditions that prompt liberals to establish (generous) restrictions on immigration. Michael Walzer, an influential civic communitarian, points out that open admissions into nations would undermine the capacity of countries to be "communities of character" in which citizens recognize and honor extensive obligations to one another and respond generously to each other's needs.[53] However, cosmopolitan theorists are more eager to pursue justice on a global scale, and they often advocate immigration policies that are more open than those advanced by civic communitarians, contemporary liberals, and other pluralists.[54] They would more readily admit economic refugees, persons who lack economic employment opportunities in their native lands and seek jobs in more developed societies.[55] Nevertheless, cosmopolitan theorists usually distinguish between opening borders to migrants seeking job opportunities and granting citizenship to migrants. Nations have fewer legitimate reasons for denying immigrants opportunities to pursue employment opportunities within their borders than for denying citizenship and corresponding political and economic rights to such immigrants.[56] Opening borders to job seekers can help reduce international inequalities in economic opportunities and circumstances, while withholding citizenship can enable nations to maintain sovereignty on the fundamental question of who comprise the citizens of a country. Of course, "guest workers" in developed societies maintain their citizenship in their native lands. But the radical left is uncomfortable with permanent guest workers within their nations, because they become second-class citizens whose deprivation of fundamental rights is experienced as an injustice and can be a source of division and instability. Thus, the radical left seeks clear criteria specifying the requirements for guest workers to become citizens and they would like to expedite naturalization processes. Although each country can determine its own criteria, the radical left emphatically rejects that people from different parts of the world and with different racial and ethnic characteristics should be subject to different standards and processes for admission to citizenship.

For the radical left, citizenship involves more extensive participation, rights, and obligations than for contemporary liberals. While liberals believe that citizens are best served by limiting their participation to voting in periodic elections, joining interest groups, and engaging in occasional acts of protest, the radical left calls for much more extensive citizen participation. Citizen participation should begin in families, schools, churches, neighborhood groups, and – most importantly – the workplaces of daily life. By actively participating in such local communities, citizens attain a greater sense of belonging, concern, and mutuality with others. Through such participation, they can use local groups as vehicles for solving common problems and thus exercise greater collective control over their lives. Greater participation in local communities and workplaces will also help to politicize the relatively disadvantaged who don't participate fully in national elections and policy-making processes. Greater and more representative participation at the national level can begin to rectify the limitations of representative democracy, bring more popular control over government, and generate citizen pressures for public provisions that are widely needed by citizens. Greater participation in global governance might result in policies that are more favorable to developing nations, labor, and environmental concerns than the easing of restrictions on global capital that has thus far occurred.

While seeking extensive citizen participation, the radical left understands the difficulties of achieving it. Orthodox pluralism presumes citizens can easily be mobilized into activists and organized into groups to pursue collective and group interests, but the radical left recognizes that there are real obstacles to such mobilization.[57]

First, and most generally, citizenship has increasingly become personalized in ways that make citizens less available for collective mobilization to achieve collective benefits. According to Matthew Crenson and Benjamin Ginsberg, political leaders and activists have restructured politics in ways that permit them to pursue their interests without mobilizing citizen support. For example, candidates for public office have learned how to turn out reliable supporters and turn off potential supporters of their opponents, and thus seldom seek to attract new voters to their campaigns. At the same time, leaders of social movements have increasingly turned to insider strategies and litigation to pursue their goals, while turning away from mass mobilization strategies.[58] As a result, America has become "a nation of emphatically private citizens – consumers and clients who find it difficult to express coherent common interests through collective political action."[59] For example, as private citizens we will take advantage of voucher programs enabling us to send our children to better schools or file lawsuits to redress discrimination against ourselves. But we are less inclined to become public citizens who pursue collective interests – for example, joining others to attain more resources and other improvements for inadequate public schools generally or to enact legislation that more harshly penalizes discriminatory practices generally.

Second, those who govern entities ranging from global institutions like the International Monetary Fund to local special districts often believe that their policies involve highly technical issues that should be resolved by experts and specialists; insofar as they are willing to consult with the public, they are more likely to listen to those who own or run businesses directly influenced by their policies than to the broader public whose concerns are seen as more peripheral.

Third, existing pluralist regimes often have narrow preconceptions about what is political. A whole host of issues are banished from consideration on governmental agendas, because they are reserved for a broader private sphere.[60] For example, it is hard for people who are having difficulties with their landlords to get governments to address such issues if relationships between renters and landlords are considered matters that are reserved for the private market (unless there is some breach of contract that might involve the courts).

Fourth, the working class, minorities, and other previously excluded groups often confront extensive informal barriers to their equal participation. Collective action problems seem to be especially acute for leaders of marginalized segments of the public. Because they seek policies that would benefit all members of marginalized groups, their followers often wish to be free-riders who receive the benefits of successful participation by others without becoming personally involved.[61] The marginalized are less likely than more advantaged citizens to belong to civic organizations that form the social capital and trust that reduce the barriers to collective action and contribute to effective citizen participation.[62]

The radical left often holds contentious models of democracy that suggest that there are certain opportunities for the formation of oppositional publics.[63] For example, they claim that international organizations like the World Trade Organization (WTO) are not democratic because they have a predetermined agenda and follow exclusionary processes, even though their policies have a wide impact on the environment and on labor and other excluded constituencies. As far as the radical left is concerned, the meetings of the WTO provide moments of opportunity for the excluded to see clearly their marginality and the oppressive outcomes that lie ahead if the WTO remains unchallenged. Such moments prompt radicals to contest globalization by organizing alternative venues like the World Social Forum (WSF), by demanding that their concerns be included in trade negotiations, and by demonstrating a willingness to fight for fairer outcomes.[64] The radical left believes that those with dominant power within existing arrangements will not give in to their challengers without a fight; thus radical democrats are committed to finding opportunities and discovering tactics to allow ordinary citizens to fight for social justice and more democracy.

Among the radical left, civic communitarians have emphasized the need to instill various civic virtues into citizens that will make them more effective participants. Citizens need to be oriented not just toward their own interests; they must also seek the public good and social justice. They must be willing to invest their time and energy for public purposes. They must develop the skills and understandings necessary to be effective in pluralist politics. They must learn how to frame issues and propose policies that address broad public concerns, and they must learn how to give sound reasons for their goals that are understandable and persuasive to the many other participants in pluralist politics who do not immediately share their goals. They must be persistent, seeing both failed protests and small successes as building blocks for more effective participation in the future.

The radical left believes that liberal governments impose inadequate obligations on citizens. At best, liberals connect citizen obligations to citizen rights, since the liberal sees the social contract as specifying that "I should pay the community back for what I receive from it." The radical left believes that citizens should take a less individualistic and more far-sighted approach to what the social contract means. A more socialist social contract is not so much an agreement among individuals about their individual rights as it is a broad understanding among citizens about their common needs and their obligations to cooperate among themselves to satisfy these needs. What people need is not just individual rights but community itself, and they are thus obligated to provide each other with the respect and support required to sustain themselves as a community.[65] Additionally, citizens must participate in a collective decision-making process that enables them to identify what all citizens need to thrive in their communities. The radical left does not try to provide a universal list of citizen obligations, because these will depend on what each community regards as common needs and necessary obligations. But the various strands within the radical left regard the communal provisions of and accompanying obligations on citizens of the American polity as inadequate.[66]

The difference between liberalism and the radical left in their views regarding citizen obligation can be illustrated by considering the issue of public service. President Clinton's proposal that young people should work for one or two years in public service jobs in order to pay back college loans was an attempt by a contemporary liberal to extend the liberal conception of citizen obligation. Citizens – but only some citizens – were asked to serve, and their obligation to serve was directly tied to the receipt of a concrete and material personal benefit (student aid) that was otherwise unavailable to them. In contrast, radical democrats often call for "a program of universal citizen service [that] would enlist every American citizen – male and female alike – in a service corps for one to two years of either military or nonmilitary training and service."[67] Participants in such universal service programs would get some individual benefits such as occupational training, but the greatest advantages would be "fellowship and camaraderie, common activity, teamwork, service for and with others, and a sense of community . . . cooperation . . . and mutuality."[68] While extensive and mandatory in comparison to liberal service, radical left proposals for public service are far less extensive and coercive than those of the fascist state, because they cover only a brief period in the lives of youths and because people are provided choices as to where they will serve.

Liberals are leery of radical left proposals for extensive citizenship. Reflecting the liberal preference for private leisure over public participation, Oscar Wilde (1854–1900) once commented: "The problem with socialism is that it takes too many evenings." The radical left replies to such a criticism by questioning the liberal belief that life can be segmented into a public life of citizenship and a private life of personal satisfaction. For the radical left, all life is necessarily social life. By recognizing and acting upon the need of people to participate in decision-making in both voluntary associations and polities and by accepting their obligations to others in the various communities to which they belong, the radical left hopes to further its goal of approaching communal harmony, social equality, and political democracy.

The Extreme Right: Restricting Citizenship

Perhaps the most well-known aspiration of the contemporary extreme right is the restriction of immigration of outsiders into their political communities. In the US, such white nationalist organizations as Stormfront have declared "immigration to be the single most destructive policy that has been implemented by the government."[69] Among the many extremist parties that have fared reasonably well in elections during the past decade by stressing their opposition to immigration are Jean-Marie Le Pen's National Front in France, Jörg Haider's Freedom Party of Austria, and the New Zealand National Front. Supporters of right-wing organizations believe that their nations have homogeneous racial and ethnic identities, that those of other ethnicities should be denied admission, and that legal and (and especially illegal) immigrants should be deported. Minimally, the extreme right emphasizes that outsiders who arrive in pluralist societies for economic reasons should be denied citizenship, excluded from many rights and services, and contained within sub-communities of the country. In some instances, the extreme right calls for the partitioning of countries to achieve racial homogeneity. For example, American white supremacists often single out the Pacific Northwest as the territory for a future all-white nation.[70] The Afrikaner Weerstandsbeweging (AWB) in South Africa is committed to the restoration of an Afrikaner (Boer) republic – often called "Boerstaat" – within South Africa.

It is more the social and political consequences – rather than the economic ones – of citizenship policies that most concern the extreme right. Their goal is to have a unified citizenry so that dominant and traditional cultural values are not challenged and so that political power will remain with (or return to) those groups that have long dominated a community. The vision of the extreme right is of political communities comprised of citizens having extensive ethnic and culturally commonalities, facilitating moral unity.

The extreme right is far from unified, however, on the importance and substance of rights and responsibilities of citizens. The American extreme right is strongly oriented toward individual rights. They believe that God or the Constitution provides many inalienable rights, such as absolute property rights and the right to bear arms. And they often deny a duty to obey laws, pay taxes, or otherwise submit to distant governmental officials who are seen as illegitimate. Some members of the Patriot movement claim that there is no obligation to obey authority above the county level.

In contrast, supporters of Islamic fundamentalism are little concerned with individual rights, and instead emphasize obligations. Since Islam means "to submit" to the will of Allah, its adherents believe that Islamic citizens should submit completely to the decrees of those Islamic leaders who understand and embody Allah's will. Islamic fundamentalists seek to follow the path of righteous living, which means surrounding themselves with others having similar conceptions of morality and faithfully executing the duties stressed by Islamic authorities. Since many Muslims live in countries whose leaders are "infidels" – either non-Muslims or corrupted Muslims – such citizens may have duties to actively oppose such impure regimes. According to some Muslim extremists, opposition to infidels may impose a duty on righteous Islamic citizens to become suicide bombers.

The Extreme Left: Changing Passive Citizens into Contentious Ones

The extreme left has little to say about such issues as restrictions on immigration, the presence of second-class citizens, the adequacy of citizen rights, or the obligations of citizens within pluralist societies. The far left would doubtlessly question and oppose the way these issues are currently handled, but its attention is focused on the character of citizens within pluralist societies and how citizen deficiencies must be overcome if the inadequacies of existing pluralist societies are to be redressed.

Elements of the extreme left sometimes provide a theory of citizenship that suggests that the deficient democracies that presently exist are the result of the nature of the citizens of these democracies. The extreme left agrees with the radical left that stronger democracy is the basic cure for the ills of the world, but they see such strong democracy as being compromised from below by deformed citizens as much as it is compromised from above by how various power agents dominate citizens. William Ophuls, for example, declares that pluralist democracy has degenerated into "mobocracy."[71] Liberalism has reduced citizenship to occasional acts of voting in which we choose among candidates for political office as we choose among soaps; we cast ballots for those with name recognition and by how well they have been marketed and sold to us. Globalization has reduced our functional choices to candidates whose commitments to neoliberal policies are only marginally different, in large part because most citizens want elected officials that will pursue policies designed to satisfy their every economic wish. When ordinary citizens join interest or protest groups to influence political decisions between elections, they behave more like consumers of governmental goods and services than as citizens.

Such a diagnosis differs little from that of the radical left, but the prescriptions offered by the radical and extreme left to cure this disease are quite different. The radical left wants citizens to become re-engaged in redistributive politics, taking part in broad-based collective actions aimed at creating public policies that improve the lives of those at the bottom of the economic ladder. Given this orientation toward social justice in the distribution of material benefits, the radical left has little sympathy for the politics of post-materialism.[72] In contrast, the extremist left sees the materialism of the radical left as evidence of a narrow vision. The extreme left stresses the importance of citizens de-emphasizing the acquisition of material goods that are zero-sum in character (the more I have, the less you have) and instead pursuing post-material goods that are non-zero-sum in character (the more I have, the more we all have). Deep greens stress the importance of "spiritual" values that involve people living in harmony with nature and humans throughout the world, even if this means significant reductions in standards of living.[73] Hardt and Negri call on citizens to be more oriented toward *immaterial* production and consumption:

When we take off the blinders of capitalist society that limit our vision, we can see with Marx that material wealth, including commodities, property, and money, is not an end in itself. This recognition should not send us to some ascetic abnegation. The real wealth, which is an end in itself, resides in the common; it is the sum of the pleasures, desires, capacities, and needs we all share. The common wealth is the real and proper object of production.[74]

While denying a commitment to the kind of asceticism that is common among deep greens, Hardt and Negri direct citizens toward the production of immaterial goods like knowledge and social relationships and toward the satisfaction that arises from having access to common property rather than being preoccupied with acquiring private property. For the extreme left, instilling in citizens a post-material ethic is of fundamental importance. From their perspective, people need to understand that their freedoms to pursue narrow and ultimately destructive material self-interests or class interests must be limited by their broader duties to others, to future generations, and to the land.[75]

Precisely how such an ethic is to take hold is a matter of disagreement among the far left. Perhaps their most distinctive attitude is a deep pessimism that such a trans-formation can take place, since the needs of global capitalism to market its goods and its capacities to dominate citizen outlooks will always make citizens materialists whose main motivation will be to acquire more wealth and material goods than others.[76] While Hardt and Negri expressed such pessimism in their first book, *Empire*, they are much more optimistic in *Multitude*. Here they find traces of more enlightened people throughout the world, especially those engaged in immaterial production of ideas and relationships who are becoming increasingly networked. This germ of "the multitude" is collaborating and cooperating to achieve social and immaterial production. While Hardt and Negri insist that such networking thus far only gener-ates the potential for a vast transformation in human consciousness, they believe that the present global system is unsustainable, in much the same way that Marx thought capitalism was unsustainable, and that the "mechanism of desire" to escape the domination of Empire "will thrust us like an arrow into that living future."[77]

Conclusions

Pluralists agree on several basic ideas about the distribution of citizenship within political communities. First, and perhaps most basically, they insist that people have the right to renounce their citizenship and leave a community. Coercion cannot be used to force people to remain in political communities against their will and without at least their tacit consent. Second, pluralists do not endorse a parallel right of out-siders to become citizens of a community simply on the basis of their own free choice. Instead, existing communities, in order to have control over their own character and destiny, have the right to determine whether or not someone who wants to be a citizen will be extended that opportunity. As a consequence, pluralists recognize the need to develop just admission standards, criteria, and processes. However, this right to establish admission policies applies only to the most broad political communities, like the United States and the European Union. Neither American states nor towns can exclude citizens, and nations within the European Union must abide by their broader agreements regarding the free movement of citizens within the Union.[78] Secondary associations – like country clubs and sororities – have the right to establish their own admission policies, though their eligibility for governmental benefits may be dependent on meeting politically defined standards of nondiscrimination and other components of just admission criteria.

Third, pluralists recognize that people who have long resided within the community are entitled to equal citizenship and the rights and obligations that citizenship entails. Perhaps recent immigrants must undergo naturalization processes and the young must undergo maturation processes, but these are required only to prepare such people for full citizenship, to familiarize them with their fundamental rights and commensurate obligations, and not to create a permanent group of second-class citizens or alien residents with lesser or no rights.[79] Of course, liberal democratic societies have not always respected these standards, as women, racial minorities, and other marginalized populations were historically treated as second-class citizens. In times of war and international insecurity, liberal democracies have also denied certain legal rights to those citizens with similar racial, ethnic, or religious backgrounds as their enemies. The forced relocation and interment of 120,000 Japanese-Americans during World War II illustrates this departure of equal rights. The social intolerance and unequal administration of legal rights of Arabic-Americans after 9/11 also has raised many questions about gaps between pluralist ideals and practices regarding equal citizenship. The removal of various barriers to full citizenship and the elimination of gaps between ideals and practices regarding equal citizenship are marks of a more mature pluralist society.

A fourth area of consensus among pluralists is that citizen rights should be fairly extensive. Political liberty (the right to vote and hold public office), freedom of thought and conscience, freedom of speech and assembly, privacy rights, legal rights (freedom from arbitrary arrest, the right to a fair trial, etc.), and various economic liberties are widely regarded as central to a pluralist society.

A fifth area of consensus is that there should be a basic correspondence between the rights that citizens have and their obligations. Most basically this means that if you possess a basic right, you are obligated to honor the equivalent right for others. When considering economic, property, and welfare rights, this correspondence rule is sometimes breeched in ways that undermine effective pluralist politics. To curry favor with voters, politicians can enact laws providing certain rights to citizens – such as the right to an adequate education or entitlements to various welfare programs – but they are often reluctant to impose corresponding tax obligations on citizens to pay for these entitlements. While it is easy to agree in the abstract on the principle that rights entail corresponding obligations, pluralist democracies are challenged to impose on citizens the just obligations that are required to provide the rights that citizens demand.

One consequence of this difficulty is that friends of pluralism will disagree on the rights that should be provided. Contemporary conservatives and those on the radical right normally argue for a reduction of welfare rights in order to minimize the tax obligations of citizens. Contemporary liberals and the radical left have argued for fewer property rights and against the right to bear arms, arguing that such rights impose risks and burdens for others in society. Such disagreements are, of course, the stuff of ordinary pluralist politics, and are resolved by appeals to political principles regarding freedom and justice and by having the political power to put one's principles and interests into law.

Another area where pluralists disagree about citizenship is on immigration policy. While contemporary liberals, the radical left, and globalists favor relatively unrestrictive admissions policies, many voices on the radical right and many contemporary conservatives seek more restrictive admissions policies. Because pluralists agree on the right of a nation to set just admission standards, there is nothing inherently wrong with denying admission and citizenship to some applicants seeking to enter a pluralist society. However, the extreme right goes too far when it advocates policies that are offensive to many citizens who are already members of pluralist societies. Demands to expel African-Americans or to deny further immigration of Blacks into America are insulting to African-Americans and others who value the racial and ethnic pluralism of our society. Radical right proposals like that of Samuel Huntington to admit only 150,000 immigrants from Latin America is arguably within the bounds of the rights of a nation to have control of its borders.[80] While pluralists could never accept efforts to exclude Mexicans and other Latinos from America, the right to self-determination of pluralist societies could justify democratic deliberation on proposals to stem the influx of Latinos so that newcomers might better reflect the existing ethnic composition of the community, are less likely to form ethnically homo-geneous sub-communities, and are unlikely to bring about an ethnically bifurcated society.[81] For pluralists, such deliberations must focus on the kind of society America is and wants to become and must remain respectful of the ethnic and cultural diversity that exists in society. Inflammatory and inaccurate characterizations of the qualities of particular ethnic and racial groups and cultures can only undermine the respect for all peoples that is essential to pluralist societies.

The extreme right and extreme left both have ideas about citizenship that pluralists reject. The extreme right's desire for racially or ethnically homogeneous political communities are unworkable and undesirable given the many historical processes – including the recent history of globalization – that have generated political communities that are now heterogeneous. Partitioning land to create ethnically homogeneous enclaves denies people the basic freedom of movement that a globalized world community expects and demands. It would also deprive political communities of the very diversity that gives the autonomous individuals within pluralist societies access to other cultures and peoples. The extreme left's desire for people to undergo a transformation of moral outlooks, rejecting the materialism and individualism that is so prevalent in pluralist societies, and adopting more spiritual and communal values, may be desirable but is probably utopian in the same way that Marx's call for a transformation of citizens into creative labors was utopian. Perhaps pluralists have no quarrel with efforts by the extreme left to bring about cultural change that prompts citizens to be more receptive to such values, but they are wary of any political or coercive effort to impose a particular moral system on citizens. The presence of a multitude of comprehensive moral doctrines among citizens is a central feature of pluralist political communities.

Chapter 11

Questions of Structure

What are the primary processes and institutions that structure political communities, giving meaning and direction to the lives of citizens and organizing them for economic, social, and political purposes? To what extent should community life be structured by market transactions, cultural norms, and such institutions as governments, corporations, labor unions, charitable organizations, churches, and families? What is the existing balance of power among these structures? Should this balance of power be modified?

The importance of structures has been emphasized by historicism, the claim that human history is best understood in terms of the dominant social structures that define major stages and transitions of civilized life.[1] Our discussion of Marxist ontology in chapter 2 described the most prominent such rendering of history. Slavery structured the ancient world, and feudalism structured the Middle Ages, but these structures and periods have been swept into the dustbins of history. According to Marx, capitalism has been the dominant structure of the modern period, but he projected a subsequent historical stage dominated by state-controlled socialism. The communist regimes in the USSR and elsewhere during the twentieth century may be seen as constituting such a stage. Fascists and Nazis proposed an alternative fourth stage of history, one dominated by a totalitarian state. Francis Fukuyama is the most influential social theorist to claim that both state-dominated socialism and fascism were utter failures. In broad historical perspective, these experiments may have been too brief to be regarded as significant separate stages in history. Indeed, Fukuyama has proposed that the modern stage of history, structured by democracy as well as capitalism, is the "end of history," an era that will not be followed by any others, because it contains governmental structures and economic processes that are superior to all conceivable alternatives.[2] Such a claim obviously contradicts that of Marx, who thought that the end of history would be marked by the development of a society without capitalism and government, rather than by a maturation of capitalist and democratic structures. Questions of structure thus continue to center on the role of capitalist economies and democratic governments. Even those ideologies that agree on the centrality of capitalism and democracy have sharply different ideas about their interrelationship and how capitalism and democracy could be better structured. Other ideologies urge a de-emphasis on capitalism and/or democracy and the pursuit of alternatives ranging from theocracies to self-sufficient and ecologically sustainable communes. Let's examine more carefully alternative views of how to structure political communities.

Classical Liberals: Designing Free Markets and Representative Democracies

Classical liberals were the first to proclaim the importance of *free markets* for structuring political communities. Free markets enable people to engage in economic activity in a voluntary and mutually beneficial manner. While slave-holding, feudal, and state-dominated economies employed coercion to get people to perform various economic tasks, free markets enable people to work, invest, trade, and consume according to their own desires. People are free to do or not do any economic activity, and their motivation for engaging in economic activity that is beneficial to others in a political community is that they, too, will benefit.

John Locke laid the foundation for liberal endorsement of free markets and capitalism by proclaiming that people have *property rights*.[3] Because individuals are the rightful owners of their own labor and because the value of goods is due to the labor that has been invested in their production, people have property rights to those goods in which they have invested their labor.[4] People can exchange their labor for a wage, and in so doing transfer their right to the goods they produced to the person who paid their wages, but such exchanges are voluntary and mutually beneficial, or else they would not be undertaken.

Adam Smith further described and analyzed the basic structures of free markets – such as the role of private property, the efficiency of a division of labor in manufacturing goods, the effectiveness of processes of supply and demand, and the benefits of free trade across national borders. Smith argued that a free enterprise system would generate much greater wealth for a political community and its citizens than was generated by previous economic systems, because it would direct economic activity toward the production of those material goods that people want, it would encourage investments in those areas that are most profitable, and it would give people incentives to innovate and be productive in order to reap personal rewards. Subsequent liberal economic philosophers elaborated on these structures and justifications, but all celebrated the rationality and efficiency of free markets.[5]

For classical liberals, free markets need to be complemented by governments that are strong enough to perform those functions necessary for a capitalist economy – such as protecting property rights, enforcing contracts, adjudicating disputes, and providing such basic infrastructure as roads and harbors.[6] However, classical liberals insisted that governmental power should be limited to avoid unjustified infringements on individual rights, over-regulation of the economy, and redistributions of wealth. Liberals, therefore, had to address the problem of how to structure governments so that they perform necessary functions without abusing their power. Their solution to this problem involved establishing *constitutional restraints on government*, dividing and balancing governmental power, and providing political accountability.[7]

According to classical liberals, social contracts should result in constitutions containing specific, written rules that organize and restrain the activities of governments. They do so in four ways. First, constitutions specify in general terms what governments can and cannot do. The American Constitution, for example, specifies that the national government can collect taxes, coin money, and declare war, but that it cannot establish a state religion, infringe on the right of people to keep and bear arms, or infringe on other liberties as specified in the Bill of Rights. Second, constitutions establish governmental institutions (such as the American presidency, Congress, and the Supreme Court) for enacting and implementing policies. Third, constitutions specify how positions in such institutions are to be filled and how occupants can be removed from these offices. Fourth, constitutions specify extraordinary procedures for their modification, such as Article V of the American Constitution requiring that three-fourths of the states ratify each amendment.

While classical liberals view these constitutional provisions as important devices for blocking governmental abuses of powers, they face the problem of ensuring that governments adhere to constitutional limitations. In America, the practice of judicial review – which enables the courts to declare legislative and administrative acts unconstitutional – may strengthen constitutional restraints, but, in general, governments are prompted to abide by constitutional limitations out of fear of loss of legitimacy. If a government ignores constitutional constraints, liberals argue, its citizens may believe that the social contract has been violated and withdraw their consent to be governed by it.

Many liberal constitutions specify federalism and the separation of powers to constrain governmental power. Federalism distributes power among national, provincial, and local governments, thus limiting the power of any one government. Although the idea of separation of powers goes back to the ancient idea of "mixed regimes,"[8] the French political philosopher Baron de Montesquieu (1689–1755) is credited with transforming this idea into a device for limiting government and preserving individual liberty. By insisting that legislative, executive, and judicial powers be distinguished and relegated to different institutions, by providing that positions within these different institutions be held by different people who may represent different interests, and by giving each institution devices for resisting encroachments and usurpations of powers by officials in other institutions, the power of all governmental officials is limited and checked. An independent judiciary ensures that legislators and executives cannot suppress their political opponents through political trials. Bicameral legislatures – requiring that laws be passed by two legislative bodies representing different interests – limit the capacity of popularly elected legislatures to enact laws that infringe on personal liberties, over-regulate the economy, or redistribute wealth.

Providing procedures of *accountability* is another liberal means of preventing abuses of governmental power. A prominent example of such accountability is the liberal practice of civilian control of the military. By having the President serve as Commander-in-Chief of the armed forces and by requiring that only Congress can declare war, the liberal founders of America hoped to limit the ability of military officers to use their control of coercive power to dominate the country.

A more general method of providing accountability is having governmental officials stand for re-election. According to James Madison, "a dependence on the people" is "the primary control on government, more important than even the separation of powers." Classical liberals do not envision elections as a means of discovering "the will of the people," dictating what governments should do in a positive sense. Classical liberals did not intend elections to be a means for forcing government to be responsive to the views of most citizens, who might have "a rage for paper money, for the abolition of debts, for an equal division of property, or for any other improper and or wicked project."[9] Instead, elections were intended to give citizens an opportunity to remove officials who violate their rights or are corrupt or incompetent. The founders of liberalism created electoral arrangements that allow citizens to replace officials who abuse their power but prevent them from using elections to install representatives who simply transform public sentiment into public policy. Lengthy and staggered terms of office (such as for US senators) are typical methods for reducing the likelihood that elections will result in policies overly responsive to majority opinion.

Classical liberals thus stressed capitalism and limited and representative government as providing the most important structures for political communities, and they saw these structures as complementing each other, rather than as countervailing forces. Classical liberals believed representative democracies provided essential needs for capitalism, and they tried to structure governments so that they would not make policies hostile to the needs of capitalism. Classical liberals did understand the importance of countervailing power, but they applied this concept to the internal structure of government, not to the relationships between government and capitalism.

Classical liberals appreciated the role of other structures beyond capitalism and representative government. They understood the separation of church and state to mean that religion would play roles in structuring society distinct from those of the state. Governments would not incorporate a particular church within the state; instead, a variety of churches should thrive within civil society. More generally, while classical liberals are known for their emphasis on individualism, they did not deny that individuals would want and need to associate with other citizens, forming many voluntary groups within civil society for these purposes.

Classical liberals also understood the cultural norms could play a useful role in structuring society. They regarded norms emphasizing the importance of hard work, thrift, investment, and other economic virtues as necessary lubricants to an effective free market economy.[10] They regarded norms emphasizing respect for the rights of others, tolerance, and vigilance over public officials as essential for effective politics.

But classical liberals rejected the notion that political communities should be structured by many of the cultural norms that had traditionally been stressed. Sheer deference to the customs and traditions that prevail in the cultures of communities can undermine the capacity of individuals to think for themselves and make choices that can lead to personal growth and social progress.

Traditional Conservatives: Emphasizing Civil Society and Cultural Norms

Traditional conservatives have no one preferred way of structuring political communities. Each polity has its own history and traditional understandings of how it should be structured. Moreover, conservatives have changed their emphasis on various structures as cultural understandings have evolved.

At its inception, traditional conservatism viewed the capitalist structuring of the economy with considerable apprehension. Appreciating the continuing roles played by remnants of slavery (as black slaves provided the labor necessary to maintain Southern plantations in America), feudalism (as peasants and commoners provided similar labor for European aristocrats), and mercantilism (where national industries in such areas as shipping and arsenals were supported by royal treasuries), conservatives were reluctant to abandon these economic institutions. While economic markets had long existed and played a role in structuring economic activities, conservatives feared that unleashing capitalism could have many deleterious effects on society, such as encouraging commoners to abandon their traditional roles, engendering excessive competition, pandering to people's basest material interests, and breaking down moral restraints. However, as market economies developed, many of these fears abated, and conservatives increasingly embraced capitalism.

Traditional conservatives opposed the liberal emphasis on limited governments, as they appreciated the pre-eminence of government in political communities. If society was an orchestra in which everyone had to play their various roles in order to achieve social harmony, government was the conductor. The royal families and aristocrats who controlled government were seen as the most effective maestros, the natural leaders who understood the importance of every role in the orchestra and who could get optimal performances out of those who occupied various roles. Traditional conservatives often viewed as unnecessary and even repugnant written constitutions that constrained governmental leaders. For Burke, the British Constitution included all acts of Parliament, the common law, and many informal traditions; it was a living and evolving set of conventions that specified what governments do and ought to do, not a written document that limits governmental authority.

Traditional conservatives originally feared that democratic structures would pander to the whims and passions of ordinary people, undermining effective government and social harmony. But as liberals succeeded in bringing democratic norms to national cultures, traditional conservatives came to embrace the republican idea that monarchs, aristocrats, and democrats should each have a role in government.

Republican structural principles call for "mixed" governmental institutions in which the interests of the various elements of a society are balanced and blended so that no faction within society can corruptly pursue its own interest, generating disharmony and conflict in the body politic. In such a mixed system, some persons and classes may lead, but all elements within society have a sufficient role to insist that policies serve society as a whole. Traditional conservatives embraced "aristocratic republicanism," limiting the role of the public in government to holding leaders accountable through elections that were structured to limit public influence, often more so than the devices used by classical liberals.[11]

This traditional conservative desire to insulate officials from citizens can be seen in their efforts to curb democracy in America during the past century. Such conservatives were critical of the Seventeenth Amendment to the US Constitution, passed in 1913, which changed the method for selecting senators. They preferred the older method of having senators selected by state legislatures, rather than by popular vote. While often hostile to the decisions of the Supreme Court, traditional conservatives remain the greatest advocates of continuing the practice of appointing judges for life rather than subjecting them to the democratic pressures of periodic elections. They still prefer employing the electoral college in presidential elections, rather than selecting the President by popular vote.[12]

Fearing that the individualism of free markets and the egalitarianism of democracy threaten the tight organization of communities that they prize, traditional conservatives, more than liberals, stress the importance of voluntary associations in civic society. Alexis de Tocqueville (1805–59) greatly admired the role that voluntary associations played in early America; he thought that such associations enabled Americans to simultaneously retain and enhance their liberties (given their voluntary character) *and* pursue collective objectives.[13]

For traditional conservatives, cultural norms are also essential to keep democratic capitalist societies from becoming unglued. As former New York Senator Daniel Patrick Moynihan (1927–2003) put it, "The central conservative truth is that it is culture, not politics, that determines the success of a society."[14] While liberals celebrate individual choice, traditional conservatives understand that social needs must have priority over individual autonomy, and that individuals need the guidance of traditions, customs, and habits to keep them from mistaking temporary passions for their real needs. Among the cultural norms that traditional conservatives admire are those that deal with sexuality and family life. Liberals might regard questions of sexual relations and whether to marry as matters of personal choice among consenting adults, but for conservatives, these matters have important implications for society. Cultural prohibitions on such things as premarital sex are needed in order that young people develop the self-discipline required of mature adults. Couples must receive the blessings of their parents before deciding to marry so as to maintain the centrality and stability of extended families. Women must stay in the home and assume as their primary role the upbringing of children in order to ensure that future generations learn their proper roles in society. Ignoring such cultural norms can lead to the decay of political communities.

Anarchists: Rejecting All Conventional Structures

Anarchists believe that conventional social structures must be abolished so that natural structures can emerge in their place. Anarchists have been unwilling to provide precise designs of these natural structures, because they understand that people will want to imagine and experiment with various alternatives.[15] Nevertheless, the social structures that are acceptable to anarchists will clearly contrast with conventional structures in the following ways.

Decentralized structures must replace centralized ones. Centralized states and other institutions have been organized from above, and they contain vertical relationships of authority in which those at the top issue commands that those below must obey. In contrast, decentralized institutions are organized from below, and they contain horizontal relationships in which all members of the organization have relatively equal power. Although different people may have different roles and responsibilities, they should not be in permanent positions of authority and subordination.

Small structures must replace large ones. The nation-state should be abolished, and our primary communities should be local. Insofar as possible, people should know other members of the social units to which they belong, and they should be in continuous face-to-face interaction with them. People should understand the particular needs of their associates.

Voluntary organizations must replace coercive ones. No one should be a member of a state or any other organization against her will. Perhaps current voluntary associations within civil society resemble the structures that they support, but anarchists regard most such associations as too coercive. Most churches, schools, and other "voluntary organizations" – as well as families – have authority structures that enable some people to dominate others, and they have practices that make leaving difficult. The voluntary organizations preferred by anarchists would be less hierarchical and coercive than most existing institutions in civil society.

Rather than emphasizing territorial associations, anarchists emphasize non-territorial associations. States are organized on the basis of people living in the same area and have coercive police powers over everyone living in that area. However, residents within the same area may have little basis for associating with each other. Only some people within a territory may wish to associate with each other because of certain collaborative economic, educational, social, or religious interests. And those who wish to associate because of such collaborative interests may come from many different geographic locations.

Anarchists wish to destroy centralized, national, coercive, and territorial social structures, and replace them with decentralized, local, voluntary, and non-territorial ones. Communities would be structured on the basis of *mutualism*. In economic life, mutualism refers to ongoing associations for the production and distribution of goods and services based on voluntary contractual arrangements between economically independent persons. In principle, capitalism's free enterprise system also provides for associations based on voluntary contracts, but anarchists insist that, in practice, capitalist agreements are coercive, because the parties to them are not genuinely independent. If one party owns the land or the equipment used to produce goods, the party that owns only his labor is in a poor bargaining position and therefore gets exploited. But if each party owns his own land or tools or if such means of production are owned in common, no one is dependent on the owners of private property. In this context of independence, parties can acknowledge that their cooperation can be mutually beneficial and they can become associates in workplaces or syndicates to produce goods more efficiently. Education could also be provided on the basis of mutualism. Rather than being organized by centralized and hierarchical public and private institutions, anarchists seek voluntary, mutually agreeable, and mutually beneficial arrangements among parents, teachers, and students. In general, a vast proliferation of mutual-interest associations could be organized in which people with common intellectual, artistic, spiritual, and recreational interests could agree to provide certain benefits to one another according to whatever arrangements they adopt for their association.

Because mutual-interest associations would be composed of individuals with similar interests and ideals and because individuals would only join those groups whose organizational arrangements they regarded as just and necessary, there would be little conflict within such associations. But anarchists are not so unrealistic as to think that no conflict would ensue. Associations could form internal "police" units to detect violations of just conduct, and they could resolve disputes among members by employing mediation and arbitration.

Anarchists also recognize that social pressure would be an important natural instrument that associations would use to ensure that individuals do not harm each other. For example, members of a workplace who fail to act responsibly toward others could be subject to criticism, chastisement, and even ostracism. Such social pressure certainly resembles the cultural norms stressed by conservatives, but anarchists reject the claim that people should comply with traditional beliefs about moral goodness, insisting on their right to reach their own moral judgments. The social pressures of an anarchistic community would impose a very thin layer of constraints on people, applying to obviously disruptive behaviors, but they would not compel adherence to norms that proscribe activities that cause no clear harm to others.

Anarchists also recognize the need for different associations to work out agreements regarding their mutual and conflicting interests. Although Proudhon often referred to a "federal principle" as a means of structuring such inter-associational relations, the term "confederation" seems to capture anarchist ideals more accurately in this regard. Anarchists did envision different local associations forming larger umbrella organizations by mutual agreement. According to Bakunin, "there may arise free unions organized from below by the free federations of communes into provinces, of provinces into nations, and of nations into the United States of Europe."[16] Nevertheless, anarchists insisted that sovereignty would be largely retained at the local level, and that the higher-level organizations would largely coordinate cooperative activity among the local associations.[17]

Marxists: Stressing the Oppression of Capitalism

Marxists believe that the central structure of modern societies is capitalism, which includes features beyond the system of free market exchange emphasized by liberals. For Marxists, capitalism also includes *private* ownership and control of the means of production, increasing monopolization (or concentration of ownership and control of property), and bourgeois domination over all other aspects of society, including family life, culture, and government. Because private industries dominate government, Marxists view governmental structures in capitalist societies as serving to reinforce the needs and values of capitalism, as having little independent influence over society, and as impossible to reform in ways that might make governments benefit society as a whole. Even the democratic aspects of governments are of little value, because they simply provide a false façade that masks capitalism's domination of government, deceiving the proletariat with talk of democracy and rights.

The relative impotence of governments means that the essential decisions about society, including what goods to produce and how to distribute them, are left to those capitalists who have the most power within the political economy. According to Marx, this structural arrangement served positive social functions during the early industrial era for several reasons. First, it enabled capitalists to "pitilessly [tear] asunder the motley feudal ties that bound man to his 'natural' superiors. . . . In a word, for exploitation, veiled by religious and political illusions, it has substituted naked, shameless, direct, brutal exploitation."[18] Second, capitalist domination generated "more massive and more colossal productive forces than have all preceding generations together," enabling humans to master nature.[19] Capitalism's productive forces include new material technologies (such as electrical and oil-based forms of power) as well as new technologies of organization (such as the assembly line and bureaucratic forms of industrial management). After capitalism has been destroyed, many of these productive forces will remain and be perfected to provide the resources needed to attain the ideal communist society. Third, competition within the capitalist marketplace drives industry to become ever more efficient, leading to innovations in the material forces of production and in the organization of production, which in turn lead to larger changes in society. According to Marx:

> The bourgeoisie cannot exist without constantly revolutionizing the instruments of production, and thereby the relations of production, and with them the whole relations of society. . . . All fixed, fast-frozen relations, with their train of ancient and venerable prejudices and opinions, are swept away, all new-formed ones become antiquated before they can ossify. All that is solid melts into air, all that is holy is profaned.[20]

For this reason, Marx claimed that the bourgeoisie have historically "played a most revolutionary part" because it has "simplified class antagonisms: Society as a whole is more and more splitting up into two great hostile camps, into two great classes directly facing each other: Bourgeoisie and Proletariat."[21]

All these developments are positive for Marx, not because of any intrinsic moral worth, but because they hasten the coming of communism. But this also means that capitalism and its illusory democratic institutions will outlive their usefulness. Capitalist modes of production can produce more goods than can be consumed, given its mode of distribution. The capitalist means of production promises abundance, but the pressure of competition and profit-seeking leads to general misery. Capitalism's waning usefulness will prompt an inevitable revolt against it that will sweep away its institutions.

After the revolution, the political economy will be structured by a *centralized proletarian state*. Contrary to the assertions of subsequent communists, Marx thought that the state, and not the party, would be the dominant institution in the transitory socialist society. He made this clear in *The Communist Manifesto*, asserting that the party would "centralize all instruments of production in the hands of the State, *i.e.*, of the proletariat organized as the ruling class." As socialism matures, however, the centralized state will also become outmoded. Having overseen the transition from capitalism to communism, the socialist state will no longer be needed, and can therefore "wither away." Society will then be organized on the basis of decentralized, voluntary organizations. Class antagonisms will no longer exist, so that the political power and institutions that are "merely the organized power of one class for oppressing another" will no longer be needed.[22] In short, Marxists endorsed the structural ideals of anarchists at "the end of history."

Communists: Emphasizing Party Organizations

Like Marxists, communists stress that capitalism has been the central oppressive structure of modern political communities. What communists add to Marxism is a much more elaborate set of ideas about how communities should be structured both domestically and internationally after capitalism is abandoned.

On the domestic side, capitalism and its weak democratic governments must be replaced by an integrated political economy under the control of the Communist Party. At least during the transitional stage, the Communist Party must control all governmental and economic institutions and processes. Under a program of nationalization, the state would assume ownership of all industrial and agricultural property. The state would then engage in economic planning, determining where investments were to be made, which consumer goods were to be produced, what prices were to be charged, what wages were to be paid, and other such matters that in capitalist economies are instead determined by market forces.

While the state structures the economy, the Communist Party structures the state, so the party in effect structures the entire political economy. According to Lenin, the Communist Party (the "vanguard of the proletariat") should be organized according to the principles of *democratic centralism*. First, all officers of the party should be elected from below; ordinary members within local organizations elect their leaders who in turn elect those at higher levels. Second all decisions must be made in free and

open debates of the party congress. Third, all decisions of the party congress are binding on all lower agencies and officials of the party and of the government. Fourth,
no factions can be allowed within the party, and no minority groups can secede from
the party or air their grievances in public. Fifth, executive officials of the party are
authorized to purge members who do not toe the official line of the party hierarchy.
In principle, this structure is democratic, because leadership is formally accountable
to the rank and file and because it allows for open debate. But this structure is also
dictatorial, because leaders make and enforce decisions from which there can be no
dissent.

The main issue among communists concerning the structure of their polities has
been centralization versus decentralization. Most communists interpreted Marx and
Lenin as claiming that the political economy of post-revolutionary societies would be
dominated by a centralized state. But others supported decentralization, even during
the transitional period, giving significant roles to labor associations that were not
controlled by the central party organs and to democratic decision-making at the local
level. Most communist regimes during the era of Stalin and his immediate successors
practiced centralization, and this produced large, inefficient bureaucracies, government waste, and poor economies. For this reason, communists in the 1970s and
1980s considered some restructuring.

The most famous effort to decentralize a communist society was *perestroika*, introduced in 1987 by Soviet leader Mikhail Gorbachev. The original aim of perestroika
was to reduce the power of the huge centralized Soviet bureaucracy. Rather than have
the bureaucracy direct all economic activity, the managers of local plants would be
free to plan production, obtain raw materials, hire workers, and establish prices.
While these reforms brought some decentralization to the Soviet political economy,
they were not intended initially to privatize it. Only when Gorbachev introduced
"revolutionary perestroika" in November 1989, and professed his intentions to
privatize ownership of the means of production and pursue a liberalized free market
system did the Soviets move decisively away from centralized state control of the
political economy.

Communists depreciated the role of civil society in structuring society. They generally regarded the Orthodox Christian Church, which had been a traditional part
of Russian society, as playing a reactionary role, inhibiting the transformation of
citizens into good communists; such churches were greatly suppressed. Communists
similarly regarded many other voluntary associations with suspicion and hostility.

Communists also depreciated the role of cultural values, because the traditional
culture was also reactionary and had to be replaced with communist ideology. Communist parties engaged in "unceasing campaigns of persuasion and indoctrination."
They "used the press, radio, television, schools, and all the arts to mold the thoughts
of their citizens" so that they conformed to the ideological doctrine established by
party leaders.[23]

Another structural issue confronting communism concerned international organization. Communism, like Marxism, was intended to be a class movement that
transcended ethnic and national boundaries. Accordingly, communists formed an

international organization, the Communist International, which debated and set policies for revolutionary and governing activities. Marx had helped organize the First International in 1864, but it was internally beset by factions and externally persecuted by hostile governments; it disbanded in 1873.[24] Engels helped to establish the Second International in 1889, which opposed working-class participation in any war; however, it dissolved after the outbreak of World War I in 1914, as most of its rank and file supported their own countries in that conflict. The Third International, or Comintern, rose to prominence in the 1920s. By 1939, Comintern, which can be seen as a tool for Soviet foreign policy, provided 60 communist parties of various nations with important ideological, financial, and organizational ties in their efforts to create a worldwide revolution. However, in 1943 the Soviets dissolved the Third International to indicate their good will toward their Western Allies in their struggle against Nazism. After the war, the Russians continued to try to dominate communist movements worldwide, but differences between them and Mao, Tito, and other communists undermined these efforts. In short, maintaining a unified international communist community was a major challenge, given the different interests among communist nations.

Fascists and Nazis: Empowering Totalitarian States

In order to gain total control over their political communities and create strong and unified states, fascists and Nazis sought to eliminate competing centers of power. The pluralist model of having countervailing structural powers within society and the republican model of having competing centers of power within government were both anathema to them.

In fascist Italy, Mussolini structured a *corporatist* political economy that permitted private ownership of the means of production but called for the owners of industry to cooperate with labor and the fascist party in structuring economic activity. The fascists formed 22 corporations that represented broad areas of economic activity. Sectors of the economy – such as transportation, steel, textiles, and grains – each had their own corporation comprising workers, unions, managers, and executives. Members of the fascist party were included in the governing structure of each corporation. This corporate structure provided fascists with a mechanism for controlling workers and managers and for directing productivity toward the goals of the state.[25]

In Germany, the Nazis emphasized *National Socialism*, which (like fascist corporatism) did not involve nationalization of the means of production. Instead, it involved close collaboration between industrialists and Nazi officials who headed the German state. Big businesses and such industrialists as Ferdinand Porsche (1875–1951) served the Nazi regime, benefiting directly from its harsh labor laws.[26] Workers (including many detainees captured abroad) became forced laborers who were required to work long hours at an accelerated pace for minimal compensation. German capitalists were offered huge profits in return for producing the arsenal that Hitler required for his expansionist military objectives.

Fascists and Nazis rejected both the separation of powers and the idea of checks and balances within governmental institutions. The Nazis employed the *Führerprinzip* ('leadership principle'), which created multiple and overlapping spheres of activity and competence (rather than vertically distinct functional and organizational structures).[27] While the presence of multiple and overlapping institutions suggests a dispersed structure of power, all institutions remained under centralized control. This structure enabled Hitler to delegate tasks to those institutions that were most effective and responsive to his will. Alternative institutions for performing tasks, coupled with the direct and personal delegation of authority from the Führer, tended to undermine bureaucratic rigidity and produce a highly mobilized set of subordinates, all eager to respond to the will of those higher up in the hierarchy. Such centralization permitted government to focus on national goals established by the Führer, rather than on accommodating factional and bureaucratic interests.[28]

Fascists and Nazis sought to eliminate secondary associations within civil society and traditional cultural norms as structural forces that might undermine unity. Emphasis was given to a single political party, rather than to the diversity of directions provided by many groups in civil society. Emphasis was also given to a single unifying ideology inculcated into all citizens through a strong propaganda machine, rather than to cultural norms that might undercut support for the regime. Destruction of (or at least domination over) all competing structural forces was a defining element of fascism and especially Nazism, making them totalitarian ideologies.

Contemporary Liberals: Balancing and Integrating Government and Capitalism

Contemporary liberals continue to appreciate the positive role of capitalism in structuring the economy, but they emphasize a reformed rather than pure form of capitalism. They recognize that capitalism is no longer well characterized as small entrepreneurs hiring workers to produce goods for sale in competitive markets; instead, current forms of corporate capitalism feature much larger economic entities with many stockholders, large managerial organizations, and vast workforces selling many products and services in global markets. Contemporary liberals recognize the need for some governmental oversight and control over such capitalism. They call on democratic governments to be countervailing structures that regulate capitalism to prevent such market failures as collusions and mergers that undermine market competition and the incentives for companies to externalize costs in ways that harm the public and the environment. But contemporary liberals also believe governments can cooperate with corporations and thus often support public–private partnerships. In this vein, governments should subsidize downtown redevelopment, because such projects often provide broad economic, social, and cultural benefits to citizens of the entire community, in addition to being places of private enterprise. Governments should share in the building of major facilities, such as sports stadiums and airports, because these bring "major league" opportunities to the community as a whole, and not just to those who purchase tickets at these facilities. Governments should bail out or provide bankruptcy protections to airlines, because they provide essential services to citizens in areas where market demand is low or when it has been eroded by such events as those of 9/11. Governments should provide tax incentives for new capital improvements or establish import tariffs on foreign competitors in such industries as steel and automotive, because of their centrality to the larger domestic economy. Such examples could be extended endlessly, but the point is clear: contemporary liberals support a mixed political economy that is structured in part by the actions of free market forces, in part by the regulations of governments, and in part by cooperative arrangements between private and public forces.

Such an economy requires a much larger and stronger governmental presence than the more limited governments of classical liberalism. These strong governments must be appropriately structured so that they can deal with the myriad problems and opportunities that arise in a contemporary political economy. One such problem is that the market justice provided by capitalism is only one component of a just society – as will be discussed in more detail in chapter 14 – and must be complemented by various governmental initiatives to generate social justice. But the stronger governments required for such tasks must be structured in such a way that this increased power is not abused. Like classical liberals, contemporary liberals recognize the need for constitutional restraints on governments. They understand that governmental power must be divided. And they hope to check abuses of governmental power through various procedures of accountability.

While recognizing the importance of constitutions, contemporary liberals do not regard them as static. Constitutions that are centuries old need not be abandoned as new problems and moral understandings emerge, but they can be amended and reinterpreted. For example, constitutional amendments (such as the Sixteenth Amendment to the US Constitution establishing the income tax) can give governments new powers to collect revenues to finance the strong state. More frequently, liberals support new interpretations of existing constitutional provisions. During the New Deal, they endorsed several Supreme Court rulings permitting an expanded role of the federal government in the areas of economic regulation and redistribution. During the 1950s and 1960s, they supported judicial reinterpretations of the Fourteenth (equal rights) Amendment in order to desegregate schools. And in 1973, they applauded when the Court ruled in *Roe v. Wade* that constitutional privacy rights implied that women have the right to abortions. In general, contemporary liberals have endorsed *judicial activism* – the practice whereby judges interpret vague and abstract wordings in the Constitution to expand the powers of government in economic matters and in promoting the political, social, and legal rights of minorities, women, and persons accused of crimes. For liberals, the practice of actively reinterpreting the Constitution is justified because the abstract vagueness of constitutional provisions requires that constitutional language be fused with contemporary moral, social, political, and economic understandings to resolve the new problems that emerge as societies evolve.[29]

One of the major areas where American liberals have reinterpreted the Constitution concerns the powers of the national government relative to state governments. Classical liberals supported the Tenth Amendment of the Constitution that reserved most powers for the states; during the nineteenth century, the states made and enforced most of the laws regarding business and finance, property, labor, welfare, and crime.[30] However, contemporary liberals (citing "the elastic clause" in the Constitution giving Congress the power "to make all laws which shall be necessary and proper") have endorsed enhancing the importance of the national government, as mentioned in chapter 9. One reason for strengthening national governments is they are much more able than regional, state, and local governments to expand welfare rights in mobile, modern societies.[31] The problem is that there are strong economic disincentives for states and localities to produce redistributive policies. States that create more generous welfare programs than other states can attract "the wandering poor" from those other states, while encouraging businesses and wealthy citizens to leave the state to avoid the high taxes needed to cover increasing welfare costs. Because national governments can restrict entry of the poor of other countries through immigration laws and because the wealthy are less inclined to give up their citizenship than to move to low-tax states, they have fewer disincentives than the states to have generous welfare-rights policies.

However, it is probably a mistake to overemphasize contemporary liberal support for national governments. As budget deficits in the US have curtailed the capacity of the federal government to expand welfare rights and provide public services, and when conservatives have captured Congress and the presidency, American liberals have turned back to the states, seeking innovative solutions to social and economic problems at that level. In short, liberal beliefs about the proper powers of national, state, and local governments are derivative rather than fundamental. Contemporary liberals are primarily concerned with using governmental power to resolve social and economic problems and to enhance social justice, and they support constitutional interpretations that enable the use of power by any government that is readily available for such purposes.

Another area where American liberals have reinterpreted the Constitution concerns the distribution of powers between the executive and the legislature. While classical liberals generally supported legislative-centered government, contemporary liberals have generally supported executive-centered and bureaucratic government.[32] At least until conservative Republicans came to power during the Reagan and Bush administrations, liberals generally sought to strengthen the executive for several reasons. First, legislatures represent diverse and parochial interests and contain many veto points, making it difficult for them to pass progressive legislation solving social problems and furthering social justice. It has often been observed that liberal legislation in the areas of civil rights and welfare policies could only pass Congress during periods when liberal democrats had supra-majorities in each house and were influenced by the prodding of liberal presidents.[33] Second, chief executives such as US presidents have developed significant informal powers to define the agenda of social problems and to convey their concerns to the public; presidents who utilize these informal powers can build broad support for policy initiatives on behalf of liberal goals. Third, as societies have become more modern, problems have become more complex, and the expertise to address these problems appears to reside in a professional bureaucracy rather than among legislative generalists. While legislators might be able to agree that certain problems require the investment of governmental resources, they seldom have the expertise to define specific policy solutions. As a result, legislative law-making amounts to little more than "expressing broad and noble sentiments, giving almost no direction at all but imploring executive power, administrative expertise, and interest-group wisdom to set the world to rights."[34]

Despite supporting strong executive-centered national governments, contemporary liberals are well aware that such governments can abuse their powers, and so they endorse structures and practices of accountability. In general, presidential initiatives and bureaucratic programs should be subjected to legislative oversight. Legislative staffs should evaluate the legality, effectiveness, and fairness of bureaucratic actions. Executive abuses of power can be investigated by the legislature, which should apply appropriate sanctions ranging from cutting off program appropriations to impeachment.

Understanding that legislators should, in turn, be accountable to citizens, contemporary liberals have endorsed a variety of reforms to enhance such accountability. For example, American liberals have sought legislative districts that are apportioned equally based on population, to ensure that legislators are as accountable to urban voters as rural ones. More recently, many liberals have called for public financing of elections, believing that such reforms would make representatives more accountable to the general public rather than to "fat cat" contributors.

Contemporary liberals support the role of secondary associations in structuring society, but they regard the voluntary nature of such organizations as limited in their capacity to deal adequately with the problems of modern communities. The Red Cross does not have adequate capacities to address large-scale catastrophes, such as those inflicted by hurricane Katrina. Only national governments have the massive capacities to deal with such matters. Only the coercive powers of governments can extract tax resources to pay for programs that deliver essential public goods and provide social justice.

Contemporary liberals also understand that many cultural norms are important in structuring political communities. They believe that public schools, secondary associations, and families are important in transmitting to the young such values as a work ethic, tolerance, civility, and compassion. But they believe that traditional cultures sometimes transmit undesirable norms that discriminate against minorities, women, gays, and others. They believe traditional cultures can be excessively supportive of practices that are no longer appropriate to current conditions (e.g., carrying hand-guns) or excessively repressive of individual choices (e.g., to form a same-sex union). Sometimes, the way traditional cultures structure life in communities must be challenged.

Contemporary Conservatives: Reining in Strong States

Contemporary conservatives believe that their pluralist friends – especially contemporary liberals and democratic socialists – have overemphasized the role of
government in structuring political communities, and that totalitarian ideologies have
been even worse in this regard. Such ideologies are guilty of creating excessive expectations about what governments can do, such as provide social justice or effectively
solve various economic and social problems. Contemporary conservatives emphasize
the failures of many governmental programs, the deleterious consequences of many
social engineering efforts by strong governments, and the destabilizing consequences
of their excessive ambitions. Because leftist ideologies create rapidly rising expectations about a glorious future, which governments find hard to meet, citizens lose faith
in government and question its legitimacy. This ultimately undermines the capacity
of government to do the essential things – like provide security and the infrastructure
of an effective market economy – that are realistically within its capability.

Contemporary conservatives think capitalism effectively structures economic activity. Excessive governmental taxation to pay for extensive public programs diverts
money away from capitalists and thus curtails investment in innovative technologies
that can make the economy grow. Excessive governmental regulations on behalf of
various social and environmental goals strangle entrepreneurial activity. The profit
motive and the competition of free markets can work to improve the programs that
governments do deliver. Thus contemporary conservatives want to privatize (contract
out to private corporations) the management of many programs that were formerly
provided by the bureaucracies created by liberal and socialist governments. Such
changes would help restore the vitality of capitalism and its capacity to effectively
structure economic life.

Contemporary conservatives accept the institutions of representative democracy
as legitimate, but they reject the suggestion that there is one best way to structure
government. In Western Europe, conservatives have worked within parliamentary
systems, and in the US, conservatives have supported the presidential system, including the separation of powers and federalism.

In the US, the structural issue of greatest concern to conservatives is the character
of American federalism, as discussed in chapter 9. Conservatives generally oppose
strong national governments and support states' rights. State and local governments
have knowledge of local problems and capacities and can thus best determine the
proper laws and policies for their communities. Contemporary conservatives believe
that local control over many policies will force citizens to recognize that public
programs are expensive and thus be willing to prune them. To finance reductions
in federal taxes, George W. Bush withdrew federal aid to the nation's cities (and the
poor within them). His most visible urban program – urging churches to sponsor
programs to provide homeless shelters, soup kitchens, and social services – illustrates
the conservative view that national governments should be minimally involved in
local matters.[35]

As pointed out in related discussions of contemporary conservative views of community, citizenship, and justice, voluntary associations are regarded as important for building the character of citizens and as alternatives to governmental welfare programs. Voluntary associations are preferable to governmental programs because the assistance they provide is not an economic entitlement and thus does not undermine incentives for the poor to take responsibility for themselves.

Contemporary conservatives are especially outraged by what they see as the liberal trashing of our cultures. They believe that liberalism is a political outlook that supports moral relativism and fails to acknowledge the moral depravity that is prominent in much popular culture. Obscene music and films crowd out wholesome family programs. Sexual promiscuity is tolerated, as liberals call for "safe sex" rather than the abstinence that is necessary for young people to achieve the self-discipline required for adulthood. While examples could be provided endlessly, the point is that conservatives believe that liberals and civil libertarians have broken down the cultural norms that previously proscribed morally offensive conduct.[36] While conservatives are reluctant to endorse a single moral outlook on society, they believe some limits on a toxic culture are necessary if political communities are to be composed of citizens with sufficient virtue to fulfill the responsibilities that pluralist politics requires.

Like their traditional precursors, today's conservatives believe that "culture makes all the difference" in redressing such social problems as poverty, sickness, and ignorance. As David Landes says, "What matters is a secular code of behavior: hard work, honesty, seriousness, the thrifty use of money and time." He urges us to replace the ideas of "working to live and living to be happy" with the norms of "living to work and getting happiness as a byproduct." Furthermore, he stresses cultural values that "accentuate the positive," because achievement and improvement require an "educated, open-eyed optimism."[37] Landes suggests that the left foolishly dismisses such cultural values as "platitudes" and fails to recognize them as "the wisdom of the ages that never become obsolete."[38]

The Radical Right: More Freedom in The Marketplace and Less Cultural Freedom

The radical right would severely reduce the range of activities that national governments perform. Giving actors more freedoms within economic markets, having individuals more deeply embedded in voluntary organizations like churches, and strengthening traditional cultural values are the sorts of structural reforms within pluralist societies sought by the radical right.

Like contemporary conservatives, the radical right criticizes contemporary liberals and the left for expanding the role of government in structuring society. Libertarians are the voice within the radical right that stresses enhancing the role of capitalism and reducing the coercive capacities of government. Most globalists also seek to enhance the role and importance of capitalism and reduce the role of the democratic state in the global political economy. As Thomas Friedman puts it, the beginning of the age of globalization "was a victory of market forces above politics," and he emphasizes how capitalism now comprises the basic "hardware" of all political economies.[39] Like classical liberals, libertarians and globalists regard capitalism as the key to economic freedom and material prosperity. Free markets allow and encourage people to specialize, innovate, invest, and make use of competitive advantages in ways that produce dramatic increases in prosperity and dramatic decreases in poverty.[40] The kind of capitalism that libertarians and globalists prescribe is free market capitalism – not "crony capitalism." Rather than economic enterprises prospering as a result of governmental privileges and protections, companies in a truly free market can only "hold on to a good economic position by improving production and offering people good products and services."[41]

Globalists generally agree that the role of government must be reduced, but they stress that they do not seek to weaken the democratic state and are instead committed to building democratic governments where they do not exist.[42] Globalists may seek reduction of governmental involvement in the political economy, for example, through the privatization of certain public programs, but they understand that free markets are highly dependent on democratic institutions to provide effective rules that govern market activity. Such rules must preserve property rights, encourage investment and risk-taking, and provide the sort of political stability that can encourage people to invest their resources and energy into productive economic activity.

Most globalists believe that countries without democratic capitalism should first give priority to developing democracy rather than creating free markets. They often suggest that democracy is a precondition for effective capitalism, as investors will not bring needed capital to countries governed either as autocracies whose arbitrary decrees make investments insecure or as "kleptocracies" where corruption is so extensive that it greatly enhances the costs of business.[43] The priority of "good government" over "free markets" is suggested by those analyses that claim that poverty and economic collapses are the result of corrupt and undemocratic governments and to misguided policies by autocratic regimes rather than the results of exploitation and bad judgments by participants in free market globalism.[44]

Other voices among the radical right stress that the problem with government is not its authority to structure political communities, but its tendency to dissipate its authority by engaging in misguided activities. The radical right agrees that governments must give priority to providing security, especially against external enemies, though there are differences of opinion as to how aggressive governments should be. American neoconservatives believe that the US national government should have military superiority in international affairs and use that power to spread democratic capitalism to those parts of the globe where it is lacking. But other conservatives, like Samuel Huntington, believe that each civilization should have its own "core state" providing regional security and that the US government should avoid involvements in conflicts and instabilities in other regions of the world.[45] And national protectionists stress that the military force of pluralist governments should be used exclusively to protect vital national interests.

American cultural conservatives and traditional communitarians believe that governmental authority should be less directed toward regulating economic activity and redistributing income and should instead look toward upholding traditional cultural values. Governments should use their authority to ensure the dominance of Anglo and Christian culture, instill moral character and virtues in citizens, strengthen families, and promote the role of churches. Traditional communitarians and the religious right are particularly upset when liberals have interpreted the constitutional prohibition of an established church to mean that our forefathers sought freedom *from* religion rather than freedom *for* religion. In their view, the doctrine of separation of church and state has resulted in governments that are excessively hostile to religious organizations, as illustrated by their banning of prayers in public schools and challenging the display of religious symbols in public spaces.

The organizations within civil society are of primary importance to the communitarian, religious, and cultural right. Pluralist polities have difficulty establishing a comprehensive moral code that directs individual behavior. However, churches and other associations in civil society can be committed to moral doctrines that sustain sub-communities and provide meaning for the individuals within such communities. Traditional communitarians stress the need for such organizations to emphasize and enforce their own moral codes among their members. The Catholic Church is well within its rights to specify and enforce its doctrines about sexual behavior among its parishioners. Individuals within pluralist societies require the moral guidance that they attain from their involvements in voluntary organizations; such moral guidance helps pluralist societies from spinning out of control.

While globalists and libertarians do not stress voluntary associations as much as other voices on the radical right, they do support such structures for at least two reasons. First, charitable groups and philanthropic foundations are an important alternative to the welfare state. Norberg believes "we have more to expect from philanthropic capitalists than from politics." According to Norberg:

> Microsoft's Bill Gates, the very personification of modern capitalism, himself devotes more to the campaign against disease in the developing countries than the American government does. Between November 1999 and 2000, through the $23 billion Bill and Melinda Gates Health Fund, $1.44 billion went to vaccinate children in developing countries from common diseases and to fund research into HIV/AIDS, malaria, and TB.[46]

In addition, voluntary organizations within civil society provide an important sense of identity and belongingness to people uprooted from local communities by the mobility and rapid change that is a part of globalization. Friedman argues that such voluntary associations provide the roots that people require to balance the forces of globalization.[47]

In summary, the radical right recognizes the importance of many structures. In general, its voices seek to shift the balance of power from governments to markets. They also want voluntary associations and cultural norms to play a much greater role in rooting individuals within political communities.

The Radical Left: Pursuing Market Socialism and Democratic Cultures

The radical left believes that the institutions, processes, and moral values of capitalism deeply characterize modern societies. Capitalist influences are excessive, having a wide variety of undesirable impacts on political communities.

First, capitalism dominates economic distributions. The radical left recognizes that capitalism has a legitimate role to play in distributing the kind of commodities that people want to purchase downtown, in shopping malls, or on eBay, but necessities are too often distributed through the free market. In the US, for example, the availability of healthcare is largely dependent on the capacity of the afflicted to pay for it, and the willingness of affluent people to pay extensively for various medical treatments prompt doctors and hospitals to set the costs of such treatments at levels beyond the reach of poor people. According to the radical left, necessities like medical care should be allocated on the basis of need, not by one's ability to pay.[48]

Second, capitalism restricts human freedom by forcing people to do things in order to survive that they would not ordinarily choose to do. Because many necessities are distributed through capitalist markets, people are often required to make "desperate exchanges" and "trades of last resort."[49] In order to obtain basic food and shelter, poor people may have to engage in dangerous, excessive, demeaning, and alienating work. When people must accept such work to purchase necessities, it is fallacious to claim that they are truly free participants in market exchanges.

Third, capitalism dominates government, influencing who has power and distorting governmental policies. Capitalism distributes wealth unequally, and those with access to wealth are well positioned to win democratic elections and to influence officeholders.[50] Issues that threaten the profitability of capitalists are usually dismissed by democratic states. Policies that increase the power and material well-being of the disadvantaged at the expense of capitalists are seldom adopted.[51] A capitalist-dominated economy creates conditions under which governments inevitably pursue policies where benefits are targeted in the first instance to the wealthy in the hope that their reinvested profits will eventually "trickle down" and benefit labor and the poor.

Fourth, capitalism enables those who own and manage capital to control their workers, consumers, and the broader public. Corporate owners and managers are granted the power to make a wide array of decisions – such as whether to adopt new labor-saving technologies and whether to relocate plants[52] – that have serious consequences for their workers and the surrounding community. Many voices within the radical left now concede that the owners of capital have the right to profit from their investments, but they question whether such ownership gives capitalists a legitimate monopoly of power over important decisions regarding the use of capital. Socialists have long argued that the absence of workplace democracy leads to illegitimate domination of employees by capitalists.[53]

Fifth, capitalism dominates family life. Families generate consumer demands for the products that capitalism produces. Fathers are disproportionately empowered when they are the primary revenue-producers who pay for these goods. Mothers are too often relegated to subordinate positions as unpaid domestic servants, while also forming a flexible workforce that is available for low-paid, part-time, and temporary jobs. Children are given little opportunity to explore their many potentialities but are instead socialized in the family to become productive and compliant men and women whose primary future function is to succeed in the capitalist system. In short, radical feminists stress how capitalism supports patriarchal families.[54]

Sixth, capitalism dominates our cultures, determining the values we hold and making material acquisition and economic advancement the unquestioned priorities in society. The radical left argues that capitalism manipulates citizen desires – directly by inducing people to want certain products through advertising and indirectly by maintaining a social system in which worth is measured by material acquisitions. As a consequence, the competitive capitalist system induces people to seek wealth, power, and status as their primary goals. We fail to appreciate adequately other values – such as engaging in meaningful and creative work, living in a healthy environment, living in harmony with others, and developing our intellectual and spiritual capacities – because they have little economic value in capitalist societies.

Finally, capitalism dominates human psychology, undermining self-esteem and self-confidence. It is difficult for people to believe that they are important if they are in a subordinate position in the workplace and engaged in repetitive, meaningless work. When capitalist values dominate life, those who fail in economic competition are inclined to view themselves not only as economic losers but as losers in life.[55]

Regarding capitalism as the root cause of such problems, the radical left "keeps a weather eye on the nastier tendencies of capitalism."[56] Still, all voices within the radical left remain within the pluralist tradition, because they tolerate capitalism. Rather than seeking its abolition, they wish to limit its domination over economic, social, and political life. Rather than abolishing private property, they wish to limit the benefits that accrue to those who own property. Rather than seeking absolute economic equality, they wish to limit the excessive pride, luxury, and power that accompany the concentration of wealth.

Being reformers, those on the radical left are willing to move down the road toward a more egalitarian and democratic society using economic, political, social, and cultural institutions that already exist within pluralist communities. Being more radical than contemporary liberals, they often seek more extensive modifications of these structures than those sought by their pluralist friends.

For the most part, the radical left has emphasized the restructuring of the broader political economy. Initially, democratic socialists sought a strong centralized state that owned most of the means of production and distributed many economic goods. More recently, egalitarian liberals and civic communitarians have stressed more decentralized structures. For example, John Rawls endorsed a *property-owning democracy*.[57] Such a political economy would seek a very broad distribution of private (productive) property so that the operations of a free market would generate much smaller inequalities of income than occur when such property is as concentrated as it is in contemporary capitalist societies.[58] While the centralized liberal welfare state modestly redistributes income after market forces have produced highly unequal outcomes, property-owning democracies would sharply reduce the inequalities in the initial ownership of productive property, so that the market would produce more equal incomes.

The term "market socialism" is often used as a label for the structure of a political economy that reduces the role of large-scale capitalist enterprises, avoids the rigidities and inefficiencies of state-run industries, and provides a major role for property-owning democracy. A mixture of public and private economic organizations all play important roles in market socialism. Central governments own and manage *nationalized* enterprises in industries like transportation and communication, where economic forces tend to produce natural monopolies. Governments can also own *socialized* enterprises, turning the management of these organizations over to private agencies and/or workers. Some workers collectively own and manage *cooperatives*. And privately owned corporations, small-scale partnerships, and individual entrepreneurs also play major roles under market socialism, though they are subject to the regulations of various governments.

Such an economy has many "market" characteristics. Most economic enterprises are privately owned. Resources must be secured within competitive markets; for example, even nationalized enterprises must attract workers from a labor market in which workers can try to secure higher wages and other benefits from other employers. There is freedom of entry and exit from various markets. Successful enterprises will encourage others to invest in the area, and unsuccessful enterprises can fail. Thus, market socialism encourages productivity and innovation. Most importantly, market socialism prices and sells *commodities* – the goods that people want but do not require – on the basis of market considerations. If some people are willing to pay extensively for luxury homes, some enterprises will emerge to supply them.

However, such an economy has various "public" characteristics. Natural monopolies are publicly owned. The public can influence private investment decisions by having the state control credit and by providing various financial incentives and disincentives for private investors. The state also regulates production through labor, safety, environmental, trade and other types of legislation. Most importantly, some goods – like public transit, basic housing, and healthcare – are supplied by state agencies as *necessities* or as welfare rights to those who cannot afford to pay for them.

Socialists have long maintained that governmental agencies should provide necessities through *nationalized distributions*. Such structures act as agents of national compatriots who are committed to providing for each others' essential needs and paying for these provisions through taxes. However, civic communitarians worry that the role played by state agencies in providing nationalized distributions undermines fraternal values; such distributions of necessities may be seen as "bureaucrats spending taxpayers' money" rather than as mutual aid. Civic communitarians want to augment nationalized distributions with *socialized distributions*, which is aid to needy individuals provided directly by citizens through helping societies, rather than through the state. Helping societies are composed of citizens who, rather than being taxed on an involuntary and impersonal basis, give of their time, energy, and money on a voluntary and personal basis.[59]

The radical left believes that pluralist communities have constitutional and institutional arrangements that incorporate political rights and democratic principles offering them opportunities to pursue market socialism and other social and environmental goals, win public support, and govern. They thus focus on strengthening those existing institutions – like labor unions and socialist and green parties – that facilitate the attainment of their goals. However, if conservative and corporate interests are entrenched in state institutions, the radical left may make proposals for "restructuring" and reorganization that allow ordinary citizens more opportunities to participate and acquire power in government. For example, radical democrats may support public funding of efforts to organize marginalized groups and support proposals that ensure that marginalized groups are represented in various policy-making arenas.[60]

Like other pluralists, the radical left appreciates the role of voluntary associations in structuring societies. Indeed, civic communitarians stress that the institutions of civil society – schools and workplaces, churches and synagogues, trade unions, and social movements – provide essential public roles.[61] The radical left often rejects the liberal distinction between public and private spheres of life, regarding associations in civil society as public and political. From their perspectives, egalitarian, communitarian, feminist, environmentalist values must be pursued in the family, in the workplace, and in various voluntary associations. Indeed, the radical left regards these as excellent places to strengthen people's commitments to the values and virtues stressed by the left.[62]

Socialists have a deeper appreciation than liberals of the role of cultural norms in structuring society. Much of what is "evolutionary" in democratic socialism, rather than revolutionary Marxism, is the transformation of cultural values in a socialist direction. In general, the radical left believes that liberal values – stressing individual achievement and material prosperity – must be complemented by values involving collective achievement, social solidarity, social justice, and environmental sustainability. They reject the Marxist belief that capitalism so dominates liberal societies that changes in cultural values in a leftward direction are impossible without destroying capitalism. Instead, they believe cultural values can be changed through education and persuasion.

The Extreme Right: Seeking Theocracies

The various voices on the extreme right seldom challenge the virtues of a market economy with capitalist ownership or reject at least some form of democracy, but they regard as deeply flawed the existing capitalist democracies that structure pluralist societies. What is most extreme about the far right, however, is their rejection of civil society as presently constituted. They loathe the wide array of racial, ethnic, and religious groups in modern pluralist societies, and they abhor the ability of organizations representing the interests of minorities, welfare recipients, and the like to influence government. Those on the extreme right see themselves as members of a particular organization (such as a church or militia) that seeks to redeem the larger political community from the many illegitimate interests that have become more prominent than themselves.

Global capitalism is seen as controlled by transnational elites who pursue trade and investment policies that undermine national interests and traditional cultural values. An effective democratic government would provide protection from such elites and would pursue policies that ensured national self-sufficiency. The extreme right usually accepts a capitalist economy, one that allows people many economic freedoms, including the right to own productive property. But to ensure that such an economy is not under foreign control, generates proper investments, and works harmoniously, they would probably endorse some state involvement in the economy. The fascist corporatist model – where corporations and labor worked harmoniously under government oversight – would be attractive, but only if government is promoting "righteous" goals.

The extreme right doubts that such governments currently exist. The democratic governments of pluralist society are viewed as far removed from citizen concerns and accountability and as dominated by foreign (often Jewish) interests, neoliberal organizations (like the Trilateral Commission), and liberal bureaucrats who are overly sympathetic to minorities, rich capitalists, those who are lazy and thus poor, and others who are parasites on society, rather than hard-working ordinary citizens. Many voices within the extreme right claim that some nefarious but difficult to identify conspiratorial elite dominates pluralist governments.

The extreme right in America believes the state should shed its neutrality among religions and embrace those Christian churches that uphold the moral culture that is central to American identity. Some right-wing extremists wish to go further and establish a Christian theocracy in which the borderlines between state and church structures become increasingly blurred and even eradicated.

Islamic fundamentalists are committed to creating a theocracy. Muslims have long sought "din wa dawla" – the integration of church and state.[63] Some Muslims have sought to liberalize or secularize the governance of Islamic societies – most famously the effort of Mustafa Kemal Atatürk to "Westernize" Turkey after the disintegration of the Ottoman Empire. However, "the Kemalist option" has been much resisted, and some Islamic theocracies have been re-established, especially after the Iranian Revolution of 1979. There are presently many movements to "Islamize" other governments in Islamic societies, such as those in Pakistan and Saudi Arabia, that are regarded as overly sympathetic to Western elites and inadequately concerned with traditional Muslim values. Such *theocracies* involve church-dominated governments that create and enforce regulations that reflect divine law and that sustain church-defined moral behavior of individuals. For some Islamic extremists, such theocracies are necessary to prepare Muslims for a future apocalypse.

The Extreme Left: Fighting Globalization and Other Forms of Domination

According to Hardt and Negri, the most prominent theorists on the extreme left, capitalism and imperialism do not fully capture the structure of the new international political economy:

> There is emerging a new form of global order that we call Empire. Our point of departure was the recognition that contemporary global order can no longer be understood adequately in terms of imperialism as it was practiced by modern powers based primarily on the sovereignty of the nation-state extended over foreign territory. Instead, a "network power," a new form of sovereignty, is now emerging, and it includes as its primary elements, or nodes, the dominant nation-states, along with supranational institutions, major capitalist corporations, and other powers.[64]

In old-fashioned imperialism, imperial powers merely controlled economic processes, but Empire involves "biopolitical production," in which all aspects of social behavior are subject to social control, and rule is "interiorized within subjects themselves."[65] Capital has become more mobile than ever, has technologies that more thoroughly pierce both mature and developing nations, and involves processes that are more able to manipulate and control citizens, orienting them to a life centered on production and consumption in ways that serve the interests of the corporate elite. Leaders and citizens in political communities throughout the world willingly participate in the global economy and enter into one-sided agreements to attract mobile capital because they believe such arrangements are the key to future affluence. The extreme left maintains that this is an illusion, that the promised affluence is often fraudulent. Even if economic growth occurs and people attain higher wages, there are enormous costs. Private material goods might be more plentiful, but common goods become scarcer and immaterial goods become less valued. Economic prosperity is always relative, as economic development creates more real and perceived material needs that can only be satisfied by more intense economic activity. People's overall sense of well-being is reduced despite their higher standards of living, as they devote more of their lives to alienated labor, as they have less leisure time, as they go into debt to pay for their higher standard of living, as they devote more of their lives to maintaining the material goods that clutter their lives, as they feel increasingly insecure and vulnerable to changing economic forces that can deprive them of their jobs and livelihoods, and as their natural environments are devastated and depleted.[66] Additionally, Empire has sustained a permanent state of war, as opponents of the current global order do not engage in conventional battle against Empire, but, like Islamic terrorists, are "a swarm of insects" that create threats everywhere and at all times, thus necessitating a continuous "state of emergency" that justifies the global policing of the world, with its curtailments of a sense of security, civil liberties, and democracy.[67]

The extreme left can find no place within pluralist communities to turn for relief from these forces. Democratic governments within pluralist nations and sub-communities are dominated by capitalist interests and see their role as facilitating the community's participation in the global capitalist system. Perhaps it is possible to envision international political organizations being responsible for constraining multinational corporations and global markets on behalf of the interests of labor and the environment, but the extreme left views existing international organizations as hopeless. The World Bank promotes economic growth in developing nations, but only under terms acceptable to developed nations and corporate interests. The International Monetary Fund aids economies undergoing financial crises, but normally imposes regulations on such countries, requiring them to implement neoliberal policies that serve the interests of global capital. The World Trade Organization is completely oriented toward securing free trade and financial investment policies that enhance economic globalization and thus the interests of transnational corporations. Other international organizations like the United Nations have neither the legitimacy nor the capacity to be of any help. While Hardt and Negri (and other left-wing extremists) may entertain experiments in global reform, they have few illusions that these would be effective and thus call for abandoning all forms of sovereign control that presently exist and "imagining a new science of democracy" – one that is yet to be defined but would clearly be different than the pluralist arrangements that exist in many political communities today.[68]

The principles of the extreme left regarding community structures are more oriented toward criticizing current arrangements than offering alternatives. The deep greens probably have the most developed ideas about alternative economic structures. Their call for decentralization is not merely territorial, but aimed at economic organization. "Small is beautiful" applies to economic activity as well as political communities.[69] "Human-scale" communes and cooperatives are proposed as alternatives to today's mega corporations. Such organizations should be concerned with producing goods for their "use-value" (i.e., their capacity to satisfy the real material needs of citizens) rather than for "exchange-value" (i.e., the capacity to profit from economic trade in ways that enable one to accumulate capital and enlarge one's bank account). By producing only what is needed in the local community, local economic organizations can be highly efficient, avoiding such unnecessary costs as those involved in advertising and marketing their goods and transporting them to faraway markets. Economic growth and development is not seen as an end in itself, and thus a prosperous local economy may be a "steady-state" one that can sustain rather than exploit the environment and that can involve humans in cooperative economic activity rather than ceaseless competition.

Conclusions

According to the pluralist underlying consensus, our political communities require a variety of social, economic, and political structures to provide order and rules of conduct over our lives. Governments (and their military forces), business organizations, unions, churches, schools, and families are among the most important institutions.

Central to pluralist societies is the notion that these structures are *countervailing powers* to one another, ensuring that no one institution dominates people's lives.[70] Pluralists believe in civilian control over the armed forces, to prevent militarism. They seek mixed political economies where governments check the power of corporations and unions, which in turn check each other. They preach separation of church and state, not simply to prevent church domination of government, but so that governments do not dominate the religious sphere. Pluralist governments must be free of control from even the most powerful families in political communities, and they must not control families (at least as long as family members do not abuse one another).

Still, pluralist public philosophy insists that democratic governments remain strong and authoritative relative to other institutions. Governments must be able to defend their communities from such outside threats as terrorism, and they must be able to attack corruption within economic markets, oppressive applications of power by voluntary associations, and intolerant cultures. Democratic governments are especially legitimate, because they are the only structures that can be controlled by the public as a whole.

However, this broad consensus on these ideas about countervailing structures and democratic sovereignty does not curtail conflict within pluralist societies about the precise balance of power among institutions. Governments may place more or fewer regulations over corporate and union activities, and these business organizations may have greater or lesser influence on government. Governments can enhance or reduce controls over religious expression, and religious organizations can seek various levels of penetration of pluralist governments. But such conflicts – when properly bounded – are all part of "politics as usual" within pluralism.

Pluralism could probably accommodate any of the structural reforms sought by the radical right and radical left. Pluralism would be restructured but pluralist societies could survive libertarian goals to reduce governmental activities, globalist goals to reduce governmental regulations on market activities, communitarian goals to strengthen traditional cultural values and voluntary organizations, efforts by the religious right to have governments be more supportive of a variety of churches, egalitarian liberal goals to work toward a greater property-owning democracy, radical green goals to give priority to environmental concerns, and radical democratic goals to more strongly include marginalized groups into community decision-making. Indeed, pluralism might be strengthened by many of these reforms.

Perhaps the criticisms of capitalism by the radical and extreme left are threatening to pluralism, but they can be viewed as efforts to make the friends of pluralism more wary of free markets, the power of capital, and the material values that drive global capitalism. Absent the old left's enthusiasm for nationalizing capital and planned economies, most perspectives among today's left lack any real program to dismantle the economic structures that pluralists accept as providing desirable economic opportunities and affluence.

The decentralized economic structures supported by the deep greens may be the greatest threat from the left to pluralism as it is currently practiced, because it is difficult to see how such an economy could emerge without the destruction of the economic institutions that are now so central to pluralist societies. Such decentralized economic structures may require political decisions to privilege one way of life – the pursuit of a nonmaterial lifestyle – while punishing alternative life styles that depend on participation in the markets of global capitalism. Because pluralism is a public philosophy that insists on political neutrality about the contents of the good life – because pluralists agree on structuring society so as to allow individual auto-nomy in the choice and pursuit of alternative lifestyles – any effort to structure the political economy in a way that reduces such autonomy would be a serious threat to pluralism.

Right-wing support for theocracies currently poses the greatest threat to the pluralist consensus that the major institutions of society should exist as counter-vailing powers that prevent an oppressive centralization of power. Unable to make significant advances toward such unified structures, and believing that the existing structures are hopelessly dominated by corrupt and alien forces, many members of the extreme right have become highly alienated from the basic structures of pluralist societies, withdrawing into their own enclaves in such places as Hayden Lake, Idaho (the home of the Aryan Nation), rural counties that are hospitable to militia and patriot groups, and fundamentalist churches like World Church of the Creator and the Church of Israel. When withdrawal is for purposes of creating training bases for hostile actions against perceived enemies, as exemplified by al-Qaeda units in the mountains of Afghanistan and Pakistan, pluralism is threatened, but when such withdrawal is only a manifestation of severe alienation, pluralists may merely shrug their shoulders. Pluralists may believe that efforts by the extreme right to isolate themselves from pluralist society are based on delusions about the structure of pluralist society, but pluralist philosophy affirms the moral autonomy of residents within their midst. If members of the extreme right withdraw from the basic struc-tures of pluralist society in ways that are not abusive of the rights of others or threatening to pluralism, their minor violations of pluralist practices may be tolerated in order to provide an uneasy peace with those whose beliefs are far removed from the pluralist underlying consensus.

Chapter 12

Questions of Rulers

Who rules and who should rule? Do ordinary citizens and their elected representatives have extensive political power, or do capitalists, special interests, or other elites really rule over political communities? Should ordinary citizens have more power? What constraints should be placed on the power of various kinds of political actors, including citizens?

The democratic idea that all citizens should participate in ruling their political communities can be traced back to ancient times, and various democratic institutions for accommodating citizen participation have long existed. Both Athens and Rome had elements of democracy more than two millennia ago, and various democratic institutions have existed elsewhere in the distant past.[1] But democracy was not highly regarded until the Enlightenment, and democracies were certainly scarce prior to the twentieth century. The instability of democracies throughout history and the realization that democracies have only recently become widely praised have led to speculation that the current "democratic era" may be just a brief interlude in history, not a permanent condition.[2]

Nevertheless, dictatorships, military regimes, and other contemporary alternatives to democracy have little appeal. Most contemporary political theorists reject guardianship – the ideal of having political communities ruled by a small elite selected and trained to exhibit uncommon wisdom, knowledge, and virtue – because guardianships seem always to descend into corruption and because even an enduring benevolent guardianship would not provide the extensive freedoms that are central to democracies.[3]

Advocates of democracy believe that citizens and their elected representatives should share extensive political power. Such power can be defined as the capacity of political actors to get what they want when community issues are established, resolved, and implemented. If you want to raise the minimum wages paid to workers, for example, you have direct power to the extent that you use your political resources to have the issue considered, get your proposed change enacted, and ensure the policy is fully implemented. You also can have indirect influence if you use your resources to get others to want what you want and induce them to apply power to get the issue on the political agenda, enacted, and implemented. Estimating the overall power of various political actors is extremely difficult.[4]

While the friends of pluralism agree that democratic forms of governance are best and that elected representatives and citizens should have more power than other actors, they often have different principles about the distribution of power between representatives and citizens. And many other voices believe that other kinds of actors – such as capitalists and others with "big money," various special interest groups, and proclaimed "hidden powers" – really dominate political communities. By considering how different ideologies look at questions of rulers, we can appreciate the commonalities and differences in how people think about democracy.

Classical Liberals: Empowering Representatives While Holding Them Accountable

Classical liberals sought an alternative to the manner in which power was distributed in Europe at the beginning of the modern period. They wanted to reduce the power of monarchs, aristocrats, and religious leaders. The intellectuals and owners of industrial property who developed and adhered to classical liberalism wanted power to devolve to the middle-classes, of which they were a part. They sought a representative democracy that empowered those who held property and only slowly were they persuaded that the working classes should also have a voice in ruling.[5] The initial motivation of classical liberals for democratizing government was to hold governmental officials accountable to property-holders, so that their property rights would not be abused. As classical liberalism matured during the nineteenth century, liberals were persuaded that democracy meant having governments that were accountable to a broader public.

Classical liberals recognized that democratic elections did not just provide accountability; they also authorized the winners to rule during their terms of office. Electoral victory legitimates elected officials having more power than other members of society. However, by endorsing representative democracy, liberals did not want to concentrate all political power in the hands of legislators and elected executives. They wanted citizens and non-elected experts to share in the distribution of power. But liberals have always assumed that elected representatives should have pre-eminent power within political communities.

For liberals, the power of representatives resides in their capacity to enact legislation. In this capacity, representatives should not be mere *instructed delegates* who decide issues on the basis of dominant public opinion. Nor should representatives be *trustees* who decide issues on the basis of their independent judgments about the good of society. Instead, liberals expect representatives to decide policy issues on the basis of expert recommendations, public discussion, debate, and bargaining among various affected interests. In order for effective and fair policies to emerge, liberals believe that a wide range of interests should be represented in the policy-making process. Thus, liberals have focused considerable attention on the question of representation.

Most early liberals rejected the idea that all citizens should be represented in the electorate, as discussed in chapter 10. They initially insisted that only property-owners were qualified to be voters, though they relaxed qualification standards during the nineteenth century. However, John Stuart Mill's scheme of weighted voting, which would give multiple ballots to the most educated, illustrates lingering fears among classical liberals that the poor and working class would be represented in greater number than the more well-to-do (but smaller) classes.

In addition to being concerned about representation in the electorate, classical liberals were concerned with representation in legislatures. Early liberals like John Locke suggested that only property-owners needed such representation, and they therefore supported property qualifications for holding elected office. While owners of rural estates, owners of emerging industries, landlords of urban property, and other property-owners had diverse interests that classical liberals thought should be represented, people without property or with interests in issues other than pre-serving and promoting their property interests remained unrepresented in early liberal governments. But as liberalism matured in the nineteenth century, liberals became more concerned with having legislatures that better represented all citizens. In *Considerations on Representative Government*, for example, John Stuart Mill advocated proportional representation. Rather than having district elections in which a party that narrowly lost in all districts would be left unrepresented, he called for a scheme (now widely adopted worldwide) that assured each party is represented in legislatures according to its proportion of the total vote.

By endorsing representative democracy, classical liberals sought a much broader distribution of power than existed in the ancient regimes of Europe, but they always stopped short of calling for populist democracy giving direct and equal power to all citizens. Classical liberals – ranging from Madison to Mill – thus joined more conservative thinkers like Alexis de Tocqueville in expressing concerns about the *tyranny of the majority*. Liberals have feared that minority rights to hold property, to exercise freedom of conscience, and to act freely in the private realm can easily be invaded by unlimited majority rule of citizens. Madison argued that minority rights must be guaranteed in order to secure minority compliance with electoral results. If elections permit majorities to enact legislation curtailing minority rights, outvoted minorities may resort to violence whenever they lose an election. To provide universal security and peace, classical liberals have argued that majority rule must yield to minority rights.

Illustrative of liberalism's aversion to populism is John Stuart Mill's call for *skilled democracy*: a three-tiered scheme regarding the distribution of political power. At the top would be a governing elite – non-elected experts who should craft legislation for the overall good of political communities as determined by utilitarian analysis. In the intermediate position would be elected representatives, who should oversee the elite, accepting or rejecting their proposals. At the bottom would be citizens, who should in turn oversee the decisions of their representatives, using the electoral process to remove representatives if they approve proposals that violate citizen rights. In short, Mill exemplified the view of classical liberals that citizens should be several steps removed from direct governing power.

Traditional Conservatives: Finding a Place for Elitism Within Democracy

In response to the initiatives of classical liberals (and radicals) to democratize political communities, traditional conservatives defended existing monarchies and aristocracies throughout much of the nineteenth century. Nostalgia for the Crown and preference for elite rule have always been central to the predispositions of traditional conservatives, but they have also been realists, ready to accommodate broader social changes. Edmund Burke, for example, accepted parliamentary supremacy over the Crown, and during the past two centuries, traditional conservatives have gradually accepted the increasing democratization of governments.

Initially, traditional conservatives maintained that there existed a *natural aristocracy* and that society was best served when those people born into established families were in positions of leadership. Over time, this belief gave way to the notion of a political hierarchy based on acquired talents obtained through education and experience. Only the elites at the top of this political hierarchy have the virtue, competence, and prudence to govern wisely. Finding a place for such elites within democracy has been a major concern of traditional conservatives.

Burke developed the theories of virtual representation and trusteeship in order to strengthen elite power within representative democracies. In response to the liberal claim that people were not represented in government unless they could vote for (or against) a particular legislator who was their representative, Burke defended the notion of *virtual representation*. According to this, all non-voting citizens (such as women or those who did not meet property qualifications) were "virtually" represented by legislators who had been duly elected by more qualified citizens, because elected officials were obligated to pursue the interests of all citizens. Many traditional conservatives applied this concept to argue that legislators from England could represent American colonists even though the colonists were not able to elect their own representatives, because it was the duty of representatives to look after the interests of all Englishmen (whether at home or in the colonies).[6]

Burke also rejected the claim that elected leaders should be delegates – mere errand boys who voted according to the passions of their constituents. Burke argued instead that elected representatives should be *trustees*, custodians of the public interest who base their positions on what is best for society as a whole, and in the long run, and who refuse to pander to popular opinion.

Behind both these theories were Burke's views that most people are too passionate, inconsistent, and incompetent to rule, and that representative democracy should merely be a device for selecting among elites who were competent to rule. At most, the role of the people should be to control the improper use of authority. In Burke's words:

[N]o legislator, at any period of the world, has willingly placed the seat of active power in the hands of the multitude; because there it admits of no control, no regulation, no steady direction whatsoever. The people are the natural control on authority; but to exercise and to control together is contradictory and impossible.[7]

Elections merely gave the people an occasion to exercise some sort of control over those who failed to govern wisely.

Anarchists: Rejecting All Rulers

Because anarchists refuse to be ruled, they reject any system of rulers. They oppose both conventional governments (such as those ruled by monarchs, aristocrats, and capitalists) and revolutionary governments (such as those ruled by a dictatorship of the proletariat), because all such governments create hierarchies of rulers and ruled. Proudhon captured this anarchistic sentiment when he proclaimed: "Whoever puts his hand on me to govern me is a usurper and a tyrant; I declare him my enemy."[8]

But what about democratic governments? At least ideally, democracy is a system of government in which the people rule themselves. Indeed, early anarchists like William Godwin argued that democracy is superior to other forms of government because, under its ideal form, every man is considered an equal and because democratic participation helps develop fellow feelings among citizens.[9] Nevertheless, subsequent anarchists stressed that even democratic governments are coercive. Even in ideal democracies where all citizens participate in making laws, the people as a collective body rule, and their laws restrict individual liberty.

Anarchists insist that each person must rule himself. To be free, each person should only obey those laws of his own making. Two aspects of democracy undermine this imperative. First, most democracies employ representatives rather than providing for direct participation by citizens. Whenever representatives vote contrary to the will of their constituents, the laws no longer reflect the will of the people. Yet, in representative democracy, citizens must obey laws that are contrary to their will. Second, most democracies employ majority rule in reaching decisions. This means that the minority must obey laws that are not of their making. Thus, only unanimous direct democracy is consistent with the anarchist principle that each person must rule himself, because only in such a process does each person speak for himself and concur with the outcome.[10] Anarchists recognize that only very small, face-to-face communities allow everyone to participate directly in decision-making and reach unanimity.

Marxists: The Need for a Temporary Dictatorship
of the Proletariat

Marx asserted that capitalists dominate liberal societies. Capitalists make important decisions about the production and distribution of material goods in market

economies, subject to little or no influence by governmental officials, let alone representatives of the proletariat. Insofar as governmental officials exercise authority, they
did so in response to the interests of capitalists and not those of ordinary citizens.
Consequently, Marx characterized even democratically elected representatives as
"the executive committee of the bourgeoisie." Democratic elections, therefore, fail
to empower citizens, because the real power-wielders in society – capitalists – are not
candidates for election, nor can they be democratically removed from office. Those
people seeking election, moreover, must respond to the interests of the capitalist class,
because capitalism could not prosper and increase the wealth of the community unless
capitalists prosper. For this reason, Marx doubted that democratic elections could
bring to power representatives who would serve the interests of the working class and
who would use their governmental power to achieve the goals of ordinary citizens.[11]

For Marx, the revolution against capitalism was to be the first genuinely democratic moment in modern society. It required widespread participation by the great
multitude of working people who previously had no voice in their political communities.
As we shall see below, subsequent communist revolutionaries advocated the concept
of "substitutionism," claiming that revolutions could be made on behalf of the proletariat, but there is no evidence that Marx shared this view. For Marx, the revolution
could not be engineered by a vanguard that acted on behalf of the proletariat but
were not of the proletariat; intellectuals and party leaders could only help to form
proletarian class-consciousness and spark widespread proletarian revolt. According to
Engels, "Marx entirely trusted to the intellectual development of the working class,"
so that "the emancipation of the working class must be an act of the working class
itself."[12]

Marx claimed that, after the revolution, the dictatorship of the bourgeoisie would
be replaced by a *dictatorship of the proletariat*. He used the term dictatorship to
emphasize the domination of the proletariat *over* the bourgeoisie, but there was to
be no dictatorship *within* the proletariat. Just as Marx envisioned no vanguard of the
proletariat during the revolution, he never mentioned a vanguard that would govern
on behalf of the proletariat after the revolution. Nor did he conceive of one-party
control of the state by leaders of the communist party. For Marx, the dictatorship of
the proletariat would be, in Tony Smith's words, "a decidedly popular affair."[13] The
bourgeoisie, however, would not be included in this popular dictatorship, because
this kind of democracy was restricted to those who accepted the idea that progress toward communist ideals could not be made by making accommodations to
capitalist ideals and the interests of the bourgeoisie.

The Paris Commune seems to have provided Marx with a model for how democracy would function during the transitory socialist society. There would be freedom
of speech and assembly; there would be open discussion and debate within neighborhoods and factories. Representatives would be selected to higher-level organizations,
but they would act as delegates, rather than as trustees, and would be subject to
recall if they failed to act according to their democratically devised instructions.
Delegates would receive few perks of office, and their salaries would be those of the
average worker.[14]

Post-Marxists now offer a revisionist account of Marx that claims he was tempera-
mentally democratic in two senses. First, he wanted to make democratic institutions
more accessible to citizen participation and increase working-class involvement. Second,
he wanted to expand the agenda of issues that could be resolved democratically. In
this regard, he rejected the liberal public–private distinction that put economic issues
and the power of capitalists beyond the reach of democratic control.[15] Believing that
capitalists would never concede their own capacity to dominate economic life, Marx
concluded that they would resist his preferred democratic reforms and had to be
overthrown by a democratic revolt.

Marxists thought that the need for the dictatorship of the proletariat would end
as the state withered away. In an ideal communist society, power would be broadly
dispersed among workers in their decentralized workplaces and associations, and
there would be genuine self-management. Changes in economic structures would
bring about transformations in both human nature and the nature of society that
would eliminate the need for some humans to be ruled by others.

Communists: The Need for a Vanguard of the Proletariat

Like orthodox Marxists, communists such as Lenin, Stalin, and Mao believed that a
ruling class dominated every existing society and ruled in its own interests. They also
agreed with Marx that changes in such a structure of power would have to occur in
two distinct stages. In the first phase, societies must be ruled by a dictatorship of the
proletariat that eradicates every trace of capitalism (and feudalism in less-developed
societies) and transforms how people think into a mode that is non-alienated and
embraces creative labor. In the second and final stage – after citizens are so transformed
– government will have no coercive tasks left to perform, and rulers will no longer be
necessary. In the ideal communist society, anarchism – a society without rulers – will
be possible.

However, communists departed from Marx in their views about who would rule
during and after the revolution. Marx did not believe that successful revolution
could occur in societies that were unprepared for it (i.e., that were not in an advanced
stage of capitalism), nor did he believe that an elite acting on behalf of the proletariat
could carry out the revolution. But Lenin, Mao, Castro, and others led revolutions in
countries that were not industrialized, had small or non-existent proletarian classes,
and thus required a *vanguard* to foment the revolution.

Following the revolution, Stalin and many other communists perceived the need
for a one-party state that ruled during the transitional period. The elite domination
that this implied was quite contrary to Marx's anticipation of a largely democratic
dictatorship of the proletariat, as discussed above. However, Lenin and other communist theoreticians suggested that the power of the party could decrease and that of
the proletariat would increase as the working class developed, both as a proportion
of the population and in its consciousness as being cooperative, creative laborers.
Thus, the distribution of power changes after the revolution, residing first with the

revolutionary vanguard, then shifting toward the proletariat proper, and finally resulting in a full communist society that eliminates any form of rule.

Fascists and Nazis: Concentrating Power in the Hands of a Single Ruler

Fascists and Nazis reject democratic forms of government for a form of elitism in which political power is concentrated in the hands of a single ruler (e.g., Il Duce in Italy and the Führer in Germany). There are three central elements to such elitism. First, it abandons the idea of electoral accountability. Second, it makes power centralized and unlimited, rather than divided and checked as in liberal democracies. Third, rather than deriving their goals and programs from consultations with the people, rulers are said to attain superior knowledge about the national interest from their own intuitions. We can understand Fascist and Nazi principles concerning questions of rulers by considering these three elements.

First, rulers should not be elected by competitive democratic elections, at least not once a true leader is installed in office. Mussolini and Hitler initially sought power by means of elections. However, shortly after attaining office, both the Italian Fascist Party and the National Socialist Party in Germany acquired dictatorial powers for their leaders from subservient legislatures, and they then suppressed political opposition. Insofar as elections were held under fascist or Nazi regimes, they were plebiscites that merely permitted citizens to affirm the power of those who had emerged as leaders of the ruling party. To allow truly competitive elections would have undermined the unity and harmony of society stressed by these ideologies.

Second, constitutional limitations and institutional checks on the powers of ruling elites are weak or nonexistent. In fascist Italy and Nazi Germany, the party controlled public opinion, education, the media, and most other groups or institutions that might have resisted elite edicts. All agencies of the state were placed in the hands of party members who were obedient to Il Duce and the Führer at the top of the party. Hitler's absolute power was enforced by a top-down administrative structure that eliminated the capacity of subordinates holding intermediate positions in the hierarchy to exercise independent judgment and influence. According to Hannah Arendt, in this ruling structure "the will of the Fuehrer can be embodied everywhere and at all times," enabling Nazis to achieve an intense concentration of power that "gives opposition or sabotage almost no chance to become effective."[16] The power of Il Duce also emanated downward through hierarchies of party and state authority, but (in contrast to Nazism) there was less emphasis on the notion that all authority was derived from Mussolini. While ultimate authority was vested in Il Duce, there was in fascism some latitude for initiative and discretion among subordinates.

The third anti-democratic feature of fascism and Nazism involved the expansive roles expected of leaders. Beyond establishing a legislative agenda, administering the executive branch of government, being the military commander-in-chief, and representing the nation in foreign affairs, Il Duce and the Führer were expected to know and articulate their nation's will and destiny. In fascist and Nazi ideology, the leader's will is the same as the will of the nation. Ideally, neither Il Duce nor the Führer acted out of personal interest or whim. Instead, both were in mystical union with all people of the nation and intuitively grasped the will of the populace and the national destiny. Having discovered and interpreted the will and destiny of the nation, it was the leader's role to communicate it to the people in ways that elicited their affirmation and obedience. Fascists and Nazis did not claim that there is a rational or objective basis for determining that the goals, policies, and programs of Il Duce or the Führer do in fact conform to the national will. Instead, these ideologies simply assumed and asserted that the leader knew it. Such an epistemological assumption greatly enhanced the power of such leaders, since the ideologies provided no basis for questioning their directives.

Such principles about rulers may seem odd to people accustomed to democratic norms, but such norms were not especially prevalent in Italy and Germany during the 1920s when fascists and Nazis came to power. Indeed, a leading school of social scientists at the beginning of the twentieth century – *the elite theorists* – were highly critical of democratic rule. Vilfredo Pareto (1848–1923) differentiated between the gifted few and the herd and claimed that the masses must follow elites like sheep. Gaetano Mosca (1858–1941) asserted that elite rule could be relatively responsive to the needs of the masses, even if elites gained power by self-legitimating myths. Robert Michels (1876–1936) proposed his well-known "iron law of oligarchy," which states that all forms of political organization tend to evolve into a small group of leaders and a large group of followers. While Pareto, Mosca, and Michels were responsible academics who opened the door to important questions about the possibilities and forms of democracy, fascists and Nazis took from them more simple conclusions: societies, quite rightly, are ruled by elites.

Beyond the elite theorists, many other European intellectuals espoused ideas that helped to justify elite rule. For example, the writings of Friedrich Nietzsche (1844–1900) were often simplistically interpreted as a call for a heroic man or "the overman," whose creative "will to power" would put him in a position to dominate the multitude. The writings of Georges Sorel (1847–1922) gave Mussolini appreciation of the use of myth for manipulating the masses and of the nobility of violence in achieving political ends. Sorel seemed to suggest that the ruler should govern by virtue of his superior ability and that he should use mythical images and employ violence to energize the masses on behalf of national goals.

Contemporary Liberals: More Representative and Responsive Democracies

Liberals have believed that, as long as all citizens have the right and opportunity to participate, democracy can function effectively and fairly even if most people choose not to participate or limit their participation to voting in periodic elections. Robert Dahl, a prominent liberal democratic theorist, divides citizens into two groups: those who participate extensively (*homo politicus*) and those who do not (*homo civicus*).[17]

The inevitable existence of these two strata makes unachievable the democratic ideal of political equality among all citizens. Therefore, contemporary liberals are satisfied with a second-best approximation of democracy, which Dahl calls *polyarchy*. In polyarchies, all citizens have fundamental political rights, including the opportunity to participate, and governments are controlled by elected officials who modify their conduct so as to win elections in political competition with other candidates and parties.[18] Contemporary liberals support such arrangements for several reasons. *Homo civicus* need not devote much time to politics. Simply by voting in periodic elections, citizens acquire "indirect influence," as elections give leaders incentives to enact policies reflecting citizen preferences and needs. *Homo civicus* need not meet ideal standards of civic virtue. He need not be well informed on all issues of the day; he need not have a sophisticated ideology; he need not know the public good and put it ahead of his personal interests. Citizens only need to evaluate the overall performance of officials based on casual observations. Have officials abused the public trust? Have prominent problems dwindled or are they accelerating? Have representatives responded to the needs of their constituents? Relatively unsophisticated citizens can remove representatives who fail these tests through the device of contested elections. Thus, elected officials have strong incentives to be responsive to citizens' preferences and needs, as they are controlled and held accountable for their performance even if only some citizens actually vote in elections and even if their information about politics is limited.[19]

Contemporary liberals, like classical liberals, are committed to representative democracy. They believe that pre-eminent power should reside with elected officials, and they have sought to increase the representativeness of such officials. They initially recognized that making the electorate more representative was a necessary prerequisite to having public officials better represent all citizens. While classical liberals focused on removing property qualifications for voting, contemporary liberals have extended voting rights to women, racial minorities, and younger people. Additionally, they have often sought other means of increasing the representativeness of legislatures. For example, liberals in the US have been concerned that Blacks and Hispanics (as well as the poor, women, and many other groups) remain significantly underrepresented on city councils, and they have sought changes in electoral arrangements – for example by having wards that are composed largely of minorities – so as to improve the prospects for electing minorities to office.[20] Liberals have also been concerned with bureaucratic representation, for example by urging city police departments to recruit and promote more Black, Hispanic, and female officers.

Despite gains in the representativeness of the electorate and of public officials, contemporary liberals believe that real power in policy-making remains distributed in ways that depart from democratic ideals. Compared to most citizens, business interests have held "a privileged position" among the interest groups that have become so influential in representative democracies.[21] To balance the interest group system, liberals have urged the formation of new groups representing consumers, the poor, minorities, women, and other relatively unorganized citizens, and they have pushed for once again strengthening labor unions.[22]

In a related vein, liberals recognize that specialized policy arenas – often called "subgovernments" – have emerged.[23] These arenas are usually dominated by business organizations that have large economic stakes in a particular issue area, agency officials who provide policy-specific expertise, and members of legislative committees whose constituencies benefit from governmental spending in the area. In the US, the most famous of these subgovernments is the "military-industrial complex," composed of defense contractors, leaders in the defense department and the military, and congressmen whose districts contain military bases or defense contractors employing many constituents. Subgovernments associated with scientific-educational, agricultural, medical, and other interests may also exist.

Contemporary liberals have ambivalent attitudes regarding such power arrangements. Subgovernments can be an effective means of bringing governmental power to bear on national problems. The expertise of interest groups and bureaucrats can be employed in specialized areas. And legislators can develop expertise in specialized policy areas, enabling them to lead other legislators to more effective decisions. Nevertheless, contemporary liberals recognize that many interests and citizens are unable to penetrate these power arrangements, resulting in policies that may better serve dominant special interests than the public interest. Such negative aspects of subgovernments have prompted some liberals to try to control their powers. Theodore Lowi argues that such control must begin with legislatures practicing the principles of *juridical democracy* by delegating fewer powers to these subgovernments.[24] Rather than passing vague legislation providing funding and directing agencies to achieve certain goals (such as improving student performance in the public schools), the rule of law must be restored. According to Lowi, legislatures must draft laws that state precisely what is to be done, how funds are to be spent, and who is to be affected. Other liberals call for greater openness and representation within subgovernments. For example, as the Federal Drug Administration (FDA) considers whether various experimental drugs should be placed on the market, liberals call for input from potential patients as well as from the drug manufacturers, physicians, and scientists who have traditionally dominated this policy arena. Finally, some liberals seek greater emphasis on performance criteria. Those programs that are not performing adequately should be terminated by "sunset clauses" in the enabling legislation. By reducing the discretionary powers delegated to administrative agencies, by opening subgovernments to a broader array of interests, and by holding these power-wielders more accountable to the legislature, contemporary liberals hope that the power of subgovernments will not be abused.

In summary, contemporary liberals support various reforms in order to make the distribution of power in liberal societies better correspond to the democratic ideal that the primary rulers in a liberal society are its elected representatives and citizens. However, liberals insist that dominant power should reside with elected representatives. They seldom support reforms that empower citizens through populist democratic procedures. They believe representatives are more able than citizens to set agendas establishing priorities among issues, to adjust competing interests through compromise, and to oversee administrative bodies.

The Radical Left: More Inclusive and Participatory Democracies

The radical left seeks *strong democracies* through greater citizen involvement – more so than other ideologies. While liberals are satisfied if most citizens confine their political participation to voting in periodic elections and becoming active on those few issues in which their primary interests are at stake, the radical left wants citizens to be more actively involved in counteracting capitalist domination and addressing community problems.[25] The radical left believes that liberal democracies do not adequately control capitalism, because representatives within governmental institutions are more often the agents of capitalism than of the public, and because corporate decision-making is, for the most part, untouched by the principles and institutions of democracy. The radical left thus seeks to weaken capitalist influence within political communities by increasing the representation of socialist, green, and other leftist parties in governments, by employing more frequently the tools of direct democracy, by democratizing workplaces, and by working toward a more equal distribution of power in the various associations of everyday life. In general, the radical left embraces "contentious democracy," a conceptualization that stresses that democracy can never be fully achieved but rather is a continuing process of movement toward political equality.[26] Such a process involves the interrogation of prevailing democratic practices and structures for their inequalities and exclusions and supporting a wide variety of struggles by the oppressed.

Democratic socialists gave the most prominent voice to advocating stronger democracy throughout the twentieth century. They believed that the realization of socialist ideals did not require the revolution predicted by Marx, but could be pursued during a long evolutionary process of strengthening democracy. The rudimentary forms and institutions of democracy that emerged in the US, Britain, and a few other European societies during the nineteenth century encouraged democratic socialists. For example, the Chartist movement, which was particularly influential in Britain between 1837 and 1848, led to universal manhood suffrage, electoral districts of equal size, the secret ballot, the abolition of property qualifications for candidates to Parliament, and the payment of members of Parliament. These changes enabled the working class to be better represented in Parliament and led to policy reforms that were responsive to labor and the poor.[27] During the twentieth century, socialist parties governed in many countries, but they made only modest progress toward achieving socialist goals. Thus, the radical left today recognizes that democratic institutions must be continuously reformed and strengthened to reduce the influence of such capitalist interests as industrialists, bankers, and realtors and to increase the influence of those groups within society that have less power than their counterparts, such as labor unions, neighborhood organizations, minority groups, feminists, and environmentalists.

The radical left recognizes the necessity of representative democracy, and thus supports many of the reforms pursued by contemporary liberals to make voters more representative of all citizens, to organize groups that might be countervailing forces to powerful business interests in the pressure group system, and to make public officials more representative of ordinary citizens. Elements of the radical left seek not only to increase the power of the working class but also to locate those groups of citizens who have been marginalized, enhancing their voting participation, their organization, and their voice in government. Even significant successes in these efforts are unlikely to dislodge capitalist and corporate concerns from governmental agendas, and so the radical left seeks means of pressuring representatives to give greater attention to their concerns.

One such tactic is to emphasize the instruments of *direct democracy*, such as initiatives, referenda, and recalls. Initiatives allow citizens to write and submit for voter approval legislation addressing concerns of low visibility and priority to legislators. Referenda deal with issues that legislatures have addressed but cannot resolve and that are thus submitted to the public. Recalls allow citizens to bring a premature end to the term of office of officials who have failed to represent their constituents effectively. Some among the radical left believe that provisions for initiatives, referenda, and recalls enlarge the power of voting rights, giving citizens the opportunity to enact directly policies that respond to the goals of socialists, environmentalist, feminists, and various marginalized populations. For example, the radical left has frequently used initiatives to thwart economic development projects that are seen as harmful to the environment or that have received extensive subsidies ("corporate welfare") from city councils.

Another tactic for marginalized groups is to turn to disruptive tactics, such as strikes, boycotts and demonstrations. Such tactics are intended to impose costs on their targets and generate publicity for issues that might broaden public support for concerns that public officials have ignored. The anti-war protests that occurred during the War in Vietnam and that now are occurring over the prolonged involvement of the U.S. military in Iraq illustrate how the radical left can use protest to gain the attention of leaders within representative democracies.

Even if the radical left is better represented and puts more pressure on democratic governments, such stronger democracies remain limited in their power within the broader political economy. Because the most powerful organizations in a capitalist economy are privately owned and controlled, *workplace democracy* is an important goal for the radical left. Workplaces are important arenas for democratic participation, because they are places where relationships of authority and subordination are most pronounced and where people spend most of their lives. G. D. H. Cole (1889–1959) emphasized the importance of workplace democracy to socialism almost a century ago, regarding the subordination of workers to their economic bosses as a form of slavery.[28] He pointed to several positive effects of enhancing the involvement and influence of workers in industrial decision-making. Workplace democracy would develop appreciation amongst workers of socialist ideals, and would enhance their participatory skills and thus train them for social democracy in the larger world. It would reduce workers' fear of authorities, increase management appreciation of the capacities of workers, and thus diminish social and class distinctions. Greater involvement of workers would unleash their suppressed talents and energies, enhancing economic productivity. Many experiments with worker participation in the governance of economic institutions provide encouragement to socialists (and even some liberals) about its effectiveness.[29] Japan's economic miracle during the 1980s has been cited as providing compelling evidence for worker participation. By having relatively egalitarian compensation structures and by providing for regular and extensive consultation between managers and workers, Japanese firms made progress toward achieving such socialist goals as fraternal harmony, recognition and utilization of unique individual talents, and social justice.[30]

The radical left also supports *grassroots democracy*. Just as the radical left wants citizens to exercise more power in their workplaces, civic communitarians in particular call for citizens to exercise more power in other organizations in which they lead their daily lives: families, neighborhoods, schools, religious groups, civic groups, and so forth.[31] Radical feminists want to democratize the family, thereby equalizing the power of husbands and wives.[32] Radical democrats want to democratize their local communities, employing neighborhood assemblies to provide opportunities for citizens to discuss their immediate problems and goals, using community boards and task forces to develop concrete policy proposals, and enacting policies through city councils that represent not just "the growth machine" but also the diversity of citizens living in urban areas.[33] Such measures taken at the grassroots levels are thought to encourage citizens to develop a fuller democratic consciousness. By learning how to promote the public good, communal harmony, and social justice locally, they can better pursue such values in larger political communities.

Contemporary Conservatives: More Formal Representative Democracy

By expressing little interest in democratizing corporations, voluntary associations in civil society, and families, contemporary conservatives are less democratic than the radical left. They are particularly wary of workplace democracy, believing that such democracy will infringe on the property rights of the owners of workplaces, especially their right to make those investments that will maximize profits.

Nevertheless, contemporary conservatives embrace representative democracy within government. Like liberals, they believe that rulers should be selected by and accountable to citizens. By believing that certain mechanisms that distance representatives from popular passions are reasonable – the Electoral College being a prime American example – conservatives are probably less democratic than liberals.

While critical of "professional politicians," conservatives expect talented individuals to hold positions of power in legislatures and executive offices. While expecting representatives to act less like Burkean trustees than advocated by traditional conservatives, today's conservatives believe that good rulers should be able to provide guidance and direction for their political communities, even while listening to the concerns of ordinary citizens.

Conservatives believe that there have been several threats to the proper functioning of representative democracy, particularly in the US. One threat is interest-group liberalism. Conservatives believe that their liberal opponents are simply made up of a gaggle of special interest groups – labor unions, racial minorities, welfare recipients, environmentalists, feminists, and the like. When liberals govern, they respond to numerous special and parochial interests at the expense of the public good. Conservatives believe that real statesmen must replace such liberal politicians.

Another threat to representative democracy, according to contemporary conservatives, is judicial activism, where liberal judges misinterpret the Constitution to justify social policies that would often be rejected by a democratically elected legislature. This threat to democracy is illustrated by the 1973 *Roe v. Wade* decision by the US Supreme Court (which has been used to declare unconstitutional many state laws prohibiting and limiting abortion) and the actions of judges in Massachusetts and California during 2004 to give gay and lesbian couples the rights of civil unions and even marriage (despite state laws and local ordinances to the contrary).

A third threat is that provided by *the New Class* – an elite of liberal professionals, intellectuals, journalists, governmental bureaucrats, and cultural megastars who are committed to various abstract values like human rights and economic egalitarianism. According to Jeane Kirkpatrick (1928–2006), the New Class draws upon intellectual speculation and artistic imagination to envision utopian possibilities, and it forgets the real limits of human nature and economic scarcity.[34] Although at odds with conventional beliefs, the New Class is nevertheless portrayed in the media as speaking for American ideals, influencing popular thinking on many issues. The realities of political life cannot live up to New Class ideals, and this breeds cynicism. In short, the New Class has power, especially over a star-struck public, that is unwarranted, undemocratic, and dysfunctional.

A fourth danger to representative democracy, from a conservative perspective, is captured by the concept of "autonarchy," a system in which government is "controlled by itself,"[35] which is to say, a government that is not controlled at all. According to the conservative commentator who coined the term autonarchy, almost all those who testify at congressional hearings support new governmental initiatives and spending. Most of these people are federal bureaucrats who administer programs in the area, state and local officials who seek funding for their initiatives, other congressmen with interests in the program, and lobbyists for groups benefited by the programs. In short, government is dominated by a "political class" of insiders who benefit from expansion of governmental programs. Taxpayers who must pay for these programs or future generations that must deal with the resulting national debt are in no position to control government-by-itself.

While interest-group liberalism, judicial activism, the New Class, and autonarchy are ideas that conservatives employ to express concerns about democratically elected leaders being overwhelmed by idealistic elites and self-interested insiders, some conservatives also fear that representatives can be overwhelmed by populist forces. Indeed, US conservatives have been divided over how much democratization is healthy in representative government. One branch of contemporary conservatism, which is prominent in the American West, has populist tendencies. They have made widespread use of referenda and initiatives to enact conservative positions in such areas as lowering property taxes, stemming immigration, and reducing gay rights. They have also used the recall to oust liberal Democrats like Gray Davis, the former Governor of California, replacing him, ironically, with a New Class megastar, Republican Arnold Schwarzenegger. Another branch of contemporary conservatism, which is more prominent among the establishment in the America East, has more aristocratic tendencies. These conservatives view populist devices as unnecessary contrivances that reduce the distance between thoughtful representation and the passions of constituencies. In general, eastern conservatives endorse republican structures and processes that distance rulers from the ruled. For example, George Will has argued that the C-SPAN 2 coverage of the Senate has deprived the institution of requisite distance and isolation from the public.[36]

Finally, conservatives have had to address the issue of the executive power in modern democracies. In the US, conservatives have long been critical of the growth in presidential power that was achieved by Franklin Roosevelt, such as his use of direct appeals to the populace to claim popular support in his battles with Congress. FDR created what has been termed "the imperial presidency." Wary of concentrated power, conservatives have defended congressional power and warned against the dangers of populist and powerful presidents. However, they applauded Ronald Reagan's use of executive power to modify and eliminate many liberal programs enacted by prior Democratic regimes, and they see in George W. Bush an effective president who is willing to use his power to enhance national security in an increasingly dangerous world. Since 9/11, Bush has declared that his authority as commander-in-chief has given him the ability to deal with terrorist threats, including engaging in surveillance of American citizens without receiving judicial approval, thereby restricting due process. Conservatives have, for the most part, accepted these aggressive actions and unilateral initiatives.

Although one can see tensions in contemporary conservative thinking about direct democracy and strong presidents, conservatives respond that these do not amount to significant inconsistencies. Conservatism is more about dispositions than firm principles. For conservatives, using populist instruments of direct democracy and electing strong and even imperial presidents are opportunistic means of achieving such conservative goals as redirecting the activities of government away from liberal social and economic programs and toward national security.

The Radical Right: Democracy as Freedom

One can find among the radical right disturbing images about the existing distribution of power. National protectionists in America, such as Pat Buchanan, share some of the left's fears of economic elitism, as they see our real rulers to be the heads of the Business Roundtable, the Council of Foreign Relations, and various transnational interests. However, for the most part, the radical right echoes and sharpens contemporary conservative criticisms that too much power now resides with interest groups (especially those having pro-labor, pro-welfare, pro-environmental, and multi-cultural agendas), liberal judges, and a "New Class" of people who feed off a bloated state. Of course, the various voices on the radical right would like to rein in these powerful actors. In contrast to the radical left, the radical right is not much concerned with generating stronger democracies that encourage greater citizen participation and that are more open to excluded citizens.

In general, the radical right's conception of democracy resembles that of classical liberals, albeit with universal and equal voting rights for all citizens. They focus not on expanding the power of ordinary citizens but, rather, on furthering political and economic freedoms.[37] Democracy provides political rights that enable citizens to participate in what are sometimes called "protective democracies" and "performance democracies."[38] Libertarians like Frederick Hayek regard (protective) democracy as nothing more – and nothing less – than a method of controlling governmental authorities and protecting freedoms by allowing citizens to get rid of tyrannical (or merely ineffective) governmental officials through free elections. Libertarians believe that more expansive conceptions of democracy that seek to open political decision-making to extensive citizen participation and influence result in governments that are more responsive to special interests than to average citizens; such particular interests provide public officials with support in return for policy benefits that the broader public must pay for, both in terms of higher taxes and losses of freedom. Other voices on the radical right seem to endorse performance democracy, a theory developed by Joseph Schumpeter that regards democracy as elite competition for power. Elites form competing parties and seek power by winning elections; as in protective democracy, the role of citizens in government is reduced to simply choosing that party whose "products" (policies and programs) they prefer. This limited role for citizens allows a professional bureaucracy to provide the expertise and steward-ship that is required to run the economy effectively and it gives elected leaders the authority to impose on citizens the obligations that are needed for social harmony and stability.

Although the power of citizens in such conceptions of democracy is limited to choosing among governmental leaders, citizens exert significant influence as parti-cipants in the free market economy, if they have the extensive economic rights that are provided under democratic capitalism. Libertarian economists assert consumer sovereignty – that economic decisions are ultimately determined by the preferences of consumers. Since we all buy goods that we need and want, we vote with our wallets, influencing what is produced and who is rewarded in the market.

Global neoliberals like Thomas Friedman also recognize that anonymous investors exercise great influence in global markets, as their decisions determine what sectors of the economy and what locations will grow and prosper; indeed, the power of investors extends into the political arena, because governmental officials must anti-cipate investor reactions to their political decisions. For example, if governments run a budget deficit or increase welfare spending, investors are likely to see an unfavor-able economic climate and invest elsewhere. In a global economy, where investors can move wealth easily across borders, governmental leaders must pursue policies that encourage investments within their borders.[39] While this may imply that the requirements of investors, not the preferences of citizens, are the greatest influence on the policies of governments, the radical right doubts that this is a significant problem. First, they assert a continuing autonomy and primacy of democratic governments, denying that governments are captured by global capitalists and thus overly responsive to the needs of investors. Their performance model of democracy affirms their belief that competitors for governmental positions will continue to try to win elections by offering voters a wide range of welfare benefits as well as policies that promise economic prosperity for all.[40] Second, the investor class is large and growing, and power is becoming increasingly dispersed throughout the global economy. Globalization has generated enough affluence that stock and bond portfolios are common holdings of many citizens, especially through retirement accounts. Thus investors are not some small, monolithic, and dominating force; investors are as diversified as citizens and consumers in their goals, and their power is highly decentralized. Additionally, they do not rule the day-to-day operations of the companies in which they invest. As Friedman has stressed, in order to survive the intense competition of the global marketplace, companies have had to become more decentralized and democratized in their internal operations.[41]

The radical right is thus less interested in deepening democracy where it exists than in spreading protective and performance democracy to those parts of the world where fundamental political and economic rights are lacking. However, neoliberals and neoconservatives emphasize different models for the diffusion of democracy.

For global neoliberals, the proper way to spread democracy around the world is to encourage the economic development that globalization provides. Jagdish Bhagwati summarizes this globalist perspective by citing the massive research linking globalization to democratization:

> Globalization promotes democracy both directly and indirectly. The direct link comes from the fact that rural farmers are now able to bypass the dominant classes and castes by taking their produce directly to the market thanks to modern information technology, thereby loosening the control of these traditionally hegemonic groups. In turn, this can start them on the way to becoming more independent actors, with democratic aspirations in the political arena. . . . The indirect link, on the other hand, comes from . . . the thesis popularly attributed to (Seymour Martin) Lipset . . . that economic prosperity produces a middle class. This emerging middle class creates, however haltingly, an effective demand for democratization of politics.[42]

In short, as countries acquire some economic investments as a result of an open global economy, they begin to demand more democratic governments, and when such governments replace dictatorships that rule by arbitrary decrees, investors are attracted to the more secure environment provided by the rule of law. Thus begins a positive causal cycle between economic development and democratic development. For neoliberals, globalization results in democratic capitalism, where power is widely dispersed among investors, consumers, and other participants in the marketplace, appropriately concentrated among elected officials in government, and ultimately provided to citizens who can hold governmental leaders accountable.

While agreeing with this theory of democratization by modernization, neoconservatives believe that military means can and should also be employed to spread democracy in some cases. America's invasion of Iraq and removal of Saddam Hussein was, at least ultimately, based on the neoconservative belief that democratic societies have both a moral duty and a practical interest in freeing people elsewhere from tyranny. Natan Sharansky, a former Soviet dissident who immigrated to Israel, co-authored *A Case for Democracy*, which is widely cited by neoconservatives in the Bush administration. Sharansky argues that all people have a right to live in a free society, one that can pass his "town square test":

> If a person cannot walk into the middle of the town square and express his or her views without fear of arrest, imprisonment, or physical harm, then that person is living in a fear society, not a free society. We cannot rest until every person living in a "fear society" has finally won their freedom.[43]

According to neoconservatives, the interests of Americans and citizens of other democracies are served by ridding countries of rulers who create an environment where people fear for their security and safety at the hands of dictators like Saddam or parties that sponsor terrorism like Hamas in Palestine. If citizens are given democratic rights, they will turn their energies to governing themselves effectively, to ensuring their economic freedoms and to using these freedoms to improve their economic well-being. Such people will be unlikely to become angry militants who, in an era of global interconnection, can lash out and inflict great damage in faraway places, as shown by the events of 9/11.

The Extreme Right: Imagining Conspiracies

Believing that the real rulers are some kind of hidden elite, the extreme right denies that the duly elected and appointed leaders of democratic governments have much real power. Most famous in this regard is the conspiratorial theory prominent among white nationalists that a diabolic clique of Jews rules America and indeed the rest of the world – that ours is an International Zionist Occupied Government (IZOG).

While the extreme right wants to dislodge such hidden leaders, they seldom seek a highly democratic alternative. Among the extreme right, there is cult of leadership, especially for charismatic spokespersons for nativist and racist ideas, that is perhaps a residue of fascist and Nazi disdain for democracy. The extreme right prefers top-down governing arrangements, where the leaders are endorsed, more than chosen, by citizens. For example, in America, white nationalists embrace charismatic and outspoken leaders such as David Duke, a former Grand Wizard of the Ku Klux Klan who has run for many political positions including the US presidency, and Matthew Hale, the leader of the Creativity Movement. Such leaders often employ Christian language and symbols to sugar-coat their white supremacy messages to enlarge their followings. As mentioned in chapter 4, Roy Moore, the defrocked Chief Justice of the Alabama Supreme Court, provides another example of the sort of charismatic leadership embraced by the extreme right.

Islam fundamentalists have related conceptions of rulers. While issues of leadership have divided Islam since the death in 632 CE of Muhammad – the prophet who received Allah's laws and established Islam – the question among fundamentalists has never been about the provision of democratic rule, but about the proper identification of rulers.[44] Historically and in principle, Sunni Muslims believe that the leaders of Islam select a caliph as a successor to Muhammad. While the caliph has great authority, due to his piety and his adhering to Islamic traditions, he is not regarded as divinely inspired or infallible, nor is he the sole political authority. In contrast, Shiite Muslims believe that their leader should be a living descendant of Muhammad; unlike the Sunnis, they believe that the first Imam is infallible in his interpretation of Allah's will and thus his authority on all political and religious matters is absolute.[45] In short, fundamentalists believe that the democratic institutions in their societies should have little real power. They believe Islamic societies are best ruled by religious authorities who are most able to understand and interpret the will of Allah. Rulers must be trained in religion, and law must be based solely on divine law rather than secular reason.

The Extreme Left: Seeing Formidable Obstacles to Radical and Global Democracy

Like the radical left, the extreme left seeks a deeper democracy, but they are more disillusioned about the prospects for realizing such a goal. They see all existing democracies as deeply flawed. Most people are effectively excluded from pluralist democratic politics. Even the social movements on behalf of labor, racial and ethnic minorities, women, and gays that liberals and the radical left applaud for widening democracy are overrated. While these movements may have resulted in the inclusion of those movement leaders who accept and work within the norms and practices that have long characterized pluralist politics, they have not much empowered the rank-and-file. Moreover, these movements have urged people to identify with the working class, African-Americans, women, or gays, but these identities can themselves be exclusionary and inadequate to the emerging forms of oppression and exclusion that occur in our society.[46] Perhaps Third World women workers are the most exploited and marginalized people in today's global economy, but getting such people to assume a common identity, effectively organize for political action, and achieve real changes can be a formidable challenge.[47]

The extreme left never accepts as given the arrangements that exist or the interests and identities that are brought to bear on democratic decisions. Every political arrangement, every interest, every identity that now prevails can reflect dominant powers in pluralist society. What people imagine as products of their autonomous concerns are really illusions, the products of manipulation and control by the powers-that-be.

Who are the powers-that-be? The contemporary far left has moved beyond the simple Marxist conviction that capitalism and those who own and control the most capital control everything else. While not discounting the influence of such forces, they have developed much more complex theories to answer the question of who rules.

One such model is that of Michel Foucault, who developed a decentralized conception of power as an antidote to what he saw as dated ideas about sovereignty.[48] According to conventional wisdom, sovereignty or supreme power in a society is monopolized in government. Of course, in a democracy, citizens should control government, giving rise to the notion of popular sovereignty. But for Foucault, a breakdown of sovereignty (and popular sovereignty) has occurred. This breakdown is not so much due to capitalists assuming the power that formerly resided in an autonomous state (or in the citizens that controlled such a state) as it is to the dispersion of power to an extended array of disciplinary agents who control individuals and society in ways that are beyond the reach of law and accountability. In the institutions of everyday life – in our factories, schools, hospitals, asylums, prisons, and numerous other institutions – a vast number of foremen, teachers, doctors, psychiatrists, wardens, and other administrators exercise enormous power over our behavior, our thoughts, and even our identities. They operate not under the rule of law but under conceptions of norms – about what is normal and how to treat the abnormal. A surveillance regime has emerged to detect anything about us that departs from an acceptable normal range. Disciplinary power has emerged to provide treatments and controls that will redirect us toward the norm. A dramatic example can occur at birth, when a doctor delivers an intersexed or hermaphrodite child and urges the parents to have the infant undergo operations that will yield the normally recognized sex characteristics of a boy or girl; in such ways are people's most basic identities controlled by an army of disciplinary agents.[49] Given such a dispersion of power, the extreme left seems to believe or suggest that meaningful popular sovereignty and democratic control are impossible.

Hardt and Negri have provided an even more chilling model of who rules everyone in our globalized society: Empire – globalization's successor to the old colonial powers that ruled in an earlier age of imperialism – rules. Empire is conceived as a network of national and supranational organisms (including multinational corporations) all united under a single logic of rule – presumably the neoliberal logic of globalists. Clearly a superpower like the United States is implicated in Empire, but it is not Empire, as this controlling force is globally constituted and has no center or boundaries. Clearly, Empire includes a capitalist system of investment, production, distribution, and consumption. It includes a liberal culture – one of "non-values" that undermines creativity, community, liberty, and humanity. While Empire has a positive face of providing order, peace, and rights, it has a more dominant negative face of exploitation, alienation, and oppression. Most importantly, Empire is a regime of control beyond Foucault's disciplinary regime, because while we often resist the efforts of disciplinary agents, we internalize the dictates of Empire. Our identities, our interests, and our behavior all reflect the power of Empire, not because Empire constantly has us under its surveillance or because it sends out an army of agents to shape us into normality, but rather because it dwells within us. The idea that we are autonomous citizens able to pursue our genuine interests through democratic means is, at least for the most part, a grand illusion.

Given these conceptions of power, an issue that divides the extreme left is the size of the cracks in the controlling system. Although we are largely controlled, there are moments of opportunity when we can overcome these controls. Those who think that the cracks in the system are fairly wide begin to resemble pluralists. They see that in everyday life, people experience oppression and they often react against it, both individually and collectively. There is nothing deep or mysterious about this. Ordinary people believe that democratic ideals preclude marginalization and oppression, so they stand up for themselves in countless ways. From this perspective, the extreme left assumes as its role that of helping the oppressed identify the injustices that are perpetuated on them, organize for collective action, and otherwise act in politically effective ways. Compared to contemporary liberals and even the radical left, the extreme left is much more militant and "bottom up" in its approach to helping the oppressed. Given their low opinion of those in power within pluralist systems, the extreme left doubts that even progressive politicians can be trusted to bring about real changes, and thus the oppressed must act on their own. Given their lack of resources, this involves putting up a fight – it means imposing costs, if necessary by inflicting disruption and even violence, on those who are comfortable within pluralist society. By employing such actions, the far left hopes that the comfortable will calculate that it is better to concede to the demands of the oppressed than to absorb the continuing costs of their disruptive actions.

Such members of the left presume that the cracks in the systems of control that are currently in place are fairly wide. But others see very little opportunity for such militant activity. They see only the most narrow of cracks in the system. They recognize the means of repression available to the powerful to control agitation. They focus on the capacity of the comfortable to isolate themselves from disruption. Most importantly, they stress the difficulty of awakening the oppressed from their misconstrued interests and identities that keep them docile. Given such constraints, the most that the oppressed can do is "strike like a snake."[50] Such attacks on controlling agents and forces, whether verbal or physical, occur in rare moments of transcendence and heightened consciousness of oppression, and they seem largely cathartic rather than political. Given the enormity of Empire, little of broad impact can be accomplished. But for the individual "snake" who strikes, there is a momentary experience of rising up to one's full humanity and perhaps the beginnings of a personal journey toward becoming a member of the extreme left who can find meaning in a life of deconstructing and confronting the world as it exists.

Conclusions

Pluralists agree that power should be widely dispersed within and across political communities. They believe that unequal power in the marketplace, civil society, and government are inevitable, but they fear great concentrations of power that approach monopolies. They believe, for example, that democratic forces must apply their resources to limit the power of economic elites when such power becomes too concentrated.

Pluralists agree that elected representatives and citizens as a whole should share the exercise of power in government. When pluralist democratic processes function effectively, elected officials will normally arrive at collective judgments that set the political agenda, enact policies, and oversee the implementation of their decisions, and these judgments will coincide with what most citizens want or will support. Representatives should strive to maximize consensus when making decisions, but persistent conflict must be normally resolved by majority rule. While the decisions of representatives should normally be consistent with dominant citizen preferences, representatives will sometimes believe they should exercise independent judgments that conflict with dominant public opinion. At such times, representatives are obligated to explain their actions and must be prepared to be held accountable for their failure to represent citizen preferences.

Pluralists disagree on whether the best system of governance is aristocratic republicanism or democratic republicanism.[51] Aristocratic republicanism, which traces its roots to Edmund Burke and Alexander Hamilton, stresses the importance of strong leadership – of empowering those with the most wisdom, knowledge, and virtue and insisting that such persons exercise independent judgment when governing rather than pandering to ill-informed public prejudices. While such ideas are relatively elitist, aristocratic republicans understand that elites are accountable to citizens through regular, fair, and competitive elections and thus remain committed to weak conceptions of pluralist democracy. Democratic republicanism, which traces its roots to Jean-Jacques Rousseau and Thomas Jefferson, stresses the importance of citizen involvement and responding to the preferences of citizens. As democratic norms have spread and deepened, democratic republicanism has also incorporated demands that marginalized groups be more fully included in the political process and that the political agenda be expanded to address their concerns.[52]

This debate between aristocratic and democratic republicans can be illustrated by those who argue for and against the use of initiatives and referenda. On the one hand, democratic republicans see such devices of direct democracy as important means of deepening democracy. On the other hand, more aristocratic republicans argue that initiatives and referenda overemphasize "vote-centric" conceptions of democracy and underemphasize "talk-centric" conceptions of democracy. Referenda may result in policies that reflect majoritarian passions and prejudices, rather than the thoughtful deliberation that is at least possible by representatives in legislative bodies. Referenda may result in policies that reflect the most popular outcome among extreme choices, while precluding reasonable compromises that are acceptable to most citizens. For pluralists, referenda and initiatives can never replace representative democracy and deliberative legislative bodies; they can only supplement such institutions under circumstances that are specified in the constitutions of pluralist societies. Debates about the extensiveness of constitutional provisions for direct democracy must always take into account the importance of minority rights in a pluralist society. Resolving some issues by referenda can be a way of deepening democracy. But issues that make vulnerable the rights of minorities – whether these be economically advantaged minorities, racial and religious minorities, or gays and other minorities whose lifestyles are unconventional – are usually better addressed through representative institutions, where principled deliberation trumps popular passions and prejudices and where institutional checks help preserve minority rights.[53]

Most ideological voices operate within the pluralist consensus about rulers, but to remain firmly within that consensus, their undemocratic tendencies must be curbed. Traditional conservatives cannot retreat from their increasing willingness to subject political leaders to the electoral accountability of citizens who are given equal and extensive political rights. Marxists cannot slip into an endorsement of a vanguard, but must rather be post-Marxists who want mainly to deepen citizen participation on issues subjecting the economy to democratic control. Contemporary liberals must ensure that their political processes do not delegate too much power to special interests or to unelected public officials like judges and bureaucrats. Contemporary conservatives and libertarians must ensure that their desire to remove constraints on free markets do not generate great concentrations of wealth that enable dominance in markets and governments. Globalists may need to rethink their resistance to democratizing global institutions.[54] And the radical left must ensure that their efforts to create strong democracy do not overly empower "the mob" that imposes anti-pluralist passions.

Finally, pluralism can be endangered by extremist beliefs about who does actually rule. Pluralists find conspiratorial theories by the extreme right about hidden rulers – such as the belief in an IZOG – to be fanciful imaginations that cannot withstand objective scrutiny. For pluralists, widespread belief in such conspiratorial theories are dangerous, because they undermine the legitimacy of the existing regime and encourage citizens to support demagogues who claim the need to work outside existing restraints to eliminate the conspiratorial threat.

Left-wing radicals have also offered conspiratorial theories that are difficult to verify and thus are a dubious guide to political reality. As discussed in chapter 1, the radical left countered pluralism with elite theory more than a half century ago, claiming that nominally democratic communities were really ruled by a narrow and hidden power elite that was removed from any democratic control. Economic elites often have disproportional influence and pluralists must be prepared to detect and resist such domination, but elite theories do more to raise anxieties about the potential for democracy to work on behalf of ordinary (and oppressed) citizens than it provides an adequate model for who rules in pluralist societies.

The work of Foucault, Hardt and Negri, and other such leftists today can be seen in a similar light. They do provide provocative insights into the complex power arrangements at work in pluralist societies. Foucault's disciplinary agents can be observed doing their work, but the extensiveness of their control may be more a matter of theoretical speculation than empirical confirmation. Hardt and Negri's *Empire* lacks the sort of operational indicators that enable intersubjective understandings of what it is, how it acts, or how much power it exerts. *Empire* is likely to give rise to conspiratorial theories of global domination that have the effect of suggesting that the quest for deeper democracy within pluralist societies is hopeless. If that is its effect, it may undermine the legitimacy of existing pluralist regimes and encourage citizens to support demagogues who claim the need to work outside existing restraints to eliminate the conspiratorial threat. Pluralists see theories of power arrangements that are open to various democratic forces as not only more accurate than more dark conspiratorial depictions, but also as providing democratic forces with hope that they can be effective. When citizens lose hope that they can be effective and retreat from political life, illegitimate power-seekers will fill the vacuum.

Chapter 13

Questions of Authority

In what realms of community life do governments exercise authority? What constraints on individual freedom in such areas as economic behavior, social interaction, religious worship, and personal lifestyles can governmental authorities legitimately impose? What extensions and restrictions on government authority are needed?

Discussions of governmental authority are often framed as a debate over the merits of "big" and "limited" government, and this issue can be further focused as a question of governmental spending. In this framing, voices on the left – liberal Democrats in the United States – are often labeled as "tax-and-spend" governmental interventionists, while those on the right – conservative Republicans in the US – are labeled as frugal opponents of governmental spending who tax less of "your money." To provide some perspective on such a debate, it is useful to consider historical trends in federal government spending, which are displayed in table 1.[1] The data show that such spending increased from $42.6 billion in 1950 to $2,050.5 billion in 2005, a 48-fold increase over a half of century, even when adjusted for inflation. However, this huge increase in federal expenditure does not look quite so extraordinary when one considers that the country's gross domestic product (GDP) was more than 34 times as large in 2005 as in 1950. Nevertheless, the data in the fifth column, showing federal outlays as a percentage of GDP, indicate that the government has indeed become significantly more involved in the economy. Whereas federal spending as a percentage of GDP was 14.4 percent in 1950, it was 20.4 percent in 2005. The table also reveals several other interesting facts. First, federal spending has never reached as high a proportion of the country's economic resources as occurred in 1945, when the country was mobilized militarily at the end of World War II. Second, subsequent federal expenditure as a percentage of GDP peaked in the mid-1980s. Third, while government spending as a proportion of GDP did rise under Democratic Presidents Kennedy, Johnson, and Carter, it rose even more under Republican Presidents Reagan and George W. Bush, and some of the sharpest reductions occurred during the 1990s under Democratic President Bill Clinton. Although

Table 1 Changes in US federal expenditures as percentage of GDP

	GDP[a]	Federal[a]	Defense[a]	Nondefense[a]	Federal % GDP	Defense % GDP	Nondefense % GDP
1945	223.2	92.7	83.0	9.7	41.5	37.2	4.4
1950	294.6	42.6	13.7	28.8	14.4	4.7	9.8
1955	415.1	68.4	42.7	25.7	16.5	10.3	6.2
1960	526.6	92.2	48.1	44.1	17.5	9.1	8.4
1965	719.1	118.2	50.6	67.6	16.4	7.0	9.4
1970	1,035.6	195.7	81.7	114.0	18.9	7.9	11.0
1975	1,630.6	332.3	86.5	245.8	20.4	5.3	15.1
1980	2,784.2	590.9	134.0	456.9	21.2	4.8	16.4
1985	4,180.7	946.4	252.8	693.6	22.6	6.1	16.6
1990	5,743.8	1,252.5	299.0	953.5	21.8	5.2	16.6
1995	7,269.6	1,519.1	275.0	1,244.1	20.9	3.8	17.1
2000	9,365.4	1,706.5	294.5	1,494.3	18.2	3.0	15.2
2005	10,043.9	2,050.5	465.9	2,013.6	20.4	3.8	16.6

[a] In billions of 1998 dollars

Republican administrations significantly increased defense spending in the early 1980s and again after 2001, Republican administrations did not succeed in cutting federal outlays on domestic spending.

While such data and observations are often used to advance claims about the appropriate size of government, they hardly provide any self-evident normative conclusions about governmental authority. Even as opponents of big government cite the huge overall increases in expenditures and the upward trend in the proportion of economic output that is consumed by the federal government, defenders of big government can argue that federal spending seems to grow (or shrink) in accordance with national needs. Even fiscal conservatives have seldom questioned the defense spending that was undertaken to win World War II, to counter Soviet power at the end of the Cold War, or in response to 9/11. And liberals would surely argue that the steady but modest increases in federal domestic outlays over the past half century have enabled the government to make many improvements in public goods and services that have been affordable given the great overall expansion of the economy. In short, although the figures given in table 1 outlines the big picture about federal governmental activities in the recent past, our ideas about the appropriate authority of government must be based on concepts and arguments that go well beyond these sorts of data.

Our thinking on governmental authority can be directed to the much more particular things that governments do or to the most general conceptions of what governments ought to do. Everyday pluralist politics deals with more particular questions. Should the recent increases in US military spending be focused on fighting the war on terrorism or should they be used to enhance the prospects for spreading democratic institutions to such countries as Iraq? Should a particular state legislature give greater priority to the needs of K-12 public schools or to higher education? Of course, the number of such questions is endless, and the answers that one might provide depend on the particular circumstances that exist in the particular political communities in which these issues arise. Conversations on questions of authority must go beyond matters concerning specific policies that governments should pursue or even whether overall governmental spending should increase. Such conversations address broad areas of governmental activity – such as whether government should have greater control over the economy, the moral choices of its citizens, or the preservation of the natural environment. The best way to understand these concerns is to see what various ideologies say about them.

Classical Liberals: Authorizing Limited Governments that Secure (Property) Rights

Classical liberals developed the concept of the social contract to clarify their thinking about governmental authority.[2] John Locke, for example, argued that it was rational for members of civil society to reach an agreement with a government, authorizing it to establish and administer laws clarifying and protecting individual rights, to adjudicate conflicts about how these laws apply in specific cases, and to punish those who violate established laws protecting the rights of others. To do these things, liberals thought governments should have military capacities to provide defense against external enemies and police forces to provide defense against criminals. They thought governments should also administer and enforce civil laws dealing with contracts between individuals. Such governmental authority would enable people to devote their energies to economic activity. Investors, workers, traders, and consumers would be assured that government would secure their property. If a person believed that an agreement made with another had been broken, he would have access to an impartial judge – the judicial authority of the state – to determine the validity of his claim and to determine an appropriate remedy. As economic exchanges became more complicated, many new civil laws were required. For example, as corporations rather than individual entrepreneurs increasingly organized economic activity, laws concerning the rights and responsibilities of corporations were enacted. As investors purchased stocks and became partial owners of corporations, financial markets were regulated. As some investments failed, putting some people deeply into debt, bankruptcy laws were developed. In short, classical liberals understood that it was the function of government to enact and enforce those civil laws that were necessary for people to engage confidently in market exchanges.[3]

Classical liberals also realized that some physical and social infrastructures served public purposes, and that using government authority for such purposes was acceptable. Roads, canals, and other public works were necessary to facilitate business activity. Safe water and sewers were necessary for public health. In addition, liberals came to believe that democracy and capitalism worked better with a reasonably well-educated citizenry, and they recognized the provision of public schools as a legitimate governmental function.

While classical liberals supported such expansions in governmental authority, it remained for contemporary liberals to stress the need for state involvement in the many functional areas where liberal governments now exercise authority. Classical liberals always emphasized *limited government*, curtailing the use of governmental authority so that it would not become oppressive. They emphasized four types of restrictions on governmental authority.

First, governments must not infringe on freedom of thought and expression. According to classical liberals, no government should "determine what doctrines or what arguments [citizens] should be allowed to hear."[4] No government should restrict religious beliefs or suppress political opinions, no matter how offensive these beliefs are to most citizens or how critical these opinions are of governmental officials. While early liberals regarded such liberty as a natural right, Immanuel Kant and John Stuart Mill provided utilitarian defenses for governmental noninterference in the freedoms of conscience, speech, and the press. According to Kant, governments should not stifle freedom of the press because, by so doing, they would lose access to vital information needed for effective governance. According to Mill, governments (and societies in general) must abide the expression of all ideas, even the most noxious ones, because only a general policy of governmental nonintervention in such freedoms allows the kinds of intellectual experimentation that produces human progress.

Second, governments should not act paternalistically by restraining self-regarding acts. Classical liberals like Mill partition human life into two spheres. The *private sphere* concerns that part of life "when a person's conduct affects the interests of no persons besides himself." In this sphere, "there would be perfect freedom, legal and social, to do the action and stand the consequences."[5] The *public sphere* concerns that part of life in which a person's conduct may injure others or when certain actions by individuals significantly affect society and its institutions. For the most part, the private and public spheres of life are distinct. Classical liberals believe governments can legitimately regulate only those individual actions that clearly fall within the public sphere. Because of dominant religious and moral sentiments, governments are often urged to regulate such "private amusements" as dancing and playing games, prohibit the consumption of alcohol, close businesses on the Sabbath, or regulate marriages (such as prohibiting polygamy, as practiced by Mormon fundamentalists). According to Mill, "the intrusively pious members of society (and their governments) should be told to mind their own business."[6]

Third, governments should not regulate economic activity beyond what is necessary for the effective functioning of free markets. Governments had long regulated economic activities that were regarded as immoral (such as usury) or contrary to the public interest (such as purchasing foreign goods). But classical liberals opposed such restrictions on free trade, arguing that the best way for a society to become economically productive and wealthy is to permit people to pursue their private interests. Among those who contributed to the liberal rejection of governmental restraints on trade were the French Physiocrats, especially François Quesnay (1694–1776) and Jacques Turgot (1727–81), who produced an economic theory showing the productivity of an economy unregulated by government, and they contributed the slogan *"Laissez-faire, laissez-passer"* (let it be, leave it alone). Adam Smith argued that when people are allowed to pursue their own economic gain, unconstrained by governmental regulations, an "invisible hand" creates social harmony and improves the condition of everyone. In *The Wealth of Nations*, Smith protested numerous state interventions in commerce, agriculture, and manufacturing.

Finally, government should not redistribute wealth by seizing the property of the wealthy or imposing extensive taxes on them in order to provide for the needs of the poor. According to Locke, "The Supreme Power cannot take from any man any part of his property without his own consent."[7] The Physiocrats and Adam Smith argued that if men were permitted to accumulate great wealth, they would reinvest it in ways that would make society as a whole wealthier. In order to gain a good reputation among other men, the wealthy would also contribute to charity. Classical liberals thus believed that governmental noninterference in inequalities generated by capitalism ultimately improves the condition of the poor. The Social Darwinist strand within nineteenth-century liberalism took a more strident position against governmental redistribution. Herbert Spencer argued that social progress depends on competition among individuals and that efforts to alleviate suffering among the poor interfere with the natural process of eliminating the weak and unfit from the species. Thus, Spencer rejected the idea that governments should "administer charity . . . adjust the prices of food . . . vaccinate children . . . or see that small dwellings are supplied with water."[8]

While classical liberals stressed such limitations on governmental authority, it is a mistake to assume that they therefore wanted a weak state.[9] Liberals like Montesquieu and Kant argued that central governments must be stronger than those social forces – like religious majorities or local strongmen – that might limit individual rights. In his famous *Federalist Paper Number 10* defending the American Constitution, James Madison argued that the central government had to be strong enough to protect citizens from the tyrannical acts of factions that often dominated smaller communities. Governments based on liberal principles have proven to be enormously powerful, as illustrated by the capacity of the British government to rule over a vast empire in the nineteenth and early twentieth centuries. Indeed, liberals believe that a government whose authority is limited to specific functions can best enlist citizen cooperation and private wealth in the pursuit of large-scale national objectives. In short, classical liberals want a government whose authority is limited to specific functions so that it has the necessary power to perform these functions effectively.

Traditional Conservatives: Orchestrating Social Harmony

Traditional conservatives reject activist governments that implement grand schemes for the improvement of society, but they also reject the limited role of governmental authority advocated by classical liberals. Government, as the head of the body politic, has important functions to fulfill. Traditional conservatives argue that governments must use their authority on behalf of the good of the community.

First, government must promote harmony in society by reducing the friction among individuals and groups. Government should not be just an "umpire," a favorite metaphor for classical liberals, because an umpire makes rulings after conflict has taken place. In the quest for social harmony, government should be active in reducing conflicts among members of society, cajoling individuals to be deferential to governmental authority – even at the expense of their immediate self-interest.

Second, government should enhance social harmony by promoting mediating institutions, such as churches and civic associations, that inculcate morality, provide for the needy, and remind individuals of their limited place within particular communities. Creation, maintenance, and expansion of voluntary groups are important responsibilities of governments.

Third, government must protect traditional norms and conventional rights. Such norms and rights have emerged over time from the specific legal and institutional arrangements that are unique to each community, and it is the responsibility of government to ensure that people continue to respect them.

The fourth role of government is to protect society from adverse changes that result from the emergence of capitalism. Market economies severed the bond between lord and serf and replaced it with a contract between owner and worker. The worker became free to sell his labor to the highest bidder, but he now finds himself bound to an employer who feels no obligation to him other than payment of a wage for contracted labor. Such free market arrangements trouble traditional conservatives, who believe that the larger community and the well-off have responsibilities to take care of needy members of society. While traditional conservatives increasingly accepted market practices, they have advocated intervention in the market to counteract extreme inequalities and the mistreatment of workers. Conservative regimes enacted policies to protect workers during rapid industrialization in the later part of the nineteenth century, regarding these policies as useful for increasing worker loyalty to existing arrangements, and thus for combating Marxist-inspired revolts against polities that harbored capitalism.

Traditional conservatives also support intervention in the market to curtail immoral or imprudent behavior. Rejecting the liberal claim that buyers and sellers always know best their own wants and interests, traditional conservatives believe people should not be able to pursue vices in a free market, and producers should not market goods that pander to people's worst instincts. They often claim, for example, that governmental authority can be legitimately used to forbid prostitution, the sale of pornography, gambling, and the use of alcohol and drugs.

In sum, traditional conservatives believe governments have a role in furthering the public good and reminding citizens of their role in this endeavor. They certainly call for governments that are more active, visible, and authoritative than the more limited governments stressed by classical liberals. But it is important to remember that traditional conservatives reject any kind of perfectionism. They do not think governments can solve all human and social problems, and they are opposed to governments becoming too zealous in efforts to do so. They thus advocate a limited style of politics.[10] In general, intrusiveness of conservative governments is diminished by an approach that seeks to guard that which exists and introduces change reluctantly.

Anarchists: Rejecting All Government Authority

Anarchists claim that governments have no authority to govern. Thus, they refute the claims of classical liberals that government authority is needed to provide security and of traditional conservatives that government authority is needed to integrate society. Anarchists offer three main arguments against these claims.

First, they argue that the existence of governments promotes struggles for power within societies that enhance social disorder. Only a small number of people can possess governmental authority, yet many are seduced by "the perks of office" to seek it, setting off endless competition to rule society. History shows that people will engage in great cruelty and violence against others to attain such authority. History also shows that transitions from one set of authorities to another are frequently times of great social instability. In short, more disorder is injected into political communities by the struggle to secure governmental authority than is created by the capacity of government to provide security.

Second, anarchists observe that governmental laws normally favor the property and liberty of the rich and powerful against the needs of the poor and powerless. Governmental laws make criminals of those who are oppressed by capitalism and traditional norms. According to Peter Kropotkin: "Three quarters of all the acts which are brought before our courts every year have their origin, either directly or indirectly, in the present disorganized state of society with regard to the production and distribution of wealth – not in the perversity of human nature."[11] Rather than protecting society from criminals, governmental laws force those who have been exploited under capitalism to engage in "crimes" in order to satisfy their basic needs. If capitalism produced the goods that were needed – rather than being organized to produce the frivolous luxuries consumed by the rich – and if society distributed these goods in a way that reflected the efforts and needs of those who have been exploited, most crime would disappear. Governmental laws also make criminals of those who challenge the traditional norms of a community but who harm no one. If governments ceased creating and enforcing laws dealing with social prejudices against such things as sexual freedom and drug use, courts and jails would be less crowded by persons made "criminals" by their lifestyle choices.

Third, anarchists assert that governmental laws lead, in the long run, to the moral depravity of humans and thus to social disorder. Anarchists claim that as governmental laws become the codes of social conduct, individuals become less governed by moral principles. Their motivation to obey governmental laws is to avoid being punished by the state; with such motivations, individuals often violate the rights of others if they think they can do so without being detected by authorities. More generally, when people believe that state laws define right conduct, they are unlikely to exercise their own moral judgment about what is right. But the laws of government often are unjust or are silent on issues involving moral judgment, thus providing inadequate moral guidance. When people rely on governmental laws rather than being guided by their own moral code, they are likely to perpetuate the injustices of government and to act on the basis of personal expedience, rather than in accordance with moral principles.

The idea that governmental authority is illegitimate because it undermines human moral development has long been part of anarchist ideology, but the argument why this is so has never been stated so succinctly and clearly as by Robert Paul Wolff in his *In Defense of Anarchism.* According to Wolff, there is an irreconcilable conflict between authority and autonomy. Authority is the right to command and be obeyed, and political theorists have produced many (spurious) justifications for why the state has such authority. Traditional conservatives pointed to the superior wisdom and virtue of those in authority and how obedience to such authority produces a stable and harmonious community. Classical liberals created the idea of a social contract in which citizens grant authority to governmental leaders in return for gaining security of their lives and property. According to Wolff, such justifications fail to address the central idea of moral philosophy: each individual must be morally autonomous. Moral autonomy is a combination of freedom and responsibility. Individuals are free because they possess free will, which gives them the capability of choosing for themselves how to act. Individuals are responsible when they acknowledge that their choices should be consistent with what is morally right. Because humans are endowed with reason, they are capable of engaging in "a process of reflection, investigation, and deliberation about how [they] ought to act."[12] Thus, there is by definition an irreconcilable conflict between governmental authority (the right of government to be obeyed) and individual autonomy (the right of each individual to choose freely and responsibly for oneself). To resolve this conflict by granting government the authority to command our obedience is to *demoralize* people. Obedience to governmental authority gives people a "moral holiday" by encouraging them to go along thoughtlessly with what authorities dictate and by discouraging them from using their human capacity to discern what is morally right for themselves and others in the particular circumstances of moral judgment. Only when people have extensive opportunities to practice moral reasoning will they develop the moral capacities to live harmoniously and naturally in community with others.

This conflict is not merely definitional but is an ever-present reality in everyday life. When governments spend tax money for programs that an individual concludes are wrong (such as military intervention in other societies), the individual's payment of taxes compromises his moral autonomy.[13] When governments prohibit actions that an individual may regard as morally required (such as euthanasia), the individual's autonomy is undermined. If humans surrender their moral autonomy and obey the commands of government in such instances, they forfeit the exercise of those capacities that define their humanity.[14]

Anarchists claim that the only legitimate authority is that which stems naturally from society. In this regard, anarchists often distinguish between the written laws of government and the unwritten laws of society. While governmental laws are tools of domination by oppressors, *social laws* are the norms of a society that support social harmony. While governmental laws are enforced by coercion, social laws are supported by much more gentle social pressures from other members of society. While governmental laws are incompatible with moral autonomy, social laws help guide individuals to make right moral choices.

Marxists: Authority As Oppressive, Then Necessary, and Finally Eliminated

Marx believed that governments in liberal society use their authority to further the interests of capitalists. Such governments have fostered capital accumulation and facilitated the concentration of wealth among an ever-smaller elite class that can invest it in more innovative and labor-saving technologies.[15] Marxists today claim that, as democratic capitalism has matured, governmental authorities now seek to ameliorate class conflict through myth-making and co-optation.[16] Governments have drawn from reigning ideologies, religious beliefs, and social customs to advance myths that induce people to believe falsely in the universal benevolence of democratic capitalism. The welfare policies and employment insurance programs provided by governments have been intended to co-opt and mollify the dispossessed.

In socialist society following the overthrow of capitalism, Marxists argued that governmental authority should properly be used to control all aspects of the economy.[17] The means of production – including banks and companies in the transportation and communication sector – should be socialized. Agriculture should be collectivized. The property of all opponents of the revolution must be confiscated.[18] Rejecting the anarchy of the market, public authorities should rationalize production through planning. Public authorities should determine social needs and organize production to meet these needs. Public management of production should ensure that private interests do not take precedence over public interests. Public authorities must also crush dissent and any counter-revolutionary activities of the bourgeoisie, and they must play a leading role in educating people to accept the egalitarian and fraternal values of a future communist society.

In such a future, governments will have only administrative functions, if any. Because citizens will be community-regarding creative laborers, because economic scarcity will be vanquished, and because a classless society will be achieved, governmental authority will no longer be needed to regulate individual behavior, distribute social goods, and serve the interests of any dominant class.

Communists: Justifying Massive Authority as a Means to Abolish the State

Like Marxists, communists believe that governmental authority in liberal societies is used to further the interests of capitalists. After the revolution, state authority, which would then reside in the Communist Party, should be used to bring about a transition to an ideal society. When this future arrives, there will no longer be a need for governmental authority, as Marx specified. Communists have augmented these Marxist ideas about state authority by developing the role of the state during the transition to the perfect society. Communists have insisted that during this period, such authority must be absolute and should be of three kinds: social, economic, and interpretive.

First, communist states must use their authority to shape social life in a manner that will enable the realization of "a new man," who must come into being in order to achieve an ideal society. The state must exercise direct control over citizens, re-socializing people away from the self-regarding and competitive norms that have defined human existence in capitalist societies; the state's social control must enable people to grasp the virtues of being community-oriented and cooperative creative laborers. The state also must control various social institutions within civil society (the family, schools, religion, and other local associations) so that they reinforce the state's efforts to develop such socialist citizens.

Second, communist states must use their authority to industrialize their pre-capitalist economies, creating the affluence that ideal communism presupposes. During the Cold War era, most communist regimes embraced a very authoritative role for the state in achieving these goals. The prototypic example is the collectivist Soviet state established by Stalin in 1929 and generally retained until Gorbachev introduced reforms in the mid-1980s. Stalin nationalized all industrial private property and collectivized agriculture. He also established strict centralized, bureaucratic control of the national economy. Central planners developed Five-Year Plans that indicated production priorities and created production goals and quotas. Pay rates for various jobs were also set by the state. Supervision of local industries was from above, by the *nomenklatura*, (the small ruling class within the Party), rather than from below by satisfied (or dissatisfied) customers.

Such state control of the economy has been subjected to many criticisms – such as its inability to reward innovation and effort[19] – but there is some evidence that a planned economy did bring about economic improvements, at least for many years. Between 1960 and 1973, for example, estimates indicate that the Soviet Union experienced an annual growth rate of 5.3 percent, a rate better than that of most capitalist societies including the United States. In addition, the Soviets were able to increase investment spending during this period, surpassing American investment levels by 1977. While Soviet consumption never reached American levels, the Soviets significantly reduced the gap between American consumption and Soviet consumption between 1955 and 1975.[20] Nevertheless, by the 1980s it became apparent that Soviet central planning and control did not sustain an economy that could produce either parity with capitalist societies or the affluence required for communism. These disappointments led citizens of communist regimes to question the sacrifices imposed on them in the name of a future ideal society, and they began to view the communist ideology justifying these sacrifices as mere myths and lies. In this environment, communist leaders began to reevaluate their commitment to state control over the economy.

It can be argued that the degree of state control of the economy is not a central principle of communism. As early as 1921, Lenin introduced the New Economic Policy (NEP) in response to extreme Bolshevik control of the Soviet economy. The NEP, which lasted until 1928, removed many restrictions on free trade, denationalized some smaller enterprises, and allowed greater market freedom in agriculture. In Yugoslavia, Tito introduced self-management Workers' Councils that allowed industrial workers to elect (and dismiss) their managers and to deliberate on many decisions of local firms. In 1986, Mikhail Gorbachev introduced perestroika in an attempt to overcome some of the rigidities of the centralized Soviet economy. These policies at first allowed local managers to gear production to consumer demand and to establish wage and bonus policies in ways that encouraged productivity; soon they were extended to allow limited private ownership and profitability in industry and agriculture. In recent years, China has also turned away from extensive state control of its economy, dismantling price controls, permitting private ownership of corporations, and allowing foreign direct investment. In 2004, fundamental changes were made in the Chinese Constitution stressing the role of the private sector in economic activity and protecting private property from arbitrary seizure.[21] Since 1992, Cuba has allowed new agricultural markets and legalized self-employment in some areas of the economy.[22] Whether or not communism requires extensive state economic planning or whether the state can give more autonomy to local enterprises may, therefore, be a question of interpretation.

Interpretative authority is thus the third and perhaps most important function that communists proclaim as vital to achieving their ideals. From the perspective of communism, the theories of Karl Marx provide the proper guidance about how to achieve the ideal communist society, but his writings are complex and unclear on specific applications of authority. The proper interpreters of Marx on these matters are neither political theorists nor ordinary citizens, but leaders of the Communist Party, and their interpretations can seem arbitrary. For example, Stalinists could point to certain passages in Marx regarding the importance of collective ownership and central control, while Gorbachev could point to other passages in Marx calling for more decentralization in making economic decisions.[23] While party leaders might draw different interpretations from Marx, it is essential to communism that only such leaders have interpretative authority. One task of the party is to eliminate all errant interpretations that might derail progress toward the ideal communist society.[24] This suggests that Gorbachev's most significant retreat from the Soviet communist model was not his policy of perestroika, but that of *glasnost*, which involved the Communist Party relinquishing its ultimate interpretive authority and permitting open debate on social and economic issues.

Fascists and Nazis: Embracing Totalitarian State Authority

Fascists and Nazis regard state authority as the means by which a nation or a race attains the power to achieve its ultimate purposes. According to fascist doctrine, governmental authority should be used to express the national will and to provide the power necessary to achieve national greatness. Since the goal of fascism is to create a powerful nation, the government must have the absolute authority necessary to achieve that end. It must instill in citizens a total devotion to the state. Gentile described such a state as a totalitarian entity:

> The relationship between State and citizen (not this or that citizen, but all citizens) is accordingly so intimate that the State exists only as, and in so far as, the citizen causes it to exist. Its formation therefore is the formation of a consciousness of it in individuals, in the mass. Hence the need of the Party, and of all the instruments of propaganda and education which Fascism uses to make the thought and will of the *Duce* the thought and will of the masses.[25]

The state must exercise total and exclusive control over all aspects of social, economic, religious, and private life to attain national unity. Family, church, and all other political, social, and private organizations or activities fall under the purview of the state.

Nazis regarded the state as an instrument that the race uses in its quest for dominance. According to Hitler:

> The state is a means to an end. Its end lies in the preservation and advancement of a community of physically and psychically homogenous creatures. This preservation itself comprises first of all existence as a race and thereby permits the free development of all the forces dormant in this race. Of them a part will always primarily serve the preservation of physical life, and only the remaining part the promotion of a further spiritual development. Actually, the one always creates the precondition for the other. . . . States, which do not serve this purpose, are misbegotten, monstrosities in fact.[26]

The Nazi doctrine of *Gleichschaltung*, the synchronization by the state of all private, social, and political institutions and activities toward the fulfillment of Nazi goals, articulated an intention of generating even greater totalitarian state control than that sought by fascism, because achieving racial purity requires even more governmental authority than does the more vague goal of national unity.

Nevertheless, fascist and Nazi principles regarding state authority are generally similar and simply stated. In principle, the state must be given unlimited authority to pursue the goals of the nation or racial group. This means that the state must be the dominant force in the lives of all citizens, controlling their beliefs, ideals, emotions, motives, and loyalties. The state must also be dominant in economic life, planning and controlling production, consumption, and investment. It must also be dominant in cultural life, controlling art, literature, and religion. In practice, neither the Nazis nor the fascists nationalized industry, as private ownership of industry remained the norm. Instead of using state authority to own industry, fascists and Nazis used it to control the economy so that its outputs conformed to national needs. Similarly, neither the Nazis nor the fascists used their authority to eliminate churches, but remained satisfied with cowing religious leaders into passive acceptance of their regimes. To comprehend the totalitarian aspects of these ideologies, however, one must understand that state authority was potentially unlimited and total, and that any limits on its use were pragmatic concessions based on the calculation that, at least in the short term, granting some latitude to individuals and subordinate organizations would not impede the realization of national or racial objectives.

Contemporary Liberalism: From Limited Government to a Strong State

Contemporary liberals agree with classical liberals that citizens must be protected from excessive governmental authority, as absolutism and arbitrariness must be restrained to protect individual liberties. But compared to classical liberals, contemporary liberals endorse a much wider role for governmental authority. Citizen rights should be expanded to ensure that they are able to make claims upon governments to provide for their welfare. Governments should enact and implement policies that provide steady, well-managed economic growth. They should employ pragmatic and scientific methods to address economic, social, and security problems.

To aid in problem identification and help establish priorities for their activities, liberal governments employ a variety of social and economic indicators measuring changes in, for example, human health, violent crime, the academic performance of students, the numbers of minorities and women attaining various prestigious positions, and climatic conditions. Particular attention is given to regular reports on the level of unemployment and other indicators of economic activity. Liberals also monitor the disparities of income and wealth between the rich and the poor, whites and minorities, and men and women. Implicit in the collection of all this data is the liberal view that governments should respond to adverse changes in economic, social, and environmental conditions.

Liberals do not, however, expect governments to solve indicated problems through omnipotent laws or programs. If inflation is high, liberals seldom call for mandatory wage and price controls. If unemployment is high, liberals seldom call on government to be the employer of last resort for those without jobs. If student test scores in mathematics are disappointing, liberals seldom call for a standardized and mandatory math curriculum. Liberals recognize that governments work within market economies and pluralist societies that vitiate the possibility and effectiveness of such authoritarian approaches. Thus, they are satisfied with modifying the laws and circumstances under which individuals, business firms, and other groups act. Rather than imposing price controls, liberal governments seek to moderate inflationary pressures by reducing the supply of money and consumer demand. Rather than imposing a mandatory math curriculum, liberal governments provide resources and incentives for local school districts to improve the quality of instruction in ways they deem appropriate. In short, liberals do not want governments to micro-manage and strongly control economic and social life. Instead, they want governments to engage in macro-level planning and produce a broad framework of laws, programs, and conditions that induce individuals and organizations to act in ways that reduce problems.

Like classical liberals, they want to honor the existence of a private sphere permitting individuals to make free choices regarding their economic and social aspirations, but unlike classical liberals, they believe that public authority can be employed effectively to induce people to make choices that serve public goals.

Contemporary liberals increasingly recognize the difficulty of maintaining a firm distinction between the private and public spheres of life. While wanting to preserve an extensive private sphere where individuals can pursue their own conception of the good life, contemporary liberals have come to recognize that some social problems can only be addressed by using governmental authority to promote certain moral positions.[27]

Discrimination on the basis of race, gender, or other ascriptive traits is an example of a moral issue that contemporary liberals believe should be addressed by government. If governments were indeed neutral, prejudiced individuals could refuse to do business with anyone they wished. However, liberals recognize that the refusal to hire women because of their sex or to sell property to Blacks because of their race constitute significant social problems, and they have legislated a morality of nondiscrimination.

Pornography, drug and alcohol abuse, family breakdown, and teenage pregnancy have become widespread – if not endemic – prompting contemporary liberals to debate among themselves the role of government in addressing such social problems. From one liberal viewpoint, the producers and consumers of pornography are acting as consenting adults in the private sphere, and their actions harm no one (other than themselves). From another liberal viewpoint, pornography involves the exploitation of certain people. On the issue of abortion, many liberals seem to endorse *some* governmental regulations, falling between the extremes of either "outlawing abortions" or permitting "abortion on demand." By endorsing restrictions on abortions after the first trimester and requiring parental consent before minors can terminate unwanted pregnancies, liberals can acknowledge their moral reservations about abortions. But liberals nevertheless have reservations about using governmental authority on matters that fundamentally concern women's rights to control their own bodies.[28]

While contemporary liberals have reluctantly endorsed some governmental intervention on moral freedom, they have more enthusiastically endorsed governmental intervention in economic life. They point out that countries such as Germany, Japan, and the "Little Tigers" of Asia have enjoyed economic success by increasing, rather than reducing, governmental intervention in business.[29] But just as liberals want to retain extensive moral choice for individuals, so do they want to retain extensive economic freedom. They want governments to shape the free market, not to abolish it.

Contemporary liberals seek steady and stable economic growth and believe that governmental authority can address the problems of business cycles that occur in uncontrolled free markets. Annual growth rates of about 3 percent allow for reasonably full employment, investment opportunities, wage increases, and additional tax revenues to expand public goods and services. A declining or even stagnate economy undermines these goals. An "overheated" economy with excessive growth has its own problems, such as high inflation. To deal with such problems, liberals have employed the *fiscal policies* developed by John Maynard Keynes (1883–1946). Although such policies are fairly complex, it is sufficient for our purposes to understand that their application requires extensive governmental involvement in economic matters. They require, on the one hand, governmental stimulation of the economy during economic downturns – by, for example, increasing public spending and/or reducing taxes – and, on the other, policies that rein in an overheated economy – by, for example, reducing government spending and/or increasing taxes.

Contemporary liberals expect governments to deal with the problem of (negative) *externalities*, which occur when people produce goods or undertake transactions in ways that are beneficial to them but which hurt (or externalize costs upon) non-participating "third parties" or the public at large. For example, in order to lower their costs of production, industries often dump their waste byproducts in ways that are detrimental to the environment; in order to maximize their profits, developers may try to build apartments that adversely affect single-family homeowners in the neighborhood. To counteract such trends, liberals have endorsed pollution controls, zoning ordinances, and many other such regulations on economic activity in order to protect the health and welfare of the broader public.

Liberals also want governments to address the problem that the market does not adequately provide *public goods*. A public good is something with benefits that are (at least partially) indivisible. The classical example of a public good is national defense. National defense is indivisible because if some citizens benefit from national defense, then all citizens benefit. There is a problem in providing public goods in the marketplace without governmental involvement. The rational, self-interested individual will want to be a "free-rider" who pays nothing but still receives the public good that is paid for by others. But within free markets, there will be few if any "suckers" who will pay private businesses to provide public goods. Liberals argue that the adequate provision of public goods requires that they are supplied by governments and that everyone is required to pay by means of mandatory taxes. Liberal economists stress that there are many undersupplied public goods.[30] Government investments in education, job training, public health, public safety, and other human resources benefit the public as a whole. Government spending on transportation systems, waste disposal systems, and other aspects of our physical infrastructure provide extensive public benefits. Government subsidies for scientific research and technological developments in many areas – from cures for cancer and AIDS to more energy-efficient automobiles – can be seen as public goods.

Finally, liberals recognize the need for governments to assist those who cannot participate in the market economy. Compared to conservatives, liberals are unlikely to believe that the poor are generally lazy, or that poverty could be solved if everyone would simply "get off the public dole and get a job." Liberals argue that many of the poor cannot work or that they already do work, but at poorly paid jobs. Many of those in poverty are children, or single-parent mothers of small children, or the disabled. Liberals also recognize that recessions and other problems that occur within capitalist economies can cause structural unemployment, throwing productive and willing workers out of jobs. In short, contemporary liberals believe that capitalism is partly responsible for the problem of poverty. They believe that a purely capitalist economy fails to supply the needs of the poor, but that abolishing capitalism would enhance – not reduce – the extent of poverty. Nor can private charity be a reliable and efficient means of responding to the needs of the poor. For the contemporary liberal, governments have extensive responsibilities toward the poor, a topic to be further explored in chapter 14, dealing with questions of justice.

Contemporary Conservatives: Limiting the Activity of Governments

Conservatives want governmental activity and authority to be limited, but within its limits government should be strong and effective. Governmental authority should not be used to solve every social problem. Indeed, conservatives think that labeling problems like the spread of AIDS and drug abuse as social problems, rather than as personal problems, is a liberal tactic to invite governmental intervention. Governmental authority should not be used to help every group that might confront problems, especially if these arise out of bad personal choices. By taking on dubious "social problems," liberal and socialist governments have spread themselves thin, weakening their capacity to accomplish their proper goals.

For contemporary conservatives, the most important tasks of government are to provide national security and domestic order. They must effectively pursue national interests in foreign policy and ensure that military forces are strong enough to deter communist expansion, international terrorism, and aggression by other adversaries. Hence, faced with enhanced security threats after 9/11/01, George W. Bush created another cabinet-level bureaucracy, the Department of Homeland Security, increased military spending, and undertook a war on terrorism. Such a response was consistent with conservative perspectives that security and military needs must take priority over welfare provisions. Conservatives also believe that governments should focus on domestic disorder. Because of their concern with the rights of criminals, liberals have, according to conservatives, shackled the police and been soft on crime. In contrast, conservatives want to expand police forces, reduce "the loopholes" in the law that allow the guilty to go free, make punishment more certain and severe, and reinstate the death penalty in cases of particularly heinous crimes.

Conservatives generally accept the need for governmental authority, but also fear that excessive authority threatens individual liberties; they thus engage in lively debates about where to draw the boundary between authority and liberty. Many conservatives rely on the ideas of Thomas Hobbes to defend the authority of the state. Hobbes's view – that individual rights must give way to the need for governmental authority that protects the broader public – can be seen in the limitations on civil liberties pursued by the Bush Administration to secure the US from terrorism. While Bush appointees to the Supreme Court – John Roberts and Samuel Alito – have seemed generally to concur with this Hobbesian stance, other conservative justices have histories of protecting individual rights against excessive authority, leading to uncertainty as to how a conservative court will resolve these issues. A similar tension within contemporary conservativism exists on the issue of using governmental authority to promote moral virtue. Social conservatives often seek strong prohibitions over activities that they regard as morally offensive, but more moderate conservatives believe that government should simply promote a more moral culture and those voluntary associations like churches that uphold traditional values.

According to contemporary conservatives, some governmental intervention in the economy is warranted, though to a much lesser degree than advocated by their ideological opponents on the left. For example, conservatives have long accepted the idea of *eminent domain*, whereby governments can take private property for public purposes, such as building highways and other essential public facilities (provided property-owners are adequately compensated for their losses). But most conservatives have been distressed by the Supreme Court ruling in the case of *Kelo v. New London* in June 2005, which allows state and city governments to use their power of eminent domain to help developers acquire land for private projects that have only indirect public benefits. Liberals have wanted to have greater eminent domain powers, and to be able to use them for public–private partnerships in order to build facilities like stadiums, arenas, and convention centers that are privately owned and operated, but which provide broad public benefits and spur economic development. Conservatives generally see such extended uses of eminent domain as yet another assault on traditional property rights.

More broadly, contemporary conservatives understand that a completely unregulated market may produce undesirable outcomes in some instances. They agree with liberals that some governmental policies must be developed to deal with the problems of externalities; for example, they understand that some regulations are needed to reduce pollution of our air, water, and soil. They argue, though, that the "command-and-control" approach of liberals – in the US, for example, having the Environmental Protection Agency require industries to use the best available technology to meet certain standards – is heavy-handed, excessively bureaucratic, and gives businesses no opportunity or incentive to develop innovative solutions that might reduce pollution *below* these standards. Conservative economists advocate allowing government agencies to set fees for units of pollution released, to monitor pollution releases, and to bill companies for the pollution they produce. In their view, this market-like approach encourages companies to develop new and efficient pollution control techniques, in order to cut costs and keep them competitive in the market.

Conservatives also understand that public goods are necessary and must be paid for by government expenditures. Inoculations that help control the spread of diseases throughout society and schools that create an informed and skilled citizenry are examples of public goods that conservatives recognize will be inadequately sought and provided for in the free market and that government must therefore fund. But conservatives do not believe that public bureaucracies must necessarily deliver public goods. For example, instead of children receiving their education at designated public schools, governments could provide parents with vouchers that they can use to send their children to the public or private schools of their choice.[31] *The voucher system* uses governmental authority to pay for (most of) the costs of education, ensuring its availability to everyone, including the poor, but it relies on a "market-like" mechanism to give incentives for schools to be innovative and effective, to be the school chosen by most parents. Bad schools would be unable to attract students and thus be unable to survive in the market created by the voucher system. But good schools would flourish, delivering better education than provided by the existing public school monopolies.

Contemporary conservatives also recognize that poverty is a problem requiring some governmental response, but they oppose the massive welfare states created by contemporary liberals and socialists. In chapter 14, we will discuss the principles of contemporary conservatives regarding how to address poverty.

The Radical Right: Starving Government While Imposing Social Regulations

The radical right believes that liberal and socialist governments have intervened too strongly in the economy and have been too inattentive to moral breakdown, and that contemporary conservatives have provided some useful corrections to these failings on the left. It argues, however, that when conservatives have governed, they have been too hesitant to limit intervention in the market and use their authority to ensure that citizens follow dominant moral understandings. But the radical right is hardly united on these matters. While libertarians want to reduce the use of governmental authority in both economic and moral issues, traditional communitarians, social conservatives, and the religious right are focused on the need for regulation on certain moral issues. And national protectionists are focused on the need for governmental regulations that will protect American workers within the global economy.

On issues of governmental intervention in the economy and restrictions on property rights, libertarians are the true heirs of the classical liberal tradition. Indeed, Robert Nozick's libertarianism can be seen as a radicalization of Lockean liberalism that had stressed limiting the role of government to providing security.[32] While Locke readily granted that the protection of individual rights required a government, Nozick argued that before creating a government to police society and adjudicate conflicts among individuals within it, more voluntary arrangements for securing individual rights should be explored. Perhaps security could be provided through voluntary market exchanges between individual customers seeking security and producers of such security. In exchange for customer fees, protective agencies – perhaps organizations like the Pinkertons or even the Mafia – could provide police protection to deter others from violating the rights of customers, apprehend and punish those who infringe upon customers' rights, and seek compensation from offenders for those customers whose rights are violated. While many such protective agencies might initially be formed, the logic of providing security would, in time, lead to the existence of a dominant protective agency. Everyone would want to be protected by the strongest protective agency – the one with the capacity to impose its views in the resolution of conflicts between customers of different protective agencies. Thus, everyone would be driven to purchase security from the strongest protective agency, which would resemble a *minimal state.*

Still, the dominant protective agency is not a government, for two reasons. First, its capacity to protect, adjudicate, and compensate is based on its power, not its authority. While a powerful organization has authority and thus becomes a government only when people believe it has *legitimacy* or the moral right to rule, the dominant protective association rules by virtue of its superior coercive power. Second, a dominant protective agency serves only its paying customers. Those individuals living within the territory where a dominant protective agency operates can be apprehended and punished by it, but they cannot expect to receive its protection unless they are paying customers. These deficiencies in strictly voluntary arrangements for providing security led Nozick to concede that a weak libertarian government legitimated by voter approval is the proper method of ensuring everyone's security. In order to cover the costs of those people who cannot afford to pay for its protective services, such a government must be (mildly) redistributive, taxing more wealthy members of the community to cover the costs of providing security for the poor. But providing equal security for all exhausts governmental authority.[33] Governments should not regulate social or economic behavior, nor should they redistribute economic goods beyond that necessary to provide equal protection for all, because they exist only to compensate for the deficiencies of having protective agencies in the free market provide security.

Some libertarians believe that Nozick's theory overly restricts governmental authority. For example, Frederick Hayek's libertarianism is directed toward limiting governmental authority to those activities that are clearly authorized by the constitutions of political communities. According to Hayek, limiting governments to constitutionally authorized activities is necessary to prevent elected officials from taxing private property to pay for programs that they believe will generate an electoral coalition that will return them to office.[34] Economists with libertarian tendencies have suggested the possibility of a few additional governmental activities that may not have occurred to the founders of older constitutions. For example, Milton Friedman recognizes that governments may be needed to provide public goods, to protect the public from externalities, and ease severe poverty (through a negative income tax), but many things that governments do – such as run social security programs, place tariffs on imports, establish minimum wages, and criminalize the sale of marijuana – cannot be justified in terms of any principles that are duly attentive to concerns of individual liberty and economic efficiency.[35] If governments stopped all unauthorized activities, the size of government would be minimized and individual freedom would flourish. Libertarians have sometimes argued that the best practical cure to curtail illegitimate programs is to starve government by cutting taxes.

Global neoliberals have libertarian tendencies but are somewhat less strident in limiting governmental intervention in the global economy. For globalists, the role of government in the political economy should focus on providing only those regulations that are necessary to secure genuine market competition, ensure the transparency of market activities, and control corruption. Among the kinds of governmental regulations that should be eliminated are those that protect and promote private interests (such as bans and tariffs on imports in order to shield domestic countries from price competition), that set restraints on entry into the market (such as workplace safety standards that price developing countries out of global markets), and that serve dubious public interests at excessive costs.[36]

Globalists believe that attaining the full benefits of globalization also requires lessening tax burdens and reducing governmental spending. They believe that a reduction in governmental spending could be accomplished by shrinking governmental bureaucracies (especially those involved in unnecessary regulations), privatizing public services (to achieve the efficiencies of market competition that monopolistic public providers now escape), and reducing welfare, both for the poor who use welfare rights to escape gainful employment and for those corporate entities that require subsidies to survive in the marketplace. However, globalists recognize that government authority is necessary for the provision of various public goods and social needs like education and healthcare.[37] Such public provisions are justified because they help everyone to have greater opportunities and capacities to participate in the global economy.[38]

Globalists have little to say about the role of governmental authority in limiting freedom in order to ensure that individual behavior accords with widely held moral ideals within a community. Perhaps this is because globalists understand that moral restraints often take the form of economic restrictions (for example, curtailing the extensive markets that exist for selling eroticism and sex).[39] Or perhaps this is because globalists are quite content to let local communities and voluntary associations like churches establish and promote moral codes, because the many moralities that exist throughout the world make raising moral questions at the level of large and pluralistic communities a volatile distraction from the business of producing economic prosperity.

Other voices on the radical right want governments to focus their authority on reversing the dilution of traditional cultural values and thus attack value relativism. Cultural conservatives doubt that a country can be strong relative to others in the international system or that it can have the unity of purpose to address internal problems effectively unless citizens have allegiance to traditional cultural values. Hence, they want governments to reverse policies like multiculturalism and weak immigration controls that have diluted strong national identities. Social conservatives have a more focused moral agenda: they endorse governmental censorship of literature, movies, art, and music that they regard as offensive, the prohibition of abortion, and restrictions on other "objectionable" behaviors, such as gay partnerships.[40]

National protectionists in the US think that governmental authority should focus on securing all Americans from the forces of globalization. They think governmental authority should protect American jobs from "unfair international competition,"[41] from the practices of transnational companies that gain benefits from US governments while they outsource jobs that were traditionally held by Americans, and – most importantly – by restricting immigration (both legal and illegal) into the country, because new arrivals take jobs away from American citizens or at least drive down the wages paid to American workers.

The Radical Left: Enhancing the Public Sphere

In contrast to contemporary conservatives and the radical right, the radical left sees most problems that people confront as social problems requiring governmental solutions. The radical left thinks that liberal governments usually fail to use their authority to attack the roots – or ultimate sources – of social problems.

Consider, for example, social problems associated with education. For contemporary liberals, an important educational problem occurs when rich white children attend better schools than poor black ones. In response, liberals in the US have used governmental authority to desegregate schools, to equalize expenditure per pupil among wealthy and poor school districts throughout a state, and to create special programs like Headstart and Upward Bound to help poor children catch up with their peers. While the radical left does not reject such liberal approaches to educational problems, it believes liberals do not go far enough. The more fundamental problems involve the inability of schools to escape the domination of traditional cultures and capitalist economies. The radical left believes that schools mold children to accept passive roles in the prevailing social and economic systems; the primary function of most schools has been to sort and label students, a process that ensures that the most advantaged children will be directed toward professional and managerial careers while the least advantaged will be trained to perform and accept low-paying jobs. For the radical left, schools must enable students to be free and equal citizens of a democratic society rather than teach them to be passive citizens who conform to traditional values and the needs of a capitalist economy. To do this, governmental authority must be used to finance an equal basic education for all children in public schools and to protect such schools from pressures to use the curriculum to advance the values of a traditional culture and a capitalist economy.[42]

While the different voices within the radical left agree that governmental authority should be used to attack the root causes of social problems, they emphasize different problems. Radical feminists have sought governmental assistance to undermine the patriarchal family. Radical greens have sought many governmental regulations to protect natural resources. Democratic socialists have been especially prominent in seeking more extensive governmental roles in the production and consumption of public goods, in regulating the market, and in redistributing the goods produced by capitalism. Radical democrats have sought governmental programs that support multiculturalism.

Radical feminists seem to challenge directly the liberal emphasis on limited government and its public–private distinction with their motto that "the personal is the political." But such feminists do not mean to proclaim that governmental authority should be applied to all family and private matters; clearly, they believe a woman's control over her own body (the right to an abortion) should be a personal decision that is beyond the reach of governmental authority.[43] Instead, this slogan brings attention to the idea that what happens in the family has political implications and can sometimes justify governmental intervention. Most obviously, incidents of domestic violence should no longer be treated as private matters between husbands and wives; the police and courts must intervene. More generally, the continuing inequalities between mothers and fathers in the rearing of children and in housekeeping justify such programs as governmental provision of childcare.

Radical greens have called on greater governmental authority to pursue programs to protect the environment. While many of these programs have been incorporated into the agendas of contemporary liberals and even become acceptable to contemporary conservatives, it remains for radical greens to push for more extensive regulations in this area. For example, many radical greens call for much higher taxes on gasoline, as incentives for drivers to develop more ecologically sustainable habits and for producers of automobiles to develop more ecologically sustainable products.

Many voices on the radical left seek to expand government authority in the economic realm, as has already been pointed in our discussion of structures in chapter 11 and as will considered in more detail when turning to questions of justice in the next chapter. The discussion here focuses on some broad principles of various radical left perspectives regarding the role of government in economic matters.

Civic communitarians respect commodity and labor markets, but they must be subordinated to broader public concerns that are subject to governmental authority. According to Michael Walzer:

> [S]ocially recognized needs are the first charge against the social product; there is no real surplus until they have been met. What the surplus finances is the production and exchange of commodities outside the sphere of need. Men and women who appropriate vast sums of money for themselves, while needs are still unmet, act like tyrants, dominating and distorting the distribution of security and welfare.[44]

In short, civic communitarians call on governmental authority to give priority to a public sphere which embraces the common needs of all members of the community and the responsibilities that all members of society have to those most in need. Only once such needs are met should citizens be able to pursue their personal desires for various unneeded but desired economic goods or commodities.

Egalitarian liberals like John Rawls also call for a strong state – a government that uses its authority more aggressively to achieve a more egalitarian society than is provided by most states today. Rawls claims that his egalitarian principles justify the familiar governmental programs pursued by contemporary liberals; governments must provide "a social minimum," pay for such welfare provisions through progressive taxes, and regulate the overall economy to ensure "reasonably full employment in the sense that those who want work can find it."[45] Still, Rawls's theory has been interpreted as calling for deeper reductions in inequality than liberals have usually sought, as we shall see in the next chapter.

Democratic socialists provide the most prominent and well-developed ideas regarding the expansive role of governmental authority in the production and distribution of economic goods. The revisionist and Fabian founders of democratic socialism focused on economic production and supported the *nationalization of industry*. They wanted the state to own and manage most industries and thus employ most workers. They believed nationalization would promote communal harmony, as production could be based on rational assessments of social needs rather than in response to market forces. Nationalization would promote real freedom because private owners of the means of production would no longer dominate workers. And nationalization would promote social and economic equality because class distinctions between the bourgeoisie and the proletariat would disappear when everyone worked for governments that could establish more equal wages than those prevailing under capitalism.

For such reasons, many socialist parties have nationalized specific industries when they have come to power. For example, in Great Britain after World War II, the Labour Party nationalized the coalmines, the railroads, and the electricity, gas, and iron and steel industries. In France in the early 1980s, the Socialist Party under François Mitterand nationalized almost all private banks, steel production, a major armaments firm, and several multinational corporations. The Swedish socialist party, the SAP, created Statsforetag AB (State Enterprise Ltd) as a conglomerate of publicly owned industries. However, in each of these cases nationalization was limited to specific industries – particularly to those in which there were natural monopolies and where national priorities justified extensive investments by national governments.

Governing socialists have never seriously contemplated wholesale nationalization of all private industry. An overwhelming constraint on nationalization is the cost of acquiring private enterprises. While communist regimes have been willing to confiscate private property by force, socialist governments understand that capitalists are constitutionally and legally protected from confiscation. Liberal laws require compensation for owners of industries nationalized by governments. Providing just compensation to the owners of *all* private industry is far beyond the means of any democratic government, and providing full compensation to former capitalists will do little to generate more equal distributions of wealth. Thus, socialists have had to be selective in choosing which industries they wish to purchase and manage.

Because of such difficulties, since the 1970s, socialists have tended to de-emphasize state ownership of the means of production and, instead, emphasize public control over economic production through partial state planning, which is less extensive than comprehensive planning, as practiced by communists in the former Soviet Union, and more extensive than the macroeconomic planning practiced by liberal governments in the US. Under partial socialist planning, the state controls capitalism by influencing major private investments through control of banking and financing. The state monitors salaries and wages, establishing equitable compensation guidelines that reduce the huge and unjustified inequalities of an unregulated labor market. Socialist planners also seek to ensure job security for workers, creating labor laws that protect them from arbitrary dismissals and facilitating their mobility to more productive industries through such programs as job retraining and relocation subsidies.

The justification for socialist state planning rests on the understanding that free markets respond well to the immediate wants of individuals but poorly to long-term social needs. Some goods like "affordable housing" are needed, but those with the need are unable to pay market prices; socialist planning is needed to help produce such goods. Other goods like a sustainable environment and education may have benefits that lie in the distant future; socialists believe that state planners can better balance short-run wants with long-run needs than can actors in an unplanned and unregulated market.

While socialists favor an extensive role for government in the production of goods and services, they have put even greater emphasis on expanding the role of government in the distribution of goods and services. Socialists understand that the market should distribute most commodities – the goods that people prefer that aren't really necessities. But socialists want the state to distribute as universal entitlements those goods that all need but are often unable to afford. While contemporary liberals also call for the state to distribute some goods as entitlements, the socialist welfare state is more expansive than the liberal welfare state in two respects. First, socialists think that people's minimal needs are much more extensive than do liberals. Second, while liberals focus on the needs of the poor and often target entitlements to specific groups, socialists stress that certain needs are universal and thus claim that entitlements must be provided to everyone.

As one moves from classical liberalism to contemporary liberalism and then to socialism, there is a steady expansion of the concept of need and of the social contract to provide for needs. Classical liberals think of people as *volitional* beings; they are defined by their many wants, and they are thought to have minimal needs. Here individuals need to secure their right to pursue their self-interests, and the social contract is an agreement among citizens to form governmental authority that provides for the need of such security. Contemporary liberals think of people as *purposive* beings; they want to pursue their own life plans, and certain social goods (especially income) are viewed as necessary means to achieving these pursuits. Here individuals need minimal amounts of these goods to have real opportunities to achieve their chosen goals, and the social contract is an agreement among citizens to have government provide baseline amounts of these goods. Socialists think of people as *social* beings whose wants and needs are socially and culturally defined. Here there is no particular list of goods that individuals need. Instead, social, economic, and cultural conditions influence what people need to live individually fulfilling and socially productive lives within these conditions. In a socialist society, "the social contract is an agreement to reach decisions together about what goods are necessary to our common life, and then to provide those goods for one another."[46]

At least in an affluent society, the goods that socialist citizens recognize as needed by everyone are likely to be much more extensive than specified by liberals. Major advances in medical treatments and capabilities, for example, have resulted in new conceptions of people's health needs, prompting the understanding that health-care ought to be communally provided rather than distributed by the market. Vast changes in how cities are physically structured – with residential, industrial, and commercial areas often miles apart – have created new transportation needs, prompting the understanding that mass transport should be communally provided. Such examples could be greatly expanded, but there is no objective or natural list of human needs. Political debate and decision are the socialist method of determining governmental entitlements. Because all citizens have a reasonable understanding of what people need to thrive in their particular societies, an open and democratic process is the appropriate method of determining entitlements.

The socialist welfare state is also more universal than the liberal welfare state.[47] For socialists, socially recognized needs become *universal entitlements* that are provided to everyone based on their common citizenship rather than on such criteria as destitution. Medicaid is a liberal program entitling the poor to certain health benefits, but socialists prefer universal healthcare programs covering all citizens regardless of how wealthy they are or how much (or how little) they pay in taxes. While liberals propose subsidies to poor families for childcare, socialists argue that day-care centers are a universal need and should be available to all families.

By targeting the poor for entitlements, it may appear that liberal welfare policies are more likely than socialist welfare policies to equalize conditions, which seems odd, because socialists value equality more than liberals. But socialists defend universal entitlements on a number of grounds. First, universal entitlements recognize common citizenship. By providing universal entitlements, everyone makes a commitment to one another to provide for common needs. For example, wealthy working mothers as well as poor mothers need quality day care. Second, socialists view universal entitlements as an important antidote to middle- and upper-class hostility toward the liberal welfare state. The affluent may resent paying higher taxes for welfare benefits targeted toward those who, they believe, contribute little to society. Because universal entitlements benefit everyone, they help generate support for the welfare state, enhancing its long-term viability. Third, socialists recognize that even universal entitlements promote equality of condition. While everyone may equally consume social provisions, such goods comprise a relatively large share of all goods available to the poor and a relatively small share of all goods available to the rich. Thus, new social provisions provide a much greater increase in the quality of life of the poor than the rich. Moreover, universal entitlements are normally paid for, in socialist states, by progressive taxes. Because the rich pay more of the costs of entitlements than do the poor, new social provisions lessen economic inequalities between the rich and the poor.

While most voices on the radical left have called for governments to exercise their authority on behalf of universal rights, some advocates of multiculturalism believe that governments must sometimes supplement universal provisions with *special group rights* for oppressed and marginalized groups. Such group rights enable minorities to engage in practices, speak languages, and affirm identities that are different from those that define the dominant culture in a political community. Perhaps the most famous example of such a minority practice is the *l'affaire du foulard* that arose in France in 1989. When Muslim girls came to school wearing headscarves (the hijab), they violated a French law (*laïcité*) that charged public schools with the task of assimilating people of diverse religions, races, and ethnicities; the *laïcité* prohibited students from wearing symbols of their specific cultures.[48] For multiculturalists, the *laïcité* invoked governmental authority illegitimately, requiring minorities to conform to dominant or traditional cultural practices. In contrast, multiculturalists believe that government authority must be used to allow minorities full access to their own cultures, for example, by backing bilingual programs in those sub-communities where minorities are concentrated. The left claims that multiculturalism allows all individuals in society, not just minorities, to gain exposure to a full array of moral outlooks, permitting them to make more informed choices among various options. Multiculturalism allows people to see the limitations of their own culture, and thus encourages efforts to improve, rather than passively accept, dominant cultural values.

However, civic communitarians have sometimes been uneasy with multiculturalism, arguing that it needs to be balanced by renewed efforts to strengthen ties to the community as a whole. Cornel West provides one expression of such an orientation when he stresses that while "race matters" greatly in American life and minorities need to strengthen their communities, "Afrocentric" orientations by African-Americans that focus solely on the social, political, and economic problems of Blacks fail to see how such problems are simply at the forefront of problems that increasingly plague all Americans. Consequently, African-Americans must identify with all Americans, and all Americans must identify with African-Americans. West insists: "We must focus our attention on the public square – the common good that undergirds our national and global destinies. The vitality of any public square ultimately depends on how much we care about the quality of our lives together".[49]

The Extreme Right: Resisting Authority that Disregards Sacred Texts

The extreme right is highly critical of how pluralist governments have used their authority. Government support for globalization, multiculturalism, public welfare, affirmative action, abortion rights, and gun control incur the wrath of right-wingers in the US. They are particularly opposed to overly lenient immigration policies that threaten to transform American culture, undermining the values of Western civilization and Christianity. White nationalists think American policies enable miscegenation, the sexual as well as social intermixing of the races that is diluting the white race. The extreme right in Europe expresses similar complaints. Islamic fundamentalists often regard their political authorities as unfaithful to Islamic law and as too hospitable to "satanic" secular interests from the West.

Whatever the specific complaints, the overall result is that the extreme right denies the legitimacy of how governmental power is currently applied. For some, constitutions are the only legitimate source of political authority, and any government actions and policies that can be construed as contrary to the intentions of the framers of a particular constitution are illegitimate. For others, God is the only legitimate source of political authority, and any government actions and policies that are thought to be contrary to God's will are illegitimate. Some on the extreme right would like to see a much less authoritative government, one that reserves more liberties to individuals and more political power to local communities. Others on the extreme right believe that an authoritative government that enacts and administers the divine law is what is needed in order to counteract the moral decay that encompasses pluralist societies. Both Islamic and Christian fundamentalists seek a theocracy that legislates morality and outlaws sinful practices, such as homosexuality, as identified by their understanding of holy texts.

The Extreme Left: Contesting Governmental Authority

The extreme left believes that the authority of governments in pluralist societies is used for misguided, if not immoral and inhumane, purposes. A deep green, Edward Abbey, provides a typical assessment:

> Representative democracy in the United States has broken down. Our legislators do not represent those who elected them but rather the minority who finance their political campaigns and who control the organs of communication – the TeeVee, the newspapers, the billboards, the radio – that have made politics a game for the rich only. Representative government in the USA represents money not people and therefore has forfeited our allegiance and moral support. We owe it nothing but the taxation it extorts from us under threats of seizure of property, or prison, or in some cases already, when resisted, a sudden and violent death by gunfire.[50]

Instead of using authority to pursue social justice, governments pursue policies that empower and enrich corporate interests. Rather than using authority to protect the environment, governments pursue policies that enable corporate interests to plunder and denude our natural resources. Rather than using authority to achieve the public good, they pursue policies that serve powerful special interests. Rather than using authority to encourage the development of democratic regimes around the globe, they prop up authoritarian regimes that are friendly to foreign investment. While the precarious balance between capitalist structures and democratic processes has always jeopardized governmental authority, globalization has increasingly shifted the balance so that pluralist governments have become "Government Incorporated."[51]

The extreme left believes that it is futile to theorize about how governmental authority should be used at the global, national, or local levels, given that such ideals would be thwarted by existing dominant powers. Specifying such principles would also be repressive, constituting an effort to declare authoritatively, universally, and permanently the proper role of government, when what governments do (indeed what politics should do) must always be contested. New and previously marginalized groups will always emerge, placing new demands on government, and such demands should not be resisted merely because they fall beyond some limit of authority as specified by pre-existing principles. New problems and opportunities will always emerge, and how governments respond to them should be based on radicalized democratic processes that are inclusive of all people in the community and that do not privilege predetermined principles.

Conclusions

Among the friends of pluralism, there is consensus that the authority of government must be sufficient to cope with various social, economic, and security problems.[52] To ensure citizens the freedom to pursue their happiness and life plans, the authority of the state in pluralist societies is limited, but pluralists understand that government authority needs to be exercised in ways that sometimes constrain freedom in order to pursue public concerns.

Influenced by liberal philosophy, pluralists of all stripes accept that governmental authority must restrict individual freedom at that point where it infringes on others' freedoms and rights. But influenced by the moral systems central to conservative and socialist thought, pluralism recognizes that it is sometimes desirable to further restrict human freedom. In order to promote human wellness, to enhance individual development, and to prevent individuals from harming themselves, pluralistic government authority can be used to enact and enforce some paternalistic laws and policies.[53] To promote social justice, pluralistic government authorities can impose some limitations on economic freedoms and property rights.[54] To protect society and the environment, pluralist societies may restrict other individual freedoms.

Within pluralism there is extensive conflict over the extensiveness of governmental authority and individual freedom. Those on the political right have generally called for more use of governmental authority to promote adherence to traditional moral values and for less use of governmental authority that regulates capitalism and constrains economic freedoms. Those on the political left have generally called for greater governmental authority in regulating economic behavior and redistributing wealth and less use of governmental authority requiring individuals to adhere to traditional cultural values. Pluralist societies have witnessed increasingly bitter and polarized politics, as people have taken ideological positions on concrete issues involving the extensiveness of governmental authority.[55] Perhaps the best hope for pluralist societies to escape this state of affairs is for political leaders and citizens to approach concrete issues through less ideological lenses, focusing instead on how proposed government programs, or cutbacks in proposed programs, will actually affect different members of the political community. Looking beyond broad ideological orientations about the role of government, and considering the economic, social, and environmental impacts of policy alternatives, might enable pluralist communities more readily to adopt certain policies because their consequences serve the common good and justice. Of course, such considerations require that people have informed understandings of what constitutes the common good and justice; the next chapter is devoted to these concepts.

In general, the radical right pushes pluralist societies to think about what governments should do to provide for greater economic freedom and to more fully regulate morality. The radical left pushes pluralist societies to think about what governments should do to more extensively regulate the economy, enhance communal provisions of various goods and services, and promote special group rights. Pluralists believes there is nothing inherently wrong with any of these aspirations, but they believe that all specific proposals must be carefully deliberated and resolved through democratic procedures.

Pluralists tolerate the extreme right's protests against the uses of political authority; such dissent is an exercise of the political freedoms that pluralism provides and defends. However, when opposition moves beyond attacks on particular policies (and the authorities who support them) and focuses instead on the pluralist regime and community, pluralists become less tolerant. They strongly resist efforts to recreate homogeneous and traditional societies or theocracies. They strongly resist basing political decisions on the interpretations of sacred texts provided by fiery fundamentalist preachers and jurists committed to "originalist" and "strict constructionist" legal philosophies.

Extreme left criticisms of how pluralist governments use their authority are certainly acceptable within pluralist politics. The dangers posed by the far left are more about the tone of their critique and possibilities of encouraging political demands that would undermine pluralism in the future. If the extreme left attains a receptive audience for its claim that pluralist authority will inevitably be used for dubious purposes, it may inadvertently discourage the kind of democratic participation that is required to pressure pluralist governments to exercise authority more legitimately. If the extreme left encourages the belief that democratic authority can be used for any and all purposes – for purposes beyond those constrained by the underlying consensus of pluralism upholding minority, privacy, and property rights – it may open the door to forms of social oppression that undermine their proclaimed goals of a more free and equal society.

Chapter 14

Questions of Justice

How fairly are money and other social goods distributed among citizens of various political communities? What principles and procedures are used and should be used to distribute income, wealth, power, education, and other resources that affect people's opportunities to achieve their goals in life? Does justice require anything other than fair distributions?

In December, 2004, an American Political Science Association (APSA) Taskforce issued a report on growing inequality, especially in the US.[1] Drawing on census data, it documented that between 1947 and 1973, the real income of families across the board roughly doubled; indeed, no group had a greater gain in their incomes than the poorest quintile (the lowest 20 percent of the population), who saw an average 115 percent increase in their real income during this period. But between 1973 and 2000, the incomes of the poor rose only 10 percent, while those of the rich rose, on average, by more than 60 percent. Other studies show stronger trends toward greater income inequality. Using census data between 1979 and 2003, Chuck Collins and his associates report that, while the incomes of the top 20 percent of all families rose by 75 percent, the poorest 20 percent had a net loss in income of 2 percent, when adjusted for inflation. As another measure of increasing inequality, Collins reports that in 1980, the average chief executive officer (CEO) of the 365 largest American corporations was paid 42 times more than the average factory worker. But this inequality became much more acute by 2003, when the average CEO was paid 301 times more than the average factory worker. In 2003, the average CEO was paid at a rate of about $3,800 an hour. Meanwhile, the average production worker earned less than $13 an hour.[2] Gar Alperovitz reports that the ten most highly paid CEOs in America averaged $3.5 million in annual income in 1980; by 2000, this figure had risen to $154 million, an increase of 4,300 percent in 20 years.[3] According to Lester Thurow, "No country not experiencing a revolution or a military defeat with a subsequent occupation has probably ever had as rapid or widespread an increase in inequality as has occurred in the United States in the past two decades [between 1976 and 1995]".[4]

Wealth, or net worth (the assets minus the liabilities of individuals and families), is even more unequally distributed than income. For example, the APSA Taskforce reports that the richest 1 percent of all families received (only) 16 percent of the nation's income in 1998, but they had 38 percent of the nation's wealth.[5] Inequalities in wealth have also greatly increased over the past few decades. In 1976 the wealthiest 1 percent held 20 percent of the nation's wealth, but by 2001 they held over 33 percent of the nation's wealth.[6]

Beyond these overall inequalities, there are important differences among racial groups. The average income of black families stands at about 62 percent of that of (non-Hispanic) white families.[7] But racial differences in income pale compared to racial inequalities in wealth. While the average white household had a net worth of $121,000 in 2001, the average African-American household had a net worth of only $ 19,000.[8] Dalton Conley puts the inequities in black wealth this way: while African-Americans owned only .5 percent of total private wealth in America in 1865, which is not surprising for people who had just been emancipated from slavery, they still owned only 1 percent of total wealth 135 years later (in 1990).[9] A racial group that comprises 13.5 percent of the country has only 1 percent of its wealth.

Finally, such inequality is not restricted to America. According to the United Nations Development Program, in 1998 the top 10 percent of the world's population was receiving almost 50 percent of the total world income, while half of the world's population was trying to survive on $2 or less a day.[10]

John Rawls, arguably the most important political philosopher during the second half of the twentieth century, asserted: "[J]ustice is the first virtue of social institutions."[11] The very definition of tyranny and oppression is the absence of a system that distributes fairly various rights and opportunities, income and wealth, power, education, status, and other important social goods. Conversely, a political community that delivers justice commands the consent and loyalty of people who live within it. However, achieving agreement on the requirements of justice has proven difficult. Many people would not necessarily regard the distributions of income and wealth described above as unjust; they argue that people often deserve very different levels of social goods because of their unequal talents, efforts, and contributions to the marketplace.

In this chapter, we will see that different ideologies stress different conceptions of justice, but perhaps these differences are the result of focusing on a small, partial portion of justice, rather than on justice in its entirety.[12] Perhaps each ideology focuses on that portion of justice that serves the interests of those who develop, defend, and become devotees of the ideology. Perhaps by hearing what each ideology sees as an important component of justice, a clearer picture of justice in all its complexity can emerge. Pluralist societies are built on the hope that justice is best achieved when the diverse interests in society express their partial views, when others listen sympathetically to these partial views, and when they then collectively set out to satisfy as many of these legitimate claims as possible.

Classical Liberals: Equal Dignity but Unequal Rewards

The American Declaration of Independence proclaims, "All men are created equal." Its author, Thomas Jefferson, is regarded as a pre-eminent classical liberal, and this declaration is regarded as a clear expression of early liberal sentiment. But what an odd declaration it is. Forget for the moment the omission of women. Jefferson may have meant to use "men" to refer to all humanity or he may have intended to ignore women (regarding them as inferior to men), as early classical liberals were wont to do. This oddity is understandable in terms of the terminology and prejudices of his times. What is less understandable is that, on its surface, this declaration seems at odds with our most basic perceptions. Surely Jefferson was not blind or naive, so we can presume he did not intend to say that men (humans) were created equal in the sense that they had equal physical and mental endowments. Rather, he meant to declare that all were to be treated as equals despite their unequal characteristics. When Jefferson subsequently declared that the Creator endowed men with "unalienable rights, among these are life liberty, and the pursuit of happiness," he meant people *ought* to have these equal rights.

While liberalism has evolved over the centuries, this fundamental belief in equal human treatment has remained central to all liberals. Early liberals had prejudices concerning who was to count as a man or a human in their philosophy, but the underlying liberal ideology has always assumed that each person's life, liberty, and happiness had equal worth.[13] And because of this, the early natural-rights liberalism of Locke and Jefferson simply declared from the start that all humans had equal natural rights. When liberals could not adequately respond to the assault on natural rights from traditional conservatives, the utilitarian liberalism of Bentham and Mill emerged as a theory of justice that still emphasized the equal treatment of all. In this theory, justice meant acting for "the greater good of the greater number," but the aggregate good was to be understood and calculated by giving equal respect to the interests of everyone. The good of the well endowed was worth no more than the good of the poorly endowed in determining what was just, what was best for the greater number in society after everyone's interests were given equal consideration.

Despite these egalitarian premises, classical liberals are weakly – not strongly – egalitarian. Because everyone is human, everyone is entitled to equal treatment in the application of laws governing individual opportunities. Anyone accused of a crime is entitled to equal treatment under the law and by the courts. Anyone wishing to express and act on their political views is entitled to equal political rights. Anyone seeking to get more education, to acquire a good job, or to hold an office is entitled to equal opportunity in the competition for such social goods. But such equal treatments do not mean that everyone will, in the end, get equal allocations of the things they desire. Equality under the law ends up acquitting some and imprisoning others. Equal treatment in politics results in some winning and some losing political conflicts. Equal opportunity in social and economic life means that some will get more education, better jobs, and more compensation, while others will get less. In short, classical liberals believed that everyone should have certain equal rights and opportunities, but they do not believe that everyone should enjoy equal amounts of economic resources or other social goods (like education, social prestige, or political power). To understand how classical liberals believed that equal human worth and equal opportunities could be consistent with unequal distributions of social goods, it is instructive to consider further the theories of John Locke, especially his *labor theory of value.*

According to Locke, the earth and its material resources have been given to humans in common. At the same time, each individual is given complete ownership of his own body and mind. Everyone thus has equal right to use his body and mind – to labor – as he wishes. Some will choose to labor more than others and some will work more productively than others, and these differences in how much and how effectively one labors result in differences in one's just holdings of property. By mixing his labor with nature, an individual creates value that did not previously exist. For example, a forest has little value until someone chops down the trees, produces lumber, and then builds a home (or some other form of property) with it.[14] Because labor gives property its value, the individual attains a property right to those aspects of nature on which he has labored. If each person is given an equal opportunity to acquire property, if each person has freedom to work in ways that increase the value of nature, all will justly end up with different amounts of private property because of the differences in the quantity and quality of labor that they expend.

Locke added two provisos to the amount of property that people can justly extract from nature and thus possess through their labor. First, they must leave enough for others. Second, they must not allow the goods they appropriate from nature to spoil. But Locke assumed that if people were assured the fruits of their labor, they would labor more diligently, multiplying the goods that are available for others, and thus reducing the scarcity implied by the first proviso. He also realized that the invention of money enables people to exchange their perishable goods for more durable forms of wealth, thus negating the second proviso. In short, Locke's labor theory of value justified unequal distributions of wealth among individuals who have equal formal rights. It also encouraged people to be productive workers and thus promoted progress toward a more affluent society.

As economic theory developed from these Lockean foundations during the eighteenth and nineteenth centuries, classical liberals embraced the more general principle of *market justice*: people should be rewarded according to their contributions in the marketplace.[15] Classical liberals believe that economic goods (money and commodities) are the primary social resources to be distributed. Economic goods should be distributed through the workings of a free market (rather than by some other agency such as government), and the market will allocate rewards according to several intrinsic or "natural" laws. First, the free choices of individuals influence the value and thus the price of commodities and labor. People will be able to command higher wages for those forms of labor that are most in demand by others. Second, the scarcity of goods or services influences prices. People will be able to command higher wages for those forms of labor that are in limited supply. Third, if workers are self-interested, instrumentally rational, and have mobility (no artificial barriers to entrance into the marketplace), they will move into those areas where there is high demand and scarce supply. The laws of supply and demand establish an equilibrium of fair prices and wages. For example, if lawyers are making huge salaries relative to teachers, students will flock to law school, increasing the supply of lawyers, increasing competition among them, and reducing their salaries. Fourth, if investors are self-interested, instrumentally rational, and have mobility, they will move their capital from areas of production where they are suffering economic losses to areas where they perceive opportunities for profits – where demand is predicted to be high but production is currently scarce. For example, if demand for automobiles declines, reducing the profits of those who have invested in the auto industry, those investors will search out better investment opportunities (say, for example, in producing ethanol). If they correctly predict that existing production of ethanol is inadequate to satisfy consumer demand, these investors may reap extensive profits by moving into the area. By increasing the supply of a highly demanded good, the investors have been economically productive, and their contribution to the market-place justifies their profits. In short, the laws of the marketplace reward those who take their labor and invest their capital in those areas of the marketplace where they increase the supply of goods that are scarce but highly demanded by others. Market justice occurs when people are rewarded to the extent that they contribute to the supply of demanded goods.

Classical liberals thought it would be unjust to interfere with the free choices of individuals in the marketplace. If one person acquires wealth by hard work and by making mutually advantageous exchanges with others, and another person becomes poor because he is unwilling to work hard or enter into mutually advantageous exchanges, their choices would be treated unequally if the justly acquired wealth of the productive person is redistributed to the unproductive person in an effort to achieve a conception of justice that emphasizes equal social goods rather than equal opportunity.

Traditional Conservatives: Unequal Rights but Commensurate Responsibilities

Like classical liberals, traditional conservatives believe that people are entitled to unequal shares of social goods. But they depart from liberal conceptions of justice in three fundamental ways. First, they reject all abstract rights, and thus they reject even the minimal or narrow egalitarian ethic of classical liberalism. Second, among the abstract rights that conservatives reject are those involving property. Because "real" property rights are based on traditional understandings and laws – not exclusively on labor or market exchanges – traditional conservatives end up having different conceptions from classical liberals about who is entitled to more extensive holdings of property. Third, traditional conservatives nevertheless embrace certain norms of fair treatment, which leads them to accept greater responsibility than classical liberals for the welfare of the poor.

Traditional conservative thinking about justice begins with the premise that the natural or unalienable rights declared by liberals are mere abstractions, the product of inventive rationalizations by Enlightenment theorists with no basis in reality. The person who generates valuable property through his labor does not gain any meaningful natural right to it. If you build a house through your labor, nature will not secure that property from those who would seize or destroy it; only social understandings and governmental rules can do that.

Burke claimed that the *real rights* of people were those that arise out of traditional understandings and agreements and that are enforced by governmental laws and institutions.[16] While classical liberals were declaring their principle of equal natural rights, the real rights of people were very complex and unequal. At the beginning of the modern era, national monarchs did not enact and enforce a uniform set of laws that applied to their subjects. Instead, they protected a large array of local rights and privileges. Villages, guilds, parishes, universities, and other such associations had developed their own understandings of the privileges and duties of their members. For example, various trades like cobblers and weavers were organized into guilds, composed of master artisans, journeymen, and apprentices, and each guild had its own rules governing the rights and responsibilities of people at different ranks. The masters had such rights as the ability to set prices, establish standards, and determine entry into a guild; they exercised these rights, the masters maintained, in ways that served the interests of everyone in the guild. Broader political communities also had hierarchical class structures that entailed different rights and responsibilities for the nobility and for commoners. For example, nobles but not commoners had the right to wear fancy clothes. In England, nobles enjoyed certain hunting and fishing privileges that were denied commoners. The landed aristocracy – made up of about 400 families in Great Britain – were entitled to send their eldest son to serve in the House of Lords, while commoners were without such representation. Most French nobles did not have to pay a land tax (the *taille*) that was levied on other property holders.[17] While liberals bristled over such inequalities, traditional conservatives regarded them as just. They arose out of many traditions and agreements that served the needs of their communities. It was presumptuous of liberals to believe that their theories of equal rights should take precedence over these complex real rights that had served people well for generations.

Locke's emphasis on the importance of labor in generating economic value threatened the "leisure classes" that regarded such labor as beneath them, and liberal stress on market justice threatened the existing distribution of property and other social goods. Traditional conservatives thus developed conceptions of justice that defended the way property and other social goods had long been distributed. In general, they held ascriptive principles of justice, claiming that goods should be distributed on the basis of social traits and traditional understandings of what people having certain traits required.[18] Russell Kirk expressed this principle as follows:

> Different types of character deserve different types of reward. The best reward for a scholar is contemplative leisure; the best reward for a soldier is public honor; the best

reward of the quiet man is the secure routine of domestic existence; the best reward of the statesman is just power; the best reward of the skilled craftsman is the opportunity to make fine things; the best reward of the farmer is a decent rural competence; the best reward of the industrialist is the sight of what his own industry has built; the best reward of the good wife is the goodness of her children. To reduce all these varieties of talents and aspirations, with many more, to the dull nexus of cash payment, is the act of a dull and envious mind; and then to make that cash payment the same for every individual is an act calculated to make society one everlasting frustration for the best men and women.[19]

Not only should people receive different rewards for their different characters, but people hold the most desirable characteristics to different degrees. According to Kirk, "There could be no greater injustice to society than to give the good, the industrious, and the frugal the same rewards as the vicious, the indolent, and the spendthrift."[20] Goods are thus to be distributed on the basis of mental, physical, and moral qualities.

Initially, traditional conservatives believed that only certain types of people – those white men born into the aristocracy and the best families – possessed the virtues that deserved the greatest rewards. But as traditional conservatism evolved within increasingly liberal cultures, conservatives accepted that people from various social origins could have talents and other virtues. They thus slowly embraced the ideals of *meritocracy*: those with the most desirable qualities – regardless of their class, race, or gender – should get the most important positions in society and be rewarded accordingly.

While traditional conservative and classical liberal views of justice seem similar in rejecting equal distributions, there is a fundamental difference between them. For conservatives, differences in property and positions should correspond to differences in abilities. But for classical liberals, differences in property and position should reflect – to a more limited degree – differences in labor and contribution to the market. Conservatives are more likely than liberals to see an injustice when those of low ability rise to the top of social hierarchies, because liberal theories of justice provide more room for luck and other imponderables to affect outcomes. If the value of your land skyrockets because it lies on the edge of a boomtown, your new wealth is due less to your work or contribution to the market than to luck. Classical liberals, unlike traditional conservatives, believe there is no injustice in getting ahead through good fortune.

There is one aspect of traditional conservative justice that would seem to appeal to those who do not enjoy great ascriptive advantages: conservatives claim that those who enjoy greater rights and privileges have greater obligations and responsibilities. While the specifics of these rights and obligations are different in each country, two examples illustrate this idea of commensurate rights and obligations.

The first example is from medieval France. In Paris, the law held that it was legal for paupers and traveling serfs to sleep under bridges at night. It was, however, illegal for royalty, no matter their condition, to sleep under bridges. Royalty had so many privileges that it would be unfair for them to displace the poor from one of these places of refuge.

The second example comes from twentieth-century Britain. In World War II, British Army officers were almost always sons of elites, and they were given privileges far superior to the common soldier. It was understood that these privileges were accompanied by commensurate obligations. The "Bomb Squads" – regiments developed to defuse German bombs that landed in England but did not detonate – were composed of both officers and common soldiers. When an unexploded bomb was discovered, common soldiers made preparations for defusing it and then exited the danger area; the officers then assumed responsibility for defusing the bomb. Mortality rates on the Bomb Squads were high, and officers were almost always the only troops killed. Officers did not complain, as they accepted the convention that their privileges must be matched by the greater danger they faced.

In summary, traditional conservatives reject claims of equal abstract rights and assert differentiating principles of justice. They believe people are unequal in the traits, talents, and importance and thus ought to be treated unequally. They believe that justice is the enforcement of rights and obligations that have developed within the institutions and conventions of particular communities.

Anarchists: Right Conduct in the Absence of Just Institutions

Anarchists reject both traditional conservative and classical liberal conceptions of justice. They believe that conservative conceptions of justice have enabled the upper classes to use their power to acquire maximum rights and impose unneeded obligations on the lower classes. They believe the property rights emphasized by liberals enable the wealthy to exploit others in market transactions. For anarchists, neither traditional societies nor capitalist economies provide justice. Justice cannot be delivered by any set of institutions, nor can it be reduced to a single precept regarding the proper distribution of social goods.

Anarchists believe justice can occur when people treat each other rightly. As we saw in the previous chapter, anarchists believe that morally autonomous individuals must make their own determinations about right conduct. Still, anarchists emphasize that morally just people should give due consideration to such values as mutual respect, honesty, reciprocity, generosity, impartiality, and equality.

According to Proudhon, justice is "respect, spontaneously felt and mutually guaranteed, for human dignity, in whatever person and under whatever circumstances we find it compromised, and to whatever risk its defense may expose us."[21] Godwin stressed honesty as a key element in the conduct of a just person; people should avoid all pretenses designed to provide an advantage for themselves. Proudhon stressed reciprocity in transactions and relations among people; a just relationship occurs when one person gives benefits to another and receives equivalent benefits, to the betterment of both. Other anarchists emphasized generosity, aiding and supporting those who are poor or whose basic needs are unfulfilled. In general, anarchists admire impartiality, not confusing one's own good with the general good. According to Godwin, if a person can promote the general good by dying rather than living, justice requires that he die.[22]

Anarchists are more egalitarian than conservatives and liberals. According to Godwin, there is justice in "an equal distribution of the good things of life,"[23] and he provides several justifications for this. First, inequality promotes a sense of dependence on others, producing a spirit "that reduces the great mass of mankind to the rank of slaves and cattle for the service of a few." Second, inequality hinders intellectual growth, because it prompts humans to emphasize sordid concerns about the accumulation of property, rather than focus on mental development. Third, inequality promotes in the wealthy a love of opulence and an insatiable desire to satisfy material appetites, and it promotes in the poor a sense of injustice, fanning the emotions of envy and anger. Such concerns demean the human spirit of both the wealthy and the poor.

Nevertheless, anarchists do not propose that all goods should be distributed equally to everyone. Only some authoritative and coercive institution could enforce an equal distribution of goods on all members of an association. Rather than claiming that everyone has a right to an equal share of social goods, anarchists affirm an egalitarian ethic whereby people accept the norms that everyone is, in general, equally deserving of most social goods and that the needs of everyone are equally important.

Students of anarchism often distinguish between individualistic anarchists who suggest that goods should ordinarily be distributed according to one's deeds, and collectivist anarchists who suggest that goods should ordinarily be distributed according to one's needs. Thus, different anarchistic associations stress different distributive patterns. Both individualistic and communistic associations can be just, as long as they are not coercive and reflect the moral principles of the persons who are members of them.

The idea that goods should be distributed according to one's deeds is the underlying principle of Proudhon, who was concerned with relatively rural communities. He believed (like Locke) that labor is the key contributor to the value of goods, that each farmer or craftsman has the right to that property (land and tools) necessary to make his own labor productive, and that each individual then deserves rewards proportionate to the productivity of his labor.

The idea that goods should be distributed according to one's needs is the underlying principle of Kropotkin, who was concerned with more urban and industrial communities. He believed that much of the value of social goods derives from complex social processes that make it impossible to assess each individual's contribution to the worth of goods. He noted, for example, that a person could build equivalent homes in St Petersburg and some Siberian hinterland, and the home in St Petersburg would have much more value because the theaters, shops, other facilities that others have built in St Petersburg enhance the value of homes there. Kropotkin focused on industrial production, understanding it as a collective process in which individual contributions become indistinct. He argued that the products of such social production should be owned in common. Individuals must nevertheless consume these products; communities composed of impartial and generous persons ought to distribute these goods to those people with the greatest need for them. Anarchists believe that distribution according to need is just, not because the poor person has a right to be supported by the community, but rather because a community committed to justice has a positive duty to support the needy.

Distributions according to deed may be very different from distributions according to need, because the most productive workers are seldom the most needy members of an association. Nevertheless, distributions according to either deed or need are likely to be much more equal than distributions based on traditional rights or provided by a capitalist economy. Both Proudhon and Kropotkin understood their distributive principles as prohibiting exploitation and domination. When distributions are based on deed or need, the mass of humanity would not be subservient to those in the upper echelons of society and would no longer be in positions where the high and mighty could exploit them.

Marxists: Transcending the Circumstances of Justice

Marxists have engaged in a lively debate over Marx's ideas regarding justice. Some commentators argue that he did not emphasize justice, as he regarded as "obsolete verbal rubbish" such ideas as equal rights and fair distribution.[24] Other commentators argue that he understood that capitalism was based on injustice – on capitalists wrongly taking what rightfully belongs to the worker – and sought an alternative, more just system for distributing social goods.[25] What is clear is that Marx believed that the issue of just distribution was much less important than having effective methods of production.[26] Whether or not it is unjust, the capitalist mode of production has ineffective elements, because it exploits and alienates workers. Eliminating private property by socializing the means of production is central to Marxist justice.

Marxists stress that capitalism involves *exploitation* because the working class does not receive the full value of its labor. While laborers provide much of the value of the commodities that they produce in a factory and that capitalists sell in the marketplace, they are paid only a minimum subsistence wage.[27] While the labor market produces some variation in the wage that workers are given, "the average price of wage-labor is the minimum wage, i.e., the quantum of the means of subsistence which is absolutely requisite to keep the labourer in bare existence as a labourer."[28] Workers receive a minimal wage not because capitalists are necessarily greedy and mean-spirited, but rather because of the logic of capitalist competition. If a capitalist were to pay his workers more than a subsistent wage, his costs would rise, the price of his product would rise, and consumers would abandon him to purchase the cheaper goods of his competitor who paid minimum wages. The threats of unemployment and eventual starvation force workers to accept this minimum wage. Each one understands that there is a large reserve of industrial workers who will be ready to accept subsistence wages to survive, so he must do so as well.

The capitalist, meanwhile, extracts *surplus value*, or profits, from the labor of his workers. As owner of the means of production, he pockets the difference between the value that workers actually produce and the wages paid to them to subsist. Much of this profit is then reinvested in labor-saving machinery so that the capitalist can reduce his costs of labor in the future and ensure his survival in the marketplace. Thus, workers provide the very surplus value that is used to bring about their future unemployment. In this way, the capitalist system exploits the working class and causes human misery.

Nevertheless, Marx did not believe that the exploitation of labor in this way is necessarily unjust, because the exchange between capitalist and worker is, in some sense, a voluntary and mutually beneficial exchange. The worker exchanges his labor for the money he needs for subsistence.[29] But Marx certainly implied that the larger capitalist system built on the private ownership of productive property is unjust.

The abolition of private property is central to Marxist justice. While Marx had no objection to personal property such as clothes, shelter, furnishings, and leisure goods, he argued that capitalists have "no moral right to the private ownership and control of productive resources," which he called capital.[30] He ridiculed the idea that capitalists have justly acquired the means of production through prudent saving and reinvestment of their earned wealth or because of the unusually great risks they have taken. Instead, he asserted that capital had typically been accumulated "by conquest, enslavement, robbery, and murder."[31]

For Marxists, abolishing private ownership of the means of production is important for several reasons. Until private property is abolished, unjustified inequalities in power will persist, as capitalists will retain control over workers. Inequalities in control of productive resources make the equal rights of classical liberals a mere formality, since such inequalities give those without private property little choice but to exchange their labor for a minimum wage. Until private property is abolished, workers will be alienated, unable to be creative, and working only as hard and as effectively as necessary to retain their meager wages and survive. Until private property is abolished, the capitalist class will continue to make the key economic decisions; they will choose to produce the luxuries that the rich can afford, rather than the minimal necessities of most workers who have difficulty paying for such goods. Without public control of the production process, there will be ruthless competition, closure of many productive enterprises, and recurring cycles of economic crises that impoverish nearly everyone. In short, Marx believed that, while industrialization enables humans to attain economic abundance, the private ownership of property instead produces economic scarcity.

Marx thus believed that the scarcity produced by capitalism, like that produced by all previous political economies, continued to provide the "circumstances of justice," because scarcity encourages people to be preoccupied with how to distribute scarce resources fairly.[32] Marx sought to move beyond these "circumstances of justice" to an affluent society. A truly good society would have no need for justice when "the springs of co-operative wealth flow more abundantly."[33] He believed that the circumstances of justice would be transcended only in the ideal communist society that had eliminated economic scarcity – after capitalism had produced immense industrial and technological improvements, after the state had turned these capacities to the production of the goods people really needed, and after humans had become creative workers.

Marx did not assume that the abolition of capitalism would immediately create conditions beyond the circumstances of justice. During the transition to communism, goods should be distributed by the *contribution principle*: those who contributed the most to production would deserve greater shares. While Marx regarded the precept of "to each according to his labor" as in improvement over the exploitation that occurred in capitalism and as a useful means of motivating people until they overcame their alienation, he did not regard distribution based on labor as just. He understood that unequal talents and unequal social conditions would lead to unequal work contributions. Because unequal talents and social circumstances are undeserved, distributions based on labor that reflects such inequalities would also be undeserved and unfair.

If scarcity could be eliminated, society would no longer need principles of justice to resolve their conflicts over the fair distribution of social goods. Marx asserted that the ideal communist society would inscribe on its banner: "From each according to his ability, to each according to his needs."[34] But this is perhaps less a principle of justice, understood as a method for distributing scarce resources, than a projection of what could happen in an affluent communist society. Without scarcity, people would simply take what they need from the stock of abundant resources.[35]

Communists: Using Social Control to Build a Society in which All Needs are Met

Communists interpreted Marx's writings as stressing the injustices of the exploitation of workers in capitalist societies. Indeed, they stress that imperialists also exploit peasants and other indigenous populations in developing countries.

Communists also relied on Marx to justify their authoritarian rule as a necessary stage to a future utopia where scarcity will be overcome and everyone's material needs will be met. The communist regimes of Lenin, Stalin, Mao, and Castro took control of all productive property, and communist governments employed all workers, compensating them in proportion to the quality and quantity of work performed. Like Marx, communists realized that the compensation workers would receive from their labor would not equal the full value of that work, but, rather, must be subject to some "social deductions." For example, the state would have to extract "forced savings" from workers to pay for the technological improvements necessary to industrialize their underdeveloped societies, to replace equipment that depreciated during the production process, and to pay for "the communal satisfaction of needs, such as schools, health services, etc."[36] Because such deductions would promote a future ideal society, they constituted no injustice. While the difference between what workers contribute to production and what they receive as compensation must be regarded as exploitative surplus value when capitalist employers retain it, this difference should be regarded as social contribution within the transitory socialist society.

To get citizens to regard such forced savings as social contributions, communists have practiced extensive social control over human thought and behavior.[37] While employing social control to transform the way people think about the distribution of resources may seem unjust to liberals, communists saw no injustice in the positive changes that occur when humans overcome their competitive and selfish characteristics and are molded into cooperative and community-serving beings.[38]

Following this transitional period, communists claimed that people would willingly engage in self-actualizing and creative labor. Government would no longer be needed to ensure fair compensation for labor, since everyone would contribute to society in accordance with his abilities, and each member of society would be provided his needs.

Fascists and Nazis: National or Racial Dominance as More Important than Justice

There is no well-defined theory of justice in either fascism or national socialism. Neither is particularly concerned with legal justice or the fair distribution of income or with the rights and well-being of the individual; they focus instead on the well-being or power of the collective.[39] Maximizing national or racial strength precludes much attention to problems of distributive justice. Any theorizing about the distribution or redistribution of resources or about the role of law in general is always done in terms of those arrangements that serve collective goals. If the state implements policies to maximize productivity and national power, fascists claim that everyone will benefit. Thus, the distribution of wealth is only a concern if it affects the productivity and power of the whole.

This is not to say that fascists and Nazis did not use the rhetoric of distributive justice in their initial efforts to come to power. In Germany and Italy, Nazis and fascists appealed to those segments of society that felt threatened either by economic instability or by the redistributive policies of left-wing parties. Fascists pledged to increase the material well-being of various needy groups, but they did not propose to increase taxes on the well-off, apparently intending to use the booty of war to finance such programs. When the fascists and Nazis came to power, these trends were sharpened, as both groups demonstrated a decided lack of concern with workers' rights and economic fairness.[40] Perhaps it can be argued that various public work projects of the fascists and Nazis were justified on the basis of utilitarian principles, and that these projects served the interests of most citizens. However, it must be remembered that public works – such as the German Autobahn (a network of highways similar to the US Interstate system) – were not created with the intention of promoting the well-being of individuals. Rather, they were built to serve military needs and to unify society around the nationalist and racist goals of Mussolini and Hitler.

Contemporary Liberals: Compensating for Undeserved Disadvantages

In 1975, Arthur M. Okun, who chaired Lyndon Johnson's Council of Economic Advisors during the development of the Great Society, wrote a book, *Equality and Efficiency: The Big Tradeoff*, that captures well the views of contemporary liberals regarding justice. Like classical liberals, Okun stressed capitalism's efficiency. The market system encourages investors and laborers to use their resources and energies productively, and the unequal distribution of rewards in capitalism stimulates individual effort. The result is that capitalism produces an ever-expanding economic pie and a higher standard of living than alternative systems. Nevertheless, Okun lamented the inequalities of wealth – the unequal slices of pie – that capitalism produces. Contemporary liberals generally doubt that capitalism slices the pie fairly.

Even if each person is rewarded according to her contribution to the marketplace, market justice may not be fair for various reasons. First, the unequal rewards of the marketplace are only partly due to the efforts that individuals expend. Differences in natural endowments (in intelligence, in health, etc.) and differences in social circumstances (for example, whether one is raised amidst the turmoil of the inner city or among the opportunities provided by a wealthy suburb) affect contributions to the market. But it is morally problematic that those who are born with special talents or who have been raised in advantageous circumstances deserve to be rewarded for their good fortune. Second, the market rewards people on the basis of the behavior and tastes of other people. A person may spend years writing a great book that fails to sell while a pulp novelist may make a fortune in the marketplace. Given such difficulties, it is hard to claim that the market distributes material goods justly. Third, everyone may be entitled to certain rights whatever their contributions to the marketplace simply because of their equal worth as humans. Perhaps everyone should have a right to a certain level of education, to adequate nutrition, to essential healthcare, or to other goods.

Okun recognized that there is a trade-off between efficiency and equality. When governments distribute the economic pie more equally, they simultaneously reduce the size of the pie. Redistribution is costly, because more equality must be financed by higher tax rates on upper-income citizens, which can reduce their tendency to save and invest, which can, in turn, reduce economic growth. Redistribution is costly, because more welfare rights can reduce the incentives for people to work. And redistribution reduces economic efficiency, because governments must absorb administrative costs as they establish and implement welfare programs. Contemporary liberals want both the efficiency (increases in aggregate wealth) generated by capitalism and more equality (through extended welfare rights) than is provided by pure capitalism. But, they have disagreed about the emphasis to be given to efficiency and equality.

Some contemporary liberals argue for the need to emphasize efficiency and an expanding economic pie. This was the position of certain American Democrats in the 1980s who feared that contemporary liberals had swung too far to the left by embracing extensive welfare rights and other redistributive schemes; its advocates, which included Bill Clinton and other moderate Democrats, became known as *neoliberals*, who were precursors to today's global neoliberals. They argued that economic growth is vital to other liberal goals and that liberals must thus pursue policies of economic renewal and reindustrialization. Economic growth is necessary for meaningful equal opportunity, as it provides new and better jobs. Growth helps avoid internal strife between those who currently have the best jobs and those who aspire to them. Growth also is a necessary prerequisite to expansion of citizen rights, as it generates the revenues to pay for the welfare state. According to Paul Tsongas (a former Democratic Senator from Massachusetts), "If the economy is expanding, we can open our hearts to the aspirations of others, since the growth can accommodate their demands."[41]

This liberal tilt toward efficiency and economic growth continues to be evident today in such organizations as the Democratic Leadership Council (DLC), whose members have included Bill Clinton, Al Gore, and John Kerry and which today comprises nearly 400 national, state, and local elected and appointed officials. The DLC has sought to revitalize liberalism through a greater emphasis on economic growth and a greater effort to reduce welfare expenditures.[42] While the DLC emphasizes efficiency over equality, its leaders argue that their principles should not be confused with those of contemporary conservatives. First, such liberals claim that they want "real growth, not just paper growth." They disapprove of policies that result in higher aggregate income, but achieve such growth by increasing the incomes of the wealthy without improving the well-being of the middle and lower classes. For example, soaring stock prices – stimulated by such conservative policies as deregulation and cuts in corporate taxes – increase the wealth of the rich, but by themselves do not increase economic productivity or provide well-paying and secure jobs for the middle class. Second, the DLC claims that, unlike contemporary conservatives, they do not wish to reduce or eliminate legitimate welfare rights. Instead, they want to use economic growth to expand citizen rights into new areas, such as national health insurance, that are targeted to the most needy members of society.

Some liberals, however, want to emphasize equality over efficiency. Beginning with the basic assumption that all people are to be treated equally – regardless of their natural or social differences – such liberals have sought to clarify the principles and policies implied by a commitment to equal treatment. A necessary but insufficient condition for equal treatment is *formal equal opportunity* – the right for everyone to compete for the best and most rewarding positions in society in a context where no one is disadvantaged in the competition because of her race or sex or social background. While laws and policies enforcing such nondiscrimination are important, they do not adequately provide for *fair equal opportunity*, because inequalities in natural talents and social circumstances provide undeserved advantages for some over others in the ensuing competition. While such differences are inevitable and cannot be erased, those liberals committed to a strong conception of equal treatment want governmental programs that provide fair equal opportunity.

Through governmental compensatory and welfare programs, liberal societies can provide certain essential goods and services as *entitlements* to those who need but cannot afford to purchase them. Programs that compensate people for their natural disabilities or for deficiencies that arise from social hardships are most often found in schools. Special education is the general label for many programs that address a variety of needs for "at risk students" within public schools; they provide remedial training for kids struggling with basic reading, writing, and mathematical skills, teach English as a second language, provide psychological counseling for those with emotional and mental health problems, and include many other efforts to generate more equal educational outcomes. Welfare programs include provision for the basic nutritional, housing, and healthcare needs of the impoverished through such measures as food stamps, housing subsidies, and Medicaid. While the liberal welfare state emphasizes programs targeted toward a relatively small number of eligible recipients based on specified criteria of need, liberals also support some important entitlements for everyone. Public schools provide the right to basic education to everyone. Public libraries entitle everyone to have access to books and other educational resources. However, contemporary liberals support fewer universal entitlements than do socialists.

Additionally, contemporary liberals normally seek to regulate access to the most desirable opportunities in ways that make it easier for the disadvantaged to compete for them. *Affirmative action* policies begin by encouraging universities and employers to exert greater efforts to recruit Blacks, women, and other disadvantaged groups. Stronger affirmative action policies may involve colleges and employers adopting preferential admissions where lower qualification standards are used to admit specific disadvantaged groups. Still stronger affirmative action policies may stipulate that a certain percentage – or quota – of new positions be filled by members of disadvantaged groups. Preferential treatment and quotas have sometimes been disparaged as reverse discrimination, because they violate the idea of formal equal opportunity – that people should not be classified by race, gender, and so forth in ways that influence their chances for success. However, contemporary liberals often respond that such policies are necessary to achieve fair equal opportunity – to give those with undeserved disabilities and social disadvantages more equal prospects of achieving the desired position.[43] Especially if the social disadvantages of some group (such as African Americans) are rooted in past injustices (from the legacies of slavery and racial discrimination), then rectifying these injustices may require such compensatory programs as affirmative action.

Some liberals also argue that affirmative action is justified on utilitarian grounds, as providing an overall gain to the community. Such was the reasoning of Supreme Court Justice Sandra Day O'Conner in her decisive opinion in the case of *Grutter v. Bollinger*, in which she sided in favor of a limited affirmative action program used by the University of Michigan School of Law.[44] In a nutshell, she argued that the school's preferential treatment of minority applicants was needed to attain a diverse student body and that a critical mass of minority students was needed to obtain the educational benefits flowing to all students from diversity. More generally, some liberals argue that affirmative action programs are needed to increase the number of minority doctors, lawyers, and other professionals who are available to otherwise underserved minority populations.

Liberals have also argued that affirmative action policies do not always involve reverse discrimination. White males have no right to equal treatment in the assignment of jobs, for example, if this means that they get positions as a result of outperforming their competitors on standardized tests when such tests are themselves arbitrary and perhaps biased standards for admission. A society can justly employ a variety of criteria for admissions to desired positions – including some prediction about how well various kinds of people will serve the public. As long as affirmative action programs employ justifiable criteria and processes to promote socially desirable equal prospects for minorities, and as long as these criteria are employed impartially to specific cases, those who are disadvantaged by the criteria cannot complain of injustice.

The Radical Left: Pursuing a More Egalitarian Society

All voices within the radical left agree that social goods should be more equally distributed than they are in pluralist societies with unregulated capitalist economies. After a discussion of the egalitarian ethos that unites the radical left, it is instructive to consider some of its different approaches to attaining justice.

The radical left seeks *social justice*, but its various voices are reluctant to describe any particular distribution of social goods as just. Drawing upon such studies as those cited in the introduction to this chapter, the radical left thinks that the distributions of income and wealth produced under capitalism – both nationally and globally – are unjust. They claim that many fortunes have been gained by exploiting others (and the environment) and that the poor have been victims of many forms of oppression. They argue that people's incomes bear little relationship to how hard people work, to their contribution to society, or to their moral merit.

One reason why capitalism fails to distribute goods fairly, according to the radical left, is that the most basic operative justice principle within pluralist societies having free markets is equal opportunity: giving everyone an equal chance of winning a competitive race to get a greater share of those goods being sought. Formal equal opportunity (the conception of justice endorsed by classical liberals) means that the hurdles that each aspirant must clear are equal. Fair equal opportunity (the conception of justice endorsed by contemporary liberals) means that social policies have been implemented that compensate socially disadvantaged competitors in ways that help bring them closer to the "starting line" where their more advantaged competitors begin. The radical left does not deny the value of formal and fair equal opportunity, but it regards equal opportunity as inadequate as a complete conception of justice.[45] When citizens value only equal opportunity, they behave as if life is simply a competitive race and devalue the intrinsic worth of the lives of all individuals. Equal opportunity encourages people to be preoccupied with succeeding more than others – rising to the top of the pyramids of education, wealth, status, and power. Equal opportunity justifies the victories and losses that occur in this struggle for success; winners think they have won a fair fight under conditions of equal opportunity, and they see themselves, and are often seen by others, as better people; meanwhile, the losers think they have lost a fair fight, and they see themselves, and are seen by others, as inferior people. Such understandings are often wrong (as winners may simply be more lucky or ruthless than losers) and lead to distorted self-esteem and social disharmony. Because equal opportunity is an inadequate conception of social justice, the radical left stresses conceptions of equality beyond equal opportunity.

Despite popular beliefs to the contrary, the radical left does not stress a simple equality of condition. It recognizes that a society in which everyone has absolutely equal amounts of education, wealth, power, or any other social good would be both undesirable and impossible. An equal distribution of any social good would restrict the liberty of those people who had the capacities and motivation to obtain more than the equal allotment. Unequal distributions of certain goods (such as advanced education for doctors and scientists) can benefit the public. Attempts to maintain equal distributions of such goods as wealth would necessitate an absolutist government that continuously meddles in individual lives. Even such governments would inevitably fail to achieve equal conditions. According to Michael Walzer: "We know that money equally distributed at twelve noon of a Sunday will have been unequally redistributed before the week is out. Some people will save it, and others will invest it, and still others will spend it (and they will do so in different ways)."[46] Creating more than equal opportunity yet less than equal conditions, the left seeks an egalitarian society, "one in which everybody would see each other as sister and brother, having equal worth and potential."[47] Several basic orientations promoting such a society seem common among the radical left.

First, inequalities should be questioned and justifications for them should be demanded. If adequate justifications are forthcoming, social friction can be reduced, because the inequality would be regarded as legitimate. If no adequate justification is provided, public policies can be adopted to reduce the inequality. The US Securities and Exchange Commission (SEC), hardly an institution filled with those on the radical left, nevertheless provides an illustration of the beginnings of such an orientation. In January 2006, it adopted rules requiring public companies to give the SEC data on the salaries and perks provided to their chief executives and directors. By requiring companies to provide dollar estimates on such things as stock options and retirement packages, the SEC sought to prompt companies to offer greater justification for why annual compensations in the hundreds of millions of dollars are deserved or necessary.[48]

Second, efforts would be made to reduce inequalities in wealth, power, and other goods, even though legitimate differences in such goods would remain. For example, wealth could be made more equal by increasing inheritance taxes and using the revenue from inheritance taxes to provide more entitlements. Political power could be made more equal through policies that encourage the organization and participation of groups of marginalized citizens.

Third, efforts could be made to contain deleterious effects of unequal distributions. Laws could block certain uses of money that permit the wealthy to have options that are unavailable to the less well-off.[49] For example, money could not be used to gain political influence or to buy better or more extensive education for the children of the rich. Efforts could also be made to make inequalities less permanent. For example, the most desired positions and honors could be widely rotated over time among the many people qualified for them. Inequalities could be made less cumulative through efforts to have those with high levels of one good receive lower levels of other goods. In this regard, it might be desirable to sever the link between, for example, between receiving the highest wages and the longest vacation.

These orientations show that the left's search for social justice does not entail any particular distribution of goods. Instead, the precise contents of social justice "would remain perpetually ambiguous, open, flexible, debatable, a moving horizon that is never quite reached, irreducible to either economic formula or legislative final solution."[50]

The most famous attempt to develop an egalitarian theory of justice is John Rawls's *A Theory of Justice*, first published in 1971. In this monumental work, Rawls focused on two basic principles of justice. The first– the equal liberty principle – provides everyone with the most extensive system of equal basic liberties compatible with a similar system of liberties for all. The second – the difference principle – specifies when equality can be abridged. Inequalities in distributions of such social goods as money and power are permissible if opportunities to receive greater amounts of these goods are equally open to all under conditions of fair equal opportunity, and when the resulting inequalities are to the advantage of the least advantaged.

The *equal liberty principle* is essential to Rawls and has been relatively uncontroversial, as it simply reaffirms the thin equalitarianism that was supported by classical liberals and eventually embraced by all friends of pluralism. This principle specifies that all members of a liberal society are guaranteed equal political liberties (the right to vote, the right to seek office, and freedoms of speech and assembly), liberty of conscience (freedom of thought and religion), property rights (the opportunity to acquire and hold personal property), and legal rights (freedom from arbitrary arrest, right to an impartial judge and jury, and so forth). Notice that this principle does not necessarily allow for unlimited amounts of these liberties. For example, the right to vote does not mean that all members of society have the right to decide who will hold each public office (e.g., judges might be appointed rather than elected) or what laws should be enacted (e.g., representative democracy may be preferable to direct democracy). Instead, the equal liberty principle states that societies should provide their citizens with the most extensive liberties that are feasible and desirable, and when such liberties are provided, they must be provided equally to all.

Moreover, according to Rawls, the equal liberty principle takes priority over the difference principle. This means that basic equal liberties can never be sacrificed or compromised. For example, the poor may be tempted to sell their voting rights or even themselves into slavery in order to acquire their minimal material needs. In order to ensure everyone's dignity, such exchanges must be banned, even though they may be economically efficient and advantageous to the poor. Having banned the capacity of the poor to sell their basic liberties in order to survive, societies incur an obligation to prevent individuals from finding themselves in such desperate conditions that they would be tempted to exchange their basic liberties to acquire those goods that are necessary to survival. The second principle is intended to achieve this goal.

The *difference principle* begins with a presumption that primary social goods – resources directly distributed by social institutions, such as wealth and power – are to be distributed equally unless an unequal distribution is to the advantage of everyone. For example, giving some people a larger share of wealth in order to give them an incentive to use fully their talents and energies to produce products that improve the quality of life for everyone would be acceptable to everyone. In short, inequalities are allowed if they add to each person's share of goods, but are disallowed if they invade anyone's share of goods.[51]

The difference principle specifies that in order for there to be acceptable inequalities, there must first be fair equal opportunity for all to achieve the larger shares. Formal equal opportunity is insufficient, because inequalities in natural endowments and in social circumstances unfairly privilege some individuals. An extensive system of compensatory programs must be in place to ensure that everyone has equal prospects of achieving larger shares and so that the larger shares are rewards for efforts and responsible choices, rather than the results of arbitrary and undeserved differences in people's natural talents of social circumstances.[52]

The difference principle also specifies that the resulting inequalities of social primary goods must benefit the representative person in the lowest socioeconomic class.[53] Although Rawls often says that inequalities must be "to everyone's advantage," his concern is clearly over the fate of the poor and disadvantaged. Policies and programs that reduce the social goods available to the advantaged while increasing the social goods available to the disadvantaged are just, because they move society toward the preferred state of equality. In contrast, policies that increase the aggregate level of social goods, that provide fair equal opportunity to all, that increase the social goods available to the advantaged, but that decrease the social goods available to the poor are unjust, because they move society away from the preferred state of equality.

Consider, for example, the economic policies of the Reagan and Bush administrations. Each claimed that economic growth is enhanced by reducing taxes on the wealthy and eliminating various welfare programs. Moreover, each has claimed that everyone – the poor as well as the wealthy – would see an improvement in their economic situation. Such claims make these economic policies appear compatible with a cursory understanding of Rawls's difference principle. However, egalitarian liberals like Rawls can make at least two counterclaims. First, these policies were not created and are not pursued in a context of fair equal opportunity. Clearly, the well-off have greater opportunities than the poor to take advantage of tax cuts for corporations and businesses. Second, the evidence suggests that such policies do not improve the conditions of the least advantaged. Studies have shown that post-tax income growth during the Reagan period "was limited mainly to the 20 percent of American households with the highest incomes. Households headed by poor persons from traditionally disadvantaged groups faired less well. The poorest black and Hispanic households actually lost 30 to 40 percent of their incomes between 1983 and 1987."[54] The effects of the economic policies of George W. Bush are still being contested, but some evidence suggests that the tax cuts of 2001 and 2002 and other policies of the Bush administration have not improved the conditions of the least advantaged. To the contrary, the bottom quintile, or poorest fifth, of all American households, experienced a 7.9 percent reduction in real income between 2000 and 2004.[55]

But why should principles of justice, and thus the social and economic policies of a society, favor the disadvantaged? In *A Theory of Justice*, Rawls employs a social contract argument to defend these principles.[56] Much like the state of nature in classical liberalism, Rawls posits an *original position*, a hypothetical situation defining the foundational ideas that must be shared in order for each person to enter voluntarily into a society governed by Rawlsian principles. Rawls argues that if everyone agreed to certain ideas, such as the following, they would enter a society governed by the equal liberty and difference principles, because such a society would serve everyone's interests.

Equal respect   The goals (or life plans) of each individual must be equally respected by everyone. The state must be neutral regarding the value of various life plans. Its principles and policies should not privilege certain life plans over others. Most importantly, no one's goals can be deemed insignificant or valueless and thus be sacrificed for the sake of the greater good of society.

Non-risky rationality   Everyone realizes that the achievement of one's life plans requires having some social goods and that these life plans will become endangered if one's social goods drop below a certain minimal level. While it is rational to seek more social goods, it is irrational to put oneself in a situation where it is possible to attain large increases in one's social goods but only by risking the availability of those minimal social goods that are needed to achieve one's life plans.

The veil of ignorance   The distributions of natural talents and social advantages that affect the chances for individuals to succeed or fail in their attempts to acquire more social goods are unknown. Everyone must be ignorant of whether they are relatively smart or healthy or energetic. No one can know whether they are born to privileged or disadvantaged social circumstances. Everyone must assume that it is possible that they are relatively disadvantaged in terms of natural talents and/or have been born into social circumstances that limit their opportunities.

Mutual disinterestedness   Everyone is unconcerned about the social goods available to others. Being concerned with their own life plans and the social goods available to them to achieve their goals, individuals will not altruistically provide needed social goods to others. At the same time, envy will not preclude people from accepting the larger holdings of social goods for others as long as they recognize that such holdings do not adversely affect, and may even enhance, their own situations.

Rawls contends that people who hold such ideas will find his two principles of justice preferable to alternative principles. For example, they will reject utilitarianism – the principle that governments should maximize the greater good for the greater number – because this principle permits some individuals and their life plans to be sacrificed for aggregate gains. They will also reject pure equality, because some inequalities can be mutually beneficial. They will accept the equal liberty and difference principles, because these principles protect the fundamental interests of each person from being sacrificed for the gains of others and because they protect each person from misfortune in the genetic lottery or in the social circumstances in which they were raised.[57]

Rawls's theory has been subjected to many criticisms and modifications, and much of contemporary political thought can be seen as answers to his equalitarian theory of justice.[58] Nevertheless, his theory continues to have a strong appeal for those on the radical left because it suggests that their egalitarian principles are not mere moral sentiments, but have philosophical foundations that are compelling to people who are willing to think deeply about the requirements of justice. Many other voices on the radical left can be seen as trying to further what they see as the implications of Rawls's egalitarianism.

Democratic socialists have provided the most basic approach. Having abandoned the idea of focusing on nationalization of industry and just production, they have turned to elaborating the socialist welfare state, as discussed in chapter 13. Essentially, they have focused on redistributing social goods after free market processes have provided extensive inequalities in income. But the socialist welfare state may be inadequate for realizing Rawlsian principles. By focusing on the *redistribution of income* and other material goods, through tax and transfer policies, the socialist welfare state may fail to attack the root causes of inequalities.

Other voices on the left call for the *redistribution of wealth*, sometimes labeled the search for a *property-owning democracy*. Jacob Hacker argues that wealth (or net assets, property, or capital) is much more important than income in determining the opportunities of individuals. Having wealth enables its possessors to make investments in education, in other property, or in pursuit of economic opportunities that enable its possessors more readily to attain disposable income to live their daily lives. As Marx noticed long ago, people without capital can only gain income by their work, and in order for work to get much more than a minimum wage, it must be capitalized by the acquisition of skills and knowledge that enhance its value and productivity. Having sufficient wealth so that one can gain the skills and knowledge to have significant *human capital* or so that one can own the property and equipment that makes one's labor more productive and valuable is necessary for people to have much opportunity in the contemporary world. Additionally, wealth provides a cushion against such setbacks as becoming unemployed, having a prolonged illness or injury, or a disruption in family life. While most people suffer such setbacks in the course of their lives, those without wealth are particularly likely to incur great debts from which they cannot recover.[59]

Having enormous wealth allows people to live as they wish without making much social contribution and enables them to exercise enormous power over others, generating the sort of domination that is antithetical to the radical left. Existing inequalities in wealth make a mockery of equal opportunity. Consequently, radical left proposals to achieve property-owning democracy have become increasingly prominent. Rather than redistributing income, these proposals would redistribute wealth. Perhaps the simplest such proposal is the call for a *stakeholder society* by Bruce Ackerman. Instead of welfare supplements to increase the income of the poor, each citizen would at maturity get a one-time lump sum of wealth (Ackerman proposed $80,000 in 1999), to be financed by a 2 percent levy annually on everyone's wealth.[60] Each person could use their capital as he or she wants: to increase her human capital, to acquire stocks and bonds that produced streams of interest and dividends, to purchase a home, to start a business, or to take a long vacation (not a good idea for capitalizing on one's wealth). Other proposals for property-owning democracy may not be as dramatic as Ackerman's stakeholder society, but they can command our attention. Dalton Conley argues that a just society must focus on policies that help stimulate asset formation, especially for blacks and other social groups that have been derived from acquiring much property due to historical and social factors.[61] While it is unclear exactly how this can be done, Conley encourages lawmakers to be inventive, for example, by allowing welfare recipients to accumulate assets without penalizing them with reduced welfare payments, by designing programs to enable residents of public housing to own their units, and by creating Individual Development Accounts that encourage the asset-poor to save for their children's future education expenses.[62] Gar Alperovitz applauds federal legislation encouraging companies to adopt Employee Stock Ownership Plans (ESOPs) that ease the access of workers to capital.[63] Insofar as such programs succeed in generating more equal distributions of wealth, they would also generate far more equal opportunities than exist when socialist welfare states try to generate more equal incomes but never enable many people to escape from indebtedness and do little to diminish the more extensive opportunities that are available to the wealthy and their children.

Radical feminists and civic communitarians point out that programs directed at providing more equal income and wealth may fail to undo the inequalities of opportunities that exist in families and local communities. Radical feminists point out that patriarchal families oppress women by burdening them with the lion's share of household chores and childcare responsibilities – hard work that is uncompensated.[64] For radical feminists, justice must begin with a fair distribution of these tasks in the home. Civic communitarians notice that where one lives is a major determinant of opportunities.[65] Compared to those in exurbia and the outer rings of suburbia, people living in inner cities and older suburbs have less access to jobs and public services (including quality education), good healthcare, better shopping, and even clean air. Unless metropolitan areas are able to develop policies that combat the class and racial segregation that accompanies urban sprawl, another unjustified inequality will undermine the overall fairness of contemporary political communities.

These voices on the radical left focus on moderating inequalities *within* nation states and local communities. Rawls makes clear that his theory of justice is one of bounded societies, and, in his later work, he denies that this theory should be extended beyond the nation-state to the global community.[66] However, cosmopolitans believe that global justice requires alleviating global inequalities, such as those noted in the introduction to this chapter. Clearly if where one resides within American metropolitan areas matters in terms of one's opportunities, where one is born throughout the world matters to a greater degree, but the resulting unequal opportunities are undeserved. One solution is for rich countries to open their borders to those living in poor countries – to allow the poor people to come to where the resources are – but such solutions violate the right of a political community to sovereign control over its borders, as discussed in chapter 10.

Thus, most cosmopolitans focus on redistributing resources from citizens in rich countries to those in poor ones. Such redistribution is usually justified in terms of *human rights*.[67] The moral case for human rights includes the argument that all people have equal capacities to suffer, and thus humans have moral duties to alleviate the suffering of others.[68] The political case for human rights is found in agreements among nations codified into international law, such as the United Nations Declaration of Human Rights in 1948. This Declaration recognizes that all people as humans, rather than as members of particular political communities, have a right to those goods needed to satisfy basic needs. These include rights to health, education, and decent living, working, and environmental conditions. However, there are enormous difficulties that undermine efforts to achieve such provisions. Proposals like the Tobin Tax – which would tax at rates of .1 to .25 percent the several trillion dollars exchanged daily by short-term currency speculators – could generate $100–300 billion annually to be used for international projects, especially those providing healthcare and educational opportunities to those in underdeveloped countries.[69] But we lack the sort of global institutions that have the authority to carry out such a global redistributive scheme, making the prospects for global justice even dimmer than those for more social justice within countries.[70]

Contemporary Conservatives: Criticizing Social Justice, Emphasizing Compassion

Like their traditional precursors, contemporary conservatives defend unequal distributions, but their views of justice differ in one important respect. Traditional conservatives believed that the stability of organic societies depended on people having the unequal privileges and responsibilities that accompanied their station in life as determined by their family origins. In contrast, contemporary conservatives believe unequal privileges (attending the best universities, acquiring the most prestigious positions, and attaining the most wealth) should be the result of fair competition, where individuals are treated equally under the law. Those with the most talent and merit, not necessarily those from the best families, should sit atop social hierarchies.

Thus contemporary conservative views of justice are closer to the ideas of classical liberals than their traditional ancestors. Government should ensure fair market competition and protect private property. A just society should provide individuals with equal treatment before the law and with (formal) equality of opportunity in education and employment. Economic inequalities are not unjust, and they do not require attention or social action, if they are the result of differences in talents and efforts. Conservatives, then, disapprove of the egalitarian tendencies in contemporary liberalism and the radical left, and are especially critical of attempts to undo inequalities by creating an extensive welfare state and using affirmative action.

Conservatives have opposed the welfare states created by contemporary liberals and democratic socialists. Their most general criticism is that welfare programs tax hard-working citizens to subsidize lazy and irresponsible ones, and by doing so welfare treats people's choices unequally. Why should one person be taxed for choosing to work hard while someone else gets a welfare check for choosing to hang out? A second general criticism is that welfare programs involve *moral hazards* that exacerbate the problems they were intended to solve. Liberal welfare programs were initially developed to alleviate the risks of life – to help those who suffered temporary unemployment, injury, illness, the death of one's bread-winning spouse, and so forth. But, conservatives assert, if people are ensured against risks by welfare programs, they are encouraged to engage in risky or morally hazardous behavior. If government provides socialized medicine, people will take less care of their health and overuse publicly provided health care facilities. If government provides a welfare check for the children of unwed mothers, women will be more sexually permissive.[71] A related criticism is that welfare creates more dependency than it eliminates. Welfare recipients lose incentives to improve their conditions and thus remain and become increasingly dependent on welfare.[72] This criticism is especially important, because it suggests that conservatives do not reject the idea that the vulnerable need assistance; it suggests that the problem with liberal and socialist welfare programs is that they do not actually help the poor, and instead make them worse off.[73] Conservative welfare policies in the US, such as those embodied in the Temporary Assistance to Needy Family (TANF) reforms of 1996, have allowed the states to experiment with many welfare programs, hoping to find those that might actually be effective at getting people off welfare rolls and into more prosperous conditions.

Contemporary conservatives also disapprove of affirmative action policies, regarding preferential treatment and quotas for underrepresented groups as unjust. They maintain that in university admission decisions, such policies deny admission to more qualified students while under-qualified preferred-group students take their places. This is unfair to both sets of students. Qualified students are victims of "reverse discrimination" and the under-qualified students are placed in settings where many are likely to struggle and perhaps fail.

Thomas Sowell, a black economist associated with the Hoover Institution at Stanford University, has been an especially provocative critic of preferential policies, because he marshals empirical evidence that challenges both the basis for affirmative action and its effects.[74] Advocates of preferential policies assume that racial discrimination is the most significant cause of different income levels between minorities and whites, but Sowell provides data suggesting that the causal relations are more complex. When other factors (such as differences in education and place of residence) are incorporated into analyses of income differentials between minorities and whites, the impact of race per se – or racism – is rather small.[75] Even if we grant that some racial discrimination remains, history suggests that this is a transitory phenomenon that will disappear over time without unnecessary preferential governmental policies. In the American experience, immigrants such as the Irish, the Jews, and the Polish suffered discrimination upon arrival, but later caught up with (and often surpassed) the descendants of Anglo-Saxon settlers in their economic standing. For example, the average family income of Jews and Asians in the US is higher than that of Anglo-Saxons.[76] Sowell argues that currently deprived groups – such as Afro-Americans,

Hispanics, and Native-Americans – were making typical progress toward average incomes before the development of preferential policies.[77]

Sowell also provides data suggesting that affirmative action policies have various negative consequences. First, preferential policies demean the achievements of individuals in preferred groups. Minorities who are successful can be viewed with suspicion, and their qualifications for positions can be overlooked. Such individuals then face the animosity that is directed against them by those who see themselves as victims of reverse discrimination.[78] Second, quotas aid the already successful members of the preferred groups, but hurt the opportunities of those minorities with fewer credentials who were supposed to be the beneficiaries of affirmative action. Even if an employer would like to hire a member of a preferred group who has attractive qualities but lacks objective credentials, he is discouraged from doing so, because affirmative action regulations can make firing such employees who don't work out costly and time-consuming. Third, preferential policies have often harmed the most deprived groups, because these policies are easily abused by democratic politics. Preferential policies are initially developed to benefit only the most victimized groups, but more and more groups gain affirmative action protection as politicians respond to interest-group demands. Affirmative action policies that were intended originally to benefit Afro-Americans, Hispanics, and Native-Americans have often been modified to extend preferential treatment to women, then to veterans, then to gays and lesbians, and so forth. According to Sowell, the extension of protected groups combined with the growth of credentialism results in "fewer job opportunities for less educated black males" than such men would otherwise have had without affirmative action programs.[79] Employers fill their quotas with women who possess the requisite credentials, and otherwise qualified black males remain unemployed.

Instead of pursuing social justice through governmental welfare and affirmative action programs, contemporary conservatives have increasingly emphasized compassion for the needy. While the term *compassionate conservatism* has sometimes been dismissed as a mere campaign slogan, Marvin Olasky, a professor of journalism who has most thoroughly developed the concept, argues that it is a "full-fledged program with a carefully considered philosophy."[80] It may be the philosophy that guided the Bush Administration in its approach toward poverty. According to Olasky, compassionate conservatives want to increase the responsibilities on both the destitute and the affluent. Society must practice "the tough love" that will enable the poor to become self-sufficient. Instead of "being given a fish," they must "learn to fish for themselves," and they must have hope that their efforts will be successful. Having the poor engage in "hard, character-building work is particularly important in this process."[81] Such learning and acquisition of hope does not take place through bureaucratic welfare programs. Instead, those who have learned to fish must mentor the poor. Rather than believing that justice has been served when they pay taxes that provide governmental welfare, the affluent must become personally involved, devoting their time and energy to helping specific individuals.[82]

The responsibility of helping the poor begins with families who must help their own. When more resources are required, charitable organizations – especially churches and other faith-based social services – should play the major role. When public resources are required, they should first be provided by local and state governments, with the federal government only helping when more local sources of support have been exhausted.

Rather than financing state welfare bureaucracies, the federal government should encourage families, charities, and local communities to take on the responsibility of helping the poor, by, for example, making charitable donations increasingly tax deductible and allowing private and religious groups to compete with public agencies for federal funding to provide services for the poor. According to Olasky, compassionate conservatism incorporates the values of pluralism, as recipients of assistance can choose among a variety of programs offered by Protestant, Catholic, Jewish, Muslim, and other religious and secular organizations. Public funding of social services would never go directly to purposes of religious proselytizing, and all social service agencies would be evaluated for their effectiveness in terms of removing the poor from dependency rather than on the basis of their moral outlook. In short, compassionate conservatism emphasizes private charity over state-administered social justice, but sees charitable and governmental programs working together to enable the poor to escape their destitution and dependency.

The Radical Right: Focusing on Fair Procedures and the Pursuit of the Common Good

As on other perennial issues, the various voices on the radical right have a wide range of views about justice. Perhaps the most important or unique contributions of the radical right to our thinking about justice come from global neoliberals, libertarians, and traditional communitarians.

Globalists emphasize procedural justice, or fair governmental rules concerning the distribution of social goods, and market justice, which claims that people are entitled to unequal holdings if these goods are attained through just processes of production and exchange. But they supplement such procedural and market justice with two additional principles: enhanced equal opportunity and the provision of safety nets.

For globalists equal opportunity means more than having anti-discrimination laws that ensure equal access of everyone – regardless of race, gender, sexual orientation, etc. – to market opportunities. Most globalists also support governmental programs like basic education and medical care that increase the market opportunities for people who cannot afford to purchase such stepping stones to market success.[83]

Second, globalists support the provision of minimal "safety nets" for those who are losers in the competition that occurs in a capitalist society and from those who are displaced when the "creative destruction" of capitalism causes corporations to relocate or go out of business. Margaret Thatcher recognizes that "a safety net of benefits for those who genuinely cannot cope" is a direct concern to the state.[84] And Thomas Friedman says that "we still need traditional safety nets – social security, Medicare, Medicaid, food stamps, and welfare," but that we must also seek a "new equilibrium point" regarding such provisions.[85] On the one hand, globalization may prompt us to increase welfare coverage where new social needs emerge; for example, universal access to the Internet may become a basic right in an era when such access is essential for learning, communicating, dealing with the government, and shopping for the best price. On the other hand, the elaborate welfare systems established in democratic societies during the Cold War era – to prevent workers from being attracted to communism – can be reduced. Wherever the new equilibrium is established, however, globalists recognize that the affluence generated by globalization should be sufficient to afford some safety nets.

Globalists are confident that their principles result in a just political order, and thus regard as totally unfounded depictions of globalism as an ideology that justifies the rich getting richer and the poor getting poorer. Their counter-attack is based both on narratives of how the processes of globalization have improved conditions of impoverished people in developing nations and on statistical studies of comparative and international political economy.

For an exemplary narrative, globalists have drawn on the work of Peruvian economist Hernando de Soto for presenting the case for property rights; the issue of property rights is crucial because they are often portrayed as legal protections of the holdings of the rich that deny the poor access to needed resources.[86] According to Soto, however, the poor in underdeveloped countries often hold extensive resources (land and buildings) worth trillions of dollars, but they encounter huge obstacles trying to convert these holdings into registered property to which they have legal rights. If these possessions of the poor cannot be claimed as their legal property, they cannot be converted to capital, used as collateral for loans, or traded, and the poor face massive disincentives to improve their property to its more productive uses. In short, Soto's work provides a basis for understanding how the conditions of the poor can be greatly improved if the forces of globalization diffuse democratic capitalism to those parts of the globe where it has yet to take hold and where its laws can result in the registration and protection of the possessions of the poor.

As for statistical evidence, globalists draw on numerous studies to document that global capitalism has greatly improved the conditions of people in the developing world, reducing inequality and poverty. Jagdish Bhagwati succinctly summarizes their case: "The scientific analysis of the effect of trade on poverty is compelling. It has centered on a two-step argument: that trade enhances growth, and that growth reduces poverty. These propositions have been supported by many economists and policy makers of very different persuasions over the years."[87] Their studies show that the growth provided by globalization benefits the poor just as much as it benefits the rich.[88] They show that wages in the developing world have risen much faster than those in more developed nations during the first stages of the globalization process.[89] Perhaps most arresting is Norberg's claim that "the general pattern of higher globalization and greater income equality holds for most countries, both in mature economies and merging markets."[90] If such evidence is credible, it does much to counter the claim that global neoliberalism is an ideology that promotes the interests of the rich and developed countries at the expense of the poor and developing nations.

Globalists are more concerned about inequality and the fate of the losers in a global capitalist economy than are libertarians. The most radical libertarians endorse Robert Nozick's *entitlement theory*, which clarifies and extends liberal principles of market justice.[91] According to Nozick, if unequal distributions of wealth result from historical processes that involve no injustice – if there is no force or fraud – the resulting inequalities are just. Consider Nozick's famous (if now dated) Wilt Chamberlain example. Imagine a situation in which everyone in society starts with equal incomes, but many people voluntarily deposit a quarter at the turnstile to the arena as payment to Wilt for the pleasure of watching him play basketball. Through these free exchanges, Wilt gets enormously wealthy and his fans get a little poorer. Nozick argues that to avoid such inequalities, government would have to "forbid capitalist acts between consenting adults."[92] Consider also inheritances. A straightforward application of the principle of market justice would suggest that it would be unfair for some people to acquire a significant inheritance; they could become very rich without having made any contribution to the market. But Nozick's entitlement theory claims that inheritances are perfectly just, as they arise from processes that infringe on the rights of no one. To prevent the inequalities that arise from inheritances, government would have to forbid people from making bequests. In short, Nozick argues that if people are given the freedom to exchange and bequeath goods and services as they wish – and only an oppressive government would limit such freedom – the results will be unequal but just distributions of economic goods.

Libertarians like Nozick seem to acknowledge only three roles for government in the pursuit of justice. First, governments must provide legal or procedural justice, which establishes fair rules for producing and exchanging goods and services in a free market. Second, they can adjudicate on claims by people who believe that such rules have been violated and that they have been treated unjustly; governments can rectify the injustices that have occurred due to force and fraud. Third, governments could provide security for all, as discussed in chapter 13. But any further governmental provision for the needy involves a system of taxation that unjustly violates the rights of people who acquired their property fairly. Libertarians reject the welfare states of liberals and socialists, the safety nets provided by globalists, and even the assistance that governments provide to the needy under compassionate conservatism as illegitimate efforts in the search for social justice.[93]

Traditional communitarians have generally regarded issues of justice as dealing with matters of the common good and virtue rather than the fair distribution of social goods. In *After Virtue*, Alasdair MacIntyre argued that before people are given rights to certain goods, we must first know what is good, and in a political community this means knowing the good that is common to all, such as becoming morally and intellectually developed. Justice thus involves political efforts to promote virtue in everyone.

Traditional communitarians have been reluctant to specify the distributive justice principles that are involved in the pursuit of the common good and virtue. For the most part, they emphasize embedding individuals deeply in cultures that emphasize the importance of living according to traditional moral understandings. But perhaps traditional communitarians imply that the state should distribute resources so as to encourage everyone to live according to "the best way of life" as revealed by cultural traditions.[94] Perhaps they want the state to distribute punishments to deter people from pursuing lifestyles that are seen as involving vices and sins by the political community, even if these lifestyles do not violate the rights of others but only violate widespread social understandings of human virtue. If so, they reject the liberal insistence on a neutral state that neither rewards nor punishes citizens for the goals or ends that individuals choose to pursue. The argument for such a traditional (non-neutral) communitarian state is that it will promote more virtuous citizens and better communities than do governments that emphasize individual rights and capitalist systems that merely deliver market justice.

The Extreme Right: Regarding Moral Goodness as the Basis of Just Outcomes

The extreme right believes that neither pluralist politics nor global capitalism produces justice. For example, white nationalists believe pluralist governments exhibit extreme bias in favor of racial minorities, welfare recipients, and other undeserving groups. Islamic fundamentalists believe that globalization has resulted in the injustices of economic exploitation – as multinational corporations have usurped common property and natural resources – and of cultural degeneration – as Muslims are encouraged to engage in "the consumption of the forbidden" and embrace materialist and secular life styles. Many Muslims believe their own political leaders have collaborated in such injustice, engaged in corrupt practices, and embraced decadent lifestyles.

Such views are hardly surprising, as extremists on both the right and the left have always claimed the prevailing system produces grave injustices. But while the left has conceived of justice in fairly egalitarian terms, the extreme right supports unequal rewards and punishments based on various conceptions of what people deserve. At least two different emphases can be detected among the extreme right about the qualities that comprise the bases for differential just deserts.

Groups like white nationalists emphasize conformity and nonconformity to the qualities and values of the dominant racial-ethnic group. They believe that a person's moral goodness is indicated by such traits as one's race and by one's allegiance to traditional values. Persons failing to display the requisite traits and allegiances should be excluded from political power, denied social recognition, and otherwise deprived of various social goods. A perhaps extreme example of such a conception of justice is the belief in capital punishment for white women who defile their race by having sexual relations with nonwhite men.[95]

Fidelity to divine law is a second emphasis among the extreme right for defining one's just deserts. Islamic extremists defend severe punishment for infidels who fail to obey divine law. In their view, the execution of infidels is not only just, but beneficial to the executed. Such punishments provide a sort of spiritual cleansing of the victims, serving their true interests by denying further opportunities to defy Allah's will.[96]

The Extreme Left: Decrying Global Injustice while Striving to Share "the Common"

The extreme left has long emphasized that global capitalism creates injustices among nations, as it engenders imperial practices allowing more developed nations (especially in the North) to exploit underdeveloped ones (especially in the South). More recently, it has argued:

> [Globalization has generalized] the perverse mechanisms of unevenness and inequality everywhere. Today there is uneven development and unequal exchange between the richest and poorest neighborhoods of Los Angeles, between Moscow and Siberia, between the center and periphery of every European city, between the northern and southern rims of the Mediterranean, between the southern and northern islands of Japan – one could continue indefinitely.[97]

In short, the extreme left emphasizes that global capitalism has degenerated into *global apartheid*, a system with an enormously complex geographical typography but which contains a deeply divided and separated class structure. At the bottom, there is a large excluded and subordinated population that is "cut-off, worthless, and disposable" to the global economy. At the top, there is a small elite that controls a "productive system of hierarchical inclusion that perpetuates the wealth of the few through the labor and poverty of the many."[98]

For deep greens, global capitalism exploits the earth's ecological system and denies the fundamental rights of all living beings. They believe human rights need to be invoked in the domestic politics of pluralist societies to counter the effort of globalists to weaken the welfare state in order to make national economies more hospitable to mobile wealth.[99] Moreover, human rights need to be incorporated into international agreements and promoted by international organizations. However, deep greens recognize that the concept of human rights cannot be interpreted too broadly, as an invitation for humans to demand extensive material provisions that can be attained only at the expense of other animals and that cannot be provided in a sustainable global community.[100] Animals as well as humans have capacities to suffer,[101] and thus humans have moral duties to restrain from inflicting pain on animals and to alleviate their suffering. Deep greens argue that we must abandon our homocentric perspectives that view nature and other non-human species as things to be valued for human use, control, and exploitation. They emphasize that the earth is a resource shared by the people of all nations and by all species. Justice demands that we preserve the earth that we share in common.

While today's extreme left seldom evokes Marxian images of an ideal communist society at the end of history, it does emphasize "the common" in ways that differentiate it from the radical left. When the radical left speaks of more equality, it is generally referring to a more equal distribution of privately held income and wealth, and when it speaks of communal provisions, it is normally referring to public facilities and services that each individual can use for their personal purposes – as when a citizen uses socialized medical facilities to take care of her personal health problems. For the radical left, such privately consumed goods are inadequately distributed. For the extreme left, this emphasis on such distribution misses larger issues. When thinking about justice, deep greens challenge us to think beyond the fair distribution of these goods and recognize our obligations to our common environment. Additionally, Hardt and Negri invite us to think beyond just distribution and consider the inadequate production and provision of what they call common immaterial goods. Knowledge, ideas, images, and feelings of pleasure, excitement, or being at ease are not so much private goods as things we share, or can share, in common.

Technological advances and globalization have enabled people everywhere (the multitude) to engage in collaborative production of new ideas and immaterial wealth, giving rise to products ranging from music to medicines that are produced through cooperative activities and can be enjoyed as nonzero-sum goods. Perhaps the Linux open-source computer operating system or the Wikipedia free online encyclopedia exemplify the common wealth that inspires Hardt and Negri to envision an alternative way of producing and consuming goods that casts aside the distributional allocations of capitalist society.[102] If not for corporations and individuals claiming intellectual property rights to such things as computer programs, music, and medications, these goods could be enjoyed in common by all, because, after they are created, they can be distributed at virtually no cost. And collaborative processes create these goods in ways that make claims on ownership of these intellectual properties highly debatable. For example, natural medications that have been used in underdeveloped countries for centuries can be "discovered" by modern drug companies, patented, and then privatized. As another example, this book draws upon thousands of ideas from many people, both dead and alive, and it could be made available over the Internet at virtually no additional costs to anyone who wanted to read it, and yet it is copyrighted to further the private interests of its authors and publishers. According to Hardt and Negri, such exploitation of the common has become the predominant new face of injustice in the world, as goods that were previously held in common or that could easily be made available to all, are being privatized despite our having more possibilities than ever for sharing these resources.

In summary, the extreme left argues that material goods are becoming increasingly polarized in their distribution, much as Marx predicted, but that the pattern of inequality is much more complex than Marx imagined. Given this complexity, the extreme left cannot propose any clear solution that might result in a just distribution of material goods. Compared to the radical left, which still invokes a variety of strategies to deal with such injustice, the extreme left has little hope of any fundamental change in such distributions. However, the extreme left argues that new ways of life centered on the common are both necessary and increasingly possible. Deep greens claim that we must sustain our common environment, and neo-anarchists like Hardt and Negri maintain that we can increasingly produce and consume immaterial goods where humans (or at least the vast multitude) live beyond the circumstances of justice, enjoying the truly good life. But while Marx's communist society was to be a singular achievement, where our material and immaterial lives were to be shared in common, the global society envisioned by the extreme left may emphasize an enlarged common sphere that sustains the earth and shares intangibles, even while a private sphere of unjust distributions of material goods continues unabated.

Conclusions

Pluralists insist that justice is a complex concept involving a variety of trade-offs. They uphold the importance of legal and procedural justice – of providing formal and regularized procedures of resolving conflict and equal treatment under the law.[103] They uphold market justice, the idea that unequal incomes and wealth are legitimate if achieved by processes of production and exchange that reflect individual choices and are free of coercion and exploitation.[104] But fair legal procedures and market exchanges must be complemented with other principles of justice involving equality, need, and desert.[105] In pluralist societies, some policies provide certain social goods (like basic education) equally to everyone, other social goods (like welfare) to those in greatest need, and still other social goods (like prized occupations) to those who deserve them given their qualifications. Pluralists insist that no single conception of justice is universally valid. Pluralist politics involves continuous conflict over the emphasis given to various justice principles. But pluralist politics is not just power politics, where political outcomes simply reflect successful applications of political resources to achieve personal and group preferences. Pluralist politics involves appeals to justice in its myriad forms.

Radical demands for simple equality – that everyone has a right to equal incomes and wealth regardless of their contributions to the production and distribution of economic goods – would clearly violate the pluralist understanding of the complexity of justice, but it is a misunderstanding to assert that anarchists, Marxists, or other voices on the radical or extreme left call for such equality.

The radical left usually initiates demands for social justice – for the provision of certain goods equally to everyone by virtue of their equal citizenship and humanity and the provision of other types of welfare services to people because of their unsatisfied needs. Such demands are simply part of pluralist politics. When leftists propose specific policies to further social justice, they must surmount two major obstacles. First, they must overcome the limited conceptions of justice – especially those focusing on market justice – that are so prevalent in pluralist societies.[106] Perhaps conversations on the meaning of justice could generate such expansions in how people think about justice, bringing greater attention to egalitarian and need-based ideals. But perhaps people would be more receptive to such ideals by hearing "sad and sentimental stories" of oppressed people and other narratives that appeal to people's senses of compassion and empathy for the poor.[107] Second, the radical left must surmount the apathy and alienation of the marginalized and oppressed people that would be benefited by greater pursuit of social justice. Such groups will have to engage in contentious politics, because those who are well-off in a pluralist society will not give up their privileges without a fight.[108]

The extreme left envisions fundamental changes in people's orientations – we must cease striving constantly for greater shares of material goods and become content with living more simply in harmony with nature and sharing intangible goods with others. These are legitimate and even laudable aspirations. Efforts to change human and cultural values would surely affect some of the content of pluralist politics, but if extremists on the left continue to recognize the need for democratic politics and economic markets and if they respect the moral autonomy of individuals, their efforts should not greatly trouble pluralists.[109]

On issues of justice, pluralists are more troubled by the extreme and radical right. The extreme right seems to believe in the justice of punishing people for who they are racially and what they believe religiously. Such beliefs are anathema to pluralists. For the most part, libertarians can be seen as just another voice in the pluralist pantheon of competing voices, but if extreme libertarians have much success in achieving their goal of a minimal state that would preclude policies aimed at furthering social justice, pluralism would be unacceptably truncated. Democratic politics pursuing social justice and the capacity of governmental authority to provide programs of social justice are essential aspects of pluralist politics.

Pluralists worry that traditional communitarians violate their commitment to individual moral autonomy and state neutrality. For pluralists, individuals have the right to choose, pursue, and revise their own conceptions of the good life, as long as their actions do not create injustices for others. The pursuit of some conceptions of the good life will be more rewarded, and others more punished, by the social processes and norms that exist in pluralist societies, and individuals are well advised to consider such matters as they make and revise their life plans. But the state should be neutral in the sense that it does not directly distribute rewards and punishments according to perfectionist ideals.[110] When traditional communitarians propose that states structure rewards and punishments on the basis of a particular comprehensive moral doctrine, they cease being friends of pluralism.

Chapter 15

Questions of Change

How much and what kind of change is desirable? By what means should change be pursued? When is it legitimate for proponents of change to employ extra-legal, disruptive, and even violent means to achieve their goals? Can defenders of the status quo repress those who agitate for change?

Political change is a certainty. But the degree and direction of change is unpredictable, despite the efforts of scholars to theorize about the conditions of change and the initiatives of political activists to achieve it.

Periodic elections in America provide occasions for most of its citizens to think about the desirability of change. Despite the institutional rigidity that impedes fundamental reorientations in political life in the aftermath of elections – the barriers to successful third parties and independent candidates, the dominance of one party in particular regions and districts, the biases favoring incumbents, and so forth – elections can serve to redirect governmental priorities and the general contours of political life. The 1932 and 1964 elections, for example, made possible the New Deal and the Great Society, programs that extended the role of government in economic and social life and gave greater emphasis to social justice. In contrast, the 1980 and 1994 elections brought more conservative regimes to power.

Whether elections in the coming decades will bring fresh orientations to politics remains to be seen, but the election of new political leaders and even the emergence of a different dominant party seldom have effects beyond issues of authority and justice. Electoral shifts can bring new policy orientations, but they are seldom the cause of larger shifts in the democratic process, broad changes in economic, cultural, and governmental structures, new conceptions of citizenship, or a reconfiguration of the political community. An exception was the election of 1860, which brought to power the new Republican Party and a fairly obscure country lawyer, Abraham Lincoln (1809–65), and sparked changes that involved fundamental questions about the American political community (whether the Union would be dissolved by the secession of Southern Confederate States), citizenship (whether to abide by the Dred Scott decision that declared blacks to be non-citizens), and structure (whether slavery would continue as an American institution).

Since the Civil War, America has witnessed many great changes that were not associated with any particular election. The territorial size of the country has more than doubled with the admission into the Union of various large states in the West, Hawaii, and Alaska. The arrival of large waves of immigrants (especially from Southern and Eastern Europe at the end of the nineteenth century and from Latin America and Asia during the last three decades of the twentieth century) and the women's and civil rights movements have generated a much more multicultural citizenry. Vast changes have occurred in economic, civic, cultural, and governmental structures that, in total, can be regarded as revolutionary, but they occurred incrementally, through many reforms that were only partially attributable to the results of elections.

Other political communities have perhaps experienced even greater changes than those that have occurred in the US during the past two centuries. Czarist Russia was replaced by a communist Soviet Union, which has since disintegrated into various smaller nations whose commitments to capitalism and democracy are still to be determined. The British Empire and Commonwealth at one time dominated world politics and have since disintegrated. China, India, South Africa, and numerous other political communities in Asia, Africa, and Latin America have gained or regained independent status and have transformed their economies, cultures, and governments. Political movements, rebellions and revolutions, war, economic developments, population migrations, and cultural transformations are just some of the causal factors that have changed global life today in ways that were unimaginable 200 years ago. Most analysts believe that the pace of change will continue to accelerate in the future. We might thus expect that the changes that occur within the next 50 years will be even more dramatic than all the changes that have occurred during the past few centuries.

If future change will be enormous, unpredictable, and of a different character from those of the past, the ideas about change contained in past, present, and emerging ideologies are unlikely to provide much guidance about the future. But careful consideration of how these ideologies envision change should deepen our awareness of the multidimensional nature of change and remind us of the need to keep our political theorizing open to the changes that are sure to come. Because the orientations of various ideologies regarding change reflect their beliefs and values on the other perennial issues, careful consideration of how ideologies envision change helps summarize their political ideas and is an appropriate way to conclude political conversations.

Classical Liberals: Seeking Economic, Intellectual, and Moral Progress

The most general statement about the ideas of classical liberals toward change is that they want continuous economic, intellectual, and moral progress. Governments that fail to provide the conditions for such improvement should be dissolved or reformed. Governments that do provide the conditions for such progress should, of course, be sought or maintained.

Classical liberals believe that *economic progress* occurs through capitalism. If individuals are given property rights and economic freedoms, they will make choices to maximize their economic well-being, the economy as a whole will become more productive, and nations will become wealthier. Government can best facilitate economic improvements by permitting economic freedoms, protecting property rights, enforcing contractual obligations, and refraining from extensive interference in the marketplace.

Classical liberalism was born in the conviction that *intellectual progress* occurs when people are freed from religious dogma and political absolutism and can pursue knowledge through scientific observation and reasoning, leading to greater inter-subjective agreement about the true nature of things. According to the Marquis de Condorcet (1743–94), increases in scientific understanding result in technological advances, improve industrial and agricultural productivity, prompt medical innovations, and provide an overall increase in physical, mental, and emotional well-being. Improved principles of social and political organization can be discovered and become part of the cumulative inheritance of humans, ensuring that each generation is more advanced intellectually than its predecessors. Classical liberals therefore focused on achieving an open society that provided the intellectual freedom to discover knowledge that improves human life and that transmits knowledge freely to all citizens. Classical liberals believed that the roles of government in fostering intellectual progress are minimal but crucial. Governments must provide secure and open environments in which people can engage in the discovery of new truths. They can support those institutions that educate the public about these discoveries.

Classical liberals came to believe that *moral progress* is possible and is fostered by citizen involvement in the democratic process. According to John Stuart Mill, democratic institutions draw citizens into the public realm, give them an interest in public issues, stimulate them to become knowledgeable about social matters, and encourage them to make better and fairer political judgments.[1] Through participation in public life, self-interested individuals can attain a clearer understanding of their obligations to others in the broader community.[2]

In short, classical liberals have sought and continue to seek progress. Their attitudes about maintaining, reforming, or dissolving existing governments are dependent on the performance of these governments in securing the conditions of progress.

For classical liberals, political revolution is justified if governments inhibit progress by limiting various freedoms. John Locke wrote that governments could be dissolved if they violated property rights. Although precursors of liberalism defended the most significant political revolutions of the seventeenth and eighteenth centuries – the "Glorious" Revolution in England, the American Revolution, and the French Revolution – their commitment to revolution in general was limited. Locke, for example, regarded his defense of the right of citizens to dissolve government as a means of deterring revolution rather than as an invitation to revolt: "This power in the people of providing for their safety anew by a new legislature when their legislators have acted contrary to their trust by invading their property is the best fence against rebellion, and the probablest means to hinder it."[3] By acknowledging that citizens have the right to revolt when governments abuse their power and by recognizing that citizens will revolt against abusive government, Locke hoped to convince legislators that their best hope of forestalling political revolution was to secure rather than abuse the rights of their citizens. Even the most radical liberal theorists, like Thomas Paine, are silent on how aggrieved citizens might go about fomenting a revolution. The image of revolutionary action that emerges from Locke and Paine is one of all members of society assembling and deciding to remove their government by majority vote. There is no manning of the barricades here.

Can regimes that come to power on the basis of liberal principles use their coercive power to repress citizens who seek to overthrow them? Classical liberals uphold the rights of opposition: the right to articulate grievances, the right to organize as an opposition party, and the right to try to convince the public that the current regime should be replaced. If liberal regimes could repress such political dissent, the democratic accountability so important to classical liberals could not be realized.

If a constitutional democracy exists and effectively preserves rights, but if laws and practices remain that depart from liberal ideals, classical liberals advocate political reform. During the beginning and middle of the nineteenth century, Jeremy Bentham and James Mill were the intellectual leaders of the *philosophical radicals*, who hoped to reform the British legal and electoral systems. Bentham focused on codifying and rationalizing British law. Where existing laws simply secured the privileges of the aristocracy, he sought their replacement with laws consistent with utilitarian principles promoting "the greatest good of the greatest number." The Benthamites – including economist David Ricardo (1772–1823) and legal theorist John Austin (1790–1859) – pushed reform in such areas as criminal justice, education, public health, and foreign trade. James Mill focused on reforming the electoral system, by, for example, extending the franchise.

John Stuart Mill argued that legislative reforms should seek to make life more humane for everyone, even if that required redistributing some of the wealth generated by the market economy. Such reforms were anathema to earlier classical liberals, and opened the door to the reform of liberalism itself. When contemporary liberals began to pursue numerous economic and social reforms that threatened property rights and expanded the role of government, their opponents often asserted classical liberal principles. Thus it was that, during the twentieth century, classical liberalism became a ideology that normally defended the status quo.

Today, of course, most industrial societies have governments that extensively regulate the economy and redistribute economic resources through welfare policies. Perhaps one of the most prominent social movements today is composed of classical liberals calling themselves conservatives and libertarians who seek economic deregulation and the dismantling of the welfare state. By seeking to return to a political economy that conforms to the principles of classical liberalism, this movement can be regarded as a proponent of reactionary change. Such classical liberals respond that only a return to these earlier principles can promote an environment of economic, intellectual, and political freedom that will revitalize the economy, unleash the intellectual energies of individuals, ensure political rights, and thus promote human progress.

Traditional Conservatives: Slowing the Winds of Change

Most basically, traditional conservatives prefer to avoid change. Deeply appreciative of various inheritances from their forefathers, they wish to conserve the traditions and practices that have long guided their societies. Michael Oakeshott, a leading British conservative philosopher during the twentieth century, famously declared:

> [Conservatives are inclined to prefer] the familiar to the unknown, the tried to the untried, fact to mystery, the actual to the possible, the limited to the unbounded, the near to the distant, the sufficient to the superabundant, the convenient to the perfect, present laughter to utopian bliss.[4]

Conservatives claim that this disposition makes them *realists*. They deeply appreciate the present "real world" that God and their ancestors have bequeathed to them, rather than longing for some alternative "ideal world." They realistically appraise the limitations of human beings and their governments that vitiate the utopian dreams of other ideologies. In short, traditional conservatives do not share the modern fascination for innovation and progress.

Nevertheless, traditional conservatives recognize that change is sometimes necessary and that states must be prepared for social changes. Despite attacking the French Revolution, Burke declared: "A state without the means of change is without the means of its conservation. Without such means it might even risk the loss of that part of the Constitution which it wished the most religiously to preserve."[5] Proper attention to serious illnesses within the body politic will prevent the need drastic interventions in the future.

Necessary change should take the form of organic evolution. Changes should aim at remedying serious and specific problems, not minor vexations. Corrections should be limited, as major changes can have unexpected costs and unanticipated consequences that do more overall harm than good. Changes should be introduced gradually, so as to fit within the traditions of society and not disrupt social stability. Tampering with complex social organisms is always dangerous, so it must be done with great prudence.

Rather than changing laws to modify traditional ways of life, changes in the law should reflect changes in cultural norms and public understandings. According to Alan Finlayson, conservatives maintain that "the only guide for political action is the slowly evolving 'spirit of the people' as manifested in its tradition and culture."[6] Traditional conservatives have not been sympathetic to social movements – such as the civil rights movement, feminism, or gay liberation – that have sought legal changes that are contrary to dominant community views and that seek to alter cultural norms.

Appreciating the status quo, traditional conservatives believe both governments and citizens must be cautious. Government must avoid adventurism in either domestic policies or foreign affairs. Citizens must avoid radical actions aimed at disrupting or overthrowing an existing government.[7]

The only time that disobedience or revolutionary action is justified is when the regime violates the traditional rights that have developed within a country. For example, Burke argued that American colonists were simply demanding their traditional rights, and that the failure of Britain to respect these rights justified the rebellious acts of the colonists during the American Revolution. But Burke opposed the French Revolution, because the proponents of change sought new abstract rights that went well beyond their traditional rights. Those who call for change in traditional understandings and rights can be repressed, for example, by imprisoning them in the Bastille.

Marxists: Predicting Revolution From Below

According to Marx, all societies have experienced fundamental and progressive change; he thought capitalist society would experience such change as well. As we have seen, he claimed that, at some point, this change would be revolutionary, but that point would occur only when objective economic conditions reach a critical conjuncture and when subjective class consciousness among the proletariat had been adequately developed. Orthodox Marxists rejected the notion that revolutions could be made before both objective and subjective conditions were ripe. Perhaps Marx thought that the political turmoil in Europe in both 1848 and 1871 were harbingers of revolutionary change and that a revolution against capitalism was imminent. But it is also possible to read his theory of political change as a projection into a future that has yet to be realized.

According to orthodox Marxists, the revolution that overthrows capitalism and inaugurates the reign of communism will occur as the laws of political economy take their course. This revolutionary process can be summarized as a deterministic sequence, having the following ten steps.[8]

1   As industrial society develops, there will be extensive competition among capitalists. To compete in the marketplace, capitalists must exploit workers, paying them only subsistence wages, thereby extracting surplus value. Capitalists must then reinvest these profits in more efficient technology in order to reduce future labor costs.

2   Some capitalist enterprises will be successful and some will fail under these conditions of competition and innovation. The unsuccessful ones will be forced out of the marketplace. Capital will become more concentrated.

3   As successful capitalist enterprises replace workers with machines and as more and more enterprises fail, there will be fewer employers, and more and more workers will be laid off, with many becoming permanently unemployed.

4   These unemployed workers will lack the purchasing power to buy the goods that are being produced by capitalist enterprises. Production will therefore slow down, and even more workers will become unemployed.

5   Cycles of unemployment and consequent slack demand (recessions) will recur over time. With each recession, there will be fewer and fewer successful capitalists who weather the economic storm. Their economic position will improve with the lack of competition, and their wealth will increase.

6   With each recession, there will be more and more unsuccessful people in the marketplace. Unsuccessful capitalists will fall into the ranks of the proletariat, and some of the proletariat will sink even further into an underclass or "lumpenproletariat." Such downward mobility will continue to swell the ranks of the proletariat and the unemployed, a phenomenon that Marx called the "immiseration of the proletariat."

7   These increasingly desperate conditions cause the proletariat and others who are being marginalized in the economic system to question the usefulness and fairness of capitalism. Working-class consciousness develops out of this questioning.

8   When the economy hits a severe depression, when proletarian misery is particularly acute, and when the proletariat finally comes to believe that the capitalist system has outlived its usefulness, a spontaneous mass uprising will occur. It will begin with unrelated small strikes, boycotts, and riots. These will coalesce into more militant and unified political action. One of several scenarios will then lead to revolution: a general strike may disempower and bankrupt capitalists; a civil war may occur between capitalists and their agents of order (the police and army) on the one side and an armed proletariat on the other; or, the bourgeoisie could be overthrown by ballots rather than bullets in a democratic election, although this is unlikely.[9]

9   After the proletariat has seized power, there will exist a state of emergency. Because the bourgeoisie will remain wedded to liberal ideology, and because their interests will be to restore their own power and wealth, they may initiate a counter-revolution. To prevent this possibility, the proletariat must establish a dictatorship of the proletariat that will forcefully suppress capitalists.

10 The proletarian defeat of the bourgeoisie will begin a socialist stage in history – a period of transition from capitalism to full communism. During this period, the remnants of capitalism will be replaced with new cooperative social arrangements, and a "new man" will emerge who is committed to socialist ideals.[10] A complete communist society will eventually arise out of this socialist interlude.

Contemporary post-Marxists believe that such a theory of history provides continuing insights into the processes of fundamental change, but they reject an interpretation that this theory is deterministic. From their perspective, revolution will not be a necessary outcome of objective economic conditions but will depend on the emergence of subjectivities – on the way that many kinds of people differentially situated in the global economy evolve their own understandings about the limitations of global capitalism and their own strategies for moving toward a society that is fundamentally different from the one we have. Post-Marxists recognize that capitalist society and liberal governments have adapted in certain ways that make necessary many revisions in Marx's scenario. For example, evolving class structures may have diminished the revolutionary role of the proletariat (defined strictly as industrial workers), and a broader array of marginalized people organized into many social movements may be instrumental as agents of revolutionary change.[11]

Post-Marxists also differentiate between a *theory of history* and a *philosophy of history*. They applaud Marx for providing an insightful theory of history that focuses on fundamental rather than marginal change. This theory claims that history was (and is) moving in the direction of a communist society, and it identifies the basic structures of oppression (such as capitalism) and the mechanisms of transformation (such as revolutionary movements). But post-Marxists assert that Marx did not have a philosophy of history that gives meaning to history, one that claims that the dislocations that occur in history can be explained and in some way justified by reference to a teleological "end of history."[12] In this way, post-Marxists seek to rescue Marxism from the twentieth-century communists who justified the oppressions that Stalin, Mao, and others inflicted on their subjects as sacrifices that were necessary to achieve a future utopia. Still, Marx's vision of an affluent, egalitarian, and communal society without the need for a coercive government remains a significant element of the changes sought by those who claim to be Marxists.

Anarchists: Calling for Rebellion rather than Revolution

Because of the radical hostility of anarchists toward the status quo – because they seek the destruction of most existing institutions and a major transformation of human values – anarchism is usually regarded as a revolutionary ideology, much like Marxism. Nevertheless, anarchists usually claim that they are more committed to *rebellion* than to revolution. From their perspective, revolutionary change involves the destruction of old institutions and their replacement with new ones; it involves replacing one oppressive state with another oppressive state. In contrast, rebellion means placing oneself in radical opposition to existing institutions. Rebels refuse to obey conventional authority. Rebels seek the destruction of conventional modes of domination without any provision for their replacement.

From the anarchist perspective, Marxists mistakenly seek revolution. Mikhail Bakunin criticized Marx for supporting a revolution in which the working class would conquer the state rather than destroy it. As we have seen, Marx did claim that the proletariat must seize state power during the revolution and use its coercive capacities during a transitional period of undetermined duration. During this transitional period, the state would abolish capitalism and promote the arrival of an anarchistic society. Anarchists generally – and Bakunin in particular – rejected such a scenario. Bakunin believed that the leaders of the new proletarian state would become corrupt and use state authority for their own purposes. If the state were merely conquered rather than destroyed, the new authorities would refuse to relinquish their power even when the state was no longer necessary.[13] Anarchists thus insist that when the old state is destroyed, arrangements involving a natural society without government must spring immediately from the void.[14]

Anarchists generally agree on four imperatives regarding rebellion. First, they believe that participation in the rebellion against conventional institutions must be *voluntary*. Each person must make a personal decision to rebel. Instead of conceiving of rebellion as a mass action in which individuals are swept away by historical circumstances or caught up in mob behavior, anarchists regard rebellion as a conscious act by each individual. Rebellion must be carefully chosen by individuals who are morally committed to the justice of their cause and who assume moral responsibility for their actions. Second, anarchists believe that rebellion must be *spontaneous*. While communists believe that a revolution can be led by a vanguard that understands when conditions are ripe for a successful revolution and that can organize the masses, anarchists reject the "claim that even the most intelligent and best-intentioned group of individuals will be capable of becoming the mind, soul and guiding and unifying will of the revolutionary movement."[15] In order for rebellion to occur voluntarily and spontaneously, anarchists perceive the need for a long period of preparation in which the desirability of destroying the old institutions is deeply etched into the consciousness of humanity.

Third, anarchists insist that only *total* rebellions can be effective. Acts of rebellion must be directed not merely at governmental authority. The French Revolution had taught anarchists that changes in government without broader social changes are of little significance. According to Proudhon, the French Revolution was political only; its "success" consisted of delivering the nation from the hands of kings and aristocrats into those of warriors and lawyers.[16] In addition to destroying the old political regime, anarchists seek to overturn simultaneously the economic system based on ownership of private property, the authority of established churches, the social system in which the upper classes demand and expect deference from the lower classes, and those cultural values that promote materialism, selfishness, and the superiority of some people over others. A total rebellion involves destroying all conventional institutions and beliefs that allow some people to dominate others.

Fourth, anarchists maintain that once rebellion begins, it should be rapidly pursued on an *international* scale. If an anarchistic society were established, it would be without the military means of defending itself against aggression. Thus, to be successful, *all* national governments must be rapidly abolished.[17] Anarchists maintain that a successful total rebellion on an international scale would leave intact nothing but peaceful natural communities.

While agreeing upon these aspects of a successful rebellion, anarchists disagree about the role of *violence*. William Godwin and Leo Tolstoy were committed to nonviolence, regarding acts of revolutionary violence to be as coercive as the violence of governments. Godwin claimed that force was no substitute for reason and that rebels should exhaust all means of moral persuasion before considering violence – which he regarded as the last desperate resort of just men. Tolstoy also urged rebels to use reason to persuade others of the validity of anarchist views, but he defended passive resistance against authority. Confronted with unjust authority, Tolstoy's nonviolent anarchist would refuse military service, jury duty, and the payment of taxes; he would refrain from cooperating with government.

Other anarchists, like Bakunin and even the gentile Kropotkin, believe that violence is a necessary, if undesirable, means of resisting authority. They differentiate between various forms of violence. Sabotage and strikes can be regarded as violence against property; since capitalist claims to property are illegitimate, acts that destroy property or disrupt its employment are not unjust. Acts of violence that result in the death of innocent people raise more difficult moral issues, because of the inherent worth of all life. Such violence can sometimes be justified, according to anarchists, if the good that results from it outweighs the evil. If the target of a political assassination practices policies that impose terror, violence, and death on many citizens, then is not the murder of that person justified?

Anarchists justify the use of violence in various ways. First, employing violence may be an act of liberation for those who have long been dominated by their oppressors; by taking up arms, the oppressed can shed their shackles and perform acts of courage and self-realization. Second, confronting oppressors through violence polarizes conflict, provoking them to over-react and use much more violence than originally used by the rebels. Such over-reactions by the oppressors often prompt uncommitted members of the public to recoil at the excesses of authorities and side with the rebels. Third, violent destruction must simply be understood as part of a continuous natural process of death and rebirth. Violence is a necessary part of the process of renewal in the natural world.

Anarchists understand that conventional authorities will use their coercive power to repress them, but they believe that such repression is morally unjustified. Repression of anarchists merely continues the oppression and domination that characterize conventional societies.

Communists: Generating Revolutions While Deviating From Marxist Orthodoxy

The Black Flag of anarchism both cooperated and competed with the Red Flag of communism during the Russian Revolution and Civil War that occurred between 1917 and 1921. By emerging victorious in these struggles, communism rather than anarchism became the dominant philosophy of the left throughout much of the twentieth century.

Like Marxists, communists believe that revolutionary change is needed. Unlike orthodox Marxists, communists do not believe that revolutionary change will occur only when economic and historical conditions are ripe or when proletarian consciousness has been fully developed. Instead, those with political acumen can provoke revolutionary change. Since change is enacted by human agency, the question for communists becomes: how can we effectively bring about the revolution that moves people throughout the world toward communism? During the twentieth century, communists employed several strategies, each having characteristics that reflect the specific society where revolutionary change was initiated.

Lenin's strategy for change in Czarist Russia at the beginning of the twentieth century called for organizing and training a relatively small, secret, professional, and disciplined Bolshevik party, led not by the proletariat, but by middle-class intellectuals (like Lenin) who understood the interests of the proletariat and the requirements of the revolution. When their enemies were weak, the Bolsheviks staged a political coup. When this succeeded, the party centralized power and initiated the transformation from capitalism to communism through massive party control of the state, economy, and society.

Mao Zedong had a different strategy for bringing change to China during a prolonged struggle that began in the 1920s and resulted in communists coming to power in 1949. First, he emphasized that the peasantry would play a critical role in the revolution. This aspect of Mao's revolutionary doctrine clearly contradicted Marx, who had stressed that the urban proletariat rather than rural peasants would lead the revolution. But Mao realized that China lacked a mature proletariat; instead, it had a large peasant population that had been exploited for centuries. Mao observed in the peasantry the virtues of innate goodness, self-sacrifice, courage, and shrewdness, and he believed they had the motivation to play a major role under the leadership of the Communist Party in the revolution.

Second, Mao believed that *guerrilla warfare* was the appropriate method of revolutionary struggle in colonial nations. While Lenin had used a small and disciplined party to seize power in a coup, Mao's doctrine of guerrilla warfare called for long-term popular effort, extensive local peasant initiatives, and numerous opportunistic skirmishes with the imperialist enemies and local authoritarian regimes. Guerrilla warfare had both military and social components. By declaring that "power comes from the barrel of a gun," and by teaching guerrilla soldiers to remain mobile and to engage in direct combat only when victory was assured, Mao demonstrated his emphasis on military effectiveness. By having party leaders build extensive social networks with the peasants, gaining their allegiance so that they would provide the guerrilla soldiers with needed information, food, shelter, and new recruits, Mao emphasized that successful guerrilla warfare depended on the support and cooperation of the local population.[18]

Mao's doctrine of *a people's war* was exported to other underdeveloped countries – like Vietnam and Cambodia – that had characteristics similar to those of China.[19] A successful export into other colonial countries was intended to serve two purposes: it would undermine the worldwide systems of capitalism and imperialism, and it would show that underdeveloped countries could "leap forward" toward communism, sidestepping the indigenous capitalist phase that Marx thought necessary in order for communism to occur.

Mao's revolutionary strategy was both adopted and modified by Fidel Castro and Che Guevara who developed *the Cuban model* for exporting communist revolutions throughout Latin America, Africa, and other developing nations. The distinctive aspect of the Cuban model was its de-emphasis of the role of communist parties. Castro had come to power in Cuba in 1959 through a popular insurrection, and did not depend on the Communist Party to govern Cuba or to initiate revolutions elsewhere. Guevara insisted that the struggle against Western domination required communists to work within a "united, anti-imperialist front,"[20] but a centralized party should not control this effort, because it would be a clear target for brutal governmental repression. Instead, revolutionaries should be organized into many spontaneous, fluid, independent, and decentralized groups that would engage the enemy in guerrilla warfare. According to Castro, such a decentralized approach to revolution would not only be more effective in defeating "Yankee imperialists," it would also reduce the danger of revolutionaries turning away from democratic principles once the revolution had succeeded.

In Western Europe, revolutionary change in accordance with the Marxist or Leninist models became increasingly unlikely during the twentieth century. Antonio Gramsci was the communist theorist who provided the most important explanation for this development. According to Gramsci, *bourgeois hegemony* made a mass-based revolution unlikely. Bourgeois hegemony meant that the processes of socialization, the institutions of education, and the means of communication all impressed on the West European mind the values of liberal democracy and capitalism. As a consequence, capitalists ruled not by force but by consent, because most citizens thoroughly embraced a bourgeois liberal ideology. Gramsci also thought that it was futile and dangerous for communist parties, acting as a vanguard, to foment a revolution on behalf of the proletariat. The excesses of Lenin and Stalin caused Western Europeans to fear that successful revolutionary vanguards brought about as much oppression and misery as existed prior to their takeover. Consequently, demolishing capitalism and establishing a democratic socialist state required an *ideological* revolution prior to a political one. The populace had to become free of bourgeois hegemony through a slow process of reforming civil society. In this way, Gramsci modified the orthodox Marxist claim that the ideological superstructure of society is entirely dependent on the economic infrastructure. He claimed that the dominant ideology in a society was somewhat independent of economic forces and could be transformed by communists working within the institutions of civil society. Gramsci gave communist parties the new roles of teaching the population about the injustices and failings of capitalist society and of modifying the orientations of old institutions. For example, communists could be active in municipal politics, blocking those proposals for economic developments that threatened citizen interests. Communists could also attempt to democratize the workplace, get churches to speak on behalf of the poor, and encourage new cultural expressions portraying the evils of capitalism. By engaging in such activities, communists hoped to transform the beliefs and values of the population prior to any political revolution.[21] Gramsci's ideas influenced communist parties throughout Europe, who sought to acquire power by means of popular acceptance and electoral victory rather than by means of revolution. Such ideas gave rise to "Eurocommunism" prior to the end of the Cold War, moving communism closer to democratic socialists than to the revolutionary founders of communism. Since 1990, most Eurocommunist parties have abandoned much of their communist rhetoric and have lost influence.

Fascists and Nazis: Revolutionary Change Toward Certain Conservative Values

Fascism and Nazism were revolutionary ideologies that arose in a context of serious social and political problems during the 1920s and 1930s; fascists and Nazis believed these problems required immediate, wide-ranging, and often violent actions. Both ideologies emphasized revolutionary action over theoretical reflection, incremental policy changes, or preservation of established social customs and institutions. They overthrew both liberal and conservative governments. In order to synchronize society and strengthen the nation, they sought to eradicate those democratic, socialist, and communist elements that they believed divided and weakened society.

Nazism was more revolutionary than fascism in its intention to transform citizens completely. Through eugenics and the elimination of those of "inferior" racial qualities, a new super-human species would emerge, the men and women of the Aryan race.

Despite these revolutionary aspects, fascists and Nazis are often placed to the right of traditional conservatism on a left–right ideological scale. Such a description implies that the left–right continuum must encompass more than the degree of change sought, for traditional conservatives are far more committed to the status quo than fascists and Nazis, who rival the far left in their enthusiasm for change. What makes fascism and Nazism far right ideologies is the kind of change they sought. They stressed strengthening the collective by severely reducing individual rights and freedoms. They stressed the advantages of a hierarchical society and resisted egalitarian distributions of power and privileges. Because of such features, some conservative political parties and politicians were somewhat sympathetic to fascists and Nazis, even cooperating with them in their rise to power. The conservatives in Weimar Germany were instrumental in shunting aside the liberal-democrats and helping the Nazis come to power. Similarly, conservative elements in Italy saw in Mussolini a counterweight to the threats from Bolsheviks and socialists, and they accepted the King's appointment of Mussolini as Prime Minister in 1922. When the fascists and Nazis came to power, however, conservatives soon realized that they had encouraged forces that sought greater changes than they could abide.

Many countries today have within them neo-fascists and neo-Nazis who engage in disruptive and violent street actions and who have organized into political parties that appeal to a small but troubling number of voters. While their ability to seize power seems unlikely in the near future, they have found various ways, including spreading their message on the Internet, to be a presence whose activities are vigilantly monitored by their many opponents within pluralist societies.

Contemporary Liberals: Achieving Fundamental Change Incrementally

Contemporary liberals believe that change is often needed to alleviate economic problems, social injustices, and governmental inadequacies. While classical liberals emphasized the role of an "invisible hand" within economic markets for transforming the self-interested actions of individuals into social progress, contemporary liberals believe that progress can best be achieved collectively through democratic processes. To a much greater degree than classical liberals, they think that the future must be socially constructed. They believe that political institutions provide forums for addressing existing problems and deliberating on future goals and that the power of the state must be applied to bring about beneficial changes.[22]

At least for those contemporary liberals living within Western democratic societies, change need not be revolutionary. The basic economic, political, and social institutions of these societies should be maintained. Small, family-owned and operated businesses may have often turned into large corporations, night-watchman states may have become strong states, and social structures may have become more heterogeneous and complex, but these aspects of modernization have largely been beneficial. While problems arise within these arrangements and need correction, the basic structures are sound.

If contemporary liberals have any desire for revolutionary change, they seek the transformation of illiberal societies. Certainly liberals applauded the revolutionary developments in Eastern Europe when communism and authoritarianism were replaced by market economies and democratic governments, however imperfect these replacements may be. And liberals would like to see the emergence of liberal democracies in such places as Iraq, North Korea, and China. Nevertheless, they are cautious in their support of revolutionary change even in illiberal societies. They realize that liberal institutions cannot be imposed on underdeveloped nations without disrupting their unique cultures. Liberals recognize that different people and thus different societies have their own goals and ways of life that may not include the materialism and individualism that are so pervasive in liberal societies.

Contemporary liberals occasionally pursue progress through *transformative reforms*, which greatly alter social life while preserving fundamental institutions. For example, Alexander II ordered the emancipation of the serfs in Czarist Russia and Abraham Lincoln freed American slaves even though such reforms were intended to maintain rather than change basic political institutions.[23] Perhaps leading examples of such transforming reforms in liberal societies during the twentieth century were the New Deal and the Great Society in the US. Seeking to preserve capitalism and employing existing governmental institutions, the New Deal brought about greater equality in the bargaining power between business and labor, and a greater role of the federal government in providing security against economic deprivation. While leaving intact basic economic and political institutions, the Great Society sought far-reaching changes in race and class relations through civil rights legislation and poverty programs.[24] Despite conservative claims about the failure of such major reforms, liberals insist that these programs have resulted in significant progress. For example, John Schwarz points out that the policies of the Great Society significantly reduced poverty, curbed flagrant malnutrition, relieved overcrowded and substandard housing, improved educational opportunities for impoverished children, gave useful skills to thousands of otherwise unemployable persons, reversed pollution trends, and accomplished all these gains without significantly increasing the taxes on American citizens as a percentage of their steadily expanding incomes.[25]

Despite the importance of such major reforms, contemporary liberals are perhaps more committed to achieving incremental changes, as they understand that progress in most areas occurs by making many small adjustments over time. Even the massive changes in international politics at the end of the Cold War did not prompt most liberal politicians to call for an immediate drastic transfer of funds from defense to domestic programs. Instead they pursued incremental reductions in military expenditures throughout the Clinton presidency. Liberals often settle for smaller changes for several reasons. First, *incrementalism* avoids intolerable dislocations; for example, a slow build-down of the armed forces avoids flooding society with unemployed soldiers and producing massive shocks to local economies that are dependent on military expenditures. Second, incrementalism is more acceptable politically than massive reform; conflicting interests can more easily be accommodated by making changes slowly. Third, incrementalism allows for remedial actions; unexpected problems may occur as reforms are implemented, but incrementalism allows for adjustments and even reversals to deal with such difficulties.[26] Because military spending had been only incrementally reduced during the 1990s, the new dangers of terrorism exposed by the attacks of 9/11/01 could be immediately addressed, and increases in military spending could replace previous policies of disinvestment in the military without causing huge social dislocations.

Liberals have thus sought to achieve progress through both transforming and incremental reforms rather than through revolutionary politics. Nevertheless, it can be argued that the effects of liberal reforms over an extended period can indeed be revolutionary. According to Theodore Lowi, the First American Republic, based largely on the principles of classical liberalism, began to erode during the New Deal, and has been replaced by a Second American Republic, based largely on the principles of contemporary liberalism.[27] The small state has given way to the strong state. Free enterprise has yielded to a regulated and mixed economy. Market justice has been complemented with social justice, at least in some areas. The separation of powers has become dominated by executive-centered government. The primacy of state governments has yielded to the dominance of national institutions. Power has become more broadly dispersed among many private and public organizations that control particular policy domains. Citizen rights have expanded enormously. Liberals laud these changes, because they enable governments to extend the positive liberty of citizens, solve social, environmental, and economic problems, and thus bring about progress.

During the Reagan Presidency of the 1980s and the Bush presidency at the beginning of the twenty-first century, conservatives sought to diminish or dismantle the changes that contemporary liberals had achieved. When out of office, liberals have found themselves on the defensive, fighting to retain the programs they had earlier implemented. To avoid being regarded as advocates of the status quo, they have proposed new initiatives in such areas as public health and environmental protection, but these initiatives have not involved any fundamental changes in liberal ideology. Yet, liberalism is a perspective that always seeks its own reform, and thus liberals are currently engaged in efforts to generate a new, revitalized liberalism for the twenty-first century.[28]

Contemporary Conservatives: Pursuing Reforms – of "Failed" Liberal Programs

At least in principle, contemporary conservatives are suspicious of fundamental changes. They draw on traditional conservative ideas about the dangers and unanticipated consequences of social engineering in complex societies. However, contemporary conservatives view change differently from traditional conservatives in several inter-related ways. Most generally, traditional conservatives were prominent in an era when they sought to protect societies from changes sought by liberals and radicals, but contemporary conservatives live in an era where their societies have been transformed by liberal and socialist regimes, and thus they want to change the policies that have moved their societies away from conservative values.

While traditional conservatives feared that free markets would undermine their values, contemporary conservatives have adopted values – such as individualism and social mobility – that are furthered by free market economies. Because many contemporary conservatives celebrate the dynamic and creative features of capitalism, they have embraced policy changes that free the marketplace from extensive governmental regulations.

While traditional conservatives were skeptical of the capacity of government to make extensive economic changes without disrupting society, contemporary conservatives are confident they can undo previous reforms that interfered with market relations and produce an effective economy without causing unanticipated and dire consequences. In the 1980s, in both Great Britain and the US, contemporary conservatives came to power and took the opportunity to reverse established socialist and liberal reforms. In Britain, conservatives re-privatized industries (such as British Petroleum) and privatized much public housing, despite the length of time these socialist programs had been in existence. In the US, they deregulated many industries that had operated within regulatory structures for 50–90 years.

Compared to traditional conservatives, contemporary conservatives have been willing to push reforms that are wide in scope and that may produce a broad range of unanticipated consequences. For example, during the 1970s, Ronald Reagan called for an end to social security as an unnecessary government infringement on citizens' rights to choose their own retirement programs. During his first term, George W. Bush sought personalized accounts within social security, though he backed away from this proposal when many people, including some conservatives, opposed it as a radical change that would subject many senior citizens to significant risks. Conservatives have also been generally supportive of adopting voucher systems for public education. Attempts to provide education on a more market-like basis would change the education system and the larger community dramatically. But because conservatives have not succeeded in creating widespread school-choice programs, the unanticipated consequences of such changes remain largely unknown, although one possibility might be that diminishing the roles of local schools would erode the sense of community that exists within neighborhoods.

George W. Bush's willingness to undo long-standing liberal programs has led some analysts to declare that he is a "radical conservative." For example, John Rauch has found in the Bush administration a commitment to redefining conservatism as change-oriented and to transforming the Republican Party into a vehicle for fundamental changes.[29] From this perspective, contemporary conservatives seek vast alterations in the society that has developed under welfare state liberalism. They want to propose reform after reform and end programs that benefit special interests – such as affirmative action policies that favor minorities, collective bargaining arrangements that support organized labor, welfare policies that coddle irresponsible behavior by the poor, and so forth. By pursuing these changes, conservatives hope to make clear that it is liberals who protect an unsatisfactory status quo.

Contemporary conservatives, then, are significantly more comfortable with change than traditional conservatives. However, they do resist certain changes, especially the egalitarian reforms sought by liberal and socialist social engineers. They are particularly resistant to liberal reforms that demand changes in behavior before citizens have been persuaded that such changes are necessary. Many reforms sought by George W. Bush were unnerving to the many conservatives who are concerned about the dislocations that these changes might provoke. While generally approving the dynamic changes produced by capitalism, contemporary conservatives think government should rarely instigate extensive change – unless it is designed to undo the damage of earlier liberal reformers.

The Radical Right: Seeking Major Changes, even if they Enhance Inequalities

Most voices on the radical right are even more eager than contemporary conservatives to turn back the many changes that occurred under liberal and socialist governments during the twentieth century. Social conservatives and traditional communitarians emphasize a return to traditional values that they believe have been de-emphasized for decades, if not centuries. The religious right questions the scientific progress that is cherished by liberals. National protectionists seek to isolate their economies from the forces of globalization. However, such reactionary views are not shared by libertarians and globalists, who wish to unleash more fully individual freedom, especially in the economic realm, to achieve more rapid advances in the material quality of life than occur in the regulated economies of pluralist societies. After considering the more reactionary voices, this section focuses on globalist views of change.

Reactionaries want extensive changes in politics, but they prefer to look backward rather than forward in history for guidance. Social, cultural, and religious conservatives view the multiculturalism, scientism, and secularism of today's pluralist societies as misguided. Individuals and entire communities have become uprooted from traditional values and structures that provide meaning and direction to life. Humans can best mature, acquiring and exhibiting important virtues, if they aim toward the good life as embodied in the traditional norms and religious beliefs that have withstood the test of time. Such voices on the radical right think they are hardly reactionary, as changes that root people in traditional and religious ways of life are both noble and within our grasp; such changes would reverse the trend that sets us adrift to pursue utopian goals in uncharted waters.

Such voices within the radical right seek changes through pluralist politics. They have mobilized voters through activism at the grassroots levels and through talk-radio, television, and the Internet. Usually, these efforts are aimed at supporting candidates committed to their positions on social issues and toward passage of referenda addressing such issues directly. To rally support, they appeal to people's fears. Cultural conservatives stress that extensive immigration and multiculturalism will weaken social bonds and national strength in international politics. Social conservatives stress that feminism and gay rights will undermine the traditional family. Traditional communitarians stress that an overemphasis on individual rights will prompt people to forget their necessary obligations to the community. The religious right stresses that governmental neutrality on religious and moral questions will lead to a godless culture where sin and vice continue to escalate. National protectionists stress that globalization will lead to economic decline and misery, as industries relocate in other countries where labor costs can be minimized.

In most pluralist societies, these radical right forces have been unable to capture enough votes to govern, but they have attained sufficient clout to be included as important forces within governing parties (such as within the Republican Party in the US) and as partners in multiparty coalitions (in other countries). Because their goals are indeed more radical than those of others in the parties and coalitions with which they align, they often become disillusioned with ordinary pluralist politics and their erstwhile allies. Leaders on the religious right, for example, sometimes threaten to withdraw from electoral politics and to retreat to organizations in civil society where they can focus on preaching cultural restoration. They believe that removing themselves from pluralist politics can allow them to remain steadfast in their positions and avoid compromises that often deflect their more moderate conservative allies from the purity of radical aims.

The term "reactionary" does not well describe the orientations of neoconservatives, libertarians, and globalists. Neoconservatives, for example, want extensive change in the international system, using military means if necessary to create democracies that will be more secure allies in the future.

Libertarians are among the strongest advocates of increasing the social liberties of gays, women, and those who espouse counter-cultural lifestyles. Because liberal positions on social issues distance them from parties on the right, and because their strong advocacy of property rights distance them from parties on the left, libertarians have sometimes formed their own political parties. Thus far, they have been unable to acquire sufficient voting strength to be much included in the governance of pluralist societies, and thus they focus on getting the public to recognize the unnecessary oppressions of traditional moral beliefs and strong governments.

Globalism can be seen as both a status quo and a revolutionary outlook. On the one hand, globalism is the governing public philosophy of much of the world, and thus a defense of its principles is a conservative enterprise that upholds the present distribution of power and material resources. Globalism is the "Washington Consensus" upheld by most leaders of Western nations, many rulers of developing countries, and the heads of international organizations. These leaders see the world as increasingly structured and governed according to the principles of democratic capitalism. To the extent that they see these principles embedded in the policies of political communities throughout the world, they seek to maintain the status quo. To the extent that they see particular departures from these principles, they seek reforms that will move political communities closer to these ideals.

On the other hand, the ideas of globalism as pursued by Margaret Thatcher, Ronald Reagan, Mikhail Gorbachev, and Deng Xiaoping led to the breakdown of the old political order. During the Cold War era, globalism could be seen as a revolutionary outlook. This does not mean that its ideas were especially new, as most had been prominent in classical liberal and libertarian thought. Nor does this mean that these "revolutionaries" had to resort to violence to achieve change. However, such globalists were revolutionary in the sense that they sought extensive changes that transformed formerly communist countries into more pluralist ones and that brought extensive changes to how developed Western nations were governed. Because the main ideas of globalism were "old wine in new bottles," globalism could be seen as incorporating the tried and true and thus were attractive to more conservative actors within political systems, leading to the seeming paradox that globalism produced revolutionary conservatives.

What is most revolutionary about globalism is not its politics but the social and economic transformations that it spurs. As new technologies such as the Internet have emerged, as trade barriers have been reduced, and as people and ideas breech the old walls and borders that contain them, we have entered a world of breathtaking innovation and change in our daily lives. Globalists admit that some of these changes are destabilizing – as people lose jobs in declining industries and as entire communities grow or collapse at a speed that was previously unimaginable. The tremendous competition within global capitalism and the great mobility of people, capital, and goods in globalized society has led to a world that Thomas Friedman aptly characterizes as "Darwinism on steroids."[30] For globalists, this is not a frightening metaphor because change under globalism can be expected to be not only rapid but also highly beneficial. Globalization brings about changes that dramatically improve the lives of most people. It is producing more economic prosperity, more access to life-enhancing and life-prolonging innovations, and more social, economic, and political freedom. While we formerly were confined to the parochial worlds that we inhabited, we increasingly have the world at our command, whether through global telecommunications in the comfort of our homes, or by our easy access to people, ideas, and goods from other cultures in our local communities, or by our capacity to move easily beyond our own towns and nations and explore the possibilities that await us throughout the globe. Such experiences will stretch individual humans, prompting them to evolve into far more complex and enlightened beings than previously, and this will lead to higher stages of evolution for the human species, at least according to globalists.

The Extreme Right: Returning to a Past of Greater Moral Certainty

The extreme right can be characterized as more deeply reactionary than the radical right. They are greatly discontented with the present and fearful that the future will result in the continued decline of society. In order to reverse existing trends, extensive or radical change is required, and such change normally involves reverting back to the practices of some prior golden age. For white nationalists this golden age existed when America was founded, when white men controlled the nation's destiny. Christian fundamentalists look back to a much more religious society in the past when people were more obedient to Christian morality. And Islamic fundamentalists recall a pre-modern era when Islam was a strong and vital force in the world. In general, the extreme right wishes to re-establish a bygone era of national (or civilizational) superiority, cultural uniformity, and moral certainty.

The extreme right has no uniform theory of how to achieve its goals. Some embrace violent means. The notion of RAHOWA (racial holy war) is much discussed among white nationalists, who draw inspiration for such a violent conflagration between whites and nonwhites from the 1978 novel by William Pierce, *The Turner Diaries*. The Islamic notion of *jihad* is sometimes given a "holy war" interpretation, as Muslims have long believed that Allah commanded His followers to struggle militarily against their oppressors. Jihad conveys the general idea that Muslims should strive, struggle, and endeavor in all aspects of their life to be faithful to the commands of Allah. Islam established itself when Mohammad and his followers returned from exile in Medina to engage the pagan and idolatrous rulers of Mecca in holy war. For many Muslims, the situation is similar today, as infidels occupy and dominate their holy lands. Islamic fundamentalists regard themselves as Allah's final attempt to establish righteousness on earth, and thus He legitimizes the use of violence in defense of the righteous community of Islam. While the doctrine of jihad is much debated and open to many interpretations and nuances, there is little question that many Islamic fundamentalists draw upon the concept to justify the use of violence to cleanse Muslim communities of the secular and impious forces of globalization and Western domination.[31] They also see in terrorism and nuclear weapons the tools that can change the current distribution of military and political power between the globalized West and the oppressed.

Some on the extreme right foresee a different process of change, one involving the guidance of a great leader or savior. In this vision, a charismatic political leader or a prophet of God will emerge who can rally the community to a moral vision and to the exercise of political power on behalf of that vision. Such a theory can involve a conception of divine intervention on behalf of necessary change.

The Radical Left: Evolutionary Change Toward More Democratic Equality

The radical left wants deeper changes than are sought by contemporary liberals. While liberals want governments to correct specific market failures, the radical left wants democratic processes to exercise greater control over capitalism at the local, national, and global levels. While liberals preach tolerance of individual differences, the radical left wants genuine communal bonds among people with many social differences. While liberals want to redress some of the starkest inequalities among people, the radical left regards as unjust many of the inequalities that remain. While liberals seek more representative and responsive democratic institutions and processes for governments, the radical left wants democratic values and processes to be much more deeply sown into the fabric of life.

The various voices within the radical left focus on different fundamental changes. Egalitarian liberals question the legitimacy of unequal distributions of social goods within pluralist societies, while cosmopolitans question the morality of unequal distributions of resources among developed, developing, and underdeveloped societies. Radical feminists and leaders of racial and ethnic minorities stress the oppression of women and people of color and call for more equal conditions between men and women in the home and between whites and nonwhites in civil society. Greens and progressive opponents of urban development call for more extensive controls on capitalism, corporate interests, and "the growth machine," in their efforts to promote a healthier environment and a variety of social values (such as the reduction of urban sprawl, less congestion, and smaller, "human-scale" living conditions).

During the twentieth century, democratic socialists pursued some of these concerns, but it remains to be seen if the many changes sought by the radical left can still be incorporated into a single coherent ideology or organized within a single political party. Perhaps antipathy toward the word "socialism" precludes rallying around that label in the US, but the orientations of democratic socialists toward change can be instructive to the various voices on the radical left if they wish to unite into a cohesive progressive force to the left of contemporary liberalism.

A century ago, Eduard Bernstein provided several reasons for the socialist preference for *evolutionary change* over the revolutionary change sought by orthodox Marxists and communists. First, Bernstein recognized that, at the beginning of the twentieth century, the objective conditions that Marx thought were necessary for a revolution were nowhere in sight. Such conditions did not arise throughout the century and remain absent today. Rather than producing massive unemployment, capitalism has created more jobs through massive economic expansion. Rather than impoverishing the working class, capitalism has produced significant increases in real wages. Rather than engaging in ruthless competition leading to the failure of many enterprises, capitalists have often pursued the advantages of mergers and other forms of cooperation. Perhaps most importantly, the ownership of capital has become more diffused rather than more concentrated, as more and more citizens have become stockholders in corporations, especially through retirement programs. The radical left recognizes that, instead of collapsing, capitalism has developed in ways that have averted the crisis predicted by Marx.

Second, Bernstein noted that the subjective conditions for a communist revolution were likewise fading more than a century ago. He argued that the working class was not becoming larger and more unified. It was not developing a class-consciousness of its exploitation and alienation under capitalism and a commitment to revolutionary change. The radical left today agrees that the class structure of capitalism has become complex, diminishing revolutionary consciousness. Rather than being composed primarily of a small exploiting class of property-owning capitalists and a large exploited class of property-less proletariat, several intermediate classes have evolved (e.g., the people who manage but do not own economic enterprises; white-collared salaried professionals like engineers, teachers, and civil servants; a "labor aristocracy" of highly skilled blue-collar workers who command high wages in the labor market). Members of such classes do not identify with the conditions and the revolutionary aims of the proletariat. However, such classes can support programs of the radical left that merely hope to tame the excesses of capitalism and promote progressive values.

Third, Bernstein argued that by the beginning of the twentieth century some Western industrial societies had become democratized in ways that facilitated the acquisition of power by socialist parties and their use of state authority to regulate capitalism and to distribute goods more fairly. The radical left point to continuing democratization throughout the world and to the successful implementation of many socialist policies to show that progress toward democracy can result in the evolution of the economy and society toward socialism.[32]

The radical left has long questioned whether revolutions produce enduring progressive change.[33] The French Revolution suggested to early socialists that revolutions, initiated in pursuit of noble ideals, become oppressive as revolutionary leaders turn to coercion and violence to solidify their hold on power and to pursue their programs against resistant populations. The Stalinist era following the Russian Revolution gave subsequent socialists additional evidence of the failures of revolutionaries to achieve their expressed goals.

For socialists, reform can be much more enduring than revolutionary change. Sounding a bit like a traditional conservative, Sidney Webb (1859–1947) argued that enduring change should be organic; it could not be imposed upon a society, but must result from internal processes within society. Organic change had to be:

(1) Democratic, and thus acceptable to a majority of the people and prepared for in the minds of all; (2) gradual, and thus causing no dislocation, however rapid may be the rate of progress; (3) not regarded as immoral by the mass of people, and thus not subjectively demoralizing to them; and in this country, at any rate; (4) constitutional and peaceful.[34]

Bernard Crick, a leading British political theorist during the second half of the twentieth century, distinguished three time periods in the process of achieving evolutionary, but ultimately radical, change. In the short run, which is the life of an existing administration or legislature, the radical left must address immediate and particular abuses in the capitalist system and provide specific material benefits for citizens in order to build political support for future social movements. Looking to the middle term (20–25 years from now), radicals must change the values of the next generation by demonstrating the deficiencies of existing institutions (such as privatized medical care) and the effectiveness and fairness of more democratic practices (such as worker participation in corporate decision-making). The long run, which is in the faraway future, concerns the ideal society. The radical left rejects claims that they are on a quest for a utopian final resting point. They know that history is but a "long march," employing democratic means toward, but probably never achieving, socialist ideals. Still, it is useful for the radical left to provide visions of a future ideal society – not in a dogmatic manner but rather in a speculative manner – so that discussions of the good society are not limited to prevailing values.[35] Such idealizations serve as reminders that deficiencies remain even in those societies that have most embraced democratic socialism. The limitations of such societies mean that they are only transitional stages in the slow and steady movement toward greater attainment of egalitarian, communal, and democratic values.[36]

Finally, we should note that the radical left – unlike Marxists – do not believe in the inevitability of realizing such a society or even progressing toward it. All that is inevitable is that the future will bring radical change. Capitalism, technology, and science – "our microbiology, phototonics, and superconductors" – are creating "epochal transformations of the very conditions of human life."[37] Such transformations could be regressive – promoting isolated individualism, reducing real freedom, increasing inequality, and empowering a few elites. Or such transformations could lead to the greater realization of socialist values. The task of the radical left is to clarify its principles in such a way as to inspire people to take many small ~~~~~~ ~~ the road toward a more socialist society.

The Extreme Left: Wholesale and Ongoing Change – Without Revolutions

The extreme left is committed to more extensive and fundamental changes than those sought by the radical left. Even the most democratic societies are seen as having deficiencies that preclude their being able to bring about necessary changes through normal pluralist politics. Despite this insistence on change, it is hard to characterize the extreme left as revolutionary – at least in the traditional sense of seeking the violent destruction of existing pluralist societies and the institutions that exist within them. The extreme left is better characterized as consisting of rebels, people committed to resisting current forces of globalization and its globalist ideology. For the most part, their resistance takes place through the sort of strategies that are familiar and acceptable to pluralist politics. For example, their organizing of local resistance against abuses that arise from neoliberal policies, their efforts to generate an anti-globalization movement, and their promoting vast changes in cultural values are all strategies that are common within pluralist politics.

The extreme left has also employed highly disruptive tactics such as the demonstrations and obstructions that were employed during the 1999 WTO ministerial meeting and the subsequent "Battle of Seattle." If the purposes of such militant tactics are to gain access to closed decision-making processes and to publicize grievances to an unaware public, it is difficult to conclude that they are unacceptable to pluralists, who have come to understand that disruption is one of the most effective resources available to the oppressed.

Three characteristics seem most clearly to define the thinking of the extreme left: a deeper cynicism about pluralist politics than is evident among the radical left; an emphasis on confronting those with power rather than participating within a more democratic pluralist politics; and an insistence on the development of a new ethic to replace the individualism and materialism that prevails in pluralist societies.

Utter disgust with pluralist societies in general and America in particular is evident in the writings and speeches of many voices on the extreme left. Richard Rorty summarizes the recent literature and philosophy of the far left as envisioning

> a history of European and American peoples since the Enlightenment [as] pervaded by hypocrisy and self-deception. Readers of Foucault often come away believing that no shackles have been broken in the past two hundred years; the harsh old chains have merely been replaced with slightly more comfortable ones. . . . Such people find pride in American citizenship impossible, and vigorous participation in electoral politics pointless. They associate American patriotism with an endorsement of atrocities: the importation of African slaves, the slaughter of Native Americans, the rape of ancient forests, and the Vietnam War.[38]

Rorty's characterizations seem accurate, as Foucault does claim that "entire populations are mobilized for the purpose of wholesale slaughter in the name of life necessary: massacres have become vital."[39] Noam Chomsky is perhaps the most prominent spokesman of the extreme left, as he typically claims

> None of these guys [Harry Truman, Winston Churchill and other unnamed Western leaders] had anything against Stalin's crimes. What's more, they had nothing against Hitler's crimes – all this talk about Western leaders principled opposition to atrocities is just a complete fabrication, totally undermined by a look at the documentary record. Its just that if you've been properly educated, you can't understand facts like these: even if the information is right in front of your eyes, you can't comprehend it.[40]

Such deep cynicism of the extreme left can verge on nihilism. For example, one commentator on the recent writings of Noam Chomsky characterizes him as an anarchist who hates all national governments – especially those of the United States and Israel – and whose writings have a nihilistic tone:

> To read Chomsky's recent political writing at any length is to feel almost physically damaged. The effect is difficult to convey in a quotation because it is cumulative. The writing is a catalogue of crimes committed by America, terrible crimes, and many of them, but it is not they that produce the sensation of blows: it is Chomsky's rage as he describes them. His sentences slice and gash, envenomed by a vicious sarcasm. . . . The sentences are accusations of guilt, but not from a position of innocence or hope for something better. Chomsky's sarcasm is a scowl of a fallen world, the sneer of Hell's veteran to its appalled naifs.[41]

Whether the writings of Chomsky or other writers on the extreme left produce in the reader a sense of nihilism is, of course, for each reader to determine. But if the effect is to convey that pluralist institutions are so riddled with injustices and problems that they are beyond repair, then the extreme left has achieved a political stance that amounts to a deep pessimism about achieving beneficial change through pluralist politics.

While not calling for revolution, the extreme left prefers rebellious protest to participation within pluralist politics. Hardt and Negri clearly exemplify the anarchistic orientation of the extreme left by stressing the importance of "refusal" and "exodus." They stress that "in politics, as in economics, one weapon that is constantly at the disposal of the ruled . . . is the threat to refuse their position of servitude and subtract themselves from the relationship" between rulers and the ruled. Rebellion, rather than revolution, can succeed because "without the active participation of the subordinated, sovereignty crumbles," and rebels then become "capable of forming society on their own."[42]

In response to the vast shortcomings and injustices of pluralist society, those on the extreme left have pursued a number of alternatives to revolution. First, they have extensively described and criticized the oppressions of pluralist societies. Second, they have urged acts of defiance – ranging from casting protest ballots to disrupting ordinary life in pluralist societies – perceiving that such actions can prompt rulers to make (minor) concessions. Third, they envision raising the consciousness – or overcoming the false consciousness that leads to acceptance or apathy of the existing system – so that people will "drop out" of conventional pluralist society. For the extreme left, rebelling against or exiting from the system can allow conscious individuals to achieve a modicum of self-respect and fulfillment as being a warrior against convention. As rebels begin to network with each other and create new social relationships, the possibility of a very different form of politics emerges – or so the extreme left hopes.

The extreme left believes that those who drop out of pluralist politics do so out of disgust with its lack of morality – its materialism, its emphasis on individual assertiveness in a competitive world, its tolerance of oppression, and so forth – and out of conviction for the need to pursue a higher morality. The radical and extreme right also call for a higher morality, but their morality is one of following traditional religious teachings and cultural values. The extreme left emphasizes socialist and ecological values that they believe have been undermined and ignored by the regressive moralities of other ideologies.

For Hardt and Negri, this new morality is one of love as a political concept:

> The modern concept of love is almost exclusively limited to the bourgeois couple and the claustrophobic confines of the nuclear family. Love has become a strictly private affair. We need a more generous and more unrestrained conception of love. . . . Love serves as a basis for our political projects in common and the construction of a new society. Without this love, we are nothing.[43]

While a new morality emphasizing love might be laudable and inspiring, another morality emphasized by the deep green strand of the extreme left may be especially urgent. This morality calls for humans – especially those in pluralist societies with advanced industrial economies – to reduce their consumption of material goods. Additionally, this morality would call on humans to practice a "land ethic" in which individuals cease exploiting the earth's resources and instead regard themselves as part of a natural ecological system. Naturalist Aldo Leopold coined the land ethic concept almost 60 years ago, imploring us to radically alter our dominant ethic:

> All ethics so far evolved rests upon a single premise: that the individual is a member of a community of interdependent parts. His instincts prompt him to compete for his place in the community, but his ethics prompt him also to co-operate (perhaps in order that there may be a place to compete for). The land ethic simply enlarges the boundaries of the community to include soils, waters, plants, and animals, or collectively: the land.[44]

Deep greens thus call for a radical change in our personal and social habits, and even that part of human nature dealing with our fundamental motivations. Rather than seeing the good life as satisfying our material wants, humans must see it as living in harmony with nature. Deep greens argue that such a change in morality will have at least two major types of benefits.[45] Widespread acceptance of the land ethic may be required if we are to have a sustainable ecological system. The earth has limited carrying capacity (it cannot sustain unlimited population growth), productive capacity (many of its resources will be exhausted at current rates of exploitation), and absorbent capacity (it cannot renew all the pollutants that are the byproducts of human production and consumption). Profound changes in the earth's climate, including global warming, are a major threat to a sustainable society, and such threats may not be manageable by various technological fixes but only by radically reduced human exploitation of the earth's ecological system. The second benefit of adopting a land ethic is that human life will better be directed at achieving real human needs rather than the fabricated wants that we have acquired from advertisers and other capitalist powers. From this perspective, our having, consuming, and maintaining material goods that ultimately fail to satisfy our more authentic human needs have excessively cluttered life in pluralist societies. In short, adopting the land ethic can enhance the spiritual dimension of life. Real joy is be found, according to deep greens, by living in harmony with others and nature.

The extreme left thus maintains that their ideas are not so much "extreme" as they are necessary if we are to survive the twenty-first century. Deep greens argue that modernity witnessed two major paradigm shifts. The liberal revolution at the beginning of modernity unleashed individual freedom, which was accompanied by capitalism and materialism. The socialist paradigm that emerged toward the end of the modern period sought to control the plundering and the inequalities of capitalism, but retained a fundamentally homocentric set of principles. The ecological paradigm shift seeks to correct the deficiencies of liberalism and socialism. While admitting that it is difficult "to stand in one paradigm and see into another," William Ophuls suggests that postmodernity requires that we replace the liberal moral code of noninterference and the socialist egalitarian moral code with "a morality that is fundamentally ecological in spirit."[46]

Ophuls goes on to list four moral tenets that are requisite to the politics of the future. First, we must abandon our tendency to be parasitic "despoilers of the biosphere" and become agents that give as much as we take from nature. Second, rather than seeing civilized life as involving the multiplication of wants, humans must deliberately and voluntarily renounce much of what we call progress. Third, rather than focusing on natural rights, we must stress obedience to "a new theory of natural law," that imposes limitations on our appetites and that respects the inescapable interdependence of humans and all living things. Fourth, we must regain the understanding of governance as something quite different from pandering to human passions and maximizing human wants. Governance must again be understood as "controlling, guiding, directing, and restraining individuals who would otherwise behave selfishly and destructively, so that they respect the interests and needs of the larger human and natural community of which they are a part." While adoption of such a moral system "does not imply a return to the Stone Age," it "will clearly entail radical changes in every aspect of our way of life."[47]

Conclusions

Pluralists recognize that economic, social, and political changes are often beneficial, and that democratic processes must be in place to bring about desirable change through peaceful means.[48] Ideas about how much change and what kind of change is needed (on issues regarding community, structure, rulers, citizens, authority, and justice) are, of course, the ordinary stuff of pluralist politics. The many disagreements over these matters, as described in this text, ensure there will be no "end of history," but perennial ideological battles within pluralist societies.

Central to change within pluralist politics are the related ideas of opposition, dissent, and protest. People have the right to oppose existing authorities and question the effectiveness and justice of their policies. People have the right to engage in peaceful protest like signing petitions and voicing their concerns at public hearings to publicize social and economic conditions that they think should be changed.[49] While pluralists accept the central role of protest as a vehicle for change, they also understand that protesters can go too far when disruption turns coercive and violent.[50]

Because pluralism is a modern public philosophy and seeks progress, the reactionary aspects of the radical and extreme right might seem dangerous to pluralism. But to believe that "the past was better than the present and should be recaptured" is not itself incompatible with pluralism. Pluralists admit that yesterday's reforms might have dysfunctional consequences for society; if so, such reforms should indeed be abandoned. Pluralists recognize that members of their society can have many visions of the good society, and some of these visions may resemble societies of a bygone era. Pluralism is only threatened in this regard by the means that people employ to pursue their vision. Those on the extreme right become dangerous to pluralism when they believe that tactics involving destruction and violence are necessary to bring about their desired changes. The belief in the necessity of violence by advocates of extreme change forgets that democracy is a peaceful means of resolving conflicts – that pluralist politics involves persuasion, voting, and other non-forceful means to bring about change.

Historically, pluralist societies have been threatened and undermined by utopianism and nihilism. Utopian thought focuses not just on an improved future but on a perfect one, and holds to the possibility that all social ills and human shortcomings can be redeemed. Utopians believe that existing institutions and practices that stand in the way of redemption should be dismantled or that the current generation should endure great hardships in order to secure utopia for their children.[51] Utopianism characterized much old left thought, which clung to a vision of an ideal communist society as the final result of political struggles and of sacrifices undergone to hurry the realization of that ideal. The fact that communist regimes justified oppressive politics as necessary means to utopian ends has not been lost on most members of today's far left. Their focus on the deconstruction of existing power structures and relationships rather than on the development of utopian schemes can thus be seen as an effort to reconcile themselves to (contentious) pluralist politics.

Nihilist thought focuses on the present, and finds pluralist institutions like capitalism and representative democracy so oppressive and/or the existing liberal culture so repulsive that any means toward their destruction is justified, regardless of what would replace them in the future. Such ideas go back at least as far as the anarchists of the nineteenth century, but they can still be detected in some of the rejection of contemporary pluralist society by extremists on both the right and left. Pluralism may be able to tolerate individual expressions of cynicism and nihilism. Indeed, pluralism is committed to providing individuals with opportunities to express dissent, no matter how nihilistic these expressions are. Perhaps the ranting of the extreme left and right is functional for pluralist societies, prompting people to look more carefully at their political failings and to pledge themselves to both correct these failings and avoid such failings in the future. But the nihilism of extremists can lead to such despair about pluralist politics that people withdraw their support for pluralism, leading to the possible replacement by far more repressive structures.

In his famous "Letter from Birmingham Jail," Martin Luther King, Jr. expressed "initial disappointment at being categorized as an extremist," but on reflection "gradually gained a measure of satisfaction from that label," and called on his followers to become "extremists for the extension of justice."[52] King's reflections remind us that "extremists" can sometimes express ideas that become necessary for positive political change and in time are incorporated into the mainstream of public philosophy. For the most part, this book has described and criticized extremist ideas as dangerous challenges to a pluralist public philosophy that has evolved and (in response to the ideas of radicals) is continuing to evolve in ways that generally bring about peaceful progress in political life. But one set of extremist ideas – the deep green plea for a new ecological ethic – may be compelling despite being antithetical to pluralism.

If an ecological ethic is to be more than one among many moral choices within a pluralist society, if it is to be an ethic that all must embrace if we are to attain a sustainable society and ecology, then central premises of pluralism must be abandoned. Pluralism insists that citizens must be morally autonomous, that they can choose freely among justice-respecting lifestyles and values. Pluralism insists that the state be neutral among various moral doctrines. From the perspective of pluralism, the ecological ethic is just one of many moral frameworks, and the state must not support a "perfectionist" politics that distributes privileges and penalties on the basis of citizens' conformity to any ethic, including an ecological one. But deep greens may seek a form of governance that would punish those who violate ecological norms and reward those who would respect the needs of the larger human and ecological communities.

Perhaps ecological needs are so urgent and compelling that pluralist autonomy must be abandoned for conformity to a communitarian ecological ethic, and pluralist neutrality must give way to enforcement of ecological morality. Perhaps pluralism as a public philosophy will need to be replaced by a new public philosophy that better fits the needs of a sustainable society. But perhaps pluralism can adopt itself to growing ecological imperatives. Just as pluralism has thus far been able to accommodate a liberal emphasis on individual freedom, a conservative emphasis on community, and a socialist egalitarian ethic, so might an evolving pluralism accommodate human desires for freedom, community, and equality to constraints that are environmentally necessary. The questions of whether pluralist public philosophy must do this and how it can be done are perhaps the most urgent topics for thoughtful political conversations today.[53]

Notes

CHAPTER 1   CONSTRUCTING OUR PUBLIC PHILOSOPHIES

1 See, for example, John Rawls, *A Theory of Justice*, and Michael Sandel, *Democracy's Discontent*. In *Why Deliberative Democracy?* Amy Gutmann and Dennis Thompson summarize a wide range of literature on the importance of deliberation in resolving political issues.

2 Kathleen Knight, "Transformations of the Concept of Ideology."

3 John Thompson, *Studies in the Theory of Ideology*, and Michael Freeden, *Ideology*, pp. 1–11.

4 In *Political Thinking*, Glenn Tinder provides a classical introduction to "the perennial questions."

5 David Easton, *A Systems Analysis of Political Life*, p. 154.

6 Karl Deutsch, "On Political Theory and Political Action," p. 18.

7 Some of these communities – such as the global community – may not exist as organized political states with governing institutions and the capacity to enforce obligations, but they can still be bases of human identity and their attainment as political communities can be important ideals for many people.

8 Valid generalizations relating two phenomena in the observable world provide both explanations and predictions. Consider, for example, the generalization that the spread of democracy is associated with a decline of war. This generalization (potentially) explains the decline of war as due to (factors associated with) the spread of democracy. This generalization (potentially) predicts a lessening of war as democratic values and institutions continue to replace non-democratic regimes throughout the world.

9 Tinder provides a typical expression of this tentativeness through the concept of "humane uncertainty" that is central to his conclusions in *Political Thinking*, pp. 237–50.

10 Most philosophers of science recognize the tentativeness of all ideas, whether they concern the natural or social world. See Thomas Kuhn, *The Structure of Scientific Revolutions*.

11 The attempt to divorce political philosophy and political science and to emphasize empirical theory and methods has been *The Tragedy of Political Science*, according to David Ricci. The centennial issue of the *American Political Science Review* (November 2006) contains a host of articles addressing such issues.

12   In response to a liberal characterization of the distribution of power in American cities provided by such "pluralists" as Robert Dahl (in *Who Governs?*), elite theorists like William Domhoff have argued on behalf of a Marxist hypothesis of domination by capitalists (in such books as *Who Really Rules?*).

13   Raymond Wolfinger, "Reputation and Reality in the Study of Community Power."

14   Domhoff, *Who Really Rules?*

15   David Ricci, "Receiving Ideas in Political Analysis."

16   Post-structuralists like Michel Foucault have emphasized additional conceptions of power. Thomas Wartenberg, *The Forms of Power*, provides an overview of this literature.

17   For a neo-Marxist acknowledgment of these three dimensions of power, see Steven Lukes, *Power: A Radical View*. For a liberal acknowledgment of these three dimensions of power, see Robert Dahl, *Democracy and Its Critics*, pp. 111–14.

18   Willis Hawley, *Nonpartisan Elections*.

19   Paul Peterson, *City Limits*.

20   Interesting recent uses of the dialectical method are found in the various conversations between democrats and their opponents in Dahl, *Democracy and Its Critics*.

21   Ricci, *The Tragedy of Political Science*, pp. 300–1.

22   The idea that there is a difference between the ideal and what is best in particular circumstances derives from *The Politics* of Aristotle (384–322 BCE). Following Aristotle, we might recognize, for example, that certain countries have political cultures that make democratic institutions undesirable for them, even though we are convinced that, generally and ideally, democratic institutions are best. The recognition that different principles may be best for different communities suggests that the members of each community should conduct their own smaller conversations about what principles are best for them.

23   This process is exemplified by Rawls's initial presentation of his *A Theory of Justice*, the enormous response that his views received in thousands of scholarly articles and books, and by his reformulation of his ideas in subsequent works such as *Political Liberalism*. This literature has greatly advanced our understanding of justice, but conversations on this perennial issue continue.

24   The classic renderings of orthodox pluralism include David Truman, *The Governmental Process*, and Dahl, *Who Governs?*

25   Recent discussions of the normative ideas of pluralism include: Michael Walzer, *Spheres of Justice*; Avigail Eisenberg, *Reconstructing Political Pluralism*; John Kekes, *Pluralism in Philosophy*; Richard Flathman, *Pluralism and Liberal Democracy*; William Connolly, *Pluralism*.

26   Overviews of this massive literature are provided by Robert Dahl in *Dilemmas of Pluralist Democracy*; John Manley, "Neopluralism"; and Donald Brand, "Three Generations of Pluralism." My *Critical Pluralism* is one effort to express an evaluative theory of pluralism.

27   Richard Hofstadter, *The American Political Tradition*; Louis Hartz, *The Liberal Tradition in America*.

28   Herbert McClosky and John Zaller, *The American Ethos*.

29   Ronald Inglehart, *Human Values and Social Change*.

30   George Klosko, *Democratic Procedures and the Liberal Consensus*.

31   Rawls, *Political Liberalism*, p. 164.

32   Bernard Crick, *In Defence of Politics*, pp. 111–39.

33   Daniel Bell proclaimed *The End of Ideology* after the demise of fascism and Nazism, while Francis Fukuyama proclaimed *The End of History* during the demise of communism as Eastern European countries broke free of Soviet domination and the Soviet Union crumbled.

34 Consensus does not mean unanimity. Public opinion polls show some people in pluralist societies reject even the most widely accepted ideas of that society. For example, the principle that "everyone should have equal opportunity to get ahead" is opposed by 2 percent of Americans. See McClosky and Zaller, *The American Ethos*, p. 83.

35 The social construction of political knowledge, and thus the possible social reconstruction of political knowledge, is emphasized by both constructivism and pragmatism. Rawls describes political constructivism as a practical procedure for selecting principles to regulate the basic structure of society; it is a social process whereby persons belonging to political communities use their moral capacities and commitments to reasonableness to achieve fair terms of social cooperation. See his *Political Liberalism*, pp. 89–99. Richard Rorty is perhaps the leading political philosopher who emphasizes pragmatic approaches. He challenges the long-standing conception of truth as occurring when humans attain an understanding that mirrors objective reality and claims instead that truth is a matter of agreement achieved in conversations with one's peers. His works in this vein include *Consequences of Pragmatism* and *Truth and Progress*.

36 Rawls, *The Law of Peoples*, p. 62. In *Pluralism in Philosophy*, Kekes argues that pluralist epistemology generally avoids skepticism.

37 Arthur Okun, *Equality and Efficiency*.

38 Utilitarians have claimed that "utility" provides a common standard for choosing among values, but utility has always been an empirically vacuous concept that fails to provide any basis for interpersonal comparisons of how much utility is gained or lost by pursuing various values. Choosing among alternative ethical values and value-systems is also complicated by many "burdens of judgment" such as those presented by William Galston in "Liberal Egalitarian Attitudes Toward Ethical Pluralism," p. 29. For a concrete example of the complexities of moral and political judgment in the evaluation of the best procedures for selecting the American President, see Paul Schumaker and Bruce Oppenheimer, "Electoral College Reform."

39 Ronald Dworkin, *Taking Rights Seriously*, pp. 180–1. In *Equalities*, Douglas Rae provides a broader discussion of the many meanings of this concept.

40 It is often argued that political science has been more successful in attaining knowledge describing and explaining the political world than political philosophy has been at producing knowledge about our political ideals. Perhaps, but much disagreement remains about empirical, as well as normative, theories of politics. The dialectical method cannot produce "truth" about political ideals, but the scientific method has not produced "truth" about political beliefs. Just as the scientific method helps produce better descriptions and explanations of politics, so does the dialectical method help produce better political idealizations, prescriptions, and evaluations.

41 Richard Madsen and Traci Strong, *The Many and the One*, p. 2.

PART I   PARTICIPANTS IN OUR POLITICAL CONVERSATIONS

1 The major work in this tradition is Robert Lane's *Political Ideology*.

2 The seminal treatment of the social bases of ideological perspectives is Karl Mannheim, *Ideology and Utopia*.

3 This assumes the need to limit these participants to more modern, Western perspectives. Of course, pre-modern contributors to the canon of Western civilization originated a number

of important ideas, but many of these have been subsumed by the ideologies covered here, especially traditional conservatism. Perhaps more limiting is the exclusion of non-Western perspectives, except for Islamic fundamentalism. Giving adequate attention to such perspectives would require another book.

4   While the differences between authoritarian and totalitarian systems will be developed below, it is sufficient for now to understand totalitarianism as calling for much more governmental control over individuals and groups in society than does mere authoritarianism. Authoritarianism claims that people should defer to the authority of rulers in matters pertaining largely to public affairs. Totalitarianism claims that people should defer to the authority of rulers in matters that are not only public but have traditionally been regarded as private or pertaining to social life in civil society.

5   Irving Kristol, *Two Cheers for Capitalism*.

CHAPTER 2   VOICES FROM THE MAJOR IDEOLOGIES OF THE NINETEENTH CENTURY

1   The term "ideology" was coined in 1797 by a group of philosophers, the *ideologues*, led by Antoine Louis Claude Destutt de Tracy. The ideologues are discussed in Schumaker et al., *Great Ideas/Grand Schemes*, pp. 12–13.

2   Max Weber, *The Protestant Ethic and the Spirit of Capitalism*.

3   John Locke, *Letter Concerning Toleration*.

4   Thomas Paine, *The Rights of Man*.

5   John Stuart Mill, *On Liberty*.

6   Thomas Hobbes, *Leviathan*, p. 262. Throughout this text, page number references are to those editions of classical works that are indicated in the bibliography. The year in brackets after these citations indicate when they were first published.

7   Mill, *On Liberty*, p. 12.

8   From the marginal notes of John Adam's *Discourses on Divila*, written in 1813 and contained in Russell Kirk, ed., *The Portable Conservative Reader*.

9   See Houston Smith, *Religions of Man*, pp. 151–74.

10   Edmund Burk, *Reflections on the Revolution in France*, in Peter Stanlis, ed., *Edmund Burke: Selected Writings and Speeches*, p. 444.

11   Burke, *Reflections*, pp. 493–9.

12   In the twentieth century, traditional conservatives accepted religious toleration and the separation of church and state, but still applauded the role of churches as social institutions. For a more detailed discussion of the various views on religion held by traditional conservatives, see Robert Nisbet, *Conservatism*, pp. 68–74.

13   See Nisbet, *Conservatism*, pp. 2–11.

14   Michael Oakeshott, "On Being Conservative," in his *Rationalism and Politics*, p. 184.

15   See José Ortega y Gasset's, *The Revolt of the Masses*, an intellectually acclaimed book, arguing that it was the duty of the masses to be guided by a properly constituted elite.

16   Oakeshott, "On Being Conservative," pp. 175–8.

17   Oakeshott, "On Being Conservative," pp. 172–3.

18   The terms "right," "left," and "center" are derived from the seating arrangements in the National Assembly that governed France during its revolutionary period, as conservatives sat to the right, moderates sat in the center, and radicals sat to the left.

19   Emma Goldman, "Anarchism: What it Really Stands For," in *Anarchism and Other Essays*, p. 50. Goldman was the most prominent of many women involved in the anarchist movement. See Margaret Marsh, *Anarchist Women, 1870–1920*.

20   As Robert Booth Fowler points out in "The Anarchist Tradition of Political Thought," most analyses of anarchism have stressed the distinction between individualist and collectivist anarchists, but other distinctions among anarchists have been proposed. For example in his *In Defense of Anarchism*, Robert Paul Wolff distinguishes between his philosophical anarchism (which urges individuals to disobey government authority when its commands conflict with their own moral judgments) and political anarchism (which stresses actions aimed at destroying existing institutions).

21   Pierre Proudhon, *The General Idea of the Revolution in the Nineteenth Century*, p. 129.

22   As suggested by David de Leon, in *The American Anarchist*, radicalism in the US may be more closely linked to the ideas of anarchism than to those of Marxism.

23   David McLellan, *Karl Marx: His Life and Thought*, pp. 407–11.

24   Marxist-Leninists and Revisionist Marxists are considered as separate communist and social democratic ideologies below. Other distinct forms of Marxism, such as neo-Marxism and post-Marxism, remain influential social theories in academia. For example, the critical theory of the Frankfurt School – especially as it is presented in the writings of Max Horkheimer and Jürgen Habermas – has been deeply indebted to Marx, insisting that philosophy must be a practical activity that aims to further human emancipation by enhancing human consciousness of oppressive social and political conditions.

25   See, for example, John Gray, *Liberalisms*.

CHAPTER 3   PROMINENT TOTALITARIAN AND PLURALIST VOICES OF THE TWENTIETH CENTURY

1   Italian fascism is emphasized here because its advocacy of totalitarianism under Mussolini was more explicit than the fascism of other societies. The extent to which communist regimes advocated and practiced totalitarianism is subject to scholarly dispute, but Soviet communism under Stalin and Chinese communism under Mao were clearly highly totalitarian. The totalitarian aspects of these fascist and communist regimes are emphasized here in order to draw attention to those ideas that most clearly differ from pluralist ones.

2   Robert Dahl, *On Democracy*, p. 8. Dahl discusses the difficulties of providing precise counts of the number of democracies over time in the appendix of this book.

3   See <www.freedomhouse.org>.

4   In his *In Defence of Politics* (pp. 130–8), Bernard Crick presents democratic socialists as the third major friend of (pluralist) politics. During the past century, socialists have certainly been prominent in international politics, and their ideas deserve a complete hearing in our conversations. However, democratic socialists are not introduced until the next chapter for three reasons. First, the political principles of socialists have indeed been more radical than those of liberals and conservatives. Second, socialist parties have reduced their radicalism in recent decades, often governing in ways that are little distinguishable from liberalism. Third, other perspectives have taken up the socialist banner of deepening democracy and constraining capitalism, and it is thus useful to consider democratic socialism along with other radical left voices that seek major transformations of pluralism.

5   For an excellent discussion of such developments throughout the world, see Jeffry Frieden, *Global Capitalism*.

6 See Barry Cooper, *The End of History*, pp. 298–327.

7 Technically, the Aryan peoples are Indo-Europeans who originated in southwestern India and Iran. Rather than celebrate such darkly complected peoples, the Nazis asserted the racial superiority of lightly complected Germanic peoples who were of Scandinavian origin. But they called these peoples "Aryans."

8 Mussolini's regime (and the fascist regime in Hungary) treated Jews much better than did the Nazis. See Hannah Arendt, *Eichmann in Jerusalem*, pp. 138–40, 176–80.

9 Cited in James Forman, *Fascism*, p. 34.

10 For Nazis, the First Reich refers to the centralizing tendencies that German kings provided to various Germanic territories between the tenth and thirteenth centuries. The Second Reich was the imperial German Empire that was shaped by the policies of Otto von Bismarck between 1871 and 1918 and that was dismantled by the Treaty of Versailles.

11 For evidence of a Jewish conspiracy, Nazis frequently cited the *Protocols of the Elders of Zion*, an alleged record of Jewish plans to conquer the world. The *Protocols* were a forgery, fabricated in the late nineteenth century by anti-Semites to provoke hatred of the Jews.

12 Arendt notes, "The Nazis did not think that the Germans were a master race, to whom the world belonged, but that they should be led by a master race, as should all other nations, and that this race was only on the point of being born." In a footnote to this observation she continues: "In a decree of August 9, 1941 . . . Hitler prohibited the further use of the term *German race*, because it would lead to the sacrifice of the racial idea as such in favor of a mere nationality principle." See her *Origins of Totalitarianism*, p. 412.

13 See Adolf Hitler, *Mein Kampf*, p. 393.

14 See Karl Brader, *The German Dictatorship*.

15 James Weinstein, *The Corporate Ideal and the Liberal State*, and Jeffrey Lustig, *Corporate Liberalism*.

16 Theodore Lowi, *The End of Liberalism*.

17 Periodicals that focus on the evolving liberal agenda include *The Nation*, *The American Prospect*, the *Brookings Review*, and the *New Republic*. In 2006, *Democracy: A Journal of Ideas* and *The Democratic Strategist* established websites to discuss similar concerns: <www.democracyjournal.org> and <www.thedemocraticstrategist.org>.

18 Paul Starr, "Liberalism After Socialism."

19 There are several types of environmentalism. Contemporary liberalism is most congenial to "managerial environmentalists" who believe that environmental problems can be resolved by governmental regulations without fundamentally altering capitalism or reducing economic prosperity. More radical environmentalists – such as "greens" – are much more critical of contemporary liberalism and are developing their own ideological perspectives, which we will consider in the next chapter. For a discussion of the distinction between liberal environmentalism and green ideology, see Andrew Dobson, *Green Political Thought*, pp. 2–35.

20 We thus absorb liberal feminism – the feminism that merely asks government to provide laws and programs that allow women to have genuinely equal opportunities with men in social, economic, and political life – into our discussions of contemporary liberalism. More radical and extreme forms of feminism will be introduced in the next chapter.

21 T. H. Green, *Lectures on the Principles of Political Obligation*. In *Four Essays on Liberty* (pp. 118–72), Isaiah Berlin analyzes negative and positive liberty.

22 Daniel Lerner, *The Passing of the Traditional Society*.

23 Mancur Olson, "Rapid Growth as a Destabilizing Force," p. 529.

24   In *How Democratic is the American Constitution?*, Robert Dahl challenges the view that the US Constitution should be viewed as a sacred text.

25   John Dewey, *The Public and Its Problems*.

26   John Dewey, *Liberalism and Social Action*, p. 51.

27   Jonathan Rauch, "The Accidental Radical."

28   A much more extensive list of ideas held by contemporary conservatives is provided by the popular talk-show host, Rush Limbaugh, *The Way Things Ought to Be*, pp. 2–3. Perhaps the first and most revered popular account of contemporary conservatism is Barry Goldwater's *The Conscience of a Conservative*.

29   Conservatives, such as England's Winston Churchill, have also been strong opponents of the totalitarian ideologies of fascism and Nazism. However, because contemporary conservatism has been most fully developed since the heyday of these ideologies, its principles have been largely defined in reaction to its opponents on the political left.

30   These forums now include: the *Public Interest*, *The National Interest*, *The American Enterprise Magazine*, the *American Spectator*, *Commentary*, and *the Weekly Standard*.

31   The label "neoconservatism" has a complex history. Whereas earlier neoconservatives of the 1960s and 1970s focused on the failures of liberal domestic programs, the new "neocons" of the Bush administration came to focus on what they regard as the failures of liberal foreign policy. Today, "neocons" believe liberals have been too unwilling to take proactive steps to disarm security threats and to create democratic regimes more aligned with American interests. In general, neoconservatives can be regarded as a fairly radical strand within contemporary conservatism and are treated as such in chapter 4 and elsewhere in this text.

32   Republic Senator Joseph McCarthy, from Wisconsin, became infamous for his "witch-hunts" in search of communist conspirators in the early 1950s. McCarthyism remains a code name for a tendency among conservatives to see governments being secretly infiltrated by those who would radically change America in a leftward direction.

33   George Gilder, *Wealth and Poverty*, pp. 135–6.

34   James O. Wilson, "The Rediscovery of Character," pp. 3–16.

35   See Allan Bloom, *The Closing of the American Mind*.

36   Wilson, "Rediscovery of Character," p. 16.

37   Conservatives coined the term "politically correct" to denigrate liberal approval of multiculturalism and the agendas and language of militant minorities and feminists. To the extent that liberals have tried to curtail insensitive racial and sexist remarks, conservatives chide liberals for betraying their free speech principles.

38   Milton Friedman's *Capitalism and Freedom* is regarded by conservatives as the most important contemporary celebration of free market capitalism.

39   The Ramsey Colloquium, "Morality and Homosexuality," *Wall Street Journal* (February 24, 1994), p. A20. The authors of this article, which first appeared in *First Things* (March 1994) were sponsored by the Institute for Religion and Public Life.

40   This thesis was most forcefully developed by Milovan Djilas in *The New Class*.

41   Francis Fukuyama, *The End of History*.

42   See Roland Pennock, "Liberalism Under Attack."

43   Michael Tomasky, "Party in Search of a Notion."

44   See the symposium entitled "Is the Common Good Good?" in *The American Prospect* (July/August 2006) containing reactions to Tomasky's arguments by William Galston and others.

CHAPTER 4 RADICAL AND EXTREME VOICES IN CONTEMPORARY POLITICS

1   Peter Saint-André includes more than 200 ideologies in *The Ism Book*, at <www.ismbook.com/ismlist.html>.

2   For example, many theorists employ two dimensions – the extensiveness of governmental control of economic life and the extensiveness of governmental regulation of moral and social matters – to generate a typology of four ideologies: libertarians, who want minimal government intervention is both economic and moral life; liberals, who want minimal government intervention in moral life but extensive control over the economy; conservatives, who want minimal government control over the economy and extensive regulation of morality; and communitarians, who want extensive public control over both economic and moral questions.

3   See, for example, Richard Rorty, *Achieving Our Country*, p. 14, and Noberto Bobbio, *Left & Right: The Significance of a Political Distinction.*

4   This typology, like any typology, may have difficulties classifying specific cases. For example, its founders have presented communitarianism as a perspective that transcends left-right politics (see Amitai Etzioni et al., *The Communitarian Reader*, p. 7). By stressing problems with the foundations of liberalism, communitarianism has appealed to those whose political ideas fall both to the left and to the right of liberalism, posing difficulties in classifying its central tendencies. To solve this problem, analysts often differentiate two branches of communitarianism. For example, in *Looking Backwards*, Derek Phillips distinguishes between "forward-looking" and "backward-looking" communitarians. We also see the need for such distinctions. Below, those on the left are designated as civic communitarians, while those on the right are designated as traditional communitarians.

5   See Andrew Dobson, *Green Political Thought.*

6   See Rosemary Tong, *Feminist Thought.*

7   For a discussion of democratic socialism as a comprehensive ideology, see Paul Schumaker et al., *Great Ideas/Grand Schemes*, ch. 9.

8   Among the leading periodicals that provide forums for radical left thought are *Dissent, The Progressive, The New Left Review, and The Socialist Review.*

9   As with liberalism, there are a variety of socialisms; see Anthony Wright, *Socialisms.* Our concern here is with core ideas and central tendencies.

10   Contemporary post-Marxists make similar claims, asserting that Friedrich Engels over-emphasized the determinism in Marxist thought, and that Marx himself was largely interested in widening democratic participation and gaining greater social control over the capitalist means of production. While democratic socialists and others on the radical left generally share these orientations, post-Marxists remain focused on the exploitive power of capitalists and remain attached to a Marxist language that has long distanced Marxists from pluralists. Introductions to post-Marxism can be found in Terrell Carver, "Marxisms and Post-Marxisms," and Stuart Sim, *Post-Marxism.*

11   This phenomenon is known as American exceptionalism, and there are various explanations for the inability of socialism to become a significant ideology in the US. Historical explanations suggest that the lack of a feudal past has made it easy for Americans to become part of the middle class, thus reducing the attractiveness of the more radical politics of socialism. Economic explanations suggest that America's great natural resources

coupled with industrial and technological developments have provided unusual economic expansion and opportunities for the vast majority of Americans. Political explanations suggest that the American Constitution was specifically designed to reduce the capacity of a class-based faction like a socialist party to dominate the political system. Sociological explanations suggest that American ethnic heterogeneity has made it difficult for the working classes of various ethnic and racial groups to unify behind a socialist party that represents their common economic interests. And cultural explanations suggest that socialism in America is hindered by the ethos of rugged individualism, the dream of upward mobility, and the fear of equality. For a discussion of American exceptionalism, see Seymour Martin Lipset and Gary Marks, *It Didn't Happen Here.*

12   See, for example, Mickey Kaus, *The End of Equality.*

13   These data are from Manfred Steger, *Globalism: Market Ideology Meets Terrorism,* p. 118.

14   Kai Nielson, *Globalization and Justice,* p. 33.

15   Leading cosmopolitan theorists include Charles Beitz, Joseph Carens, Charles Jones, Thomas Pogge, and Kok-Chor Tan.

16   Josh Tyrangiel, "The Constant Charmer," *Time* (December 26, 2005): 46.

17   John Rawls, *The Law of Peoples,* p. 106.

18   Michel Sandel, "America's Search for a New Public Philosophy," p. 74. Sandel developed his civic communitarianism in *Democracy's Discontent.*

19   Robert Putnam, *Bowling Alone.*

20   Michael Walzer, *Spheres of Justice.*

21   Catharine MacKinnon, *Feminism Unmodified* and *Toward a Feminist Theory of the State.*

22   See Susan Okin, *Justice, Gender, and the Family.*

23   Anna Marie Smith, "Democratic Theory for a New Century."

24   John Guidry and Mark Sawyer, "Contentious Pluralism."

25   Iris Marion Young, *Justice and the Politics of Difference.*

26   Simone Chambers, *Reasonable Democracy.*

27   Benjamin Barber, *Strong Democracy.*

28   Some factions within the Green Party, especially in New England, thought that Nader had stolen its nomination.

29   In *A Brief History of Neoliberalism,* David Harvey provides an excellent overview of the people and processes involved in the rise of globalism.

30   Steger, *Globalism: Market Ideology Meets Terrorism,* pp. 47–90.

31   Steger, *Globalism: Market Ideology Meets Terrorism,* pp. 85–9.

32   Thomas Friedman, *The Lexus and the Olive Tree,* pp. 44–72.

33   Thomas Friedman, *The World is Flat.*

34   Margaret Thatcher, *Statecraft,* p. 441.

35   Johan Norberg, *In Defense of Global Capitalism,* pp. 38–40.

36   Norberg, *In Defense of Global Capitalism,* p. 40. This proposition is corroborated by Bruce Russett's *Controlling the Sword,* and other work on "the democratic peace."

37   Francis Fukuyama, *The End of History.*

38   Harvey, *A Brief History of Neoliberalism,* p. 119.

39   See Norman Podhoretz, "World War IV."

40   He received less than half of 1 percent of the votes and – unlike Ralph Nader – was not a factor in George W. Bush's narrow and contested victory over Al Gore.

41   Pat Buchanan, *State Of Emergency.*

42   Samuel Huntington, *Who Are We?,* pp. 225–7.

43 Huntington, *Who Are We?*, pp. 161–2 and 242.

44 Despite his characterization as a communitarian, Alasdair MacIntyre rejects ordinary distinctions between individualist and collectivist doctrines in ways that suggest that he also rejects being labeled a communitarian. See, for example, *After Virtue*, pp. 34–5.

45 Mary Ann Glendon, *Rights Talk*.

46 Mary Ann Glendon, *Abortion and Divorce in Western Law*.

47 For an excellent overview of communitarianism, see Robert Booth Fowler, *The Dance with Community*.

48 Damon Linker, *The Theocons*.

49 For an interesting, intellectually nuanced overview of these issues, see Christian Smith, *Christian America*.

50 Overviews of Islam and politics are provided by Carl Brown, *Religion and State*; Bernard Lewis, *The Crisis of Islam*; Ahmad Moussalli, *Moderate and Radical Islamic Fundamentalism*; and Emmanuel Sivan, *Radical Islam*.

51 Gilles Kepel, *War for Muslim Minds*.

52 James Risen and Judy Thomas, *Wrath of Angels*.

53 Rawls, *Political Liberalism*, pp. 58–62.

54 Joshua Green, "Roy and His Rock."

55 Carol Swain, *The New White Nationalism*.

56 Carol Gallaher, *On the Fault Line*.

57 Rorty, *Achieving Our Country*, pp. 35–8.

58 Steger calls Michael Hardt and Antonio Negri's *Empire* "the communist manifesto of our time" in his review of the book in the *American Political Science Review* (March, 2002), p. 264.

59 Hardt and Negri would insist that Marx only claimed that certain economic forces *could* result in a revolution.

60 Chantel Mouffe, *The Return of the Political*, pp. 152–4.

61 See Judith Butler, "Contingent Foundations."

62 Dobson, *Green Political Thought*, pp. 2–10.

63 William Ophuls, *Requiem for Modern Politics*.

64 E. F. Schumacher, *Small is Beautiful*.

65 For a compilation of Chomsky's writings, see *Understanding Power*, edited by Peter Mitchell and John Schoeffel.

66 Gillis Kepel, *The Revenge of God*; and Philip Jenkins, "The Next Christianity."

PART II PHILOSOPHICAL ASSUMPTIONS: THEIR IMPORTANCE AS FOUNDATIONS FOR POLITICAL PRINCIPLES

1 In this brief introduction, the importance of philosophical assumptions to political principles is illustrated by contrasting justice principles of the egalitarian liberal John Rawls and the libertarian Robert Nozick, both of whom were introduced in chapter 4. These ideas will be elaborated in chapter 14.

2 The Rawls–Nozick debate was so framed for broad public understanding in *Esquire* magazine by Randall Rothenberg: "Robert Nozick vs. John Rawls: Give me Liberty or Give me Equality." The interpretation that Rawls's principles of justice emphasize equality is due to his claim that an equal distribution of social goods is to be preferred, unless inequalities are justified. The interpretation that Nozick's principles emphasize freedom is

due to his claim that unequal distributions are justified if they arise from one's free choices about working and exchanging goods with others. But on deeper reflection, such interpretations are oversimplifications. Rawls's theory calls for extensive equal liberties for everyone, including the liberty to choose one's own life plan. Nozick's theory calls for the equal treatment of all people in at least one important sense: we are all treated equally if each of us has equal rights to the fruits of our own labor.

3   Both Rawls and Nozick seem to have so understood their adversary in this debate. In such later work as *Political Liberalism*, Rawls is usually interpreted as de-emphasizing his strong egalitarianism and allowing more space for those committed to libertarian principles in his conception of stable liberal community. In *The Examined Life*, Nozick explicitly states: "[T]he libertarian position I once propounded now seems to me seriously inadequate, in part because it did not fully knit the humane considerations and joint cooperative activities it left room for more closely into its fabric" (p. 287).

4   See, for example, Will Kymlicka, *Contemporary Political Philosophy*, pp. 5–7.

CHAPTER 5   QUESTIONS OF ONTOLOGY

1   See, for example, Tim Hayward, "Ecologism and Environmentalism," p. 353.

2   Michael Hardt and Antonio Negri, *Multitude*, p. 19.

3   Stephen White, "Affirmation and Weak Ontology in Political Theory: Some Rules and Doubts," available at <http://muse.jhu.edu/journals/theory_and_event/v0004/4.2white.html>. This article draws from White's *Sustaining Affirmation*.

4   John Rawls, *A Theory of Justice*, pp. 26–30. Deontological approaches employ a wide variety of foundational assumptions, such as those identified as part of Rawls's original position, as the basis of theories of political justice and individual rights. In this usage, such assumptions are deontological only in that they avoid any assumptions about a universal conception of the good.

5   Michael Oakeshott, "On Being Conservative," in *Rationalism in Politics*, pp. 182–4.

6   Leo Tolstoy, *The Kingdom of God is Within You*.

7   The concept of collective consciousness has received much attention in recent years, and not only in anarchist thought. See, for example, Attila Grandpierre, "The Physics of Collective Consciousness," available at <http://philsci-archive.pitt.edu/archive/00001210/01/PCC.pdf>.

8   Peter Kropotkin, *Mutual Aid*.

9   Alexander Herzen, *From the Other Shore*, p. 107.

10 Kropotkin, *Mutual Aid*, pp. 81–2.

11 For a brief account of such schemes, see Norman Cohn, *The Pursuit of the Millennium*, pp. 108–11.

12 Some interpreters of Hegel have understood him to mean that states embodying the ideas of democratic liberalism have achieved such perfection. See Barry Cooper, *The End of History*, and Francis Fukuyama, *The End of History*.

13 Karl Marx, "Afterword" of *Kapital*, cited by Robert Tucker in *The Marx-Engels Reader*, p. xxi.

14 Marx was indebted to Ludwig Feuerbach (1804–72), a German philosopher and moralist, for thinking that history is determined by material conditions, rather than ideas.

15 These contradictions include the tension between the social mode of production and the individualistic mode of appropriation within capitalism and the conflict of interests between the proletariat and the bourgeoisie.

16 See David McLellan, *Marxism after Marx*, pp. 9–17. Among neo-Marxists, Louis Althusser (1918–90) was the foremost proponent of "hard" economic determinism, while Nicos Poulantzas (1937–79) argued for a softer interpretation of Marx's ontology.

17 V. I. Lenin, "What Is To Be Done?" in *The Lenin Anthology*, pp. 49–54 and 72–9.

18 This transfer indicates the distance between Nietzsche and fascism. Although certain of his ideas were appropriated by them, Nietzsche was neither a fascist nor a "proto-fascist." He looked forward to the rule of a cultural aristocracy, and he abhorred the notion of any sort of mass participation in politics. He was, moreover, sharply critical of anti-Semitism, nationalist chauvinism, and Darwinian theories of race or social competition.

19 Benito Mussolini, "The Doctrine of Fascism," p. 10.

20 There are many reasons for rejecting such a "scientific" basis for racism, but we will mention only two here. First, race and species must be demonstrated to be scientifically equivalent concepts – which they are not, because inter-species breeding is almost never possible, while inter-racial breeding is possible and fairly common. Second, one must also show how either the genetic material of a race or its physiological manifestations determine a variety of fundamental racial differences among humans, such as differences in intellect. The bulk of science has shown just the opposite – that individual differences are far greater within a racial type than between races and that the independent impact of race on most human characteristics is negligible.

21 Gobineau's writings attracted others who coarsened his ideas further. Gobineau was not specifically anti-Semitic, arguing that the present inferiority of the Jews was the result of mingling with black races, and not an inherent fault in the race itself.

22 This doctrine of race was rarely disseminated in such a pure form to the German masses.

23 John Rawls, "Justice as Fairness: Political not Metaphysical," and John Gray, *Liberalisms*, p. 240.

24 John Maynard Keynes, for example, saw belief in "some law of nature" precluding intervention as "nonsense." See *Collected Writings*, vol. 9, pp. 90–1.

25 Classical liberalism did emphasize that government was based on the "consent of the people," rather than divine will, so these terms may have become confused over time. To say that governmental authority is based on popular consent is not to say that governments must always act in accordance to what most people prefer. See Hannah Pitkin, *The Concept of Representation*.

26 William Riker, *Liberalism against Populism*.

27 Riker particularly emphasized this conclusion from the theory of public choice.

28 William Galston, "Civic Education in a Liberal State," p. 93.

29 John Kenneth Galbraith discussed the determinant power of organizations in *The New Industrial State*.

30 Robert Nozick, *Anarchy, State, and Utopia*, ch. 1.

31 Francis Fukuyama, *The End of History*, pp. xiv–xv. See also Ulrich Beck, *What is Globalization?*, p. 122.

32 Thomas Friedman, *The Lexus and the Olive Tree*.

33 Manfred Steger, *Globalism: Market Ideology Meets Terrorism*, pp. 60–6.

34 Fukuyama, *The End of History*, p. xvi.

35 Johan Norberg, *In Defense of Global Capitalism*, pp. 286–91.

36 Religious conservatives are most likely to stress God as a foundational force, though many do not thereby insist that theocracies are implied by their ontological beliefs.

37 See the *Left Behind* series of novels by Tim LaHaye and Jerry Jenkins.

38 Another somewhat less encompassing version of divine determinism is prominent among Islamists. Some believe that Allah will reward martyrs in the service of His Will with a

home in eternal paradise (Heaven), which may encourage suicide bombers to endanger pluralist societies.

39   McLellan, *Marxism after Marx*, pp. 33–8. Philosophers working in this Kantian tradition sought to synthesize Hegel and Marx almost a century after Kant produced his work.

40   Eduard Bernstein, *Evolutionary Socialism*, pp. 13–14.

41   T. H. Huxley, "Evolution and Ethics."

42   Hardt and Negri emphasize this term, and it is important in this context, because it refers to individuals having unique properties that preclude any sort of characterization as normal or abnormal. In a community of "singularities," individuals are not dominated by others.

43   The extreme left thus rejects the economic determinism of orthodox Marxists. But it might argue that Marx's ontology is not so different from its own. Even orthodox Marxists assume that strict economic determinism only applied to humanity's historical stage, and in the post-historical stage, humanity would be free from economic determination. The extreme left might claim that the fundamental realities that it perceives in the current situation resemble the economic forces that Marx thought were foundational to the historical period, and all such forces can be escaped in the future.

44   Hardt and Negri, *Multitude*, pp. 351–2.

45   William Ophuls, *Requiem for Modern Politics*, pp. 7–12.

46   Ophuls, *Requiem for Modern Politics*, p. 8.

47   Gilles Kepel, *The Revenge of God*.

48   During Fall 2005, Pat Robertson made such claims when voters in Dover, Pennsylvania removed from office a group of fundamentalists who had supported intelligent design. Most conservatives repudiated Robertson.

CHAPTER 6   QUESTIONS OF HUMAN NATURE

1   For an historical treatment of various theories of human nature, see Louis Pojman, *Who are We?*

2   C. B. Macpherson, *The Life and Times of Liberal Democracy*, p. 24.

3   For a discussion of instrumental reason and its problems, see Thomas Spragens, *The Irony of Liberal Reason*.

4   Most classical liberals really thought that only men were capable of such self-development and that their principles thus applied only to men. But early liberal feminists insisted on the equal developmental capacities of women. Mary Wollstonecraft's *Vindication of the Rights of Women* is the classical statement in this regard.

5   Emile Durkheim, *Suicide*, esp. pp. 241–360.

6   Alexander Herzen, *From the Other Shore*, pp. 139–40.

7   Emma Goldman, "Anarchism: What It Really Stands For," in *Anarchism and Other Essays*, p. 51.

8   Peter Kropotkin, *Mutual Aid*, pp. 194–251.

9   Goldman, "Anarchism," p. 62.

10   Kropotkin, *Mutual Aid*, pp. 83–193.

11   Hannah Arendt, *The Human Condition*, p. 86, n14.

12   Fourier was a French utopian socialist whose ideas about the intrinsic enjoyment of work influenced both anarchists and Marxists. His ideas are available in Jonathan Beecher and Richard Bienvenu, *The Utopian Vision of Charles Fourier*.

13 Karl Marx, "Economic and Philosophical Manuscripts of 1844," in *The Marx-Engels Reader*, p. 72.

14 Marx, "Economic and Philosophical Manuscripts," in *The Marx-Engels Reader*, p. 72.

15 Antonio Gramsci, "The Study of Philosophy," in *Selections from the Prison Notebooks*, p. 351.

16 Jonathan Rauch, "The Forgotten Millions."

17 From *Castro Speaks*, quoted in Tony Smith, *Thinking Like a Communist*, p. 154.

18 See René Descartes, *Meditation on First Philosophy*, p. 81.

19 Among the "burdens of freedom" are the psychic costs of weighing difficult alternatives, the intellectual costs of informing ourselves about our alternatives and their likely consequences, and the emotional costs of fearing that we could choose poorly. Erich Fromm discusses the willingness of individuals to try to escape such costs and submit to fascist leaders in *Escape from Freedom*.

20 Benito Mussolini, "The Doctrine of Fascism," p. 15.

21 Giovanni Gentile, "The Philosophical Basis of Fascism," p. 48.

22 By emphasizing the centrality of the will in human nature, by recognizing that the human will is not always rational, and by stressing the capacity to motivate people with emotional appeals, both fascism and Nazism have been labeled as ideologies of irrationality. This label may be somewhat misleading, because fascist and especially Nazi regimes incorporated various technologies in a manner that was effective for their goals, and thus rational in that sense. Death camps are irrational with respect to ethical and humanistic principles but they were an efficient tool for genocide and medical experimentation. See Hannah Arendt, *Origins of Totalitarianism*, pp. 437–59; and Jay Lifton, *The Nazi Doctors*.

23 Robert Dahl, *Democracy and Its Critics*, pp. 84–8.

24 Liberals recognize that different life plans will be subject to different evaluations socially and economically. If I choose to be a surfer and you choose to be a heart surgeon, I should expect you to be more honored by others and more rewarded in the market. However, I should not expect the state to subsidize or penalize my life plan any more than it subsidizes or penalizes yours.

25 Will Kymlicka, "Liberalism and Communitarianism."

26 Emily Gill, "Goods, Virtues, and the Constitution of the Self."

27 Dahl calls this imperative the "presumption of personal autonomy" in *Democracy and Its Critics*, pp. 97–105.

28 William Galston, *Liberal Purposes*, pp. 121–4.

29 John Schaar, "Equal Opportunity and Beyond," p. 248.

30 Michael Sandel, *Liberalism and the Limits of Justice*, pp. 55–9.

31 The virtue of public reasonableness is discussed by John Rawls in *Political Liberalism*, pp. 213–56.

32 James Q. Wilson, *The Moral Sense*.

33 William Mitchell, "Efficiency, Responsibility, and Democratic Politics," pp. 343–73.

34 The concept of "rent-seeking" derives from the work of Gordon Tullock (*Public Goods, Redistribution, and Rent-seeking*).

35 Alasdair MacIntyre, *After Virtue*, pp. 204–25.

36 Charles Taylor, *Hegel and Modern Society*, p. 157.

37 Norberg, *In Defense of Global Capitalism*, pp. 136–44. This assumption seems important to counter the Marxist argument that the productive capacities of free market capitalism will outstrip our demand for economic goods and services and that over-supply will eventually lead to the downfall of the capitalist system.

38   Neil Postman, *Amusing Ourselves to Death*.
39   Thomas Friedman, *The World is Flat*, pp. 103–13.
40   Francis Fukuyama, "The Great Disruption."
41   The extreme right has developed a very tortured theory about the linkages between Jesus and the first Christians and the Anglo-Saxons and Aryan peoples. See Michael Barkun, *Religion and the Racist Right*.
42   This reference is from the Nation of Islam literature, as cited by Carol Swain, *The New White Nationalism*, p. 66.
43   Judith Butler, "Contingent Foundations," p. 344; Terrill Carver, "Marxisms and Post-Marxisms," p. 20.
44   Frederick Hacker, *Crusaders, Criminals, Crazies*, p. 162.
45   Psychologists working in the area of affective forecasting stress that people often are mistaken about the intensity and duration of the pleasure experienced by attaining an object of our desire (like a luxury car or a promotion). See, for example, Daniel Gilbert, *Stumbling on Happiness*. People mistakenly believe that increases in wealth bring proportionate increases in happiness, though there is considerable research showing that beyond a certain point, increases in wealth provide little if any increase in happiness.
46   Much criticized in this regard is *The Bell Curve*, by Charles Murray and Richard Hernstein.

CHAPTER 7   QUESTIONS OF SOCIETY

1   John Locke, *Two Treatises of Government*, p. 362.
2   Locke, *Two Treatises*, p. 375.
3   Thomas Hobbes, *Leviathan*, p. 186.
4   Locke, *Two Treatises*, p. 311.
5   Locke, *Two Treatises*, p. 367.
6   While the first social contract forming civil society is among individuals residing in the state of nature, the second social contract is between these individuals now acting as a collectivity and a governing regime.
7   Edmund Burke, *Reflections on the Revolution in France*, in Peter Stanlis, *Edmund Burke*, p. 471.
8   Robert Nisbet, *Conservatism*, pp. 35–8.
9   Alexander Herzen, *From the Other Shore*, p. 139.
10   The importance of friendship and face-to-face interconnections is discussed by Jane Mansbridge, *Beyond Adversarial Democracy*, p. 20.
11   Jean-Jacques Rousseau, "Discourse on the Origin of Inequality," in his *Basic Writings*. This essay was first published in 1755.
12   Rousseau, "Discourse on the Origin of Inequality," p. 60.
13   Marx, "The Grundrisse," in *The Marx-Engels Reader*, p. 262. "The Grundrisse" comprise Marx's notebooks produced in 1857–8.
14   Karl Marx, *Capital, Volume One*, in *Marx-Engels Reader*, p. 433.
15   Friedrich Engels, *The Origins of Family, Private Property, and State*, in *Marx-Engels Reader*, p. 753. The *Origins* was written in 1884.
16   *Communist Manifesto*, in *Marx-Engels Reader*, pp. 473–4.
17   V. I. Lenin, "Introducing the New Economic Policy," in *The Lenin Anthology*, p. 504. Lenin presented this report in 1921.
18   According to Theodore Lowi in *The End of Liberalism*, pp. 31–41, pluralists like Arthur Bentley and David Truman played a key role in the emergence of contemporary

liberalism. Initially, such pluralists believed that organized groups are simply the product of the common interests of particular kinds of individuals, but recent pluralists recognize that ongoing associations play a large role in defining the interests and life plans of individuals. See, for example, Charles Anderson, "Pragmatic Liberalism," p. 210.

19   These benefits are analyzed in Robert Putnam's *Bowling Alone*.

20   Liberals are less clear about extending toleration to groups that oppose liberal institutions and principles. Rawls suggests that intolerant groups, like fascist and communist organizations, should be tolerated if they are weak and liberal institutions are strong. But one of the primary obligations of a liberal citizen is to preserve and protect liberal institutions, and this can mean repressing those groups that become genuine threats to the persistence of liberalism. See *Theory of Justice*, pp. 216–21.

21   Roger Scruton has been particularly forceful about the lack of philosophical foundations for conservatism. See his *The Meaning of Conservatism*.

22   Michael Tomasky, "A Perfect Storm?," p. 24.

23   The metaphor of the "delicate watch" had been used by classical liberals. They emphasized the delicate qualities to point out that interference with the economy should be carried out carefully and precisely, and only when it is not keeping its own time. Conservatives here, once again, draw on the ideas of classical liberalism. A discussion of the watch as a metaphor in the history of classical liberal political economy can be found in Albert Hirschman, *The Passions and the Interests*, esp. pp. 81–93.

24   Samuel Huntington, *Who Are We?*

25   Michael Walzer, "The Community."

26   Thomas Bottomore, *Classes in Modern Society*, p. 29.

27   This image is stressed by Samuel Huntington in *The Clash of Civilizations*. For a chauvinistic celebration of the West, see Charles Murray, *Human Accomplishment*.

28   Sherri Berman, "Islamism, Revolution, and Civil Society."

29   Judith Butler, "Sexual Inversions."

30   Chandra Mohanty, "Women, Workers, and Capitalist Scripts."

31   Michael Hardt and Antonio Negri, *Multitude*, pp. 351–8.

32   Putnam, *Bowling Alone*.

33   William Ophuls, *Requiem for Modern Politics*, p. 268.

34   Rawls, *Political Liberalism*, pp. 36–40.

35   Paul Schumaker, *Critical Pluralism*, pp. 174–202

CHAPTER 8   QUESTIONS OF EPISTEMOLOGY

1   Plato presented the classical case for guardianship. See Robert Dahl, *Democracy and Its Critics*, pp. 52–64.

2   For an excellent discussion of the debt that liberalism owes to Descartes, see Benjamin Barber, *Strong Democracy*, pp. 46–66.

3   Jeremy Bentham, *An Introduction to the Principles of Morals and Legislation*, p. 153.

4   John Stuart Mill, *Utilitarianism*, p. 14.

5   Michael Oakeshott, "Rationalism in Politics," in *Rationalism and Politics*, p. 8.

6   Sam Dolgoff, *Bakunin on Authority*, p. ix.

7   Some contemporary political theorists insist that scientific and positivist modes of inquiry unnecessarily restrict political thought. See, for example, Sheldon Wolin, "Political Theory as a Vocation" and Henry Kariel, "Creating Political Reality."

8   In *The Ego and His Own*, Max Stirner emphasized that no individual should be a servant to truths outside of those of their own construction.

9   Robert Booth Fowler, "The Anarchist Tradition," p. 748.

10 George Woodcock, *Anarchism*, p. 204.

11 William Godwin, *Enquiry Concerning Political Justice*, pp. 168–77.

12 While rejecting anarchism, Robert Dahl concedes that the Inuit in Northern Canada provide such evidence. See his *Democracy and Its Critics*, p. 46.

13 Friedrich Engels, *Socialism: Utopian and Scientific*, in *The Marx-Engels Reader*, pp. 695–6. This essay was part of *Anti-Dühring*, published in 1878; it was published independently in 1880.

14 Friedrich Engels, *Socialism*, pp. 683–717; Karl Marx and Friedrich Engels, *Communist Manifesto*, in *The Marx-Engels Reader*, pp. 491–500.

15 Karl Marx, *Economic and Philosophic Manuscripts*, in *The Marx-Engels Reader*, p. 67.

16 Tony Smith, *Thinking Like a Communist*, p. 54.

17 Marx and Engels, *Communist Manifesto*, pp. 474–480.

18 Marx, *German Ideology*, in *The Marx-Engels Reader*, p. 159; *Communist Manifesto of the Communist Party*, p. 489.

19 Joseph Stalin, *Dialectical and Historical Materialism*, pp. 26–30.

20 While criticisms of forms of politics that give subordinates a "moral holiday" go back at least as far as Aristotle, the most important critic of this aspect of such authoritarianism has been Hannah Arendt. See her *Eichmann in Jerusalem*.

21 Charles Fecher, *The Philosophy of Jacques Maritain*, p. 22.

22 Henri Bergson, *The Two Sources of Morality and Religion*, esp. pp. 312–17 and 209ff.

23 For a discussion of Nazi rallies, see Albert Speer, *Inside the Third Reich*, pp. 58–62.

24 For an exception to this, see the foundational approach to justifying liberalism provided by Alan Gewirth in "The Epistemology of Human Rights."

25 A good overview of the limitations of utilitarianism is provided by Will Kymlicka in *Contemporary Political Philosophy*, pp. 20–45.

26 John Rawls, *A Theory of Justice*.

27 Rawls, *Theory of Justice*, pp. 26–7. Rawls is introduced as a contemporary liberal at this point, because his philosophical foundations are certainly within the liberal tradition and these assumptions have influenced extensive work within contemporary liberalism. It is Rawls's strong egalitarianism that provides a radical perspective within pluralism and prompts us to classify and discuss egalitarian liberalism as part of the radical left.

28 Classical liberals also emphasized the subjectivity of the good, but their initial conception of the good incorporated a sensual understanding of utility that liberals have long abandoned. Rawls conception of a "good life" is much closer to Mills's "enlightened utilitarianism," and this more complex conception of human motivation made Rawls's contractual defense of a form of contemporary liberalism quite different from the one provided by classical liberals.

29 John Rawls, "Justice as Fairness: Political, not Metaphysical."

30 Rawls himself came to this conclusion in *Political Liberalism*.

31 John Gray, *Liberalisms*, p. 254. Gray attributes this argument to John Stuart Mill, T. H. Green, K. W. von Humbolt, and Earnest Barker. He finds it wanting.

32 Brian Barry, "How Not to Defend Liberal Institutions," pp. 4–5.

33 See, for example, John Schwarz, *America's Hidden Success*.

34 David Ricci, *The Tragedy of Political Science*, p. 104.

35 Charles Anderson, *Pragmatic Liberalism*.

36 Among Richard Rorty's many articles and books in this vain are "Human Rights, Rationality, and Sentimentality," and *Achieving Our Country*.

37 Albert Hirschman, *The Rhetoric of Reaction*.

38 James Coleman and Sara Kelly, "Education."

39 George Stigler, "Director's Law of Public Income Distribution."

40 Thomas Sowell, *Preferential Policies*.

41 For detailed and explicit criticisms of this type applied to political science research, see *Essays on the Scientific Study of Politics*, edited by Herbert Storing.

42 Thomas Sowell, *Inside American Education*, esp. pp. 70–4.

43 Ayn Rand, *The Fountainhead*.

44 Alasdair MacIntyre, *After Virtue*, pp. 201–7.

45 Francis Fukuyama, *The End of History*, p. xv.

46 Thomas Friedman describes many such managerial improvements in *The World is Flat*, pp. 49–172.

47 Even an ascetic monk whose only ultimate end is divine grace would benefit from the possession of money, since money can be used to buy time and the material necessities that would enable him to devote even more attention to the pursuit of God.

48 Francis Fukuyama, *The End of History*, pp. 71–81.

49 Rawls, *Theory of Justice*.

50 William Julius Wilson, *Bridge Over the Racial Divide*.

51 Aldo Leopold, *The Sand County Almanac*.

52 Michael Sandel, *Democracy's Discontent*.

53 The seminal discussion of the importance of openness in agenda-setting is that of Peter Bachrach and Morton Baratz, *Power and Poverty*.

54 See, for example, Amy Gutmann and Dennis Thompson, *Why Deliberative Democracy?*

55 Rawls invented the veil of ignorance as one device for helping individuals see beyond their immediate self-interests to imagine what would be desirable for others; see his *Theory of Justice*, pp. 118–23.

56 Iris Marion Young, *Justice and the Politics of Difference*.

57 For a discussion of public reason, see Rawls, *Political Liberalism*, pp. 131–80. For a discussion of the importance of addressing the consequences of political alternatives, see Theodore Lowi, *The End of The Republican Era*, pp. 245–8.

58 Dennis Thompson, *Just Elections*.

59 The first of these assumptions seems reasonable, but the second two are certainly contestable. See Robert Dahl, *How Democratic is the American Constitution?*

60 According to *The Militant Ideology Atlas*, compiled by the Combating Terrorist Center at West Point, the most influential Islam Fundamentalist theorist is Abu Muhammad al-Maqdisi. His ideas are referenced at <https://www.hsdl.org/hslog/?q=node/3207>.

61 Michel Foucault, *Power/Knowledge*.

62 John Rawls, *Political Liberalism*, pp. 133–72.

CHAPTER 9   QUESTIONS OF COMMUNITY

1 Plato, "Apology," in *Five Dialogues*, p. 41.

2 Robert Dahl, *Democracy and Its Critics*, pp. 193–209.

3 Ashutosh Varshney, "Nationalism, Ethnic Conflict, and Rationality," p. 85.

4 Conor O'Brien, "Thomas Jefferson: Radical and Racist."

5 Samuel Huntington, *Who Are We?* pp. 59–80.

6 The communists in the USSR created and controlled some sub-communities such as youth groups.

7 Z (anonymous), "To the Stalin Mausoleum."

8 See, for example, Robert Reich, "The Nationalism We Need." The theme of increasing the obligations of American citizens *primarily* to other Americans is more often implied than expressly stated in the literature on a new liberal American nationalism. See, for example, John Judis and Michael Lind, "For a New American Nationalism."

9 This is Gunnar Myrdal's term in his groundbreaking work on racial problems, *The American Dilemma*.

10 Michael Sandel provides these terms to stress the difference between individuals who become deeply embedded in the moral system of a communitarian group and individuals who become involved in political communities simply to find procedures for resolving their differences. See his "Morality and the Liberal Ideal," pp. 15–17.

11 Robert Dahl, *How Democratic is the American Constitution?*

12 Mary Ann Glendon, *Rights Talk*, pp. 109–12.

13 Pat Buchanan, "Address to Chicago Council on Foreign Relations," quoted in Manfred Steger, *Globalism: The New Market Ideology*, p. 92.

14 Huntington emphasizes that, to avoid conflicts, the core states of each civilization must abstain from intervening in conflicts in other civilizations, and they must negotiate with each other to deal successfully with conflicts between states from different civilizations. See his *Clash of Civilizations*, pp. 312–21.

15 Thomas Friedman, *The Lexus and the Olive Tree*, p. 31. See also Margaret Thatcher, *Statecraft*, p. xviii.

16 Johan Norberg, *In Defense of Globalization*, pp. 104–11 and 163–8.

17 Jeff Spinner-Halev and Elizabeth Theiss-Morse, "National Identity and Self-Esteem," pp. 521–2.

18 Francis Fukuyama, "The Great Disruption," p. 80.

19 Norberg, *In Defense of Globalization*, pp. 278–285.

20 See, for example, Kai Nielsen, *Globalization and Justice* and the various essays in *Global Justice*, edited by Thomas Pogge.

21 A good brief overview of the international left is provided by Manfred Steger, *Globalism: Market Ideology Meets Terrorism*, pp. 120–6.

22 John Rawls, *The Law of Peoples*, pp. 38–9.

23 John Rawls, *Political Liberalism*.

24 Michael Sandel, "America's Search for a New Public Philosophy," pp. 73–4.

25 Sandel, "America's Search," p. 74.

26 Benjamin Barber is the American political theorist who perhaps best exemplifies this socialist conception of social solidarity; see, for example, his *Strong Democracy*.

27 Carol Swain, *The New White Nationalism in America*, pp. 16–22.

28 See, for example, Noam Chomsky, *Imperial Ambitions*.

29 Micahel Hardt and Antonio Negri, *Multitude*.

30 Hardt and Negri, *Multitude*, pp. 290–6.

31 See, for example, David Korten, "A Planetary Alternative to the Global Economy."

32 Theodore Roszak, *Person/Planet*; Robert Goodin, *Green Political Theory*, p. 400.

33 Hardt and Negri, *Multitude*, pp. 306, 312.

34 Hardt and Negri, *Multitude*, p. 336.

35 Hardt and Negri, *Multitude*, p. 336.

36   Hardt and Negri, *Multitude*, pp. 341–2.

37   For example, see John Sullivan, James Pierson, and John Marcus, *Political Tolerance and American Democracy*; Robert Putnam, *Bowling Alone*; Allan Cigler, and Mark Joslyn, "The Extensiveness of Group Membership and Social Capital."

38   In *Rethinking Multiculturalism* (pp. 165–8), Bhikhu Parekh discusses the various intellectual justifications for people being exposed to views and values outside their own parochial communities.

39   Spinner-Halev and Theiss-Morse, "National Identity and Self-Esteem."

40   Pluralist societies have witnessed significant migration of political authority from the national level to local communities and to larger regional communities such as the European Union. These changes are discussed in Elizabeth Gerber and Ken Kollman, "Introduction – Authority Migration."

41   Samuel Huntington, *Who Are We?* Huntington argues that strong community identities can come from four types of unity: racial, ethnic, political, and cultural. He claims that ethnicity and race are no longer relevant to the question of American national identity, but that our national identity requires considerable cultural unity as well as political allegiance.

42   Liberal nationalism is discussed by Will Kymlicka, *Contemporary Political Philosophy*, pp. 261–8.

43   Insofar as neoconservatives deny the importance of international institutions and agreements, they can be accused of straying from the pluralist consensus on this matter.

CHAPTER 10   QUESTIONS OF CITIZENSHIP

1   C. B. Macpherson discusses this issue in *The Life and Times of Liberal Democracy*, pp. 23–76.

2   Samuel Huntington, *Who are We?*, p. 54.

3   Republican theories, which date back to Aristotle and include such eminent philosophers as Machiavelli and Montesquieu, stress instilling in citizens the virtue of seeking the common good rather than narrow self-interest. In contrast, liberal theorists thought citizens would inevitably pursue their self-interests, but they claimed that political competition, like economic competition, contained an "invisible hand" that transforms self-interested actions into outcomes that are good for the community as a whole. If citizens vote according to their own self-interests, incumbents and opposing candidates would take positions corresponding to the interests of most citizens to win a competitive election. The winning candidate would then be the one that supported the interests of most people, which, by liberal reasoning, would approximate the public interest understood in utilitarian terms.

4   Steven DeLue provides this quote by John Stuart Mill in *Political Thinking, Political Theory, and Civil Society*, p. 215.

5   DeLue, *Political Thinking*, pp. 14–15.

6   DeLue, *Political Thinking*, pp. 18–21.

7   John Locke, *Two Treatises of Government*, p. 392.

8   In "Conservatisms," Alan Finlayson stresses that traditional conservatives have "predispositions" but not "principles."

9   These quotes are drawn from W. Wesley McDonald, "Russell Kirk on Immigration," available at <http://www.vdare.com/misc/mcdonald_041031_immigration.htm>.

10   William Godwin, *Enquiry Concerning Political Justice*, p. 207.

11   Godwin, *Enquiry*, pp. 185–6. In his *Nicomachean Ethics*, Aristotle provided similar prescriptions regarding virtuous conduct.

12   Jürgen Habermas, *Legitimation Crisis*, p. 37.

13   Post-Marxists have continued to debate the potential of such vehicles. See Ernesto Laclau and Chantal Mouffe, *Hegemony and Socialist Strategy*.

14   Marx's ideas about the political community that could be constructed in revolutionary circumstances are conveyed in his admiration of "The Paris Commune," which he discussed in his essay on "The Civil War in France," pp. 618–52 in *The Marx-Engels Reader*. Marx wrote this essay in 1871.

15   See Michael Walzer, "A Day in the Life of a Socialist Citizen," pp. 229–38.

16   While such an abstract vision of a self-governing citizenry may seem attractive, it obviously rests on ignoring the two problems that make for politics: the diversity of interests that make people self-regarding rather than public-regarding and the scarcity of resources that intensifies the diversity of interests.

17   See Helena Sheehan, *Marxism and the Philosophy of Science*, ch. 5.

18   An extended diatribe against such "heretics" along with a thorough discussion of revolutionary principles and tactics may be found in Lenin's "Left-Wing Communism: An Infantile Disorder," pp. 550–618 in *The Lenin Anthology*. This work was published in 1920.

19   Edwin Black discusses Hitler's exclusionary immigration laws in *War Against the Weak*.

20   Benito Mussolini, "The Doctrine of Fascism," p. 10.

21   Alfredo Rocco, "The Political Doctrine of Fascism," p. 36.

22   Robert Dahl, *Democracy and Its Critics*, pp. 119–31.

23   Paul Schuck, "The Great Immigration Debate," pp. 100–17.

24   Mary Ann Glendon, quoted in a symposium on drafting a bill of duties entitled "Who Owes What to Whom?" edited by Gerald Marzorati, p. 45.

25   President Clinton's call for a "new covenant" during the 1992 presidential campaign is the most visible recent attempt to stress citizen responsibilities as well as rights.

26   Lawrence Tribe, "Ways Not to Think About Plastic Trees," pp. 1314–48.

27   Dahl, *Democracy and Its Critics*, pp. 91–3.

28   Seminal treatments of civil disobedience are provided by Christian Bay, "Civil Disobedience," and John Rawls, *A Theory of Justice*, pp. 319–43.

29   Martin Luther King, Jr., "Letter from Birmingham Jail," in *Why We Can't Wait*.

30   See Kenneth Lee, "Republicans Support Immigration Too," available at <http://www.speakout.com/activism/opinions/5672-1.html>.

31   Joseph Schumpeter, *Capitalism, Socialism, and Democracy*.

32   Samuel Huntington, "The Democratic Distemper."

33   Elaine Spitz, "Citizenship and Liberal Institutions."

34   George Gilder, *Wealth and Poverty*, pp. 13–16.

35   Jonathan Rauch, "The Accidental Radical."

36   Leo Strauss, "The New Political Science," p. 426.

37   David Hoeveler, *Watch on the Right*, p. 37.

38   James Buckley, *The Jeweler's Eye*, pp. 257–9.

39   George Will, "A Poverty of Thought," *Washington Post*, September 13, 2005, p. A33.

40   James Q. Wilson, *The Moral Sense*,

41   Joseph Carens, "Aliens and Citizens."

42 John Fonte, "Dogmatic Libertarians," available at <www.nationalreview.com/comment/comment-fonte050902.asp>.

43 Anthony Gregory, "In Defense of Open Immigration," available at <www.fff.org/freedom/fd0410e.asp>.

44 Johan Norberg, *In Defense of Globalization*, pp. 148–9.

45 Margaret Thatcher, *Statecraft*, p. 415.

46 Thomas Friedman, *The Lexus and the Olive Tree*, pp. 139–42.

47 Huntington, *Who are We?*, ch. 9.

48 Pat Buchanan, *State of Emergency*.

49 Huntington, *Who are We?*, pp. 37–40.

50 The contributions of such members of the radical right as Allan Bloom, and Alasdair MacIntyre to this conception of citizenship are discussed by Robert Booth Fowler, *The Dance with Community*, pp. 80–120.

51 This quote from Tocqueville is provided by Mary Ann Glendon, *Rights Talk*, p. 120.

52 Gerald Marzorati, "Who Owes What to Whom?" pp. 44–54.

53 Michael Walzer, *Spheres of Justice*, pp. 31–62.

54 Valeria Ottonelli, "Immigration: What does Global Justice Require?"

55 See Adam Przeworski. *Democracy and the Market*.

56 Ottonelli, "Immigration," p. 232.

57 Jeffrey Henig, *Neighborhood Mobilization*, pp. 140–56.

58 Matthew Crenson and Benjamin Ginsberg, *Downsizing Democracy*, pp. 182–97.

59 Crenson and Ginsberg, *Downsizing Democracy*, p. 234.

60 Peter Bachrach and Morton S. Baratz, *Power and Poverty*.

61 Mancur Olson, *The Logic of Collective Action*.

62 American Political Science Association Task Force Report, "American Democracy in an Age of Rising Inequality."

63 Contentious pluralism and the example of opposition groups mobilizing against the WTO are drawn from John Guidry and Mark Sawyer, "Contentious Pluralism."

64 See Francis Houtart and François Polet, *The Other Davos*.

65 Michael Walzer, *Spheres of Justice*, pp. 64–5.

66 Walzer, *Spheres of Justice*, p. 84.

67 Benjamin Barber, Strong *Democracy*, pp. 298–303. See also Michael Walzer, "Socializing the Welfare State," pp. 298–9.

68 Barber, *Strong Democracy*, p. 302.

69 This quote by Stormfront leader Don Black is provided by Carol Swain, *The New White Nationalism in America*, p. 99. Swain points out that many black nationalists are as opposed to nonrestrictive immigration policies as are white nationalists.

70 James Ridgeway, *Blood in the Face*, pp. 168–9.

71 William Ophuls, *Requiem for Modern Politics*, esp. pp. 88–91.

72 Crenson and Ginsberg, *Downsizing Democracy*, p. 237. For a discussion of post-material values, see Ronald Inglehart, *Culture Shift in Advanced Industrial Societies*.

73 Andrew Dobson, *Green Political Thought*, pp. 2–35.

74 Michael Hardt and Antonio Negri, *Multitude*, p. 149.

75 For an early statement of the land ethic, see Aldo Leopold, *The Sand County Almanac*.

76 In *Achieving Our Country*, Richard Rorty accuses the far left with "spectatorship," a deep disillusionment about the capacity for change that results in their merely generating deep philosophical systems of despair while avoiding doing anything constructive to improve political life.

77 Hardt and Negri, *Multitude*, pp. 356–8.

78 See "Free Movement of persons, asylum, and immigration," available at <http://europa.eu/scadplus/leg/en/s17000.htm>.

79 This discussion is highly influenced by Walzer's *Spheres of Justice* (esp. pp. 31–62), which prompted a revival of interest in these questions of citizenship. In *Contemporary Political Philosophy* (pp. 284–326), Will Kymlicka has discussed much of this work.

80 Huntington, *Who Are We?*, p. 243.

81 Huntington, *Who Are We?*.

CHAPTER 11   QUESTIONS OF STRUCTURE

1   Civilization is often said to have begun when humans formed permanent settlements, resulting in urban centers. "Civilization" is derived from the Latin term *civitas*, which means an inhabitant of a city and a citizen. Societies become civilized when they feature a division of labor, the development of security systems, the designation of rulers, the establishment of rules, and the development of systems of collective memory, especially systems of writing. Such features structure societies.

2   Francis Fukuyama, *The End of History*.

3   While free market economies and capitalism are often equated, these structures can be differentiated. Capitalism stresses the private ownership of the means of production, but privately owned enterprises can operate in heavily regulated (rather than laissez-faire) markets. Free markets are usually dominated by privately owned firms, but publicly owned enterprises and cooperatives can also participate in markets that actors can enter and exit as they wish and that are minimally regulated.

4   John Locke, *Two Treatises of Government*, pp. 327–344.

5   See Robert Heilbroner, *The Worldly Philosophers*.

6   In 1776, Adam Smith's *Wealth of Nations* spelled out capitalism's need for government. Karl Polanyi's *The Great Transformation* provides a more thorough account of why a "free enterprise" system requires governmental rules.

7   In *Freedom's Power*, pp. 29–52, Paul Starr argues that classical liberal restrictions on government did not weaken government but, rather, prevented governmental abuse of power. He notes, for example, that the British and US governments became enormously powerful in the nineteenth century while operating under constitutional constraints.

8   See, for example, Plato's *Laws* and Aristotle's *Politics*.

9   James Madison, "*Number 10*," in Alexander Hamilton et al., *The Federalist Papers*, p. 128.

10 See Steven DeLue, *Political Thinking, Political Theory, and Civil Society*, pp. 18–21.

11 For a discussion of the difference between aristocratic republicanism and democratic republicanism, see Robert Dahl, *Democracy and Its Critics*, pp. 24–8.

12 Perhaps many political scientists are traditional conservatives in this respect, as there is widespread support in the profession for the Electoral College. See Paul Schumaker and Burdett Loomis, *Choosing a President*.

13 Alexis de Tocqueville, *Democracy in America*, vol. 2, bk 2, ch. 5.

14 Quoted by Huntington, in Lawrence Harrison and Samuel Huntington, *Culture Matters*, p. xiv.

15 Robert Nozick, *Anarchy, State, and Utopia*, pp. 312–17.

16   Quoted in George Woodcock, *Anarchism*, p. 163.

17   Anarchists have never resolved the problem of conflicts among local associations. Federal inter-associational agreements typically empower some central authority to control and adjudicate conflicts among local associations, but anarchists regard such central authorities as potentially coercive and thus unsatisfactory. Nozick discusses this issue in *Anarchy, State, and Utopia*, pp. 326–31, but he is unable to propose a solution to the problem that would be compatible with anarchist ideals.

18   *Communist Manifesto* in *The Marx-Engels Reader*, p. 475.

19   *Communist Manifesto*, p. 477.

20   *Communist Manifesto*, p. 476.

21   *Communist Manifesto*, pp. 474–5.

22   *Communist Manifesto*, pp. 490–1.

23   These quotes are from Howard Mehlinger, *Communism in Theory and Practice*, p. 82. For discussion of ideological control, see also Alfred Meyer, *Communism*, pp. 103–19.

24   For detailed histories of the First International, see David McClellan, *Karl Marx*, pp. 360–411.

25   In Eduard Tannenbaum's estimation, corporatism was an abject failure in Italy. The corporations served to discipline workers, but did not seriously limit the power of capitalists. See Tannenbaum, *The Fascist Experience*, pp. 89–100.

26   Frederic Clairmont, "Volkswagens' history of forced labor," in *Le Monde Diplomatique* (January 1998), available at <http://mondediplo.com/1998/01/11volkswag>.

27   Paul Brooker, "The Nazi Fuehrerprinzip."

28   Hannah Arendt, *The Origins of Totalitarianism*, chs. 11–13.

29   Ronald Dworkin, *Taking Rights Seriously*, p. 149.

30   Theodore Lowi, *The End of Liberalism*, p. 272.

31   Paul Peterson, *City Limits*, pp. 210–22.

32   Lowi, *End of Liberalism*, pp. 274–9.

33   James Sundquist, *Policies and Politics*.

34   Lowi, *End of Liberalism*, p. 276.

35   See Peter Dreier, "Urban Neglect: George W. Bush and the Cities," *Shelterforce Online* (Sept/Oct. 2004), available at <www.nhi.org/online/issues/137/urbanneglect.html>.

36   Charles Krauthammer, "A Social Conservative Credo."

37   David Landes, "Culture Makes Almost All of the Difference," p. 11.

38   Landes, "Culture Makes Almost all the Difference," p. 13.

39   Thomas Friedman, *The Lexus and the Olive Tree*, p. 107.

40   Johan Norberg, *In Defense of Globalization*, pp. 72–94.

41   Norberg, *In Defense of Globalization*, p. 90.

42   Francis Fukuyama, *State-Building*.

43   Friedman, *Lexus and the Olive Tree*, pp. 145–66.

44   Margaret Thatcher, *Statecraft*, pp. 441 and 463.

45   Samuel Huntington, *Clash of Civilizations*.

46   Norberg, *In Defense of Globalization*, p. 189.

47   Friedman, *Lexus and the Olive Tree*, pp. 468–75.

48   Bernard Williams, "The Idea of Equality," p. 122.

49   Michael Walzer, *Spheres of Justice*, p. 102.

50   Greg Palast, *The Best Democracy Money Can Buy*.

51   Joshua Cohen and Joel Rogers, *On Democracy*, pp. 51–3.

52   The tyranny of allowing capitalists to determine the fate of local communities through their plant relocation decisions is discussed by Barry Bluestone and Bennett Harrison, *The Deindustrialization of America*.

53   Walzer, *Spheres of Justice*, pp. 291–303.

54   For a review of radical feminist literature, see Rosemary Tong, *Feminist Thought*.

55   John Schaar, "Equal Opportunity and Beyond," pp. 238–9.

56   Robert Kuttner, "Socialism, Liberalism, and Democracy," p. 7.

57   John Rawls, *Theory of Justice*, p. 242.

58   Richard Krouse and Michael McPherson, "Capitalism, 'Property-Owning Democracy,' and the Welfare State."

59   Michael Walzer, "Socializing the Welfare State." Walzer points out that helping societies should not be confused with more conservative philanthropic organizations that provide aid as charity. Conservative charities, like the United Way, are more bureaucratic and impersonal than socialist helping societies.

60   Iris Marion Young, "Polity and Group Difference."

61   Michael Sandel, *Democracy's Discontent*, p. 348.

62   G. D. H. Cole, *Social Theory*, pp. 6–11. Such ideas are developed by Carole Pateman in *Participation and Democratic Theory*.

63   David Ingersoll, Richard Matthews, and Andrew Davison, The *Philosophical Roots of Modern Ideology*, p. 278.

64   Michael Hardt and Antonio Negri, *Multitude*, p. xii.

65   Michael Hardt and Antonio Negri, *Empire*, pp. 22–41.

66   William Ophuls, *Requiem for Modern Politics*, pp. 121–76.

67   Hardt and Negri, *Multitude*, pp. 3–95.

68   Hardt and Negri, *Multitude*, pp. 289–358.

69   E. F. Schumacher, *Small is Beautiful*.

70   See John Galbraith, *American Capitalism*, and Walzer, *Spheres of Justice*. This idea is also supported by public opinion research showing most Americans have sufficient support for both capitalism and democratic government and that they seek marginal adjustments when their values conflict, rather than unregulated capitalism or pure democracy. See Herbert McClosky and John Zaller, *The American Ethos*, pp. 184–8.

CHAPTER 12   QUESTIONS OF RULERS

1   A brief history of democracy is provided by Robert Dahl, *On Democracy*, pp. 7–27. There are claims that some Native American nations – such as the Iroquois – have long practiced democracy. See Donald Grinde and Bruce Johnson, *Exemplar of Liberty: Native America and the Evolution of Democracy*, available at <www.ratical.org/many_worlds/6Nations/>.

2   Robert Kaplan, "Was Democracy Just a Moment?"

3   Robert Dahl, *Democracy and Its Critics*, pp. 77–9.

4   My *Critical Pluralism* attempts to provide estimates of the power of various types of actors in one community.

5   C. B. Macpherson, *The Life and Times of Liberal Democracy*, pp. 1–43.

6   Burke, however, argued that the colonies should be given some representation.

7   Edmund Burke, "An Appeal from the New to the Old Whigs," p. 537 in Peter Stanlis, ed., *Edmund Burke: Selected Writings*.

8   Quoted in George Woodcock, *Anarchism*, p. 34.

9   Woodcock, *Anarchism*, p. 81.

10   Robert Paul Wolff, *In Defense of Anarchism*, pp. 21–67.

11   Some democratic socialists have questioned this orthodox Marxist interpretation, point-ing to some letters that Marx wrote toward the end of his life that suggested that under certain conditions, socialism could occur through democratic elections.

12   Friedrich Engels, "Preface to the 1888 English Edition" of *The Communist Manifesto*, cited in Tony Smith, *Thinking Like a Communist*, pp. 57–8.

13   Smith, *Thinking Like a Communist*, p. 24.

14   Engels, Introduction to *The Civil War in France*, in *Marx-Engels Reader*, pp. 627–8.

15   Terrill Carver, "Marxisms and Post-Marxisms."

16   Hannah Arendt, *Origins of Totalitarianism*, pp. 404–5.

17   Robert Dahl, *Who Governs?* pp. 223–8.

18   Dahl, *Democracy and Its Critics*, pp. 218–24.

19   V. O. Key, *The Responsible Electorate*.

20   For a discussion of related research, see Susan Welch and Timothy Bledsoe, *Urban Reform and its Consequences*, pp. 35–53.

21   Charles Lindblom, *Politics and Markets*, pp. 170–88.

22   Thomas Geoghegan, *Whose Side Are You On?*.

23   These arrangements have also been labeled as iron triangles and issue networks.

24   Theodore Lowi, *The End of Liberalism*, pp. 295–313.

25   For an excellent analysis of the limitations of liberal democracy and a description of populist democracy, see Benjamin Barber's *Strong Democracy*.

26   John Guidry and Mark Sawyer, "Contentious Pluralism."

27   The Chartist Movement emphasized radical democratic politics, but it did not embrace socialism. For example, the Chartists wanted unemployed workers to be provided with smallholdings of land and capital, and believed that such reforms would produce a more competitive market system of small proprietors.

28   G. H. D. Cole, *Self-Government in Industry*, p. 33.

29   In *A Preface to Economic Democracy*, Dahl argues that worker-controlled enterprises "are likely to tap the creativity, energies, and loyalties of workers to an extent that stockholder-owned corporations probably never can, even with profit-sharing schemes" (p. 132).

30   Alan Blinder, "More Like Them?"

31   Harry Boyte, *The Backyard Revolution*.

32   One discussion of democratizing the family is provided by Anne Phillips, *Engendering Democracy*, pp. 101–4.

33   Barber, *Strong Democracy*, pp. 267–78. The need to balance the power of capitalists, developers, realtors, and other components of "the growth machine" in city politics by mobilizing left-leaning groups and movements has been most thoroughly analyzed by John Logan and Harvey Molotch, *Urban Fortunes*.

34   Jeane Kirkpatrick, "Politics and the 'New Class'."

35   James Payne, "The Congressional Brainwashing of Congress," p. 12.

36   Will's views on US political institutions are presented in David Hoeveler, *Watch on the Right*, pp. 53–80.

37   Social conservatives have made use of instruments of direct democracy to regulate such vices as sexual deviance, illicit use of drugs, and respect for the lives of the unborn and terminally ill, and these efforts have been strongly opposed by libertarians who see these as infringements on social rights.

38   See Ronald Terchek and Thomas Conte, *Theories of Democracy*, pp. 91–121 and 141–63.

39   Thomas Friedman calls the subservience of governmental officials to investors "the golden straightjacket." See his *Lexus and the Olive Tree*, pp. 101–11.

40   Johan Norberg, *In Defense of Globalization*, p. 274.

41   Friedman, *Lexus and the Olive Tree*, pp. 85–9.

42   Jagdish Bhagwati, *In Defense of Globalization*, pp. 93–4.

43   Natan Sharansky, with Ron Dermer, *The Case for Democracy*, pp. 40–1.

44   Most Muslims – the vast majority who reject fundamentalism – have democratic beliefs that are much like those of followers of other religions.

45   In The *Philosophical Roots of Modern Ideology*, pp. 261–3, David Ingersoll et al. summarize Muslim ideas about rulers. In *Religion and the State*, Carl Brown argues that such conceptions of rulers are modern departures from traditional Shiite doctrines. It should also be noted that neither Ayatollah Khomeini nor anyone else (such as Osama bin Laden) is thought to be an identifiable Imam, and thus it is necessary for the Shiites to be led by the most eminent of ayatollahs until some living Imam ("in hiding") is identified.

46   Judith Butler, "Sexual Inversions."

47   Chandra Talpade Mohanty, "Women, Workers, and Capitalist Scripts."

48   Michel Foucault, *The History of Sexuality, Volume 1: An Introduction*.

49   This example is provided by Anne Marie Smith, "Democratic Theory for a New Century," pp. 563–4.

50   Alan Wolfe stresses this metaphor in his review of *Empire* in *The New Republic* (Oct. 1, 2001), p. 31.

51   Dahl, *Democracy and its Critics*, pp. 24–8.

52   John Guidry and Mark Sawyer, "Contentious Pluralism," pp. 273–89.

53   Some analysts suggest that minority rights are no more vulnerable through referenda and initiatives than when resolved by legislatures. See Thomas Cronin, *Direct Democracy*.

54   It is not clear whether the globalist preference for the current practice of holding leaders of global institutions accountable to the leaders of nation-states that they represent is sufficiently democratic to satisfy the broad norms of pluralism regarding rulers. See Will Kymlicka, *Contemporary Political Philosophy*, pp. 312–15.

CHAPTER 13   QUESTIONS OF AUTHORITY

1   These data are derived from various editions of the *Statistical Abstract of the United States* and from the <www.infoplease.com/year>. This popular website is a useful addition to the more detailed data in the *Abstract*, because it reports gross domestic product (GDP) with annual figures adjusted to 1998 dollars, while the *Abstract* reports gross national product (GNP) for earlier years and a variety of years are used to adjust for inflation. To provide comparability, the 2000 and 2005 figures for GDP and federal spending are also adjusted to provide estimates in 1998 dollars.

2   There are variations in the liberal social contracts of such theorists as Hobbes, Locke, and Kant, but each begins with an agreement among individuals not to violate the legitimate moral claims of other individuals. Such contracts are fundamentally different from more communitarian social contracts, such as that of Rousseau. In a communitarian social contract, the parties agree to put aside their self-interests and pursue the common good, as long as others agree to do likewise.

3 In *The Great Transformation*, Karl Polanyi points out, "Regulations and markets, in effect, grew up together" (p. 68).

4 John Stuart Mill, *On Liberty*, p. 15.

5 Mill, *On Liberty*, pp. 72–3.

6 Mill, *On Liberty*, p. 85. Despite the belief of classical liberals that governments should not legislate morality, it does not follow that such liberals were uninterested in morality or promoting the virtue of citizens. They believed that citizens should exhibit such virtues as self-denial, civility, industry, and truthfulness in order for liberal institutions to function well. However, they believed that enlightened individuals and such non-governmental institutions as churches – not government – should promote such virtues. See William Galston, "Liberalism and Public Morality."

7 John Locke, *Two Treatises of Government*, p. 406.

8 Herbert Spencer, *The Man Versus The State*, pp. 79–120.

9 Paul Starr, *Freedom's Power*, pp. 29–52.

10 Noel O'Sullivan, *Conservatism*.

11 Peter Kropotkin, *Revolutionary Pamphlets*, pp. 68–75.

12 Robert Paul Wolff, *In Defense of Anarchism*, pp. 13–14.

13 The classical statement of these difficulties remains Henry David Thoreau's *Essay on Civil Disobedience*, written in 1849 to protest his arrest for failing to pay taxes that supported the Mexican-American War.

14 For a rebuttal of this argument, see Jeffrey Reiman, *In Defense of Political Philosophy*.

15 See Robert Alford and Roger Friedland, *Powers of Theory*, pp. 288–307.

16 Tony Smith, *Thinking Like a Communist*, p. 44.

17 Karl Marx and Friedrich Engels, *Communist Manifesto*, pp. 490–1.

18 Marx and Engels, *Communist Manifesto*, p. 490.

19 An extensive critical evaluation of the Soviet planned economy is provided by Alec Nove, *The Economics of Feasible Socialism Revisited*, pp. 73–126.

20 The initial success of the Soviet planned economy is discussed by Charles McCoy, *Contemporary ISMs*, pp. 70–94, and Jeffry Frieden, *Global Capitalism*, pp. 326 and 337–8. In "To the Stalin Mausoleum," Z provides a more critical assessment.

21 Organization for Economic Co-operation and Development, Economic *Survey of China, 2005*. Available at <www.oecd.org/document/7/0,2340,en_2649_201185_35343687_1_1_1_1,00.html>.

22 Antonio Gayoso, "The Rule of Small and Medium Size Enterprise in Cuba's Future." Accessed at <http://lanic.utexas.edu/la/cb/cuba/asce/cuba9/gayoso.pdf>.

23 For Mikhail Gorbachev's attempt to interpret Marx and Lenin as supporters of perestroika, see his "The Socialist Idea and Revolutionary Perestroika."

24 V. I. Lenin, " 'Left-Wing' Communism: An Infantile Disorder," in *The Lenin Anthology*, p. 609.

25 Giovanni Gentile, "The Philosophic Basis of Fascism," p. 60.

26 Adolf Hitler, *Mein Kampf*, p. 393.

27 David Callahan, *The Moral Center*.

28 Richard Flathman, *Toward a Liberalism*, pp. 168–205.

29 Lester Thurow, *The Zero Sum Society*.

30 See, for example, John Kenneth Galbraith, *The Affluent Society*.

31 For a thoughtful approach to school vouchers, see John Chubb and Terry Moe, *Politics, Markets and America's Schools*. For a useful critique of school vouchers, see Jeffrey Henig, *Rethinking School Choice*.

32   Robert Nozick, *Anarchy, State, and Utopia*, pp. 10–28.

33   Nozick acknowledges that government authority might also rectify distributions of goods that have been acquired unjustly – by force or fraud – but the purpose of any such rectification is to secure the property of those unjustly deprived of it.

34   Friedrich Hayek, *Law, Legislation, and Liberty, Volume III*.

35   Milton Friedman, *Capitalism and Freedom*, especially pp. 22–36.

36   Johan Norberg, *In Defense of Global Capitalism*, pp. 192–7.

37   Margaret Thatcher, *Statecraft*, p. 431.

38   In his *Defense of Globalization*, Jagdish Bhagwati argues "the fear that globalization puts total social spending at risk because globalization punishes such spending needs to be discounted" (p. 101). He claims that politicians in globalizing countries have incentives to promote social spending to protect their citizens from the volatility of the global economy.

39   The producers of *60 Minutes* estimated that Americans alone spend about $10 billion each year on adult entertainment. Accessed on September 25, 2005, at <www.cbsnews.com/stories/2003/11/21/main585049.shtml>.

40   In *What's the Matter with Kansas?*, Thomas Frank discusses the increasing role of social conservatism in American electoral politics. He argues that social conservatives seldom achieve their policy goals, as elected representatives turn the bulk of their attention to economic questions and sustaining capitalism once they are elected.

41   For example, it is argued that Japanese and other Asian products can sometimes be sold at prices lower than similar American products, because the Japanese economy is so structured that many costs are nationalized.

42   Michael Walzer, *Spheres of Justice*, pp. 204–6.

43   Anne Phillips, *Engendering Democracy*, pp. 110–13.

44   Walzer, *Spheres of Justice*, pp. 75–6.

45   John Rawls, *Theory of Justice*, p. 244.

46   Walzer, *Spheres of Justice*, p. 65.

47   The importance of universal social provisions is discussed by William Julius Wilson, *The Truly Disadvantaged*, pp. 149–64.

48   *L'affaire du foulard* and various justifications for multiculturalism are discussed by Bhikhu Parekh, *Rethinking Multiculturalism*, pp. 165–8 and 249–54.

49   Cornel West, *Race Matters*, p. 7.

50   Edward Abby, in "Forward" to *Ecodefense*, p. 7.

51   William Ophuls, *Requiem for Modern Politics*.

52   Despite believing that they are over-taxed, most citizens continue to believe that government should be committing more resources to such problems as protecting the environment, promoting the nation's health, solving the problems of big cities, reducing crime, improving education, and providing assistance to the poor. See, for example, Richard Niemi, John Mueller, and Tom Smith. *Trends in Public Opinion*, pp. 73–91. For a theoretical defense of sufficient governmental authority, see Theda Skocpol, *Social Revolution in the Modern World*.

53   The willingness of citizens in pluralist societies to support laws restricting freedoms and upholding dominant moral values is discussed by Herbert McClosky and John Zaller in *The American Ethos*, pp. 52–9. Although the World Values Survey seldom asks about support for laws regulating moral standards, Ronald Inglehart, Miguel Basanez, and Alejandro Moreno (*Human Values and Beliefs: A Cross-National Sourcebook*) report that abortion (V227–240), the use of marijuana/hashish (V301), prostitution (V309),

divorce (V310), euthanasia (V312), and other such activities are seen as wrong by many, and often by most, citizens in many pluralist countries.

54 McClosky and Zaller, *The American Ethos*, pp. 146–7; William Mayer, *The Changing American Mind*, p. 459.

55 In *Culture War?*, Morris Fiorina and his associates argue that it is political leaders, not citizens, who are most polarized in their approaches and stances to policy issues.

CHAPTER 14   QUESTIONS OF JUSTICE

1 APSA Taskforce, "American Democracy in an Age of Rising Inequality."

2 Chuck Collins and Felice Veskel, *Economic Apartheid in America*, pp. 38–45.

3 Gar Alperovitz, *America Beyond Capitalism*, p. 10.

4 Lester Thurow, *The Future of Capitalism*, p. 42.

5 APSA Taskforce, "American Democracy," p. 654.

6 Collins and Veskel, *Economic Apartheid*, p. 51.

7 This is from the 2004 census, which reports median white family incomes of $48,979. See <www.census.gov/Press–Release/www/releases/archives/income_wealth/005647. html>. Hispanics have average family incomes that are 70 percent of those of whites, while Asian–Americans have incomes that are 117 percent of those of whites.

8 Collins and Veskel, *Economic Apartheid*, p. 50.

9 Dalton Conley, *Being Black, Living in the Red*, p. 23.

10 Collins and Veskel, *Economic Apartheid*, pp. 59–60. These figures are for 1998 and come from reports of the United Nations Development Program and from Branko Milanovic's *Worlds Apart.*

11 John Rawls, *A Theory of Justice*, p. 3.

12 Manfred Steger uses the analogy of an elephant and many blind men feeling the elephant to convey a similar predicament in our understanding of globalization. See his *Globalism: Market Ideology Meets Terrorism*, pp. 21–3. For our purposes, justice is the elephant, the various ideologies are the various blind men, and each feels a part of the elephant and proclaims that the part that he touches is the whole. This analogy suggests that each ideology is correct to insist on the reality of the part of justice that it feels, but each is wrong to insist that the whole can be reduced to the part emphasized by any ideology.

13 Non-liberals may assert that, from a social viewpoint outside each individual, some lives have greater worth than others and thus are worthy of more social resources, but liberals deny the existence of any such social viewpoint.

14 John Locke maintained that about 99 percent of the value of material goods comes from the labor that goes into them. See his *Two Treatises*, p. 338.

15 A contemporary understanding of market justice is provided by Robert Lane, "Market Justice, Political Justice."

16 Edmund Burke distinguished real from abstract rights in his *Reflections on the Revolution in France* (ed. Peter Stanlis), pp. 451–6.

17 A useful discussion of the unequal privileges of pre-liberal society is available in Donald Kagan, Steven Ozment, and Frank Turner, *The Western Heritage*, pp. 546–52.

18 For a discussion of the ascriptive norm of distributive justice, see Jennifer Hochschild, *What's Fair?*, pp. 70–5.

19 Russell Kirk, *A Program for Conservatives*, pp. 170–1.

20 Kirk, *A Program for Conservatives*, p. 170.

21   Quoted in Mulford Sibley, *Political Ideas and Ideologies*, p. 540.

22   William Godwin, *Political Justice*, p. 170.

23   William Godwin, *Enquiry Concerning Political Justice*, pp. 725–35

24   Karl Marx, "Critique of the Gotha Program," in *The Marx–Engels Reader*, p. 531. This essay was originally published in 1875.

25   This debate is summarized in Steven Lukes, *Marxism and Morality*, pp. 48–59.

26   See Robert Tucker, *The Marxian Revolutionary Idea*, pp. 33–53.

27   It is often asserted that Marx accepted a Lockean labor theory of value – that labor alone creates value. In *History, Labour, and Freedom*, G. A. Cohen suggests that Marx merely claimed that workers produce some value for which they are not rewarded, and that this constitutes exploitation (pp. 226–7).

28   Karl Marx and Friedrich Engels, *Communist Manifesto*, in *Marx–Engels Reader*, p. 485.

29   Marx, "Grundrisse," in *Marx–Engels Reader*, p. 249.

30   Cohen, *History, Labour, and Freedom*, p. 298.

31   John Roemer, *Free to Lose*, pp. 58–9.

32   Will Kymlicka, *Contemporary Political Philosophy*, p. 164.

33   Karl Marx, "Critique of the Gotha Program," p. 531.

34   Marx, "Critique of the Gotha Program," p. 531.

35   Kymlicka, *Contemporary Political Philosophy*, p. 183. Kymlicka points out that if the unrealistic assumption of complete abundance is dropped, the principle of distributing goods according to need is not very clear or helpful. The principle can then be interpreted in two different ways. First, needs could be interpreted narrowly – everyone would be provided the basic material necessities. In this interpretation, communist societies would not be significantly more egalitarian than existing welfare states. Second, needs could be interpreted much more broadly – different people would have different needs to sustain the different kinds of lives they pursue. Because the needs a person who sails yachts for recreation are on a different order than the needs of a jogger, its not clear that the principle of "to each according to his needs" means that each has equal justice claims.

36   Marx, "Critique of the Gotha Program," p. 529.

37   For discussions of the dictatorship of the proletariat and of the Communist Party in Russia after the 1917 Revolution, see Leszek Kolakowski, *Main Currents in Marxism*, pp. 485–91.

38   V. I. Lenin, "State and Revolution," in *Lenin Anthology*, pp. 378–84.

39   Ingo Mueller, *Hitler's Justice*.

40   See Eduard Tannenbaum, *The Fascist Experience*, pp. 89–116.

41   Paul Tsongas, *The Road from Here*, p. 129.

42   The policy orientations of the Democratic Leadership Council can be found on their website at <www.dlc.org>.

43   Ronald Dworkin, *Taking Rights Seriously*, pp. 223–39.

44   *Grutter v. Bollinger*, 536 U.S. 306 (2003).

45   See John Schaar, "Equal Opportunity and Beyond."

46   Michael Walzer, *Spheres of Justice*, p. xi.

47   Bernard Crick, *Socialism*, p. 90.

48   "SEC Tightens Rules for Executive Pay," available at <www.forbes.com/columists/business/2006/02/09/sec–rules–execpay–cx_0210oxford_e>.

49   Walzer, *Spheres of Justice*, pp. 100–2.

50   Crick, *Socialism*, p. 90.

51   Kymlicka, *Contemporary Political Philosophy*, p. 55.

52   In "What is Equality?" Ronald Dworkin takes up this concern with having distributions that are "endowment insensitive," and tries to do a better a job than Rawls of balancing endowment insensitivity with "ambition sensitivity."

53   Rawls, *Theory of Justice*, p. 78.

54   "Growing Inequality in America's Income Distribution," *The Urban Institute Policy and Research Report* (Winter–Spring 1991), p. 1. The most extensive statistics about income inequalities and fairness of American society are available in *The Green Book*, published annually since 1981 by the House Ways and Means Committee. These data clearly show that the new wealth generated during the 1980's went mostly to the most privileged members of society.

55   These figures are supplied by the Democrats on the Joint Economic Committee, in their September 2005 report "Household Income Unchanged in 2004, But Down Since 2000," available at <jec.senate.gov/democrats/Documents/Reports/income7sep2005.pdf>.

56   Rawls, *Theory of Justice*, ch. 3.

57   Of course, it can be objected that the foundational ideas that people must hold in the original position are themselves problematic. Why, for example, should people be expected to ignore their natural endowments or social circumstances in choosing principles of justice? Or why should people be expected to prefer a risk–free situation where they are guaranteed access to minimal social goods rather than prefer to gamble such a situation for one that provides the possibility for extensive wealth, power, and so forth? Rawls's response to such criticisms is that the ideas in the original position are consistent with our considered judgments about the good life and morality. In 1993, Rawls conceded that his theory may not be universally applicable and applies only to liberal societies where there is a commitment to the fundamental ideas of liberty and equality.

58   In *Contemporary Political Philosophy*, Kymlicka discusses and analyzes many of the outlooks considered here in terms of their relationship to Rawls's *Theory of Justice*.

59   Jacob Hacker, *The Great Risk Shift*.

60   Bruce Ackerman and Anne Alstott, *Stakeholder Society*.

61   As Conley points out, black people have not been able to increase their wealth as rapidly as white people by simply owning homes, because racism has prompted most of them to own homes in locations where the resale value of property is relatively depressed.

62   Conley, *Being Black*, pp. 149–50.

63   Alperovitz, *America Beyond Capitalism*, pp. 81–9.

64   Susan Moller Okin, *Justice, Gender, and Family*.

65   Peter Dreier, John Mollenkopf, and Todd Swanstrom, *Place Matters*.

66   John Rawls, *The Law of Peoples*.

67   James Nichol, *Making Sense of Human Rights*.

68   In *Global Justice*, Charles Jones provides more sustained defenses of the morality of cosmopolitan justice.

69   Important as the Tobin Tax might be for generating global justice, many of its advocates see its primary function as discouraging currency speculation, which introduces crisis-generating volatility in the value of national currencies.

70   According to most advocates, global justice is not economically impossible but only politically unachievable. However, in *Globalization and Justice* (pp. 243–80), Kai Nielsen makes the more optimistic claim that global poverty can be greatly reduced in the not too distant future.

71 For a discussion of the concept of moral hazard, see George Gilder, *Wealth and Poverty*, p. 132.

72 See Lawrence Mead, *Beyond Entitlement*.

73 Nathan Glazer, *The Limits of Social Policy*.

74 See, for example, Thomas Sowell, *Affirmative Action Around the World*.

75 Liberals and the radical left would argue that Sowell's analysis is suspect because factors beyond direct measures of race that produce unequal outcomes (his control variables) are themselves unjustly distributed because of racist practices.

76 Thomas Sowell, *Ethnic America*, pp. 5–7.

77 Sowell, *Ethnic America*, pp. 273–96.

78 Thomas Sowell's discussion of "new racism" at US universities is outlined in his *Inside American Education*, pp. 132–73. Sowell neglects to mention that this racism has also been aimed at Jews, Arabs, and Asians, despite the lack of preferential treatment for members of these groups.

79 Thomas Sowell, *Preferential Policies*, p. 171.

80 Marvin Olasky, *Compassionate Conservatism*, p. 1.

81 Olasky, *Compassionate Conservatism*, p. 18.

82 In *Who Really Cares?*, Arthur Brooks reports extensive charitable contributions by the affluent.

83 Margaret Thatcher, *Statecraft*, p. 431.

84 Thatcher, *Statecraft*, p. 424.

85 Thomas Friedman, *The Lexus and the Olive Tree*, pp. 449–51.

86 Hernando de Soto, *The Mystery of Capital*. Soto's work is discussed by Thatcher in *Statecraft* (p. 416) and by Johan Norberg in his *In Defense of Global Capitalism* (pp. 90–4).

87 Jagdish Bhagwati, *In Defense of Globalization*, p. 53.

88 David Dollar and Aart Kraay, "Trade Growth and Poverty."

89 Gary Burtless et al., *Globalphobia*.

90 Norberg, *In Defense of Global Capitalism*, p. 89.

91 Robert Nozick, *Anarchy, State, and Utopia*, pp. 149–82.

92 Nozick, *Anarchy, State, and Utopia*, p. 163.

93 Hayek, *Law, Legislation, and Liberty*, vol. II.

94 Kymlicka, *Contemporary Political Philosophy*, pp. 209–21.

95 Quoted in Swain, *The New White Nationalism in America*, p. 38.

96 This is not to suggest that devout Christians and Muslims generally have views of justice that lack compassion. To the contrary, there are also many egalitarian aspects in political Islam, such as *Zakat*, which mandates graduated taxes and redistribution of material goods to those in direst need. Islam sees extremes in income and wealth as intolerable.

97 Miahael Hardt and Antonio Negri, *Multitude*, p. 164.

98 Hardt and Negri, *Multitude*, pp. 160–7.

99 Cass Sunstein, "Economic Security: A Human Right."

100 Hayward, "Ecologism and Environmentalism," pp. 358–60.

101 Thomas Regan, *The Case for Animal Rights*.

102 Linux is a powerful and free version of the Unix operating system. The source code for Linux is freely available to everyone, allowing users continuously to refine the system in a collaborative manner. Wikipedia is a set of encyclopedic entries that has been produced collaboratively, where readers can add and amend entries to produce and make available knowledge on a massive number of topics to any Internet user.

103 The underlying consensus in a liberal pluralist society is largely built around the concept of procedural justice, according to Klosko, *Democratic Procedures and the Liberal Consensus*.

104 Widespread support for market justice is reported by Lane, "Market Justice, Political Justice." Related evidence of widespread support for market–based distributions is reported by Herbert McClosky and John Zaller, *The American Ethos*, pp. 80–94.

105 Walzer, *Spheres of Justice*; David Miller and Michael Walzer, *Pluralism, Justice, and Equality*; David Miller, *Principles of Social Justice*.

106 Lane, "Market Justice, Political Justice."

107 Richard Rorty, "Human Rights, Rationality, and Sentimentality"; Grant Reeher, *Narratives of Justice*.

108 John Guidry and Mark Sawyer, "Contentious Pluralism."

109 Hardt and Negri's emphasis on retaining "singularities" suggest an effort on their part to honor the moral autonomy that is central to pluralism. See *Multitude*, pp. 99, 125–9.

110 As discussed in chapter 8, there is a distinction to be made between state neutrality among comprehensive moral doctrines and particular issues where different conceptions of morality come into play. For example, the state must not as a general policy favor Christian morality over the moralities of other religions or secular traditions. But on a specific issue like miscegenation, states must choose among conflicting moral doctrines. Such issues cannot be resolved by appealing to the morality of one particular doctrine but should instead be resolved by appeals to the values that comprise the underlying consensus of pluralism and the consequences of alternative policies for a pluralist society.

CHAPTER 15   QUESTIONS OF CHANGE

1 C. B. Macpherson, *The Life and Times of Liberal Democracy*, pp. 50–64.

2 The limited and sporadic citizen participation in politics that is endorsed by classical liberals may seem unlikely to promote much moral development. In *Personality and Democratic Politics*, Paul Sniderman provides one pessimistic empirical assessment.

3 John Locke, *Two Treatises of Government*, p. 464.

4 Michael Oakeshott, *Rationalism in Politics and Other Essays*, p. 408.

5 Edmund Burke, *Reflections on the Revolution in France* (edited Pater Stanlis), p. 434.

6 Alan Finlayson, "Conservatisms," p. 156.

7 Roger Scruton, *The Meaning of Conservatism*, pp. 37–42.

8 Presenting this orthodox Marxist theory of revolution in such a nutshell is inspired by Roy Macridis, *Contemporary Political Ideologies*, p. 102.

9 There is some evidence that, near the end of his life, Marx thought that the revolution could be achieved by parliamentary means in democratized societies such as England, the United States, Belgium, and the Netherlands.

10 This agenda is outlined in Karl Marx, "Critique of the Gotha Program," in the *Marx–Engels Reader*, pp. 525–41.

11 Ernesto Laclau and Chantel Mouffe, *Hegemony and Socialist Strategy*.

12 Alex Callinicos, *Theories and Narratives*.

13 Mikhail Bakunin, "Letter to La Liberté." Bakunin's criticisms of Marx were published in 1872, when Bakunin and Marx struggled for leadership of the First International Workingmen's Association.

14   Before the split between anarchists and Marxists in the 1870s, some anarchists thought that a minimal government might be needed following the destruction of the old state. For example, Proudhon urged anarchists to make temporary use of the state, because it would remain "the mainspring of society" following a revolution.

15   Bakunin, "Letter to La Liberté," p. 275.

16   Pierre Proudhon, *The General Idea of the Revolution*, p. 44.

17   Robert Dahl stressed the vulnerability of anarchist societies to "gangster states" in *Democracy and Its Critics*, pp. 44–7.

18   Chalmers Johnson, *Autopsy on People's War*, pp. 14–15, 47–53.

19   Johnson, *Autopsy*, pp. 22–30.

20   George Lavan, ed., *Che Guevara Speaks*, p. 31.

21   Antonio Gramsci, "Problems of Marxism," in *Selections from the Prison Notebooks*, pp. 381ff.

22   Paul Starr, *Freedom's Power*.

23   James MacGregor Burns, *Leadership*, pp. 181–95.

24   See, for example, Sidney Verba and Gary Orren, *Equality in America*, pp. 41–8.

25   John Schwarz, *America's Hidden Success*.

26   David Braybrooke and Charles Lindblom defended the rationality of incrementalism in *A Strategy of Decision*.

27   Theodore Lowi, *The End of Liberalism*. Lowi disapproves of these changes.

28   *The Next Agenda*, edited Robert Borosage and Roger Hickey, is an example of such an effort.

29   Jonathan Rauch, "The Accidental Radical."

30   Thomas Friedman, *The Lexus and the Olive Tree*, p. 81.

31   An example of differences in interpretation is provided by Osama bin Laden's apparent doctrine of creating a union of faithful and "non–righteous" followers of Islam to do battle against infidels. Rather than stress jihad as a practice of only those truly faithful to Islam, he has deemphasized the failings of some decadent regimes under which Muslims live in order to have them take part in the struggle against the greater infidels from the West.

32   Francisco Weffort, "The Future of Socialism"; Peter Russell, *The Future of Social Democracy*.

33   A landmark analysis of the repressive aftermath of revolutions remains Albert Camus, *The Rebel*.

34   Sidney Webb, *Socialism in England*, quoted in Bernard Crick's, *Socialism*, p. 68.

35   Crick, *Socialism*, p. 113.

36   Irving Howe, "The First 35 Years Were the Hardest," p. 136.

37   Michael Harrington, "Toward a New Socialism," p. 163.

38   Richard Rorty, *Achieving Our Country*, p. 7.

39   Michel Foucault, "Right of Death and Power over Life," in *The History of Sexuality*.

40   Quoted in *Understanding Power: The Indispensable Chomsky*, edited by Peter Mitchell and John Schoeffel, p. 145.

41   Larissa MacFarquhar, "The Devil's Accountant," p. 75.

42   Michael Hardt and Antonio Negri, *Multitude*, pp. 333, 334, 336.

43   Hardt and Negri, *Multitude*, pp. 351–2.

44   Aldo Leopold, *The Sand County Almanac*.

45   Among the many discussions of a "sustainable society" and the need to reorient human ethics toward ecological values is Andrew Dobson, *Green Political Thought*, pp. 62–111.

46 William Ophuls, *Requiem for Modern Politics*, p. 271.

47 Ophuls, *Requiem for Modern Politics*, pp. 276–7, 278.

48 The World Values Survey shows widespread support for reform, as opposed to revolutionary change or maintenance of the status quo. See Ronald Inglehart, Miguel Basanez, and Alejandro Moreno, *Human Values and Beliefs*, V249.

49 As shown in V242–244, most citizens in the World Values Survey indicate that they have either engaged in peaceful protest or might do so. However, there is considerably less acceptance of disruptive forms of protest among the public than there is among theorists of pluralist democracy. For such theorists, people have the right to engage in disruptive tactics such as demonstrations, boycotts, and strikes and to engage in civil disobedience in order to apply pressure on authorities to respond to their concerns. Such ideas are often contested by more conservative pluralists and thus are not part of the underlying consensus of pluralism.

50 Long ago, I presented evidence suggesting that moderate protest is not only within the bounds of pluralist acceptability but also effective. But when protest becomes too militant, its effectiveness diminishes in pluralist societies. Violence seems most effective in non–pluralist societies. See my "Policy Responsiveness to Protest Group Demands."

51 For a theoretical discussion of the difficulties of "the politics of redemption," see Glenn Tinder, *Political Thinking*, pp. 198–206. In "To the Stalin Mausoleum," Z (an anonymous observer of the Soviet scene) suggests that communism may have been the deadliest utopian fantasy, as its atrocities were responsible for 60–100 million deaths.

52 Martin Luther King, Jr., "Letter from Birmingham Jail," in *Why We Can't Wait*.

53 The first step in this endeavor is to convince leaders and the public that "the green scare" is real and based on compelling scientific evidence. George Bush's refusal to respond more strongly to environmental concerns is sustained by various writings, such as Michael Crichton's *State of Fear*, discounting evidence that ecological doom is on the horizon.

References

Abby, Edward, and David Foreman. *Ecodefense: A Field Guide to Monkeywrenching*. Tuscan, AZ: Ned Ludd, 1987.

Ackerman, Bruce, and Anne Alstott. *Stakeholder Society*. New Haven, CN: Yale University Press, 1999.

Alford, Robert, and Roger Friedland. *Powers of Theory: Capitalism, the State, and Democracy*. Cambridge MA: Cambridge University Press, 1985.

Alperovitz, Gar. *America Beyond Capitalism*. New York: John Wiley, 2005.

American Political Science Association Taskforce. "American Democracy in an Age of Rising Inequality," *Perspectives on Politics 2* (December 2004): 651–66.

Anderson, Charles. *Pragmatic Liberalism*. Chicago: University Press of Chicago, 1990.

Anderson, Charles. "Pragmatic Liberalism: Uniting Theory and Practice," pp. 201–19 in *Liberals on Liberalism*, edited by Alfonso Damico. Totowa NJ: Rowman and Littlefield, 1986.

Arendt, Hannah. *Eichmann in Jerusalem*. New York: Penguin, 1963.

Arendt, Hannah. *The Human Condition*. Chicago: University of Chicago Press, 1958.

Arendt, Hannah. *The Origins of Totalitarianism*. New York: Harcourt, Brace, Jovanovich, 1951.

Bachrach, Peter, and Morton S. Baratz. *Power and Poverty*. New York: Oxford University Press, 1970.

Bakunin, Mikhail. "Letter to La Liberté," pp. 274–85 in *Bakunin on Authority*, edited by Sam Dolgoff. New York: Alfred A. Knopf, 1972 [1872].

Barber, Benjamin. *Strong Democracy*. Berkeley: University of California Press, 1984.

Barkun, Michael. *Religion and the Racist Right*. Chapel Hill: University of North Carolina Press, 1994.

Barry, Brian. "How Not to Defend Liberal Institutions," *British Journal of Political Science 20* (June, 1990): 1–14.

Bay, Christian. "Civil Disobedience: Prerequisite for Democracy in Mass Society," in *Political Theory and Social Change*, edited by David Spitz. New York: Atherton, 1967.

Beck, Ulrich. *What is Globalization?* Cambridge: Polity, 2000.

Beecher, Jonathan, and Richard Bienvenu. *The Utopian Vision of Charles Fourier*. Boston, MA: Beacon, 1971.

Bell, Daniel. *The End of Ideology*. Glencoe, IL: Free Press, 1960.

Bentham, Jeremy. *An Introduction to the Principles of Morals and Legislation*, edited by Wilfred Harrison. Oxford: Basil Blackwell, 1967 [1789].

Bergson, Henri. *The Two Sources of Morality and Religion*, translated by R. Ashley Audra and Cloudesley Brereton. Garden City, NY: Doubleday, 1954 [1935].

Berlin, Isaiah. *Four Essays on Liberty*. London: Oxford University Press, 1969.

Berman, Sherri. "Islamism, Revolution, and Civil Society," *Perspectives on Politics* 1 (June 2003): 257–72.

Bernstein, Eduard. *Evolutionary Socialism*. New York: Schocken, 1961 [1899].

Bhagwati, Jagdish. *In Defense of Globalization*. New York: Oxford University Press, 2004.

Black, Edwin. *War Against the Weak*. New York: Four Walls, Eight Windows, 2003.

Blinder, Alan. "More Like Them?" *The American Prospect* (Winter, 1992): 51–62.

Bloom, Allan. *The Closing of the American Mind*. New York: Simon and Schuster, 1987.

Bluestone, Barry, and Bennett Harrison. *The Deindustrialization of America: Plant Closings, Community Abandonment, and the Dismantling of Basic Industry*. New York: Basic, 1982.

Bobbio, Norberto. *Left & Right: The Significance of a Political Distinction*, translated by Allan Cameron. Chicago: University of Chicago Press, 1996.

Borosage, Robert, and Roger Hickey, eds. *The Next Agenda: Blueprint for a New Progressive Movement*. Boulder, CO: Westview, 2001.

Bottomore, Thomas. *Classes in Modern Society*, 2nd edn. London: HarperCollins Academic, 1991.

Boyte, Harry. *The Backyard Revolution: Understanding the New Citizen Movement*. Philadelphia: Temple University Press, 1980.

Brader, Karl Dietrich. *The German Dictatorship*. New York: Praeger, 1970.

Brand, Donald. "Three Generations of Pluralism," *Political Science Reviewer* 15 (1985): 109–43.

Braybrooke, David, and Charles Lindblom. *A Strategy of Decision*. New York: Free Press, 1963.

Brooker, Paul. "The Nazi Fuehrerprinzip: A Weberian Analysis," pp. 193–9 in *Political Ideologies and Political Philosophies*, edited by H. B. McCullough. Toronto: Wall and Thompson, 1989.

Brooks, Arthur C. *Who Really Cares? The Surprising Truth About Compassionate Conservatism*. New York: Basic, 2006.

Brown, Carl. *Religion and State: The Muslim Approach to Politics*. New York: Columbia University Press, 2000.

Buchanan, Patrick J. *State of Emergency: The Third World Invasion and Conquest of America*. New York: Thomas Dunne Books/St. Martin's Press, 2006.

Buckley, James. *The Jeweler's Eye: A Book of Irresistible Political Reflection*. New York: Putnam, 1968.

Burns, James MacGregor. *Leadership*. New York: Harper and Row, 1978.

Burtless, Gary, Robert Z. Lawrence, Robert E. Litan, and Robert Shapiro. *Globalphobia: Confronting Fears about Open Trade*. Washington DC: Brookings, 1998.

Butler, Judith. "Contingent Foundations: Feminism and the Question of 'Postmodernism'," in *Feminists Theorize the Political*, edited by Judith Butler and Joan Scott. London: Routledge, 1992.

Butler, Judith. "Sexual Inversions," in *Discourses of Sexuality: From Aristotle to Aids*, edited by Domna C. Stanton. Ann Arbor: University of Michigan Press, 1992.

Callahan, David. *The Moral Center*. Orlando, FL: Harcourt, 2006.

Callinicos, Alex. *Theories and Narratives: Reflections on the Philosophy of History*. Cambridge: Polity, 1995.

Camus, Albert. *The Rebel*. New York: Vintage, 1953.

Carens, Joseph H. "Aliens and Citizens: The Case for Open Borders," *Review of Politics* 49 (Spring, 1987): 251–73.

Carver, Terrill. "Marxisms and Post-Marxisms," pp. 198–208 in *Contemporary Political Thought*, edited by Alan Finlayson. New York: New York University Press, 2004.

Chambers, Simone. *Reasonable Democracy: Jürgen Habermas and the Politics of Discourse*. Ithica, NY: Cornell University Press, 1996.

Chomsky, Noam. *Understanding Power: The Indispensable Chomsky*, edited by Peter R. Mitchell and John Schoeffel. New York: New Press, 2002.

Chomsky, Noam. *Imperial Ambitions: Conversations on the Post-9/11 World*, interviews with David Barsamian. New York: Metropolitan, 2005.

Chubb, John E., and Terry M. Moe. *Politics, Markets and America's Schools*. Washington, DC: Brookings, 1990.

Cigler, Allan J., and Mark R. Joslyn. "The Extensiveness of Group Membership and Social Capital: The Impact on Political Tolerance," *Political Research Quarterly* 55 (March 2002): 7–25.

Cohen, G. A. *History, Labour, and Freedom: Themes from Marx*. Oxford: Oxford University Press, 1988.

Cohen, Joshua, and Joel Rogers. *On Democracy*. Hamondsworth, UK: Penguin, 1983.

Cohn, Norman. *The Pursuit of the Millennium*. New York: Oxford University Press, 1970.

Cole, G. D. H. *Self-Government in Industry*. London: G. Bell and Sons, 1919.

Cole, G. D. H. *Social Theory*. London: Frederick A. Stokes Company, 1920.

Coleman, James S., and Sara D. Kelly. "Education," pp. 231–80 in *The Urban Predicament*, edited by William Gorham and Nathan Glazer. Washington DC: The Urban Institute, 1976.

Collins, Chuck, and Felice Veskel. *Economic Apartheid in America*. New York: New Press, 2005.

Conley, Dalton. *Being Black, Living in the Red*. Berkeley: University of California Press, 1999.

Connolly, William E. *Pluralism*. Durham NC: Duke University Press, 2005.

Cooper, Barry. *The End of History: An Essay on Modern Hegelianism*. Toronto: University of Toronto Press, 1984.

Crenson, Matthew A., and Benjamin Ginsberg. *Downsizing Democracy*. Baltimore, MD: Johns Hopkins University Press, 2002.

Crichton, Michael. *State of Fear*. London: HarperCollins, 2004.

Crick, Bernard. *In Defence of Politics*. New York: Penguin, 1962.

Crick, Bernard. *Socialism*. Minneapolis: University of Minnesota Press, 1987.

Cronin, Thomas E. *Direct Democracy*. Cambridge, MA: Harvard University Press, 1989.

Dahl, Robert A. *Democracy and Its Critics*. New Haven, CT: Yale University Press, 1989.

Dahl, Robert A. *Dilemmas of Pluralist Democracy*. New Haven, CT: Yale University Press, 1982.

Dahl, Robert A. *How Democratic is the American Constitution?*, 2nd edn. New Haven, CT: Yale University Press, 2003.

Dahl, Robert A. *On Democracy*. New Haven, CT: Yale University Press, 1998.

Dahl, Robert A. *A Preface to Economic Democracy*. Berkeley, CA: University of California Press, 1985.

Dahl, Robert A. *Who Governs?* New Haven, CT: Yale University Press, 1961.

De Leon, David. *The American Anarchist*. Baltimore, MD: Johns Hopkins University Press, 1971.

DeLue, Steven. *Political Thinking, Political Theory, and Civil Society*, 2nd edn. New York: Longman, 2002.

Descartes, René. *Discourse on Method*, translated by Donald A. Cress. Indianapolis: Hackett Publishing Company, 1980 [1637].

Descartes René. *Meditation on First Philosophy*, translated by Donald A. Cress. Indianapolis: Hackett, 1980 [1641].

Deutsch, Karl. "On Political Theory and Political Action," *American Political Science Review* 65 (March, 1971): 11–27.

Dewey, John. *Liberalism and Social Action*. New York: Putnam, 1935.

Dewey, John. *The Public and Its Problems*. Chicago: Swallow Press, 1954 [1926].

Djilas, Milovan. *The New Class: An Analysis of the Communist System*. New York: Praeger, 1957.

Dobson, Andrew. *Green Political Thought*, 3rd edn. London: Routledge, 2000.

Dolgoff, Sam. *Bakunin on Authority*. New York: Alfred A. Knopf, 1972.

Dollar, David, and Aart Kraay. "Trade Growth and Poverty," World Bank Working Paper 2615. Washington DC: World Bank, 2001.

Domhoff, G. William. *Who Really Rules?* Santa Monica, CA: Goodyear, 1978.

Dreier, Peter, John Mollenkopf, and Todd Swanstrom. *Place Matters*, 2nd edn. Lawrence: University Press of Kansas, 2004.

Durkheim, Emile. *Suicide: A Study in Sociology*, edited by George Simpson. New York: Free Press, 1966 [1897].

Dworkin, Ronald. *Taking Rights Seriously*. Cambridge, MA: Harvard University Press, 1977.

Dworkin, Ronald. "What is Equality?" *Philosophy and Public Affairs* (July and September, 1981): 185–246, 283–345.

Easton, David. *A Systems Analysis of Political Life*. New York: John Wiley, 1965.

Eisenberg, Avigail I. *Reconstructing Political Pluralism*. Albany: State University of New York Press, 1995.

Etzioni, Amitai, Andrew Volmert, and Elanit Rothschild. *The Communitarian Reader: Beyond the Essentials*. Lanham. MD; Rowman and Littlefield, 2004.

Fecher, Charles A. *The Philosophy of Jacques Maritain*. New York: Greenwood, 1953.

Fiorina, Morris P., Samuel J. Abrams, and Jeremy Pope. *Culture War? The Myth of a Polarized America*. New York: Pearson Longman, 2005.

Finlayson, Alan. "Conservatisms," pp. 154–68 in *Contemporary Political Thought*, edited by Finlayson. New York: New York University Press, 2004.

Flathman, Richard, *Pluralism and Liberal Democracy*. Baltimore, MD: Johns Hopkins University Press, 2005.

Flathman, Richard. *Toward a Liberalism*. Ithaca, NY: Cornell University Press, 1992.

Forman, James D. *Fascism: The Meaning and the Experience of Reactionary Revolution*. New York: Dell, 1974.

Foucault, Michel. *Power/Knowledge: Selected Interviews and Other Writings, 1972–1977*, edited by Colin Gordon. New York: Pantheon, 1980.

Foucault, Michel. *The History of Sexuality, Volume 1: An Introduction*, translated by Robert Hurley. London: Penguin, 1978.

Fowler, Robert Booth. "The Anarchist Tradition of Political Thought," *Western Political Quarterly* 26 (December 1973): 738–52.

Fowler, Robert Booth. *The Dance with Community: The Contemporary Debate in American Political Thought*. Lawrence: University Press of Kansas, 1991.

Frank, Thomas. *What's the Matter with Kansas?* New York: Metropolitan Books, 2004.

Freeden, Michael. *Ideology: A Very Short Introduction*. Oxford: Oxford University Press, 2003.

Frieden, Jeffrey A. *Global Capitalism: Its Fall and Rise in the Twentieth Century*. New York: W.W. Norton, 2006.

Friedman, Milton. *Capitalism and Freedom*. Chicago: University of Chicago Press, 1962.

Friedman, Thomas L. *The Lexus and the Olive Tree*. New York: Anchor, 1999.

Friedman, Thomas L. *The World Is Flat*. New York: Farrar, Straus, and Giroux, 2005.

Fromm, Erich. *Escape from Freedom*. London: Farrar & Rinehart, 1941.

Fukuyama, Francis. *The End of History and the Last Man*. New York: Avon, 1992.

Fukuyama, Francis. "The Great Disruption: Human Nature and the Reconstruction of the Social Order," *Atlantic Monthly* (May 1999): 55–80.

Fukuyama, Francis. *State-Building: Governance and World Order in the 21st Century*. Ithaca, NY: Cornell University Press, 2004.

Galbraith, John Kenneth. *The Affluent Society*. Boston, MA: Houghton-Mifflin, 1958.

Galbraith, John Kenneth. *American Capitalism: The Concept of Countervailing Power*. Boston, MA: Houghton-Mifflin, 1952

Galbraith, John Kenneth. *The New Industrial State*. Boston, MA: Houghton-Mifflin, 1967.

Gallaher, Carolyn. *On the Fault Line: Race, Class, and the American Patriot Movement*. Lanham, MD: Rowman & Littlefield, 2003.

Galston, William. "Civic Education in a Liberal State," pp. 89–101 in *Liberalism and the Moral Life*, edited by Nancy Rosenblum. Cambridge, MA: Harvard University Press, 1989.

Galston, William. "Liberal Egalitarian Attitudes Toward Ethical Pluralism," pp. 25–41 in *The Many and the One: Religious and Secular Perspectives on Ethical Pluralism in the Modern World*, edited by Richard Madsen and Traci Strong. Princeton, NJ: Princeton University Press, 2003.

Galston, William. *Liberal Purposes*. New York: Cambridge University Press, 1991.

Galston, William. "Liberalism and Public Morality," pp. 129–47 in *Liberals on Liberalism*, edited by Alfonso J. Damico, Totowa, NJ: Rowman & Littlefield, 1986.

Gentile, Giovanni. "The Philosophical Basis of Fascism," pp. 48–61 in *Readings on Fascism and National Socialism*. Chicago: The Swallow Press, 1952 [1928].

Geoghegan, Thomas. *Whose Side Are You On? Trying to be for Labor when It's Flat on Its Back*. New York: Farrar, Straus, Giroux, 1991.

Gerber, Elizabeth R., and Ken Kollman. "Introduction – Authority Migration: Defining an Emerging Research Agenda," *PS: Political Science and Politics* 2 (July 2004): 397–400.

Gewirth, Alan. "The Epistemology of Human Rights," *Social Philosophy and Policy* 1 (1984).

Gilbert, Daniel. *Stumbling on Happiness*. New York: Alfred A. Knopf, 2006.

Gilder, George. *Wealth and Poverty*. New York: Bantam, 1981.

Gill, Emily. "Goods, Virtues, and the Constitution of the Self," pp. 111–28 in *Liberals on Liberalism*, edited by Alfonso Damico. Totowa NJ: Rowman & Littlefield, 1986.

Glazer, Nathan. *The Limits of Social Policy*. Cambridge, MA: Harvard University Press, 1988.

Glendon, Mary Ann. *Abortion and Divorce in Western Law*. Cambridge, MA: Harvard University Press, 1987.

Glendon, Mary Ann. *Rights Talk*. New York: Free Press, 1991.

Godwin, William. *Enquiry Concerning Political Justice*. Middlesex, UK: Penguin Classics, 1985 [1793].

Goldman, Emma. *Anarchism and Other Essays*. New York: Dover, 1969.

Goldwater, Barry. *The Conscience of a Conservative*. New York: Macfadden, 1960.

Goodin, Robert. *Green Political Theory*. Cambridge: Polity, 1992.

Gorbachev, Mikhail. "The Socialist Idea and Revolutionary Perestroika," *National Affairs* (November 17, 1989): 70–80.

Gramsci, Antonio. *Selections from the Prison Notebooks of Antonio Gramsci*, edited and translated by Quinton Hoare and Geoffrey Nowell Smith. New York: International Publishers, 1971 [1929–36].

Gray, John. *Liberalisms: Essays in Political Philosophy*. London: Routledge, 1989.

Green, Joshua. "Roy and His Rock," *Atlantic Monthly* (October 2005): 70–82.

Green, Thomas Hill. *Lectures on the Principles of Political Obligation*. London: Longman, Green, 1907 [1886].

Guidry, John A., and Mark Q. Sawyer. "Contentious Pluralism: The Public Sphere and Democracy," *Perspectives on Politics* 1 (June 2003): 273–89.

Gutmann, Amy, and Dennis Thompson. *Why Deliberative Democracy?* Princeton NJ: Princeton University Press, 2003.

Habermas, Jürgen. *Legitimation Crisis*, translated by Thomas McCarthy. Boston, MA: Beacon, 1975.

Hacker, Frederick. *Crusaders, Criminals, Crazies: Terror and Terrorism in Our Time*. New York: Norton, 1996.

Hacker, Jacob S. *The Great Risk Shift*. New York: Oxford University Press, 2006.

Hamilton, Alexander, James Madison, and John Jay. *The Federalist Papers*, edited by Issac Kramnick. New York: Penguin, 1987.

Hardt, Michael, and Antonio Negri. *Empire*. Cambridge, MA: Harvard University Press, 2000.

Hardt, Michael, and Antonio Negri. *Multitude: War and Democracy in the Age of Empire*. New York: Penguin, 2004.

Harrington, Michael. "Toward a New Socialism," *Dissent* (Spring 1989): 153–63.

Harrison, Lawrence E., and Samuel P. Huntington. *Culture Matters: How Values Shape Human Progress*. New York: Basic Books, 2000.

Hartz, Louis. *The Liberal Tradition in America*. New York: Harcourt, Brace, 1955.

Harvey, David. *A Brief History of Neoliberalism*. New York: Oxford University Press, 2005.

Hawley, Willis. *Nonpartisan Elections and the Case for Party Politics*. New York: John Wiley, 1973.

Hayek, Friedrich A. von. *Law, Legislation, and Liberty, Volume II. The Mirage of Social Justice*. Chicago: University of Chicago Press, 1976,

Hayek, Friedrich A. von. *Law, Legislation, and Liberty, Volume III. Political Order of a Free People*. Chicago: University of Chicago Press, 1979.

Hayward, Tim. "Ecologism and Environmentalism," pp. 351–63 in *Contemporary Political Thought*, edited by Alan Finlayson. New York: New York University Press, 2004.

Heilbroner, Robert L. *The Worldly Philosophers*. New York: Simon and Schuster, 1953.

Henig, Jeffrey. *Neighborhood Mobilization*. New Brunswick, NJ: Rutgers University Press, 1982.

Henig, Jeffrey. *Rethinking School Choice*. Princeton, NJ: Princeton University Press, 1994.

Herzen, Alexander. *From the Other Shore*, translated by Moura Budberg. London: Weidenfeld and Nicolson, 1956 [1850].

Hirschman, Albert O. *The Passions and the Interests: Political Arguments for Capitalism Before its Triumph*. Princeton: Princeton University Press, 1977.

Hirschman, Albert O. *The Rhetoric of Reaction: Perversity, Futility, and Jeopardy*. Cambridge, MA: Belknap Press, 1991.

Hitler, Adolf. *Mein Kampf*, translated by Ralph Mannheim. Boston, MA: Houghton Mifflin, 1971 [1925–6].

Hobbes, Thomas. *Leviathan*, edited by C. B. Macpherson. New York: Penguin, 1968 [1651].

Hochschild, Jennifer. *What's Fair?* Cambridge, MA: Harvard University Press, 1981.

Hoeveler, David. *Watch on the Right*. Madison: University of Wisconsin Press, 1991.

Hofstadter, Richard. *The American Political Tradition and the Men Who Made It*. New York: Vintage, 1948.

Houtart, Francis, and Francois Polet. *The Other Davos: The Globalization of Resistance to the New World Economic System*. New York: Zed Books, 2001.

Howe, Irving. "The First 35 Years Were the Hardest," *Dissent* (Spring 1989): 133–6.

Huntington, Samuel P. "The Democratic Distemper," *The Public Interest* (Fall 1975): 9–38.

Huntington, Samuel P. *The Clash of Civilizations*. New York: Simon and Schuster, 1996.

Huntington, Samuel P. *Who Are We? The Challenge to American National Identity*. New York: Simon and Schuster, 2004.

Huxley, T. H. "Evolution and Ethics," in *Selections from the Essays of Huxley*, edited by Alburey Castell. Arlington Heights, IL: Crofts Classics, 1948 [1893].

Ingersoll, David E., Richard K. Matthews, and Andrew Davison. *The Philosophic Roots of Modern Ideology: Liberalism, Communism, Fascism*, 3rd edn. Upper Saddle River, NJ: Prentice-Hall, 2001.

Inglehart, Ronald. *Culture Shift in Advanced Industrial Societies*. Princeton, NJ: Princeton University Press, 1990.

Inglehart, Ronald. *Human Values and Social Change*. Lieden, Netherlands: Brill, 2003.

Inglehart, Ronald, Miguel Basanez, and Alejandro Moreno. *Human Values and Beliefs: A Cross-National Sourcebook*. Ann Arbor: University of Michigan Press, 1998.

Jenkins, Philip. "The Next Christianity," *Atlantic Monthly* (October 2002): 53–68.

Johnson, Chalmers. *Anatomy on People's War*. Berkeley: University of California Press, 1973.

Jones, Charles. *Global Justice: Defending Cosmopolitanism*. New York: Oxford University Press, 1999.

Judis, John B., and Michael Lind. "For a New American Nationalism," *The New Republic* (March 27, 1995): 27–30.

Kagan, Donald, Steven Ozment, and Frank Turner. *The Western Heritage*, 6th edition. Upper Saddle River, NJ: Prentice-Hall, 1998.

Kaplan, Robert. "Was Democracy Just a Moment?" *Atlantic Monthly* (December 1997): 55–80.

Kariel, Henry. "Creating Political Reality," *American Political Science Review* 64 (December 1970): 1088–98.

Kaus, Mickey. *The End of Equality*. New York: Basic, 1992.

Kekes, John. *Pluralism in Philosophy: Changing the Subject*. Ithaca, NY: Cornell University Press, 2000.

Kepel, Gilles. *The Revenge of God: The Resurgence of Islam, Christianity and Judaism in the Modern World*, translated by Alan Braley. University Park: Pennsylvania State University Press, 1994.

Kepel, Gilles. *War for Muslim Minds: Islam and the West*, translated by Pascale Ghazalch. Cambridge, MA: Belknap Press, 2004.

Key, V. O. Jr. *The Responsible Electorate*. Cambridge, MA: Harvard University Press 1966.

Keynes, John Maynard. *The Collected Writings of John Maynard Keynes*, edited by Donald Moggridge. London: Macmillan, 1980.

King, Martin Luther, Jr. *Why We Can't Wait*. New York: Harper & Row, 1963.

Kirk, Russell, ed. *The Portable Conservative Reader*. New York: Penguin, 1982.

Kirk, Russell. *A Program for Conservatives*. Chicago: Henry Regnery, 1954.

Kirkpatrick, Jeane. "Politics and the 'New Class'," *Society* 16: (January/February 1979): 42–48.

Klosko, George. *Democratic Procedures and the Liberal Consensus*. New York: Oxford University Press, 2000.

Knight, Kathleen. "Transformations of the Concept of Ideology in the Twentieth Century," *American Political Science Review* 100 (November 2006): 619–26.

Kolakowski, Leszek. *Main Currents in Marxism, Volume 2. The Golden Age*, translated by P. S. Falla. Oxford: Oxford University Press, 1978.

Korten, David C. "A Planetary Alternative to the Global Economy," *Synthesis/Regeneration* (Winter 2000).

Krauthammer, Charles. "A Social Conservative Credo," *The Public Interest* (Fall 1996): 15–22.

Kristol, Irving. *Two Cheers for Capitalism*. New York: Basic Books, 1978.

Kropotkin, Peter. *Revolutionary Pamphlets*. New York: Vanguard, 1927.

Kropotkin, Peter. *Mutual Aid: A Factor in Evolution*. New York: New York University Press, 1972.

Krouse, Richard, and Michael McPherson. "Capitalism, 'Property Owning Democracy' and the Welfare State," pp. 79–106 in *Democracy and the Welfare State*, edited by Amy Gutmann. Princeton, NJ: Princeton University Press, 1988.

Kuhn, Thomas. *The Structure of Scientific Revolutions*. Chicago: University of Chicago Press, 1962.

Kuttner, Robert. "Socialism, Liberalism, and Democracy," *The American Prospect* (Spring 1992): 7–12.

Kymlicka, Will. "Liberalism and Communitarianism," *Canadian Journal of Philosophy*, 118 (June 1988): 181–203.

Kymlicka, Will. *Contemporary Political Philosophy*, 2nd edn. New York: Oxford University Press, 2002.

LaHaye, Tim F., and Jerry B. Jenkins. *Left Behind: A Novel of the Earth's Last Days*. Wheaton, ILL: Tyndale House, 1995.

Laclau, Earnesto, and Chantel Mouffe. *Hegemony and Socialist Strategy*. London: Verso, 1985.

Landes, David. "Culture Almost Makes All the Difference," in *Culture Matters: How Values Shape Human Progress*, edited by Lawrence E. Harrison and Samuel P. Huntington. New York: Basic Books, 2000.

Lane, Robert. *Political Ideology: Why the Common Man Believes What He Does*. New York: Free Press, 1962.

Lane, Robert. "Market Justice, Political Justice," *American Political Science Review* 80 (June 1986): 383–402.

Lavan, George, ed. *Che Guevara Speaks*. New York: Pathfinder, 1983.

Lenin, Vladimir I. *The Lenin Anthology*, edited by Robert C. Tucker. New York: Norton, 1975.

Leopold, Aldo. *The Sand County Almanac*. New York: Oxford University Press, 1947.

Lerner, Daniel. *The Passing of the Traditional Society*. Glencoe, IL: Free Press, 1959.

Lewis, Bernard. *The Crisis of Islam: Holy War and Holy Terror*. New York: Modern Library, 2003.

Lifton, Jay. *The Nazi Doctors: Medical Killing and the Psychology of Genocide*. New York: Basic, 1986.

Lijphart, Arend. *Democracy in Plural Societies*. New Haven, CN: Yale University Press, 1977.

Limbaugh, Rush. *The Way Things Ought to Be*. New York: Pocket Star, 1992.

Lindblom, Charles E. *Politics and Markets*. New York: Basic Books, 1977.

Linker, Damon. *The Theocons: Secular America Under Siege*. New York: Doubleday, 2006.

Lipset, Seymour Martin, and Gary Marks. *It Didn't Happen Here*. New York: Norton, 2000.

Locke, John. *Letter Concerning Toleration*, edited by Patrick Romanell. Indianapolis, IN: Bobbs-Merrill, 1950 [1689].

Locke, John. *Two Treatises of Government*, edited by Peter Laslett. New York: Mentor, 1960 [1690].

Logan, John R., and Harvey Molotch. *Urban Fortunes*. Berkeley: University of California Press, 1987.

Lowi, Theodore J. *The End of Liberalism: The Second Republic of the United States*. New York: Norton, 1979.

Lowi, Theodore J. *The End of the Republican Era*. Norman: University of Oklahoma Press, 1995.

Lukes, Steven. *Marxism and Morality*. Oxford: Oxford University Press, 1987.

Lukes, Steven. *Power: A Radical View*. London: Macmillan, 1974.

Lustig, R. Jeffrey. *Corporate Liberalism*. Berkeley: University Press of California, 1982.

MacFarquhar, Larissa. "The Devil's Accountant," *The New Yorker* (March 31, 2003): 64–79.

MacIntyre, Alasdair. *After Virtue*, 2nd edn. Notre Dame, IN: University of Notre Dame Press, 1984.

MacKinnon, Catherine. *Feminism Unmodified: Discourses on Life and Law*. Cambridge, MA: Harvard University Press, 1977.

MacKinnon, Catherine. *Toward a Feminist Theory of the State*. Cambridge, MA: Harvard University Press, 1989.

Macpherson, C. B. *The Life and Times of Liberal Democracy*. New York: Oxford University Press, 1977.

Macridis, Roy. *Contemporary Political Ideologies*, 3rd edn. Boston, MA: Little, Brown, 1986.

Madsen, Richard, and Traci Strong, eds. *The Many and the One: Religious and Secular Perspectives on Ethical Pluralism in the Modern World*. Princeton, NJ: Princeton University Press, 2003.

Manley, John. "Neopluralism: A Case Analysis of Pluralism I and Pluralism II," *American Political Science Review* 77 (June 1983): 368–89.

Mannheim, Karl. *Ideology and Utopia*. London: Routledge and Kegan Paul, 1936.

Mansbridge. Jane. *Beyond Adversarial Democracy*. Chicago: University of Chicago Press, 1980.

Mao Zedong. "On Practice," in *The Collected Works of Mao Tse-tung*. Arlington, VA: Joint Publication Research Service, 1978 [1937].

Marsh, Margaret S. *Anarchist Women, 1870–1920*. Philadelphia, PA: Temple University Press, 1981.

Marx, Karl, and Friedrich Engels. *The Marx-Engels Reader*, 2nd edn., edited by Robert C. Tucker. New York: Norton, 1978.

Marzorati, Gerald et al. "Who Owes What to Whom?" *Harper's Magazine* 282 (February 1991): 44–54.

Mayer, William G. *The Changing American Mind*. Ann Arbor: University of Michigan Press, 1992.

McClosky, Herbert, and John Zaller. *The American Ethos: Public Attitudes Toward Capitalism and Democracy*. Cambridge, MA: Harvard University Press, 1984.

McCoy, Charles. *Contemporary ISMS: A Political Economy Perspective*. New York: Franklin Watts, 1982.

McLellan, David. *Karl Marx: His Life and Thought*. New York: Harper and Row, 1973.

McLellan, David. *Marxism after Marx*. Boston, MA: Houghton Mifflin, 1979.

Mead, Lawrence M. *Beyond Entitlement: The Social Obligations of Citizenship*. New York: Free Press, 1986.

Mehlinger, Howard. *Communism in Theory and Practice*. San Francisco, CA: Chandler, 1964.

Meyer, Alfred. *Communism*, 4th edn. New York: Random House, 1984.

Milanovic, Branko. *Worlds Apart*. Princeton, NJ: Princeton University Press, 2005.

Mill, James. *Essay on Government*, edited by Jack Lively and John Rees, Oxford: Clarendon Press, 1978 [1820].

Mill, John Stuart. *On Liberty*, edited by Elizabeth Rapaport. Indianapolis: Hackett, 1978 [1859].

Mill, John Stuart. *Utilitarianism*, edited by Oskar Piest. Indianapolis: Bobbs-Merrill, 1957 [1861].

Miller, David, and Michael Walzer, eds. *Pluralism, Justice, and Equality*. New York: Oxford University Press, 1995.

Miller, David. *Principles of Social Justice*. Cambridge, MA: Harvard University Press, 1995.

Mills, C. Wright. *The Power Elite*. New York: Oxford University Press, 1956.

Mitchell, William C. "Efficiency, Responsibility, and Democratic Politics," pp. 343–73 in *Liberal Democracy, Nomos XXV*, edited by J. Roland Pennock and John W. Chapman. New York: New York University Press, 1983.

Mohanty, Chandra Talpade. "Women, Workers, and Capitalist Scripts," in *Feminist Genealogies, Colonial Legacies, Democratic Futures*, edited by M. Jacqui Alexander and C. T. Mohanty. New York: Routledge, 1997.

Mouffe, Chantel. *The Return of the Political*. London: Verso, 1993.

Moussalli, Ahmad. *Moderate and Radical Islamic Fundamentalism*. Tallahassee: University of Florida Press, 1999.

Mueller, Ingo. *Hitler's Justice*. Cambridge, MA: Harvard University Press.

Murray, Charles A. *Human Accomplishment: The Pursuit of Excellence in the Arts and Sciences, 300 BC to 1950*. New York: Harper Collins, 2003.

Murray, Charles A. and Richard Hernstein. *The Bell Curve*. New York: Free Press, 1994.

Mussolini, Benito. "The Doctrine of Fascism," pp. 7–25 in *Readings on Fascism and National Socialism*. Chicago: Swallow, 1952 [1928].

Myrdal, Gunner. *The American Dilemma: The Negro Problem and American Democracy*. New York: Harper & Brothers, 1944.

Nichol, James W. *Making Sense of Human Rights*, 2nd edn. Malden, MA: Blackwell Publishing, 2007.

Nielsen, Kai. *Globalization and Justice*. Amherst, NY: Humanities Books, 2003.

Niemi, Richard G., John Mueller, and Tom W. Smith. *Trends in Public Opinion*. New York: Greenwood, 1989.

Nisbet, Robert. *Conservatism: Dream and Reality*. Minneapolis: University of Minnesota Press, 1986.

Norberg, Johan. *In Defense of Global Capitalism.* Washington, DC: Cato, 2003.

Nove, Alec. *The Economics of Feasible Socialism Revisited.* London: Harper Collins, 1991.

Nozick, Robert. *Anarchy, State, and Utopia.* New York: Basic Books, 1974.

Nozick, Robert. *The Examined Life.* New York: Simon and Schuster, 1989.

O'Brien, Conor Cruise. "Thomas Jefferson: Radical and Racist," *Atlantic Monthly* (October 1999): 53–66.

O'Sullivan, Noel. *Conservatism.* London: J. M. Dent, 1976.

Oakeshott, Michael. *Rationalism in Politics and Other Essays.* New York: Basic Books, 1962.

Okin, Susan Moller. *Justice, Gender, and the Family.* New York: Basic Books, 1989.

Okun, Arthur. *Equality and Efficiency: The Big Tradeoff.* Washington, DC: Brookings, 1975.

Olasky, Marvin. *Compassionate Conservatism.* New York: Free Press, 2000.

Olson, Mancur. *The Logic of Collective Action.* Cambridge, MA: Harvard University Press, 1971.

Olson, Mancur. "Rapid Growth as a Destabilizing Force," *Journal of Economic History* 23 (1963): 529–58.

Ophuls, William. *Requiem for Modern Politics.* Boulder, CO: Westview, 1997.

Ortega y Gasset, José. *The Revolt of the Masses.* New York: Norton, 1957 [1930].

Ottonelli, Valeria. "Immigration: What Does Global Justice Require?" pp. 231–41 in *Global Citizenship: A Critical Introduction,* edited by Nigel Dower and John Williams. New York: Routledge, 2002.

Paine, Thomas. *The Rights of Man.* New York: Penguin, 1984 [1791].

Palast, Greg. *The Best Democracy Money Can Buy.* New York: Plume/Penguin, 2002.

Parekh, Bhikhu. *Rethinking Multiculturalism: Cultural Diversity and Political Theory.* London: Macmillan, 2000.

Pateman, Carole. *Participation and Democratic Theory.* New York: Cambridge University Press, 1970.

Payne, James. "The Congressional Brainwashing of Congress," *The Public Interest* (Summer 1990): 3–13.

Pennock, J. Roland. "Liberalism Under Attack," *The Political Science Teacher* 3 (Winter 1990): 6–9.

Peterson, Paul. *City Limits.* Chicago: University of Chicago Press, 1981.

Phillips, Anne. *Engendering Democracy.* University Park: Pennsylvania State University, 1991.

Phillips, Derek L. *Looking Backward: A Critical Appraisal of Communitarian Thought.* Princeton, NJ: Princeton University Press, 1993.

Pitkin, Hannah F. *The Concept of Representation.* Berkeley: University of California Press, 1967.

Plato. *Five Dialogues,* translated by G. M. A. Grube. Indianapolis IN: Hackett, 1981.

Podhoretz, Norman. "World War IV: How it Started, What it Means, and Why we Have to Win," *Commentary* 118 (September 2004): 17–38.

Pogge, Thomas, ed. *Global Justice.* Malden, MA: Blackwell, 2001.

Pojman, Louis, P. *Who Are We? Theories of Human Nature.* New York: Oxford, 2006.

Polanyi, Karl. *The Great Transformation: The Political and Economic Origins of Our Time.* Boston, MA: Beacon, 1944.

Postman, Neil. *Amusing Ourselves to Death.* New York: Penguin, 1985.

Proudhon, Pierre. *The General Idea of the Revolution in the Nineteenth Century,* translated by John B. Robinson. New York: Haskell House, 1923 [1851].

Przeworski, Adam. *Democracy and the Market: Political and Economic Reform in Eastern Europe and Latin America.* Cambridge: Cambridge University Press, 1991.

Putnam, Robert. *Bowling Alone*. Cambridge, MA: University of Harvard Press, 2000.

Rae, Douglas. *Equalities*. Cambridge, MA: Harvard University Press, 1981.

Rand, Ayn, *The Fountainhead*. The New American Library, 1943.

Rauch, Jonathan. "The Accidental Radical," *National Journal* (July 26, 2003): 2404–10.

Rauch, Jonathan. "The Forgotten Millions," *Atlantic Monthly* (December 2003): 27–8.

Rawls, John. "Justice as Fairness: Political not Metaphysical," *Philosophy and Public Affairs* 14 (1985): 223–51.

Rawls, John. *Political Liberalism*. New York: Columbia University Press, 1993.

Rawls, John. *A Theory of Justice*, rev. edn. Cambridge, MA: Harvard University Press, 1999.

Rawls, John. *The Law of Peoples*. Cambridge, MA: Harvard University Press, 1999.

Reeher, Grant. *Narratives of Justice*. Ann Arbor: University of Michigan Press, 1996.

Regan, Thomas. *The Case for Animal Rights*. Berkeley: University of California Press, 1985.

Reich, Robert. "The Nationalism We Need," *The American Prospect* (December 1999): 64.

Reiman, Jeffrey H. *In Defense of Political Philosophy: A Reply to Robert Paul Wolff's In Defense of Anarchism*. New York: Harper Torchbacks, 1972.

Ricci, David. "Receiving Ideas in Political Analysis: The Case of Community Power Studies, 1950–1970," *Western Political Quarterly* 33 (December 1980): 451–75.

Ricci, David. *The Tragedy of Political Science: Politics, Scholarship and Democracy*. New Haven, CT: Yale University Press, 1984.

Ridgeway, James. *Blood in the Face: The Ku Klux Klan, Aryan Nations, Nazi Skinheads, and the Rise of New White Culture*. New York: Thunder Mouth Press, 1995.

Riker, William. *Liberalism Against Populism*. San Francisco, CA: Freeman, 1982.

Risen, James, and Judy L. Thomas. *Wrath of Angels: The American Abortion War*. New York: Basic Books, 1998.

Rocco, Alfredo. "The Political Doctrine of Fascism," pp. 25–47 in *Readings on Fascism and National Socialism*. Chicago: Swallow, 1952.

Roemer, John. *Free to Lose: An Introduction to Marxist Economic Philosophy*. Cambridge, MA: Harvard University Press, 1988.

Rorty, Richard. *Achieving Our Country*. Cambridge, MA: Harvard University Press, 1998.

Rorty, Richard. "Human Rights, Rationality, and Sentimentality," pp. 111–34 in *Human Rights: Oxford Humanities Lectures*, edited by Stephen Shute and Susan Hurley. New York: Basic Books, 1993.

Rorty, Richard. *Consequences of Pragmatism*. Minneapolis: University of Minnesota Press, 1982.

Rorty, Richard. *Truth and Progress*. New York: Cambridge University Press, 1998.

Roszak, Theodore. *Person/Planet*. New York: Anchor Press/Doubleday, 1978.

Rothenberg, Randall. "Nozick v. Rawls," *Esquire* (March 1983): 201–9.

Rousseau, Jean-Jacques. *Basic Writings*, translated and edited by Donald A. Cress. Indianapolis: Hackett, 1978 [1755–62].

Russell, Peter, ed. *The Future of Social Democracy: Views of Leaders from Around the World*. Toronto: University of Toronto Press, 1999.

Russett, Bruce. *Controlling the Sword: The Democratic Governance of National Security*. Cambridge, MA: Harvard University Press, 1990.

Sandel, Michael J. *Liberalism and the Limits of Justice*. New York: Cambridge University Press, 1982.

Sandel, Michael J. "Morality and the Liberal Ideal," *New Republic* (1984): 15–17.

Sandel, Michael J. *Democracy's Discontent: America in Search for a Public Philosophy*. Cambridge, MA: Harvard University Press, 1996.

Sandel, Michael J. "America's Search for a New Public Philosophy," *Atlantic Monthly* (March 1996): 57–84.

Schaar, John. "Equal Opportunity and Beyond," in *Equality: Nomos IX*, edited by J. Roland Pennock and John W. Chapman. New York: Atherton, 1967.

Schuck, Paul H. "The Great Immigration Debate," in *The American Prospect* (Fall 1990): 100–17.

Schumacher, E. F. *Small is Beautiful*. New York: Harper and Row, 1975.

Schumaker, Paul. *Critical Pluralism, Democratic Performance, and Community Power*. Lawrence: University Press of Kansas, 1991.

Schumaker, Paul. "Policy Responsiveness to Protest Group Demands," *Journal of Politics* 37 (May 1975): 488–521.

Schumaker, Paul, Dwight Kiel, and Thomas Heilke, *Great Ideas/Grand Schemes: Political Ideologies in the 19th and 20th Centuries*. New York: McGraw-Hill, 1996.

Schumaker, Paul, and Burdett Loomis, eds. *Choosing a President: The Electoral College and Beyond*. New York: Chatham House, 2002.

Schumaker, Paul, and Bruce Oppenheimer. "Electoral College Reform at the State Level: Options and Tradeoffs," pp. 192–212 in *Counting Votes: Lessons from the 2004 Election in Florida*, edited by Robert Watson. Tallahassee: University Press of Florida, 2004.

Schumpeter, Joseph. *Capitalism, Socialism, and Democracy*. New York: Harper and Row, 1942.

Schwarz, John. *America's Hidden Success*. New York: Norton, 1983.

Scruton, Roger. *The Meaning of Conservatism*. London: Macmillan, 1984.

Sharansky, Natan. *The Case for Democracy*. New York: Public Affairs, 2004.

Sheeham, Helena. *Marxism and the Philosophy of Science: A Critical History*. Atlantic Highlands, NJ: Humanities Press International, 1993.

Shklar, Judith. *After Utopia: The Decline of Political Faith*. Princeton, NJ: Princeton University Press, 1957.

Sibley, Mulford Q. *Political Ideas and Ideologies: A History of Political Thought*. New York: Harper & Row, 1970.

Sim, Stuart. *Post-Marxism: An Intellectual History*. London: Routledge, 2000.

Sivan, Emmanuel. *Radical Islam: Medieval Theology and Modern Politics*. New Haven, CT: Yale University Press, 1990.

Skocpol, Theda. *Social Revolution in the Modern World*. New York: Cambridge University Press, 1994.

Smith, Adam. *The Wealth of Nations*, in *Adam Smith's Moral and Political Philosophy*, edited by Herbert W. Schneider. New York: Hafner, 1948 [1776].

Smith, Anna Marie. "Democratic Theory for a New Century," pp. 559–70 in *Contemporary Political Theory*, edited by Alan Finlayson. New York: New York University Press, 2004.

Smith, Christian. *Christian America: What Evangelicals Really Want*. Berkeley: University of California Press, 2000.

Smith, Houston. *The Religions of Man*. New York: Mentor, 1958.

Smith, Rogers M. *Civic Ideals*. New Haven, CT: Yale University Press, 1997.

Smith, Tony. *Thinking Like a Communist: State and Legitimacy in the Soviet Union, China, and Cuba*. New York: Norton, 1987.

Sniderman, Paul. *Personality and Democratic Theory*. Berkeley: University of California Press, 1975.

Soros, George. *The Crisis of Global Capitalism*. New York: Public Affairs, 1998.

Soto, Hernando de. *The Mystery of Capital: Why Capitalism Triumphs in the West and Fails Everywhere Else*. New York: Basic Books, 2000.

Sowell, Thomas. *Affirmative Action Around the World*. New Haven, CT: Yale University Press, 2004.

Sowell, Thomas. *Ethnic America: A History*. New York: Basic Books, 1981.

Sowell, Thomas. *Inside American Education: The Decline, the Deception, and the Dogma*. New York: Free Press, 1993.

Sowell, Thomas. *Preferential Policies: An International Perspective*. New York: Quell, 1990.

Speer, Albert. *Inside the Third Reich: Memoirs*, translated by Richard and Clara Winston. New York: Macmillan, 1970.

Spencer, Herbert. *The Man Versus The State*. Caldwell, ID: Caxton Press, n.d. [1892].

Spinner-Halev, Jeff, and Elizabeth Theiss-Morse. "National Identity and Self-Esteem," *Perspectives on Politics* 1 (September 2003): 515–32.

Spitz, Elaine. "Citizenship and Liberal Institutions," pp. 185–90 in *Liberals on Liberalism*, edited by Alfonso J. Damico. Totowa, NJ: Rowman and Littlefield, 1986.

Spragens, Thomas. *The Irony of Liberal Reason*. Chicago: University of Chicago Press, 1981.

Stalin, Joseph. *Dialectical and Historical Materialism*. Tirana: The "8 Nentori" Publishing House, 1979 [1938].

Stanlis, Peter J., ed. *Edmund Burke: Selected Writings and Speeches*, Garden City, NY: Anchor, 1963.

Starr, Paul. *Freedom's Power: The True Force of Liberalism*. New York: Basic Books, 2007.

Starr, Paul. "Liberalism After Socialism, *The American Prospect* (Fall 1991): 70–80.

Steger, Manfred B. *Globalism: The New Market Ideology*. Lanham, MD: Rowman & Littlefield, 2002.

Steger, Manfred B. *Globalism: Market Ideology Meets Terrorism*. Lanham, MD: Rowman & Littlefield, 2005.

Stigler, George. "Director's Law of Public Income Distribution," *Journal of Law and Economics* 13 (April 1970): 1–10.

Stirner, Max (Johann Kaspar Schmidt). *The Ego and His Own*, translated by S. T. Bylington. London: Jonathan Cape, 1921 [1843].

Storing, Herbert J., ed. *Essays on the Scientific Study of Politics*. New York: Holt, Rinehart, and Winston, 1962.

Strauss, Leo. "The New Political Science," *American Conservative Thought in the 20th Century*, edited by William F. Buckley, Jr. Indianapolis: Bobbs-Merrill, 1970.

Sullivan, John, James Piereson, and George E. Marcus. *Political Tolerance and American Democracy*. Chicago: University of Chicago Press, 1982.

Sundquist, James. *Policies and Politics: The Eisenhower, Kennedy, and Johnson Years*. Washington, DC: Brookings, 1968.

Sunstein, Cass. "Economic Security: A Human Right," *The American Prospect* (October 2004): A24–A26.

Swain, Carol. *The New White Nationalism in America: Its Challenge to Integration*. New York: Cambridge University Press, 2002.

Tannenbaum, Eduard. *The Fascist Experience: Italian Society and Culture, 1922–1945*. New York: Basic Books, 1972.

Taylor, Charles. *Hegel and Modern Society*. New York: Cambridge University Press, 1979.

Terchek, Ronald, and Thomas Conte, eds. *Theories of Democracy*. Landon, MD: Rowman & Littlefield, 2001.

Thatcher, Margaret. *Statecraft*. New York: Harper Collins, 2002.

Thompson, Dennis F. *Just Elections: Creating a Fair Electoral Process in the United States*. Chicago: University of Chicago Press, 2003.

Thompson, John B. *Studies in the Theory of Ideology*. Cambridge: Polity, 1984.

Thurow, Lester. *The Future of Capitalism*. New York: William Morrow, 1996.

Thurow, Lester. *The Zero Sum Society*. New York: Penguin, 1980.

Tinder, Glenn. *Political Thinking: The Perennial Questions*, 6th edn. New York: Pearson Longman, 2004.

Tocqueville, Alexis de. *Democracy in America*, translated by Gerald E. Bevan. New York: Vintage, 1945 [1835–40].

Tolstoy, Leo. *The Kingdom of God is Within You*, translated by Leo Wiener. New York: Noonday Press of Farrar, Straus, and Giroux, 1961 [1905].

Tomasky, Michael. "A Perfect Storm," *The American Prospect* (October 2005): 23–6.

Tomasky, Michael. "A Party in Search of a Notion," *The American Prospect* (May 2006): 20–8.

Tong, Rosemary. *Feminist Thought: A More Comprehensive Introduction*. Boulder, CO: Westview, 1998.

Tribe, Lawrence. "Ways Not to Think About Plastic Trees: New Foundations for Environmental Laws." *Yale Law Review* 83 (Fall 1974): 1314–48.

Truman, David. *The Governmental Process*. New York: Knopf, 1951.

Tsongas, Paul. *The Road from Here: Liberalism and Realities in the 1980s*. New York: Knopf, 1981.

Tucker, Robert C. *The Marxian Revolutionary Idea*. New York: Norton, 1969.

Tullock, Gordon. *Public Goods, Redistribution, and Rent-Seeking*. Northampton, MA: Edward Elgar, 2005.

Varshney, Ashutosh. "Nationalism, Ethnic Conflict, and Rationality," *Perspectives On Politics* 1 (March 2003), 85–99.

Verba, Sidney, and Gary Orren. *Equality in America*. Cambridge, MA: Harvard University Press, 1985.

Walzer Michael. "A Day in the Life of a Socialist Citizen," pp. 229–38 in *Obligations: Essays on Disobedience, War, and Citizenship*. Cambridge, MA: Harvard University Press, 1970.

Walzer, Michael. "The Community," *New Republic* (March 31, 1982): 11–14.

Walzer, Michael. "Socializing the Welfare State," *Dissent* (Summer 1988): 292–300.

Walzer, Michael. *Spheres of Justice*. New York: Basic Books, 1983.

Wartenberg, Thomas. *The Forms of Power*. Philadelphia: Temple University Press, 1990.

Weber, Max. *The Protestant Ethic and the Spirit of Capitalism*, translated by Talcott Parsons. New York: Scribner, 1976 [1904].

Weffort, Francisco. "The Future of Socialism," *Journal of Democracy* 3 (July, 1992): 90–9.

Weinstein, James. *The Corporate Ideal and the Liberal State*. Boston, MA: Beacon, 1966.

Welch, Susan, and Timothy Bledsoe. *Urban Reform and its Consequences: A Study in Representation*. Chicago: University of Chicago Press, 1988.

West, Cornel. *Race Matters*. Boston, MA: Beacon, 1993.

White, Stephen. *Sustaining Affirmations: The Strength of Weak Ontology in Political Theory*. Princeton: Princeton University Press, 2000.

Williams, Bernard. "The Idea of Equality," in *Philosophy, Politics, and Society*, edited by Peter Laslett and W. G. Runciman. Oxford: Basil Blackwell, 1962.

Wilson, James Q. *The Moral Sense*. New York: Free Press, 1993.

Wilson, James Q. "The Rediscovery of Character: Private Virtue and Public Policy," *The Public Interest*, 81 (Fall 1985): 3–16.

Wilson, William Julius. *Bridge Over the Racial Divide*. Berkeley: University of California Press, 1999.

Wilson, William Julius. *The Truly Disadvantaged*. Chicago: The University of Chicago Press, 1987.

Wolff, Robert Paul. *In Defense of Anarchism*. New York: Harper and Row, 1970.

Wolfinger, Raymond. "Reputation and Reality in the Study of Community Power," *American Sociological Review* 25 (October 1960): 636–44.

Wolin, Sheldon. "Political Theory as a Vocation," *American Political Science Review* 63 (December 1969): 1062–82.

Wollstonecraft, Mary. *Vindication of the Rights of Woman*. New York: Penguin, 2006 [1792].

Woodcock, George. *Anarchism: A History of Libertarian Ideas and Movements*. Cleveland: World Publishing, 1962.

Wright, Anthony. *Socialisms: Theory and Practice*. New York: Oxford University Press, 1986.

Young, Iris Marion. "Polity and Group Difference," *Ethics* 99 (January 1989): 250–74.

Young, Iris Marion. *Justice and the Politics of Difference*. Princeton, NJ: Princeton University Press, 1990.

Z (an anonymous observer of the Soviet scene). "To the Stalin Mausoleum," *Daedalus* (Winter 1990): 295–343.

Index

Index